P R O C E E D I N G S

Symposium on
LOGIC IN COMPUTER SCIENCE

Ithaca, New York

June 22-25, 1987

Sponsored by the Computer Society of the IEEE
Technical Committee on
Mathematical Foundations of Computing

In cooperation with:
ACM SIGACT
Association for Symbolic Logic
European Association for Theoretical Computer Science

Support provided by:
Odyssey Research Associates
Cornell Mathematical Sciences Institute

Local arrangements supported by:
Cornell University

Computer Society Order Number 793
Library of Congress Number 87-45360
IEEE Catalog Number 87CH2464-6
ISBN 0-8186-0793-9
SAN 264-620X

THE COMPUTER SOCIETY OF THE IEEE
IEEE THE INSTITUTE OF ELECTRICAL AND ELECTRONICS ENGINEERS, INC.
IEEE COMPUTER SOCIETY PRESS

Published by Computer Society Press of the IEEE
1730 Massachusetts Avenue, N.W.
Washington, D.C. 20036-1903

Computer Society Order Number 793
Library of Congress Number 87-45360
IEEE Catalog Number 87CH2464-6
ISBN 0-8186-0793-9 (paper)
ISBN 0-8186-4793-0 (microfiche)
ISBN 0-8186-8793-2 (case)
SAN 264-620X

Order from:

Computer Society of the IEEE
Post Office Box 80452
Worldway Postal Center
Los Angeles, CA 90080

IEEE Service Center
445 Hoes Lane
P.O. Box 1331
Piscataway, NJ 08855-1331

Computer Society of the IEEE
Avenue de la Tanche, 2
B-1160 Brussels
BELGIUM

IEEE

THE INSTITUTE OF ELECTRICAL AND ELECTRONICS ENGINEERS, INC.

FOREW0RD

The purpose of this second annual conference on Logic in Computer Science (LICS) is to bring together a wide range of issues in computer science broadly relating to logic, including algebraic and topological approaches. The LICS conferences evolved from the Logics of Programs workshops and have a substantially broader scope. The call for papers for this second annual LICS symposium included the following topics of interest: abstract data types, computer theorem proving, verification, concurrency, type theory and constructive mathematics, constructive proofs as programs, data base theory, foundations of logic programming, program logics and semantics, knowledge and belief, software specifications, logic-based programming languages, logic in complexity theory.

Organizing Committee:

K. Jon Barwise
Woodrow W. Bledsoe
Ashok K. Chandra (Chair)
Edsger W. Dijkstra
Erwin Engleler
Joseph A. Goguen
Dexter C. Kozen
Zohar Manna
Albert R. Meyer
Rohit Parikh
Gordon D. Plotkin
Dana S. Scott

CONFERENCE PROGRAM

The thirty-four papers in these Proceedings were selected by the Program Committee on January 19, 1987, from 126 extended abstracts submitted in response to the call for papers. A large number of worthy abstracts had to be rejected because of size limitations. The program committee wishes to thank all who submitted papers for consideration.

Neither the extended abstracts submitted to the Program Committee nor the final papers in these Proceedings went through a formal refereeing process. Selections were based on several criteria, including quality and originality, but also including presentability, appropriateness, and completeness. Many of the papers are preliminary reports of on-going research, and it is expected that many authors will publish more polished and complete versions in scientific journals.

Program Committee:

Stephen Brookes
Luca Cardelli
Robert Constable
Melvin Fitting
Joseph A. Goguen
David Gries (Chair)
Yuri Gurevich
David Harel
Jean-Pierre Jouannaud
Richard E. Ladner
Vladimir Lifschitz
Giuseppe Longo
Anil Nerode
Gordon Plotkin
Amir Pnueli
Philip Scott

CONFERENCE ORGANIZATION

Conference Chair

Ashok K. Chandra
IBM T.J. Watson Research Center

Program Chair

David Gries
Cornell University

Local Arrangements Chair

Dexter Kozen
Cornell University

Publicity Chair

David W. Bray
Clarkson University

Table of Contents

Session 7

(Chair: A Nerode, *Cornell University*)

Thursday, June 25, 1987

Session 8

(Chair: G. Longa, *Universita di Pisa*)

Session 9

(Chair: J.-P. Jouannaud, *Universite Paris-Sud-Orsay*)

Invited Speaker

Chair

A. Pnueli

Weizmann Institute of Science

Speaker

R. Milner

University of Edinburgh

Some Uses of Maximal Fixed Points

(Abstract of Invited Lecture)

R. Milner
Department of Computer Science
University of Edinburgh, Hope Park Square
Meadow Lane
Edinburgh EH8 9NW
SCOTLAND

The notions of indistinguishability and "lack of discrepancy" are captured by maximal fixed points. Results in concurrent processes and operational semantics will be discussed.

Session 1

Chair

L. Cardelli

Digital Equipment Corporation

Polymorphism is conservative over simple types
(Preliminary Report)

Val Breazu-Tannen *Albert R. Meyer*

Laboratory for Computer Science
MIT
Cambridge, MA 02139

Abstract. We prove that the addition of the Girard-Reynolds polymorphic constructs to arbitrary simply typed equational lambda theories is *conservative.* This implies that polymorphism can be superimposed on familiar programming languages without changing their behavior.

Using a purely syntactic method, we give an effective proof of conservative extension in the case of equational reasoning that is complete when all types are assumed non-empty. When polymorphic types may be empty, we prove the stronger result that any model of the simply typed lambda calculus can be *fully and faithfully embedded* in a model of the polymorphic lambda calculus.

1 Introduction

This paper is a sequel to a previous one, [BM87], where the main result presented here was briefly announced. We will not, however, assume that the reader is familiar with [BM87]; we now recapitulate some of our motivation.

In programming languages of universal power, the *computational* data type domains must be distinguished from the *classical* data types because of the "divergent" element. This is illustrated in [MR86], [BM87], by a typical example in which one starts with a straightforward algebraic specification (for an integer data type with a conditional operator) and adds to it the ability to have recursive function declarations. Using the "copy rule" (on recursive calls) and the axioms of the specification one can then prove equations between (algebraic) data type terms that the specification alone cannot prove [1]. Thus, the equational theory of the programming language with recursion is *not* a *conservative extension* of the data type specification.

In order to reason about the underlying data types in a semantics that accommodates recursion, we need a logic that takes non-termination into account. LCF [GMW79] or the partial lambda calculus [Plo85], [Mog], are such logics that take recursion as a must and try to reason about the resulting data domains. In both logics, however, when reasoning about expressions of data element type one needs to worry about *more* than the data type specification, namely about whether certain subexpressions terminate or whether they are defined.

In [BM87], we took a different course: we aimed to preserve classical reasoning about the data by achieving the kind of conservative extension that fails above. Instead of recursion, we added to the data type the constructions made possible by procedural and polymorphic abstraction.

Following familiar tradition [Lan65], we take lambda calculi with reduction rules as models of programming languages and their evaluation, and in particular the Girard-Reynolds polymorphic lambda calculus, denoted by $\lambda^{\forall}$, [Gir72], [Rey74], *cf.* [FLO83] or

This work was supported in part by NSF Grant DCR-8511190 and in part by ONR Grant N00014-83-K-0125. The first author was partially supported by an IBM Graduate Fellowship.

[1] In fact, in the example in [MR86] [BM87] such reasoning is *inconsistent*, i.e., *any* equation is provable.

[Mit84] as a formal model of polymorphic programming [2]. Its syntax is reviewed in Section 2. First, we modeled data type specifications by algebraic theories [GTW78]. Let $\alpha(\Sigma, E)$ be a many-sorted algebraic theory , where Σ is a many-sorted signature and E is a set of algebraic axioms. Let $\lambda^{\forall}(\Sigma, E)$ be the polymorphic lambda theory (an extension of $\lambda^{\forall}$) in which the sorts of Σ are added as type constants, the function symbols of Σ are added as constants (of suitably curried type), and the equations in E are added to the axioms of $\lambda^{\forall}$.

In [BM87], we proved that the addition of the polymorphic constructs to any algebraic data type specifications is conservative, *i.e.*, $\lambda^{\forall}(\Sigma, E)$ is a *conservative extension* of $\alpha(\Sigma, E)$.

We now go further and enrich our model for specifications from many-sorted algebras to certain higher-order theories, specifically *simply (finitely) typed lambda theories.* We will denote the (pure) simply typed lambda calculus [Fri75], [Bar84] with $\lambda^{\rightarrow}$. A simply typed theory $\lambda^{\rightarrow}(\Sigma, E)$ consists of base (ground) types out of which one builds simple (finite) types using the $\rightarrow$ operator, of a signature Σ of constant symbols of arbitrary simple type out of which one builds simply typed lambda terms and of a set E of arbitrary equational axioms between simply typed lambda terms which are added to the axioms of $\lambda^{\rightarrow}$. Let $\lambda^{\forall}(\Sigma, E)$ be the polymorphic lambda theory in which the base types, the constants in Σ and the additional axioms in E are added to $\lambda^{\forall}$ ($\lambda^{\rightarrow}$ is already contained in $\lambda^{\forall}$). The main result of this paper is

Theorem 1
For any simply typed theory $\lambda^{\rightarrow}(\Sigma, E)$, the extension $\lambda^{\forall}(\Sigma, E)$ is conservative over $\lambda^{\rightarrow}(\Sigma, E)$. That is, for any $\lambda^{\rightarrow}(\Sigma)$-terms M and N,

$$E \vdash^{\lambda^{\forall}} M = N \iff E \vdash^{\lambda^{\rightarrow}} M = N \,.$$

We remark that since adding $\lambda^{\rightarrow}$ to arbitrary algebraic theories is conservative [MR86], Theorem 1 implies the earlier result of [BM87].

In our view, what makes Theorem 1 considerably more interesting than the earlier result is the fact that more features, such as function and data type declarations, can be better and more naturally modeled by simply typed lambda theories than by algebraic theories. Indeed, while the pure simply typed lambda calculus does not get very far, the capability of having extra constants and extra equations to govern their behavior is quite powerful. For example, simply typed theories can be used to model full-fledged programming languages [THM84] by modeling unrestricted recursion via higher-order fixed point operators. Even arbitrary recursively defined types can be modeled, by axioms asserting isomorphism between types. For example, the untyped lambda calculus can be captured by declaring a type u together with constants $rep : (u \rightarrow u) \rightarrow u$ and $abs : u \rightarrow (u \rightarrow u)$ and axioms asserting that *rep* and *abs* are inverse to each other (*cf.* [GMW79] or [Sco80]).

Polymorphic type disciplines have recently enjoyed increased attention as the naturalness and usefulness of the types-as-values paradigm which they embody was recognized. As a result, the design of programming languages has witnessed the widespread adoption of polymorphic type systems. A number of examples and a survey of this field can be found in [CW85]. Theorem 1 shows that polymorphic constructs and reasoning can be added to any programming language features that can be described within the simple type discipline without changing the familiar behavior of these features. From this perspective, the adoption polymorphic type systems is *safe*.

There are two technical variants of the main theorem because there are two related proof systems for polymorphic lambda-calculus which in general yield set-theoretically incomparable theories from the same axioms. The systems differ in the assumption of whether polymorphic types may be empty. The original polymorphic proof system is sound and complete for deriving semantic consequences over all models with all types non-empty [BM84]. But this system is *not sound* in models with empty types. After arguing that such models are of interest, [MMMS87] gives a new proof system that is sound and complete for deriving semantic consequences over *all* models.

The bulk of this paper (Section 3) focuses on establishing conservative extension for the older, nonempty-types, proof system of [BM84]. Using purely syntactic methods, we give an *effective* proof

[2] The version we consider here has *universal* types but it does not have *existential* types.

of conservative extension, *i.e.*, we describe a procedure that transforms any proof of $M = N$ from E in $\lambda^{\forall}$ into a proof of the same in $\lambda^{\rightarrow}$.

For the new, empty-types, proof system of [MMMS87] we give a quite different, *semantic*, proof of conservative extension (Section 4) by showing that any model of the simply typed lambda calculus can be *fully and faithfully embedded* in a model of the polymorphic lambda calculus. The desired models are constructed using a general method, the *extensional collapse*, developed in [BC87]. (Familiarity with [BC87] is desirable for understanding Section 4.)

In [BM87] we showed that adding the constructs of the Girard-Reynolds polymorphic lambda calculus to algebraic theories was not only safe but also that this could be done in a manner that guarantees substantial additional computing power on the original *algebraic* data types. Contrary to the announcement in [BM87], it remains open whether conservative extension of *simply typed theories* by polymorphism *with transfer of computing power* is true. We examine this conjecture in Section 5.

2 Basic syntax

Let K be a set of *(ground* or *base) type constants.* The *K-polymorphic type expressions* are defined by

$$\tau ::= k \mid t \mid \sigma \rightarrow \tau \mid \forall t.\, \sigma$$

where k ranges over K and t ranges over an infinite set of *type variables.* The set of free type variables of σ will be denoted $fv(\sigma)$.

Let C be a set of *constants.* By definition, each constant $c \in C$ comes equipped with its type, $Type(c)$ which must be a *closed* K-type expression. The (K, C)*-raw terms* are defined by

$$M ::= c \mid x \mid MN \mid \lambda x{:}\sigma.\, M \mid M\sigma \mid \lambda t.\, M$$

where c ranges over C and x ranges over a separate infinite set of *variables.* The set of free variables of M will be denoted $FV(M)$ while the set of free *type* variables of M will be denoted $fv(M)$. We identify the expressions or terms that differ only in the names of bound variables.

A *type assignment*, Δ, is a partial function that maps variables to type expressions such that $dom\Delta$ is *finite.* We write $\Delta, x{:}\sigma$ for $\Delta \cup \{x{:}\sigma\}$ and, by convention, the use of this notation implies that $x \notin dom\Delta$. *Typing judgments* have the form

$$\Delta \vdash M : \sigma\,.$$

The rules for deriving typing judgments (the *type-checking* rules) are

$$(constants) \qquad \Delta \vdash c : Type(c) \qquad c \in C$$

$$(projection) \qquad \Delta \vdash x : \Delta(x) \qquad x \in dom\Delta$$

$$(\rightarrow elim) \qquad \frac{\Delta \vdash M : \sigma \rightarrow \tau \quad \Delta \vdash N : \sigma}{\Delta \vdash MN : \tau}$$

$$(\rightarrow intro) \qquad \frac{\Delta, x{:}\sigma \vdash M : \tau}{\Delta \vdash \lambda x{:}\sigma.\, M : \sigma \rightarrow \tau}$$

$$(\forall\ elim) \qquad \frac{\Delta \vdash M : \forall t.\, \sigma}{\Delta \vdash M\tau : \sigma[t := \tau]}$$

$$(\forall\ intro) \qquad \frac{\Delta \vdash M : \sigma}{\Delta \vdash \lambda t.\, M : \forall t.\, \sigma} \qquad t \notin fv(ran\Delta)$$

When $\Delta \vdash M : \sigma$ is derivable by these rules, we say that M *type-checks under* Δ *with type* σ. In this case, σ is *uniquely* determined by M and Δ. Moreover, only the restriction of Δ to the variables that occur (free) in M matters. By convention, the *empty* type assignment is omitted.

The *polymorphic integers* and *booleans* are

$$\tilde{n} \stackrel{\text{def}}{=} \lambda t.\, \lambda f{:}t \rightarrow t.\, \lambda x{:}t.\, f^n x$$

of type

$$polyint \stackrel{\text{def}}{=} \forall t.\, (t \rightarrow t) \rightarrow t \rightarrow t$$

and

$$True \stackrel{\text{def}}{=} \lambda t.\, \lambda x{:}t.\, \lambda y{:}t.\, x$$

$$False \stackrel{\text{def}}{=} \lambda t.\, \lambda x{:}t.\, \lambda y{:}t.\, y$$

of type

$$polybool \stackrel{\text{def}}{=} \forall t.\, t \to t \to t\,.$$

Equations have the form

$$\Delta\,;\, M = N$$

thus are tagged with a type assignment whose role is to keep the equational reasoning type-correct. By convention, empty type assignments are again omitted.

As noted in Section 1, we are interested in two proof systems for deriving equations, which we will call "$\neg\emptyset$" and "*all*". We begin by presenting the rules which are common to the two systems. These rules form a proof system of independent technical interest, which we will call "*core*". .

The proof system "*core*" consists of

$$(\textit{extension}) \qquad \frac{\Delta\,;\, M = N}{\Delta, x{:}\tau\,;\, M = N} \qquad x \notin dom\Delta$$

reflexivity, symmetry, transitivity, congruence w.r.t. application,

$$(\xi) \qquad \frac{\Delta, x{:}\sigma\,;\, M = N}{\Delta\,;\, \lambda x{:}\sigma.\, M = \lambda x{:}\sigma.\, N}$$

β, η, congruence w.r.t. polymorphic application, *type* ξ, *type* η and

$$(\textit{type } \beta) \qquad \Delta\,;\, (\lambda t.\, M)\tau = M[t := \tau]$$

$$\text{where } \Delta \vdash M\,,\; t \notin fv(ran\Delta)$$

The proof system "$\neg\emptyset$" has the additional rule

$$(\textit{discharging}) \qquad \frac{\Delta, x{:}\sigma\,;\, M = N}{\Delta\,;\, M = N}$$

$$\text{where } x \notin FV(M) \cup FV(N)$$

This presentation of "$\neg\emptyset$"is equivalent to that in [BM84].

The proof system "*all*" uses a more complicated syntax [MMMS87]. The *extended* equations have the form

$$L\,;\, \Delta\,;\, M = N$$

where L is a finite set of assertions of the form $empty(\tau)$. The proof rules are those of the "*core*" system, adapted to the extended equations (by ignoring L), plus

(*empty-extension*)

$$\frac{L\,;\, \Delta\,;\, M = N}{L'\,;\, \Delta\,;\, M = N} \qquad L \subseteq L'$$

(*empty-trivial*)

$$empty(\sigma)\,;\, x{:}\sigma\,;\, True = False$$

(*empty-discharging*)

$$\frac{L, empty(\sigma)\,;\, \Delta\,;\, M = N \quad L\,;\, \Delta, x{:}\sigma\,;\, M = N}{L\,;\, \Delta\,;\, M = N}$$

$$\text{where } x \notin FV(M) \cup FV(N)$$

If E is a set of (extended) equations and e is an (extended) equation, we write $E \vdash_p^{\lambda^\forall} e$ when e is derivable in p using additional premises from E, where p is one of $\neg\emptyset$, *all* or *core*. An (extended) equation

$$(L\,;\,)\Delta\,;\, M = N$$

is *type-correct* if M and N both type-check under Δ with the same type. It is easy to see that for each p, $\vdash_p^{\lambda^\forall}$ preserves type-correctness.

Models are like in [BM84] and empty types are allowed. Note that (*discharging*) is not sound, in general, in models with empty types.

Since models are needed only in Section 4 we omit the definition here and refer the reader to [BC87]. Nonetheless, we recapitulate the basic completeness results:

Theorem 2 [BM84]

Let E, e be equations. $E \vdash_{\neg\emptyset}^{\lambda^\forall} e$ *if and only if e is valid in all models of E that have all types non-empty.*

Theorem 3 [MMMS87]

Let E, e be extended equations. $E \vdash_{all}^{\lambda^\forall} e$ *if and only if e is valid in all models of E.*

In contrast, the system "*core*" is *not* complete for deriving semantic consequences neither over all models with all types non-empty (obvious) nor over all systems [MMMS87] [3].

The K*-simple type expressions* (a.k.a. simple types) are all closed:

$$\tau ::= k \mid \sigma \to \tau \ .$$

By definition, the constants have simple type. The (K, C)*-simple raw terms* are defined by:

$$M ::= c \mid x \mid MN \mid \lambda x{:}\,\sigma.\, M \ .$$

From what we described for the polymorphic calculus, it is straightforward to define simple type-checking and simple equational reasoning (we use $\lambda^{\to}$ instead of $\lambda^{\forall}$) just by keeping those axioms and rules that deal only with the simply typed constructions *except* that the axiom (*empty-trivial*) is to be *replaced* with (*empty-trivial-simple*):

$$empty(\sigma)\ ;\ x{:}\,\sigma\ ;\ (\lambda y{:}\,\tau.\,\lambda z{:}\,\tau.\,y\ =\ \lambda y{:}\,\tau.\,\lambda z{:}\,\tau.\,z)$$

Simply typed models are like in [Fri75] where the analog of Theorem 2 is shown. The analog of Theorem 3 also holds. The system "*core*" while incomplete for simply typed models with or without empty types [MMMS87] is however complete for deriving semantic consequences over simply typed Kripke-style models [MM87].

3 An effective proof

Theorem 4 (conservative extension)
If E, e are simple equations then

$$E \vdash^{\lambda^{\forall}}_{\neg\emptyset} e \iff E \vdash^{\lambda^{\to}}_{\neg\emptyset} e\ .$$

Moreover, any derivation of e from E in the polymorphic proof system can be effectively transformed into a derivation of the same in the simple proof system and conversely.

[3] See however the note on simply typed Kripke-style models below.

One direction is trivial because the simple proof system is contained in the polymorphic one. For the other direction, we need to review some facts about proofs.

Equational reasoning in $\neg\emptyset$ without additional premises can be analyzed with the *reduction* system that we denote by $\lambda^{\forall}$ and that consists of the union of the four *pure* notions of reduction: β, η, *type* β and *type* η. $\lambda^{\forall}$-reduction preserves type-checking, and is strongly normalizing and Church-Rosser on terms that type-check [Gir72]. Our notation for reduction follows [Bar84].

For proofs with additional premises in $\neg\emptyset$, we have an alternative characterization of the derivable equations by means of chains of "replacements of equals by equals" Without loss of generality, we will assume that any additional premise, e, is a *type-correct* equation of the form

$$Left(e)\ =\ Right(e)$$

(thus $Left(e)$ and $Right(e)$ are *closed*).

We define on raw terms the relation of $\lambda^{\forall}$-*replacement* by $M \overset{\lambda^{\forall}}{\longleftrightarrow} N$ iff $M \overset{\lambda^{\forall}}{\longrightarrow} N$ or $N \overset{\lambda^{\forall}}{\longrightarrow} M$. For any additional premise e, we define, again on raw terms, e*-replacement* by: $M \overset{e}{\longleftrightarrow} N$ iff there exists a term P and a variable z occurring *exactly once* in P such that $M \equiv P[z := Left(e)]$ and $N \equiv P[z := Right(e)]$ or the other way around.

Let E be a set of additional premises. A *proof by replacements from* E is a vector

$$(\Delta, P_0, r_1, P_1, \ldots r_n, P_n)$$

such that $P_0, \ldots, P_n$, type-check under Δ, all with the same type, each r_j is either $\lambda^{\forall}$ or in E and, for $j = 1, \ldots, n$

$$P_{j-1} \overset{r_j}{\longleftrightarrow} P_j\ .$$

Instead of the tuple notation, we will use, for proofs by replacements, the following, more suggestive, notation:

$$\Delta\ ;\ P_0 \overset{r_1}{\longleftrightarrow} \cdots \overset{r_n}{\longleftrightarrow} P_n\ .$$

Proposition 5

$$E \vdash^{\lambda^{\forall}}_{\neg\emptyset} \Delta\ ;\ M\ =\ N$$

if and only if $\Delta\ ;\ M = N$ *is type-correct and there exists a proof by replacements from* E

$$\Delta'\ ;\ P_0 \leftrightarrow \cdots \leftrightarrow P_n$$

such that $P_0 \equiv M$, $P_n \equiv N$ *and* $\Delta \subseteq \Delta'$. *Moreover, the proof by replacements can be* effectively *obtained from the derivation and conversely.*

The proof consists of an induction on derivations and an induction on the length of proofs by replacements, both routine.

An analog alternative characterization of provability holds for $\lambda^{\rightarrow}$.

Proof of the Theorem. In view of Proposition 5, we will work with proofs by replacements instead of derivations. Fix a polymorphic proof by replacements from E for $e \equiv \Delta\ ;\ M = N$,

$$\Delta'\ ;\ M \leftrightarrow \cdots \leftrightarrow N \quad (\Delta \subseteq \Delta')\ .$$

We will deal only with terms that type-check under Δ' or with their *subterms*. These subterms type-check under well-determined extensions of Δ' that add the type declarations of the bound variables in whose scope the subterm lies. To simplify notation, when we will talk about *the* type of these terms or subterms, we will mean their type under Δ' or the appropriate extension of Δ'.

The general strategy will be to "normalize" the terms of this proof hoping to get rid of the polymorphic constructions and steps. This is complicated by the fact that Δ' may declare additional free variables of non-simple type which can then occur in the intermediate terms of the proof. (The normal form of a polymorphic term of simple type with free variables of simple type is a simple term but this is not necessarily so if there are free variables of non-simple type.) Hence the following definition:

A term Q is *quasi-simple* if it is of simple type, if it contains no *type* β-redexes and if any β-redexes $(\lambda x{:}\,\sigma.X)Y$ that occur in Q are such that σ is simple and X is of simple type. The name is justified by the following

Lemma 6
Any quasi-simple term Q *can be uniquely described as* $Q \equiv C[Z_1, \ldots, Z_m]$ *where* $C[\ ,\ldots,\ ]$ *is a simply* typed context *(see* [Bar84]*) with* m *holes of simple type, each hole occurring exactly once, and each of* $Z_1, \ldots, Z_m$ *is of the form* $z\ \alpha_1\ \cdots\ \alpha_k$ *where* z *is a variable that is free in* Q *and is of non-simple type,* $k \geq 1$ *and* α_k *is either a type expression or, if it is a term, then it has non-simple type.*

The proof is by induction on the *length* of Q and is omitted here.

Clearly, simple terms are quasi-simple and any normal form of simple type is quasi-simple. It is not hard to see that the class of quasi-simple terms is closed under application, abstraction by a variable of simple type, substitution of quasi-simple terms, e-replacement ($e \in E$) and $\lambda^{\forall}$-reduction.

Lemma 7
Any polymorphic proof by replacements from E,

$$\Delta'\ ;\ X \leftrightarrow \cdots \leftrightarrow Y$$

can be effectively transformed into a (still polymorphic) proof by replacements from E,

$$\Delta'\ ;\ U \leftrightarrow \cdots \leftrightarrow V$$

such that $X \xrightarrow{\lambda^{\forall}}\!\!\!\!\!\rightarrow U$, $Y \xrightarrow{\lambda^{\forall}}\!\!\!\!\!\rightarrow V$ *and all the terms in the second proof are* quasi-simple.

Proof of the Lemma. By induction on proofs by replacements.

Proofs of length 0. Take $U \stackrel{\text{def}}{=} V \stackrel{\text{def}}{=} nf(X)$ and notice that normalization is effective.

Proofs of length 1. Let $\Delta'\ ;\ X \stackrel{r}{\longleftrightarrow} Y$ be the proof. There are two cases:

1. $r = \lambda^{\forall}$. Take $U \stackrel{\text{def}}{=} nf(X) \equiv nf(Y) \stackrel{\text{def}}{=} V$.
2. $r = e \in E$. Then, there exists a term P and a fresh variable z occurring *exactly once* in P such that $X \equiv P[z := \mathit{Left}(e)]$ and $Y \equiv P[z := \mathit{Right}(e)]$ (or the other way around). P can be effectively found from X, Y and e (up to renaming z). Let $Q \stackrel{\text{def}}{=} nf(P)$. Take $U \stackrel{\text{def}}{=} Q[z := \mathit{Left}(e)]$ and $V \stackrel{\text{def}}{=} Q[z := \mathit{Right}(e)]$ (or the other way around). U and V are quasi-simple and one can transform U into V by as

many successive e-replacements as there are occurrences of z in Q (maybe none). This gives the desired proof by replacements built of quasi-simple terms.

Concatenation of proofs. We will assume that the claim holds for Δ' ; $X \leftrightarrow \cdots \leftrightarrow Y$ and Δ' ; $Y \leftrightarrow \cdots \leftrightarrow Z$ and show that it holds for their concatenation Δ' ; $X \leftrightarrow \cdots \leftrightarrow Y \leftrightarrow \cdots \leftrightarrow Z$. Let Δ ; $U \leftrightarrow \cdots \leftrightarrow V$ and Δ ; $V' \leftrightarrow \cdots \leftrightarrow W$ be the corresponding proofs by quasi-simple terms.

Since $V' \overset{\lambda^\vee}{\twoheadleftarrow} Y \overset{\lambda^\vee}{\twoheadrightarrow} V$ there exists, by the Church-Rosser property, a V'' such that $V \overset{\lambda^\vee}{\twoheadrightarrow} V'' \overset{\lambda^\vee}{\twoheadleftarrow} V'$. Once we now that such a V'' exists, we can effectively find one by, say, systematically trying all reduction paths (certain proofs of the Church-Rosser property probably yield better algorithms). Since V and V' are quasi-simple, all the terms that occur in the two reduction chains $V \overset{\lambda^\vee}{\twoheadrightarrow} V''$ and $V' \overset{\lambda^\vee}{\twoheadrightarrow} V''$ are also quasi-simple. The desired proof is then

$$\Delta\,;\, U \leftrightarrow \cdots \leftrightarrow V \overset{\lambda^\vee}{\longrightarrow} \cdots$$

$$\cdots \overset{\lambda^\vee}{\longrightarrow} V'' \overset{\lambda^\vee}{\longleftarrow} \cdots \overset{\lambda^\vee}{\longleftarrow} V' \leftrightarrow \cdots \leftrightarrow W\ .$$

End of Proof.

Applying this lemma to the original proof Δ' ; $M \leftrightarrow \cdots \leftrightarrow N$ we can construct a proof by quasi-simple terms Δ' ; $U \leftrightarrow \cdots \leftrightarrow V$ such that $M \overset{\lambda^\vee}{\twoheadrightarrow} U$ and $N \overset{\lambda^\vee}{\twoheadrightarrow} V$. But M and N are simple so all the terms that occur in the two reduction chains $M \overset{\lambda^\vee}{\twoheadrightarrow} U$ and $N \overset{\lambda^\vee}{\twoheadrightarrow} V$ are quasi-simple. We get a proof by replacements from E that contains only quasi-simple terms:

$$\Delta'\,;\, M \overset{\lambda^\vee}{\longrightarrow} \cdots \overset{\lambda^\vee}{\longrightarrow} U \leftrightarrow \cdots \leftrightarrow V \overset{\lambda^\vee}{\longleftarrow} \cdots \overset{\lambda^\vee}{\longleftarrow} N\ .$$

The point of all this is that quasi-simple terms can be "simplified". Let us fix, for each simple type σ, a *fresh* variable w_σ. If $Q \equiv C[Z_1, \ldots, Z_m]$ is a quasi-simple term then we construct a *simple* term out of it: $s(Q) \overset{\text{def}}{=} C[w_{\sigma_1}, \ldots, w_{\sigma_m}]$. Let $s(\Delta')$ be obtained from Δ' by restriction to the variables to which Δ' gives simple type. Then, $s(Q)$ type-checks under

$$s(\Delta'), w_{\sigma_1}\!:\sigma_1, \ldots, w_{\sigma_m}\!:\sigma_m$$

with same type that Q has under Δ'.

Clearly, if Q is already simple then $s(Q) \equiv Q$. It is easy to see that $s(MN) \equiv s(M)s(N)$, $s(\lambda x\!:\sigma.\, M) \equiv \lambda x\!:\sigma.\, s(M)$ and $s(M[x := N]) \equiv s(M)[x := s(N)]$.

Lemma 8
Let P and Q be quasi-simple.

(i) If $P \overset{e}{\longleftrightarrow} Q$ then $s(P) \overset{e}{\longleftrightarrow} s(Q)$ or $s(P) \equiv s(Q)$.

(ii) If $P \overset{\lambda^\vee}{\longleftrightarrow} Q$ then $s(P) \overset{\lambda^-}{\longleftrightarrow} s(Q)$ or $s(P) \equiv s(Q)$.

Now, recall that we had obtained a proof

$$\Delta'\,;\, M \leftrightarrow \cdots \leftrightarrow N$$

which contained only quasi-simple terms. By applying s to all the terms of this proof we get a *simple* proof by replacements from E

$$\Delta''\,;\, M \leftrightarrow \cdots \leftrightarrow N$$

where Δ'' is obtained by adding to $s(\Delta')$ the type assumptions $w_\sigma\!:\sigma$ about the fresh variables that are introduced throughout the proof. **End of Proof.**

4 Full and faithful embedding

Let $\mathcal{E}$ be a *polymorphic* model. There is a "canonical" way to extract a *simply typed* model, $s(\mathcal{E})$, out of $\mathcal{E}$ by selecting only the domains (of the meanings) of the simple types. Given a simply typed model $\mathcal{D}$ and a polymorphic model $\mathcal{E}$ we say that $\mathcal{D}$ is *fully and faithfully embedded* in $\mathcal{E}$ if $\mathcal{D}$ is isomorphic to $s(\mathcal{E})$. (Here, an *isomorphism* is a bijection that preserves types and meaning; hence, in particular, it will preserve also application and the interpretation of constants.) The crucial property of full and faithful embeddings is that for any simple extended equation e, $\mathcal{D} \models e$ iff $\mathcal{E} \models e$.

This section will be devoted to proving

Theorem 9
Any simply typed model can be fully and faithfully embedded in a polymorphic model.

This, together with the completeness result for $\vdash_{all}^{\lambda^{\rightarrow}} e$ immediately implies

Corollary 10 (conservative extension)
If E, e are simple extended equations then

$$E \vdash_{all}^{\lambda^{\forall}} e \iff E \vdash_{all}^{\lambda^{\rightarrow}} e\ .$$

Proof of the Theorem. Fix a set K of base types and a set C of constants of *simple* type. Let $\mathcal{D}$ be a (K, C)-simply typed model. For each element d of $\mathcal{D}$ we introduce a new constant q_d of the same type. Let $C' \stackrel{\text{def}}{=} C \cup \{q_d \mid d \in \mathcal{D}\}$. For each closed (K, C')-simply typed term M of type σ that is *not* a q_d, we introduce an equation

$$M = q_{[M]}\ .$$

We will denote by H the set formed by these equations.

The first step is to construct the closed type/closed term (K, C')-*polymorphic lambda interpretation* (p.l.i.) [BC87], $\mathcal{I}$, associated with the theory determined by H. The type expressions are interpreted in the structure formed by the closed type expressions. The rest of the definition follows the usual "term model" technique, *i.e.*, the domains consist of congruence classes of closed (K, C')-polymorphic terms modulo [4]

$$M \cong_{\omega} N \ \text{ iff } \ H \vdash_{core}^{\lambda^{\forall}} M = N\ .$$

We claim that, as a (K, C')-interpretation, $\mathcal{D}$ is fully and faithfully embedded in $\mathcal{I}$ via the map that takes d to the congruence class of q_d. In particular, at simple types, functional application in $\mathcal{I}$ is *extensional* (because application in $\mathcal{D}$ is extensional).

Indeed, first note that for any closed (K, C')-polymorphic term M of simple type, $nf(M)$ is simple hence M is provably equal to $q_{[nf(M)]}$.

[4] We chose *core* for simplicity, but, using Lemma 11 and Theorems 2 and 3, it can be shown that it does not matter which of the three proof systems we use.

Then, consider the reduction system $\lambda^{\forall}H$ consisting of the usual reductions of $\lambda^{\forall}$ plus the notion of reduction H defined as the union of all the equations in H oriented from left to right.

Lemma 11
$\lambda^{\forall}H$ is Church-Rosser on terms that type-check.

The proof uses the Hindley-Rosen Lemma [Bar84].

Since H-reduction also preserves type-checking, provability in $\lambda^{\forall}$ from H can be characterized by $\lambda^{\forall}H$-reduction. Thus, if

$$H \vdash_{core}^{\lambda^{\forall}} q_d = q_{d'}$$

then $d \equiv d'$ since q_d and q'_d are both $\lambda^{\forall}H$-normal forms..

While it is true that $\mathcal{D}$ is fully and faithfully embedded in $\mathcal{I}$, $\mathcal{I}$ is not extensional and hence not a model. We will therefore continue with what is called in [BC87] an *extensional collapse* and show that the full and faithful embedding "survives" it.

There are two ideas to the extensional collapse construction. The first idea is that if we have a second-order logical relation [MM85] on a p.l.i. which is the identity on types and which is a partial equivalence relation (p.e.r.) on the domain of each type, then the *quotient* p.l.i. whose elements are the p.e.r. classes is actually extensional, thus, a *model*. The second idea is how to construct such a logical p.e.r. on any given p.l.i. and we will illustrate it with our $\mathcal{I}$.

We construct from $\mathcal{I}$ a new p.l.i., $\mathcal{I}^{per}$, that has as types the set of pairs $<\omega, R>$ where ω is a type of $\mathcal{I}$ and R is a p.e.r. on the domain of ω. The rest of $\mathcal{I}^{per}$ is defined from $\mathcal{I}$ by "taking the first projection". To make $\mathcal{I}^{per}$ into a (K, C')-p.l.i., we need an interpretation for the base types, and we will assign to each base type k the p.e.r. that is the *identity* on the domain of k. Now, we have a collection $\mathcal{R}^{per}$ of p.e.r.'s, one at each type, namely R at type $<\omega, R>$ which is a logical p.e.r. on $\mathcal{I}^{per}$. The extensional collapse of $\mathcal{I}$ is the quotient $\mathcal{E} \stackrel{\text{def}}{=} \mathcal{I}^{per}/\mathcal{R}^{per}$.

Lemma 12
$R_{[\sigma]}^{per}$ is the identity for any *simple type σ.*

This follows by induction on simple types from the fact that functional application in $\mathcal{I}$ is extensional at simple types.

One consequence of the lemma is that $\mathcal{R}^{per}$ relates the constants in C' since they are all of simple type. Thus, $\mathcal{E}$ is a (K, C')-model. Another consequence is that the extensional collapse leaves the domains of (the meanings of) simple types unchanged, which was exactly the part of $\mathcal{I}$ onto which $\mathcal{D}$ was fully and faithfully embedded. Thus, $\mathcal{D}$ is fully and faithfully embedded in $\mathcal{E}$. The desired (K, C)-model is obtained by "forgetting" about the interpretation of the q_d's.

End of Proof.

Our full and faithful embedding construction always produces polymorphic models that have some empty types, even if the embedded simple model had all types non-empty [BC87]. Thus, we cannot use Theorem 9 to prove our other conservative extension formulation, Theorem 4.

John Mitchell and Eugenio Moggi have discovered how to do full and faithful embeddings of many-sorted *algebras* with all sorts non-empty into polymorphic models that have all types nonempty [Mit86] [5]. One direction for further investigation is to see if their idea could be used to embed simply typed models thus providing a semantic proof for Theorem 4 also.

5 Transferring computing power

As we said in Section 1, we argue in favor of eliminating all potentially divergent constructs such as unrestricted recursion. Clearly, this restriction commits us to programming in a language of less than universal power.

Nevertheless, it is known that an enormous class of total computable functions is programmable in the polymorphic lambda calculus, and the loss of universal power may not be noticeable. This calculus is strongly normalizing, and hence incapable of representing *all* computable functions. However, using the polymorphic integers as numerals, $\lambda^{\forall}$ can represent all the recursive functions that are provably total in second-order Peano arithmetic [Gir72]; see also [Sta81] [FLO83].

Unfortunately, the setting of Theorem 1 and that of its analog for algebraic theories [BM87] do not take advantage of this built-in computational power: the addition of just the polymorphic constructions does not cause any gain at all in the computing power over the specified data types. Indeed, all closed polymorphic terms of simple type can be "normalized" to simply typed terms.

As we have shown in [BM87], for the case of algebraic theories, there is a way to strengthen the results that *does* guarantee a gain in computing with the algebraically specified data types. The corresponding result for simply typed theories remains open [6]; we proceed to state it precisely.

The gain in computing power that we hope to achieve can be explained in terms of computable functions over an arbitrary simply typed specification. Assume that among the objects (of some ground type) specified there exists a set of *observables*—say character strings or lists or trees—and we care only about computational behavior on the observables. Moreover, assume there is some standard way of enumerating the distinct observables. This is true for all the familiar data type examples. The enumeration of observables yields a correspondence with nonnegative integers and hence a correspondence between functions on observables and functions on integers.

Conjecture 13
Let $\lambda^{\rightarrow}(\Sigma, E)$ be a simply typed lambda theory. Let $c_0, c_1, c_2, \ldots$ be a sequence of distinct closed $\lambda^{\rightarrow}(\Sigma)$-terms, called observables, *of some base type* obs, *such that no two distinct observables are provably equal in $\lambda^{\rightarrow}(\Sigma, E)$. Then, there is a uniform way of extending $\lambda^{\rightarrow}(\Sigma, E)$ to a larger theory, $\lambda^{\forall}IO(\Sigma, E)$, which is also an extension of $\lambda^{\forall}(\Sigma, E)$ such that*

1. *$\lambda^{\forall}IO(\Sigma, E)$ is a conservative extension of $\lambda^{\rightarrow}(\Sigma, E)$, and*

[5] Full and faithful embeddings of algebras into polymorphic models with empty types had been already obtained, see [BC87].

[6] Contrary to the announcement in [BM87], which is now withdrawn.

2. every computable function on observables which is provably total in second-order Peano arithmetic is representable by a closed $\lambda^{\forall}IO(\Sigma)$-term.

What we have in mind for for the *IO* (for Input-Output) extension are two typed function constants, $In : obs \rightarrow polyint$ and $Out : polyint \rightarrow obs$ and the axiom schemes $In\ c_n = \tilde{n}$ and $Out\ \tilde{n} = c_n$.

The corresponding result for algebraic theories [BM87] is proved via semantic methods (full and faithful embedding) developed in [BC87]. Specifically, it is shown there that any algebra with distinct observables can be fully and faithfully embedded into a model of the polymorphic lambda calculus in which we also find a sound interpretation for the *IO* part.

However, such an embedding is *not possible* for simply typed models. Indeed, if the *IO* part is sound then the model will contain, say at type $obs \rightarrow obs$, all the computable functions that are provably total in second-order Peano arithmetic. These functions may not be in the simply typed model to be embedded. Hence, the embedding cannot be *full*.

Nevertheless, there is an easy way to prove the conjecture for a large class of simply typed theories. This is the case when the additional axioms E can be made into rewrite rules which, together with the $\lambda^{\forall}$-reduction rules and the *IO* axioms (oriented from left to right) form a *Church-Rosser reduction system.* For example, this is true when the rules E are *delta rules* [Klo80], [Bar84] since this is already the case for the *IO* axioms. Note that the rules must preserve type-checking therefore the reduction system characterizes provability in $\lambda^{\forall}IO(\Sigma, E)$. That is, a type-correct equation is provable iff its two terms reduce to some common reduct. Now, if these terms are simply typed then they contain neither polymorphic constructs nor *In* and *Out*, thus the two reduction chains provide a simply typed proof.

While the Church-Rosser assumption gives such an easy proof, it also excessively undercuts the generality of the result. As seen in Section 3, a considerably more complicated argument, which makes also use of normalization, proves conservative extension for arbitrary additional axioms E but, of course, without the *IO* part. Thus, the obvious direction for further investigation is to try to extend the methods of Section 3 toward a proof of Conjecture 13.

References

[Bar84] H. P. Barendregt. *The Lambda Calculus: Its Syntax and Semantics.* Volume 103 of *Studies in Logic and the Foundations of Mathematics*, North-Holland, Amsterdam, second edition, 1984.

[BC87] V. Breazu-Tannen and T. Coquand. Extensional models for polymorphism. In *Proceedings of TAPSOFT'87 - Colloquium on Functional and Logic Progarmming and Specifications, Pisa, March 1987*, Springer-Verlag, Berlin, 1987. To appear.

[BM84] K. B. Bruce and A. R. Meyer. The semantics of second order polymorphic lambda calculus. In G. Kahn, D. B. MacQueen, and G. Plotkin, editors, *Semantics of Data Types*, pages 131–144, Springer-Verlag, Berlin, June 1984.

[BM87] V. Breazu-Tannen and A. R. Meyer. Computable values can be classical. In *Proceedings of the 14th Symposium on Principles of Programming Languages*, ACM, 1987.

[CW85] L. Cardelli and P. Wegner. On understanding types, data abstraction and polymorphism. *Computing Surveys*, 17(4):471–522, 1985.

[FLO83] S. Fortune, D. Leivant, and M. O'Donnell. The expressiveness of simple and second-order type structures. *Journal of the ACM*, 30(1):151–185, January 1983.

[Fri75] H. Friedman. Equality between functionals. In R. Parikh, editor, *Logic Colloqium, '73*, pages 22–37, Springer-Verlag, 1975.

[Gir72] J.-Y. Girard. *Interprétation fonctionelle et élimination des coupures dans l'arithmétique d'ordre supérieure.* PhD thesis, Université Paris VII, 1972.

[GMW79] M. J. Gordon, R. Milner, and C. P. Wadsworth. *Edinburgh LCF.* Volume 78 of *Lecture Notes in Computer Science*, Springer-Verlag, Berlin, 1979.

[GTW78] J. A. Goguen, J. W. Thatcher, and E. G. Wagner. An initial algebra approach to the specification, correctness, and implementation of abstract data types. In R.T. Yeh, editor, *Current Trends in Programming Methodology*, Prentice-Hall, 1978.

[Klo80] J. W. Klop. *Combinatory reduction systems.* Tract 129, Mathematical Center, Amsterdam, 1980.

[Lan65] P.J. Landin. A correspondence between ALGOL 60 and church's lambda notation. *Communications of the ACM*, 8:89–101; 158–165, 1965.

[Mit84] John C. Mitchell. *Lambda Calculus Models of Typed Programming Languages.* PhD thesis, Massachusetts Institute of Technology, Cambridge, Massachusetts, August 1984.

[Mit86] J. C. Mitchell. Personal communication, August. 1986. Unpublished.

[MM85] J. C. Mitchell and A.R. Meyer. Second-order logical relations (extended abstract). In R. Parikh, editor, *Logics of Programs*, pages 225–236, Springer-Verlag, Berlin, June 1985.

[MM87] J. C. Mitchell and E. Moggi. Kripke-style models for typed lambda calculus. In *Proceedings of the 2nd Symposium on Logic in Computer Science*, IEEE, 1987. This volume.

[MMMS87] A. R. Meyer, J. C. Mitchell, E. Moggi, and R. Statman. Empty types in polymorphic λ-calculus. In *Proceedings of the 14th Symposium on Principles of Programming Languages*, ACM, 1987. To appear.

[Mog] E. Moggi. Ph.D. thesis, Edinburgh University. Forthcoming, 1987.

[MR86] A. R. Meyer and M. B. Reinhold. 'Type' is not a type: preliminary report. In *Conf. Record Thirteenth Ann. Symp. Principles of Programming Languages*, pages 287–295, ACM, January 1986.

[Plo85] G. D. Plotkin. Personal communication, March. 1985. Unpublished.

[Rey74] J. C. Reynolds. Towards a theory of type structure. In B. Robinet, editor, *Programming Symposium*, pages 408–425, Springer-Verlag, Berlin, 1974.

[Sco80] D. Scott. Relating theories of the lambda calculus. In *To H.B. Curry: Essays on Combinatory Logic, Lambda Calculus and Formalism*, pages 403–450, Academic Press, 1980.

[Sta81] R. Statman. Number theoretic functions computable by polymorphic programs. In *22nd Symposium on Foundations of Computer Science*, pages 279–282, IEEE, 1981.

[THM84] B. Trakhtenbrot, J. Y. Halpern, and A. R. Meyer. From denotational to operational and axiomatic semantics for ALGOL-like languages: an overview. In *Logic of Programs, Proceedings 1983*, pages 474–500, Springer-Verlag, 1984.

Order-Sorted Algebra Solves the Constructor-Selector, Multiple Representation and Coercion Problems[1]

Joseph A. Goguen and José Meseguer
SRI International, Menlo Park CA 94025
Center for the Study of Language and Information,
Stanford University, Stanford CA 94305

Abstract: Structured data are generally composed from constituent parts by *constructors* and decomposed by *selectors*. We prove that the usual many-sorted algebra approach to abstract data types *cannot* capture this simple intuition in a satisfactory way. We also show that order-sorted algebra *does* solve this problem, and many others concerning ill-defined and erroneous expressions, in a simple and natural way. In particular, we show how order-sorted algebra supports an elegant solution to the problems of multiple representations and coercions. The essence of order-sorted algebra is that sorts have *subsorts*, whose semantic interpretation is the *subset* relation on the carriers of algebras.

1 Introduction

The goal of the research reported in this paper is to significantly expand the expressiveness and utility of abstract data types, both for programming languages, whether imperative of functional, and for specification languages, while preserving a rigorous initial algebra semantics and a simple first order proof theory. Although the many-sorted algebra (hereafter, MSA) approach to abstract data types has an attractive theory and many successful applications, it can lead to some very awkward specifications in practice, primarily because of its difficulties in handling erroneous expressions, such as dividing by zero in the rationals, or taking the top of an empty stack. In fact, there is no really satisfying MSA specification for stacks (see, for example, the two stack specifications in [2]). This is a special case of what we call the **constructor-selector problem**: for a given constructor, define functions that retrieve its components. This paper proves that the constructor-selector problem is insoluble in MSA, and shows that it can be solved with order-sorted algebra (hereafter, OSA).

There are many problems where one wants to represent data in more than one way, and convert freely between representations, using whichever representation is most convenient or efficient. This is the problem of **multiple representations**; for example, think of Cartesian and polar coordinates for points. There are other problems where one wants to convert from one sort of data to another in an irreversible way; for example, to apply integer addition to two rational numbers, one might first round them off; this illustrates the problem of **coercions**. The multiple representation problem is a special case of the coercion problem, since the selectors for one representation, when applied to a data item of another, can be thought of as mediated by coercions that change the representation. The difference is that conversions between multiple representations are necessarily reversible. OSA provides an initial algebra semantics for all these constructions.

The essence of OSA is that sorts have *subsorts*, semantically interpreted as subsets among the carriers of an algebra. OSA's rich type system supports many other features, including overloading, and total functions that would otherwise have to be partial by using sort constraints (see [6]). This paper gives a number of examples, using a syntax based on OBJ2 [3], a language with an initial OSA semantics for executable "objects," and a loose semantics for non-executable "theories." We begin with some basic OSA, including order-sorted deduction.

[1] Supported in part by Office of Naval Research Contracts N00014-82-C-0333, N00014-85-C-0417 and N00014-86-C-0450, National Science Foundation Grant No. MCS8201380 and a gift from the System Development Foundation.

2 Order-Sorted Algebra

Assuming familiarity with S-sorted sets and functions (for S a family of sorts) and with MSA signatures (S,Σ), Σ-algebra,s and Σ-homomorphisms (as in [10]), the following generalizes these concepts to OSA.

Definition 1: An **order-sorted signature** is a triple $(S,\leq,\Sigma)$ such that (S,Σ) is an MSA signature, $(S,\leq)$ is a partially ordered set[2], and the operators satisfy the following **monotonicity condition**[3]:

$$\sigma\in\Sigma_{w1,s1}\cap\Sigma_{w2,s2} \text{ and } w1\leq w2, \text{ imply } s1\leq s2 .$$

When the sort set S is clear, we may write Σ for (S,Σ), and when the partial order $(S,\leq)$ is clear, we may write Σ for $(S,\leq,\Sigma)$. Also, we may write σ: w→s for $\sigma\in\Sigma_{w,s}$ to emphasize that σ denotes a function with **arity** w and co-arity (or **value sort**) s. An important special case is $w=\lambda$, the empty string; then $\sigma\in\Sigma_{\lambda,s}$ denotes a **constant** of sort s. □

Regular signatures allow one to define the least sort of a term, and to give an order-sorted generalization of the usual term algebra construction. Intuitively, regularity means that any set of instances of an overloaded operator σ whose arities are bounded below (by w0) has a member with least arity and least sort.

Definition 2: An order-sorted signature Σ is **regular** iff given $w0\leq w1$ in S^* and σ in $\Sigma_{w1,s1}$ there is a least $\langle w,s\rangle\in S^*\times S$ with $w0\leq w$ such that $\sigma\in\Sigma_{w,s}$. If, in addition, each connected component[4] of the sort poset has a top element, then a regular signature is called **coherent**[5]. □

[2]We extend the ordering $\leq$ on S to strings of equal length in S^* by $s_1...s_n\leq s'_1...s'_n$ iff $s_i\leq s'_i$ for $1\leq i\leq n$. Similarly, $\leq$ extends to pairs $\langle w,s\rangle$ in $S^*\times S$ by $\langle w,s\rangle\leq\langle w',s'\rangle$ iff $w\leq w'$ and $s\leq s'$.

[3]Although not needed for validity of our results, this very natural condition rules out some bizarre models.

[4]Given a poset $(S,\leq)$, let $\equiv$ denote the transitive and symmetric closure of $\leq$. Then $\equiv$ is an equivalence relation whose equivalence classes are the **connected componets** of $(S,\leq)$.

[5]The notion of coherent signature can be made even more general: instead of requiring a top element, it is enough to require that each connected component be **filtered**, i.e., for any s and s' in the same component, there is always an s'' such that $s\leq s''$ and $s'\leq s''$. Every result in this paper also holds for this generalized notion.

Definition 3: Let $(S,\leq,\Sigma)$ be an order-sorted signature. Then an $(S,\leq,\Sigma)$**-algebra** is an (S,Σ)-algebra A such that

(1) $s\leq s'$ in S implies $A_s\subseteq A_{s'}$ and

(2) $\sigma\in\Sigma_{w1,s1}\cap\Sigma_{w2,s2}$ with $s1\leq s2$ and $w1\leq w2$ implies $A_\sigma: A_{w1}\rightarrow A_{s1}$ equals $A_\sigma: A_{w2}\rightarrow A_{s2}$ on A_{w1}.

When $(S,\leq)$ is clear, $(S,\leq,\Sigma)$-algebras may be called **order-sorted Σ-algebras**. We may write $A^{w,s}_\sigma$ instead of $A_\sigma: A_w\rightarrow A_s$. □

Definition 4: Let $(S,\leq,\Sigma)$ be an order-sorted signature, and let A and B be order-sorted $(S,\leq,\Sigma)$-algebras. Then a $(S,\leq,\Sigma)$**-homomorphism** h: A→B is a (S,Σ)-homomorphism satisfying the following **restriction** condition

$$s\leq s' \text{ and } a\in A_s \text{ imply } h_s(a)=h_{s'}(a) .$$

When the partially ordered set $(S,\leq)$ is clear, $(S,\leq,\Sigma)$-homomorphisms are also called **order-sorted Σ-homomorphisms**. The $(S,\leq,\Sigma)$-algebras and $(S,\leq,\Sigma)$-homomorphisms form a category that we denote $\mathbf{OSAlg}_\Sigma$. □

OSA *strictly generalizes* MSA, in the sense that any many-sorted (S,Σ)-algebra is an order-sorted $(S,\leq,\Sigma)$-algebra for $\leq$ the **trivial** ordering on S, defined by $s\leq s'$ iff $s=s'$; then $\mathbf{OSAlg}_\Sigma=\mathbf{Alg}_\Sigma$ and the forgetful functor $\mathbf{OSAlg}_\Sigma\rightarrow\mathbf{Alg}_\Sigma$ is the identity. Similarly, the rules of OSA deduction given later specialize to MSA rules for this ordering.

Definition 5: For $(S,\leq,\Sigma)$ an order-sorted signature and A an order-sorted Σ-algebra, an **order-sorted Σ-congruence** $\equiv$ on A is a many-sorted Σ-congruence $\equiv=\{\equiv_s \mid s\in S\}$ such that

$$s\leq s' \text{ in S and } a,a'\in A_s \text{ imply } a\equiv_s a' \text{ iff } a\equiv_{s'} a' .$$

□

Let f: A→B be an order-sorted Σ-homomorphism. Then the **kernel** of f, denoted ker(f), is an S-sorted family of equivalence relations $\equiv_f$ defined by $a\equiv_{f,s}a'$ iff $f_s(a)=f_s(a')$. It is easy to check that ker(f) is an order-sorted Σ-congruence. For $(S,\leq,\Sigma)$ a coherent order-sorted signature, A an order-sorted Σ-algebra, and $\equiv$ an order-sorted Σ-congruence on A, the **quotient** of A by $\equiv$ is the order-sorted Σ-algebra $A/\equiv$ defined as follows: for each sort s, the carrier of maximal sort in its connected component is $(A/\equiv)_{max(s)} = A_{max(s)}/\equiv_{max(s)}$ and the carrier of sort s is $(A/\equiv)_s = q_{max(s)}(A_s)$, for $q_{max(s)}: A_{max(s)}\rightarrow(A/\equiv)_{max(s)}$ the natural projection of each element a into its $\equiv_{max(s)}$-equivalence class. The operations are defined by: $(A/\equiv)_\sigma([a1],...,[an]) = [A_\sigma(a1,...,an)]$ for σ in $\Sigma_{s1,...,sn,s}$ and ai in A_{si}, which is well-defined since $\equiv$ is an order-sorted Σ-congruence. The order-sorted algebra $A/\equiv$ has a natural surjective order-sorted Σ-homomorphism q: $A \to A/\equiv$ defined by restricting the $q_{max(s)}$ to the remaining sorts and such that ker(q) = $\equiv$. This homomorphism is called the **quotient map** associated to the congruence $\equiv$.

Proposition 6: Universal Property of Quotients: Let Σ be a coherent order-sorted signature, A an order-sorted Σ-algebra and R an S-sorted family of binary relations R_s on A_s, $s \in S$. Then the quotient map q: $A \to A/R$ satisfies

(1) $R \subseteq ker(q)$ and

(2) if f: $A \to B$ is any order-sorted Σ-homomorphism such that $R \subseteq ker(f)$, then there is a unique Σ-homomorphism u: $A/R \to B$ such that $u \circ q = f$.

Proof: (1) follows from ker(q) being the smallest congruence containing R. For (2), let f: $A \to B$ be an order-sorted Σ-homomorphism such that $R \subseteq ker(f)$. Then $ker(q) \subseteq ker(f)$ and both are congruences (thus, families of equivalence relations), so we know that there are unique functions $u_{max(s)}: (A/R)_{max(s)} \to B_{max(s)}$ such that $u_{max(s)} \circ q_{max(s)} = f_{max(s)}$ for each maximal sort max(s), and that $u_{max(s)}$ is defined by $u_{max(s)}([a]) = f_{max(s)}(a)$. It remains only to check that u, extended to nonmaximal sorts by restriction, is an order-sorted Σ-homomorphism. Property (2) for order-sorted homomorphisms follows by construction. Let $\sigma \in \Sigma_{w,s}$ with w=s1...sn and let $ai \in A_{si}$ for i=1,...,n. Then (omitting subscripts throughout) we have, $u((A/R)_\sigma([a1],...,[an])) = u([A_\sigma(a1,...,an)]) = f(A_\sigma(a1,...,an)) = B_\sigma(f(a1),...,f(an)) = B_\sigma(u([a1]),...,u([an]))$. We leave the case $w=\lambda$ to the reader. □

We remark that the Universal Property characterizes the quotient map uniquely up to isomorphism. Now the following is an easy consequence of Proposition 6:

Proposition 7: Homomorphism Theorem: Let Σ be a coherent order-sorted signature and f: $A \to B$ and order-sorted Σ-homomorphism. Then $A/ker(f) \approx f(A)$ (isomorphism as order-sorted Σ-algebras).

Proof: Let f′: $A \to f(A)$ denote the corestriction of f to f(A). Then by the universal property of the quotient with R=ker(f′)=ker(f), there is a (unique) u: $A/ker(f) \to f(A)$ such that $q \circ u = f'$; then u is surjective since f′ is, and it remains to show that u is injective. To this end (omitting subscripts again,) suppose that u([a1])=u([a2]). Then f(a1)=f(a2), so [a1]=[a2]. □

Given an order-sorted signature Σ, we construct the **order-sorted Σ-term algebra $\mathcal{T}_\Sigma$** as the least family $\{\mathcal{T}_{\Sigma,s} \mid s \in S\}$ of sets satisfying the following conditions (note our somewhat pedantic, but temporary, use of ⦅ and ⦆ for parentheses as formal syntactic symbols):

- $\Sigma_{\lambda,s} \subseteq \mathcal{T}_{\Sigma,s}$ for $s \in S$;
- $\mathcal{T}_{\Sigma,s'} \subseteq \mathcal{T}_{\Sigma,s}$ if $s' \leq s$;
- if $\sigma \in \Sigma_{w,s}$ and if $ti \in \mathcal{T}_{\Sigma,si}$ where $w=s1...sn \neq \lambda$ then (the string) σ⦅t1...tn⦆$\in \mathcal{T}_{\Sigma,s}$.
- Also, for $\sigma \in \Sigma_{w,s}$ let $\mathcal{T}_\sigma: \mathcal{T}_w \to \mathcal{T}_s$ send t1,...,tn to (the string) σ⦅t1...tn⦆.

These terms are **ground terms**, i.e., they involve no variables. Terms with variables arise from ground terms by enlarging the signature Σ with additional constants for the variables, giving an extended signature $\Sigma(X)$ and an algebra $\mathcal{T}_{\Sigma(X)}$ which is denoted $\mathcal{T}_\Sigma(X)$ when viewed as a Σ-algebra. Although a term in an order-sorted term algebra may have many different sorts, we still have,

Fact 8: For Σ a regular signature, each term t in $\mathcal{T}_\Sigma$ has a *least* sort, denoted LS(t). □

Definition 9: Let Σ be an order-sorted signature. Then an order-sorted Σ-algebra I is **initial** in the class of all order-sorted Σ-algebras iff there is a unique order-sorted Σ-homomorphism from I to any other order-sorted Σ-algebra. □

Theorem 10: Let Σ be a regular order-sorted signature. Then $\mathcal{T}_\Sigma$ is an initial order-sorted Σ-algebra. □

The proof is a straightforward structural induction on the obvious construction of the order-sorted algebra of terms; see [6] for the details.

Corollary 11: Let A be an order-sorted Σ-algebra and let f: $X \to A$ be an S-sorted function (with X disjoint from Σ); such a function is called an **assignment** from X to A. Then, by initiality, there is a unique order-sorted Σ-homomorphism $f^*: \mathcal{T}_\Sigma(X) \to A$ that extends f. □

This fact is usually expressed by saying that $\mathcal{T}_\Sigma(X)$ is the **free** order-sorted Σ-algebra on X.

In an MSA equation t=t′, we are forced to require that t and t′ have the same sort. OSA allows more flexibility. Since a coherent signature allows comparison of terms in a common supersort, it is enough to require that the sorts of t and t′ lie in the same connected component.

Definition 12: For $(S, \leq, \Sigma)$ a coherent order-sorted signature, a **Σ-equation** is a triple ⟨X,t,t′⟩, where X is a variable set and t,t′ are in $\mathcal{T}_{\Sigma(X)}$ with LS(t) and LS(t′) in the same connected component of $(S, \leq)$; we may write $(\forall X)$ t=t′. An order-sorted Σ-algebra A **satisfies** a Σ-equation $(\forall X)$ t=t′ iff $\underline{a}^*_{LS(t)}(t) = \underline{a}^*_{LS(t')}(t')$ in A for every assignment $\underline{a}$: $X \to A$. Similarly, A **satisfies** a set Γ of Σ-equations iff it satisfies each member. The case of conditional equations and their satisfaction is entirely similar. □

3 Order-Sorted Equational Deduction

For $(S,\leq,\Sigma)$ a coherent order-sorted signature and X,Y two S-sorted variable sets, a **substitution** is an S-sorted map $\theta: X \rightarrow \mathcal{T}_\Sigma(Y)$; this is a special assignment, where the values of variables lie in a term algebra. The unique order-sorted Σ-homomorphism $\theta^*: \mathcal{T}_\Sigma(X) \rightarrow \mathcal{T}_\Sigma(Y)$ induced by θ will also be denoted θ.

Given an order-sorted signature Σ and a set Γ of conditional Σ-equations, the following are the rules for deriving (unconditional) equations:

(1) Reflexivity. Each equation $(\forall X)\ t=t$ is derivable.

(2) Symmetry. If $(\forall X)\ t=t'$ is derivable, then so is $(\forall X)\ t'=t$.

(3) Transitivity. If the equations $(\forall X)\ t=t'$, $(\forall X)\ t'=t''$ are derivable, then so is $(\forall X)\ t=t''$.

(4) Congruence. If $t \in \mathcal{T}_\Sigma(X)$ and if $\theta,\theta': X \rightarrow \mathcal{T}_\Sigma(Y)$ are substitutions such that for each x in X, the equation $(\forall Y)\ \theta(x)=\theta'(x)$ is derivable, then $(\forall Y)\ \theta(t)=\theta'(t)$ so is.

(5) Substitutivity. If $(\forall X)\ t_1=t_2$ if C is in Γ, and if $\theta: X \rightarrow \mathcal{T}_\Sigma(Y)$ is a substitution such that for each u=v in C the equation $(\forall Y)\ \theta(u)=\theta(v)$ is derivable, then so is $(\forall Y)\ \theta(t_1)=\theta(t_2)$.

When the equations in Γ are unconditional, rule (5) becomes

(5′) Unconditional Substitutivity. If $(\forall X)\ t_1=t_2$ is in Γ, and if $\theta: X \rightarrow \mathcal{T}_\Sigma(Y)$ is a substitution, then $(\forall Y)\ \theta(t_1)=\theta(t_2)$ is derivable.

Theorem 13: Completeness Theorem: For an order-sorted signature Σ and a set Γ of conditional Σ-equations, the following are equivalent:

- $(\forall X)\ t=t'$ is derivable from Γ using rules (1)-(5).
- $(\forall X)\ t=t'$ is satisfied by all order-sorted Σ-algebras that satisfy Γ.

When the equations in Γ are unconditional, the same holds replacing rule (5) by (5′). □

Derivability from Γ using the above rules of deduction defines a congruence relation on $\mathcal{T}_\Sigma(X)$; let $\mathcal{T}_{\Sigma,\Gamma}(X)$ denote the quotient under that equivalence relation.

Corollary 14: Initiality Theorem: For Σ a coherent order-sorted signature and Γ a set of conditional Σ-equations, $\mathcal{T}_{\Sigma,\Gamma}(\emptyset)$ (henceforth denoted $\mathcal{T}_{\Sigma,\Gamma}$) is an initial (Σ,Γ)-algebra and $\mathcal{T}_{\Sigma,\Gamma}(X)$ is a free (Σ,Γ)-algebra on X. □

This subsection concludes with an executable OSA specification whose initial model is the rational numbers. As noted in Section 6.10 of [2], there is no way to avoid heavy use of hidden functions and error constants in specifying the rational numbers, due to problems such as division by zero; a satisfactory MSA specification of the rationals is not possible.

Here, **Int < Rat** indicates the subsort relation, and **protecting INT** asserts that the given operations and equations do not add new elements to the built-in integer sort, and also do not identify any two different integers. We indicate "mix-fix" notation using the underbar character "_" to mark places where arguments go; the first such place should have an argument of the first sort in the sort list between the : and ->; the second such place should have an argument of the second sort in this list; etc. Thus, _*_ is binary infix, while top_ would be unary prefix. Note that the operators _/_, -_, and _*_ are "overloaded," and that [assoc comm] declares _+_ and _*_ to be associative and commutative.

```
obj RAT is
  protecting INT .
  sorts NzRat Rat .
  subsorts Int < Rat .
  subsorts NzInt < NzRat < Rat .
  op _/_ : Rat NzRat -> Rat .
  op _/_ : NzRat NzRat -> NzRat .
  op -_  : Rat -> Rat .
  op -_  : NzRat -> NzRat .
  op _+_ : Rat Rat -> Rat [assoc comm] .
  op _*_ : Rat Rat -> Rat [assoc comm] .
  op _*_ : NzRat NzRat -> NzRat [assoc comm] .
  vars R S : Rat .
  vars R' S' T' : NzRat .
  eq : R / (R' / S') = (R * S') / R' .
  eq : (R / R') / S' = R / (R' * S') .
  eq : (R' * T') / (S' * T') = R' / S' .
  eq : R / 1 = R .
  eq : 0 / R' = 0 .
  eq : R / (- R') = (- R) / R' .
  eq : - (R / R') = (- R) / R' .
  eq : R + (S / R') = ((R * R') + S) / R' .
  eq : R * (S / R') = (R * S) / R' .
endo
```

We note that an operational semantics has been given for OSA, using order-sorted rewriting [7].

3.1 Retracts

Strong typing, even with overloading, has some disadvantages. For example, the term **top pop push(7,push(3,empty))** is not well-formed according to the syntax of **STACK-OF-INT**, since **top**'s arguments should have sort **NeStack**, whereas the term

pop push(7,push(3,empty)) literally has sort **Stack**, even though we can see that **pop push(7,push(3,empty))** will evaluate to the nonempty stack **push(3,empty)**. A simple solution is to transform ill-formed Σ-terms into well-formed terms over an extended signature $\Sigma^{\bullet}$ having the same sorts as Σ, plus new operator symbols $r_{max(s),s}$: max(s)$\rightarrow$s for each s$\neq$max(s), called **retracts** (where max(s) denotes the top of the connected component of s). The semantics of retracts is given by new equations of the form $r_{max(s),s}(x)=x$, for x a variable of sort s.

The OBJ2 implementation uses retracts to handle ill-formed OSA terms, such as **top pop push(7,push(3,empty))**, that might become well-formed after reduction, giving them the benefit of the doubt at parse time by filling the gaps between actual sorts and required sorts with retracts. For example, the above term is parsed as **top r.Stack.NeStack(pop push(7,push(3,empty)))** and since it reduces to **3** under the rules in **STACK-OF-INT** plus a retract rule, it is vindicated by the reduction. Also, truly erroneous terms reduce to very informative error messages. This kind of runtime type checking, together with the polymorphism provided by subsorts and parameterization, gives most of the syntactic flexibility of untyped languages with all the advantages of strong typing. Moreover, adding retracts is *safe*, since, under extremely general hypotheses, it is a conservative extension [6]. Retracts can also be seen as rewrite rules, following a very nice theory that has been developed jointly with Jean-Pierre Jouannaud [7]

4 Constructors and Selectors

Let us consider the following simple executablespecification for **STACK-OF-INT**:

```
obj STACK-OF-INT is
  protecting INT .
  sorts Stack NeStack .
  subsorts NeStack < Stack .
  op empty : -> Stack .
  op push : Int Stack -> NeStack .
  op top_ : NeStack -> Int .
  op pop_ : NeStack -> Stack .
  var I : Int .
  var S : Stack .
  eq : top push(I,S) = I .
  eq : pop push(I,S) = S .
endo
```

Intuitively, **constructors** create data elements; thus, **push** creates **Stack** elements, **cons** creates (say) **List-of-Bool** elements, and **succ** creates **Nat** elements. A constructor generally has associated **selectors** to "pull out" underlying components of the created data element; for example, **top** and **pop** do this for **Stack**, **head** and **tail** for **List-of-Bool**, and **pred** for **Nat**. Such selectors should collectively act as an inverse to their constructor, in the sense of satisfying equations like

```
eq : top push(N,S) = N .
eq : pop push(N,S) = S .

eq : head(cons(B,L)) = B .
eq : tail(cons(B,L)) = L .

eq : pred(succ(N)) = N .
```

The problem is that expressions like **top(empty)**, **head(nil)**, and **pred(0)** are well-formed in MSA, but are intuitively erroneous, since there is no reasonable **Int** value for **top(empty)**, or **Bool** value for **head(nil)**. Thus, one must either make the selectors partial and abandon MSA, or else introduce new "erroneous" elements, say **error**. However, this gives rise to strange expressions like **3 + error** and **push(3,push(error,empty))**. A desperate attempt to minimize the (generally infinite) number of erroneous elements by adding a few seemingly innocent equations, can easily collapse all elements into a single point [8]. In fact, the well-intentioned but hopeless attempt to solve the constructor-selector problem within MSA has produced many inconsistent specifications in the abstract data type literature. As shown in **STACK-OF-INT**, introducing a subsort like **NeStack** as the target sort of **push** removes these difficulties. Similarly, subsorts **NeList-of-Bool < List-of-Bool** and **NzNat < Nat** as targets for **cons** and **succ** solve the problem for lists of Booleans and for natural numbers. Theorem 22 below shows that the approach just sketched solves the constructor-selector problem. But first, we need some further concepts.

Definition 15: A Σ-algebra A is **Σ-reachable** iff the unique Σ-homomorphism $\mathcal{T}_\Sigma \rightarrow A$ is surjective. $\square$

Definition 16: Let Σ be a coherent order-sorted signature and let Γ be a set of conditional Σ-equations. Then a **signature of canonical constructors** for Σ with respect to Γ is a subsignature Π of Σ (i.e., $\Pi_{w,s} \subseteq \Sigma_{w,s}$ for all w$\in$S* and s$\in$S) such that for every $t \in \mathcal{T}_\Sigma$ there is a *unique* $t' \in \mathcal{T}_\Pi$ with LS(t')$\leq$LS(t) and such that the equation $(\forall\emptyset)$ t=t' can be deduced from Γ by OSA deduction. Equivalently, Π is a subsignature of canonical constructors for Σ with respect to Γ iff the unique order-sorted Π-homomorphism $\mathcal{T}_\Pi \to \mathcal{T}_{\Sigma,\Gamma}$ is an isomorphism. We call elements of Π **canonical constructors.** □

The condition LS(t′)≤LS(t) is needed for $\mathcal{T}_\Pi \to \mathcal{T}_{\Sigma,\Gamma}$ to be surjective. For example, for the signature Σ with two sorts s′≤s and just two constants, a′ of sort s′ and a of sort s, and with Γ consisting of the single equation (∀∅) a=a′, the subsignature Π with the same sorts and only the constant a induces $\mathcal{T}_\Pi \to \mathcal{T}_{\Sigma,\Gamma}$ not surjective.

Definition 17: Let Π be a signature of canonical constructors for Σ with respect to Γ and let $\kappa \in \Pi_{w,s}$ be a canonical constructor with $w=s_1...s_n$. Then a family of operators $\sigma_i \in \Sigma_{s,s_i}$ for $1 \leq i \leq n$ is called a **family of selectors** for κ with respect to Π and Γ iff every Σ-reachable Σ-algebra that satisfies Γ also satisfies the equation

$$(\forall X)\ \kappa(\sigma_1(x),...,\sigma_n(x))=x$$

with X consisting of a single variable x of sort s; then σ_i is called the **i-th selector** of κ. □

With obvious changes, Definitions 16 and 17 also apply to MSA; we will use the MSA forms in showing that MSA cannot solve the constructor-selector problem. Although the definition of selector only requires a one-sided inverse, Lemma 18 below shows that we get the other inverse equation for free in any Σ-reachable algebra satisfying Γ.

In the stack example, the subsignature Π containing **push** and **empty** is a signature of canonical constructors. Theorem 22 below will show that **top** and **pop** are the first and second selectors for **push**, using the equations

(i) `top(push(x1,x2)) = x1` .

(ii) `pop(push(x1,x2)) = x2` .

Thus constructors "put data elements together," and selectors decompose data elements into their components, and these two processes are inverse to each other.

Lemma 18: Let Π be a signature of canonical constructors for Σ with respect to Γ, let $\kappa \in \Pi_{w,s}$ be a canonical constructor with $w=s_1...s_n$ and let $\sigma_i \in \Sigma_{s,s_i}$ for $1 \leq i \leq n$ be a family of selectors for κ with respect to Π and Γ. Then every Σ-reachable Σ-algebra that satisfies Γ also satisfies the equations

$$(\forall X)\ \sigma_i(\kappa(x_1,...,x_n))=x_i$$

for $1 \leq i \leq n$ and for X consisting of the variables $x_1,...,x_n$ of sorts $s_1,...,s_n$ respectively.

Proof: By the definitions of satisfaction and quotient, if an order-sorted algebra A satisfies a given equation, then any quotient of A also satisfies that equation. The algebras mentioned in the lemma are the reachable Σ-algebras that satisfy the equations Γ. Of course, $\mathcal{T}_{\Sigma,\Gamma}$ is one such algebra, and any other such algebra is isomorphic to a quotient of it. Thus it is enough to prove that $\mathcal{T}_{\Sigma,\Gamma}$ satisfies the equations

$$(\forall X)\ \sigma_i(\kappa(x_1,...,x_n))=x_i$$

for $1 \leq i \leq n$, where X contains variables $x_1,...,x_n$ of sort $s_1,...,s_n$ respectively. In other words, we have to show that for each t_1 in $\mathcal{T}_{\Sigma,s_1}$,..., t_n in $\mathcal{T}_{\Sigma,s_n}$ the equations

$$(\forall \emptyset)\ \sigma_i(\kappa(t_1,...,t_n))=t_i$$

for $1 \leq i \leq n$ follow from Γ by order-sorted equational deduction. By hypothesis there is for each Σ-term t of lowest sort s a unique Π-term can(t) of same lowest sort such that

$$(\forall \emptyset)\ t=\mathrm{can}(t)$$

follows from Γ by order-sorted equational deduction. Thus, it is enough to show the term identities

$$\mathrm{can}(\sigma_i(\kappa(t_1,...,t_n)))=\mathrm{can}(t_i)$$

for $1 \leq i \leq n$. All such identities will follow from the term identity

$$(*)\ \kappa(\mathrm{can}(\sigma_1(\kappa(t_1,...,t_n))),...,\mathrm{can}(\sigma_n(\kappa(t_1,...,t_n))))= \kappa(\mathrm{can}(t_1),...,\mathrm{can}(t_n))$$

since κ is a canonical constructor. By the congruence property of order-sorted equational deduction and by κ being a constructor, we necessarily have (using Γ and the uniqueness of canonical forms) the term identity

$$\kappa(\mathrm{can}(\sigma_1(\kappa(t_1,...,t_n))),...,\mathrm{can}(\sigma_n(\kappa(t_1,...,t_n)))) = \mathrm{can}(\kappa(\sigma_1(\kappa(t_1,...,t_n)),...,\sigma_n(\kappa(t_1,...,t_n))))$$

from which (*) follows, using the equation

$$(\forall \emptyset)\ \kappa(\sigma_1(\kappa(t_1,...,t_n)),...,\sigma_n(\kappa(t_1,...,t_n)))=\kappa(t_1,...,t_n)$$

which by hypothesis follows from Γ by order-sorted deduction. □

The following shows that selectors are unique:

Lemma 19: Let ρ be an i-th selector with respect to Σ and Γ for a canonical constructor κ of sort s which has a family σ_i for $1 \leq i \leq n$ of canonical selectors with respect to Σ and Γ. Then every reachable Σ-algebra that satisfies Γ also satisfies (∀∅) $\rho(x)=\sigma_i(x)$.

Proof: By the definition of selector, every reachable (Σ,Γ)-algebra will satisfy

$$(\forall x)\ \kappa(\sigma_1(x),...,\rho(x),...,\sigma_n(x))=x$$

where ρ is in the i-th position and x is of sort s, and also

$$(\forall x)\ \kappa(\sigma_1(x),...,\sigma_i(x),...,\sigma_n(x))=x\ .$$

Thus, any such algebra will satisfy

$$(*)\ (\forall x)\ \kappa(\sigma_1(x),...,\rho(x),...,\sigma_n(x))= \kappa(\sigma_1(x),...,\sigma_i(x),...,\sigma_n(x))\ .$$

Also, by Lemma 18, for each i=1,...,n, all reachable (Σ,Γ)-algebras will satisfy

$(\forall X)\sigma_i(\kappa(x_1,\ldots,x_n))=x_i$

and in particular will also satisfy

$(\forall x)\ \sigma_i(\kappa(\sigma_1(x),\ldots,\sigma_n(x)))=\sigma_i(x)$

and, using (*) and soundness of the rule of congruence,

$(\forall x)\ \sigma_i(\kappa(\sigma_1(x),\ldots,\rho(x),\ldots,\sigma_n(x)))=\rho(x)$

where ρ is in the i-th position; thus, all reachable (Σ,Γ)-algebras satisfy

$(\forall x)\ \sigma_i(x)=\rho(x)$,

as claimed. □

As further motivation for Theorem 22, we give a somewhat more complex example:

Example 20: Arithmetic Expressions:

```
obj EXPRESSION is
  sorts Epression Sum Product .
  subsorts Sum Product < Expression .
  ops 0 1 : -> Expression .
  op _+_ : Expression Expression -> Sum .
  op _*_ : Expression Expression -> Product .
  ops 1s 2s : Sum -> Expression .
  ops 1p 2p : Product -> Expression .
  vars E1 E2 : Expression .
  eq : 1s(E1 + E2) = E1 .
  eq : 2s(E1 + E2) = E2 .
  eq : 1p(E1 * E2) = E1 .
  eq : 2p(E1 * E2) = E2 .
jbo
```

Here the signature Π of canonical constructors contains **0,1,+,***, while **1s** and **2s** are (respectively) first and second selectors for **+**, and **1p** and **2p** are (respectively) first and second selectors for *****. Notice that the domain of **1s** and **2s** is the sort **Sum** of trees having a **+** on top, while the domain of **1p** and **2p** is **Product**, the trees having a ***** on top. Of course, we could have given a simpler one-sorted signature of constructors, as in

```
obj EXPRESSION-0 is
  sorts Expression .
  ops 0 1 : -> Expression .
  op _+_ : Expression Expression -> Expression .
  op _*_ : Expression Expression -> Expression .
jbo
```

but then there is no satisfactory way to define the selectors. For example, if

s1 s2 : Expression -> Expression were the first and second selectors for **_+_**, then we would have to have

s1(0) + s2(0) = 0,

contradicting that both **+** and **0** are canonical constructors.

□

The above argument generalizes to show the following, which is a more precise statement of the inherent impossibility of expressing constructors in MSA:

Theorem 21: In MSA with more than one constructor of some sort s, no constructor of sort s can have selectors. The only possible MSA selectors are untupling operators for the rather trivial case of a tupling operator that is the only constructor of its value sort. □

Note that any **EXPRESSION**-algebra $A=\{A_{\mathtt{Expression}}, A_{\mathtt{Sum}}, A_{\mathtt{Product}}\}$ can be viewed as a **EXPRESSION-0**-algebra by forgetting about the operators **1s**, **2s**, **1p**, **2p**, extending the range of **+** to **Expression** using $A_{\mathtt{Sum}}\subseteq A_{\mathtt{Expression}}$ and similarly for *****. This motivates the following general method of associating an order-sorted signature Σ with constructors and selectors for operators to each many-sorted signature Σ^0 without overloading[6], with many-sorted canonical constructors Π^0 of canonical constructors relative to a set Γ^0 of Σ^0-equations:

1. Define a partially ordered set S^1 to have the sorts S^0 of Π^0 together with a new sort $s_\kappa \leq s$ for each constructor κ: $s_1 \ldots s_n \rightarrow s$ in Π^0 with $n \geq 1$;
2. Define an order-sorted signature Π^1 over S^1 to have the same constants as Π^0, plus a new operator κ: $s_1 \ldots s_n \rightarrow s_\kappa$ for each κ: $s_1 \ldots s_n \rightarrow s$ in Π^0 with $n \geq 1$; in Example 20, starting with Π^0 as the signature of **EXPRESSION-0** yields Π^1 as the subsignature of canonical constructors of **EXPRESSION**.
3. Now enlarge Π^1 to a signature Π by adding a new selector operator i_κ: $s_\kappa \rightarrow s_i$ for $1 \leq i \leq n$ for each operator κ: $s_1 \ldots s_n \rightarrow s$ in Π^0; in Example 20, Π is the signature of **EXPRESSION**.
4. Finally, define SEL to be the set of Π-equations $(\forall X)\ i_\kappa(\kappa(x_1,\ldots,x_n))=x_i$ for i=1,...,n, where X consists of x_i of sort s_i for $s_1 \ldots s_n$ the arity of κ in Π with $n \geq 1$.

The following says that this construction works as desired.

Theorem 22: Let Σ^0 be a many-sorted signature (without overloading) having $\Pi^0 \subseteq \Sigma^0$ as canonical constructors with respect to Γ^0. Then for Π^1, Π, SEL defined as above, the following properties hold:

---

[6]This means that the sets $\Sigma_{w,s}$ are disjoint.

(1) Π^1 is a signature of canonical constructors for the order-sorted signature $\Sigma=(\Sigma^0-\Pi^0)\cup\Pi$ relative to $\Gamma=\mathrm{SEL}\cup\Gamma^0$, and for each nonconstant κ in Π^1, i_κ is its i-th selector with respect to Σ and Γ.

(2) By extending the range of its operators and forgetting about the selectors, each Σ-algebra A can be viewed as a Σ^0-algebra U(A) in such a way that initial algebras are preserved, i.e., such that $U(\mathcal{T}_{\Sigma,\Gamma})=T_{\Sigma^0,\Gamma^0}$.

Proof: To prove (1), define $\Sigma^1=(\Sigma^0-\Pi^0)\cup\Pi^1$ and consider the OSA specification inclusions

$$(S_1,\leq,\Pi^1,\emptyset)\subseteq(S_1,\leq,\Pi,\mathrm{SEL})\subseteq(S^1,\leq,\Sigma,\Gamma)$$

and

$$(S_1,\leq,\Pi^1,\emptyset)\subseteq(S_1,\leq,\Sigma^1,\Gamma^0)\subseteq(S^1,\leq,\Sigma,\Gamma).$$

Then we have to show the following isomorphism for the restriction of $\mathcal{T}_{\Sigma,\Gamma}$ to the operations in Π^1,

(i) $\mathcal{T}_{\Sigma,\Gamma}|_{\Pi^1}\simeq\mathcal{T}_{\Pi^1}$.

If we had already proved

(ii) $\mathcal{T}_{\Pi,\mathrm{SEL}}|_{\Pi^1}\simeq\mathcal{T}_{\Pi^1}$

and

(iii) $\mathcal{T}_{\Sigma^1,\Gamma^0}|_{\Pi^1}\simeq\mathcal{T}_{\Pi^1}$

then we could establish (i) by the following argument: Without loss of generality, we may assume that (ii) and (iii) are actual equalities, and define a Σ-algebra structure $\mathcal{T}_{\Pi,\mathrm{SEL}}+\mathcal{T}_{\Sigma^1,\Gamma^0}$ with $(\mathcal{T}_{\Pi,\mathrm{SEL}}+\mathcal{T}_{\Sigma^1,\Gamma^0})_s = (\mathcal{T}_{\Pi,\mathrm{SEL}})_s=(\mathcal{T}_{\Sigma^1,\Gamma^0})_s$ for each sort s and each operation in Σ coinciding with the one in $\mathcal{T}_{\Pi,\mathrm{SEL}}$ or in $\mathcal{T}_{\Sigma^1,\Gamma^0}$. Therefore, the equations Γ are satisfied by construction since $\Gamma=\mathrm{SEL}\cup\Gamma^0$. We claim that $\mathcal{T}_{\Pi,\mathrm{SEL}}+\mathcal{T}_{\Sigma^1,\Gamma^0}$ is an initial Σ,Γ-algebra. Let B be any Σ,Γ-algebra; then we have at most one homomorphism h: $\mathcal{T}_{\Pi,\mathrm{SEL}}+\mathcal{T}_{\Sigma^1,\Gamma^0}\to B$ since as an S^1-sorted function, h must coincide with the unique Π^1-homomorphism h: $\mathcal{T}_{\Pi,\mathrm{SEL}}+\mathcal{T}_{\Sigma^1,\Gamma^0}|_{\Pi^1}=\mathcal{T}_{\Pi^1}\to B|_{\Pi^1}$. But by (ii) and (iii), h is also a Π-homomorphism h: $\mathcal{T}_{\Pi,\mathrm{SEL}}\to B|_\Pi$ and a Σ^1-homomorphism h: $\mathcal{T}_{\Sigma^1,\Gamma^0}\to B|_{\Sigma^1}$ and therefore a $\Pi\cup\Sigma^1=\Sigma$-homomorphism, as desired; thus (i) follows.

(ii) follows by noticing that the equations SEL are Church-Rosser (there are no critical pairs) and terminating (an easy inductive argument) rewrite rules, and then using basic results about order-sorted term rewriting [7], [9]. (iii) follows by noticing that for any s among the sorts of Σ^0 we have $t\in\mathcal{T}_{\Sigma^1}$ iff $t\in T_{\Sigma^0}$ and checking that many-sorted and order-sorted replacement of equals for equals under Γ^0 coincide; since closure under context[7] is then superfluous, this is enough to establish (iii). Now, (2) also follows by (iii), since $\mathcal{T}_{\Sigma,\Gamma}|_{\Sigma^1}=\mathcal{T}_{\Sigma^1,\Gamma^0}$. □

Definitions 16 and 16 for constructors and selectors, can be made more general by dropping the requirement that the constructors be "canonical." Thus, we just define a signature Π of **constructors** for Σ relative to equations Γ by dropping the requirement that for each term t the Π-term t_0 such that $(\forall\emptyset)$ $t=t_0$ be ***unique*** (i.e., canonical), leaving the rest of the definition unchanged. Using this weaker condition, the concatenation operation on lists is a constructor for lists, though not canonical. The notion of selector also generalizes, so that **head** and **tail** become first and second selectors in the generalized sense for list concatenation. Given a constructor κ: $s_1...s_n\to s$ with $n\geq1$ in a signature Π of constructors for Σ relative to Γ, a string $w'=s'_1...s'_n$ with $s'_i\leq s_i$ and a sort $s'\leq s$, let us say that the operators σ_i: $s'\to s'_i$ for $1\leq i\leq n$ are a family of $\langle w',s'\rangle$-**selectors** for κ if all Σ-reachable algebras that satisfy Γ also satisfy the equation

$$(\forall x)\ \kappa(\sigma_1(x),...,\sigma_n(x))=x$$

for x of sort s'.

5 Degenerate Cases, Multiple Representations, and Coercions

Order-sorted algebra provides a simple and elegant analysis of degenerate cases, multiple representations, and coercions[8]. **Degenerate cases** are simply constructors that have lower dimension, i.e., involve fewer parameters, than some other constructor; this can be a particular nuisance in computational geometry. For example, in a **LINE** object, the sort **Line** might have two cases, one **General** and the other **Vertical**, with the latter being degenerate. Consider the following specification for lists of integers:

```
obj LIST-INT is
  protecting INT .
  rep List by case(Emtpy) is: {}
    or by case(NonEmpty) is: _._
      with head : Int and tail : List .
endo
```

where {} and _._ are *constructors*, while the functions **head** and **tail** following the keyword **with** are the *selectors* for _._; since {} is degenerate, it has no selectors. We will say more about this notation later. The intended order-sorted semantics for this is given by the

[7]This is an additional condition to the replacement of equals for equals that is in general required for order-sorted deduction [9].

[8]This discussion follows the development in [5].

following (of course, OSA is *needed* here, since MSA is not strong enough to define the selectors):

```
obj LIST-INT is
  protecting INT .
  sorts Empty NonEmpty List .
  subsorts Empty  < List .
  subsorts  NonEmpty < List .
  op {} : -> Empty .
  op _._ : Int List -> NonEmpty .
  op head : NonEmpty -> Int.
  op tail : NonEmpty -> List .
  var I : Int .
  var L : List .
  eq : head(I . L) = I .
  eq : tail(I . L) = L .
endo
```

This reveals that **Empty** and **NonEmpty** are *subsorts* of **List** (perhaps they could more clearly be designated **EmptyList** and **NonEmptyList**). This translation is very convenient, since it allows us to use the full machinery of order-sorted algebra, for example, **sort predicates**, which are **Bool**-valued operations that are true iff their argument has the appropriate sort. Thus,

```
Empty({}) = true .
```

while

```
NonEmpty({}) = false .
```

A "case analysis" for **rep** statements is also useful in the righthand sides of equations. For example, given

```
rep S by case(A) is: ...
   or by case(B) is: ... .
```

we may translate an equation of the form

```
t = t'(case(A X) is: t1 or case(B X) is: t2) .
```

where **t**, **t'(_)**, **t1**, and **t2** are expressions, and where **X** occurs in **t**, into the following two conditional equations using sort predicates

```
t = t'(t1) if A(X) .
t = t'(t2) if B(X) .
```

Here, **t1** can use the selectors associated with the constructor for case **A**, while **t2** can use the selectors associated with **B**, but **t1** cannot use those associated with **B** and **t2** cannot use those associated with **A**. Case analyses may also involve more than one variable, with syntax like

```
case(A X,Y ; B Z) is: ...
```

which will generate the condition

```
... if A(X) and A(Y) and B(Z) .
```

The **rep** construction is useful even when there are no degenerate cases, as illustrated in the specification of points with Cartesian coordinates in the object **POINT** below.

Let us now consider **multiple representations**. Interestingly, and perhaps surprisingly, using a selector does not *require* the corresponding representation, since its value could be computed from any underlying representation where it is defined. Let us consider an example, points represented *either* by Cartesian *or* by Polar coordinates. The following module declares both representations, together with *coercions* (i.e., implicit conversions or translations) between them; we name each representation to help distinguish between the two coercions that are given. Two new subsorts of **Real** are needed (namely, **Pos** and **Angle**) for positive elements and for angles, and are defined by sort constraints (see [6] for details about this concept). Also, a number of auxiliary functions that are used, including square root, some trigonometric functions and the constant **pi**, are assumed to be already defined in the module **REAL**, which provides some kind of real arithmetic.

```
obj POINT is
  protecting REAL .
  sort Pos < Real if P > 0 .
  sort Angle < Real if 0 <= A < 2 * pi .
  rep(Cart) Point by <_;_>
     with x : Real and y : Real .
  rep(Polar) Point by case(General) is: [_;_]
     with theta : Angle and rho : Pos
   or by case(Origin) is: * .
  coerce(Cart to Polar) by
   if x =/= 0 then
     [ arctan(y / x) ; sqrt((x **2)+(y **2))]
     else if y == 0 then * else if y > 0
     then [ pi / 2 ; y ] else
     [ 3 * pi / 2 ; - y ] fi fi fi .
  coerce(Polar to Cart) by
   case(General) is:
     < rho * cos(theta) ; rho * sin(theta) >
   or case(Origin) is: < 0 ; 0 > .
  op d : Point Point -> Real .
  vars P Q : Point .
  eq : d(P,Q) =
    sqrt(((x(P) - x(Q))**2)+((y(P) - y(Q))**2)).
jbo
```

There is no need for variables in the coercion definitions, since there is just one item involved that has the indicated representation, and the selectors implicitly take it as their argument. An interesting point about this example is that one representation has a degenerate case, while the other does not; however, the two representations are completely intertranslatable.

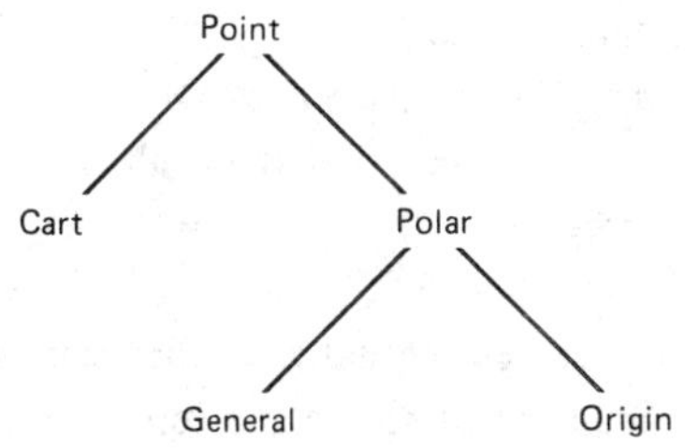

Figure 1: Subsorts for the Point Representations

Given this **POINT** object, any of the four selectors can be used anywhere in a program, without having to worry about what the underlying representation might actually be. Semantically, each representation of a given sort defines a new subsort of it, and each case of a given representation defines a new subsubsort. Thus, **Point** has subsorts **Cart** and **Polar**, and **Polar** has subsorts **General** and **Origin**. Figure 1 shows all the subsorts involved here. Operations involving points should use the sort **Point**, rather than the sort of one of the representations, in order to obtain the full benefits of this facility. (If one wants to use the same name for cases that belong to different representations, a qualification notation can be used to distinguish them; for example, if we had a **General** case of **Cart**, the two different **General** cases would be named **General.Cart** and **General.Polar**, respectively.)

Although this example has just two representations and one coercion from each representation to the other, the construction also allows any number of representations, and also *one-way* coercions, whereby some representations can be more expressive than others; however, the construction syntactically enforces that there is *at most* one coercion from any given representation to another. In addition, we must require that the coercions *compose correctly*, in the sense that if there is a coercion c from representation R1 to representation R2, and another c' from R2 to R3, and a third c'' from R1 to R3, then the composition $c \circ c'$ must equal c''. In particular, if c goes from R1 to R2 and c' goes from R2 to R1, then $c \circ c'$ must be the identity, and in fact, R1 and R2 must be isomorphic representations; this case corresponds to what Wadler [12] calls *views*. (In fact, our coercions resemble the default views of [4], in that they form a category with at most one morphism from any given object to another.) This imposes a preorder structure on the sort set, and ensures that each item has at most one translation, i.e., that the implicit conversions are consistent.

It might seem that this construction assumes that the representations are "free" (or one might say, "anarchic"), i.e., do not satisfy any non-trivial equations. However, the only disadvantage to adding equations for constructors is that it may be harder to ensure the consistency of operations defined over them, including coercions; this might require some theorem proving, whereas it is automatic in the anarchic case.

We now give an initial OSA semantics for this feature, by regarding coercion definitions as equations. This ensures, model theoretically, that the sorts **Cart**, **Polar** and **Point** have *identical* carriers in the initial algebra, thus achieving *representation independence*, since the different representations are identified, and appear in the same equivalence class. Under this view, it is necessary to use different constructors for each representation, and non-injective one-way coercions cannot be handled (these restrictions can be relaxed using a somewhat different semantics given below). The intended semantics is the initial algebra of the following OSA specification (we use a variant of the **rep** notation for single constructors, with selectors following the keyword **with**, and the corresponding subsorts and equations implicit):

```
obj POINT is
  protecting REAL .
  sort Pos < Real if P > 0 .
  sort Angle < Real if 0 <= A < 2 * pi .
  sorts Point Cart Polar General Origin .
  subsorts Cart Polar < Point .
  subsorts General Origin < Polar .
  op <_;_> : Real Real -> Cart with x and y .
  op [_;_] : Angle Pos -> General
                 with theta and rho .
  op * : -> Origin .
  op d : Point Point -> Real .
  vars X Y X' Y' : Real .
  var Rho : Pos .
  var Theta : Angle .
  eq : < X ; Y > = if X =/= 0 then
        [ arctan(Y / X) ; sqrt((X **2)+(Y **2))]
        else if Y == 0 then * else if Y > 0 then
        [ pi / 2 ; Y ] else
        [ 3 * pi / 2 ; - Y ] fi fi fi .
  eq : [ Rho ; Theta ] =
        < Rho * cos(Theta) ; Rho * sin(Theta) > .
  eq : * = < 0 ; 0 > .
  eq : d(< X ; Y >,< X' ; Y' >) =
         sqrt(((X - X')**2)+((Y - Y')**2)) .
jbo
```

Operationally, the coercion equations should not be treated as rewrite rules, but rather, the remaining equations should be matched *modulo* the coercion equations. For example, the equation

```
d(< X ; Y >,< X' ; Y' >) =
  sqrt(((X - X') **2)+((Y - Y') **2)) .
```

matches the expression `d(< 7 ; 0 >,[ pi ; - 6 ])` modulo the equation

```
[ Rho ; Theta ] =
  < Rho * cos(Theta) ; Rho * sin(Theta) > .
```

and rewrites to

```
sqrt(((7 - ((- 6) * cos(pi))) **2)+
   ((0 - ((- 6) * sin(pi))**2))
```

and eventually simplifies to 1.

Let us now consider a more complex example, the ASCII coercion from natural numbers to characters. Here, neither sort **Nat** nor **Char** is a subsort of the other, and the coercion function, let us denote it **ascii**, is defined only on a subset of the naturals, those between 0 and 127 (inclusive); let us denote this subsort **Nat[0..127]**, and assume it is already defined by a sort constraint in a module **NATS**. Then the code involved looks like the following:

```
obj CHAR is
  protecting NATS .
  sort Char .
  sort Nat[0..127] < Char .
  rep Char by nul, ........
  coerce(Nat[0..127] to Char) by
    0 is: nul
    .........
jbo
```

Thus, the sort **Char** is defined by a large list of cases, and the coercion is, in effect, defined by a large table.

Coercions are also meaningful in more general cases than multiple representation, but here the simple approach of regarding the coercion definitions as equations may break down. For example, suppose that `Int < Rat` and that we want a coercion from rationals to integers, taking the integer part of a rational; since this operation (let's denote it `int-part : Rat -> Int`) is not injective, dividing by the congruence relation generated by `R = int-part(R)` would simply destroy the rationals! What we really want here, is to apply **int-part** iff some function needs an integer but has been supplied a rational. This kind of behavior is familiar from the retracts that we have already considered: the parser inserts a special function symbol **r.rat.int** when it gets a subexpression of sort **Rat** but needs one of sort **Rat**. All we have to do then, is provide the conditional equation

```
r.rat.int(R) = int-part(R) if not Int(R) .
```

in addition to the equation that we already have for retracts, namely

```
r.rat.int(I) = I .
```

where **I** has sort **Int**; actually, in this case, we don't need the second equation at all, or the condition in the first equation, since `int-part(I) = I`. Thus, in the most general case, we may regard coercions as operation symbols having empty syntax that are invoked iff run-time type checking fails to yield an argument of the right sort; they are defined by conditional equations whose lefthand side is a retract and whose righthand side is a coercion definition. In fact, this gives a fully general way to handle coercions, since retracts will only arise inside of expressions that do not, properly speaking, parse anyway. This guarantees correctness, since the coercion equations only affect expressions outside the initial algebra of well-sorted terms. It also provides a more efficient operational semantics. However, it is less satisfying when applied to the multiple representation case, since the corresponding representations are not actually identified. Nevertheless, we can just add the relevant equations in such cases, and get the advantages of both approaches.

We conclude this section with a discussion of related work. Our coercions resemble Wadler's "views" [12], except that our coercions can be one-way, i.e., mutual inter-translatability is not required; also, we use order-sorted algebra to get selectors, we allow any number of representations, and we do not restrict to anarchic representations. The work of Reynolds [11] on "category-sorted algebra" is also closely related; however, Reynolds does not support user-defined coercions (although Wadler does), does not use order-sorted algebra to get selectors, and his category-sorted algebra may be too general, since it allows any number of coercions between a given pair of representations[9]. Our work on coercions is also related to some preliminary work of Bruce and Wegner [1], and all three of these works have influenced our approach.

---

[9] It may be worth remarking that Reynolds' category-sorted algebra is a special case of ordinary many-sorted algebra, in the sense that there is a simple translation which preserves the models, and that no special rules of deduction are required. The case of order-sorted algebra is quite different, since new rules of deduction really are needed to account for the requirement that some carriers *must* be contained in others.

6 Conclusions

We have presented some basics of order-sorted universal algebra, and shown how it generalizes the usual many-sorted algebra. Moreover, we have shown that order-sorted algebra permits an elegant solution to the constructor-selector problem, whereas this problem cannot be solved in many-sorted algebra, and we have also given some examples to illustrate the issues involved. Finally, we have discussed and given examples for the multiple representation and coercion problems, and shown how they can be solved and given an initial algebra semantics using order-sorted algebra.

References

1. Kim Bruce and Peter Wegner. "An Algebraic Model of Subtypes in Object-Oriented Languages (Draft)". *SIGPLAN Notices 21*, 10 (October 1986), 163-172.

2. Hartmut Ehrig and Bernd Mahr. *Fundamentals of Algebraic Specification 1: Equations and Initial Semantics*. Springer-Verlag, 1985.

3. Kokichi Futatsugi, Joseph Goguen, Jean-Pierre Jouannaud and José Meseguer. Principles of OBJ2. In *Proceedings, Twelvth Symposium on Principles of Programming Languages*, Brian K. Reid, Ed., Association for Computing Machinery, 1985, pp. 52-66.

4. Joseph Goguen. "Parameterized Programming". *Transactions on Software Engineering SE-10*, 5 (September 1984), 528-543. Early versions in *Proceedings, Workshop on Reusability in Programming*, Thomas Biggerstaff and Thomas Cheatham, Eds., ITT, pages 138-150, 1983 and in Technical Report CSLI-84-9, Center for the Study of Language and Information, Stanford University, September 1984.

5. Joseph Goguen. Modular Algebraic Specification of Some Basic Geometrical Constructions. In *AI Journal, Special Issue on Computational Geometry*, Joseph Mundy, Ed., , 1987, pp. to appear. Also to appear as a technical report from the Center for the Study of Language and Information at Stanford University, March 1987.

6. Joseph Goguen and José Meseguer. Order-Sorted Algebra I: Partial and Overloaded Operations, Errors and Inheritance. To appear, SRI International, Computer Science Lab, 1987. Given as lecture at Seminar on Types, Carnegie-Mellon University, June 1983.

7. Joseph Goguen, Jean-Pierre Jouannaud and José Meseguer. Operational Semantics of Order-Sorted Algebra. In *Proceedings, 1985 International Conference on Automata, Languages and Programming*, W. Brauer, Ed., Springer-Verlag, 1985. Lecture Notes in Computer Science, Volume 194.

8. Joseph Goguen, James Thatcher and Eric Wagner. An Initial Algebra Approach to the Specification, Correctness and Implementation of Abstract Data Types. RC 6487, IBM T. J. Watson Research Center, October, 1976. Appears in *Current Trends in Programming Methodology, IV*, Raymond Yeh, Ed., Prentice-Hall, 1978, pages 80-149.

9. Claude Kirchner, Helene Kirchner and José Meseguer. Operational Semantics of OBJ3. Paper in preparation.

10. José Meseguer and Joseph Goguen. Initiality, Induction and Computability. In *Algebraic Methods in Semantics*, Maurice Nivat and John C. Reynolds, Eds., Cambridge University Press, 1985, pp. 459-541. Also SRI Computer Science Lab Technical Report CSL-140, December 1983.

11. John Reynolds. Using Category Theory to Design Implicit Conversions and Generic Operators. In *Semantics Directed Compiler Generation*, Neal D. Jones, Ed., Springer-Verlag, 1980, pp. 211-258. Lecture Notes in Computer Science, Volume 94.

12. Philip Wadler. Views: A Way for Pattern Matching to Cohabit with Data Abstraction. In *Proceedings, 14th Symposium on Principles of Programming Languages*, Steve Munchnik, Ed., ACM, 1987, pp. 307-312.

Recursive Types and Type Constraints in Second-Order Lambda Calculus

N.P. Mendler
Cornell University
Computer Science Department
Ithaca NY, 14853

Abstract

We add to the second-order lambda calculus type constructors μ and ν, which give the least and greatest solutions to positively defined type expressions. Strong normalizability of typed terms is shown using Girard's *candidates for reduction* method. Using the same structure built for that proof, we prove a necessary and sufficient condition for when a collection of type constraints admit the typing of only strongly normalizable terms.

1 Introduction

In the first half of this paper, we give an extension to the second-order lambda calculus [7,3], which permits the definition of least and greatest solutions to positively defined type expressions using type constructors μ and ν, respectively. With μ, one can easily define inductive types such as the natural numbers, constructive ordinals, lists, and trees; with ν, "lazy" types such as streams, and potentially infinite trees can be defined. The focus of this paper is not on model theory as in [6,1], but on the proof theory: the central result is a proof of strong normalizability, using Girard's method [9,8], which we extend to exploit the fact that the collection of ground sets forms a complete lattice, and that recursive types can be viewed as least and greatest fixed points of monotonic (but not necessarily continuous) operations on it. This proof isolates the central arguments in the proof of the intuitionistic consistency of the extension of the Nuprl logic by recursive types [5,4,11,10].

Using the structures built in the first half of the paper, in second half we consider typing terms in the presence of type constraints [2]. The general problem can be stated as follows. *Given a collection of constraints $A = B$ between types and the rule*

$$\frac{a : A, \quad A = B}{a : B},$$

when are the resulting typed terms strongly normalizable? We consider the subcase where we have type constants τ_i for i in index set I and are given the constraints $\tau_i = T_i$, for closed type expressions T_i, which we close under reflexivity, symmetry, transitivity and substitution. We give a necessary and sufficient syntactic condition on the collection of type constraints for strong normalizability of the resulting terms. Thus we see, for example, that the constraints

$$\begin{aligned} \tau_0 &= \tau_1 \to \tau_0 \\ \tau_1 &= \tau_0 \to \tau_1 \end{aligned}$$

yield only strongly normalizable typed terms, but

$$\begin{aligned} \tau_0 &= \tau_1 \to \tau_0 \\ \tau_1 &= \tau_2 \to \tau_1 \\ \tau_2 &= \tau_0 \to \tau_2 \end{aligned}$$

will allow a diverging term to be typed.

Proofs omitted in this paper can be found in [10].

2 Recursive types

The goal of this section is to prove the strong normalizability of typed terms in a second order lambda calculus equipped with recursive types. First, the types, terms and reductions of this calculus are defined. Then the rest of the section consists of the proof of strong normalization, which we now outline.

1. Let $\top$ be the set of strongly normalizable untyped terms. A collection of sets of untyped terms, Ξ, is defined, so that $\xi \in \Xi \Rightarrow \xi \subseteq \top$.

2. In proposition 2, operations on Ξ corresponding to the type constuctors $\to, \Delta, \mu$ and ν are defined.

[0] This research supported in part by the National Science Foundation under grant MCS-81-04018.

3. These operations are employed to extend an environment ρ, a function from type variables to Ξ, to $[\![\cdot]\!]\rho$, a function from types to Ξ, by structural induction on types.

4. We define the untyped terms $\hat{a}$ that are instances of a typed term a, with respect to a given environment, and note that the untyped term corresponding to a is an instance of a. Truth for judgements is defined as:

$$\models a : A \quad \equiv \quad \forall \rho.\ \forall \text{ instances } \hat{a}.\ \hat{a} \in [\![A]\!]\rho$$

5. In proposition 7, by an induction on the derivation of judgements, all judgements are shown to be true.

6. In lemma 8, we note that a typed term is strongly normalizable, if the corresponding untyped term is strong normalizable. Now our conclusion, theorem 9, follows easily: by 5, if $\vdash a : A$, then $\models a : A$; and by 4, this implies $\hat{a} \in [\![A]\!]\rho$, where we take $\hat{a}$ to be the untyped term corresponding to a. By 1 and 3 this implies that $\hat{a} \in \top$. Thus all typed terms are strongly normalizable.

2.1 Types, terms and reductions

Assume a denumerably infinite list of type variables $V_1, V_2, V_3, \ldots$, and let X, Y and Z range over them. Define the types as follows.

- X is a type.
- If A and B are types, then so are $A \rightarrow B$ and $\Delta X.A$
- If X occurs positively in type A, then $\mu X.A$ and $\nu X.A$ are types.

Where "X occurs positively in A," $Pos(A, X)$, iff each free occurrence of X in A is on the lefthand side of an even number of $\rightarrow$'s; similarly $Neg(A, X)$ iff each free occurrence is on the lefthand side of an odd number of $\rightarrow$'s. As one would expect (hope?), in the standard encodings [12]:

$$\begin{aligned} A \times B &\equiv \Delta Z.(A \rightarrow B \rightarrow Z) \rightarrow Z \\ A + B &\equiv \Delta Z.(A \rightarrow Z) \rightarrow (B \rightarrow Z) \rightarrow Z \\ \Sigma Y.A &\equiv \Delta Z.(\Delta Y.A \rightarrow Z) \rightarrow Z \end{aligned}$$

X occurs positively in them iff X occurs positively in A and B.

Define the untyped terms to be the set of untyped lambda terms with possible occurrences of the constants R, in, Ω and out. Let a and b range over untyped terms. Untyped terms of the following syntactic forms are called *critical*[1] and we let t range over them.

$$\lambda x.a \quad R\,a \quad R \quad in\,a \quad in \quad \Omega\,a\,b \quad \Omega\,a \quad \Omega \quad out$$

Typed terms are defined in figure 1. Let a and b range over typed terms, also, letting the context determine which is meant. As usual, we identify types or terms which are alphabetic variants in their bound variables.

Figure 1: *Definition of typed terms*
For each type $\mu \equiv \mu X.A$, there are constants:

$$\vdash in^{\mu} : A[\mu/X] \rightarrow \mu$$
$$\vdash R^{\mu} : \Delta Y.\ (\Delta X.(X \rightarrow \mu) \rightarrow (X \rightarrow Y) \rightarrow A \rightarrow Y) \rightarrow \mu \rightarrow Y$$

and for each type $\nu \equiv \nu X.A$, there are constants:

$$\vdash out^{\nu} : \nu \rightarrow A[\nu/X]$$
$$\vdash \Omega^{\nu} : \Delta Y.\ (\Delta X.(\nu \rightarrow X) \rightarrow (Y \rightarrow X) \rightarrow Y \rightarrow A) \rightarrow Y \rightarrow \nu$$

where Y does not occur free in A and is distinct from X. Complete the definition with the following.

$$\vdash x^A : A$$

$$\frac{\vdash b : B}{\vdash \lambda x^A.b : A \rightarrow B} \qquad \frac{\vdash b : B}{\vdash \Lambda X.b : \Delta X.B}\ *$$

$$\frac{\vdash c : A \rightarrow B \quad \vdash a : A}{\vdash c\,a : B} \qquad \frac{\vdash b : \Delta X.B}{\vdash b\,A : B[A/X]}$$

$*$ *X is not free in A for any x^A free in b.*

The reductions for typed terms are:

1. $(\lambda x^A.a)\,b \longmapsto a[b/x^A]$
2. $\lambda x^A.a\,x^A \longmapsto a$
3. $(\Lambda X.a)\,B \longmapsto a[B/X]$
4. $\Lambda X.a\,X \longmapsto a$
5. $R^{\mu} B\, a\, (in^{\mu} b) \longmapsto a\,\mu(\lambda x^{\mu}.x^{\mu})(R^{\mu} B\, a)\, b$
6. $out^{\nu}(\Omega^{\nu} B\, a\, b) \longmapsto a\,\nu(\lambda x^{\nu}.x^{\nu})(\Omega^{\nu} B\, a)\, b$

Reduction 2 requires x to not occur free in a, and reduction 4 requires X to not occur free in a. Untyped terms have the analogous reductions (3 and 4 being

[1]Critical terms will be used to generalize the standard definition of ground sets in the presence of additional reductions.

inapplicable). Define $a > b$ to mean a reduces to b in one step, $a >^* b$ to mean a reduces to b, and let $\top$ be the set of strongly normalizable untyped terms. Reduction is Church-Rosser [13].

2.2 Strong normalization

Define the following predicates for $\xi \subseteq \top$, and the collection of the so-called ground sets, Ξ:

$$\begin{aligned} G_1(\xi) &\equiv \forall a, b.\, (a \in \xi \wedge a >^* b) \Rightarrow b \in \xi \\ G_2(\xi) &\equiv \forall a \in \top.\, (\forall t.\, a >^* t \Rightarrow t \in \xi) \Rightarrow a \in \xi \\ \Xi &\equiv \{\xi \subseteq \top \mid G_1(\xi) \wedge G_2(\xi)\} \end{aligned}$$

Proposition 1 *Ξ is a complete lattice under $\subseteq$, with $\bot = \{c \in \top \mid \neg\exists t.\ c >^* t\}$, and the lub's and glb's of chains being their union and intersection, respectively.*

Let $\Xi \overset{\text{mon}}{\to} \Xi$ be the monotonic functions in $\Xi \to \Xi$. Give these function spaces the usual pointwise orderings.

Proposition 2 *The operations given in figure 2 are well-defined. Moreover, $\to$ is anti-monotonic in its first and monotonic in its second argument, and $\boldsymbol{\Delta}$, $\boldsymbol{\mu}$ and $\boldsymbol{\nu}$ are all monotonic.*

Define *environments* to be mappings ρ, from type variables to Ξ. If $\xi \in \Xi$, then let $\rho[\xi/X]$ be the environment where

$$\rho[\xi/X](Y) \equiv \begin{cases} \xi & \text{If } X \text{ is } Y \\ \rho(Y) & \text{otherwise} \end{cases}$$

For a given environment ρ, we extend it to a mapping $[\![\cdot]\!]\rho$, from types to Ξ, by structural induction:

$$\begin{aligned} [\![X]\!]\rho &\equiv \rho(X) \\ [\![A \to B]\!]\rho &\equiv [\![A]\!]\rho \to [\![B]\!]\rho \\ [\![\Delta X.A]\!]\rho &\equiv \boldsymbol{\Delta}(\lambda\xi.[\![A]\!]\rho[\xi/X]) \\ [\![\mu X.A]\!]\rho &\equiv \boldsymbol{\mu}(\lambda\xi.[\![A]\!]\rho[\xi/X]) \\ [\![\nu X.A]\!]\rho &\equiv \boldsymbol{\nu}(\lambda\xi.[\![A]\!]\rho[\xi/X]) \end{aligned}$$

The following proposition verifies this definition.

Proposition 3 *For all types A, and environments ρ*

1. *If Y does not occur free in A, $[\![A]\!]\rho = [\![A[Y/X]]\!]\rho[\rho(X)/Y]$.*
2. *If distinct $Y_1, Y_2, \ldots$ do not occur free in A, then $[\![A]\!]\rho = [\![A]\!]\rho[\xi_1, \xi_2, \ldots / Y_1, Y_2, \ldots]$, for $\xi_1, \xi_2, \ldots \in \Xi$.*
3. *$[\![A]\!]\rho \in \Xi$.*
4. *$\lambda\xi.[\![A]\!]\rho[\xi/X]$ is a monotonic operation on Ξ, if $Pos(A, X)$.*
5. *$\lambda\xi.[\![A]\!]\rho[\xi/X]$ is an anti-monotonic operation on Ξ, if $Neg(A, X)$.*

Note that $\lambda\xi.[\![A]\!]\rho[\xi/X]$ may be monotonic without being continuous: consider $\lambda\xi.[\![\mathbf{1}+X+\boldsymbol{N} \to X]\!]\rho[\xi/X]$, where $\boldsymbol{N} \equiv \mu Y.\mathbf{1}+Y$ and $\mathbf{1} \equiv \Delta Z.Z \to Z$.

We now define a notion of truth for judgements. Fix environment ρ; an untyped term $\hat{a}$ is an *instance* of typed term a, with respect to ρ, if

$$\hat{a} = a[b_1, \ldots, b_n / x_1^{B_1}, \ldots, x_n^{B_n}]$$

with $n \geq 0$, and $b_i \in [\![B_i]\!]\rho$, for $1 \leq i \leq n$. Define *truth*, for judgements, by:

$$\models a : A \quad \equiv \quad \forall\rho.\ \forall\hat{a}.\ \hat{a} \in [\![A]\!]\rho$$

Here are two standard technical lemmas and a corollary we will need in proposition 7.

Lemma 4 *For $\xi \in \Xi$, $a[b/x] \in \xi$ and $b \in \top$ imply $(\lambda x.a)b \in \xi$.*

Lemma 5 *For types A, B and environment ρ, $[\![A[B/X]]\!]\rho = [\![A]\!]\rho[[\![B]\!]\rho/X]$.*

Corollary 6 *For $\mu \equiv \mu X.A$ and $\nu \equiv \nu X.A$,*

$$\begin{aligned} [\![\mu]\!]\rho &= \{c \in \top \mid \forall a.\ c >^* in\, a \Rightarrow a \in [\![A[\mu/X]]\!]\rho\} \\ [\![\nu]\!]\rho &= \{c \in \top \mid out\, c \in [\![A[\nu/X]]\!]\rho\} \end{aligned}$$

Now we show soundness.

Proposition 7 $\vdash a : A \ \Rightarrow\ \models a : A$

Proof.

Proof by induction on the derivation of judgements. We consider each axiom and rule in turn. Here we show the justifications for the constants; the other clauses are proven as in the standard proof.

$$\models in^{\mu} : A[\mu/X] \to \mu$$

Fix $\mu \equiv \mu X.A$, ρ and $a \in [\![A[\mu/X]]\!]\rho$. It suffices to show $in\, a \in [\![\mu]\!]\rho$. Since $a \in \top$, $in\, a \in \top$. If $in\, a >^* in\, a'$ then $a >^* a'$, and $a' \in [\![A[\mu/X]]\!]\rho$ by G_1, hence $in\, a \in [\![\mu]\!]\rho$, by corollary 6. Conclude $\models in^{\mu} : A[\mu/X] \to \mu$.

$$\models R^{\mu} : \Delta Y.\ (\Delta X.(X \to \mu) \to (X \to Y) \to A \to Y) \to \mu \to Y$$

Fix $\mu \equiv \mu X.A$, ρ, $\xi \in \Xi$ and let $\rho_1 \equiv \rho[\xi/Y]$. We can think of the least fixed point construction as building the transfinite chain:

$$\begin{aligned} \xi_0 &\equiv \bot \\ \xi_{\alpha+1} &\equiv \{c \in \top \mid \ \forall a.\ c >^* in\, a \Rightarrow \\ &\qquad a \in [\![A]\!]\rho_1[\xi_\alpha/X]\} \\ \xi_\lambda &\equiv \textstyle\bigcup_{\alpha<\lambda} \xi_\alpha, \quad \text{for limit } \lambda \end{aligned}$$

Figure 2: *Operations on* Ξ

$$\begin{aligned} \rightarrow &\in \Xi \times \Xi \rightarrow \Xi, & \xi_1 \rightarrow \xi_2 &\equiv \{c \in \top \mid \forall a.\ a \in \xi_1 \Rightarrow c\,a \in \xi_2\} \\ \boldsymbol{\Delta} &\in (\Xi \rightarrow \Xi) \rightarrow \Xi, & \boldsymbol{\Delta}(f) &\equiv \bigcap\{f(\xi) \mid \xi \in \Xi\} \\ \boldsymbol{\mu} &\in (\Xi \overset{\text{mon}}{\rightarrow} \Xi) \rightarrow \Xi, & \boldsymbol{\mu}(f) &\equiv \text{lfp of } \lambda\xi.\{c \in \top \mid \forall a.\ c >^* in\, a \Rightarrow a \in f(\xi)\} \\ \boldsymbol{\nu} &\in (\Xi \overset{\text{mon}}{\rightarrow} \Xi) \rightarrow \Xi, & \boldsymbol{\nu}(f) &\equiv \text{gfp of } \lambda\xi.\{c \in \top \mid out\, c \in f(\xi)\} \end{aligned}$$

whose limit is $[\![\mu]\!]\rho_1$. Fix $a \in [\![\Delta X.(X \rightarrow \mu) \rightarrow (X \rightarrow Y) \rightarrow A \rightarrow Y]\!]\rho_1$. It suffices to prove:

$$\forall b \in [\![\mu]\!]\rho_1.\ R\,a\,b \in \xi$$

which we will do by induction on this chain.

Base case: $b \in \xi_0$. Since b and a are in $\top$, and since b cannot reduce to a term of the form $in\,b'$, $R\,a\,b \in \bot$, so $R\,a\,b \in \xi$ by $G_2(\xi)$.

Inductive case: $b \in \xi_{\alpha+1}$. If b cannot reduce to a term of the form $in\,b'$, the argument is as above. Otherwise, let $\rho_2 \equiv \rho_1[\xi_\alpha/X]$. Note $[\![\mu]\!]\rho = [\![\mu]\!]\rho_1 = [\![\mu]\!]\rho_2$ by proposition 3. $R\,a\,b \in \top$: an infinite reduction of it must begin:

$$R\,a\,b >^* R\,a'\,(in\,b') > a'(\lambda x.x)(R\,a')b' > \cdots \quad (1)$$

where $a >^* a'$ and $b >^* in\,b'$. Since $b \in \xi_{\alpha+1}$, $b' \in [\![A]\!]\rho_2$. But *(i)* a is in $[\![(X \rightarrow \mu) \rightarrow (X \rightarrow Y) \rightarrow A \rightarrow Y]\!]\rho_2$ by the definition of $\boldsymbol{\Delta}$, and so is a', by G_1; *(ii)* since $\xi_\alpha \subseteq [\![\mu]\!]\rho_2$, $\lambda x.x \in [\![X \rightarrow \mu]\!]\rho_2$ by lemma 4; *(iii)* $R\,a$ is in $[\![X \rightarrow Y]\!]\rho_2$, by induction, and so is $R\,a'$, by G_1; and by these facts, $a'(\lambda x.x)(R\,a')b' \in \xi$, so (1) is finite and $R\,a\,b \in \top$. Now suppose $R\,a\,b >^* t$. The reduction sequence must look like (1), so there is a $a'(\lambda x.x)(R\,a')(in\,b') \in \xi$ that reduces to t. Thus $t \in \xi$ by $G_1(\xi)$, and therefore $R\,a\,b \in \xi$ by $G_2(\xi)$. Conclude $\models R^\mu : \Delta Y.(\Delta X.(X \rightarrow \mu) \rightarrow (X \rightarrow Y) \rightarrow A \rightarrow Y) \rightarrow \mu \rightarrow Y$.

(We can note here that an induction combinator over simultaneously defined recursive types, where each defining type expression is positive in all the type variables being bound, will be valid by this same argument.)

$$\models out^\nu : \nu \rightarrow A[\nu/X]$$

Fix $\nu \equiv \nu X.A$, ρ and $c \in [\![\nu]\!]\rho$. It suffices to show $out\,c \in [\![A[\nu/X]]\!]\rho$, but that is immediate from lemma 6. Conclude $\models out^\nu : \nu \rightarrow A[\nu/X]$.

$$\models \Omega^\nu : \Delta Y.\ (\Delta X.(\nu \rightarrow X) \rightarrow (Y \rightarrow X) \rightarrow Y \rightarrow A) \rightarrow Y \rightarrow \nu$$

Fix $\nu \equiv \nu X.A$, ρ, $\xi \in \Xi$, $a \in [\![(\Delta X.(\nu \rightarrow X) \rightarrow (Y \rightarrow X) \rightarrow Y \rightarrow A)]\!]\rho[\xi/Y]$, and $b \in \xi$. It suffices to show

$$\Omega\,a\,b \in [\![\nu]\!]\rho[\xi/Y]$$

which is shown by induction on the descending chain with limit $[\![\nu]\!]\rho[\xi/Y]$, in a similar argument to the proof for R.
Qed.

Lemma 8 *A typed term is strongly normalizable if the corresponding untyped term is strongly normalizable.*

Now, this section's result follows easily:

Theorem 9 *All typed terms are strongly normalizable.*

3 Type constraints

The goal of this section is to give a syntactic condition **P** on type constraints which holds exactly when the resulting typed terms are strongly normalizable. The section is organized as follows. First, types, terms and reduction are defined. Second, we state condition **P** for the type constraints, and show how its violation leads to the typing of diverging terms. Third, we give an equivalent formulation of **P** which identifies equivalence classes $[i]$ on I and a total ordering $\prec$ of these classes. We wish to repeat the previous proof, using $\prec$ in defining a variation, $[\![\cdot]\!]'$, of $[\![\cdot]\!]$, but two complications appear: $\prec$ may not be well-founded, so we cannot induct on it; and in defining certain $[\![\tau_i]\!]'$ simultaneously, we have to find fixed points of sets of functions which may not be monotonic, with respect to the $\subseteq$-ordering on Ξ. Fortunately, each complication can be overcome in turn and we outline the proof of strong normalization as follows.

1. Let the definitions of $\top$, Ξ, $\rightarrow$, $\boldsymbol{\Delta}$, $\boldsymbol{\mu}$ and $\boldsymbol{\nu}$ stand as in section 2.

2. Fix a derivation of $\vdash' a^* : A^*$ and let I' be the union of classes $[i]$ for which τ_i appears in this derivation. Define level ordinals for type expressions with respect to I'.

3. Environments ρ are extended to mappings $[\![\cdot]\!]'\rho$ from types to Ξ by level induction.

4. Define instances $\hat{a}$ as before and truth by:

$$\models' a : A \quad \equiv \quad \forall \rho. \forall \hat{a}.\ \hat{a} \in [\![A]\!]'\rho$$
$$\models' A = B \quad \equiv \quad \forall \rho.\ [\![A]\!]'\rho = [\![B]\!]'\rho$$

5. We can not expect soundness to hold, since we have made no effort to ensure $\models' \tau_i = T_i$ for $i \notin I'$. However, by proposition 12, the other axioms and rules are sound so we may conclude $\models' a^\star : A^\star$.

6. As in the first section, from 5 we can argue that $a^\star$ is strongly normalizable. Since $a^\star$ was arbitrary we can immediately generalize to conclude all typed terms are strongly normalizable (under the assumption **P**).

3.1 Types, terms and reductions

We define types as in the previous section, with the addition of atomic types τ_i for i in some infinite index set I. For notational simplicity, assume the type variables V_i are indexed by I. We are then given closed type expressions T_i for $i \in I$ and define judgements by figure 3. Note we have extended the typing rules given in figure 1 by adding six more rules to define and use equality judgements. The reduction rules are as before.

3.2 A condition on the constraints

The required condition **P** is that τ_i occurs positively in all types C that are equal to τ_i, that is:

$$\mathbf{P} \qquad \forall C, \tau_i.\ (\vdash' C = \tau_i) \Rightarrow Pos(C, \tau_i)$$

If **P** is violated, C can be used in typing a diverging term. We illustrate now by assuming that $\vdash' \tau = C$ for some C built using only $\rightarrow$, where τ occurs non-positively in C. Then C is C_{2k+1}, which is in the following form:

$$\begin{aligned} C_{2k+1} &\equiv A^1_{2k+1} \rightarrow \cdots \rightarrow A^{n_{2k+1}}_{2k+1} \rightarrow (C_{2k}) \rightarrow B_{2k+1} \\ &\vdots \\ C_1 &\equiv A^1_1 \rightarrow \cdots \rightarrow A^{n_1}_1 \rightarrow (C_0) \rightarrow B_1 \\ C_0 &\equiv A^1_0 \rightarrow \cdots \rightarrow A^{n_0}_0 \rightarrow \tau \end{aligned}$$

Some abbreviations are called for:

$$\begin{aligned} \lambda \vec{x}_i.a &\equiv \lambda x^1_i. \cdots \lambda x^{n_i}_i.a \\ t\,\vec{a}_i &\equiv t\,a^1_i \cdots a^{n_i}_i \end{aligned}$$

Assume in the following that a^j_i and x^j_i are variables of type A^j_i, y_i is a variable of type C_i and f^j_i is a

Figure 3: *Definition of typed terms with constraints For each type $\mu \equiv \mu X.A$, there are constants:*

$$\vdash' in^\mu : A[\mu/X] \rightarrow \mu$$
$$\vdash' R^\mu : \Delta Y.\ (\Delta X.(X \rightarrow \mu) \rightarrow (X \rightarrow Y) \rightarrow A \rightarrow Y) \rightarrow \mu \rightarrow Y$$

and for each type $\nu \equiv \nu X.A$, there are constants:

$$\vdash' out^\nu : \nu \rightarrow A[\nu/X]$$
$$\vdash' \Omega^\nu : \Delta Y.\ (\Delta X.(\nu \rightarrow X) \rightarrow (Y \rightarrow X) \rightarrow Y \rightarrow A) \rightarrow Y \rightarrow \nu$$

where Y does not occur free in A and is distinct from X. Complete the definition with the following.

$$\vdash' x^A : A$$

$$\frac{\vdash' b : B}{\vdash' \lambda x^A.b : A \rightarrow B} \qquad \frac{\vdash' b : B}{\vdash' \Lambda X.b : \Delta X.B}\ *$$

$$\frac{\vdash' c : A \rightarrow B \quad \vdash' a : A}{\vdash' c\,a : B} \qquad \frac{\vdash' b : \Delta X.B}{\vdash' b\,A : B[A/X]}$$

$$\frac{}{\vdash' \tau_i = T_i}\ i \in I \qquad \vdash' A = A$$

$$\frac{\vdash' A = B}{\vdash' B = A} \qquad \frac{\vdash' A = B \quad \vdash' B = C}{\vdash' A = C}$$

$$\frac{\vdash' A = B}{\vdash' C = C'}\ \dagger \qquad \frac{\vdash' a : A \quad \vdash' A = B}{\vdash' a : B}$$

$*$ *X is not free in A for any x^A free in b.*
$\dagger$ *C' is C with some occurences of A replaced by B.*

variable of type $B_j \rightarrow B_i$. For the case $k = 0$ we define the terms c_i of type C_i as follows:

$$\begin{array}{rcl} c_1 & \equiv & \lambda\vec{x}_1.\lambda y_0.f_1^1(y_0\,\vec{a}_0\,\vec{a}_1\,y_0) \\ c_0 & \equiv & \lambda\vec{x}_0.c_1 \end{array}$$

Now we reduce $c_1\,\vec{a}_1\,c_0$:

$$>^* \quad f_1^1(c_0\,\vec{a}_0\,\vec{a}_1\,c_0) \quad >^* \quad f_1^1(c_1\,\vec{a}_1\,c_0)$$

And we conclude this term is not normalizable. For the case $k > 0$ we define the terms c_i of type C_i as follows:

$$\begin{array}{rcl} c_1 & \equiv & \lambda\vec{x}_1.\lambda y_0.f_1^{2k+1}(y_0\,\vec{a}_0\,\vec{a}_{2k+1}\,y_{2k}) \\ c_3 & \equiv & \lambda\vec{x}_3.\lambda y_2.f_3^2(y_2\,\vec{a}_2\,c_1) \\ & \vdots & \\ c_{2k+1} & \equiv & \lambda\vec{x}_{2k+1}.\lambda y_{2k}.f_{2k+1}^{2k}(y_{2k}\,\vec{a}_{2k}\,c_{2k-1}) \\ & & \\ c_0 & \equiv & \lambda\vec{x}_0.c_{2k+1} \\ c_2 & \equiv & \lambda\vec{x}_2.\lambda y_1.f_2^1(y_1\,\vec{a}_1\,c_0) \\ & \vdots & \\ c_{2k} & \equiv & \lambda\vec{x}_{2k}.\lambda y_{2k-1}.f_{2k}^{2k-1}(y_{2k-1}\,\vec{a}_{2k-1}\,c_{2k-2}) \end{array}$$

Now we reduce $c_{2k+1}\,\vec{a}_{2k+1}\,c_{2k}$:

$$\begin{array}{l} >^* f_{2k+1}^{2k}(c_{2k}\,\vec{a}_{2k}\,c_{2k-1}[c_{2k}/y_{2k}]) \\ >^* \cdots(c_{2k-1}[c_{2k}/y_{2k}]\,\vec{a}_{2k-1}c_{2k-2})\cdots \\ \vdots \\ >^* \cdots(c_2\,\vec{a}_2\,c_1[c_{2k}/y_{2k}])\cdots \\ >^* \cdots(c_1[c_{2k}/y_{2k}]\,\vec{a}_1\,c_0)\cdots \\ >^* \cdots(c_0\,\vec{a}_0\,\vec{a}_{2k+1}\,c_{2k})\cdots \\ >^* \cdots(c_{2k+1}\vec{a}_{2k+1}\,c_{2k})\cdots \end{array}$$

And we conclude this term is not normalizable.

The following states a more useful formulation of **P**, that we will use in the next subsection.

Theorem 10 *Condition* **P** *is equivalent to the existence of an equivalence relation on I, whose classes $[i]$ are ordered by a relation $\prec$ such that if τ_i appears in T_j then $[i] = [j]$ or $[i] \prec [j]$. Furthermore, each class $[i]$ is divided in two parts, $[i]^+$ and $[i]^-$, and $j \in [i]^+ \Rightarrow Pos(T_i, \tau_j)$ and $j \in [i]^- \Rightarrow Neg(T_i, \tau_j)$.*

3.3 Strong normalization

In this subsection we assume **P** holds and from that argue that all typed terms are strong normalizable. Let the definitions of Ξ, $\rightarrow$, $\boldsymbol{\Delta}$, $\boldsymbol{\mu}$, and $\boldsymbol{\nu}$ stand as in 2.2. We would like to again extend the environment ρ to a mapping $[\![\cdot]\!]'\rho$ from types to Ξ, but we cannot simply do structural induction on types, because of atomic types τ_i. Order $\prec$ of theorem 10 should be involved in the induction, but it is not necessarily well-founded. The solution is to fix a derivation of $\vdash a^\star : A^\star$, and only be concerned with atomic types that occur there. Once we have concluded $a^\star$ is strongly normalizable, we can generalize immediately to prove the final result.

So, fix a derivation of $\vdash' a^\star : A^\star$. Let I' be the union of classes $[i]$ for which τ_i appears in this derivation. For $i \in I'$, let its rank, $\#i$, be 1 plus the finite number of distinct classes $[j] \subseteq I'$ for which $[j] \prec [i]$. Now we can define a level ordinal for each type expression:

$$\begin{array}{rcll} \mathcal{L}(X) & \equiv & 0 & \\ \mathcal{L}(\tau_i) & \equiv & 0 & i \notin I' \\ \mathcal{L}(B \rightarrow C) & \equiv & sup(\mathcal{L}(B), \mathcal{L}(C))+1 & \\ \mathcal{L}(\sigma X.B) & \equiv & \mathcal{L}(B)+1 & \sigma \in \{\Delta, \mu, \nu\} \\ \mathcal{L}(\tau_i) & \equiv & \omega * (\#i) & i \in I' \end{array}$$

We wish to extend an environment ρ by level induction to a mapping $[\![\cdot]\!]'\rho$, but here we encounter the second complication: at level $\omega * (\#i)$ we want to find a fixed point of operation $f \in \Xi^{[i]} \rightarrow \Xi^{[i]}$, where:

$$f(\langle \xi_j \rangle_{j\in[i]}) \equiv \langle [\![T_k[V_j/\tau_j]_{j\in[i]}]\!]'\rho[\xi_j/V_j]_{j\in[i]} \rangle_{k\in[i]} \quad (2)$$

This is not monotonic, if we order $\Xi^{[i]}$ by the usual product ordering:

$$\langle \xi_j \rangle_{j\in[i]} \sqsubseteq \langle \xi'_j \rangle_{j\in[i]} \Leftrightarrow \forall j \in [i].\xi_j \subseteq \xi'_j$$

but f *is* monotonic if we choose the ordering

$$\begin{array}{rcl} \langle \xi_j \rangle_{j\in[i]} \sqsubseteq \langle \xi'_j \rangle_{j\in[i]} & \Leftrightarrow & \forall j \in [i]^+.\xi_j \subseteq \xi'_j \\ & & \wedge \forall j \in [i]^-.\xi_j \supseteq \xi'_j. \end{array}$$

which means that taking the least fixed point of f will yield the least solutions of ξ_j for $j \in [i]^+$ and the greatest solutions for $j \in [i]^-$, but, as it will turn out, *any* fixed point will suffice. Now, we can finally define $[\![\cdot]\!]'\rho$ by level induction:

$$\begin{array}{rcl} [\![\tau_i]\!]'\rho & = & \bot, \quad \text{for } i \notin I' \\ [\![X]\!]'\rho & = & \rho(X) \\ [\![A \rightarrow B]\!]'\rho & = & [\![A]\!]'\rho \rightarrow [\![B]\!]'\rho \\ [\![\Delta X.A]\!]'\rho & = & \boldsymbol{\Delta}(\lambda\xi.[\![A]\!]'\rho[\xi/X]) \\ [\![\mu X.A]\!]'\rho & = & \boldsymbol{\mu}(\lambda\xi.[\![A]\!]'\rho[\xi/X]) \\ [\![\nu X.A]\!]'\rho & = & \boldsymbol{\nu}(\lambda\xi.[\![A]\!]'\rho[\xi/X]) \end{array}$$

And at level $\omega * (\#i)$, let $\langle [\![\tau_j]\!]'\rho \rangle_{j\in[i]}$ be the least fixed point of f, as defined in (2). Reinterpreting proposition 3, lemma 5 and corollary 6 in the context of this section, we see they hold by the same arguments. We may draw another corollary from lemma 5:

Corollary 11 *If $i \in I'$, then $\forall\rho.\ [\![\tau_i]\!]'\rho = [\![T_i]\!]'\rho$.*

We define *instance* as before and define truth by:

$$\models' a : A \quad \Leftrightarrow \quad \forall \rho . \forall \hat{a}.\ \hat{a} \in [\![A]\!]'\rho$$
$$\models' A = B \quad \Leftrightarrow \quad \forall \rho.\ [\![A]\!]'\rho = [\![B]\!]'\rho$$

Proposition 12 *Except for $\vdash' \tau_i = T_i$ when $i \notin I'$, all the axioms and rules given in figure 3 are sound.*

Now, by induction on the fixed proof of $\vdash' a^\star : A^\star$, we find $\models' a^\star : A^\star$, and as before, from this we can conclude $a^\star$ is strongly normalizable. Since $a^\star$ was arbitrary we have shown:

Theorem 13 *All typed terms are strongly normalizable (under the assumption* **P***).*

Conclusions

We have shown how to add recursive types to second-order lambda calculus while preserving the strong normalizability of terms, and to determine when a collection of type constraints admits the typing of only strongly normalizable terms. In both cases a similar method of proof, based on Girard's method, was used to solve the given problem.

In the case of the μ types of the first half of the paper, one may opt to dispense with $in^{\mu X.A}$ and have $\mu X.A$ and $A[\mu X.A/X]$ be equal - rather than just isomorphic - types. But then strong normalizibility is lost, since the induction combinator for $\mu X.X$ will essentially be taking a fixed point of an indentity function. What still holds is the head reducibility of closed typed terms to outermost normal form (by a slight variation on the proof given here). This is exactly the normalization property of the Nuprl logic and this property is enough to show the intuitionistic consistency of the extension of the Nuprl logic by recursive types, which is why this option is a natural choice there.

Acknowledgements

We would like to thank Robert Constable, Albert Meyer, John Mitchell and Prakash Panangaden for helpful discussions.

References

[1] R. Amadio, K.B. Bruce, and G. Longo. The finitary projection model for second order lambda calculus and solutions to higher order domain equations. In *Symposium on Logic in Computer Science*, IEEE Computer Society, 1986.

[2] V. Breazu-Tannan and A. R. Meyer. Lambda calculus with constrained types. In R. Parikh, editor, *LNCS #193: Logics of Programs*, pages 23–40, Springer-Verlag, 1985.

[3] K.B. Bruce and A.R. Meyer. The semantics of second order polymorphic lambda-calculus. In *Symposium on Semantics of Data Types, LNCS 173*, Springer-Verlag, 1984.

[4] R.L. Constable and N.P. Mendler. Recursive definitions in type theory. In Rohit Parikh, editor, *Logics of Programs, LNCS 193*, Springer-Verlag, 1985.

[5] Constable, R.L. et al. *Implementing Mathematics with the Nuprl Proof Developement System.* Prentice Hall, 1986.

[6] M. Coppo and M. Zacchi. Type inference and logical relations. In *Symposium on Logic in Computer Science*, IEEE Computer Society, 1986.

[7] S. Fortune, D. Leivant, and M. O'Donnell. The expressiveness of simple and second-order type structures. *Journal of the Association for Computing Machinery*, 30(1):151–185, January 1983.

[8] J.-Y. Girard. *Interprétation fonctionelle et elimination des coupures dans l'arithmetique d'order superieur.* PhD thesis, Paris, 1972.

[9] J.-Y. Girard. Une extension de l'interprétation de Gödel à l'analyse, et son application à l'élimination des coupures dans l'analyse et la théorie des types. In J. E. Fenstad, editor, *Proceedings of the Second Scandinavian Logic Symposium*, pages 63–92, North-Holland, 1971.

[10] N.P. Mendler. *Recursive Definition in Type Theory.* PhD thesis, Cornell, 1987. In preparation.

[11] N.P. Mendler, P. Panangaden, and R.L. Constable. Infinite objects in type theory. In *Symposium on Logic in Computer Science*, IEEE Computer Society, 1986.

[12] D. Prawitz. *Natural Deduction.* Almqvist and Wiksell, Stockholm, 1965.

[13] S. Stenlund. *Combinators, λ-terms and Proof Theory.* D. Reidel, Dordrecht, 1972.

Complete Type Inference for Simple Objects

Mitchell Wand

College of Computer Science
Northeastern University
360 Huntington Avenue, 161CN
Boston, MA 02115, USA

Abstract

We consider the problem of strong typing for a model of object-oriented programming systems. These systems permit values which are records of other values, and in which fields inside these records are retrieved by name. We propose a type system which allows us to classify these kinds of values and to classify programs by the type of their result, as is usual in strongly-typed programming languages. Our type system has two important properties: it admits multiple inheritance, and it has a syntactically complete type inference system.

1. Introduction

An important characteristic of object-oriented systems is *inheritance*, in which a type t_1 is said to *inherit* from type t_0 if it is an extension of t_0, that is, if it has all the fields of t_0, plus perhaps some others. Any function that takes an argument of type t_0 should be able to take an argument of type t_1 as well.

We think of objects as records with named fields. This gives a *structural* treatment of inheritance: a function which expects a record with certain fields should be applicable to *any* record containing those fields. For example, consider the following pseudocode.

```
type movable-object = [mass: real, position: point,
                       velocity: real];
     car = [id-number: string, mass: real,
            position: point, velocity: real];
     submarine = [id-number: integer,
                  available-missiles: integer,
                  owner: country,  captain: person,
                  mass: real,
                  position: point, velocity: real];
     weapons-system = [id-number: integer,
                       available-missiles: integer,
                       position: point];

function momentum (x) = x.mass*x.velocity;
```

This Material is based on work supported by the National Science Foundation under grant numbers MCS 8303325, MCS 8304567, and DCR 8605218.

The function `momentum` should be applicable to both cars and submarines. We can think of cars and submarines as inheriting from movable objects. This model also permits multiple inheritance: a submarine is both a movable object and a weapons system, because any function applicable to a weapons system will be applicable to a submarine.

Cardelli [Cardelli 84] has proposed a type system (which we call C84) that accounts for inheritance of this sort. He proved the soundness of a semantics for this system. Unfortunately, C84 sacrifices a useful property of the simply-typed lambda-calculus (as exemplified by the ML system [Gordon *et al.* 78]): the solvability of the type *inference* problem. That is, we would like to write our programs without having to include any type information, and then let the compiling system infer the types of all the bound variables.

In this paper, we present a variant of the simply-typed lambda calculus which handles simple objects, that is, records with named fields. Following Cardelli, it also handles variants with named alternatives. Our version includes some minor variations on C84, which allow parameterized type inheritance and which permit a more obvious semantics.

We then give a complete type inference algorithm for this system. That is, we show that it is decidable whether a term has a type in our system, and we furthermore generate the principal type of a term. The method for proving the completeness of the type inference algorithm may be generalized to other type inference problems.

We close with some remarks about the differences between our system and Cardelli's, and on the applicability of this type-checking scheme to practical object-oriented programming systems.

2. The Type System

Records with named fields are a generalization of pairs. The generalization of the simply typed lambda-calculus to pairs and binary unions is easy, and is shown in Figure 1. For product types, we have a pair operator and two projection operators. For union types, we have two injection operators (which conceptually "add a tag bit") and a selection operator. The selection operator takes an element of $\tau_1+\tau_2$ and two functions, one of type $\tau_1 \to \tau_3$ and one of type $\tau_2 \to \tau_3$. It examines the first argument, strips off the "tag bit", and applies one or the other function to the underlying datum. This can be expressed by the axioms

$$\mathbf{case}(\mathbf{inL}\, x)fg = fx$$
$$\mathbf{case}(\mathbf{inR}\, y)fg = gy$$

$$\langle\text{type}\rangle ::= \langle\text{base type}\rangle \mid \langle\text{type}\rangle \to \langle\text{type}\rangle \mid \langle\text{type}\rangle\times\langle\text{type}\rangle \mid \langle\text{type}\rangle+\langle\text{type}\rangle$$

$$\frac{A \vdash M_1 : \tau_1 \quad A \vdash M_2 : \tau_2}{A \vdash \mathbf{pair}\, M_1 M_2 : \tau_1 \times \tau_2}$$

$$\frac{A \vdash M : \tau_1 \times \tau_2}{A \vdash \mathbf{lson}\, M : \tau_1}$$

$$\frac{A \vdash M : \tau_1 \times \tau_2}{A \vdash \mathbf{rson}\, M : \tau_2}$$

$$\frac{A \vdash M : \tau_1}{A \vdash \mathbf{inL}\, M : \tau_1 + \tau_2}$$

$$\frac{A \vdash M : \tau_2}{A \vdash \mathbf{inR}\, M : \tau_1 + \tau_2}$$

$$\frac{A \vdash M : \tau_1 + \tau_2 \quad A \vdash N : \tau_1 \to \tau_3 \quad A \vdash P : \tau_2 \to \tau_3}{A \vdash \mathbf{case}\, M N P : \tau_3}$$

Figure 1. Rules for binary products and unions

It is easy to show, using the techniques sketched in Section 4, that the principal typing problem for this system is solvable. In fact, most existing implementations of simply typed lambda-calculus (eg ML [Gordon *et al.* 78], SPS [Wand 84]) tacitly make this extension.

We extend the rules for binary unions and products to arbitrary labelled unions and products as follows:

Let L be a fixed countable set of *labels* $a_1, a_2, \ldots$. If $\rho : D \to X$, where D is a finite subset of L, (that is a family of elements of X indexed by a finite subset of L) then we call ρ a *row* of X's. (This terminology is stolen from Algol 68). If we fix an ordering on L, then any row has a canonical finite representation $\langle (a_{i_1}, x_1), \ldots, (a_{i_n}, x_n) \rangle$, where the a_{i_k} are in increasing order.

In this paper, we use the word "type" to refer to certain syntactic objects, which may be thought of as expressions or finite trees in which rows are replaced by their canonical representations.

Definition. The set of types T is the smallest set of expressions such that:

(1) T contains the base types.

(2) T is closed under the binary operation $\to$.

(3) If ρ is a row of types, then $\Sigma\rho$ and $\Pi\rho$ are in T.

It is easy to give semantics to these syntactic objects. Given an assignment of sets to the base types, we interpret $\to$ as the function space (as usual), we interpret $\Sigma\rho$ as the disjoint union $\sum_{a \in \operatorname{dom}\rho} \rho(a)$, and we interpret $\Pi\rho$ as the product $\prod_{a \in \operatorname{dom}\rho} \rho(a)$.

Let $\rho[a \leftarrow \tau]$ denote the usual extension operation on partial functions.

We can now give the syntactic constructions dealing with records and state their typing rules:

$$\emptyset \vdash \mathbf{null} : \Pi\emptyset$$

$$\frac{A \vdash M : \Pi\rho \quad A \vdash N : \tau}{A \vdash (M \;\mathbf{with}\; a := N) : \Pi(\rho[a \leftarrow \tau])}$$

$$\frac{A \vdash M : \Pi\rho \;\; a \in \operatorname{dom}\rho}{A \vdash M.a : \rho a}$$

The first rule creates a record with no fields. The second rule allows us to extend an arbitrary record by adding a new field or changing the value of an existing field. (By contrast, C84 allows only the creation of records of fixed length. This is like only having the primitive `list` instead of having `cons` and `nil`.) The last rule provides selection in the obvious way.

We may write down the operations for labelled unions similarly:

$$\frac{A \vdash M : \tau}{A \vdash \mathbf{inj}\, a\, M : \Sigma\rho[a \leftarrow \tau]}$$

$$\frac{A \vdash M : \Sigma\rho \quad a \in \operatorname{dom}\rho \quad A \vdash N : \rho(a) \to \tau \quad A \vdash P : \tau}{A \vdash \mathbf{ifcase}\, a M N P : \tau}$$

These rules are simply extensions of the corresponding rules for binary unions. The first allows injection of a quantity into an arbitrary labelled union. The second selects one case of a labelled union: if the value of M arises from an injection along label a, then N is applied to the value; otherwise the value of the entire expression is that of P. The intended semantics may be captured by the axioms:

$$\mathbf{ifcase}\, a\, (\mathbf{inj}\, a\, v) f y = f v$$
$$\mathbf{ifcase}\, a\, (\mathbf{inj}\, b\, v) f y = y \quad (b \neq a)$$

The typing rules are obviously sound with respect to the coproduct semantics for Π. We thus avoid the rule for $[M\;\mathbf{as}\;a]$ in C84, which causes the only semantic difficulties in that system.

3. The Type Inference Problem

The type inference problem may be stated as follows:
Given a term M, for which A and τ do we have $A \vdash M : \tau$?

Following [Cardelli 85] and [Milner 78], we solve this problem by reducing it to a unification problem. We do this by using type expressions to keep track of the possible types that might occur at each node of the derivation tree. We then generate equations between the type expressions which will ensure that the tree is a legal derivation tree. Then the solutions to the equations are in correspondence with all the possible derivation trees. To do this, we must first state the appropriate notions of terms, equations, and solutions.

Since we need to represent both types and rows of types, we define type-expressions ($\langle\text{TE}\rangle$) and row-expressions ($\langle\text{RE}\rangle$).

$$\begin{aligned}\langle\text{TE}\rangle &::= \langle\text{base type}\rangle \mid \langle\text{type variable}\rangle \mid \langle\text{TE}\rangle \rightarrow \langle\text{TE}\rangle \\ &\quad \mid \Sigma\langle\text{RE}\rangle \mid \Pi\langle\text{RE}\rangle \\ \langle\text{RE}\rangle &::= \textbf{emptyrow} \mid \langle\text{row variable}\rangle \mid \langle\text{RE}\rangle[\langle\text{label}\rangle \leftarrow \langle\text{TE}\rangle]\end{aligned}$$

In the last production, $(*[* \leftarrow *])$ is just a 3-place syntactic operation, which we write using infix notation.

Define a *model* to be a map from type- and row- variables to types and rows, respectively. Given a model μ, we can interpret type- and row-expressions, as types and rows, interpreting $\rightarrow$, Σ, and Π in the obvious way, **emptyrow** as the empty row, and interpreting $(*[* \leftarrow *])$ as function extension. This gives us a meaning for $\mu \models E$, where E is a set of equations between type- and row-expressions. (We call these just sets of equations, for short).

We also need to consider *substitutions*, which are maps from type- and row- variables to type- and row-expressions. A substitution is called a *ground* substitution if its range consists of expressions without variables. Clearly each ground substitution determines a model, and each model determines a ground substitution obtained by using the canonical representation for each row. We will therefore use models and ground substitutions interchangeably below.

Composition of substitutions is defined in the usual way: $\sigma \circ \tau$ has domain $\text{dom}\,\sigma \cup \text{dom}\,\tau$, and $(\sigma \circ \tau)(v)$ is $\tau(v)$ for $v \notin \text{dom}\,\sigma$, and $(v\sigma)\tau$ otherwise.

Lemma *(Substitution Lemma): Let E be a set of equations, μ a model, v a variable, and t an expression, such that $v \notin \text{dom}(\mu)$. Then $\mu \models E[v \leftarrow t]$ iff $[v \leftarrow t] \circ \mu \models E$.*

Proof: Easy induction on the structure of terms.

If σ and τ are two substitutions, we say $\sigma \leq \tau$ iff there exists some substitution ρ such that $\tau = \sigma \circ \rho$. We say that σ is *more general* than τ.

If E is a set of equations, and σ is a substitution, we say that σ is the *most general unifier* of E iff for all models μ with $\text{dom}(m) = \text{vars}(E)$, $\mu \models E$ iff $\sigma \leq \mu$.

This asserts that σ is at least as general as any model of E. We cannot say directly that σ unifies E, as we do in the usual case of unification. Instead we require that the result of performing substitution σ on E leaves us with a *valid* set of equations: one in which any model is a solution. This leads us to the definition above.

We then have:

Theorem. *The language of type- and row-expressions has a decidable most general unification problem.*

Proof: We present an algorithm which has as its input a set E_0 of equations and has as its output either a most general unifier for E_0 or a signal that E_0 has no solutions. The algorithm has two variables, a set E of equations and a substitution σ. The algorithm will satisfy the following invariant:

INVARIANT :

$(1)(\forall\mu)(\mu \models E_0 \Rightarrow (\exists\nu)(\nu \models E \wedge \sigma \circ \nu = \mu))$

$(2)(\forall\mu)(\mu \models E \wedge \text{dom}(\mu) = \text{vars}(E) \Rightarrow \sigma \circ \mu \models E_0)$

The algorithm is given as follows:

Initialization: Set $E = E_0$ and σ to be the identity substitution on $\text{vars}(E_0)$.

Loop Step: If E is empty, then halt and return σ. Otherwise, choose an equation from E and transform E according to an algorithm to be given later.

Clearly, the initialization establishes the invariant. If E is empty and the invariant holds, then we claim that σ is a most general unifier of E_0. The first clause in the invariant guarantees that σ is at least as general as any model of E_0. To get the converse implication, assume that μ is a model such that $\sigma \leq \mu$. Then there is a substitution μ' such that $\sigma \circ \mu' = \mu$. Since μ is a model, we can choose μ' to be a model also. Now, since E is empty, $\mu' \models E$, so, by the second clause in the invariant, $\sigma \circ \mu' \models E_0$. But $\sigma \circ \mu' = \mu$, so we have $\mu \models E_0$, as desired.

It remains to give the loop step, to show that it preserves the invariant, and to show that the algorithm halts. The halting measure will be the lexicographic ordering $\langle$number of variables in E, number of symbols in $E\,\rangle$, as in the conventional unification algorithm. We now give each possibility. We begin with the cases for equations between type expressions. These are effectively the same as in the case of ordinary unification; we write them out in detail to illustrate the use of the invariant.

(1) The equation is of the form $\langle\text{base type}\rangle = \langle\text{base type}\rangle$. If the two sides are identical, delete the equation. If they are not identical, halt: there is no solution. Since there is no solution for E, by the first clause of the invariant there is no solution for E_0.

(2) The equation is of the form $t_1 \rightarrow t_2 = u_1 \rightarrow u_2$. Delete this equation from E and add the two equations $t_1 = u_1$ and $t_2 = u_2$. This is the usual step in the conventional case.

This clearly decreases the halting measure. To check the preservation of the first clause of the invariant, let E' denote the new set of equations, and let μ be a solution of E_0. By the first clause, there is a model ν such that $\sigma \circ \nu = \mu$ and $\nu \models E$. But clearly $\nu \models E'$ as well. To check that the second clause is preserved, let μ be a solution of E'. Then μ is clearly a solution to E. Hence, by the invariant, $\sigma \circ \mu \models E_0$, and the invariant is preserved.

(3) The equation is of the form $\Sigma\rho = \Sigma\rho'$ or $\Pi\rho = \Pi\rho'$. In either case, replace the equation by $\rho = \rho'$. The proof is as in the preceding case.

(4) The equation is of the form $v = t$ or $t = v$, where v is a type variable. If v appears in t, halt: there is no solution. Otherwise, replace σ by $\sigma \circ [v \leftarrow t]$, delete the equation from E, and then substitute t for all occurrences of v in the resulting set of equations.

Let E^- denote the set of equations after the selected equation has been deleted. Then the new set of equations is $E' = E^-[v \leftarrow t]$. Since v does not appear in t, it does not appear in the new set of equations. Therefore this step decreases the number of variables, and therefore decreases the halting measure. To confirm that the first clause of the invariant is preserved, let μ be a solution to E_0. Hence there is a solution ν to E such that $\sigma \circ \nu = \mu$. Since E contains $v = t$, ν must be of the form $[v \leftarrow t] \circ \nu'$, where $v \notin \mathrm{dom}(\nu')$. Hence there exists ν' such that $\mu = \sigma \circ [v \leftarrow t] \circ \nu' = \sigma' \circ \nu'$ and $[v \leftarrow t] \circ \nu' \models E^-$. Since $v \notin \mathrm{dom}(\nu')$, by the substitution lemma we have $v' \models E^-[v \leftarrow t]$, as desired.

To confirm that the second clause of the invariant is preserved, let μ' be a model such that $\mu' \models E'$ and $\mathrm{dom}(\mu') = \mathrm{vars}(E')$. Since v does not appear in t, we know that $v \notin \mathrm{vars}(E') = \mathrm{dom}(\mu')$. Hence we can use the substitution lemma to reason as follows:

$$\begin{aligned}
&\mu' \models E' \\
&\Rightarrow \mu' \models E^-[v \leftarrow t] \\
&\Rightarrow [v \leftarrow t] \circ \mu' \models E^- \\
&\Rightarrow [v \leftarrow t] \circ \mu' \models E \\
&\Rightarrow \sigma \circ [v \leftarrow t] \circ \mu' \models E_0 \\
&\Rightarrow \sigma' \circ \mu' \models E_0
\end{aligned}$$

as desired.

(5) Any other equation between type-expressions has no solution. Halt and report no solution.

The remaining possibility is that the chosen equation is an equation between row-expressions. In this case, the first step is to transform each expression into the form

$$t_0[a_1 \leftarrow t_1][a_2 \leftarrow t_2] \ldots [a_n \leftarrow t_n]$$

where t_0 is either a row-variable or the constant **emptyrow**, and the a_i are distinct, using the familiar identities:

$$\begin{aligned}
\rho[a \leftarrow t][a \leftarrow u] &= \rho[a \leftarrow u] \\
\rho[a \leftarrow t][b \leftarrow u] &= \rho[b \leftarrow u][a \leftarrow t] \qquad (a \neq b)
\end{aligned}$$

We now consider the possibilities, depending on whether each side of the equation begins with a variable or a constant.

(6) The equation is of the form $\rho = t$, where ρ is a row variable. If ρ appears in t, then halt and report no solution, as before, as this equation is unsatisfiable. Otherwise, proceed as in step 4 above.

(7) The equation is of the form

$$\begin{aligned}
&\mathbf{emptyrow}[a_1 \leftarrow t_1] \ldots [a_n \leftarrow t_n] \\
&\quad = \mathbf{emptyrow}[b_1 \leftarrow u_1] \ldots [b_m \leftarrow u_m]
\end{aligned}$$

This equation has a solution only if $n = m$ and each $a_i = b_i$, since the a_i and b_i completely determine the domains of the rows. If this condition is not met, halt and report no solution. Otherwise, delete this equation from E and add the equations $t_i = u_i$ for $i = 1, \ldots, n$. This step is justified in the same way as case (2) above.

(8) The equation is of the form

$$\mathbf{emptyrow}[a_1 \leftarrow t_1] \ldots [a_n \leftarrow t_n] = \rho[b_1 \leftarrow u_1] \ldots [b_m \leftarrow u_m]$$

Let A denote the set of labels $\{a_i\}$ and B denote the set of labels $\{b_i\}$. In any model of this equation, the domain of the row is exactly A, so in order to have a solution we must have $B \subseteq A$. If this condition is not met, halt and report no solution. Otherwise, without loss of generality assume that $a_1 = b_1, \ldots a_p = b_p$. Delete the current equation from E and add to E the equations $t_i = u_i$, for $1 \leq i \leq p$ and also the equation $\rho = \mathbf{emptyrow}[a_{p+1} \leftarrow t_{p+1}] \ldots [a_n \leftarrow t_n]$. This step is justified in the same way as case (2) above.

(9) The equation is of the form

$$\rho[a_1 \leftarrow t_1] \ldots [a_n \leftarrow t_n] = \rho'[b_1 \leftarrow t_1] \ldots [b_m \leftarrow t_m]$$

Again, let A denote the set of labels $\{a_i\}$ and B denote the set of labels $\{b_i\}$, and assume without loss of generality, that $a_1 = b_1, \ldots a_p = b_p$, and all labels appearing to the right of these are distinct. In any solution μ of this equation, the domain of the term must be a superset of $A \cup B$. Therefore, any solution must be of the form

$$\begin{aligned}
\rho &= \rho_0[b_{p+1} \leftarrow u_{p+1}] \ldots [b_m \leftarrow u_m] \\
\rho' &= \rho_0[a_{p+1} \leftarrow t_{p+1}] \ldots [a_n \leftarrow t_n]
\end{aligned}$$

where ρ_0 is a fresh row variable. If ρ appears on the right-hand side of the first equation or ρ' appears on the right-hand side of the second equation, then halt and report no solution. Otherwise, delete the current equation from E, add the equations $t_1 = u_1, \ldots, t_p = u_p$, and perform the substitution

$$\begin{aligned}
[\rho &\leftarrow \rho_0[b_{p+1} \leftarrow u_{p+1}] \ldots [b_m \leftarrow u_m], \\
\rho' &\leftarrow \rho_0[a_{p+1} \leftarrow t_{p+1}] \ldots [a_n \leftarrow t_n]]
\end{aligned}$$

on the resulting set of equations.

Since this step is a combination of decomposition and substitution, it preserves the invariant by the same argument as steps (2) and (4) above. It decreases the halting measure because it eliminates two variables ρ and ρ' and introduces a single fresh variable ρ_0, thus decreasing the number of variables by one.

These are all the possible cases, so the algorithm is finished. *QED.*

4. Reducing Type Inference to Unification

We next turn to the reduction of type inference to unification. We next give the algorithm, in two levels of refinement. We first give its control structure and state the invariant which its inner loop must maintain. We then state the actions of the inner loop and show that they maintain this invariant. The presentation is similar to that for the unification algorithm above. Instead of analyzing a set E of equations and producing a substitution σ, the reduction algorithm analyzes a set G of subgoals which are *type-expression assertions*, and produces a set E of equations.

If M is a term, A is a set of type hypotheses whose domain is the set of free variables of M, and t is a type expression, we call the tuple (A, M, t) a *type-expression assertion*. These type-expression assertions are the basic quantities manipulated by the reduction algorithm.

Typing Rules:

$$A \vdash x : \tau \quad (A(x) = \tau)$$

$$\frac{A[x \leftarrow \tau_1] \vdash M : \tau_2}{A \vdash (\lambda x.M) : \tau_1 \rightarrow \tau_2}$$

$$\frac{A \vdash M : \tau_1 \rightarrow \tau_2 \quad A \vdash N : \tau_1}{A \vdash (M\ N) : \tau_2}$$

Action Rules:

$$\langle A, x, t\rangle \Rightarrow t = A(x)$$

$$\begin{aligned}\langle A, (\lambda x.M), t\rangle \Rightarrow\ & t = \tau_1 \rightarrow \tau_2 \\ & \langle (A[x \leftarrow \tau_1])_M, M, \tau_2\rangle \\ & (\tau_1, \tau_2 \text{ fresh})\end{aligned}$$

$$\begin{aligned}\langle A, (M\ N), t\rangle \Rightarrow\ & \langle A_M, M, \tau_1 \rightarrow t\rangle \\ & \langle A_N, N, \tau_1\rangle \\ & (\tau_1 \text{ fresh})\end{aligned}$$

Figure 2. Typing and Action Rules for Simple Types

Theorem. *Given any (A_0, M_0, t_0), we can effectively construct a set E of equations such that for any set B of type assumptions and any type t,*

$$B \vdash M : t \Leftrightarrow (\exists\mu)(\mu \models E \wedge B = A_0\mu \wedge t = t_0\mu)$$

Proof: The algorithm mimics the construction of the derivation. At every step it keeps track of a set G of subgoals, which are type-expression assertions to be proved, and set E of equations between type expressions, which are verification conditions which must be satisfied for the derivation to be legal.

We need to state the invariant relating the possible completions of the derivation with the possible typings of M_0. To do this, we need to formulate the notion of a *solution* of (E, G):

Let μ be a model. If (A, M, t) is a type-expression assertion, we write $\mu \models (A, M, t)$ iff $A\mu \vdash M : t\mu$, and if G is a set of type-expression assertions, we write $\mu \models G$ iff $\mu \models (A, M, t)$ for each $(A, M, t) \in G$. Finally, we say μ *solves* (E, G) (and write $\mu \models (E, G)$) iff $\mu \models E$ and $\mu \models G$.

Thinking of μ as representing an instance of the derivation represented by (E, G), we see that $\mu \models (E, G)$ iff μ is a solution to E and μ yields a provable typing for each subgoal in G.

We can now state the invariant for our algorithm. It is just the proposition that the solutions for (E, G) generate exactly the typings of (A_0, M_0, t_0):

INVARIANT :

(1) $(\forall\mu)(\mu \models (E, G) \Rightarrow A_0\mu \vdash M_0 : t_0\mu)$

(2) $B \vdash M_0 : t \Rightarrow (\exists\mu)(\mu \models (E, G) \wedge B = A_0\mu \wedge t = t_0\mu)$

The first clause states that any solution for (E, G) generates only correct typings for (A_0, M_0, t_0) (soundness), and the second clause states that every typing of M_0 is generated by some solution for (E, G) (completeness). This is not quite an if-and-only-if, since (E, G) may involve type variables not in the initial assertion.

We may now state the top-level structure of the algorithm:

Initialization: Set $E = \emptyset$ and $G = \{(A_0, M_0, t_0)\}$. variables.

Loop Step: If $G = \emptyset$, then halt and return E. Otherwise, choose a subgoal (A, M, t) from G, delete it from G, and add to E and G new verification conditions and subgoals, as specified in an *action table* (to be supplied later).

The invariant is clearly established by our initialization step. At termination, when $G = \emptyset$, we have

(1) $(\forall\mu)(\mu \models E \Rightarrow A_0\mu \vdash M_0 : t_0\mu)$

(2) $B \vdash M_0 : t \Rightarrow (\exists\mu)(\mu \models E \wedge B = A_0\mu \wedge t = t_0\mu)$

so that the solutions of E give the typings of M_0, as desired.

We next turn to the creation of the action table. Figure 2 illustrates the typing rules and actions for the simply-typed lambda-calculus. (Here A_M denotes A restricted to the free variables of M). Since the rules always decrease the size of the terms M, they are guaranteed to terminate.

We next must show that these action rules preserve the invariant. We repeat the argument from [Wand 87]: It is easy to show that the algorithm generates only correct typings (the first clause of the invariant). We therefore only consider the

$$\begin{aligned}
\langle A, M\,\textbf{with}\,a := N, t\rangle &\Rightarrow t = \Pi(\rho[a \leftarrow \tau]) \\
&\quad\ \langle A_M, M, \Pi\rho\rangle \\
&\quad\ \langle A_N, N, \tau\rangle \\
&\quad\ (\rho, \tau \text{ fresh})
\end{aligned}$$

$$\langle A, \textbf{null}, t\rangle \Rightarrow t = \Pi\,\textbf{emptyrow}$$

$$\begin{aligned}
\langle A, M.a, t\rangle &\Rightarrow \langle A, M, \Pi(\rho[a \leftarrow t])\rangle \\
&\quad\ (\rho, \tau \text{ fresh})
\end{aligned}$$

$$\begin{aligned}
\langle A, \textbf{inj}\,a\,M, t\rangle &\Rightarrow t = \Sigma(\rho[a \leftarrow \tau]) \\
&\quad\ \langle A, M, \tau\rangle \\
&\quad\ (\rho, \tau \text{ fresh})
\end{aligned}$$

$$\begin{aligned}
\langle A, \textbf{ifcase}\,a\,M N P, t\rangle &\Rightarrow \langle A, M, \Sigma\rho[a \leftarrow \tau]\rangle \\
&\quad\ \langle A, N, \tau \rightarrow t\rangle \\
&\quad\ \langle A, P, t\rangle \\
&\quad\ (\rho, \tau \text{ fresh})
\end{aligned}$$

Figure 3. Action Rules for Labelled Records and Variants

second clause of the invariant (completeness). In each case, we assume that clause (2) holds before the action is taken, and we need to show that it holds afterwards. To do this, assume that $B \vdash M_0 : t$. By the induction hypothesis, we know that

$$(\exists\mu)(\mu \models (E, G) \wedge B = A_0\mu \wedge t = t_0\mu)$$

and we need to show that

$$(\exists\mu')(\mu' \models (E', G') \wedge B = A_0\mu' \wedge t = t_0\mu')$$

where (E', G') is the state after the action step. In each case, let G_1 denote G after the selected goal has been deleted. Then we know that $\mu \models E$, $\mu \models G_1$, and $\mu \models g$, where g is the selected subgoal. We consider each case of the action table in turn.

(1) The selected subgoal is of the form (A, x, t), where x is a variable. Then $\mu \models (A, x, t)$. Hence $A\mu \vdash x : t\mu$. By the typing rules, it must be true that $A\mu(x) = t\mu$, hence $\mu \models A(x) = t$. So $\mu \models (E', G')$ as desired.

(2) The selected subgoal is of the form $(A, (M\,N), t)$. Hence $A\mu \vdash (M\,N) : t\mu$. By the typing rules, there must be some type t_1 such that $A\mu \vdash M : t_1 \rightarrow t\mu$ and $A\mu \vdash N : t_1$. So let τ_1 be a fresh type variable (not in the domain of μ), and let μ' be defined by $\mu' = \mu[\tau_1 \leftarrow t_1]$. Then $\mu' \models (A, M, \tau_1 \rightarrow t)$ and $\mu' \models (A, N, \tau_1)$, so $\mu' \models G'$, as desired.

(3) The selected subgoal is of the form $(A, (\lambda x.M), t)$. Hence $A\mu \vdash (\lambda x.M) : t\mu$. By the typing rules, there must be some types t_1 and t_2 such that $A\mu[x \leftarrow t_1] \vdash M : t_2$ and $t\mu = t_1 \rightarrow t_2$. So let τ_1 and τ_2 be fresh type variables, and let $\mu' = \mu[\tau_1 \leftarrow t_1][\tau_2 \leftarrow t_2]$. Then $\mu' \models ((A[x \leftarrow \tau_1])_M, M, \tau_2)$ and $\mu' \models t = \tau_1 \rightarrow \tau_2$, as desired.

We can now proceed to give the action rules for records and variants. These are shown in Figure 3. Here A ranges over type-expression assumptions, M, N, P range over terms, t ranges over type expressions, and ρ, τ are fresh row and type variables as they are introduced.

The reasoning for these rules is analogous to those for the simple case, comparing Figure 3 with the typing rules in Section 2. The only trick is in the rules for field selection and **ifcase**, where we have written $\rho[a \leftarrow \tau]$ to require that a be in the domain of the row in question and to have a placeholder τ for the value of a row-application ρa. Again, termination is guaranteed, since the rules always replace a term by some of its subterms. *QED.*

We can now state the solution for the type inference problem:

Theorem. *Given a term M, we can decide whether there is any A and τ such that $A \vdash M : \tau$. Furthermore, if there is, we can effectively produce a set A_0 of type hypotheses, a substitution σ and a variable $t_0 \in \operatorname{dom}\sigma$ such that for any set B of type assumptions and any type t,*

$$B \vdash M : t \Leftrightarrow (\exists\mu)(\sigma \leq \mu \wedge B = A_0\mu \wedge t = t_0\mu)$$

Proof: Let A_0 bind each free variable of M to a fresh type variable, and let t_0 be a fresh type variable. We then use the reduction algorithm to produce a set of equations E such that

$$B \vdash M : t \Leftrightarrow (\exists\mu)(\mu \models E \wedge B = A_0\mu \wedge t = t_0\mu)$$

We can without loss of generality assume that $\operatorname{dom}(\mu) = \operatorname{vars}(E)$. We then use the unification algorithm to produce the substitution σ such that $\mu \models E \Leftrightarrow \sigma \leq \mu$. *QED.*

Let us do a short example to illustrate this. Consider the term $\lambda u.2 \times (u.a)$. We trace the algorithm by giving a table. Each line in the table consists of two entries. The first is the current set G of subgoals. At each step we apply the action table to the first subgoal in the current goal list. This yields the goal list in the next line and some equations, which are displayed in the second entry of the next line. Interspersed are comments on the actions performed.

We will need to expand the algorithm slightly to deal with integers. To do this, we will assume the existence of a constant *twice* of type int → int. We therefore set the initial type environment A_0 to $\{(twice : (\text{int} \to \text{int}))\}$. When we begin, the goal list consists of a single goal, consisting of the type assumption A_0, the term to be typed, and a single type variable.

initial configuration
$\{((twice : (\text{int} \to \text{int})), \lambda u.twice\,(u.a), t_0)\}$
analyzing λ
$\{((u : t_1,\ twice : (\text{int} \to \text{int})), twice\,(u.a), t_2)\};\quad t_0 = t_1 \to t_2$
splitting combination
$\{((twice : (\text{int} \to \text{int})), twice, t_3 \to t_2), ((u : t_1), u.a, t_3)\}$
deleting goal for *twice*
$\{((u : t_1), u.a, t_3)\};\quad t_3 \to t_2 = \text{int} \to \text{int}$
analyzing selection
$\{((u : t_1), u, \Pi(\rho[a \leftarrow t_3]))\}$
deleting goal for u
$\emptyset;\quad \Pi(\rho[a \leftarrow t_3]) = t_1$

Thus the equations generated are:

$$\begin{aligned} t_0 &= t_1 \to t_2 \\ t_3 \to t_2 &= \text{int} \to \text{int} \\ \Pi(\rho[a \leftarrow t_3]) &= t_1 \end{aligned}$$

Solving these equations using the algorithm of the previous section yields

$$\Pi(\rho[a \leftarrow \text{int}]) \to \text{int}$$

as the principal type of the term, as desired.

5. Polymorphic Definitions

The system as described so far is entirely *monomorphic*: though terms may have more than one type, the only binding mechanism is lambda-binding, which, just as in the simply-typed lambda-calculus, allows only monomorphic values to be passed. Thus there is no way to take advantage of the polymorphism in the notation.

This capability is provided in ML through the **let** mechanism. For the purposes of this paper, we will present a simplified version of this mechanism which will work only at the top level. Define the set of *programs* as follows:

$$\begin{aligned} \langle\text{program}\rangle &::= \langle\text{definition}\rangle; \langle\text{program}\rangle \mid \langle\text{term}\rangle \\ \langle\text{definition}\rangle &::= \langle\text{identifier}\rangle\ =\ \langle\text{term}\rangle \end{aligned}$$

For type-checking purposes, a definition associates the identifier with the principal type of the term on the right-hand side. The scope of the definition is the ⟨program⟩ that follows it. In this scope, the identifier is polymorphic, and may be used at any of the instances of its principal type. Consider, for example, the program:

$twicea = \lambda u.2 \times (u.a);$
$\quad twicea[a := 3, b := \text{true}] + twicea[a := 4, b := 7]$

where $[a := M, b := N]$ abbreviates **null with** $a := M$ **with** $b := N$. Here *twicea* gets assigned principal type $\Pi(\rho[a \leftarrow \text{int}]) \to \text{int}$, and is used with two different instances of ρ: with $\rho = \Pi((a,\text{int}),(b,\text{bool}))$ and with $\rho = \Pi((a,\text{int}),(b,\text{int}))$.

This is how polymorphism allows us to deal with inheritance: *twicea* may be applied to any object (that is, any record) containing an a component which is an integer. Thus *twicea* is applicable to any descendant of $\Pi((a,\text{int}))$.

One might wish to rewrite the typing rule for definitions as

$$\frac{A \vdash M[N/x] : \tau}{A \vdash (x = N; M) : \tau}$$

While this rule gives the same typings in this system, it is not equivalent in general. The issue is whether the type system provides enough types to abstract the possible uses of x; re-expanding each occurrence of x, as if it were a macro, prevents any sort of separate compilation of M and prevents us from addressing this issue at all. In the next section, we shall see how this makes a difference.

This mechanism for introducing polymorphism has been used successfully by ML [Gordon *et al.* 78] and by SPS [Wand 84]. In practice, it seems quite adequate for ordinary programming. More complicated situations, such as separate compilation of polymorphic modules, require full-fledged quantified types, for which type inference is a long-standing open problem.

6. Comparison with Cardelli's System

The system C84 uses the same types as ours. It does not use type expressions to express polymorphism, but instead adds a subtype relation between types, which is defined as follows:

$$\begin{aligned} \rho_1 < \rho_2 &\iff \operatorname{dom}\rho_1 \subset \operatorname{dom}\rho_2 \\ &\qquad \wedge (\forall a \in \operatorname{dom}\rho_1)[\rho_1 a < \rho_2 a] \\ \tau_1 \to \tau_2 < \tau_1' \to \tau_2' &\iff \tau_1' < \tau_1 \wedge \tau_2 < \tau_2' \\ \Sigma\rho < \Sigma\rho' &\iff \rho < \rho' \\ \Pi\rho < \Pi\rho' &\iff \rho' < \rho \end{aligned}$$

C84 uses explicit types on all lambda variables ($\lambda x{:}\,\tau.M$ instead of $\lambda x.M$). Polymorphism is obtained by altering the rule for typing of individual variables to read:

$$A \vdash x : \tau' \quad (A(x) = \tau, \tau < \tau')$$

To see how this deals with inheritance, let us consider again the program we wrote before:

$twicea = \lambda u.2 \times (u.a);$
$\quad twicea[a := 3, b := \text{true}] + twicea[a := 4, b := 7]$

This program is well-typed; we assign *twicea* the type

$$\Pi((a,\text{int})) \to \text{int}$$

and we use it at the two types $\Pi((a,\text{int}),(b,\text{bool})) \to \text{int}$ and $\Pi((a,\text{int}),(b,\text{int})) \to \text{int}$, each of which is greater than the original type.

One can still ask about type inference, however: when is an untyped term M the image under type-erasing of a typed term? One can then begin to compare the properties of the two systems.

The original version of C84 included some things which are not relevant to our current concerns (such as recursive type definitions), and had a somewhat different treatment of record construction and case selection (as noted in Section 2). In order to be precise, for the remainder of this section, we will define C84 to be our system with the rule for typing identifiers modified as shown. This will allow us a moderately fair comparison between the systems and their treatment of polymorphism.

For the pure systems (without definitions), the terms typed by our system are a subset of those typed by C84. To show the inclusion is proper, simply consider

$$((\lambda f. f([a := 3, b := \text{true}]) + f([a := 4, b := 7]))\ \mathit{twicea})$$

which is well typed in C84 (assign f the type $\Pi((a, \text{int})) \rightarrow \text{int}$), but is not well-typed in the current system, since the two instances of f require different values of ρ in $\Pi(\rho[a \leftarrow \text{int}]) \rightarrow \text{int}$.

We next turn to a comparison of the systems with polymorphic definitions. Since C84 provides no type expressions, we choose to interpret definitions as simple lambda-bindings, as follows:

$$\frac{A \vdash M : \tau \quad A[x \leftarrow \tau] \vdash N : \tau'}{A \vdash (x = M; N) : \tau'}$$

The polymorphism is provided by the standard identifier-lookup mechanism.

This is not equivalent to using the "macro-expansion" rule for definitions. The interesting issue is precisely whether there is a type τ which allows for all the uses of x in N; macro-expanding each occurrence of x avoids the issue completely.

For the systems with definitions, there are programs which are well-typed in the the current system but which have no type in C84. Consider, for example

$$\mathit{doublea} = \lambda u. u \ \mathbf{with}\ a := 2 \times (u.a);$$
$$(\mathit{doublea}[a := 1; b := 2]).b + (\mathit{doublea}[a := 3; c := 4]).c$$

This is well-typed in the current system, since *doublea* has principal type

$$\Pi(\rho[a \leftarrow \text{int}]) \rightarrow \Pi(\rho[a \leftarrow \text{int}])$$

but it is not well-typed in C84. To see this, consider the types of the two occurrences of *doublea*:

$$\Pi((a, \text{int}), (b, \text{int})) \rightarrow \Pi((a, \text{int}), (b, \text{int}))$$

and

$$\Pi((a, \text{int}), (c, \text{int})) \rightarrow \Pi((a, \text{int}), (c, \text{int}))$$

The greatest lower bound of these two types is

$$\Pi((a, \text{int})) \rightarrow \Pi((a, \text{int}), (b, \text{int}), (c, \text{int}))$$

which is not a possible type for *doublea*. Hence this program has no type in C84.

Hence the systems with polymorphic definition are incomparable.

We can sharpen these observations somewhat by considering the pure expressiveness of the two kinds of polymorphism. Let us say a set S of types is definable in our system iff there exists a type t such that $u \in S$ iff u is a substitution instance of t. Say a set S of types is definable in C84 iff there exists a type t such that $u \in S$ iff $t < u$. Then the definitional power of the two systems is incomparable. The previous example shows that there is a set of types which is definable in the current system but not in C84. Similarly, the set of types defined in C84 by

$$\Pi((a, \text{int}), (b, \text{int})) \rightarrow \Pi((a, \text{int}), (b, \text{int}))$$

is not definable in the current system, since it has no way to specify a class of rows containing *fewer* elements than $((a, \text{int}), (b, \text{int}))$ using only a single principal type.

It is straightforward to add inclusions to the algorithm which generates the verification conditions, but it is no longer obvious that the resulting set of equalities and inclusions has a decidable satisfiability problem.

The system we have proposed seems adequate for use in programming systems relying on "structural" inheritance through shared field names. On the other hand, it is by no means clear that this is an appropriate model of inheritance for other object-oriented systems. For example, in our introductory example, there is no guarantee that the `id-number` fields for submarines and weapons systems will be compatible. Hence a function that manipulates the `id-number` field might not really be applicable to both submarines and weapons-systems. Many real object-oriented programming systems use *name* inheritance, in which the inheritance can be more tightly controlled. This leads to a somewhat different theory, which we hope to present elsewhere.

References

[Cardelli 84]
Cardelli, L. "A Semantics of Multiple Inheritance," *Semantics of Data Types, International Symposium*, Springer Lecture Notes in Computer Science *173* (1984), 51–68.

[Cardelli 85]
Cardelli, L. "Basic Polymorphic Typechecking," *Polymorphism Newsletter 2*,1 (Jan, 1985). Also appeared as Computing Science Tech. Rep. 119, AT&T Bell Laboratories, Murray Hill, NJ.

[Gordon, *et al.* 78]
Gordon, M., Milner, R., Morris, L., Newey, M., and Wadsworth, C. "A Metalanguage for Interactive Proof in LCF," *Proc. 5th Annual ACM Symp. on Principles of Programming Languages* (1978) 119–130.

[Milner 78]
Milner, R. "A Theory of Type Polymorphism in Programming," *J. Comp. & Sys. Sci. 17* (1978), 348–375.

[Wand 84]
Wand, M. "A Semantic Prototyping System," *Proc. ACM SIGPLAN '84 Compiler Construction Conference* (1984) 213–221.

[Wand 86]
Wand, M. "A Simple Algorithm and Proof for Type Inference," *Fundamenta Informaticae 10* (1987), to appear.

Session 2

Chair

D. Harel

Carnegie-Mellon University

DOMAIN THEORY IN LOGICAL FORM

Samson Abramsky

Department of Computing
Imperial College of Science and Technology
180 Queen's Gate, London SW7, England

Abstract. A metalanguage for denotational semantics is given a logical interpretation: types are interpreted as propositional theories; terms (in an extended typed λ-calculus, denoting elements of types) are embedded in an endogenous program logic, which characterises their behaviour in terms of which properties they satisfy; terms (in an extension of the algebraic metalanguage of cartesian closed categories, denoting morphisms between types) are embedded in an exogenous logic, which characterises their behaviour as predicate transformers or modal operators. This interpretation is related to the standard domain-theoretic one via the machinery of Stone duality, and an exact correspondence is obtained. Some applications to logics for specific computational situations (e.g. concurrency) are mentioned.

1 Introduction

The classic Stone Representation Theorem for Boolean algebras [25] is the prototype for a wide class of "Stone-type duality theorems" [11]. The general form of these theorems is to assert an equivalence between a category of topological spaces and (the opposite of) a category of lattices and lattice-homomorphisms. In one direction, we pass from a space X to a lattice derived from the topology on X; we can think of this as a lattice of *properties* over X, since its elements are just subsets of X. In the other direction, starting from an abstract lattice A, which we can think of as a logical theory of properties or "observable quantities", we pass to a space whose points are the consistent, complete theories over A, i.e. the "point-like" bundles of properties over A.

The importance of Stone Duality for computer science is that *it provides the right framework for understanding the relationship between denotational semantics and program logic.* (As far as I know, this point was first made in [22], and also in unpublished work of Gordon Plotkin.)

Denotational semantics is always based, more or less explicitly, on a typed functional metalanguage. The types are interpreted as topological spaces (usually domains in the sense of Scott [20,21], but sometimes metric spaces, as in [3,16]), while the terms denote elements of or functions between these spaces. A *program logic* comprises an assertion language of formulas for expressing properties of programs, and an interface between these properties and the programs themselves. Two main types of interface can be identified [18]:

Endogenous logic In this style, formulas describe properties pertaining to the "world" of a single program. Notation:

$$P \models \phi$$

where P is a program and ϕ is a formula. Examples: temporal logic as used e.g. in [18]; Hennessy-Milner logic [8]; type inference [5].

Exogenous logic Here, programs are embedded in formulas as *modal operators.* Notation:

$$[P]\phi$$

where P is now a program denoting a function or relation. Examples: dynamic logic [7], including as special cases Hoare logic [10], since "Hoare triples" $\{\phi\}P\{\psi\}$ can be represented by

$$\phi \rightarrow [P]\psi,$$

and Dijkstra's wlp-calculus [6], since $wlp(P, \psi)$ can be represented as $[P]\psi$. (Total correctness assertions can also be catered for; see [7].)

Extensionally, formulas denote sets of points in our denotational domains, i.e. ϕ is a syntactic description of $\{x | x \text{satisfies} \phi\}$. Then $P \models \phi$ can be interpreted as $x \in U$, where x is the point denoted by P, and U is the set denoted by ϕ. Similarly, $[M]\phi$ can be interpreted as $f^{-1}(U)$, where f is the function denoted by M (and elaborations of this when M denotes a relation or multifunction). In this way, we can give a topological interpretation of program logic.

But this is not all: duality cuts both ways. We can also use it to give a *logical interpretation of denotational semantics.* Rather than starting with the denotational domains as spaces of points, and then interpreting formulas as sets of points, we can give an axiomatic presentation of the topologies on our spaces, viewed as abstract lattices (logical theories), and then reconstruct the points from the properties they satisfy. In other words, we can present denotational semantics in axiomatic form, as a logic of programs. This has a number of attractions:

- It unifies semantics and program logic in a general and systematic setting.
- It extends the scope of program logic to the entire range of denotational semantics – higher-order functions, recursive types, powerdomains etc.
- The syntactic presentation of recursive types, powerdomains etc. makes these constructions more "visible" and easier to calculate with.
- The construction of "points", i.e. denotations of computational processes, from the properties they satisfy is very compatible with work currently being done in a mainly operational setting in concurrency [8,26] and elsewhere [4], and offers a promising approach to unification of this work with denotational semantics.

2 Domains As Propositional Theories

The setting we take for our work in this paper is **SDom**, the category of Scott domains [20,21], i.e. the consistently complete algebraic cpo's. (However, everything should carry over to **SFP** [17].) Such domains D can also be viewed as spaces with the Scott topology $\Omega(D)$, with subbasic open sets of the form $\uparrow b \equiv \{d \in D | b \sqsubseteq d\}$, b a finite element of D. These spaces are *coherent* [11], meaning that they are determined by the distributive lattice of compact-open subsets $(K\Omega(D), \subseteq)$, i.e. sets of the form $\uparrow X$, where X is a finite set of finite elements of D. The advantage of the coherent case for our purposes is that we can present our logic in a finitary form. Given a distributive lattice A, its space of points is constructed as $\mathrm{Spec}\, A$, the set of prime filters over A, with topology generated by basic sets

$$U_a \equiv \{x \in \mathrm{Spec}\, A | a \in x\} \quad (a \in A).$$

The domain ordering can be recovered as the *specialisation ordering*, which in terms of this representation of Spec A is just inclusion of filters.

Some Trade Secrets of Domains

An algebraic domain is coherent (in the sense of [11]) iff it is "2/3 SFP" in the terminology of [17]. The topological significance of the "MUB axioms" [17] is that they ensure that the compact-open sets are closed under finite intersections, and hence form a distributive lattice which generates the topology. Moreover, we can recover $K(D)$, the poset of finite elements of the domain D, from $A = K\Omega(D)$ as follows: an element $a \in A$ is *prime* if $a \leq b \vee c$ implies $a \leq b$ or $a \leq c$; and a is *consistent* if $a \neq 0$. The sub-poset of consistent primes is denoted by $CPR(A)$. Now the consistent primes of $K\Omega(D)$ have the form $\uparrow b$, $b \in K(D)$. Thus:

$$K(D) \cong (CPR(K\Omega(D)))^{\mathrm{op}}.$$

Also, there are "enough" primes, in the sense that each $U \in K\Omega(D)$ can be written as a disjunction of primes:

$$\uparrow X = \bigcup\{\uparrow b | b \in X\}.$$

We begin by introducing the first part of a metalanguage for denotational semantics, the *type expressions*, with syntax

$$\begin{aligned}\sigma \; ::= \; & \mathbf{1} \mid \sigma \times \tau \mid \sigma \to \tau \mid \sigma \oplus \tau \mid (\sigma)_\perp \mid \\ & P_u\sigma \mid P_l\sigma \mid t \mid \mathrm{rec}\, t.\sigma\end{aligned}$$

where t ranges over type variables, and σ, τ over type expressions.

The standard way of interpreting these expressions is as objects of **SDom** (more generally as cpo's, but **SDom** is closed under all the above constructions as a subcategory of **CPO**). Thus for each type expression σ we define a domain $\mathcal{D}(\sigma) = (D(\sigma), \sqsubseteq_\sigma)$ in **SDom**; $\sigma \times \tau$ is interpreted as product, $\sigma \to \tau$ as function space, $\sigma \oplus \tau$ as coalesced sum, $(\sigma)_\perp$ as lifting, $P_u\sigma$ and $P_l\sigma$ as the upper and lower (or Smyth and Hoare) powerdomains, and $\mathrm{rec}\, t.\sigma$ as the solution of the domain equation

$$t = \sigma(t),$$

i.e. as the initial fixpoint of an endofunctor over **SDom**. Other constructions (e.g. strict function space, smash product) can be added to the list.

So far, all this is standard ([17,23]). Now we begin our alternative approach. For each type expression σ, we shall define a propositional theory $\mathcal{L}(\sigma) = (L(\sigma), \leq_\sigma, =_\sigma)$, where:

- $L(\sigma)$ is a set of formulae

- $\leq_\sigma$, $=_\sigma$ are the relations of logical *entailment* and *equivalence* between formulae.

$\mathcal{L}(\sigma)$ is defined inductively via formation rules, axioms and inference rules in the usual way. We give *selected examples* of the definitions.

Formation Rules (selected)

$$t, f \in L(\sigma)$$

$$\frac{\phi, \psi \in L(\sigma)}{\phi \wedge \psi, \phi \vee \psi \in L(\sigma)}$$

$$\frac{\phi \in L(\sigma),\ \psi \in L(\tau)}{(\phi \times \psi) \in L(\sigma \times \tau),\ (\phi \to \psi) \in L(\sigma \to \tau)}$$

$$\frac{\phi \in L(\sigma),\ \psi \in L(\tau)}{(\phi \oplus \psi) \in L(\sigma \oplus \tau)}$$

$$\frac{\phi \in L(\sigma)}{\Box\phi \in L(P_u\sigma),\ \Diamond\phi \in L(P_l\sigma)}$$

$$\frac{\phi \in L(\sigma[\mathrm{rec}\, t.\sigma/t])}{\phi \in L(\mathrm{rec}\, t.\sigma)}$$

We should think of $(\phi \to \psi)$, $\Box\phi$ etc. as "constructors" or "generators", which build basic formulae at complex types from arbitrary formulae at simpler types. Note that no constructors are introduced for recursive types; we are taking advantage of the observation, familiar from work on information systems [14], that if we work with preorders it is easy to solve domain equations up to *identity*.

Auxiliary Predicates

Before proceeding to the axiomatisation proper, we shall define some auxiliary predicates on formulas. These will be used as side-conditions on a number of axioms and rules (e.g. $(\to - \vee - R)$ below). Thus it is important that they are recursive predicates, defined syntactically on formulae. The main predicates we define are:

- PNF(ϕ): ϕ is in *prime normal form*, defined by the conditions that disjunctions only occur in ϕ immediately under $\Box$, and that occurrences of $\oplus$ are of one of the forms $(\phi \oplus f)$, $(f \oplus \psi)$.

Then for ϕ in PNF, we define:

- CON(ϕ): ϕ is *consistent*, i.e. so that we have

$$\mathrm{CON}(\phi) \Leftrightarrow \neg(\phi \leq f) \Leftrightarrow [\![\phi]\!] \neq \emptyset$$

(where $[\![\,]\!]$ is the semantics to be introduced below).

- T(ϕ): ϕ requires *termination*, i.e. so that we have

$$\mathrm{T}(\phi) \Leftrightarrow \neg(t \leq \phi) \Leftrightarrow \bot \notin [\![\phi]\!].$$

Of these, the idea of formal consistency, and its definition for function spaces, go back to [12], and also play a major role in [20,21]. The other predicates, as syntactic conditions on expressions, are apparently new (and in the presence of the type constructions we are considering, specifically function space and coalesced sum, the definitions of CON and T are *mutually recursive*). We illustrate the definitions of CON and T by giving the clauses for function types and coalesced sum:

- $\mathrm{CON}(\bigwedge_{i\in I}(\phi_i \to \psi_i) \Leftrightarrow \forall J \subseteq I.$

$$\mathrm{CON}(\bigwedge_{j\in J}\phi_j) \Rightarrow \mathrm{CON}(\bigwedge_{j\in J}\psi_j)$$

- $\mathrm{T}(\phi \to \psi) \Leftrightarrow \mathrm{CON}(\phi)\ \&\ \mathrm{T}(\psi)$

- $\mathrm{CON}(\bigwedge_{i\in I}(\phi_i \oplus f) \wedge \bigwedge_{j\in J}(f \oplus \psi_j)) \Leftrightarrow$

$$\neg(\mathrm{T}(\bigwedge_{i\in I}\phi_i)\ \&\ \mathrm{T}(\bigwedge_{j\in J}\psi_j))$$

$$\&\ \mathrm{CON}(\bigwedge_{i\in I}\phi_i)\ \&\ \mathrm{CON}(\bigwedge_{j\in J}\psi_j)$$

- $\mathrm{T}(\phi \oplus f) \Leftrightarrow \mathrm{T}(f \oplus \phi) \Leftrightarrow \mathrm{T}(\phi)$.

Once we have defined CON and T, we can introduce a predicate CPR(ϕ), which holds if ϕ is a disjunction of formulae ϕ_i in PNF such that for some i CON(ϕ_i) holds.

Now we turn to the axiomatization. The axioms of our logic are all "polymorphic" in character, i.e. they arise from the type constructions uniformly over the types to which the constructions are applied. Thus we omit type subscripts.

The axioms fall into two main groups.

Logical Axioms (selected)

These give each $\mathcal{L}(\sigma)$ the structure of a distributive lattice.

$(\leq -ref)\quad \phi \leq \phi$

$(\leq -trans)\quad \dfrac{\phi \leq \psi,\ \psi \leq \chi}{\phi \leq \chi}$

$(= -I)\quad \dfrac{\phi \leq \psi,\ \psi \leq \phi}{\phi = \psi}$

$(\wedge - I)\quad \dfrac{\phi \leq \psi_1,\ \phi \leq \psi_2}{\phi \leq \psi_1 \wedge \psi_2}$

$(\wedge - E - L)\quad \phi \wedge \psi \leq \phi$

$(\wedge - dist)\quad \phi \wedge (\psi \vee \chi) \leq (\phi \wedge \psi) \vee (\psi \wedge \chi)$

Type-specific Axioms (selected)

These articulate each type construction, by showing how its generators interact with the logical structure.

$$(\to - \leq) \quad \frac{\phi' \leq \phi, \ \psi \leq \psi'}{(\phi \to \psi) \leq (\phi' \to \psi')}$$

$$(\to - \wedge) \quad (\phi \to \bigwedge_{i \in I} \psi_i) = \bigwedge_{i \in I} (\phi \to \psi_i)$$

$$(\to - \vee - L) \quad (\bigvee_{i \in I} \phi_i \to \psi) = \bigwedge_{i \in I} (\phi_i \to \psi)$$

$$(\to - \vee - R) \quad (\phi \to \bigvee_{i \in I} \psi_i) = \bigvee_{i \in I} (\phi \to \psi_i)$$

$$(CPR(\phi))$$

$$(\Box - \leq) \quad \frac{\phi \leq \psi}{\Box\phi \leq \Box\psi}$$

$$(\Box - \wedge) \quad \Box \bigwedge_{i \in I} \phi_i = \bigwedge_{i \in I} \Box \phi_i$$

$$(\Box - f) \quad \Box f = f$$

The axiom $(\Box - f)$ exemplifies the possibilities for fine-tuning in our approach. It corresponds exactly to the *omission* of the empty set from the upper powerdomain.

To make precise the sense in which this axiomatic presentation is equivalent to the usual denotational construction of domains we define, for each (closed) type expression σ, an interpretation function

$$[\![]\!]_\sigma : L(\sigma) \longrightarrow K\Omega(\mathcal{D}(\sigma))$$

by

$$[\![\phi \wedge \psi]\!]_\sigma = [\![\phi]\!]_\sigma \cap [\![\psi]\!]_\sigma$$

$$[\![t]\!]_\sigma = D(\sigma) = 1_{K\Omega(\mathcal{D}(\sigma))}$$

$$[\![(\phi \to \psi)]\!]_{\sigma \to \tau} = \{f \in D(\sigma \to \tau) | f([\![\phi]\!]_\sigma) \subseteq [\![\psi]\!]_\tau\}$$

$$[\![\Box\phi]\!]_{P_u\sigma} = \{S \in D(P_u\sigma) | S \subseteq [\![\phi]\!]_\sigma\}$$

$$[\![\Diamond\phi]\!]_{P_l\sigma} = \{S \in D(P_l\sigma) | S \cap [\![\phi]\!]_\sigma \neq \emptyset\}$$

$$\vdots$$

etc. Then for $\phi, \psi \in L(\sigma)$, we define

$$\mathcal{D}(\sigma) \models \phi \leq \psi \ \equiv \ [\![\phi]\!]_\sigma \subseteq [\![\psi]\!]_\sigma.$$

Theorem 1 (Soundness and Completeness) *For all $\phi, \psi \in L(\sigma)$:*

$$\mathcal{L}(\sigma) \vdash \phi \leq \psi \iff \mathcal{D}(\sigma) \models \phi \leq \psi.$$

Now we define

$$\mathcal{LA}(\sigma) \equiv (L(\sigma)/=_\sigma, \leq_\sigma/=_\sigma),$$

the *Lindenbaum algebra* of $\mathcal{L}(\sigma)$.

Theorem 2 (Stone Duality) *$\mathcal{LA}(\sigma)$ is the Stone dual of $\mathcal{D}(\sigma)$, i.e.*

$$(i) \quad \mathcal{D}(\sigma) \cong \text{Spec } \mathcal{LA}(\sigma)$$
$$(ii) \quad K\Omega(\mathcal{D}(\sigma)) \cong \mathcal{LA}(\sigma).$$

The proofs of these results are rather long, and will be presented elsewhere. They involve the following main steps, for each type construction:

- A *Normal Form* lemma, to the effect that every formula can be proved equivalent to a disjunction of consistent primes (in the syntactic sense of our auxiliary predicates). This is the syntactic counterpart of the semantic "Trade Secret" mentioned above.
- The auxiliary predicates are proved *adequate*, i.e. sound and complete with respect to the semantic interpretation.
- One then proves a *prime completeness theorem*, using the standard description of the ordering on finite elements of $\mathcal{D}(\sigma)$ to prove completeness for syntactically prime formulae. Combined with the normal form lemma, this easily yields the full Completeness Theorem. This in turn, combined with the fact that all elements of $K\Omega(\mathcal{D}(\sigma))$ are definable by formulae in $L(\sigma)$, yields the Stone Duality theorem.
- Finally, to carry these results over to recursive types, we must ensure that our syntactic type constructions on theories are functorial, and commute with the corresponding semantic constructions on domains. Fortunately, this needs to be done only with respect to embeddings induced by a partial ordering on theories, following ideas of [14].

3 Programs As Elements: Endogenous Logic

We extend our metalanguage for denotational semantics to include typed terms.

Syntax (selected examples)

We have a set of variables $Var(\sigma)$ for each σ.

$$\frac{x \in Var(\sigma),\quad M : \tau}{\lambda x.M : \sigma \to \tau}$$

$$\frac{M : \sigma \to \tau,\quad N : \sigma}{MN : \tau}$$

$$\frac{M : \sigma}{\{\!|M|\!\}_u : P_u\sigma}$$

$$\frac{M : \sigma \to P_u\tau}{M_u^\dagger : P_u\sigma \to P_u\tau}$$

$$\frac{M, N : P_u\sigma}{M \uplus_u N : P_u\sigma}$$

$$\frac{M : P_u\sigma,\quad N : P_u\tau}{M \otimes_u N : P_u(\sigma \times \tau)}$$

We write $\Lambda(\sigma)$ for the set of terms of type σ. Note that $\{\!|.|\!\}$, $\_^\dagger$ arise from the adjunction defining the powerdomain construction; $\uplus$ is the operation of the free algebras for this adjunction; while $\otimes$ is the universal map for the tensor product with respect to this operation [9].

We now introduce an endogenous program logic with assertions of the form

$$M, \Gamma \vdash \phi$$

where $M : \sigma$, $\phi \in L(\sigma)$, and $\Gamma \in \prod_\sigma\{Var(\sigma) \to L(\sigma)\}$ gives *assumptions* on the free variables of M.

Axiomatisation (Selected Examples)

$$x, \Gamma[x \mapsto \phi] \vdash \phi$$

$$\frac{M, \Gamma \vdash \phi \quad \mathcal{L} \vdash \phi \le \psi}{M, \Gamma \vdash \psi}$$

$$\frac{M, \Gamma[x \mapsto \phi] \vdash \psi}{\lambda x.M, \Gamma \vdash (\phi \to \psi)}$$

$$\frac{M, \Gamma \vdash (\phi \to \psi) \quad N, \Gamma \vdash \phi}{MN, \Gamma \vdash \psi}$$

$$\frac{M, \Gamma \vdash \phi}{\{\!|M|\!\}_u, \Gamma \vdash \Box\phi}$$

$$\frac{M, \Gamma \vdash (\phi \to \Box\psi)}{M_u^\dagger, \Gamma \vdash (\Box\phi \to \Box\psi)}$$

$$\frac{M, \Gamma \vdash \Box\phi \quad N, \Gamma \vdash \Box\phi}{M \uplus_u N, \Gamma \vdash \Box\phi}$$

$$\frac{M, \Gamma \vdash \Box\phi \quad N, \Gamma \vdash \Box\psi}{M \otimes_u N, \Gamma \vdash \Box(\phi \times \psi)}$$

Following standard ideas, we can give a denotational semantics for this metalanguage, in the form of a map

$$[\![\,]\!]_\sigma : \Lambda(\sigma) \longrightarrow Env \longrightarrow \mathcal{D}(\sigma)$$

where $Env \equiv \prod_\sigma\{Var(\sigma) \to \mathcal{D}(\sigma)\}$ is the set of *environments*. We can use this to give a semantics for assertions:

$$M, \Gamma \models \phi \;\equiv\; \forall \rho \in Env.\, \rho \models \Gamma \Rightarrow [\![M]\!]_\sigma\rho \models \phi$$

where

$$\rho \models \Gamma \;\equiv\; \forall x \in Var.\, \rho x \models \Gamma x$$

and for $d \in D(\sigma)$, $\phi \in L(\sigma)$:

$$d \models \phi \;\equiv\; d \in [\![\phi]\!]_\sigma.$$

Theorem 3 *The Exogenous logic is sound and complete: for all M, Γ, ϕ:*

$$M, \Gamma \vdash \phi \iff M, \Gamma \models \phi.$$

We can state this result more sharply in terms of Stone Duality: it says that

$$\eta_\sigma(\{[\phi]_{=_\sigma} \mid M, \Gamma \vdash \phi\}) = [\![M]\!]_\sigma\rho,$$

where

$$\eta_\sigma : \mathrm{Spec}\; \mathcal{LA}(\sigma) \cong \mathcal{D}(\sigma)$$

is the component of the natural isomorphism arising from Theorem 2; i.e. that we recover the point of $\mathcal{D}(\sigma)$ given by the denotational semantics of M from the properties we can prove to hold of M in our logic.

4 Programs As Morphisms: Exogenous Logic

Now we introduce a second extension of our denotational metalanguage, which is based on the algebraic metalanguage for cartesian closed categories [19,13], just as the language of the previous section is an extended typed λ-calculus. Terms are sorted on *morphism types* (σ, τ), with formation rules exemplified by

$$\frac{f : (\sigma \times \tau, v)}{\Lambda(f) : (\sigma, \tau \to v)}$$

$$Ap : ((\sigma \to \tau) \times \sigma, \tau).$$

We then form a *dynamic logic* $\mathcal{DL}$, with syntax given by

- $L(\sigma) \subseteq DL(\sigma)$
- $\dfrac{f : (\sigma, \tau) \ \psi \in DL(\tau)}{[f]\psi \in DL(\sigma).}$

We illustrate the axiomatisation of $\mathcal{DL}(\sigma)$ by two examples:

$$\frac{(\phi \times \psi) \ \leq \ [f]\chi}{\phi \ \leq \ [\Lambda(f)](\psi \to \chi)}$$

$$(\phi \to \psi) \times \phi \ \leq \ [Ap]\psi$$

We write the set of (closed) terms of morphism type (σ, τ) as $\Lambda(\sigma, \tau)$. Once again, using standard ideas we can define a semantic function

$$[\![]\!]_{\sigma,\tau} : \Lambda(\sigma, \tau) \longrightarrow \mathbf{SDom}(\mathcal{D}(\sigma), \mathcal{D}(\tau))$$

which interprets each term as a morphism in the appropriate hom-set. Now we define

$$\models \phi \ \leq_\sigma \ [f]\psi \ \equiv \ [\![\phi]\!]_\sigma \subseteq ([\![f]\!]_{\sigma,\tau})^{-1}([\![\psi]\!]_\tau).$$

A *Hoare triple* in $\mathcal{DL}(\sigma)$ is a formula $\phi \leq [f]\psi$ such that ϕ and ψ do not contain any program modalities.

Theorem 4 (Completeness For Hoare Triples) *Let $\phi \leq [f]\psi$ be a Hoare triple. Then*

$$\vdash \phi \leq [f]\psi \iff \models \phi \leq [f]\psi.$$

The restricted form of this Theorem is necessary, since we have

Theorem 5 *The validity problem for $\mathcal{DL}$ is Π^0_2-complete.*

5 Applications: The Logic Of A Domain Equation

A denotational analysis of a computational situation results in the description of a domain which provides an appropriate semantic universe for this situation. Canonically, domains are specified by type expressions in a metalanguage. We can then use our approach to "turn the handle", and generate a logic for this situation in a quite mechanical way. Two substantive case studies of this kind have been carried out, in the areas of concurrency [1] and the λ-calculus [2].

For example, in [1] we define a domain equation for synchronisation trees, and generate a logic which can be applied to the whole class of labelled transition systems. This logic subsumes Hennessy-Milner logic [8], and can be taken as a rational reconstruction of it. Furthermore, we *automatically* get a compositional proof theory for this logic, along the lines indicated above. Since one can define a denotational semantics for, e.g., SCCS [15] in our denotational metalanguage, we get a compositional proof system along the lines of those developed by Stirling and Winskel [24,27]. Moreover, this proof system is guaranteed to be in harmony with our semantics.

References

[1] S. Abramsky, *A Domain Equation For Bisimulation*, unpublished manuscript, 1986.

[2] S. Abramsky, *The Lazy λ-Calculus*, unpublished manuscript, 1986.

[3] J. de Bakker and J. Zucker, Processes and the Denotational Semantics of Concurrency, *Information and Control* **54** (1982) 70-120.

[4] G. Berry, P.-L. Curien and J.-J. Levy, Full Abstraction For Sequential Languages: The State Of The Art, in: M. Nivat and J. Reynolds, eds., *Algebraic Semantics* (Cambridge University Press, 1985).

[5] H. B. Curry and R. Feys, *Combinatory Logic, Vol. 1* (North Holland, Amsterdam, 1958).

[6] E. W. Dijkstra, *A Discipline Of Programming* (Prentice Hall, New York, 1976).

[7] D. Harel, *First Order Dynamic Logic*, Lecture Notes in Computer Science **68** (Springer, Berlin, 1979).

[8] M. Hennessy and R. Milner, On Observing Non-determinism and Concurrency, in: J. de Bakker and J. van Leeuwen, eds., *Automata, Languages and Programming. Proceedings 1980*, Lecture Notes in Computer Science **85** (Springer, Berlin, 1980), 299-309.

[9] M. Hennessy and G. Plotkin, Full Abstraction for a simple parallel programming language, in: J. Becvar, ed., *Mathematical Foundations of Computer Science. Proceedings 1979*, Lecture Notes in Computer Science **74** (Springer, Berlin, 1979).

[10] C. A. R. Hoare, An Axiomatic Basis For Computer Programming, *Comm. of the ACM* **12** (1969) 576-580.

[11] P. Johnstone, *Stone Spaces* (Cambridge University Press, 1982).

[12] G. Kreisel, Interpretation of analysis by means of functionals of finite type, in: *Constructivity in Mathematics* (North Holland, Amsterdam, 1959).

[13] J. Lambek and P. Scott, *Introduction to Higher Order Categorical Logic* (Cambridge University Press, 1986).

[14] G. Winskel and K. G. Larsen, Using Information Systems To Solve Recursive Domain Equations Effectively, in: G. Kahn, D. B. MacQueen and G. Plotkin, eds., *Semantics of Data Types*, Lecture Notes in Computer Science **173** (Springer, Berlin, 1984).

[15] R. Milner, Calculi for Synchrony and Asynchrony, *Theoretical Computer Science* (1983) 267-310.

[16] M. Nivat, Infinite words, infinite trees, infinite computations, in: J. de Bakker, and J. van Leeuwen, eds., *Foundations of Computer Science III.2*, Mathematical Centre Tracts **109** (1979) 3-52.

[17] G. Plotkin, *Lecture Notes In Advanced Domain Theory*, University of Edinburgh, 1981.

[18] A. Pnueli, The temporal logic of programs, in: *Proceedings of the 19th Annual Symposium on Foundations of Computer Science* (IEEE, New York, 1977) 46-57.

[19] A. Poigne, On Specifications, Theories and Models with Higher Types, *Information and Control* (1986).

[20] D. Scott, *Lectures on a Mathematical Theory of Computation*, Programming Reseach Group Monograph (Oxford, 1981).

[21] D. Scott, Domains for Denotational Semantics, in: M. Nielsen and E. M. Schmidt, eds., *Automata, Languages and Programming. Proceedings 1982*, Lecture Notes in Computer Science **140** (Springer, Berlin, 1982).

[22] M. Smyth, Powerdomains and Predicate Transformers: A Topological View, in: J. Diaz, ed., *Automata, Languages and Programming. Proceedings 1983*, Lecture Notes in Computer Science **154** (Springer, Berlin, 1983) 662-675.

[23] M. Smyth and G. Plotkin, The Category-Theoretic Solution Of Recursive Domain Equations, *SIAM J. On Computing* **11, 4** (1982).

[24] C. Stirling, Modal Logics for Communicating Processes, Edinburgh University Computer Science Department Report, 1985.

[25] M. H. Stone, The Theory Of Representations For Boolean Algebras, *Trans. Amer. Math. Soc.* **40** (1936) 37-111.

[26] G. Winskel, *Events In Computation*, Ph.D. Thesis, University of Edinburgh 1980.

[27] G. Winskel, A Complete Proof System For SCCS with Modal Assertions, Cambridge University Computer Laboratory Report, 1985.

On the Formal Semantics of Statecharts

(Extended Abstract) †

D. Harel[1,2,3] A. Pnueli[1,2,4] J. P. Schmidt[1,5] R. Sherman[1,6]

Abstract: Statecharts have been introduced recently [H] as a visual formalism for specifying the behavior of complex reactive systems. They extend classical state transition diagrams in several ways, while retaining, and even enhancing, their visual appeal. In particular, statecharts cater for hierarchical descriptions, high-level and low-level events, and notably, multi-level concurrency with a broadcast communication mechanism that can give rise to chain-reaction effects. In this paper we provide a formal syntax and (operational) semantics for statecharts. The semantics appears to be novel in a number of ways, among which are its treatement of shared variables, chain reactions and simultaneous multiple messages.

1. Reactive systems and State Diagrams

The literature on software and systems engineering is almost unanimous in recognizing the existence of a major problem in the specification and design of large and complex *reactive systems.* A reactive system (see [P, HP]), in contrast with a *transformational system*, is characterized by being, to a large extent, event-driven, continuously having to react to external and internal stimuli. Examples include telephones, communication networks, computer operating systems, avionics systems, VLSI circuits, and the man-machine interface of many kinds of ordinary software. The problem is rooted in the difficulty of describing reactive behavior in ways that are clear and realistic, and at the same time formal and rigorous, sufficiently so to be amenable to detailed computerized simulation. The behavior of a reactive system is really the set of allowed sequences of input and output events, conditions, and actions, perhaps with some additional information such as timing constraints.

Notable among the solutions proposed for this problem are Petri nets [R], CSP [Ho] CCS [M], ESTEREL [BC], and Temporal Logic [P]. A more recent approach involves *statecharts* [H], which constitute an attempt to revive the classical formalism of finite state machines (FSM's) and their visual counterpart, state transition diagrams, and make it fitting for use in large and complex applications. Indeed, people working on the design of really complex systems have all but given up on the use of conventional FSM's and their state diagrams, and for several reasons.

1. State diagrams are 'flat'. They provide no natural notion of depth, hierarchy or modularity, and therefore do not support stepwise, top-down or bottom-up development.
2. State diagrams are uneconomical when it comes to transitions. An event that causes the very same transition from a large number of states, such as a high-level interrupt, must be attached to each of them separately, resulting in an unneccesary multitude of arrows.
3. State diagrams are extremely uneconomical, indeed quite infeasible, when it comes to states. As the system under description grows linearly, the number of states grows exponentially, the conventional FSM formalism forcing one to explicitly represent them all.
4. Finally, state diagrams are inherently sequential in nature, and do not cater naturally for concurrency.

There have been attempts to remove some of these drawbacks, by using various kinds of hierarchical or communicating state machines, but we consider these solutions to be unsatisfactory. Typically, the hierarchies are merely structural and do not provide real savings in the size of the resulting description, and the communication is usually one-to-one, being channel- or processor-based, allowing for only a single set of communicating machines on the highest level of the description. Moreover, for the most part, these extensions are not diagrammatic, and hence one loses the advantages that a visual medium might offer.

2. Statecharts

Statecharts were proposed to overcome these drawbacks while preserving, and even enhancing, the visual appeal of conventional state diagrams. We shall only review

[1] Ad Cad, Inc., Cambridge, MA.
[2] The Weizmann Inst., Rehovot, Israel.
[3] Carnegie-Mellon Univ., Pittsburgh, PA.
[4] Univ. of Texas, Austin, TX.
[5] Courant Inst., NYU, New York.
[6] USC/ISI, Marina del Ray, CA.

† See note at the end of the paper.

the essentials of the formalism very briefly here, referring the reader to [H] for more details and examples. More examples, as well as several related developments, appear in [BDH, DH1, DH2]. In a nutshell we might say:

$$\text{statecharts} = \text{state-diagrams} + \text{depth} + \text{orthogonality} + \text{broadcast-communication}$$

The idea of depth is illustrated in Fig. 1, where (ii) may replace (i). The symbols e, f, g, and h stand for events that trigger the transitions, and the bracketed c is a condition. Thus, $g[c]$ triggers the transition from A to C if and when g occurs, but only if c is true at that time. State D is the XOR of A and C, so that being in D is tantamount to being either in A or in C, but not in both. The main point here is the f-arrow, which leaves the contour of D and hence, by definition, applies to both A and C, as in (i). This simple idea, when applied to large collections of states in a multi-level manner, overcomes points 1 and 2 above. Notice the way the small *default arrows* depend on their scope: in (i) state A is singled out as being the default, or start-state, of the three, a fact represented in (ii) by the top default arrow; the bottom one, however, states that C is default among A and C if we are already in D, and hence alleviates the need for continuing the h-arrow beyond D's boundary.

Orthogonality is the dual of the XOR decomposition of states, being, in essence, an AND decomposition. Fig. 2 illustrates this. In (ii) state Y consists of two orthogonal components, A and D, related by AND: to be in Y is tantamount to being in both A and D, and hence the two default arrows. The intended semantics of (ii) is given by its equivalent 'flat' version (i), which represents a sort of automata product. Notice the simultaneity of transitions that takes place when event e occurs in state configuration (B, F), and the merging and splitting transitions that lead to and from Y. Notice also the special condition $in(G)$ attached to the f-transition from C, and the way it is reflected in (i). Fig. 2 is, of course, somewhat misleading, since (ii) may not seem to be any better than (i). However, this is obviously the heart of the exponential blow-up problem, the number of states in the (i) version being the product of the numbers in the (ii) version. If the orthogonality construct is used often, and on many levels, difficulties 3 and 4 above are overcome in a reasonable way, as can be further observed by studying the examples in the aforementioned references.

Another feature of statecharts is the ability to 'remember' a previous visit to a state. Fig. 3 shows a *history entrance* into A, which overrides the default arrow that leads to D. The default is taken when the entrance is via the

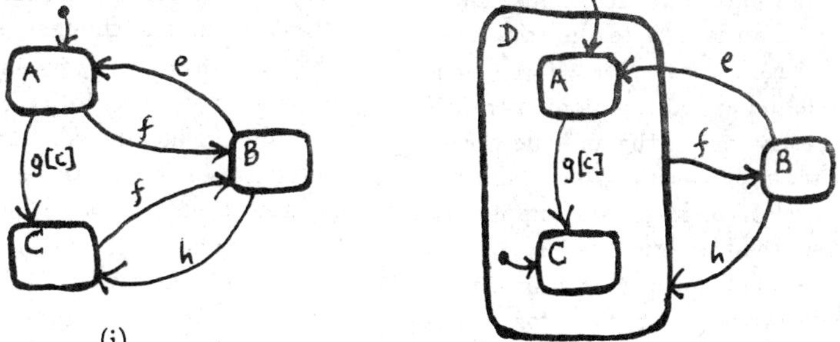

(i) (ii)

Figure 1

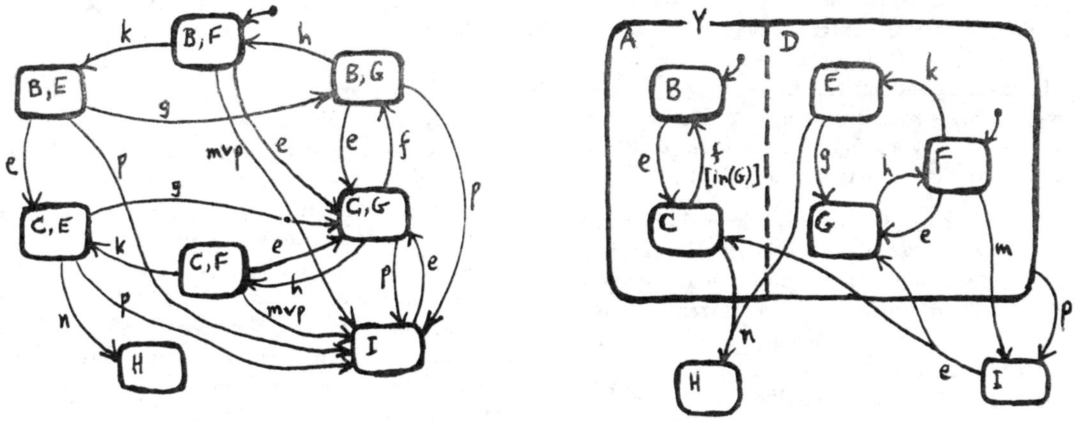

(i) (ii)

Figure 2

f-arrow, whereas if A is entered via the e-arrow the state entered is that one of B, C or D that the system happened to be in when it was most recently in A. If the state thus entered has its own substates, then the default arrows that must appear therein are used to determine the lower-level states actually entered.

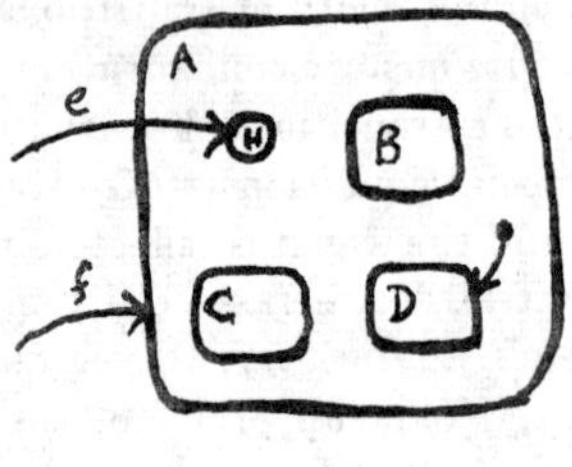

Figure 3

Now, Figs. 1–3 do not contain any outputs, and hence, so far, orthogonal components can synchronize only through common events (like e in Fig. 2), and can affect each other only through *in*(*state*) conditions. The real subtlety of the way statecharts model concurrency is in their *output* events. Here statecharts can be viewed as an extension of Mealy machines, as we allow output events, which we call *actions*, to be attached optionally to the triggering event along a transition. However, in contrast with conventional Mealy machines, an action appearing along a transition in a statechart is not merely sent to the 'outside world' as an output. Rather, it can, and typically *will*, affect the behavior of the statechart itself in orthogonal components. This is achieved by a simple broadcast mechanism: just as the occurrence of an external event causes transitions in all components at which it is relevant (see Fig. 2, for example), if event e occurs and a transition labelled e/f is taken, the action f is immediately activated, and is regarded as an (internal) event, possibly causing further transitions in other components.

Fig. 4 shows a simple example of this. If we are in (B, F, J) and along comes the external event m, the next configuration should be (C, G, I), by virtue of e being generated in H and triggering the two transitions in components A and D. This is a *chain reaction* of length 2. If now external event n occurs, the new configuration will be (B, E, J), by virtue of a similar chain reaction of length 3.

This concludes our brief discussion of the main features of the language, as discussed at length in [H]. Statecharts have been used in the design of a complex avionics system in the Israel Aircraft Industries, and are currently being used experimentaly in a number of additional industrial projects. Statecharts are also at the heart of a commercial product, STATEMATE1, that is intended as a graphical working environment for the engineers involved in reactive systems. Such an implementation is impossible without a formal semantics, and the current paper actually grew out of our work on STATEMATE1.

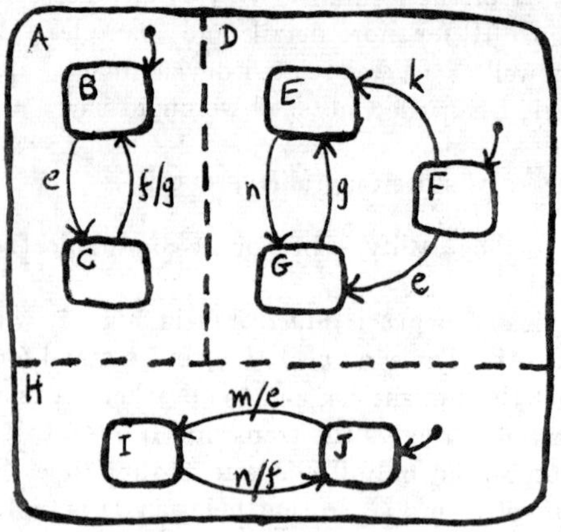

Figure 4

3. The Semantics: A Discussion

It is quite obvious that even the basic features presented here raise interesting semantic problems. For one, an instantaneous description of the system specified by a statechart must contain a state configuration whose length is not fixed, but changes as orthogonal states are entered and left. Moreover, we would like chain reactions to satisfy two seemingly contradictory properties. On the one hand, they should ideally take 'zero time'; that is, the new state configuration ought to be obtained in the very next step, so that other external events will not be able to interrupt, and perhaps alter, the inevitable chain reaction. On the other hand, the *order* of the transitions taking place within a chain reaction is important, even though they really do not take time. This is one of the main issues that our semantics addresses.

The appendix to this extended abstract contains the formal syntax and the operational semantics that we propose. It first presents a detailed syntax of a rather powerful version the statecharts language, complete with compound events and conditions, and shared variables that can be assigned to and tested. Thus, $e \wedge f$ and $e \vee f$ are events, and similarly for conditions (which are also closed under negation). Apart from e's and f's, the actions that can appear to the right of the '/' along transitions include $c :=$*true* and $c :=$*false* for a condition c, and $v := \tau$ for a variable v and an appropriate algebraic expression τ. In addition, there are several special kinds of events and conditions. For example, $en(s)$ and $ex(s)$ are events that occur upon entering and exiting state s, respectively, and $in(s)$ is the corresponding condition. Also, for expressions τ and σ we have conditions such as $\tau = \sigma$ and $\tau < \sigma$, as well as the event $ch(v)$, which occurs when v changes value. Any condition gives rise to the two events $tr(c)$ and $fs(c)$, which occur when c changes from false to true and vice versa. (Thus, for example, the events $en(s)$ and $tr(in(s))$ will always occur together.) Also, any event gives rise to the condition $ny(e)$, which stands for 'e has *not-yet* occurred.' This condition, as we shall see later, refers only to what is happening inside the currently evaluated chain reaction. And so, while events are not closed under negation, one *can* state that an event has not yet occured since the beginning of the latest chain reaction. Another special condition is $cr(c)$, which stands for 'the current value of c', and refers to the value of condition c within the current chain reaction. Similarly, we have $cr(v)$ for a variable or expression v, representing its current value within a chain reaction.

The reader who is well-versed in the semantic difficulties raised by such languages as CCS and CSP will no doubt realize the potential difficulties this syntax raises. Not only do we have high level events (like f in Fig. 1(ii) and p in Fig. 2(ii)), concurrency on all levels, and defaults and history entrances that bubble control down to the states on the lowest levels, but we also have simultanteous reactions to events broadcast throughout the system, and shared variables that can, in principle, be assigned simultaneously, possibly generating conflicting values. Some of the decisions that have to be made here involve protecting chain reactions from incoming external events, while complying with the order implicit in them, and resolving conflicts, either by an undefined outcome or by nondeterminism.

The bulk of the appendix is devoted to presenting a formal operational semantics to this version of statecharts. Our approach can be superficially described as follows. To make the explanation simple we shall assume that we are in a configuration **C** and that a single external event e that has just occurred. Our intention is to define the set of next configurations, $next(\mathbf{C})$, the elements of which are the legal outcomes of applying all transitions triggered by e, followed by all their consequences, including newly enabled transitions, followed by all *their* consequences, etc. (This sequence will not be able to become infinite, as a study of the semantics reveals.)

Given **C** and e, we first find all transitions T that are 'relevant' to the event e in configuration **C**, in the sense that (i) T originates in some ancestor of a subconfiguration of **C** in the state-tree, and (ii) its triggering event indeed occurs when e does. In doing so one must keep track of those T's that are mutually inconsistent, and therefore cannot be taken simultaneously; they will give rise to nondeterminism, as consistent ones must be taken together. Figuring out (i) above entails computing appropriate *least common ancestors* (LCA's) in the state-tree, and (ii) requires a careful definition, mutually inductive in events and conditions, and further complicated by the ny and cr constructs. Haven found such a T, we must 'apply' it, with all its consequences.

Here is where the semantics becomes really intricate. We proceed by defining *micro-steps*, with a 'real' step being a maximal sequence of them. Micro-steps thus capture the internal order in which the simultaneous transitions and actions of a single step are carried out. Micro-steps are not directly transparent to the user, although, as we exemplify below, the ny and cr constructs can be used to exploit them beneficially. In a micro-step the system nondeterministically selects any consistently executable subset of the enabled transitions (in particular, a subset with no conflicting assignment statements), and executes them at one and the same time, adding their immediate consequent actions to the events and transitions awaiting execution, and hands this remaining set to the next micro-step for execution. Note that history and default entrances in states that appear in the target sub-configurations of the transitions that are taken have to be taken into account, and their effects on the lowest-level states have to be calculated. A sequence of micro-steps terminates, and thus becomes an externally observable step, if and when there are no posible consistent choices left. Hence the term 'maximal'.

During micro-step execution, $cr(c)$ and $cr(v)$ are updated to contain the current values of conditions, variables and expressions, and $ny(e)$ is updated to reflect whether or not e has already been executed in the present step, i.e., since the first micro-step in the sequence. In contrast, the status and values of events, conditions and expressions that do *not* involve cr and ny do not noticably change within the micro-steps of a single step. Thus, cr and ny are the only mechanisms for detecting the order in which micro-steps are carried out inside a step.

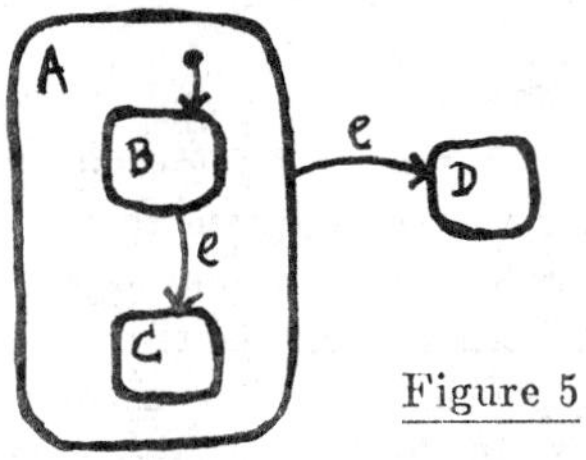

Figure 5

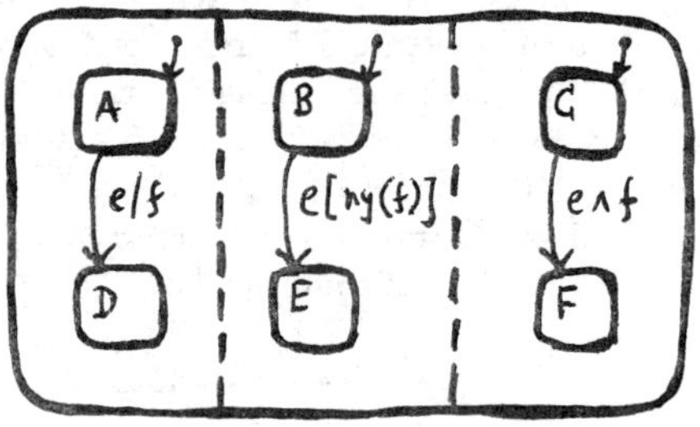

Figure 6

4. Some Examples

A few simple examples are now in order. Fig. 5 shows a simple kind of 'structural' nondeterminism, where if in B and e occurs the two possible outcomes are C and D. Fig. 6 shows nondeterminism caused by the freedom of selecting subsets in micro-steps. Here, if in (A, B, C), event e can cause the system to reach (D, B, F) if the transitions are considered in the order $A \rightarrow D, B \rightarrow E, C \rightarrow F$, since the condition in the second one will be false. However, (D, E, F) is also possible, if the transitions are considered in the order $B \to E, A \to D, C \to F$. Note that the $e \wedge f$ event occurs in both cases, as the conjunction is not sensitive to the ordering within a step.

The definition of conflicting actions forces an order to be put on two assignments to the same variable, but not on assignments to different variables. Thus, in Fig 7, if the initial values of x and y are both 0, then while the final value of both will be 1 after the step resulting from e in configuration (A, B, C), there are two nondeterministic resulting configurations: (D, E, C) (if both leftmost transitions are considered together, since x and y havn't just become equal; they were equal all along), and (D, E, F) (if they are taken separately, since one of the two variables became 1 while the other remained 0, thus making $tr(x = y)$ happen).

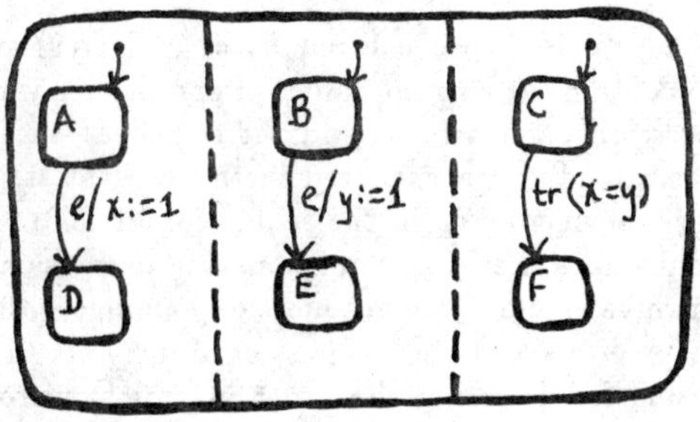

Figure 7

Here are two examples of using the *cr* and *ny* constructs to one's advantage. The first is in forcing *exclusivity* of the effect of an event e, and the second is in specifying *priority* of e over f in case they both occur simultaneously. Fig. 8 shows how the two conflicting assignments force the micro-steps to be taken in sequence, with the consequence that once one of them is taken in the first micro-step the guarding condition on the second one prevents *it* from being taken, as it tests the system's current whereabouts in the first component. The result is that when e occurs in (A, B) the systems reacts nondeterministically, entering either (A, D) (with $x = 2$) or (C, B) (with $x = 1$). Notice that omitting the *cr*'s gives a quite different behavior, with the final configuration being deterministically (C, D), but the final value of x being similarly 1 or 2.

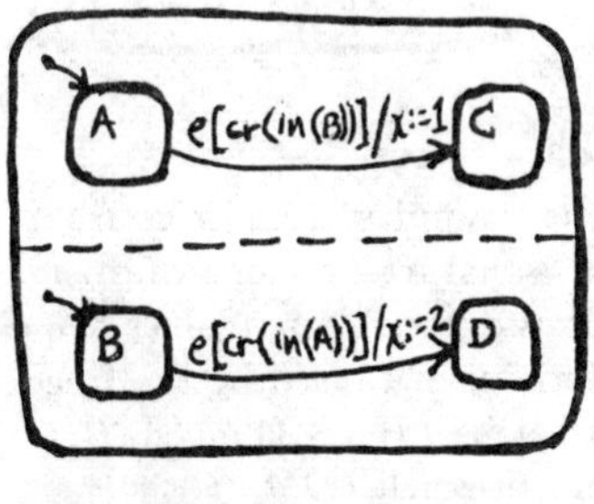

Figure 8

In Fig. 9 we are interested in specifying that in state A event e leads to B and f leads to C, but that if e and f occur *simultaneously* the e-transition is to have priority. This is achieved by the *ny* operator as illustrated.

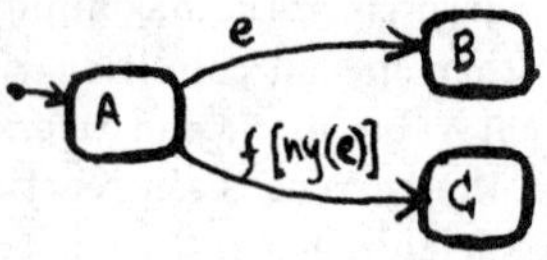

Figure 9

Finally, a somewhat more elaborate kind of priority specification appears in Fig. 10. Here we want to specify that if e occurs when in (E, C), i.e., there is a nondeterministic choice to be made in going to F or B in the top component, then in the bottom component we want to go from C to D only if the former choice was taken. Of course, this might be achieved simply by eliminating the '$/f$' action from the arrow leading to B, but for the sake of the example we may assume that f has other purposes, and has to be carried out whenever e occurs. We could have used a new action symbol, but the example shows how the *cr* alone can be used to achieve th edesired effect.

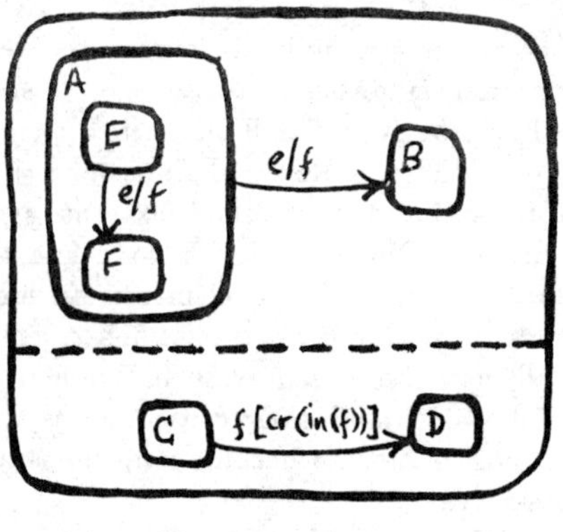

Figure 10

It should be noted that statecharts with no appearences of *cr* and *ny* behave in the intuitive way expected. Thus, the semantics prescribes the behavior described above for the likes of Figs. 1–4. An interesting question is whether this semantics can be easily extended to deal with a number of additional features described informally in [H]. One of the most promising of these is *overlapping states*, the importance of which has been argued in [DH1]. A preliminary attempt at providing a formal syntax and semantics for statecharts with overlapping states appears in [K], but it does not contain any actions, assignments, special events and conditions, or the special constructs *ny* and *cr*. It would be interesting to know if the two semantics are compatible on the rather primitive version obtained by taking the common features only, and whether our semantics can be easily extended to deal with overlapping states using the ideas of [K].

Appendix : Formal Syntax and Semantics

1. Syntax

The syntax of statecharts is defined over the following basic sets of elements: states, transitions, primitive events, primitive conditions and variables. Using these basic sets of elements we define the extended sets of: events, conditions, expressions and labels and the interrelations connecting them.

a. **States** : The set of *states*, S, is defined together with a hierarchy function ρ, a type function ψ, a set of history symbols H and a default function δ.

The *hierarchy function* $\rho : S \rightarrow 2^S$, defines for each state its *substates*. If $\rho(x)=\rho(y)$ then $x=y$. There exists a unique state $r \in S$ such that $\forall s \in S \; r \notin \rho(s)$, r is the *root* of the statechart. ρ^*, ρ^+ are extensions of ρ defined by : $\rho^*(s)=\bigcup_{i\geq 0}\rho^i(s)$, $\rho^+(s)=\bigcup_{i\geq 1}\rho^i(s)$.

The *type function* $\psi : S \rightarrow \{AND, OR\}$ defines for each state its type. If $\rho(s)\neq\emptyset$ and $\psi(s)=OR$ then $\rho(s)$ is a *xor* decomposition of s. This means that when the system is in a state s it is in one and only one of the substates of s. If $\rho(s)\neq\emptyset$ and $\psi(s)=AND$ then $\rho(s)$ is an *and* decomposition of s. This means that when the system is in a state s it is simultaneously in all the substates of s.

The set of *history symbols*, H, is related to the set of states by a function $\gamma : H \rightarrow S$ such that : $\gamma(h_1)=\gamma(h_2)$ implies $h_1=h_2$ and $\gamma(H)$ is a subset of the set of OR states, that is only an OR state may have a history symbol associated with it. It is useful to define $\omega : S \cup H \rightarrow S$ by : $\omega(x)$ is x if $x \in S$ and $\omega(x)$ is $\gamma(x)$ if $x \in H$.

The *default function*, $\delta : S \rightarrow 2^{S\cup H}$, defines for a state s a set of states and history symbols which are contained in the state. If $x \in \delta(s)$ then: for $x \in S, x \in \rho^+(s)$, and for $x \in H, \gamma(x) \in \rho^*(s)$.

$\delta(s)$ is the *default set for* s.

b. **Expressions** : The set of variables is denoted by V_p. The set of *expressions*, V, is defined inductively as follows :

1. If k is a number then $k \in V$.
2. If $v \in V_p$ then $v \in V$.
3. If $v \in V$ then $current(v) \in V$.
4. If $v_1, v_2 \in V$ and op is an algebraic operation then $op(v_1, v_2) \in V$.

$current(v)$ is abbreviated to $cr(v)$.

c. **Conditions** : The set of primitive conditions is denoted by C_p. The set of *conditions*, C, is defined inductively as follows :

1. $T, F \in C$, T, F stand for *true*, *false*, respectively.
2. If $c \in C_p$ then $c \in C$.
3. If $s \in S$ then $in(s) \in C$.
4. If $e \in E$ then $not\_yet(e) \in C$.
5. If $u, v \in V$, $R \in \{=,>,<,\neq,\leq,\geq\}$ then $u \; R \; v \in C$.
6. If $c \in C$ then $current(c) \in C$.
7. If $c_1, c_2 \in C$ then $c_1 \vee c_2, c_1 \wedge c_2, \neg c_1 \in C$.

$current(c)$ is abbreviated to $cr(c)$, $not\_yet(e)$ is abbreviated to $ny(e)$.

d. **Events** : The set of primitive events is denoted by E_p. The set of *events*, E, is defined inductively as follows :

1. $\lambda \in E$, λ is the *null event.*
2. If $e \in E_p$ then $e \in E$.
3. If $c \in C$ then $true(c), false(c) \in E$.
4. If $v \in V$ then $changed(v) \in E$.
5. If $s \in S$ then $exit(s), entered(s) \in E$.
6. If $e_1, e_2 \in E$ then $e_1 \vee e_2, e_1 \wedge e_2 \in E$.
7. If $e \in E, c \in C$ then $e[c] \in E$.

$true(c), false(c)$ are abbreviated to $tr(c), fs(c)$, respectively. $exit(s), entered(s)$ are abbreviated to $ex(s), en(s)$, respectively. $changed(v)$ is abbreviated to $ch(v)$. e is *atomic* if e is of the form 1-5.

e. **Actions** : The set of *actions*, A, is defined inductively as follows :

1. $\mu \in A$, μ is the *null action.*
2. If $c \in C_p, d \in C$ then $c := d \in A$.
3. If $v \in V_p, u \in V$ then $v := u \in A$.
4. If $a_i \in A$, $i=0,\ldots,n$ then $a_0; \cdots ; a_n \in A$

$a \in A$ is *atomic* if it is of the form 1-3.

f. **Labels** : The set of *labels*, L, is the set of pairs $E \times A$, and for $l=(e,a)$ we write e/a. Informally, if e/a is a label of a transition t, then t is triggered by e and a is executed when t is taken.

g. **Transitions** : The set of *transitions*, T, is defined as the set of triples $T \subset 2^S \times L \times 2^{S\cup H}$. A transition $t=(X,l,Y)$ is composed of: a *source set* X, a *target set* Y, denoted *source* (t), *target* (t), respectively, and a label l. Informally, if $l=e/a$, the system is in X and e occurs then t is enabled and can be taken. If t is taken, a is executed and the system is than at Y.

2. Notations and Definitions

Following are formal definitions of basic terms used in the next section. In appendix A we give diagrams illustrating these definitions.

a. A state s is *basic* if $\rho(s)=\emptyset$.

b. For a set of states X, the *Lowest Common Ancestor* of X, denoted $LCA(X)$ is defined as follows: $LCA(X)=x$ iff :

1. $X \subseteq \rho^*(x)$
2. $\forall s \in S \;\; X \subseteq \rho^*(s) \Rightarrow x \in \rho^*(s)$

For a set of states X, the *strict Lowest Common OR Ancestor* of X, denoted $LCA^+(X)$ is defined as follows: $LCA^+(X)=x$ iff :

1. $X \subseteq \rho^+(x)$
2. $\psi(x)=OR$
3. $\forall s \in S$ if $\psi(s)=OR$ then $X \subseteq \rho^*(s) \Rightarrow x \in \rho^*(s)$

c. For a transition $t \in T$, $LCA(t)$ is defined as the LCA^+ of its source and target sets of states. That is if $t=(X,l,Y)$ then $LCA(t)=LCA^+(X \cup \omega(Y))$.

d. Two states x,y are *orthogonal*, denoted $x \perp y$, if either $x=y$ or their LCA is an AND state, that is $\psi(LCA(\{x,y\}))=AND$.

e. A set of states X, is an *orthogonal set* if $\forall x,y \in X \;\; x \perp y$. Note that $\{x\}$ is an orthogonal set for every $x \in S$.

f. A set X is an *orthogonal set relative to s* if.

1. $X \subset \rho^*(s)$
2. X is an orthogonal set

g. A set X is a *maximal orthogonal set relative to s* if :

1. X is an orthogonal set relative to s.
2. $\forall y \in \rho^*(s),\; y \notin X \Rightarrow X \cup \{y\}$ is not orthogonal.

Note that for every $s \in S$, $\{s\}$ is a maximal orthogonal set relative to s.

h. A *state configuration of s* is an orthogonal set relative to s all of whose members are basic states.

i. A *maximal state configuration of s* is a maximal orthogonal set relative to s all of whose members are basic states.

j. Given a sequence of maximal state configurations relative to the root, $(X_0,\ldots,X_n)$, and a history symbol h with $\gamma(h)=s$ the *history function* $\tau(h,(X_0,\ldots,X_n))$ defines the substate of s which is the "last visit" of the system in s according to $(X_0,\ldots,X_n)$. Formally, let $I=\{i \mid \rho^*(s) \cap X_i \neq \emptyset\}$. If $I=\emptyset$ then $\tau(h,(X_0,\ldots,X_n))=\delta(s)$, otherwise let j be the maximal number in I. Then since s is an OR state there exists a unique $s' \in \rho(s)$ such that $\rho^*(s') \cap X_j \neq \emptyset$, we define $\tau(h,(X_0,\ldots,X_n))=s'$.

k. The target set of a transition may contain non basic states and history symbols. Each step of the system is defined by a set of transitions which should define a maximal state configuration of the root state. Thus, we have to define a state configuration corresponding to a target set of a transition. The function $C(s,X,(X_0,\ldots,X_n))$ where: X is an orthogonal set realtive to s and $(X_0,\ldots,X_n)$ is a sequence of maximal state configurations of the root state, is defined recursively. $C(s,X,(X_0,\ldots,X_n))$ is a maximal state configuration of s computed by repeatedly applying the default and history functions and completing the orthogonal set into a maximal orthogonal set by taking the defaults in orthogonal components. For the formal definition of $C(s,X,\overline{X})$ see appendix B.

l. The *initial state configuration* X_0, is defined to be $C(root,\{root\},\emptyset)$. The initial state configuration is a maximal state configuration of the root state.

m. A set of transitions Υ is *structurally consistent* if $\forall$ $t_1,t_2 \in \Upsilon \;\; LCA(t_1) \perp LCA(t_2)$. A consistent set of transitions can be taken simultaneously.

n. A transition $t=(Y,l,Z)$ is *structurally relevant* to a state configuration X if for every $y \in Y$ there exists $x \in X$ such that $x \in \rho^*(y)$. If t is structurally relevant to X and the system is in X then t can be taken.

3. Semantics

The semantics is based upon a sequence of time *instants* $\{\sigma_i\}_{i \geq 0}$, corresponding to the sampling rate of the *System Under Desciption* (SUD). The basic time *intervals* are defined by $I_i=[\sigma_i,\sigma_{i+1})$. At σ_{i+1} the SUD *reacts* to *external stimuli* occuring in the interval I_i. The semantics of statecharts is defined by providing the formal definition for changes occuring in the SUD as a reaction to external stimuli. An *external stimulus* associated with σ_{i+1} is a triple (Π,Θ,ξ) where : Π is a set of external primitive events occuring in I_i, Θ is a set of external primitive conditions whose value is *true* at $[\sigma,\sigma_{i+1})$ for some $\sigma \geq \sigma_i$, and ξ is a function, determined by the external environment, such that for a variable v, $\xi(v)=x$ if v's value is x in $[\sigma,\sigma_{i+1})$ for some $\sigma \geq \sigma_i$. A *system configuration* associated with an instant σ_{i+1} is a tuple (X,Π,Θ,ξ) where X is a maximal state configuration of the root state and (Π,Θ,ξ) is an external stimulus associated with σ_{i+1}.

The system reaction at some instant is composed of the set of transitions taken at that instant and the set of events generated when these transitions are taken. Thus, a *system reaction* is a pair (Υ,Π^g) where Υ is a set of transitions called a *step* and Π^g is the set of atomic events *generated* by Υ. Given a system configuration $SC=(X,\Pi,\Theta,\xi)$ we define in this section the set $\{SR=(\Upsilon,\Pi^g)\}$ of *possible system reactions* to SC

Intuitively a step is a set of consistent transitions that are structurally relevant to a given system configuration and enabled under the given external stimuli. The set of generated events is the set of events occuring as a result of taking the step's transitions and executing the actions associated with these transitions. All the transitions participating in a step Υ are taken simultaneously. In our formal definition of a step we sequence the set of taken transitions into *micro-steps* each of which is a subset of Υ. Thus, a step is defined as a sequence of micro-steps. It is important to understand that although micro-steps are essential for the precise definition and understanding of the semantics they are considered as an internal mechanism for computing steps and actually should be hidden from the user. Sophisticated users may use their knowledge about this internal mechanism of micro-steps to define complicated and unusual system reactions. However, in the simplest and most often used cases the system reaction as defined in the following is identical to the intuitive understanding of a step, above. Because of the very rich syntax allowing shared variables and simultaneous assignments to variables in actions the terms "consistent" and "enabled" in the above naive definition should be defined very carefully, and this is the reason for introducing the concept of micro-steps. The reader should remember this simple definition as an intuitive understanding of a step.

Definition : Given a system configuration $SC=(X,\Pi,\Theta,\xi)$ we define below an extension of ξ to V, and we say that v is *evaluated to* x *under* SC if $\xi(v)=x$. ξ is extended to V as follows:

1. If k is a number then $\xi(k)=k$.
2. If $v_1,v_2 \in V$ then $\xi(op(v_1,v_2))=op(\xi(v_1),\xi(v_2))$.
3. If $v \in V$ then $\xi(cr(v))=\xi(v)$.

Definition : Given a system configuration $SC=(X,\Pi,\Theta,\xi)$, SC *satisfies* $c \in C$, denoted $SC \rightarrow c$, is defined inductively as follows :

1. $SC \rightarrow T$, $not(SC \rightarrow F)$.
2. If $c \in C_p$ then $SC \rightarrow c$ iff $c \in \Theta$.
3. If $s \in S$ then $SC \rightarrow in(s)$ iff $X \cap \rho^*(s) \neq \emptyset$
4. If $e \in E$ then $SC \rightarrow ny(e)$ iff $not(SC \rightarrow e)$.
5. If $u,v \in V, R \in \{=,>,<,\neq,\geq,\leq\}$ then $SC \rightarrow u\ R\ v$ iff $\xi(u)\ R\ \xi(v)$.
6. If $c \in C$ then $SC \rightarrow cr(c)$ iff $SC \rightarrow c$.
7. If $c_1,c_2 \in C$ then
   7.1. $SC \rightarrow c_1 \wedge c_2$ iff $SC \rightarrow c_1$ and $SC \rightarrow c_2$.
   7.2. $SC \rightarrow c_1 \vee c_2$ iff $SC \rightarrow c_1$ or $SC \rightarrow c_2$.
   7.3. $SC \rightarrow \neg c_1$ iff $not(SC \rightarrow c_1)$.

Definition : Given a system configuration $SC=(X,\Pi,\Theta,\xi)$, $e \in E$ *occurs at* SC, denoted $SC \rightarrow e$, is defined inductively as follows :

1. $SC \rightarrow \lambda$.
2. If $e \in E_p$ then $SC \rightarrow e$ iff $e \in \Pi$.
3. If $c \in C$ then $not(SC \rightarrow tr(c))$, $not(SC \rightarrow fs(c))$.
4. If $v \in V$ then $not(SC \rightarrow ch(v))$.
5. If $s \in S$ then $not(SC \rightarrow ex(s))$, $not(SC \rightarrow en(s))$.
6. If $e_1,e_2 \in E$ then
   6.1. $SC \rightarrow e_1 \wedge e_2$ iff $SC \rightarrow e_1$ and $SC \rightarrow e_2$.
   6.2. $SC \rightarrow e_1 \vee e_2$ iff $SC \rightarrow e_1$ or $SC \rightarrow e_2$.
7. If $e \in E, c \in C$ then $SC \rightarrow e[c]$ iff $SC \rightarrow e$ and $SC \rightarrow c$.

Given a system configuration SC as above, the SUD reaction is composed of a sequence of micro steps. The first micro step is defined as a set of transitions whose trigger occurs at SC. This first micro step results in a *micro system configuration* to which the SUD may react by another micro step and so forth. A system configuration is a full description of the SUD status in a time instance. The micro system configuration is an abstract term in the sense that it does not describe an actual status of the SUD. In the following it is defined as an extension of the system configuration term, used to defined the abstract SUD status *between* micro steps. Note that by the following definition the only operators that are "sensitive" to the micro step mechanism are the cr, ny operators. A user who does not use these operators will in most cases get a system reaction corresponding to the simple intuitive definition introduced in the begining of this section. In the following, we formally define the micro system configuration term and the terms of satisfy and occur for conditions and events, with respect to a micro system configuration.

Definition : A *micro system configuration* μSC with respect to a system configuration $SC=(X,\Pi,\Theta,\xi)$ is a quadruple $\mu SC=(\mu X,\mu\Pi,\mu\Theta,\mu\xi,\mu Y)$ where :

1. μX is a partial state configuration, $\mu X \subseteq X$.
2. $\mu\Pi \subset E_p \cup \{ex(s),en(s) | s \in S\}$, $\Pi \subseteq \mu\Pi$.
3. $\mu\Theta \subseteq \{cr(c) | c \in C_p\}$.
4. $\mu\xi$ is a function assigning values to current-variables,
5. μY is a partial state configuration. i.e. $\mu\xi$ is a function from $\{cr(v) \mid v \in V_p\}$ to the set of numbers.

Definition : Given $\mu SC=(\mu X,\mu\Pi,\mu\Theta,\mu\xi,\mu Y)$ with respect to a system configuration $SC=(X,\Pi,\Theta,\xi)$, we define below an extension of $\mu\xi$ to V, and we say that v is *evaluated to* x *under* μSC if $\mu\xi(v)=x$. $\mu\xi$ is extended to V as follows:

1. If k is a number then $\mu\xi(k)=\mu\xi(cr(k))=k$.
2. If $v\in V_p$ then $\mu\xi(v)=\xi(v)$.
3. If $v_1,v_2\in V$ then $\mu\xi(op(v_1,v_2))=op(\mu\xi(v_1),\mu\xi(v_2))$.
4. If $v_1,v_2\in V$ then $\mu\xi(cr(op(v_1,v_2)))=op(\mu\xi(cr(v_1)),\mu\xi(cr(v_2)))$.

Note that for any cr-free expression v, $\mu\xi(v)=\xi(v)$.

Definition : Given $\mu SC=(\mu X,\mu\Pi,\mu\Theta,\mu\xi,\mu Y)$ with respect to a system configuration $SC=(X,\Pi,\Theta,\xi)$, μSC *satisfies* $c\in C$, denoted $\mu SC\rightarrow c$, is defined inductively as follows :

1. $\mu SC\rightarrow T$, $not(\mu SC\rightarrow F)$.
2. If $c\in C_p$ then:
   - 2.1. $\mu SC\rightarrow c$ iff $SC\rightarrow c$.
   - 2.2. $\mu SC\rightarrow cr(c)$ iff $cr(c)\in\mu\Theta$.
3. If $s\in S$ then:
   - 3.1. $\mu SC\rightarrow in(s)$ iff $SC\rightarrow in(s)$
   - 3.2. $\mu SC\rightarrow cr(in(s))$ iff $\mu X\cap\rho^*(s)\neq\emptyset$ or $\mu Y\cap\rho^*(s)\neq\emptyset$
4. If $e\in E$ then:
   - 4.1. $\mu SC\rightarrow ny(e)$ iff $not(\mu SC\rightarrow e)$.
   - 4.2. $\mu SC\rightarrow cr(ny(e))$ iff $\mu SC\rightarrow ny(e)$.
5. If $u,v\in V, R\in\{=,>,<,\neq,\geq,\leq\}$ then:
   - 5.1. $\mu SC\rightarrow u\ R\ v$ iff $\mu\xi(u)\ R\ \mu\xi(v)$.
   - 5.2. $\mu SC\rightarrow cr(u\ R\ v)$ iff $\mu SC\rightarrow cr(u)\ R\ cr(v)$.
6. If $c_1,c_2\in C$ then :
   - 6.1. for $c_1\wedge c_2\in C$:
     - 6.1.1. $\mu SC\rightarrow c_1\wedge c_2$ iff $\mu SC\rightarrow c_1$ and $\mu SC\rightarrow c_2$.
     - 6.1.2. $\mu SC\rightarrow cr(c_1\wedge c_2)$ iff $\mu SC\rightarrow cr(c_1)$ and $\mu SC\rightarrow cr(c_2)$.
   - 6.2. for $c_1\vee c_2\in C$:
     - 6.2.1. $\mu SC\rightarrow c_1\vee c_2$ iff $\mu SC\rightarrow c_1$ or $\mu SC\rightarrow c_2$.
     - 6.2.2. $\mu SC\rightarrow cr(c_1\vee c_2)$ iff $\mu SC\rightarrow cr(c_1)$ or $\mu SC\rightarrow cr(c_2)$.
   - 6.3. for $\neg c_1\in C$:
     - 6.3.1. $\mu SC\rightarrow\neg c_1$ iff $not(\mu SC\rightarrow c_1)$.
     - 6.3.2. $\mu SC\rightarrow cr(\neg c_1)$ iff $not(\mu SC\rightarrow cr(c_1))$.

Note that for cr,ny-free condition c, $\mu SC\rightarrow c$ iff $SC\rightarrow c$.

Definition : Given two micro system configurations $\mu SC_1=(\mu X_1,\mu\Pi_1,\mu\Theta_1,\mu\xi_1,\mu Y_1)$, $\mu SC=(\mu X,\mu\Pi,\mu\Theta,\mu\xi,\mu Y)$, both with respect to a system configuration $SC=(X,\Pi,\Theta,\xi)$ we say that μSC is a *possible successor* of μSC_1 if:

1. $\mu X\subseteq\mu X_1$.
2. $\mu\Pi_1\subseteq\mu\Pi$.
3. $\mu Y_1\subseteq\mu Y$.

Definition : Given $\mu SC=(\mu X,\mu\Pi,\mu\Theta,\mu\xi,\mu Y)$ which is a possible succesor of $\mu SC_1=(\mu X_1,\mu\Pi_1,\mu\Theta_1,\mu\xi_1)$ both with respect to a system configuration $SC=(X,\Pi,\Theta,\xi)$, $e\in E$ *occurs at* μSC, denoted $\mu SC\rightarrow e$, is defined inductively as follows :

1. $\mu SC\rightarrow\lambda$.
2. If $e\in E_p$ then $\mu SC\rightarrow e$ iff $e\in\mu\Pi$.
3. If $c\in C$ then:
   - 3.1. $\mu SC\rightarrow tr(c)$ iff either $\mu SC_1\rightarrow tr(c)$ or $\mu SC_1\rightarrow cr(\neg c)$ and $\mu SC\rightarrow cr(c)$.
   - 3.2. $\mu SC\rightarrow fs(c)$ iff either $\mu SC_1\rightarrow fs(c)$ or $\mu SC_1\rightarrow cr(c)$ and $\mu SC\rightarrow cr(\neg c)$.
4. If $v\in V$ then $\mu SC\rightarrow ch(v)$ iff either $\mu SC_1\rightarrow ch(v)$ or $\mu\xi_1(cr(v))\neq\mu\xi(cr(v))$.
5. If $s\in S$ then :
   - 5.1. $SC\rightarrow ex(s)$ iff either $\mu SC_1\rightarrow ex(s)$ or $ex(s)\in\mu\Pi$
   - 5.2. $SC\rightarrow en(s)$ iff either $\mu SC_1\rightarrow en(s)$ or $en(s)\in\mu\Pi$.
6. If $e_1,e_2\in E$ then
   - 6.1. $\mu SC\rightarrow e_1\wedge e_2$ iff $\mu SC\rightarrow e_1$ and $\mu SC\rightarrow e_2$.
   - 6.2. $\mu SC\rightarrow e_1\vee e_2$ iff $\mu SC\rightarrow e_1$ or $\mu SC\rightarrow e_2$.
7. If $e\in E, c\in C$ then $\mu SC\rightarrow e[c]$ iff $\mu SC\rightarrow e$ and $\mu SC\rightarrow c$.

Note that since $\lambda[c]\equiv c$ we have $C\subseteq E$.

Lemma : For any $e\in E$, if $\mu SC_1\rightarrow e$ then $\mu SC\rightarrow e$.

In the following, we define the micro step term. Informally, a micro step is a set of transitions whose trigger occur at a given micro system configuration and which can be taken simultaneously without causing any conflicts, either structurally or in values assigned to variables and conditions.

Lemma : If $SC=(X,\Pi,\Theta,\xi)$ is a system configuration then $\mu Sc=(X,\Pi,\Theta,\xi,\emptyset)$ is a micro system configuration with respect to SC. Also, μSC is a possible successor of itself.

Definition : Given a micro system configuration $\mu SC=(\mu X,\mu\Pi,\mu\Theta,\mu\xi,\mu Y)$, two atomic actions a,b are *inconsistent* under μSC if:
either $a\equiv c:=d_1$ and $b\equiv c:=d_2$ for some $c\in C_p$
or $a\equiv v:=u_1$ and $b\equiv v:=u_2$ for some $v\in V_p$
Two atomic actions a,b are *consistent* under μSC if they are not inconsistent.
An action $a=a_0;...;a_n$ is *consistent* under μSC if $\forall i,j$ if $i\neq j$ then a_i,a_j are consistent under μSC.

Note that an atomic action is always consistent.

Definition : Given a set of transitions $\mu\Upsilon=\{t_0,...,t_n\}$, where $t_i=(X_i,(e_i,a_i),Y_i)$, $a=a_0;...;a_n$ is the action *caused* by $\mu\Upsilon$.

Definition : Given a micro system configuration μSC, a set of transitions $\mu\Upsilon$ is *consistent* under μSC if:

1. $\mu\Upsilon$ is structurally consistent.
2. the action caused by $\mu\Upsilon$ is consistent under μSC.

Definition : Given two micro system configuration μSC_1 and $\mu SC=(\mu X,\mu\Pi,\mu\Theta,\mu\xi,\mu Y)$ both with respect to SC, where μSC is a possible successor of μSC_1, and a transition t labeled by $l=e/a$, t is *enabled* under μSC if :

1. t is structurally relevant to μSC.
2. $\mu SC \rightarrow e$.

Definition : Given two micro system configurations μSC_1 and $\mu SC=(\mu X,\mu\Pi,\mu\Theta,\mu\xi,\mu Y)$ both with respect to SC, where μSC is a possible successor of μSC_1 and a nonempty set of transitions $\mu\Upsilon$, $\mu\Upsilon$ is a *micro step* from μSC if :

1. $\mu\Upsilon$ is consistent under μSC.
2. $\forall t \in \mu\Upsilon$, t is enabled under μSC.

A micro step causes changes in the current values of conditions and variables and occurrances of new events. These changes are formally defined as follows :

Definition : Given two micro system configuration μSC_1 and $\mu SC=(\mu X,\mu\Pi,\mu\Theta,\mu\xi,\mu Y)$ both with respect to SC, where μSC is a possible successor of μSC_1 and a micro-step $\mu\Upsilon$ from μSC, where $a=a_0;...;a_n$ is the action caused by $\mu\Upsilon$, with a_i being atomic actions:

1. $\mu\Upsilon$ *generates* $e \in E_p$ iff $a_i \equiv e$ for some i.
2. $\mu\Upsilon$ *generates* $ex(s)$ iff $\rho^*(s) \cap \mu X \neq \emptyset$ and there exists $t \in \mu\Upsilon$ s.t. $s \in \rho^+(LCA(t))$.
3. Given a sequence of state configurations $\overline{X}=(X_0,...,X_n)$ where $X_n=X$, $\mu\Upsilon$ *generates* $en(s)$ iff there exists $t \in \mu\Upsilon$ s.t. $\rho^*(s) \cap C(LCA(t), target(t), \overline{X}) \neq \emptyset$ and $s \in \rho^+(LCA(t))$.
4. $\mu\Upsilon$ *assigns* T to $c \in C_p$ iff $a_i \equiv c := d$ and $\mu SC \rightarrow d$ for some i.
5. $\mu\Upsilon$ *assigns* F to $c \in C_p$ iff $a_i \equiv c := d$ and $\mu SC \rightarrow \neg d$ for some i.
6. $\mu\Upsilon$ *assigns* x to $v \in V_p$ iff $a_i \equiv v := u$ and $\mu\xi(u)=x$ for some i.

Lemma : If $\mu\Upsilon$ is a micro step from μSC then :

1. if $\mu\Upsilon$ assigns T (resp. F) to $c \in C_p$ it does not assign F (resp. T) to c.
2. if $x \neq y$ and $\mu\Upsilon$ assigns x to $v \in V_p$ then it does not assign y to v.

Proof : Follows from the consistency of micro-steps.

A micro step also results in a new micro system configuration :

Definition : Let $\overline{X}=(X_0,...,X_n)$ be a sequence of state configurations. Let SC be a system configuration whose state configuration is X_n. Let μSC_1 be a micro system configuration with respect to SC, and let $\mu\Upsilon$ be a micro-step from μSC_1. Then $\mu SC=(\mu X,\mu\Pi,\mu\Theta,\mu\xi,\mu Y)$ is the micro system configuration *reached* by $\mu\Upsilon$ from μSC_1 if:

1. $\mu X=\mu X_1 - \mu X_1 \cap \{\cup \rho^*(LCA(t)) | t \in \mu\Upsilon\}$
2. $\mu\Pi=\mu\Pi_1 \cup \{e \mid \mu\Upsilon \text{ generates } e\}$.
3. $\mu\Theta=\mu\Theta_1 \cap \{cr(c) | \mu\Upsilon$ does not assign F to $c\} \cup \{cr(c) | \mu\Upsilon$ assigns T to $c\}$
4. $\mu\xi(v)=x$ iff $\mu\xi_1(v)=x$ and $\mu\Upsilon$ does not assign any value to v or $\mu\Upsilon$ assign x to v.
5. $\mu Y=\mu Y_1 \cup \{\cup C(LCA(t), target(t), \overline{X}) | t \in \mu\Upsilon\}$

Lemma : If μSC is reached by $\mu\Upsilon$ from μSC_1 then:

1. for $e \in E_p \cup \{ex(s), en(s) | s \in S\}$, $\mu SC \rightarrow e$ iff either $\mu SC_1 \rightarrow e$ or $\mu\Upsilon$ generate e.
2. for $c \in C_p$
   - 2.1. $\mu SC \rightarrow cr(c)$ iff either $\mu SC_1 \rightarrow cr(c)$ and $\mu\Upsilon$ does not assign F to c or $\mu SC_1 \rightarrow cr(\neg c)$ and $\mu\Upsilon$ assign T to c.
   - 2.2. $\mu SC \rightarrow tr(c)(fs(c))$ iff either $\mu SC_1 \rightarrow tr(c)(fs(c))$ or $\mu SC_1 \rightarrow cr(\neg c)(cr(c))$ and $\mu\Upsilon$ assign $T(F)$ to c.
3. for $v \in V_p$
   - 3.1. $\mu\xi(cr(v))=x$ iff either $\mu\xi_1(cr(v))=x$ and $\mu\Upsilon$ does not assign any value to v or $\mu\Upsilon$ assign x to v.
   - 3.2. $\mu SC \rightarrow ch(v)$ iff either $\mu SC_1 \rightarrow ch(v)$ or $\mu\Upsilon$ assign x to v and $\mu\xi_1(cr(v)) \neq x$.

A step is a maximal sequence of micro steps as formally defined in the following :

Definition : Let SC be a system configuration. A *step* Υ from SC is a sequence $(\mu\Upsilon_0, \ldots, \mu\Upsilon_m)$ where :

1. $\mu SC_0=SC$.
2. $\mu\Upsilon_i$ is a micro step from μSC_i, for $i=0,...,m$
3. μSC_{i+1} is the micro system configuration reached by $\mu\Upsilon i$ for $i=0,...,m$.
4. The set $\mu\Upsilon_0 \cup \cdots \cup \mu\Upsilon_n$ is a structurally consistent set of transitions.
5. If t is enabled under μSC_{m+1} then $\{t\} \cup \mu\Upsilon_0 \cup \cdots \cup \mu\Upsilon_n$ is not structurally consistent (i.e. the sequence is maximal).

A step causes the system to reach a new system configuration, which is actually similar to the last micro system configuration reached by the sequence of micro steps composing the step. Since there are no enabled transitions from this last micro system configuration the SUD "waits" there a time interval for new external stimuli. A step also causes some events to occur. These events together with the new values assigned to conditions and variables are the output of the SUD to the external environment.

Definition : Let SC' be a system configuration and let $\Upsilon=(\mu\Upsilon_0, \ldots, \mu\Upsilon_m)$ be a step from SC' taken at time instant σ_i. $SC=(X,\Pi,\Theta,\xi)$ is the system configuration *reached* by Υ if:

1. $X=\mu X_{m+1} \cup \mu Y_{m+1}$
2. Π is the set of primitive events occuring at time interval i.
3. For $c \in C_p$, c holds at σ_i iff $\mu SC_{m+1} \rightarrow cr(c)$.
   Θ is the set of primitive conditions holding at $[\sigma,\sigma_{i+1})$ for some $\sigma \geq \sigma_i$.
4. For $v \in V_p$, v's value at σ_i is x iff $\mu\xi_{m+1}(cr(v))=x$.
   $\xi(v)=x$ if v's value at $[\sigma,\sigma_{i+1})$ is x for some $\sigma \geq \sigma_i$.

Definition : Let SC be a system configuration at instant i and let $\Upsilon=(\mu\Upsilon_0, \ldots, \mu\Upsilon_m)$ be a step from SC taken at σ_i. The set of *generated events* by Υ is $\Pi^g=\{e \mid e$ generated by $\mu\Upsilon_i$ for some $i\}\cup\{e \mid \mu SC_{m+1}\rightarrow e, e$ atomic $\}$.

Definition : A *run* of the SUD is a sequence $\{(SC_i, \Upsilon_i, \Pi_i^g)\}_{i\geq 0}$ where :

1. $SC_0=(X_0, \Pi_0, \Theta_0, \xi_0)$, X_0 is the initial state configuration, and (Π_0, Θ_0, ξ_0) are the external stimuli occuring at the first time interval I_0.
2. Υ_i is a step taken from SC_i at time instant σ_{i+1} for $i\geq 0$.
3. SC_{i+1} is the system configuration reached from SC_i by Υ_i for $i\geq 0$.
4. Π_i^g is the set of generated events by Υ_i for $i\geq 0$.

Definition : Let SC be a system configuration. The SUD is *non deterministic* in SC if there exist two different reactions $(\Upsilon_1, \Pi_1^g), (\Upsilon_2, \Pi_2^g)$ such that $\Pi_1^g\neq\Pi_2^g$ or $\Upsilon_1\neq\Upsilon_2$.

References

[BDH] A. Bar-Tur, D. Drusinsky and D. Harel, "Using Statecharts for Describing the Communication between Complex Systems". Submitted.

[BC] G. Berry and I. Cosserat, "The ESTEREL Synchronous Programming Language and its Mathematical Semantics", in *Seminar on Concurrency* (S. Brookes and G. Winskel, eds.), Lect. Notes in Comput. Sci., Vol 197, Springer-Verlag, Berlin, 1985.

[DH1] D. Drusinsky and D. Harel, "Using Statecharts for Hardware Description", CS85-06, The Weizmann Inst. of Science.

[DH2] D. Drusinsky and D. Harel, "Statecharts as an Abstract Model for Digital Control Units", CS86-12, The Weizmann Inst. of Science. Submitted.

[H] D. Harel, "Statecharts: A Visual Formalism for Complex Systems", *Science of Computer Programming*" **8** (1987). (Early version appeared as "Statecharts: A Visual Approach to Complex Systems", Weizmann Inst. Tech Report, Feb. 1984.)

[HP] D. Harel and A. Pnueli, "On the Development of Reactive Systems", in *Logic and Models of Concurrent Systems* (NATO ASI Series, Vol. 133, K. R. Apt, ed.), Springer-Verlag, Berlin, 1985, pp. 477-498.

[Ho] C. A. R. Hoare, "Communicating Sequential Processes", *Comm. ACM* **21** (1978), 666-677.

[K] H.-A. Kahana, "Statecharts with Overlapping States", M.Sc. Thesis, Bar-Ilan University, 1986. (In Hebrew.)

[M] R. Milner, *A Calculus of Communicating Systems*, Lecture Notes in Computer Science, Vol. 92, Springer-Verlag, Berlin, 1980.

[P] A. Pnueli, "Applications of Temporal Logic to the Specification and Verification of Reactive Systems: A Survey of Current Trends", in *Current Trends in Concurrency* (de Bakker et al. eds.), Lect. Notes in Comput. Sci., Vol. 224, Springer-Verlag, Berlin, 1986, pp. 510-584.

[R] W. Reisig, *Petri Nets: An Introduction*, Springer-Verlag, Berlin, 1985.

(**Note:** This paper is actually incomplete, being essentially an extended abstract, and describing only one approach to the formal semantics of statecharts. There are a number of reasons for considering alternative approaches, among which is the desire that a full symmetry exist between the way orthogonal components relate to each other and the way an entire statechart relates to its environment. The present proposal can be seen to fall short of achieving this goal in its entirety. The full version of this paper, which we unfortunately did not manage to complete in time for inclusion in the proceedings, contains a slightly different approach that overcomes this anomaly. On the majority of standard examples, however, both semantics are equivalent.)

MODELLING COMPUTATIONS: A 2-CATEGORICAL FRAMEWORK

R.A.G. SEELY

Dept. of Mathematics, John Abbott College, P.O. Box 2000
Ste. Anne de Bellevue, Québec H9X 3L9
and
Dept. of Mathematics, McGill University, Montréal, Québec

ABSTRACT

An introduction to 2-categories is given by illustrating how the structure of typed lambda calculus may naturally be viewed as a 2-category. In this vein, the structure of computations or conversions gives rise to notions of lax 2-adjointness.

0. Introduction

It has become standard, when modelling the lambda calculus (first or higher order), to treat beta conversion as equality (and frequently eta conversion as well.) In particular, all categorical semantics (eg. for lambda calculus, in terms of C-monoids -- for untyped -- or cartesian closed categories -- for typed -- (LAMBEK-SCOTT [1986]), and for polymorphic lambda calculus, in terms of PL categories (SEELY [1986])) have this property. However, there is no doubt that something is lost with such an approach, since beta conversion

$$(\lambda\ x \text{ in } A.\ a)\ (b) = a[x{:=}b]$$

explicitly equates each stage in a computation process with the result of the computation.

There are several standard approaches to semantics of lambda calculus which do not make such identifications, particularly for the untyped lambda calculus, and particularly in the setting of domain models. For example, a model of untyped lambda calculus may be given by a triple (D,h,k), where D is a domain, h a map $D \longrightarrow (D \Rightarrow D)$ and k a map $(D \Rightarrow D) \longrightarrow D$, satisfying suitable conditions. (For the moment, let me not specify what "domain" means, nor what kinds of maps h and k are.) In such a context, if h and k are inverse isomorphisms, then D is an extensional model, where both beta and eta conversions are interpreted as identities. Non-extensional models arise from weakening the condition on h, k: for instance, if

$$hk = id(D \Rightarrow D) \quad \text{and} \quad kh \leq id(D)$$

where $\leq$ is defined, usually pointwise, in terms of the order on D, then we get a non-extensional model in which beta conversion is identity, and eta conversion is increasing:

$$(\lambda\ x.\ a(x)) \leq a \quad (\text{for } x \text{ not free in } a).$$

Categorically, we would say that k is left adjoint to h, and so $(D \Rightarrow D)$ is a coreflective subcategory (or subdomain) of D. (SCOTT [1972] calls $(D \Rightarrow D)$ a projection of D.)

Alternatively,

$$hk = id(D \Rightarrow D) \quad \text{and} \quad id(D) \leq kh$$

gives a non-extensional model in which eta conversion is decreasing: ie. h is a left adjoint to k and so $(D \Rightarrow D)$ is a reflective subcategory of D. This is essentially the situation of Scott's $\mathcal{P}\omega$ model, SCOTT [1976].

Finally, replacing $hk = id(D \Rightarrow D)$ with, for instance,

$$hk \leq id(D \Rightarrow D)$$

yields a lambda structure with increasing beta conversion:

$$(\lambda\ x.\ a)(b) \leq a[a{:}\ {=}b].$$

Pairing with this a decreasing eta conversion, $id(D) \leq kh$, yields an adjunction: h is left adjoint to k, (but $(D \Rightarrow D)$ need not be a subcategory of D.)

This last will be the motivating example for the structures of this paper. However, we generalise the usual domain framework by replacing poset structure with categorical structure. We shall work with the typed lambda calculus, for simplicity -- however, I shall indicate at the end how this extends to polymorphic lambda calculus, which is why we use the typed structure. The lambda structure we wish to abstract in this way consists of the types, the terms, and the conversions. This will produce a 2-category, rather than just a category: the types will be the objects, the terms the morphisms, and the conversions will be the 2-cells of this 2-category. The point of this is that the structure of $\Rightarrow$ given by beta and eta conversion amounts to a weak ("lax") notion of adjunction, corresponding in the usual categorical setting to cartesian closedness.

The main purpose of this paper is to introduce 2-categories to computer scientists as a suitable framework for certain types of semantics. Hence a few words of introduction about 2-categories might be suitable. A 2-category is a category enriched with some extra structure: the hom-sets are themselves categories. (This generalises the familiar context in which one has a category, e.g of domains, in which each hom-set inherits a partial order from the orders on the domains. Since a poset is a category, every such category of domains is in fact a 2-category.) The morphisms between morphisms are called "2-cells". There are various axioms which guarantee that the categorical structures on the hom-sets "mesh" well with the original categorical structure (of objects and morphisms). Of course it is my point that the general flavour of this may be gleaned from considering the (typed) lambda calculus: thinking of types as "objects", it is easy to see how a term a of type A with exactly one free variable x of type B may be considered as a map ("morphism") $B \longrightarrow A$. Given another term b of type A with exactly one free variable x of type B, so $b: B \longrightarrow A$ also, then a "2-cell" $p: a \Longrightarrow b$ would be a reduction from a to b. (Notice that p does not affect A, B, though A, B are implicit in any description of p ; p only acts on a to produce b.)

There is an identity reduction $a \Longrightarrow a$ for any term a, and one can compose reductions, in fact in two ways: given terms

$$a,b,c : B \longrightarrow A \quad \text{and} \quad d,e : C \longrightarrow B$$

and given reductions

$$p : a \Longrightarrow b, \; q : b \Longrightarrow c, \quad \text{and} \quad r : d \Longrightarrow e$$

there are evident compositions

$$qp : a \Longrightarrow c \text{ (between terms } B \longrightarrow A\text{), and}$$
$$pr : ad \Longrightarrow be \text{ (between terms } C \longrightarrow A\text{),}$$

where ad and be are defined by composition in the category of types and terms -- ie. by substitution:

$$ad = a[x:=d] \quad \text{and} \quad be = b[x:=e].$$

The main axiom of 2-categories is the "interchange law", which asserts that these two kinds of composition must commute with each other.

A final remark: initially we shall suppose that eta conversion is decreasing, rather than increasing. This follows the proof theorist's view that eta conversion is an expansion:

$$a \leq (\lambda\, x \text{ in } A.\ a(x)) \text{ (for } x \text{ not free in } a)$$

rather than a reduction. As indicated above, this will allow us to regard beta and eta conversions as defining a (lax) adjunction in a fairly standard way. Later, we shall consider the effect of reversing the sense of eta conversion; this allows a different formulation of lax adjunction, but the notion of lax functor becomes less satisfactory.

Acknowledgement: As stated above, this paper is primarily intended as propoganda - 2-categories occur naturally as structures in computer science. (The interested reader should pursue this in more mathematically serious works in "2-categorical logic", particularly those from the "Australian school"; some references are given here.) I have not used the heading "Theorem", but rather "Example", since there are in fact no particularly new ideas or theorems here; this paper is based on SEELY [1979], which gives a similar analysis of first order logic. The main difference between that paper and this, is that in [1979], implication is not successfully treated, whereas here, by concentrating only on implication, those difficulties are avoided.

This work was completed with partial support from Fonds F.C.A.R., Québec.

1. 2-categorical preliminaries

We summarise here the basic notions we need from the general body of 2-category theory; a more comprehensive introduction may be found in KELLY-STREET [1974].

1.1 Definition: A 2-category $\underline{A}$ has the following structure:

(i) a collection $Ob(\underline{A})$ of objects, or 0-cells: A,B, etc.

(ii) a collection $Mor(\underline{A})$ of morphisms, or arrows or 1-cells: $a: B \longrightarrow A$, etc.

(iii) a collection $Cell(\underline{A})$ of 2-cells: $p: a \Longrightarrow b : B \longrightarrow A$, etc. also denoted

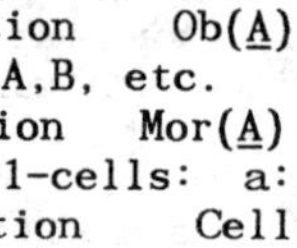

The objects and morphisms form a category $\underline{A}_o$, the "underlying category of $\underline{A}$". For fixed A,B, the morphisms $B \longrightarrow A$ and the 2-cells between them form a category Hom(B,A), also denoted $\underline{A}$(B,A). Composition in this category is known as "vertical composition":

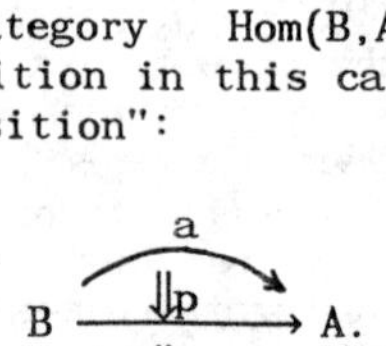

This composite is denoted $q \cdot p$, or qp if no confusion results. Furthermore, given 2-cells

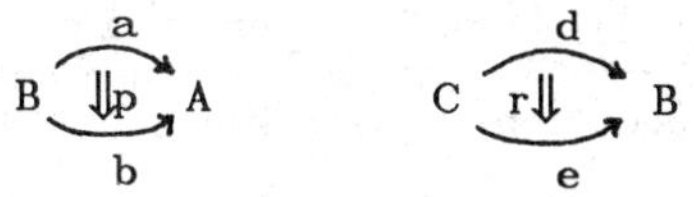

we have a "horizontal composition" giving a 2-cell

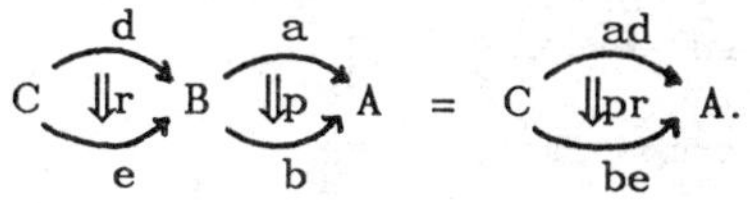

This composite is denoted $p*r$, or pr if no confusion results. (Here ad and be are given by composition in the category $\underline{A}_o$.)

The composition $*$ must be associative and have as identities the evident identity 2-cells.

Finally, the compositions must be compatible: given

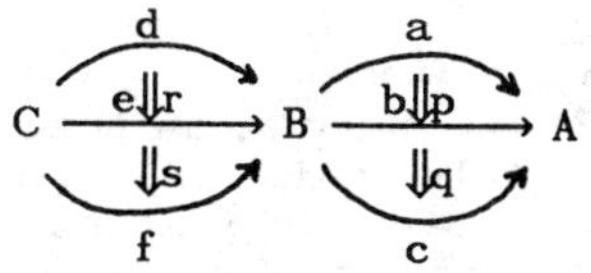

then $(q \cdot p)*(s \cdot r) = (q*s)\cdot(p*r)$, (this is known as the "interchange law".) (If we view a 2-category as a CAT-enriched category, KELLY [1982], this is part of the "functorality" of composition: $\underline{A}(B,A) \times \underline{A}(C,B) \longrightarrow \underline{A}(C,A)$.)

1.2 Examples: The paradigmatic example (for category theorists) is the 2-category CAT of categories, functors, and natural transformations. Indeed, there is an equation (categories: 2-categories) = (SET : CAT), where SET is the (paradigmatic) category of sets and functions.

Other examples can be constructed from various categories of ordered objects, where the hom-sets are themselves ordered naturally, and so are categories. For instance, the category $\underline{QD}_o$ of qualitative domains and stable functions (GIRARD [1986]) becomes a 2-category $\underline{QD}$ by saying there is a 2-cell $f \Longrightarrow g$ just if $f \leq g$ in the Berry order, for stable functions $f,g : X \longrightarrow Y$, (ie. if $f \leq g$ in $X \Rightarrow Y$.)

Finally, as stated in the introduction, the typed lambda calculus may naturally be viewed as a 2-category, as discussed in section 2.

1.3 Definition: A (strict) 2-functor $F : \underline{A} \longrightarrow \underline{B}$ sends objects (respectively morphisms, 2-cells) of $\underline{A}$ to objects (respectively morphisms, 2-cells) of $\underline{B}$, preserving domains, codomains, identities, and compositions.

1.4 Similarly, we can define 2-natural transformations. $K:F \Longrightarrow G:\underline{A} \longrightarrow \underline{B}$ assigns to each object A of $\underline{A}$ a morphism $K(A): F(A) \longrightarrow G(A)$ in $\underline{B}$, natural in the usual sense (for $a:B \longrightarrow A$, $K(A)\cdot F(a) = G(a)\cdot K(B)$), and 2-natural, in that for a 2-cell $p:a \Longrightarrow b:B \longrightarrow A$ in $\underline{A}$, we have

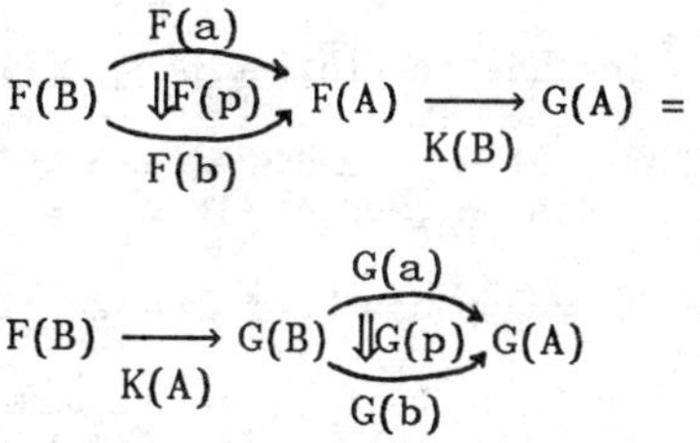

(where this notation means in fact the horizontal composite of, on the left hand side, the identity 2-cell $id(K(B))$ with $F(p)$, and similarly on the right.) (Note that one frequently identifies an object with its identity map.)

1.5 Definition: A modification $\eta:K \longrightarrow L: F \Longrightarrow G: \underline{A} \longrightarrow \underline{B}$ is a morphism of 2-natural transformations, and assigns to each object A of $\underline{A}$ a 2-cell $\eta(A):K(A) \Longrightarrow L(A)$ so that for $a:B \longrightarrow A$ in $\underline{A}$,

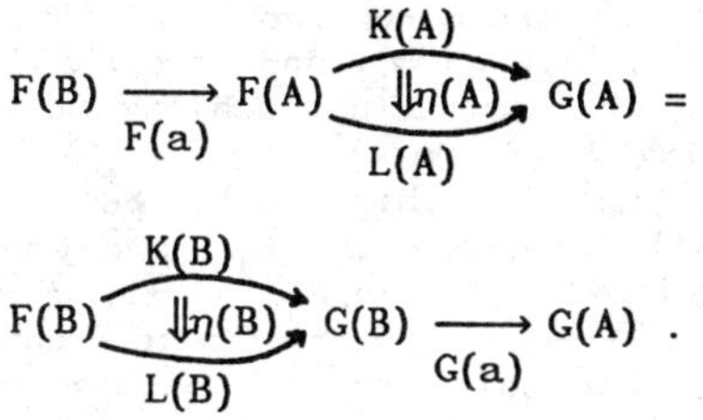

(Again, $F(a)$ means the identity 2-cell, and the equation is between horizontal composite 2-cells.)

(So, 2-CAT is really a 3-category!...)

1.6 In sections 3, 4, we shall also examine weakenings of these notions, in discussing lax functors, weak adjunctions, and so on. For a fuller discussion, see KELLY-STREET [1974], KELLY [1982] and GRAY [1974].

2. The 2-category LAMBDA

2.1 I outlined the structure in the introduction, so now I shall be brief, mainly fixing notation and clarifying some technical points. I assume the reader is familiar with the typed lambda calculus, as in LAMBEK-SCOTT [1986]; the following is a brief summary.

Types are closed under the operations $A \,\&\, B$, and $A \Rightarrow B$.

Terms include variables for each type, and are closed under:

(& I) If a in A, b in B, then ⟨a,b⟩ in A & B.
(& E) If c in A & B, then (1st c) in A, (2nd c) in B.
(⇒ I) If b in B, x a variable in A, then (λ x in A. b) in A ⇒ B.
(⇒ E) If c in A ⇒ B and a in A, then c(a) in B.

Conversions include the following:

(& beta) 1st⟨a,b⟩ = a, 2nd⟨a,b⟩ = b.
(& eta) c = ⟨1st c, 2nd c⟩.

(See below why = appears here instead of ⟹.)

(⇒ beta) (λ x in A. b) (a) ⟹ b[x:=a].
(⇒ eta) c ⟹ λ x in A. c(x) , (where x not free in c).

2.2 LAMBDA is defined as outlined in the introduction: objects are types, morphisms a: B ⟶ A are terms of type A with exactly one free variable x of type B, and a 2-cell between such morphisms is a composition of conversions (a "reduction" -- I shall use this term even though it may seem inappropriate for the increasing eta conversions.)

2.3 I shall treat alpha conversions as identities. Furthermore, for simplicity, I shall concentrate solely on ⇒, and thus shall collapse the 2-categorical structure dealing only with & by regarding (& beta) and (& eta) as identities also. This could be avoided by dropping all reference to &, and generalising the categorical structure to allow morphisms A, B, C,... ⟶ Z with finite sequences of objects as domains: such a morphism should be thought of as an ordinary morphism A & B & C &... ⟶ Z, or equivalently, A ⟶ B ⇒ C ⇒ ... ⇒ Z.

Such notions have been considered by others, but I think that cartesian closed categories are so much more natural that it would be a mistake to omit finite products, (or even a terminal object, for that matter.)

A consequence of this will be that we shall frequently use ordered pairs $\langle x_A, y_B \rangle$ to denote variables of type A & B.

2.4 It is straightforward to check that LAMBDA is in fact a 2-category; most of the details are either implicitly or explicitly in LAMBEK-SCOTT [1986]. Only the interchange law needs comment: in effect we just assume it to be true, introducing an equivalence on reductions. (The validity of this may be checked by considering the corresponding situation in the & ⇒ fragment of first order logic, via the Curry-Howard "types as formulae" isomorphism, where interchange is valid; see SEELY [1979].) The key to the interchange law is this:

2.5 Definition/"Lemma": For p:a ⟹ b:B ⟶ A, r:d ⟹ e:C ⟶ B (as in the introduction), the following reduction sequences are the same:

$$a[x:=d] \overset{p[d]}{\Longrightarrow} b[x:=d] \overset{b[r]}{\Longrightarrow} b[x:=e]$$

$$a[x:=d] \overset{a[r]}{\Longrightarrow} a[x:=e] \overset{p[e]}{\Longrightarrow} b[x:=e].$$

The common composite is p*r.

2.6 Remark: Notice that the associativity of composition of morphisms is equivalent to the equality

$$a[x_B:=b][y_C:=c] = a[x_B:=b[y_C:=c]]$$

for terms $D \xrightarrow{c} C \xrightarrow{b} B \xrightarrow{a} A$.

3. Laxity

3.1 Definition: Given two 2-categories A and B, by a lax functor F: A ⟶ B we mean a function that sends objects, morphisms, 2-cells of A to, respectively, objects, morphisms, 2-cells of B, which is strictly functorial on 2-cells; instead of functorality for morphisms, we have "comparison 2-cells" as follows:

if a: B ⟶ A, b: C ⟶ B in A, there are 2-cells in B

$$\gamma(F;\ a,b):\ F(a)F(b) \Longrightarrow F(ab)$$

$$\iota(F;\ A):\ id(FA) \Longrightarrow F(idA)$$

(Coherence conditions for these will be discussed in the appendix.)

3.2 Example: Fix a type E: then this induces a lax functor

G: LAMBDA ⟶ LAMBDA, G(A) = (E ⇒ A).

(Exercise: define G on morphisms and 2-cells. Then show that in this case γ is (⇒ beta) and ι is (⇒ eta) .)

3.3 Definition: Given two lax functors F: A ⟶ B , G: B ⟶ A, by a lax semantic adjunction F ⊣ G we mean there is a pair of lax 2-natural transformations

K:B(F-,-) ⟶ A(-,G-) and L:A(-,G-) ⟶ B(F-,-)

so that L is weakly left adjoint to K; this means the following:

(i) (laxity of K,L) Instead of strict naturality of K,L, there are comparison 2-cells. For morphisms $a:A_1 \longrightarrow A$ in A, $b:B \longrightarrow B_1$ in B, there are natural transformations (2-cells in CAT) k,l as shown in figure 1.

(Note that K and L are strict in their first coordinate, lax only in the second.)

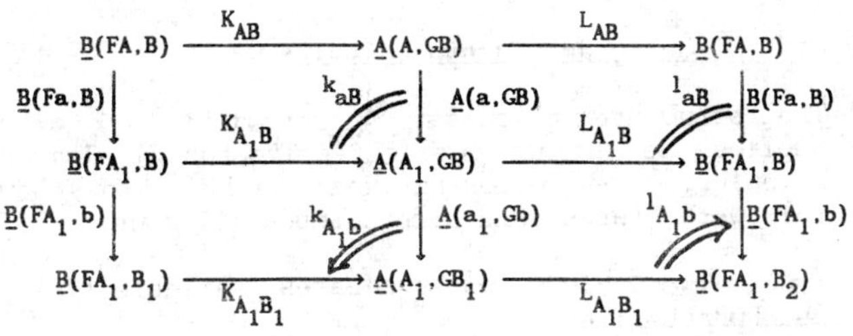

Figure 1

(ii) (L ⊣ K) There are (lax) modifications

$$\eta : id(\underline{A}(-,\ G-)) \Longrightarrow KL$$

$$\epsilon : LK \Longrightarrow id\ (\underline{B}(F-,\ -))$$

so that $(K\epsilon)\cdot(\eta K) = K$ and $(\epsilon L)\cdot(L\eta) = L$.

(Again, coherence is relegated to the appendix, where also the meaning of "lax modification" is given.)

3.4 Example: Fix a type E. If G: LAMBDA ⟶ LAMBDA is the lax functor (E ⇒ A) of 3.2, and if F: LAMBDA ⟶ LAMBDA is the (strict) functor F(A) = (A & E), then F ⊣ G.

It is a pity, but setting out this structure in full would take much too much space here; a summary of the relevant ingredients is given in Table 1. As an example, consider η and ϵ: Given objects (types) A,B and a morphism (term) c: A ⟶ (E ⇒ B),

$$K_{AB}L_{AB}(c) = \lambda\ z \text{ in } E.\ c[x_A := 1st\langle x,z\rangle](2nd\langle x,z\rangle)$$

$$= \lambda\ z \text{ in } E.\ c(z).$$

So $\eta_{AB}(c)$ is the eta conversion

$$c \Longrightarrow \lambda\ z \text{ in } E.\ c(z).$$

Similarly, for a term d: (A & E) ⟶ B, with free variable $\langle x_A,\ z_E\rangle$, $\epsilon_{AB}(d)$ is the beta conversion $(\lambda\ z \text{ in } E.\ d)\ (z) \Longrightarrow d$.

The "triangle identities" are the following principle, which may be viewed as an analogue to beta conversion at the level of reductions:

(BETA) An eta conversion of an occurrence of a logical symbol followed by beta conversion of the same occurrence is an identity operation, (provided the composite is an "endo-operation", so this makes sense.)

F:	(- & E)	k_{aB}:	(& beta)
G:	(E ⇒ -)	k_{Ab}:	(⇒ beta)
ι_G:	(⇒ beta)	l_{aB}:	(& beta)
γ_G:	(⇒ eta)	l_{Ab}:	(⇒ beta)
K:	(&I, ⇒I)	η:	(⇒ eta)
L:	(&E, ⇒E)	ϵ:	(⇒ beta)

TABLE 1

3.5 Usually in defining a notion of adjunction, it is expected that equivalent "semantic" and "syntactic" formulations exist, (the former being in terms of hom-sets, the latter of units and counits.) For lax adjunctions the situation is rather more complicated, and depends on the precise details of the notion of "laxity". In particular, for the notion of 3.3, although no doubt one could "fudge" an equivalent syntactic formulation, what is striking is that the natural such formulation fails. (Section 4 gives a variant - see SEELY [1977] for a discussion of this case.) Further, it is curious to note the role eta conversion plays: for if we reverse the sense of (⇒ eta), then although LAMBDA is no longer an example of 3.3, it gives nevertheless an example of a natural notion of lax syntactic adjunction (which has no natural semantic equivalent.)

4. Reversing eta

4.1 In this section, we briefly consider the situation when eta conversion is increasing. The first remark, of course, is that we must alter the definition (3.1) of lax functor by reversing ι ; γ remains the same.

(It must be admitted that from a 2-categorical viewpoint, this is highly unsatisfactory, in that ι and γ are now going in reversed senses. Indeed, on this observation could be based a fairly convincing argument that this illustrates just why eta ought not to be increasing.)

However, nevertheless, we can give a neat description of the adjoint structure enjoyed by ⇒ in this context as well.

4.2 Definition: Given two lax functors (as in 4.1) F: $\underline{A} \longrightarrow \underline{B}$, G: $\underline{B} \longrightarrow \underline{A}$, by a lax syntactic adjunction F ⊣⊢ G, we mean that there are lax 2-natural transformations

$$\alpha\colon id(\underline{A}) \longrightarrow GF \quad\text{and}\quad \beta\colon FG \longrightarrow id(\underline{B})\ ,$$

lax in the sense that for morphisms a: $A_1 \longrightarrow A$

of $\underline{A}$, $b: B \longrightarrow B_1$ of $\underline{B}$, there are 2-cells

$$n(a) : FG(a)\cdot\alpha(A_1) \Longrightarrow \alpha(A)\cdot a$$
$$e(b) : \beta(B_1)\cdot FG(b) \Longrightarrow b\cdot\beta(B) .$$

Furthermore, there are (lax) modifications

$$\rho : \beta F\cdot F\alpha \Longrightarrow id(F)$$
$$\sigma : G\beta\cdot\alpha G \Longrightarrow id(G)$$

so that

$$\iota G\rho\cdot\alpha = (\sigma F\cdot\alpha)(G\beta F\cdot n\alpha) : G\beta F\cdot GF\alpha\cdot \alpha \Longrightarrow \alpha$$

and

$$\beta\cdot F\sigma = (\beta\cdot\rho G)(e\beta\cdot F\alpha G) : \beta\cdot FG\beta\cdot F\alpha G \Longrightarrow \beta .$$

(Again, coherence is discussed in the appendix.)

4.3 Remark: This situation is somewhat irregular, in that one would expect ρ, σ to have opposite senses. (Indeed, if one were interested in setting up equivalent semantic and syntactic notions of adjunction, in the notations of 3.3 and 4.2, one would expect α, β to correspond to K, L; n, e to correspond to k, l; ρ, σ to correspond to η, ϵ; and the triangle identities to correspond to each other. So in this sense, ρ, σ ought to be unit and counit, and ρ ought to be reversed.) However, for the structure of LAMBDA, this simply is not the case. (However, the above correspondances are more or less correct, and give rise to Table 2.)

4.4 Example: As in 3.4, if F(A) = (A & E), G(A) = (E ⇒ A), then F ⊣ G. Again, the details are but summarized, in Table 2. It seems this formulation is less perspicuous, as may be seen by considering ρ and σ; (part of the "problem" is that in 3.4, our objects are terms, since we are working with hom-categories, whereas here the objects are types.)

Given object A, $\beta(F(A))\cdot F(\alpha(A)) = (\lambda\ z'$ in E. $\langle x_A, z'\rangle)(z_E)$ and id(F(A)) is $\langle x_A, z_E\rangle$; $\rho(A)$ is the beta conversion

$$(\lambda\ z' \text{ in E. } \langle x_A, z'\rangle)(z_E) \Longrightarrow \langle x_A, z_E\rangle.$$

Given object B, $G(\beta(B))\cdot\alpha(G(B)) = \lambda z$ in E. (1st(λz' in E.⟨y,z'⟩)(z))(2nd(λz' in E.⟨y,z'⟩)(z)), where y is of type E ⇒ B, so that id(G(B)) = y; σ(B) is the reduction: beta applied to each occurrence of (λ z' in E. ⟨y,z'⟩)(z) to produce λ z in E.y(z), (note that (& beta) is also used), and then eta conversion to yield y.

α : (&I, ⇒ I)	e : (& beta, ⇒ beta)
β : (&E, ⇒ E)	ρ : (& beta, ⇒ beta,) & eta
n : (& beta, ⇒ beta)	σ : (& beta, ⇒ beta,) & eta

TABLE 2

5. Higher order lambda calculus

The structure discussed in sections 3,4 also applies to higher order (polymorphic) lambda calculus. The following brief outline shows how this works for second order lambda calculus.

Types also include indeterminates (variable types) and FORALL t. A.

Terms are also closed under

(FORALL I) If a in A, t not free in the type of a free variable of a, then (Λ t. a) in (FORALL t. A).

(FORALL E) If c in (FORALL t. A), B a type, then c(B) in A[t:=B].

Conversions include

(FORALL beta) (Λ t. a)(B) ⟹ a[t:=B].
(FORALL eta) c ⟹ Λ t. c(t).

We then define an indexed 2-category POLYLAMBDA, along the lines of the PL categories of SEELY [1986]: now each "fibre" will be a 2-category like LAMBDA in section 2 above. The base category will consist, as in SEELY [1986], of "orders" (ie. "kinds" -- in the second order case, just finite powers of TYPE) and "operators" (ie. "constructors"). Over a kind (e.g. TYPE) will be the 2-category of types with the appropriate free indeterminates (eg. exactly one, over TYPE), terms, and reductions.

In such a context, FORALL t.( ) defines a lax functor between fibres (ie. from the fibre over K × TYPE to the fibre over K, for any kind K.) This functor has a lax left adjoint (strict) functor, viz. "add a dummy indeterminate", (this is essentially the K-combinator, as discussed in SEELY [1986].)

APPENDIX (Coherence considerations)

A.1 It is usual, when considering "lax" concepts, to require a host of coherence conditions for the various comparison 2-cells. Without being too precise, it turns out that insofar as LAMBDA is concerned, these can generally be subsumed under two principles: (BETA) of 3.4, and:

(beta comm) Beta conversions applied to different occurrences of logical symbols commute, (ie. it doesn't matter what order the beta conversions are done.)

Although a related notion is considered in BARENDREGT [1981], from our point of view this principle seems rather more dubious than, say, (BETA): surely one ought to distinguish the order of steps in making a computation, and not merely the steps themselves. However, all the various naturality and coherence conditions suitable for sections 3,4 do seem to require (beta comm).

A.2 For the record, the coherence conditions referred to are the following. We suppose ι decreasing, as in section 3, and use the notation there for objects, morphisms, and 2-cells.

(For γ, ι):

$$\gamma(id(A),a)\cdot\iota(A)F(a) = id(F(a))$$
$$\gamma(a,id(B))\cdot F(a)\iota(B) = id(F(a))$$
$$\gamma(ab,c)\cdot\gamma(a,b)F(c) = \gamma(a,bc)\cdot F(a)\gamma(b,c)$$
$$\gamma(a',b')\cdot F(p)F(r) = F(pr)\cdot\gamma(a,b)$$

(and similarly for G.)

(For k): $k(A,id(B))\cdot\underline{A}(A,\iota(B))K(A,B) = K(A,B)$

$$k(A,b'b)\cdot\underline{A}(A,\gamma(b',b))K(A,B_2) = k(A,b')\underline{B}(FA,b)\cdot\underline{A}(A,Gb')k(A,b)$$

$$k(A,b')\cdot\underline{A}(A,G(p))K(A,B) = K(A,B_1)\underline{B}(FA,p)\cdot k(A,b)$$

(and similarly for l.)

(For η): $k(A,b)L(A,B)\cdot\underline{A}(A,Gb)\eta(A,B) = K(A,B_1)l(A,b)\cdot\eta(A,B_1)\underline{A}(A,Gb)$

(and similarly for ϵ; these give the "laxity" of the modifications η,ϵ.)

A.3 Similar conditions apply for the situation of section 4, with increasing ι.

(For e): $e(id(B)) = \beta(B)\iota(B)$

$$e(b'b)\cdot\beta(B_2)\gamma(b',b) = b'e(b)\cdot e(b')FG(b)$$
$$p\beta(B)\cdot e(b) = e(b')\cdot\beta(B_1)FG(p)$$

(and similarly for n; note the similarity with the conditions for k,l.)

(for ρ): $\rho(A)F(a)\cdot\beta(F(A))F(n(a)) = F(a)\rho(A_1)\cdot e(F(a))F(\alpha(A_1))$

(and similarly for σ; these give the "laxity" of the modifications ρ,σ.)

REFERENCES

H.P. BARENDREGT, The Lambda Calculus, (North-Holland, 1981).

J.-Y. GIRARD, The system F of variable types, fifteen years later, Theoretical Comp. Sci. 45 (1986) 2, 159-192.

J.W. GRAY, Formal Category Theory: Adjointness for 2-categories, (Springer LNM 391, 1974).

G.M. KELLY, ed., Category Seminar, (Springer LNM 420, 1974).

G.M. KELLY, R. STREET, Review of the elements of 2-categories, in KELLY [1974], 75-103.

G.M. KELLY, Basic Concepts of Enriched Category Theory, London Math. Soc. Lecture Note Series 64, (Cambridge University Press, 1982).

J. LAMBEK, P.J. SCOTT, Introduction to Higher Order Categorical Logic, (Cambridge University Press, 1986).

D.S. SCOTT, Continuous lattices, in F.W. Lawvere, ed., Toposes, Algebraic Geometry and Logic, (Springer LNM 274, 1972).

D.S. SCOTT, Data types as lattices, SIAM J. Comput. 5 (1976) 522-587.

R.A.G. SEELY, Hyperdoctrines and Natural Deduction, Ph.D. Thesis, (University of Cambridge, 1977).

R.A.G. SEELY, Weak adjointness in proof theory, in M.P. Fourman, C.J. Mulvey, and D.S. Scott, eds., Applications of Sheaves, (Springer LNM 753, 1979), 697-701.

R.A.G. SEELY, Categorical semantics for higher order polymorphic lambda calculus, Math. Report 86-2, (McGill University 1986). (To appear in J. Symbolic Logic, 1987.)

PARTIAL ORDER MODELS OF CONCURRENCY AND THE COMPUTATION OF FUNCTIONS

Haim Gaifman
Mathematics and CS, Hebrew University Jerusalem, visiting CS Stanford
and
Vaughan Pratt
Stanford University, Department of Computer Science
Stanford, CA 94304
gaifman@navajo.stanford.edu, pratt@navajo.stanford.edu

Abstract

We shall describe an abstract approach, based on structures of partially ordered events, for specifying and analyzing concurrent processes. Within this approach, one framework is the pomset model. Another is based on structures called "prossets" (preorder specification sets) which include, in addition to the <-relation, a relation for denoting simultaneity of events. Some of the results apply to both, with almost identical proofs, others necessitate the use of prossets. We show how within a framework of this kind general abstract definitions can be given to concepts such as: fairness, input event, a location of the process (which can store members of some given, arbitrary cpo), input-location, and the relation computed by the process in a given location. Process composition and formation of loops are defined using a fusion operation, by which several locations are fused into one. Kahn's network semantics turns out to be a rather particular case, derived from an abstract theorem which establishes a connection between operations on processes and the least fixpoint operator on the functions defined by them.

§1 Background

In 1974 Gilles Kahn [Ka] gave a very appealing formal definition of the behavior of a system of communicating deterministic processes, based on the least fixpoint of a system of equations over finite and infinite strings. Faustini [Fau] demonstrated the consistency of this semantics with respect to a plausible operational semantics. In attempting to generalize Kahn's approach to nondeterministic processes, Brock and Ackerman encountered certain "anomalies" [BA77,BA81], which they diagnosed as a consequence of absence of interchannel order information. To cure these anomalies they proposed an extension of Kahn's model called scenarios in which interchannel order was specified. However they did not succeed in supplying a corresponding definition of the meaning of a system in terms of its components together with their interconnections.

Since then there have been a number of approaches to extending Kahn's semantics to treat nondeterminism [KS,Pa, SN,St], most of which have been alternatives to rather than extensions of the Brock-Ackerman scenario notion. The second author of this paper has proposed a definition of composition [Pr82,Pr85,Pr86] in which the scenario notion is retained essentially intact, formalizing a scenario as a partially ordered multiset or pomset, defined as a labelled partial order up to isomorphism. This notion appears to have originated with J. Grabowski [Gra], where it arose naturally in studies of Petri nets. It is noteworthy that Petri's and Kahn's very different semantics have led investigators to this common framework.

An obvious question is whether the partial order approach yields a conservative extension of Kahn's model, by which we mean: is the notion of system connection the same in this extension as Kahn's notion, for the cases that Kahn's model can treat? One of the corollaries of our main results gives a positive answer to this question. A positive answer of this nature has been obtained independently by A. Rabinovich [Rab] under strong assumptions tailored particularly to fit Kahn's original model.

The present paper is concerned with a much wider range of problems than those arising out of the above-mentioned question. In parallel to the pomset model we develop a theory of structures called "prossets," obtained by including a simultaneity relation. We show how in the general framework concepts such as input location, fairness, and computation can be given general abstract definitions which lead to insights translatable into mathematical results. We get an abstract theorem for a fixpoint semantics under very general conditions. It holds for nets of arbitrary (finite or infinite) cardinality, with arbitarily many (finite or infinite) communication channels for each component. We provide for any data type which forms a cpo (complete partial order), and for computations which extend beyond ω (probably of less practical significance than the other extensions). We provide also for input-order-sensitive computing devices, a notion which lies entirely outside the scope of Kahn semantics and which we have only been able to model with prossets.

Processes arising in Kahn's network form a very particular case of the scope of the main theorems. In addition questions concerning fairness can be treated and analyzed.

The one limitation is that time be discrete and well-founded. For non-well-founded computations our model continues to be well-defined, and we believe in agreement with reasonable operational semantics, but with no meaningful correspondence with least-fixpoint semantics.

§2 Framework

2.1 Multisets and Order

A *multiset* on a nonempty set Σ is a structure of the form (V, Σ, μ) where V is the underlying set of the multiset, Σ constitutes its *alphabet*, and $\mu : V \to \Sigma$ assigns to each element of V a letter $a \in \Sigma$. In our application V is a set of *events* conceived as particular occurrences of *actions* drawn from Σ.

The basic structures treated in this work, referred to by the general term *behaviors*, are structures of the form:

$$(V, \Sigma, \Im, \mu)$$

where (V, Σ, μ) is a multiset and $\Im$ is a set of constraints, to be interpreted conjunctively, which provides partial information on the temporal ordering of V. We will consider three possible types of constraints:

$u < v$ (read: u precedes v)

$u \equiv v$ (read: u is simultaneous with v)

$u \leq v$ (read: u is not later than v)

If '$\leq$' is provided in $\Im$ then '$\equiv$' is not considered primitive; '$u \equiv v$' is reduced by definition to the conjunction '$u \leq v$ and $v \leq v$', i.e., to the presence of both inequalities in $\Im$.

It is required that $<$ be irreflexive, that is to say $(u < u) \notin \Im$ and that $\Im$ be closed under the following rules: (i) Transitivity for $<$; (ii) Equivalence for $\equiv$ (if '$\equiv$' is available) and its congruence with respect to $< : u \equiv v < w \Rightarrow u < w$, $w < u \equiv v \Rightarrow w < v$. (iii) Reflexivity and transitivity for $\leq$ (if '$\leq$' is available) and $u \leq v < v' \Rightarrow u < v'$, $w < u \leq v \Rightarrow w < v$. (Note that (iii) implies (ii) via the definition of $\equiv$ in terms of $\leq$.)

Pomsets (partially ordered multisets) are behaviors in which only '$<$' is available. A *linear pomset* is by definition one in which $<$ totally orders V. *Prossets* (preorder specification sets) are behaviors with either '$\equiv$' or '$\leq$' available. A *linear prosset* is by definition one in which $<$ induces a total ordering on the equivalence classes of $\equiv$, that is to say: one of $u < v$, $v < u$, $u \equiv v$ must be in $\Im$. Thus a linear prosset amounts to a total preordering of V. It does *not* entail that $<$ is a linear order.

Whether the prossets are based on '$\equiv$' or on '$\leq$' does not matter – as far as the present work is concerned. But the distinction might become useful in other developments.

If $p = (V, \Sigma, \Im, \mu)$ then we put $V_p = V(p) = V$, $\Sigma_p = \Sigma(p) = \Sigma$, $\Im_p = \Im(p) = \Im$, $\mu_p = \mu$. We also use $<_p$ etc. for the various relations determined by $\Im_p$.

For a constraint $\gamma(u, v)$ we put:

$$p \vdash \gamma(u,v) \Leftrightarrow_{Df} \gamma(u,v) \in \Im_p$$

Furthermore if p is a prosset based on $\equiv$, then $p \vdash u \leq v \Leftrightarrow_{Df} (p \vdash u \equiv v \text{ or } p \vdash u < v)$. Pomsets can be identified with a special kind of prossets, one in which $\equiv$ is just the identity. For some purposes this identification might do. However certain basic concepts, for example linearity, have different interpretations in the pomset and prosset frameworks. For this reason results for prossets (e.g. the results of the last part of the work) do not carry over to the pomset framework. Since on the other hand much of what we say here applies equally to both, we use the term *behavior* as a generic term for such structures.

Isomorphism of behaviors is defined, as usual, as a bijection of the one set of events onto the other which preserves the complete structure.

Processes. A *process* P is a class of behaviors closed under isomorphism on a common alphabet Σ_P. Just as we regard each behavior as a conjunction of conditions, so can we regard a process as the disjunction of those conjunctions.

We take $P, Q, P_0, P', \ldots$ to denote processes and $p, q, r, \ldots$ behaviors throughout.

Note: Lamport [La] has also used a pair of orders in modelling concurrency, but with different properties and for different purposes.

2.2 Basic Relations and Operations

We call p a *subbehavior* of q, written $p \subset q$, if $V_p \subseteq V_q$, $\Sigma_p = \Sigma_q$, and $\Im_p$ and μ_p are the restrictions of $\Im_q$ and μ_q to V_p.

Definition. (i) $p \sqsubseteq q$ if $p \subset q$ and for all $u \in V(p)$ $v \in V(q)$, $v \leq_q u \Rightarrow v \in V(p)$.

(ii) $p \preceq q$ if $p \subset q$ and for all $u \in V(p)$, $v \in V(q)$, $v <_q u \Rightarrow v \in V(p)$.

If $p \sqsubseteq q$ we say that p is a *prefix* of q and q *extends* p. For $p \preceq q$ the terms are $\preceq$-*prefix* and $\preceq$-*extends*. The difference between a prefix and a $\preceq$-prefix is, essentially, that the latter must include all events preceding an event in it, but can omit events simultaneous with it. For pomsets the two concepts coincide, $\sqsubseteq$ being defined in this case as $\preceq$.

Definition. $\pi(P) = \{q : q \sqsubseteq p \text{ for some } p \in P\}$. $\pi(P)$ is the *prefix closure* of P and P is *prefix closed* if $P = \pi(P)$.

If the members of P represent computations that we choose to regard as complete, those of $\pi(P)$ can be viewed as representing stages. Prefix closure is desirable only if the difference between stage and completed behavior is of no concern.

Example. Let P_1 consist of the two behaviors a, $a \to b$ and let P_2 consist only of $a \to b$. In P_1 the process can do a and either quit or follow it by b. In P_2 a must be followed by b. Closing under prefixes adds a to P_2 and obliterates the distinction.

Λ_Σ is the behavior with the empty set of events over alphabet Σ. We shall occasionally omit 'Σ'.

Limits. A $\subset$-chain of behaviors is a set of behaviors totally ordered by $\subset$. If $(p_i)_{i\in I}$ is a $\subset$-chain, lim p_i is the $\subset$-minimal behavior p such that $p_i \subset p$ for all $i \in I$. It is also given by $V(p) = \bigcup V(p_i)$, $\Im(p) = \bigcup \Im(p_i)$, $\mu_p = \bigcup \mu_{p_i}$.

A $\sqsubseteq$-chain is one in which all inclusions are $\sqsubseteq$. Evidently, for $\sqsubseteq$-chains, $p_i \sqsubseteq \lim p_i$. "Chain" in this work without qualification means $\sqsubseteq$-chain.

$\lim P = \{q : q = \lim p_i$ for a chain $(p_i)_{i\in I}$ in $P\}$.

Definition. q is an *augment of* p, written $p \propto q$, just when $(V_p, \Sigma_p, \mu_p) = (V_q, \Sigma_q, \mu_q)$ and $\Im_p \subset \Im_q$.

$$\propto (P) = \{q : q \text{ augments some } p \in P\}$$

$\propto (P)$ is the *augment closure* of P. (Of course, in augmenting we can add only constraints appropriate for the given framework. We cannot add $u \equiv v$ in the pomset setting.) P is *augment closed* if $\propto (P) = P$.

If the absence of a constraint between two events is interpreted as ignorance then an augment of p is a stronger conjunction logically implying p. Hence adding the augment to a disjunction containing p makes no difference. From this point of view augment closure is a natural requirement. If on the other hand we do not want our framework to depend on this interpretation then we may try for results not depending on augment closure. As we shall see, augment closure is on the whole needed in this work.

A *linearization* of p is an augment of p which is linear.

$$\lambda(P) = \{q : q \text{ linearizes some } p \in P\}$$

2.3 Well-foundedness and Fairness

A behavior p is *well-founded* if $<_p$ is a well-founded relation (i.e. there are no infinite descending $<_p$-chains). If p is well-founded we define inductively, for $u \in V(p)$:

$$\text{rank}_p(u) = \{\text{rank}_p(v) : v <_p u\}$$

$$\text{rank}(p) = \{\text{rank}_p(u) + 1 : u \in V(p)\}$$

A process is *well-founded* if all its behaviors are well-founded.

A behavior p is *weakly fair* if $\text{rank}(p) \le \omega$. It is *fair* if the following holds.

Let $u_\equiv = \{v \in V(p) : p \vdash v \equiv u\}$, then for all $v \in V(p)$, $\{u_\equiv : u \le_p v\}$ is finite.

Note that in the case of pomsets $u_\equiv = \{u\}$ and the condition means that the prefix determined by u is finite. For prossets it can be infinite provided that the number of simultaneity classes is constrained to be finite. For linear behaviors weak fairness and fairness coincide. In this case we get the usual concept of fairness - no action is performed after an infinite ascending sequence of events.

A process is *fair* if all its behaviors are fair.

In the case of prossets we can linearize according to rank. The *rank linearization* of a well-founded prosset p is the augment p' obtained by adding the set of constraints $\{u \equiv v : \text{rank}_p(u) = \text{rank}_p(v)\}$ (and closing under the constraint rules). There is no pomset analog for this.

It is easily seen that:

Well-foundedness, weak fairness, and fairness are each preserved under limits of chains.

2.4 Restriction and Disjoint Sums.

Definition. If Σ is a set of actions then p/Σ (read: p restricted to Σ) is the behavior over alphabet $\Sigma_p \cap \Sigma$ obtained by deleting from V_p all events u such that $\mu_p(u) \notin \Sigma$. Thus p/Σ is the result of hiding away all actions not in Σ.

We define: $p/-\Sigma =_{Df} p/(\Sigma_p - \Sigma)$.

Let P_i, $i \in I$, be a process with alphabet Σ. Then

$$\sum P_i = \{p : \Sigma_p = \bigcup \Sigma_i \text{ and } p/\Sigma_i \in P_i \text{ for all } i \in I\}.$$

If the alphabets Σ_i are pairwise disjoint then $\sum P_i$ is said to be a disjoint sum. This corresponds to disjoint processes running concurrently. In the present work '$\sum P_i$' is always employed under the presupposition of disjointness.

Proposition 1. *For* $P = \sum_{i\in I} P_i$, *given* $p \in \pi P$ *and* $q_i \in P_i$ *such that* $p/\Sigma_i \sqsubseteq q_i$ *for all* $i \in I$., *there exists* $q \in P$ *such that* $p \sqsubseteq q$ *and* $q_i = q/\Sigma_i$ *for all* $i \in I$.

$$\begin{array}{ccc} p & \sqsubseteq & q \\ \downarrow /X_i & & \downarrow /X_i \\ p/X_i & \sqsubseteq & q_i \end{array}$$

Proof. Left to the reader.

Note: This implies $\pi(\sum P_i) = \sum(\pi P_i)$.

2.5 Fusion.

We wish to express the consequence of forming connections as per Figure 1.

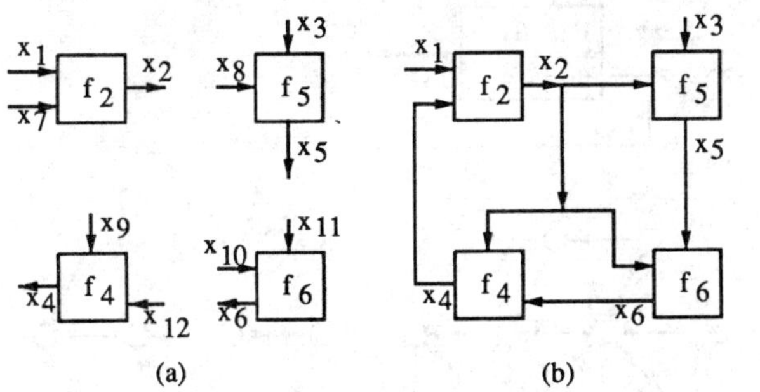

Figure 1. (a) Before Connection (b) After Connection.

We will actually define a more general concept independent of the notion of location (port). This may be illustrated with the situation of four individuals John, Mary, Bill, and Ann shaking hands. Figure 2 shows in the lower portion three events instantiating two actions: John shaking hands with Mary twice in succession, and in parallel Bill and Ann shaking hands once.

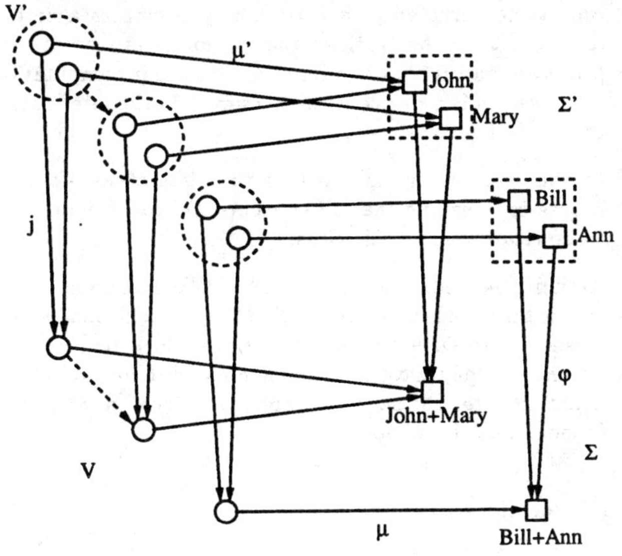

Figure 2. Three Handshakes

Events are solid circles on the left, actions solid squares on the right. In the upper portion are six events John shaking hands, Mary shaking hands, etc. instantiating four actions. The solid arrows describe functions; more abstractly we have:

$$\begin{array}{ccc} V' & \xrightarrow{\mu'} & \Sigma' \\ \downarrow{\scriptstyle j} & & \downarrow{\scriptstyle \varphi} \\ V & \xrightarrow{\mu} & \Sigma \end{array}$$

In such a situation of fusion we have two behaviors – one before fusion (e.g. the upper portion of Figure 2) and one after it – obtained by fusing together certain events. The terms "before" and "after" are somewhat misleading because we can go in either direction. Mathematically it is easier to go from the fused behavior to the unfused one. All that we do is to split single events, substituting each by a cluster of events (simultaneous in the case of prossets, order-incomparable in the case of pomsets). Here is how the construction works.

Given $\varphi : \Sigma' \to \Sigma$, a mapping of Σ' onto Σ (the translation which fuses actions) and a behavior $p = (V, \Sigma, \Im, \mu)$ (the "fused" behavior), put

$$\begin{aligned} V' &= \{(u,a) : u \in V, \varphi(a) = \mu(u)\} \\ \Im' &= \{\gamma((u,a),(u',b)) : \gamma(u,v) \in \Im\} \\ \mu' : V' \to \Sigma' &= \text{ the function } \mu'(u,a) = a \\ p' &= (V', \Sigma', \Im', \mu') \end{aligned}$$

Let $j : V' \to V$ be defined by $j(u,a) = u$. We call j a *φ-fusion* of p' to p and say that p' is the *φ-prefusion* of p, via j. The definition is naturally extended to isomorphic copies of p.

The general nonconstructive definition treats the two behaviors at the same time. Let φ be given as above and suppose we are given two arbitrary behaviors $p = (V, \Sigma, \Im, \mu)$, $p' = (V', \Sigma', \Im', \mu')$. Then a map $j : p' \to p$ is a *φ-fusion* and p' is a *prefusion* of p via j, if the following holds.

(i) $j : V' \to V$ is a map of V' onto V

(ii) $p' \vdash \gamma(u,v) \Leftrightarrow p \vdash \gamma(j(u), j(v))$ for all $u, v \in V'$.

(iii) For all $u \in V$, $\{\mu'(u') : u' \in j^{-1}(u)\} = \varphi^{-1}(\mu(u))$ and μ' is one-to-one on this set.

(Note that (ii) implies, in the case of prossets, that $j(u) = j(v) \Rightarrow u \equiv_{p'} v$. In the case of pomsets u and v are only order-incomparable.)

Evidently every behavior over Σ has a φ-prefusion (where $\varphi : \Sigma' \to \Sigma$) and all are isomorphic. We use $\varphi^{-1}(p)$ to denote such a prefusion. On the other hand not every p' over Σ' can be fused. (It is far less obvious, but true, that if it can be fused then all fusions are isomorphic – a fact which we shall not need in this work.) It is often the case that fusibility can be achieved by adding constraints so as to satisfy (ii). Thus in the handshake example we should include all constraints which are implied by the existing ones and by the requirement that fused events should behave indistinguishably. (For prossets this is simply achieved by adding $u \equiv v$ for all u, v that we are going to fuse.)

(Prefusion and fusion are called respectively restriction and utilization in section 4 of [Pr85], which applies the notion more broadly by not requiring translations to be onto; for example we may obtain our notion of the restriction $/Y$ as the fusion induced by an inclusion map from Y into a given alphabet. In more recent work in collaboration with Ross Casley and Roger Crew we have expressed the above definition categorically by defining the comma category $V \downarrow$ **Set** for the forgetful functor V : **Poset**$^=$ $\to$ **Set**, **Poset**$^=$ being the subcategory of **Poset** with just the nonaugmenting monotone maps. We define the translation functor mapping $\mu : V(p) \to \Sigma$ to the composition of $\varphi : \Sigma \to \Sigma'$ with μ, and take prefusion (restriction) to be the right adjoint of translation. This also works with the category of prosset orders, i.e. pairs $(<, \leq)$, in place of $\mathbf{Poset}^{=}$, with no requirement that the maps be nonaugmenting, which provides an interesting independent confirmation of the general utility of prossets.)

For a process P and a mapping φ on Σ_P we write $P[\varphi]$ for the set of all φ-fusions of prossets in P. When $\varphi(a) = b$ and $\varphi(x) = x$ otherwise we express $P[\varphi]$ as $P[a := b]$. If a family $\varphi(a_i) = b_i$ of such assignments is intended we write $P[a_i := b_i, i \in I]$.

When φ is one-to-one no real fusion takes place but only a renaming of actions, in which case we call $P[\varphi]$ an *action renaming.*

As an example of fusion more closely related to the motivation provided by Figure 1, consider a process with inputs X, Y and output Z which first emits 0 and then iteratively reads a pair of numbers one from each port and emits their sum. This computes the function $f : N^{\varpi} \times N^{\varpi} \to N^{\varpi}$ given by:

$$f(x, y) = 0 f_0(x, y)$$

where

$$f_0(x, \Lambda) = f_0(\Lambda, x_2) = \Lambda$$

$$\textit{For } x_1, x_2 \in N^+, f_0(mx_1, nx_2) = (n + m) f_0(x_1, x_2)$$

$$\textit{For } x_1, x_2 \in N^{\omega} : \textit{defined by limits.}$$

Fusing the output with the input then yields an accumulator, which computes the function g which maps a string of numbers to a string of numbers whose n-th element is the sum of the first n numbers in the input string.

A typical behavior of this accumulator is shown in Figure 3.

Proposition 2. *Let $\varphi : \Sigma' \to \Sigma$ be a translation and let M be an arbitrary set of behaviors over Σ. Then we can lift M by prefusion, getting a family of fusions $j_p : \varphi^{-1}(p) \to p$ such that all following diagrams are commutative.*

$$\begin{array}{ccc} V(\varphi^{-1}(p)) & \subset & V(\varphi^{-1}(q)) \\ \downarrow j_p & & \downarrow j_q \\ V(p) & \subset & V(q) \end{array}$$

Also $pRq \Rightarrow \varphi^{-1}(p) R \varphi^{-1}(q)$ where R is any of $\subset, \sqsubseteq, \preceq, \propto$.

Proof. Left to the reader.

2.6 Relativizations to Classes of Behaviors

Let $\mathcal{L}$ be a class of behaviors. The notions introduced so far can be relativized to $\mathcal{L}$ by restricting in the definitions the behavior variables to range over $\mathcal{L}$. Thus, if $\mathcal{L}$ is the class

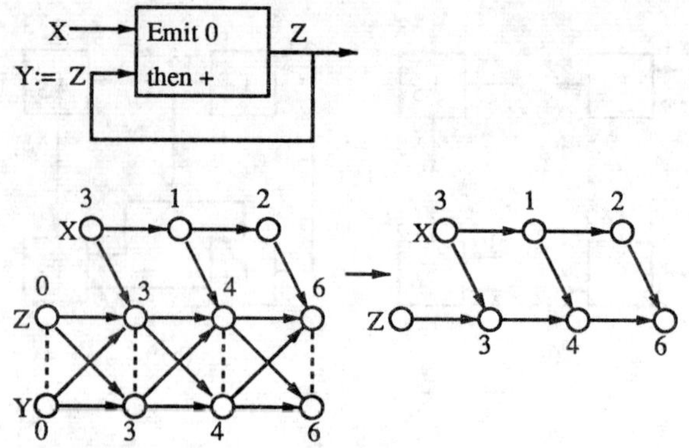

Figure 3. Typical Accumulator Behavior.

of well-founded behaviors then, for a well-founded process $P \propto^{\mathcal{L}} (P) = \{q : q$ is well founded and $p \propto q$ for some $p \in P\}$ and $\lambda^{\mathcal{L}}(P)$ consists of all well founded linearizations of members of P. Similarly we can relativize to the class of fair processes, or linear processes. The question whether a relativized version of some result is valid can be highly significant. Suppose for example that one proves that a process constructed in a certain way computes a certain function, then the truth of the version relativized to fair processes means that the function has a fair computation. Relativation is a device we shall employ in the later part of the work.

In this work we remain within the class of well-founded processes, meaning that all concepts and constructions are to be relativized to this class.

Actually we need not assume full well-foundedness. It will suffice that the restrictions to Σ, P/Σ, be well-founded processes, where Σ is the set of actions which figure in the proofs. P may have additional non-well-founded components. But for the sake of simplicity we shall assume well-foundedness throughout.

2.7 Locations and Data

The events that take place in the course of a computation may contribute to the accumulation of data. For example, if (n, X) is the action of the arrival of symbol n at location X then the events of the behavior

$$(0, X) \to (0, X) \to (1, X) \to (0, X)$$

have the effect of producing the string 0010.

And, in the case of two ports, the behavior:

$$\begin{array}{ccccccc} (0, X) & \longrightarrow & (0, X) & \longrightarrow & (1, X) & \longrightarrow & (0, X) \\ \downarrow & & & & & & \uparrow \\ (1, Y) & \longrightarrow \; \longrightarrow & (1, Y) & & \longrightarrow \; \longrightarrow & & (0, Y) \end{array}$$

will produce the pair (0010,110). Note that, in the second case, the constraints given by $(0, X) \to (1, Y)$ and $(0, Y) \to (0, X)$ are obliterated in the data — temporal cross orderings are ignored. (We could have included them, changing thereby the data domain from pairs of strings to pairs of strings augmented with additional arrows.)

These examples illustrate situations where a given perspective on a behavior induces an abstract and/or local view of that behavior. The common features of the variety of possible perspectives are abstracted in the following notion of a *location*.

Let $\mathcal{D}$ be a cpo (complete partial ordering), with $\leq = \leq_{\mathcal{D}}$ as the partial order, and with a minimal element $\perp = \perp_{\mathcal{D}}$.

Definition. A *location for* $\mathcal{D}$ is a pair $(X, \mathrm{dat}())$ where X is a process and $\mathrm{dat} : X \to \mathcal{D}$ maps the behaviors of X to members of $\mathcal{D}$ such that following holds.

(i) $\Lambda \in X$ and $\mathrm{dat}(\Lambda) = \perp$.

(ii) X is augment closed and for $p \in X$, if $p \propto p'$ then $\mathrm{dat}(p) = \mathrm{dat}(p')$.

(iii) For $p, q \in X$, $p \sqsubseteq q \Rightarrow \mathrm{dat}(p) \leq \mathrm{dat}(q)$.

(iv) X is closed under limits of chains and $\mathrm{dat}(\lim p_i) = \lim(\mathrm{dat}(p_i))$, the limit on the right side being that of $\mathcal{D}$.

(v) Given $x \leq y$ in $\mathcal{D}$ and $p \in \overline{X}$ such that $\mathrm{dat}(p) = x$ there exists $q \sqsupseteq p$ with $\mathrm{dat}(q) = y$.

$$\begin{array}{ccc} p & \sqsubseteq & q \\ \big\downarrow \mathrm{dat} & & \big\downarrow \mathrm{dat} \\ x & \leq & y \end{array}$$

We put $X = (X, \mathrm{dat}())$ using 'X' both for the location and for the underlying process.

The members of X can be thought of as just those behaviors that fit into location X. Thus we say "p fits into X" to mean $p \in X$.

Examples. (1) $\mathcal{D} = D^{\leq\omega}$ where D is some flat domain of data values (i.e. not a cpo, e.g. the integers) and X is the abstract representation of some port $\hat{X}$. Then $\Sigma_X = D \times \{\hat{X}\}$, X consists of all totally ordered behaviors of rank $\leq \omega$, and $\mathrm{dat}((d_1, \hat{X}) \to (d_2, \hat{X}) \to \cdots) = d_1 d_2 \ldots$. In this case a behavior which is not totally ordered does not fit into X, meaning that we are representing a port at which all behaviors are serialized. Note that the structure of $\mathcal{D}$ imposes this restriction.

(2) $\mathcal{D}$ is a continuous image of $D^{\leq\omega}$ under $f : D^{\leq\omega} \to \mathcal{D}$, X is as in (1), and dat() is obtained by combining the dat() of (1) with f.

(3) $\mathcal{D}$ = set of multisets over Σ ordered by multiset inclusion. $\Sigma_X = \Sigma$, X consists of all behaviors over Σ and $\mathrm{dat}(p)$ is the multiset obtained by removing the order constraints.

Definition. If X_i, $i = 1, 2$, are locations with disjoint alphabets, with X_i a location for $\mathcal{D}_i$, then $X_1 + X_2$ is the location for $\mathcal{D}_1 \times \mathcal{D}_2$ defined by putting

$$\mathrm{dat}(p) =_{Df} (\mathrm{dat}_1(p/X_1), \mathrm{dat}_2(p/X_2))$$

It is easily verified that $X_1 + X_2$ is indeed a location (for property (v) use Proposition 1).

This generalizes to arbitrary disjoint sums of locations: $\sum X_i$ is a location for $\prod \mathcal{D}_i$.

Definition. $X = (X, \mathrm{dat}())$ is a location in the process P if $\Sigma_X \subset \Sigma_P$ and $P/\Sigma_X \subset X$.

Note: We do not require $P/\Sigma_X = X$; the process can miss some behaviors fitting into X.

The actions in Σ_X and the events they label are referred to as *actions* and *events at* X.

Two locations in P are *disjoint* if their alphabets of actions are disjoint.

Notation: If X is a location in P then for $p \in P$, $p|X =_{Df} \mathrm{dat}(p/X)$.

Similarity of Locations. Two locations $X = (X, dat())$, $(X' = (X', dat'())$ for data $\mathcal{D}, \mathcal{D}'$ are *similar*, or *of the same type*, if $\mathcal{D} = \mathcal{D}'$ and there is a renaming (bijection) of actions $t : \Sigma \to \Sigma'$ such that the following holds:

The associated mapping of behaviors maps X onto X' and commutes with the data functions:

$$\mathrm{dat}(p) = \mathrm{dat}'(t(p))$$

We call t the *similarity map* of X to X'.

When speaking of similarity of locations we shall always presuppose some fixed similarity map.

Notation. If X and Y are similar locations of a process P then $P[X := Y]$ is defined to be $P[\varphi]$, where φ maps every action at X to its corresponding action at Y and φ is the identity on the rest. This is extended in the obvious way to: $P[X_i := Y_{\tau(i)}, i \in I]$ where $X_i, i \in I$ are pairwise disjoint locations and $Y_{\tau(i)}$ has the same type as X_i.

Definition. If X is a location for data $\mathcal{D}$ in P then the *subset of* $\mathcal{D}$ *computed by* P is $\{p|X : p \in P\}$.

In case $X = X_1 + X_2$, X_i a location for $\mathcal{D}_i$, we shall speak of the *relation computed by* P *at* locations X_1, X_2. Finally if this relation happens to be a partial function $f : \mathcal{D}_1 \to \mathcal{D}_2$ we shall say that $P : X_1 \to X_2$ *computes the function* $f : \mathcal{D}_1 \to \mathcal{D}_2$.

§3 Inputs

3.1 Free Input Sets

Intuitively an action of a process is an input action when it is one that the process' environment decides whether to perform. The effect of nonperformance on the behavior of the process is that the process can continue without erasing the preceding events. The simplest formalization of this intuition is given in the following definitions. The reason for the attribute "free" will appear in a later section where the more general "non-free" concepts will be defined.

Definition. A subset $\Sigma \subset \Sigma_P$ is a *free input set for* P if for all $p \in \pi(P)$ we have the following two conditions.

(1) (Free Input Stopping.) p has an extension q in P such that $p/\Sigma = q/\Sigma$.

That is, any prefix of a behavior in P can be extended to a behavior of P without adding any actions from Σ — we can stop the input at any point and the computation will eventually arrive at a member of P.

(2) (Free Input Deletion.) For all $p' \preceq p$, if $p'/-\Sigma = p/-\Sigma$ then $p' \in \pi(P)$.

That is, from any stage we can delete any actions from Σ which do not precede any of the remaining actions, and the result will remain a stage. Note that $p' \preceq p$ allows for the possibility that we have deleted some actions from Σ which are simultaneous with actions in p'. The effect of input deletion is to force an explicit display of all causal relationships by means of $<$.

Example. Let $\Sigma = \{a, b, c\}$ and let $P_1 = \{a \to b \sim c\}$, $P_2 = \{\Lambda,\quad a \to b \sim c\}$, $P_3 = \{a \to b \sim c,\quad a \to b \to b\}$, where "$\sim$" is used for simultaneity. The in P_1 none of $\{a\}$, $\{b\}$, $\{c\}$ is a free input set, e.g. $\Lambda \in \pi(P_1)$ but there is no extension of Λ which avoids any of a, b, c. In P_2 $\{a\}$ is a free input set and in P_3 $\{c\}$ is a free input set.

Proposition 3. *If Σ is a free input set then every $\Sigma' \subset \Sigma$ is a free input set.*

Proof. Immediate.

In general the union of free input sets need not be a free input set, since we may be able to stop each of two input sets without being able to do so for the set consisting of both. But if they come from unrelated components then their union is a free input set.

Proposition 4. *If $P = \Sigma_{i \in I} P_i$ and A_i is a free input set for P_i, then $\bigcup_{i \in I} A_i$ is a free input set for P.*

Proof. Let Σ_i be the alphabet of P_i and let $p \in \pi(P)$. (i) Let p_i denote p/Σ_i. Then $p_i \in \pi(P)$, whence p_i can be extended to q_i in P_i such that $q_i/A_i = p_i/A_i$. The behavior q such that $V(q) = \bigcup_{i \in I} V(q_i)$ and $\Im(q)$ is generated by $\bigcup_{i \in I} \Im(q_i)$ is an extension of p in P and $q/A = p/A$. (ii) If $p' \preceq p$ and $p'/-A = p/-A$, then for $p'_i = p_i/\Sigma_i$, we have $p'_i \preceq p_i$ and $p'_i/-A_i = p_i/-A_i$. Hence $p'_i \in \pi(P_i)$, implying $p' \in \pi(P)$.

Proposition 5. *If Σ is a free input set for P and $\varphi : \Sigma \to \Sigma_0$ is a translation, then*

(i) $\pi(P[\varphi]) = (\pi(P))[\varphi]$.

(ii) Σ_0 is a free input set for $P[\varphi]$.

Proof. The inclusion $\pi(P[\varphi]) \subset \pi(P)[\varphi]$ holds in general (a prefix of a fused behavior is a fusion of a prefix). Now given $p_0 \in \pi(P)[\varphi]$ we shall show that for some q_0 in $P[\varphi]$ such that $q_0/\Sigma_0 = p_0/\Sigma_0$, $p_0 \sqsubseteq q_0$. This will prove the reverse inclusion as well as the first condition in the definition of free input set, for Σ_0.

q_0 is constructed as follows. For some $p \in \pi(P)$ we have a ϕ-fusion $j : p \to p_0$. Extend p to $q \in P$ such that $q/\Sigma = p/\Sigma$. Augment q to $\bar{q}$ by adding all constraints $u < v$ where $u \in V(p)$, $v \in V(q) - V(p)$. This has the effect of constraining all new events to come after all events in $V(p)$. Since $p \sqsubseteq q$ it is easily seen that $p \sqsubseteq \bar{q}$. Also $\bar{q} \in P$, by augment closure. Now extend j to $\bar{j}$ by mapping every member of $V(q) - V(p)$ to itself. Since no new events labeled by action from Σ have been added it is easily seen that $\bar{j}$ fuses $\bar{q}$ to some behavior q_0. Now $p \sqsubseteq \bar{q}$ is easily seen to imply $p_0 \sqsubseteq q_0$. Thus $p_0 \sqsubseteq q_0 \in P[\varphi]$ and $q_0/\Sigma_0 = p_0/\Sigma_0$.

Finally, if p_0 is as before and $p'_0 \preceq p_0$ satisfies $p'_0/-\Sigma_0 = p_0/\Sigma_0$ then the prefusion, say p', of p'_0 under j satisfies $p' \preceq p$ and $p'/\Sigma = p/\Sigma$. Hence $p' \in \pi(P)$. Thus $p'_0 \in \pi(P)[\varphi]$.

We are now ready for the main theorem concerning free input sets.

Given monotone $f : D' \times D \to D$, let $f^* : D' \to D$ denote the least fixpoint of f, that is, $f^*(x) = \mu y(y = f(x, y))$.

Theorem 1. (Minimality) *Let Y, Z be locations of P of the same type, for data D, such that the actions of Y form a free input set. Let X be a location of P, disjoint from Y, for data D'. Then if P computes a partial monotone function $f : D' \times D \to D$, $P[Y := Z]$ computes a partial monotone function $g : D' \to D$ such that $g \subset f^*$.*

Proof. Let $p \in P[Y := Z]$ and let $x = p|X$, $z = p|Z$. Say p is a fusion of $q \in P$ under $j : V_q \to V_p$. Evidently $q|X = x$, $q|Y = q|Z = z$. Consequently $z = f(x, z)$. So $z^* \leq z$ where z^* denotes the least solution. We now show $z \leq z^*$.

Let p_α denote the prefix of p consisting of all events of p of rank $< \alpha$, let q_α denote the prefix of q of which p_α is the fusion, and let z_α denote $p_\alpha|Z$. (So each of $(p_\alpha)_\alpha$ and $(q_\alpha)_\alpha$ is an ascending chain indexed by α, with $p_0 = q_0 = \Lambda$.) We prove by induction on α that $z_\alpha \leq z^*$.

For $\alpha = 0$, $p_\alpha = \Lambda$ and $z_\alpha = \bot$ (the minimal element of D). For α a limit ordinal, $p_\alpha = \lim_{\beta<\alpha} p_\beta$, hence $z_\alpha = \lim_{\beta<\alpha} z_\beta$, and if $z_\beta \leq z^*$ for all $\beta < \alpha$ then also $z_\alpha \leq z^*$. The essential passage is from α to $\alpha + 1$.

Assume therefore that $z_\alpha \leq z^*$. Let $\tilde{q}_\alpha$ be the $\preceq$-prefix of $q_{\alpha+1}$ generated by all events in $q_{\alpha+1}$ which are not at Y, i.e. $u \in V(\tilde{q}_\alpha) \Leftrightarrow u < u'$ or $u = u'$ for some $u' \in V(q_{\alpha+1}/\text{-}Y)$. Then $\tilde{q}_\alpha/\text{-}Y = q_{\alpha+1}/\text{-}Y$. Hence by free input deletion $\tilde{q}_\alpha \in$

$\pi(P)$. (This is the crucial step – all input not preceding some member of $q_{\alpha+1}/\text{-}Y$ can be removed.)

$$\begin{array}{ccccc} q_\alpha & \sqsubseteq & \tilde{q}_\alpha & \preceq & q_{\alpha+1} \\ \downarrow j & & & & \downarrow j \\ p_\alpha & & \sqsubseteq & & p_{\alpha+1} \end{array}$$

Now consider an event $u \in V(\tilde{q}_\alpha)$ at Y. If $u < u'$ where $u' \in V(q_{\alpha+1})$ is not at Y then $j(u) < j(u')$, so $\text{rank}(j(u)) < \text{rank}(j(u')) \leq \alpha$. Consequently $u \in j^{-1}(V_{p_\alpha})$. This shows that the events at Y in $\tilde{q}_\alpha$ are in q_α, i.e. $\tilde{q}_\alpha/Y = q_\alpha/Y$.

All in all:

$$\tilde{q}_\alpha/Y = q_\alpha/Y, \quad \tilde{q}_\alpha/Z = q_{\alpha+1}/Z$$

hence

$$\tilde{q}_\alpha/Y = z_\alpha, \qquad \tilde{q}_\alpha/Z = z_{\alpha+1}$$

Since the actions at Y form a free input set, by free input stopping there must exist $r \in P$ such that $\tilde{q}_\alpha \sqsubseteq r$ and $\tilde{q}_\alpha/Y = r/Y$. Then $r|Z = f(r|Y) = f(z_\alpha)$ and $z_{\alpha+1} = \tilde{q}_\alpha|Z \leq r|Z$. Hence $z_{\alpha+1} \leq f(z_\alpha) \leq f(z^*) = z^*$. ∎

So we always stay below the least fixpoint.

3.2 Free Input Locations.

We turn now from the nonperformance of free input to the dual concern of performance, which deals with the liveness of processes, for which we wish to be able to always add input. This condition is formalized via the notion of a *free input location*. The chief consequence of the condition is that it yields an upper bound complementing the lower bound of our previous theorem, namely that we actually attain the least fixpoint.

Whereas nonperformance of input is a straightforward notion, performance is more delicate. Input addition may be restricted in various ways. We shall start with the simplest and strongest input addition condition. This condition requires the process to accept input at any moment and in a way which need not reflect the entire temporal order.

Definition. A location X is a *free input location in* P if its actions form a free input set and for every $p \in \pi(P)$, if $p \preceq q$, q/X fits into X, and $q/-X = p/-X$ then $q \in \pi(P)$.

The condition $q/-X = p/-X$ means that only events at X have been added to p. The condition $p \preceq q$ means that we cannot stipulate an added event to precede an event in p, but it allows us to stipulate simultaneity between added events and old events. Thus we can add input simultaneously with existing events of the process.

Proposition 6. *Let X be a free input location in P. Then:*

(i) For every $p' \in X$ there exists $p \in P$ such that $p/X = p'$.

(ii) If $p_1 \in P$, $p'_1 = p_1/X$ and $p'_1 \sqsubseteq p'_2$ where $p'_2 \in X$ then there exists $p_2 \in P$ such that $p'_2 = p_2/X$ and $p_1 \sqsubseteq p_2$.

$$\begin{array}{ccc} p_1 & \sqsubseteq & p_2 \\ \downarrow /X & & \downarrow /X \\ p'_1 & \sqsubseteq & p'_2 \end{array}$$

Proof. We show (ii) first. Let p be the "union" of p_1 and p'_2, i.e. $V(p) = V(p_1) \cup V(p'_2)$, $\Sigma_p = \Sigma_P$, the labels in p are as in p_1 and p'_2 (since $p'_1 \sqsubseteq p'_2$ the labels agree on the common part) and the constraints are generated by those of p_1 and p'_2. It is not difficult to see that $p_1 \sqsubseteq p$ and, *a fortiori*, $p_1 \preceq p$. By free input addition, $p \in \pi(P)$. Take $p_2 \in P$ extending p such that $p_2/X = p/X$. This has the desired property.

To prove (i) observe that the empty behavior Λ is in $\pi(P)$. Extend it to $p_1 \in P$ such that $p_1/X = \Lambda$. Now use (ii), with $p'_2 = p'$.

Corollary. If $P : X \to Y$ computes $f : \mathcal{D} \to \mathcal{D}'$ and X is a free input location then f is monotone.

Proof. Let $x_1, x_2 \in \mathcal{D}$, $x_1 \leq x_2$. By the properties of dat() we have two behaviors p'_1, p'_2 in X such that $p'_1 \sqsubseteq p'_2$, $p'_1|X = x_1$, $p'_2|X = x_2$. Using the last proposition we get $p_1, p_2 \in P$ such that $p_i/X = p'_i, i = 1, 2$ and $p_1 \sqsubseteq p_2$. Since $p_i|Y = f(x_i)$ we have $f(x_1) \leq f(x_2)$.

Proposition 7. *Let $X_i, i \in 1, 2$, be disjoint locations in P. Then*

(i) If $X_1 + X_2$ is a free input location then each X_i is a free input location.

(ii) If X_1, X_2 are free input locations and the action set of $X_1 + X_2$ is a free input set then $X_1 + X_2$ is a free input location.

Proof. (i) is immediate. For (ii) observe that addition of input at $X_1 + X_2$ can be done in two stages: first add events at X_1 then at X_2. (It is only when we come to stopping input that the property does not pass from the components to their sum.)

(ii) can be generalized to an infinite product if we assume $\pi(P)$ to be closed under limits of $\preceq$-chains.

Proposition 8. *If $P = \Sigma_{i \in I} P_i$ and X_i is a free input location in P_i, then $\sum_{i \in I} X_i$ is a free input location in P.*

Proof. The condition of free input set is satisfied via Proposition 4. Free Input addition is assured because we can add input independently at each X_i (Formally: Let $p \in P$ and let $p \preceq q$ with $p/-\sum_{i \in I} X_i = q/-\sum_{i \in I} X_i$. If $p_i = p/\Sigma_i$ and $q_i = q/\Sigma_i$, then $p_i \in \pi(P_i)$, $p \preceq q_i$, and $q_i/-X_i = p_i/-X_i$. Hence $q_i \in \pi(P_i)$. Since we have a disjoint sum this implies $q \in \pi(P)$.) ∎

Proposition 9. (Input Fusibility.) *Let $X_i, i \in J$, be disjoint locations in P such that $\sum_{i \in J} X_i$ is a free input location. Let $I \subset J$ and let $\tau : J \to I$ be such that $\tau(i) = i$ for $i \in I$ and $X_{\tau(i)}$ has the same type as X_i. Then $\sum_{i \in I} X_i$ is a free input location in $P[X_i := X_{\tau(i)}, i \in I]$.*

This means that within an all inclusive free input location we can fuse disjoint sublocations to yield a free input location in the fused process.

Proof. Free Input stopping and deletion are satisfied via Proposition 5. Let P_0 be the result of the fusion. Let $p_0 \in \pi(P_0)$ and let q_0 be a behavior with $\Sigma(q_0) = \Sigma(p_0)$ such that $p_0 \preceq q_0$ and $q_0 / \sum_{i \in I} X_i = p_0 / \sum_{i \in I} X_i$. Let p, q be the prefusions of p_0, q_0 respectively. Then $p \preceq q$ since prefusion preserves prefixes. Also $p \in \pi(P)$ and $q / \sum_{i \in J} X_i = p / \sum_{i \in J} X_i$. Hence $q \in \pi(P)$. By Proposition 5, $q_0 \in \pi(P)$. ∎

Propositions 8 and 9 enable us to represent any wiring of arbitrarily many (including infinitely many) components as a single fusion of two "big" locations in one "big" component, as follows.

We assume that each component is represented by a process and that its designated input locations combine into one free input location. Form the disjoint sum of these processes. By Proposition 8 the combined location made of all input locations contributed by the components is a free input location in the sum. Fuse together each bunch of input locations which are to be wired to the same "output location." By Proposition 9 the resulting combined location is a free input location in the fused process. Now one big fusion of the combined free input location with combined output location achieves the wiring.

3.3 The Fixpoint Theorem for the Free Input Case

For the fused process $P[X := Y]$ to compute the least fixpoint it is necessary to impose a continuity condition on P. The simplest one is that P be closed under limits:

(C) $\lim P \subset P$, i.e. for every chain $(p_i)_{i \in I}$ of members of P, $\lim p_i \in P$.

Actually a weaker condition suffices.

(C_0) (Weak continuity) $\lim P \subset \pi(P)$.

Proposition 10. *If $P = \sum_{i \in I} P_i$ is a disjoint sum then P satisfies (C) (satisfies (C_0)) if each P_i does.*

Proof. This follows easily from $\pi(\Sigma_i P_i) = \Sigma_i \pi(P_i)$.

Proposition 11. *If P is weakly continuous, $\Sigma \subset \Sigma_P$ is a free input set, and $\varphi : \Sigma \to \Sigma_0$ is a translation of actions, where $\Sigma_0 \subset \Sigma$, then $P[\varphi]$ is weakly continuous.*

Proof. Given a chain $(p_i)_{i \in I}$ in $P[\varphi]$, with $p = \lim_i p_i$, lift it to the prefusion chain, say $(q_i)_{i \in I}$, via Proposition 2:

$$\begin{array}{ccccccccc} \cdots & \sqsubseteq & q_i & \sqsubseteq & \cdots & \sqsubseteq & q_{i'} & \sqsubseteq & \cdots \\ & & \downarrow j_i & & & & \downarrow j_{i'} & & \\ \cdots & \sqsubseteq & p_i & \sqsubseteq & \cdots & \sqsubseteq & p_{i'} & \sqsubseteq & \cdots \end{array}$$

For $q = \lim q_i$ we have a φ-fusion $j : q \to p$. By weak continuity for P, $q \in \pi(P)$. Hence $p \in \pi(P)[\varphi]$. By Proposition 5 $p \in \pi(P[\varphi])$.

The following proposition states some basic properties of (C). We shall not use (C) but we bring it in its own right.

Proposition 12. *Assume that P satisfies (C). Then*

(i) If $P : X \to Y$ computes $f : D \to D'$ where X is a free input location then f is continuous.

(ii) If φ is any translation of actions, $P[\varphi]$ satisfies (C).

Proof. (i) Given $x_1 \leq x_2 \leq \cdots$ with $x_i \in D$, get by the properties of dat() a chain $p'_1 \sqsubseteq p'_2 \sqsubseteq \cdots$ of behaviors in X with $\text{dat}(p'_i) = x$. By Proposition 6 lift it to a chain $p_1 \sqsubseteq p_2 \sqsubseteq \cdots$ in P such that $p_i / X = p'_i$. Put $x = \lim x_i$, $p = \lim p_i$, $y_i = f(x_i)$. Then $y_i = p_i | Y$ and $\lim y_i | Y = p | Y$. By (C) $p \in P$, hence $\lim y_i = P | Y = f(x)$.

(The argument works for chains of length $> \omega$ - at limit ordinals take limits and continue the construction of the p'_i and the p_i.)

(ii) Given a chain of behaviors in $P[\varphi]$, lift it to a chain of prefusions in P, via Proposition 2. Then the limit of the prefusions is, by (C), in P. It fuses to the limit of the given chain.

It can be easily shown that neither (i) nor (ii) holds for weak continuity. Proposition 10 shows that (i) holds for weak continuity provided that we fuse within a free input set. It will be a part of the main theorem that weak continuity is preserved under fusion of inputs with outputs.

We come now to our main theorem for the case of free input locations. We assume the processes to be augment closed.

Theorem 2. *Let P be weakly continuous with free input location $X + Y$ and a location Z of the same type as Y. Let D_X, D_Y be the data for locations X, Y. If $P : X + Y \to Z$ computes $f : D_X \times D_Y \to D_Y$ then*

(1) $P[X := Y]$ computes the least fixpoint $g : D_X \to D_Y$, namely

$$g(x) = \mu y (y = f(x, y))$$

(2) X is a free input location in $P[Y := Z]$

(3) $P[Y := Z]$ is weakly continuous.

The general case of an arbitrary family of processes to be connected is covered by the following expansion of Theorem 2. For this theorem we first assume the following. Let P_i, $i \in I$, be a family of weakly continuous disjoint processes. Assume that for each $i \in I$, $\Sigma_{j \in J_i} X_j$ is a free input location in P_i and Y_k, $k \in K_i$ are locations in P_i disjoint from each other and from the X_j's. For convenience choose a disjoint family of index sets J_i, $i \in I$, and a disjoint family of index sets K_i, $i \in I$.

Assume that for $i \in I$, $k \in K_i$,

$$P_i : \sum_{j \in J_i} X_j \to Y_k \text{ computes } f_k : \prod_{j \in J_i} D_j \to D'_k.$$

Put $J = \bigcup_{i \in J_i} J_i$, $K = \bigcup_{i \in K_i} K_i$, and let $J' \subset J$ and $\tau : J' \to K$ be such that X_j has the same type as $Y_{\tau(j)}$. Let $P = \Sigma_{i \in I} P_i$, and let $\bar{P} = P[X_j := Y_{\tau(j)}, j \in J']$.

Theorem 3. *With the above definitions:*

(1) $\bar{P} : \sum_{j \in J - J'} X_j \to Y_k$ *computes the k-th function in the least solution of:*

$$(y_k = f_k(\ldots, x_l, \ldots, y_{\tau(m)}, \ldots))_{k \in K}$$

where l *ranges over* $J - J'$ *and* m *over* J'.

(2) $\sum_{j \in J'} X_j$ *is a free input location in* $\bar{P}$.

(3) $\bar{P}$ *is weakly continuous.*

To get Theorem 3 from Theorem 2 use Proposition 10 to conclude that P is weakly continuous and Proposition 11 to conclude that it remains so after fusing inputs together. Then use the construction described in the previous section to pass, via Propositions 8 and 9 from this many component situation to the single "big fusion" situation.

Note that it is essential to ensure the invariance of the properties which are necessary for the theorem, so that after the fusion we get again a component which can be combined and fused with other components with the same properties. We do not want to make (1) and (2) part of the definition of "computes a function." These are properties of the process which guarantee its nice behavior under fusions, whereas computing a function means simply getting its graph (i.e. the relation) in the given location.

Proof (of Theorem 2). The main lemma which we need is:

Continuation Lemma. If $j : q \to q/\text{-}Y$ is a $Y := Z$ fusion and $q \in \pi(P)$ then there exists $q^* \in P$, with $q \sqsubseteq q^*$, and a fusion $j^* : q^* \to q^*/\text{-}Y$ extending j.

Proof. Keeping the input at X fixed, we want to imitate the recursive procedure of getting new output at Z and feeding it back in at Y. At the limit we will get the desired behavior. This however implies a progression through stages – i.e., through $\pi(P)$, and we did not assume $\lim \pi(P) \subset \pi(P)$. Therefore we take care to construct the progression in such a way that the limit is also a limit of a chain in P.

Call $j : p \to p/\text{-}Y$ a *weak fusion* if $j : V(p) \to V(p/\text{-}Y)$ and, for some augment $\bar{p}$ of p, $j : \bar{p} \to \bar{p}/\text{-}Y$ is a $Y := Z$ fusion and $\bar{p}/\text{-}Y = p/\text{-}Y$. (Note that $\bar{p}$ is uniquely determined.)

We now prove:

Next-Step Claim. Given $p \in \pi(P)$ and a weak fusion $j : p \to p/\text{-}Y$ there exists $\hat{p} \in P$ and $p_1 \in \pi(P)$, satisfying $p \sqsubseteq \hat{p} \sqsubseteq p_1$, and a weak fusion $j_1 : p_1 \to p_1/\text{-}Y$ extending j.

For the proof consider the following diagram, where $\bar{p}$ in the left column and $\bar{p}_1$ in the right column are the augments required to make j and j_1 into fusions, and r is an auxiliary construct to be defined. Given the left column our aim is to produce the right one.

$$\begin{array}{ccccc}
 & & r & & \\
 & \nearrow & \downarrow{\scriptstyle \propto''} & & \\
p & \sqsubseteq & \hat{p} & \sqsubseteq & p_1 \\
\downarrow{\scriptstyle \propto} & & & & \downarrow{\scriptstyle \propto_1} \\
\bar{p} & & \sqsubseteq & & \bar{p}_1 \\
\downarrow{\scriptstyle j} & & & & \downarrow{\scriptstyle j_1} \\
p/\text{-}Y & & \sqsubseteq & & p_1/\text{-}Y
\end{array}$$

We complete the diagram as follows:

Take r to be an extension $r \sqsupseteq p$ in P such that $r/X + Y = p/X + Y$, provided by free input stopping.

Take $\hat{p}$ to be the augment of r obtained by adding all constraints $\gamma(u, v)$ such that (i) $u \in V(p)$, $v \in V(r) - V(p)$ and (ii) $\Im(r) \cup \Im(\bar{p}) \vdash \gamma(u, v)$ for prossets, and for pomsets $\Im(r) \cup \Im(\bar{p}) \cup \ker j \vdash \gamma(u, v)$ but under the prosset axioms, where $\ker j$ denotes $\{u \equiv v : j(u) = j(v)\}$.

Since $p \propto \bar{p}$ and $p \sqsubseteq r$ it is easily seen that $p \sqsubseteq \hat{p}$. As the construction will show we will have $\hat{p}/\text{-}Y = p_1/\text{-}Y$.

Take $\bar{p}_1$ to be $\varphi^{-1}(\hat{p}/\text{-}Y)$, with j_1 a $Y := Z$ fusion extending j.

Take p_1 to be the result of removing from $\bar{p}_1$ all constraints of the form $\gamma(u, v)$, $u \in V(p_1) - V(\hat{p})$, $v \in V(\hat{p}) - V(p)$. (In other words we take out all constraints between the new inputs added to match the new outputs in $\hat{p}$, and the events produced in passing from p to $\hat{p}$.) It follows from this construction that $\hat{p} \sqsubseteq p_1$.

We now have $p \sqsubseteq p_1$, whence $p/\text{-}Y \sqsubseteq p_1/\text{-}Y$ and $\varphi^{-1}(p/\text{-}Y) \sqsubseteq \varphi^{-1}(p_1/\text{-}Y)$, i.e. $\bar{p} \sqsubseteq \bar{p}_1$. It can be easily seen that $\bar{p}_1/\text{-}Y = p_1/\text{-}Y = \hat{p}/\text{-}Y$. This completes the Next-Step claim.

To prove the lemma start with $q_0 = q$ and $j_0 = j$. Using the next-step claim construct a chain $q_0 \sqsubseteq \hat{q}_0 \sqsubseteq q_1 \sqsubseteq \hat{q}_1 \sqsubseteq \cdots$ with weak fusions $j_n : q_n \to q_n/\text{-}Y$ such that $j_0 \subset j_1 \subset \cdots$, $q_n \in \pi(P)$, $\hat{q}_n \in P$. Put $q_\omega = \lim q_n$, $j_\omega = \cup j_n$. Since $q_\omega = \lim \hat{q}_n$ we have $q_\omega \in \pi(P)$.

Now it follows that $j_\omega : q_\omega \to q_\omega/\text{-}Y$ is a weak fusion. This can be seen by considering the chain $\bar{q}_0 \sqsubseteq \bar{q}_1 \sqsubseteq \cdots$ of augments of the q_n such that $j_n : \bar{q}_n \to q_n/\text{-}Y$ is a fusion and noting that $j_\omega : \bar{q}_\omega \to q_\omega/\text{-}Y$ is a fusion where $\bar{q}_\omega = \lim \bar{q}_n$. Hence if $q_\omega \notin P$ we can continue until we finally get $q_\alpha \in P$. Put $q^* = \bar{q}_\alpha$ and $j^* = j_\alpha$. Then we get a fusion $j^* : q^* \to q^*/\text{-}Y$ extending the original $j : q \to q/\text{-}Y$. Since $q/\text{-}Y \sqsubseteq q_\alpha/\text{-}Y = q^*/\text{-}Y$ we have $q \sqsubseteq q^*$. ∎(lemma)

Proof of (1). We have to show that for each $x \in \mathcal{D}_X$ there exists $p \in P[Y := Z]$ with $p|X = x$. The rest is guaranteed by the minimality theorem.

Let $r \in X$ be such that $\text{dat}(r) = x$. Using free input addition for X get $q_0 \in P$ such that $q_0/X = r$ and $q_0/\text{-}X = \Lambda$. Let j_0 be the identify over $V(q_0)$. Trivially j_0 is a $Y := Z$ fusion (there are no events at $Y + Z$). Now using the lemma get $q^* \in P$ which fuses to $q^*/\text{-}Y$ such that $q_0 \sqsubseteq q^*$ and $q^*/X = q_0/X$. Then $q^*/\text{-}Y$ is the desired p.

Proof of (2). To show that X satisfies free input addition, take $p \in \pi(P[Y := Z])$ and let $p' \sqsupseteq p$ satisfy $p'/\text{-}X = p/\text{-}X$. Applying prefusion to the pair $p \sqsubseteq p'$, lift it to $q \sqsubseteq q'$, so that $p = q/\text{-}Y$, $p' = q'/\text{-}Y$, and we have $Y := Z$ fusion maps $j : q \to q/\text{-}Y$, $j' : q' \to q'/\text{-}Y$. It is easily seen that $q'/\text{-}X = q/\text{-}X$. Now $q \in \pi P$, by the general inclusion $\pi(P[\varphi]) \subset (\pi P)[\varphi]$). By free input addition for X in P we have $q' \in \pi(P)$. We can now use $j' : q' \to q'/\text{-}Y$ as a starting point for applying the continuation lemma and getting $q^* \in P$ which fuses to $q^*/\text{-}Y$ such that $q'/\text{-}Y \sqsubseteq q^*/\text{-}Y$. This proves that $p' = q'/\text{-}Y \in \pi(P[Y := Z])$. The requirements for a free event set are satisfied via Proposition 5.

Proof of (3). Given a chain $(p_i)_{i \in I}$ in $P[Y := Z]$, lift it up to a chain of prefusions $(q_i)_{i \in I}$ with fusion maps $j_i : q_i \to p_i$ so that the diagram is commutative. Taking limits we get a fusion $j : \lim q_i \to \lim p_i$. Put $q = \lim q_i$, $p = \lim p_i$. Applying the continuation lemma get $q \sqsubseteq q^* \in P$, $p \sqsubseteq p^*$ with a fusion $j^* : q^* \to p^*$. Thus $p \sqsubseteq p^* \in P[Y := Z]$, implying $p \in \pi(P[Y := Z])$. ∎

3.4 Relativization to Fair Processes

The results of the last section relativize in full to the domain of fair prossets. (For pomsets the situation is somewhat different.) In order to relativize one has to check that all the constructions used in the proofs do not carry us out of the domain of fair prossets and that all the arguments apply. This is in fact the case.

The reader may verify for example that the main construction used in the proof of Theorem 2 generates no unfair behaviors. For the basis, P is simply a process with input location X, which is fair by hypothesis. The construction proceeds inductively by applying restrictions and prefusions, removing constraints, and appealing to input stopping. We will not go into further details, but only show as an example the following.

If p is a fair prosset and $\varphi : \Sigma \to \Sigma_p$ is a translation then the prefusion of p, $\varphi^{-1}(p)$ is fair.

Recall that a simultaneity class of a prosset q is a set of the form $\{v : v \equiv_q u\}$ and that fairness means that, for all u, $\{v : v \leq_q u\}$ is a union of finitely many simultaneity classes. Let $q = \varphi^{-1}(p)$ and let $j : q \to p$ be a φ-fusion. Since for all $u \in V(p)$, $j^{-1}(u)$ is included in a simultaneity class, it follows that for every simultaneity class, $V \subset V(p)$, of p, $j^{-1}(V)$ is a simultaneity class of q.

Given $u \in V(q)$, $\{v : v \leq_q u\}$ is a union of finitely many simultaneity classes because $\{v : v \leq_q u\} = j^{-1}(\{v : v \leq_p j(u)\})$.

Operations such as $\sum P_i$ should of course be relativized to our domain, i.e. we should use $\sum_{i \in I}^{F} P_i =_{Df} \{p \in \sum_{i \in I} P_i : p \text{ is fair}\}$. All in all we get (assuming prossets):

Theorem 4. If in Theorem 3 all the P_i's are fair and Σ is replaced throughtout by Σ^F, then $\bar{P}$ is a fair process satisfying claims (1), (2), (3) of the theorem.

3.5 Non-Free Input Locations

The condition of free input location is quite strong. It indicates an insensitivity of the process to temporal ordering of input events. Here is a simple example where this condition does not hold.

Let M be a computing device which takes input characters at locations X_1, X_2 and outputs them at locations Y_1, Y_2 respectively. Assume moreover that the order between input events at different locations affects the order of the corresponding output events. Say, if $(0, X_1) < (0, X_2)$ (i.e. if 0 at X_1 precedes 0 at X_2) then also $(0, Y_1) < (0, Y_2)$. The corresponding process P will include the following behaviors – in this case prossets (here $\wr$ indicates simultaneity).

$$\Lambda \quad (0,X_1) \to (0,Y_1) \quad (0,X_1) \to (0,Y_2)$$

$$\begin{array}{ccc} (0,X_1) & \longrightarrow & (0,Y_1) \\ \downarrow & & \downarrow \\ (0,X_2) & \longrightarrow & (0,Y_2) \end{array} \qquad \begin{array}{ccc} (0,X_1) & \longrightarrow & (0,Y_1) \\ \wr & & \\ (0,X_2) & \longrightarrow & (0,Y_2) \end{array}$$

$$\begin{array}{ccc} (0,X_1) & \longrightarrow & (0,Y_1) \\ \uparrow & & \\ (0,X_2) & \longrightarrow & (0,Y_2) \end{array}$$

Suppose that by adding input to Λ we get the behavior $q = (0, X_1) || (0, X_2)$ (i.e. we specify no order between $(0, X_1)$ and $(0, Y_2)$). There is no prefix extension $r \sqsupseteq q$ in P. Because every behavior which contains the two input events with their corresponding output events and which does not constrain the order of inputs has an augment which contradicts the specifications $(0, X_1) < (0, X_2) \Rightarrow (0, Y_1) < (0, Y_2)$. Note also that this process cannot be described by pomsets, because in order to cover all the 4-event cases it will have to contain a 4-event pomset which does not constrain the order of inputs. (We can describe the process by pomsets if we give up augment closure.)

Of course the same difficulty arises if we specify in addition $(0, X_2) < (0, X_1) \Rightarrow (0, Y_2) < (0, Y_1)$.

In order for P to continue p to its conclusion we have to include additional order information concerning the events of p, i.e. we have to augment p. This leads to the following more general concept of input. Instead of free input addition we shall have the weaker:

Input addition: For all $p \in \pi(P)$, if $p \preceq q$, and $p/-X = q/-X$ then some augment of q is in $\pi(P)$.

In the last example, if $p = \Lambda$ and $q = (0, X_1)||(0, X_2)$ then q' can be obtained by adding any of the constraints $(0, X_1) < (0, X_2)$, $(0, X_2) < (0, X_1)$, or $(0, X_1) \equiv (0, X_2)$.

By the same token we weaken also the conditions concerning input stopping and deletion. For a given P and $\Sigma \subset \Sigma_P$ the conditions are:

Input Stopping. For each $p \in \pi(P)$ there exists an augment p' of p and a behavior $q \in P$ such that $p' \sqsubseteq q$ and $p'/\Sigma = q/\Sigma$.

Input Deletion. For each $p \in \pi(P)$, if $q \preceq p$ and $q/-\Sigma = p/-\Sigma$ then some augment q' of q is in $\pi(P)$.

(The omission of input events may require additional order information just as their addition does. For it may happen that the presence of a certain event makes certain order information irrelevant which would have been relevant had this event been omitted.)

Definition. A set Σ is an *input set* if it satisfies Input Stopping and Input Deletion. A location X is an *input location* if its set of actions is an input set and it satisfies Input Addition.

Our main aim is to extend the results of the previous section to the general case of input locations. This calls for the following somewhat different continuity requirement.

Definition. P is *prefix-continuous* if, for every chain $(p_i)_{i \in I}$ in $\pi(P)$, some augment of $\lim p_i$ is in $\pi(P)$. Formally, $\lim(\pi(P)) \subset\!\propto (\pi(P))$.

That is to say: a limit of computational stages is, modulo augmentation, a computational stage. This is weaker than the simpler requirement $\lim(\pi(P)) \subset \pi(P)$. But since we are in the non-free case it is this weaker version which we need in order to get an invariant property preserved under disjoint sums and fusions of inputs with outputs.

An example of a process satisfying (C) which is not prefix continuous is $P = 0^*1$, i.e. P consists of all strings (finite pomsets) $0 \to 0 \to \cdots \to 0 \to 1$. Since for $p, q \in P$, $p \sqsubseteq q \Rightarrow p = q$, weak continuity ($C_0$) holds (there are no non-trivial chains in P). Prefix continuity however is violated because $0^* \subset \pi(P)$ but $0^\omega \notin P$. (Since 0^ω is already linear the augmentation is vacuous here.)

We can now state the main result for non-free input locations.

Theorem 2*. *Theorem 2 holds under the following substitutions.*

"free input location" $\to$ *"input location"*

"weakly continuous" $\to$ *"prefix-continuous"*

This theorem is false when formulated for pomsets, as simple counterexamples show. Henceforth we assume prossets throughout.

Since the analogous versions of Propositions 10, 11, 8, and 9 hold in our new setup we get:

Theorem 3*. *Theorem 3 holds under the same substitutions as used to obtain Theorem 2* from Theorem 2.*

Thus we can wire together computing devices which have capabilities beyond those of the devices of our Theorem 2, which in turn considerably extend the capabilities of Kahn modules, provided only that we satisfy prefix-continuity. As before there is no limit on the cardinality of either the set of components or the set of locations at each component.

The main device used in these proofs is that of linear prossets. Recall that in a linear prosset the ordering is not a total order but a total preorder. It is this feature which distinguishes it from pomsets and which makes prossets useful in the non-free case.

Proposition 13. *(i) If $p \sqsubseteq q$ and p' is a linearization of p then there exists a linearization q' of q such that $p' \sqsubseteq q'$.*

(ii) If $p \preceq q$ then there are linearizations p', q' of p and q such that $p' \preceq q'$.

Proof. (i) Let q_1 be the augment of q obtained by adding $\Im(p') \cup \{u < v : u \in V(p), v \in V(q) - V(p)\}$. Then let q' be a linearization of q_1 (say according to rank).

(ii) If $p \preceq q$, members $u \in V(p), v \in V(q) - V(p)$ may exist such that $u \equiv v$ in q (or more generally, in the case of a prosset with $\leq$ as primitive, $q \vdash v \leq u$). The idea is to collect all such "overlapping" members into a single layer of simultaneous events and to get a linearization with the mixed layer forming an interface between $V(p)$ and $V(q) - V(p)$.

Formally, put $M_1 = \{u \in V(p) : \exists v \in V(q) - V(p), v \leq_q u\}$, $M_2 = \{u \in V(q) - V(p) : \exists v \in V(p), u \leq_q v\}$, $M = M_1 \cup M_2$. Add to $\Im_q$ all constraints:

$u \equiv v$ for $u, v \in M$;

$u < v$ for $u \in V(p) - M$, $v \in M$;

$v < u$ for $u \in V(q) - M$, $v \in M$.

Then linearize.

Note. If p is of rank ω and $q \neq p$ then the lifting of $p \sqsubseteq q$ to a linearized pair yields a prosset q' of rank $> \omega$. We may thus loose fairness. This section does not relativize to fair processes in the way the previous one does. There is however an interesting way of getting the analogous results for fair processes, which we hope to present in a subsequent paper.

Proposition 14. *P satisfies input addition for X iff for all linear p, q, if $p \preceq q$ and $q/\text{-}X = p/\text{-}X$ then $p \in \pi(P) \Rightarrow q \in \pi(P)$.*

Proof. This condition is implied by input addition because linear prossets have no other augments. On the other hand, assume that $p \preceq q$ and $q/-X = p/-X$ where $p \in \pi(P)$. Lifting by linearization we get $p' \preceq q'$, $q'/-X = p'/-X$, where $p' \in \pi(P)$ (because p' augments p). By the present condition $q' \in \pi(P)$. Thus q has an augment in $\pi(P)$.

Recall the definition of $\lambda(P)$ for prossets. Since we assume augment closure throughout we have $\lambda(P) \subset P$, that is, $\lambda(P) = \{p \in P : p \text{ is linear}\}$.

The first part of Proposition 13 implies easily that

$$\pi(\lambda(P)) = \lambda(\pi(P))$$

Note that in the case of linear processes, i.e. fixpoints of λ, the free and non-free properties coincide, because every $p \in \lambda(P)$ has only one augment, namely itself.

Proposition 15. *(i) Input addition holds for X in P iff it holds for X in $\lambda(P)$.*

(ii) A set $\Sigma \subset \Sigma_p$ is an input set in P iff it is an input set in $\lambda(P)$.

And, consequently: *X is an input location in P iff it is an input location in $\lambda(P)$.*

Of course, for $\lambda(P)$ "input addition" can be replaced by "free input addition" etc.

The proof is via the same kind of argument used in Proposition 14. For example, assume that Σ is an input set in $\lambda(P)$. Let $p \preceq q \in \pi(P)$ be such that $p/-\Sigma = q/-\Sigma$. Lift $p \preceq q$ to a linearized pair $p' \preceq q'$, via Proposition 13. Since no event in $V(q) - V(p)$ has an action label in Σ (and $V(q') = V(q)$, $V(p') = V(p)$), we have $p'/-\Sigma = q'/-\Sigma$. Consequently an augment of p', which must in this case be p' itself, is in $\pi(\lambda(P))$ hence in $\pi(P)$. Thus p has an augment in $\pi(P)$.

The same transfer to the linear case holds with respect to prefix-continuity.

Proposition 16. *P is prefix continuous iff λP is prefix continuous.*

Proof. The implication from P to λP is trivial. For the other direction let $(p_\beta)_{\beta<\alpha}$ be a chain in πP. Using the first part of Proposition 13 and taking limits at limit ordinals, lift it to a chain of linearized prossets $(p'_\beta)_{\beta<\alpha}$. Then $p'_\beta \in \pi(\lambda P)$ and, by prefix continuity for λP, $\lim p'_\beta \in \pi(\lambda P)$. Evidently $\lim_{\beta<\alpha} p'_\beta$ is an augment of $\lim_{\beta<\alpha} p_\beta$.

Consider now the class of $\mathcal{L}$ of linear prossets and relativize the concpets and operations used in the proofs of the previous section to $\mathcal{L}$. Notice that for $P \subset \mathcal{L}$, $\pi_{\mathcal{L}}(P) = \pi P$ and $P[\varphi]^{\mathcal{L}} = P[\varphi]$, i.e. if the process consists of members of $\mathcal{L}$ then in the definitions of π and $[\varphi]$ we can restrict the prosset variable to $\mathcal{L}$. On the other hand $\sum_{i\in I}^{\mathcal{L}} P_i = \sum_{i\in I}^{\lambda} P_i$, where $\sum_{i\in I}^{\lambda} P_i = \{p : p/\Sigma_{P_i} \in P_i \text{ for all } i, \text{ and } p \in \mathcal{L}\}$ $= \lambda(\sum_{i\in I} P_i)$. Note also that:

$$\lambda(P[\varphi]) = (\lambda P)[\varphi]$$

(This is obvious upon observing that the prefusion of a linear prosset is a linear prosset.) Also $\lambda(\sum P_i) = \sum^{\lambda} \lambda P_i$. The propositions in this section show that the general picture is as follows.

General Prosset Processes	$\xrightarrow{\lambda}$	*Linear Prosset Processes*
P		λP
$P[\varphi]$		$(\lambda P)[\varphi]$
πP		$\pi(\lambda P)$
$\sum P_i$		$\sum^{\lambda} \lambda P_i$
Σ an Input Set in P	$\Leftrightarrow$	Σ a free Input Set in λP
X an input loc. in P	$\Leftrightarrow$	λX a free input loc. in λP
P prefix-cont.	$\Leftrightarrow$	λP prefix-cont.

Note also that P computes R in location X just when λ computes R in location λX. This follows from the fact that $\text{dat}(p') = \text{dat}(p)$ whenever $p \propto p'$.

Using this and relativizing the proofs of the previous section to $\mathcal{L}$ we get the starred version of Propositions 8 and 9 in which "free input location" is changed to "input location." To get the starred version of Propositions 10 and 11, in which "weakly continuous" is replaced by "prefix-continuous," one proves the corresponding statement for linear processes where the continuity in question is the satisfaction of (C) for $\pi(P)$. The proofs are easy. This establishes the propositions which are needed to carry us from Theorem 2* to Theorem 3*.

Finally to prove Theorem 2* it suffices to prove it for linear processes; for λP compute the needed function iff P does, and the other claims of the theorem follow via the transfer principle from linear to general processes and the fact that for linear processes the free and non-free concepts are the same. The proof follows the same schema as the proof of Theorem 2, with the important difference that a different construction is used to prove the Continuation Lemma:

If $j : q \to q/\text{-}Y$ is a fusion where $q \in \pi(P)$ then there exists $q^* \in P$, $q^* \sqsupseteq q$, $q^*/X = q/X$, with a fusion $j^* : q^* \to q^*/\text{-}Y$ extending j.

In the present case all prossets are assumed to be linear and the following claim establishes the iterative procedure.

Next Step Claim. Given a fusion $j : q \to q/\text{-}Y$, where $q \in \pi(P)$, there exists $q' \sqsupseteq q$, $q'/X = q/X$ and a fusion $j' : q' \to q'/\text{-}Y$ extending j such that either $q' \in P$ or $q' \in \pi P$ and $\text{rank}(q'/Z) > \text{rank}(q/Z)$.

Proof. Since $q \in \pi(P)$ there exists by input addition for linear prossets (i.e. free input addition) a prosset $r \in P$, such that $r \sqsupseteq q$ and $r/X+Y = q/X+Y$. If $r/Z = q/Z$ (i.e. no new output events) put $q' = r$ and extend j to j' by putting $j'(u) = u$ for all $u \in V(r) - V(q)$. Then j' is a fusion (recall again that we are working here with linear prossets, hence no further augmentation is needed to make j' a fusion). If $r/Z \neq q/Z$ let u' be an event in $V(r/Z) - V(q/Z)$ of minimal rank and let $r_0 \sqsubseteq r$ be the prosset whose events are all u such that $u \leq u'$.

Thus $\text{rank}(r_0/Z) = \text{rank}(q/Z) + 1$ and the new output events are in the last layer of r_0. Let q' be the linear prosset obtained by adding to this layer input events at Y which match the new output events. Then $r_0 \leq q'$ and, by input addition, $q' \in \pi(P)$. Extend j to j' by mapping any new input event to its match, and any event in $V(r_0) - V(q)$ to itself. It is easy to see that j' is a fusion.

The continuation lemma is proved by starting the induction with $j_0 : q_0 \to q_0/\text{-}Y$ and iterating the next step procedure to get a sequence $j_n : q_n \to q_n/\text{-}Y$, $q_0 \sqsubseteq \cdots \sqsubseteq q_n \sqsubseteq \cdots$, $j_0 \subset j_1 \subset \cdots \subset j_n \subset \cdots$, such that for all q_n, $q_n \in \pi P$. Hence by prefix continuity $\lim q_n \in \pi P$ (here is where we need it!). If $\lim q_n \in P$ we are done, else continue, taking limits at limit ordinals. Since $\text{rank}(q_n/Z)$ increases at each step (except possibly the last) we eventually reach a prosset in P.

The rest of the proof is as in that of Theorem 2. ∎

Bibliography

[BA77] Brock, J.D. and W.B. Ackerman, An anomaly in the specifications on nondeterministic packet systems, Computation Structures Group Note CSG-33, MIT-LCS, Nov. 1977.

[BA81] Brock, J.D. and W.B. Ackerman, Scenarios: A Model of Non-Determinate Computation. In: **Formalization of Programming Concepts**, J. Diaz and I. Ramos, Eds., Springer-Verlag LNCS 107, New York, 1981, 252-259.

[Fau] Faustini, A.A., An Operational Semantics for Pure Dataflow, *Automata, Languages and Programming* (editors M. Nielsen and L.E.M. Schmidt), Aarhus, Springer-Verlag, LNCS 140, 1982.

[Gra] Grabowski, J., On Partial Languages, *Fundamenta Informaticae* IV.2, 427-498, 1981.

[Ka] Kahn, G., The Semantics of a Simple Language for Parallel Programming, IFIP 74, North-Holland, Amsterdam, 1974.

[KS] Kearney, P. and Staples, J., An Extensional Fixed Point Semantics for Nondeterministic Data Flow, Research Report 12, Computing and Information Studies, Griffith University, QLD, Australia, Sept. 1986.

[La] Lamport, L., On Interprocess Communication, DEC Systems Research Center, Report No. 8, 1985.

[Pa] Park, D., The "fairness" problem and nondeterministic computing networks, *Foundations of Computer Science IV*, 133-162, Mathematisch Centrum, Amsterdam 1983.

[Pr82] Pratt, V.R., On the Composition of Processes, Proceedings of the Ninth Annual ACM Symposium on Principles of Programming Languages, Jan. 1982.

[Pr85] Pratt, V.R., Some Constructions for Order-Theoretic Models of Concurrency, Proc. Conf. on Logics of Programs, Springer-Verlag LNCS 193, Brooklyn, 1985.

[Pr86] Pratt, V.R., Modelling Concurrency with Partial Orders, International Journal of Parallel Programming, **15**, 1, 33-71, Feb. 1986.

[Rab] Rabinovich, A., Pomset Semantics is Consistent with Data flow Semantics, Manuscript, Dept. of Computer Science, Tel-Aviv University, 1986.

[SN] Staples, J., and V.L. Nguyen, A Fixpoint Semantics for Nondeterministic Dataflow, JACM, **32**, 2, 411-444, 1985.

[St] Stark, E.W., Concurrent Transition System Semantics of Process Networks, Proceedings of the Fourteenth Annual ACM Symposium on Principles of Programming Languages, Munich, Jan. 1987.

Session 3

Chair

Y. Gurevich

University of Michigan

MINIMALISM SUBSUMES DEFAULT LOGIC AND CIRCUMSCRIPTION IN STRATIFIED LOGIC PROGRAMMING

N. BIDOIT - C. FROIDEVAUX

L.R.I. , U.A. 410 du CNRS, Université Paris Sud, 91405 ORSAY Cedex, France

Abstract

Logic programs and databases are studied from the point of view of Default Logic. A specific class of programs, namely stratifiable programs, are considered. For stratifiable logic programs and databases, we show that:
(a) Default Logic, Perfect models, Circumscription and Iterated Fixed Points all lead to equivalent semantics, and
(b) The minimal model semantics is sufficient to define the semantics of logic programs and databases.

1. Introduction

In the past few years, a number of non-monotonic logics have been introduced for default reasoning[15,16,19]. These logics have recently received a great deal of attention, especially in the fields of logic programming and deductive databases. The purpose of this paper is twofold.

First, we show that Reiter's Default Logic is a well-suited formalism for specifying logic programs and databases. The advantage of using default logic lies in its simplicity and modular structure, its disadvantage in its semantics. We provide here a clear semantics for default theories in the context of logic programming and deductive databases. To do this, we use the well-known concept of stratification (i.e. no recursion on negation)[1,13, 17, 18, 21].

Second, we compare the expressiveness of default logic with other formalisms, of course again in the context of logic programming and databases. In this context, three approaches namely the "iterative fixed point"[1], the perfect model semantics[18] and Circumscription[13] have been shown equivalent[13,18]. We prove that default logic is equivalent to the others by establishing the equivalence with the perfect model semantics. Moreover, we provide a really simplified definition of the semantics of logic programs and databases. This definition is based on a stratification of the language rather than of the program (or database). The stratification of the program (or database) is induced by the stratification of the language. As a consequence, our definition uses exclusively the concept of minimal model as defined in [6]. It follows that the notions of supported model[1], preferability[18] and (pointwise) circumscription[13] introduce unnecessary complications in the context of logic programming and deductive databases.

Most results of the paper have long complex and technical proofs. For lack of space, these proofs will not be given in details. Complete proofs will appear in a journal version of this paper; they are already avaible in [3].

2. Default Logic

In the following, we assume that the reader is familiar with propositional and first order logic. In order to make the discussion clear, we review some concepts of logic and introduce Default Logic. We also present the notations used throughout the paper.

Let L be a first order language. A set of formulas of L is said to be *consistent* if it has at least one (first order) model, and is said *complete* if it is maximal consistent. First order provability is denoted |--. The logical closure of a set E of formulae, denoted Th(E), is $\{\alpha \mid \alpha \in L \text{ and } E \vdash \alpha\}$. By convention, a model M of a set of formulas is represented by enumerating the ground atomic formulas true for M. Finally, let M and M' be two models of a set W of formulas, we say that M' is *less than* M, denoted $M' \leq M$, iff $M' \subseteq M$, and that M is a *minimal model* [6] of W iff there exists no model M' of W such that $M \neq M'$ and $M' \leq M$.

Default Logic has been introduced by Reiter[19] in order to formalize non-monotonic inferences of the form: "in absence of any information to the contrary, assume ...", or more precisely, "if certain information cannot be deduced from the given knowledge base, then conclude...". In order to formally represent such a type of inference, default rules are introduced.

A *default rule* d over L is any expression of the form $\alpha : M\beta_1, \dots, M\beta_n / \gamma$ where $n \geq 1$ and α, called prerequisite, $\beta_1, \dots, \beta_n$, called justifications and γ, called consequent, are well-formed formulae in L. Note here that M is simply a new symbol to be read as "it is consistent".We denote prer(d) the formula α, just(d) the set $\{\beta_1, \dots, \beta_n\}$, cons(d) the formula γ and for a set D of default rules $JUST(D) = \cup_{d \in D} just(d)$. A default rule d is *normal* iff just(d)={cons(d)}.

Example 2.1: Let us consider the famous AI example about birds that fly except for penguins, ostriches etc. Given a particular bird, unless we happen to know that it is a penguin, or an ostrich, or more generally that it satisfies one of the exceptions, we will conclude that it flies.

Thus, the general rule to apply to birds is: "If x is a bird then in absence of any information to the contrary, infer that x can fly" or "if x is a bird and it is consistent to assume that x can fly, then infer that x can fly". For short, we would write the default rule:

BIRD(x) : M FLY(x) / FLY(x).

On the other hand, the knowledge base would classicaly

contain the first order formulas

BIRD(Tweety),

PENGUIN(x)→¬FLY(x),

OSTRICH(x)→¬FLY(x), etc.

A *default theory* Δ over L consists of a pair (D,W) where W is a set of closed formulae in L (W is a possibly incompletely specified knowledge base) and D is a set of default rules over L (D is a set of meta-rules used to enrich W). In fact a default theory Δ induces a set of first order theories, called extensions of Δ. For the purpose of our discussion, we prefer to the least fixed point definition of Reiter, the more intuitive characterization:

A set E of sentences of L is an *extension* for the default theory Δ=(D,W) iff $E=\cup_{i=0..\infty} E_i$ where:

E_0 = W and, for i≥0

$E_{i+1}=Th(E_i) \cup \{ \gamma \mid d\in D, cons(d)=\gamma, prer(d)\in E_i$, and $\forall\beta\in just(d), \neg\beta\notin E \}$.

Let us point out that E occurs in the definition of E_{i+1}. The generating defaults of E with respect to Δ are: GD(Δ,E)={d∈D | prer(d)∈E and ∀ β∈just(d), ¬β∉ E}.

In general, a default theory may not have extensions and if it does, these extensions may not be complete.

Theorem 2.1:[19]: Every normal default theory has an extension.

Notation: Let T_1 ... T_t be a sequence of sets. By convention, $T_{\to i}$ denotes $\cup T_j$ for j in [1..i].

3.Positivist default theories and stratification

The purpose of this section is to describe the declarative semantics of logic programs and deductive databases using Reiter's default logic. The two main issues raised by this are: for logic programs, it is largely recognized that their expressive power should be increased by the ability to express negation[7,9]; for deductive databases, both expressing negation in the premises of rules and allowing the inference of disjunctive information have to be combined[4]. Before starting our presentation, let us recall that the advantage of using default logic rather than circumscription[13] or "supported" model[1] lies in its well-recognized simplicity and modularity. Also, we want to stress that, only a subset of default logic is considered for which we provide a clear semantics.

In order to make the discussion clear, the concepts and results of the paper are stated in the propositional case. A short discussion at the end of the paper explains how to generalize these concepts and results to encompass full first order languages.

We first show how to express in default logic, a simple form of negation related to the Closed World Assumption. Roughly speaking, the Closed World Assumption (CWA) simplifies tremendously the representation of information by restricting it to positive (true) one. Thus, under CWA, in order to derive negative information, for example in order to derive the negative fact ¬A, one resorts to the following default inference process: "if ¬A is consistent with the knowledge base, then infer that ¬A is part of the knowledge base" or in terms of default rules: :M¬A / ¬A. Formally, we have:

Definition 3.1: Let L be a propositional language and A∈L. The *closed world default rule* associated with the proposition A is the expression :M¬A/¬A. The set of closed world default rules associated with the language L, denoted CWA_L, is:

$$CWA_L=\{ : M\neg A / \neg A \mid A\in L \}.$$

Default theories expressing the CWA have nice properties:

Lemma 3.1: Let L be a propositional language and Δ=(D,W) be a default theory over L such that $CWA_L \subseteq D$ and W is consistent. Then each extension E of Δ=(D,W) is complete.

Proof: Let E be an extension of (D,W). W consistent implies that E is consistent[19]. Now in order to show that E is maximal, it suffices to show that for each proposition A in L, either A is in E or ¬A is in E. Assume that neither A nor ¬A belongs to E. Because E=Th(E), E∪{¬A} is consistent. Hence the CWA-default rule :M¬A/¬A can be "applied" to infer that ¬A is in E, a contradiction.

Since the extensions of a default theory Δ incorporating the CWA are complete, the extensions of Δ can be easily identified with their model. It allows an easy study of the semantics of such a default theory. Indeed a strong correspondence between CWA-default logic and minimalism[5] was exhibited in [4]. For the purpose of our further discussion, we formally recall this result here:

Theorem 3.2 :[4] Let $\Delta=(CWA_L,W)$ be a default theory over L such that W is a set of positive clauses (*Recall that the disjunctive form of a positive clause has at least one positive literal.*). The three assertions are equivalent:

a. E is an extension of Δ,

b. E=Th(W ∪ {¬P | ¬P∈E}), and

c. The first order model M of E is a minimal model of W.

Intuitively, part b. says that W and the negative "facts" in E are sufficient to imply all (true) facts in E, hence E contains as much "false" facts as possible (part c.).

We are now interested in expressing negation in the premises of deductive rules (or formulas of a logic program). Assume, for example, that we want to express the following information: "If Ted has vacation and does not go to China then Ted is unhappy". The use of negation in logic programming, based on "negation as failure"[7], suggests that the meaning of the above sentence can be more accurately captured by: "if it is known that Ted has vacation and if there is no contradiction to assume that he is not going to China then infer that Ted is unhappy". And thus, using default logic, we would naturally express this by the following default rule:

VACATION_TED: M¬GO_CHINA_TED / UNHAPPY_TED.

The general form of default rules corresponding to deductive rules with negative premises is defined below :

Definition 3.2: A default rule d over L is a *positivist default rule* if prer(d) is a conjunction (possibly empty) of positive literals, just(d) is a non empty set of negative literals, and cons(d) is a disjunction of positive literals (at least one).

Now we are able to syntactically specify logic programs and deductive databases in the framework of default logic. This is done by restricting our attention to positivist default theories:

Definition 3.3: A default theory $\Delta=(D,W)$ over a language L is a *positivist default theory* iff $CWA_L \subseteq D$, $D-CWA_L$ is a set of positivist default rules, and W is a set of positive clauses.

By convention, a logic program is specified by a positivist default theory with no disjunction.

Example 3.1: (A Logic Database) Assume we want to express the following information about the two individuals TED and ANN:
TED has VACATION,
if TED or ANN has VACATION then they will either visit CHINA or PARIS,
if TED is not visiting CHINA, as well as
if he is not visiting PARIS then he will be UNHAPPY.

This database is specified by the following positivist default theory (In order to be coherent with the formal discussion, the default theory presented is built using a propositional language. It is clear that a first order language would be more convenient):

CWA_default rules:

:M¬VACATION_TED | ¬VACATION_TED
:M¬VACATION_ANN | ¬VACATION_ANN
:M¬GO_CHINA_TED | ¬GO_CHINA_TED
:M¬GO_CHINA_ANN | ¬GO_CHINA_ANN
:M¬GO_PARIS_TED | ¬GO_PARIS_TED
:M¬GO_PARIS_ANN | ¬GO_PARIS_ANN
:M¬UNHAPPY_TED | ¬UNHAPPY_TED
:M¬UNHAPPY_ANN | ¬UNHAPPY_ANN

:M¬ GO_CHINA_TED | UNHAPPY_TED
:M¬ GO_PARIS_TED | UNHAPPY_TED

Positivist default rules
D

VACATION_TED
VACATION_TED→GO_CHINA_TED∨GO_PARIS_TED
VACATION_ANN→GO_CHINA_ANN∨GO_PARIS_ANN

Positive clauses
W

It is easy to verify that the positivist default theory (D,W) admits two extensions:

E = Th(W ∪ { VACATION_TED, ¬VACATION_ANN, GO_CHINA_TED, ¬GO_CHINA_ANN, ¬GO_PARIS_TED, ¬GO_PARIS_ANN, UNHAPPY_TED, ¬UNHAPPY_ANN }),

and

E'= Th(W ∪ { VACATION_TED , ¬VACATION_ANN , ¬GO_CHINA_TED , ¬GO_CHINA_ANN , GO_PARIS_TED , ¬GO_PARIS_ANN , UNHAPPY_TED , ¬UNHAPPY_ANN })

Using default logic allows us to clearly distinguish rules that involve negation from those that do not. This distinction is of particular interest because first order logic is not sufficient for defining the semantics of the first kind of rules, while it is sufficient for the second one.

Let us discuss two more examples in order to illustrate well-known problems that arise when one increases the expressive power of logic program and database with negation.

Example 3.2: Consider the two positivist default theories $\Delta_1=(D_1,W_1)$ and $\Delta_2=(D_2,W_2)$ where:
$D_1=\{:M\neg A/\neg A,\ :M\neg B/\neg B,\ :M\neg A/B,\ :M\neg B/A\}$, $W_1=\{\}$;
and
$D_2=\{:M\neg A/\neg A,\ :M\neg B/\neg B,\ :M\neg C/\neg C,\ :M\neg A/B,\ :M\neg B/C,\ :M\neg C/A\}$, $W_2=\{\}$.
Δ_1 has two extensions, namely $Th(\{\neg A,B\})$ and $Th(\{A,\neg B\})$ but Δ_2 has no extension.

The example above shows that a positivist default theory (Δ_2) may not have an extension: "inconsistent" programs can be written. Intuitively, this arises when a certain type of recursion occurs on negation. Note that recursion does not necessarily lead to inconsistencies. The default theory Δ_1 does not contain (syntactically) any disjunctive consequences, neither in D_1 nor in W_1. Intuitively, this suggests that Δ_1 does not contain incomplete informations. However, Δ_1 has two extensions (as a matter of fact the same extensions as the "disjunctive" default theory $(\{:M\neg A/\neg A,\ :M\neg B/\neg B\},\ \{A\vee B\})$. In this case, we say that the logic program Δ_1 is "ambiguous".

In the following, we restrict our attention to non-inconsistent and non-ambiguous logic programs or databases, that is, to default theories with no recursion on negative literals. For this, it is sufficient to use the notion of stratification which has been simultaneously introduced by [1,21] and extended by [18]. In the context of default logic, the concept of stratification which generalizes the concept of taxonomy introduced in [11], is defined by:

Definition 3.4: A positivist default theory $\Delta=(D,W)$ over the language L is *stratifiable* iff there exists a sequence $S=L_1...L_s$, called a *stratification* for Δ, such that $L_1...L_s$ is a partition of the set of propositions in L satisfying:

i) $\forall\ (P_1\wedge \dots \wedge P_p : M\neg Q_1, \dots, M\neg Q_q / R_1\vee \dots \vee R_r) \in D,\ \exists\, k\in[1..s] \mid$
$\forall j\in[1..r],\ R_j\in L_k,$
$\forall j\in[1..p],\ \exists\, i\in[1..k] \mid P_j\in L_i,$
$\forall j\in[1..q],\ \exists\, i\in[1..k[\mid Q_j\in L_i,$ and

ii) $\forall\ (P_1\wedge \dots \wedge P_p \rightarrow R_1\vee \dots \vee R_r)\in W,\ \exists\, k\in[1..s] \mid$
$\forall j\in[1..r],\ R_j\in L_k,$
$\forall j\in[1..p],\ \exists\, i\in[1..k] \mid P_j\in L_i.$

Example 3.1 (continued): Two possible stratifications for (D,W) are given below:
$S=L_1L_2$ is a stratification for (D,W):
L_1={ VACATION_TED, VACATION_ANN, GO_CHINA_TED, GO_CHINA_ANN, GO_PARIS_TED, GO_PARIS_ANN},
L_2={ UNHAPPY_TED, UNHAPPY_ANN },
and

$S'=L'_1L'_2L'_3\ L'_4$ is also a stratification for (D,W):
L'_1={UNHAPPY_ANN}, L'_2={VACATION_TED, VACATION_ANN}
L'_3={GO_CHINA_TED,GO_PARIS_TED}, and
L'_4={GO_PARIS_ANN, GO_CHINA_ANN, UNHAPPY_TED}.

This example shows that there may be several different stratifications for a positivist default theory. Note also that in our example, the "smallest" (in the number of strata) stratification for (D,W) has two strata. Intuitively, (D,W) is stratifiable because the "definitions" of GO_CHINA_TED and of GO_PARIS _TED can be totally "isolated" from the definitions of UNHAPPY_TED in which GO_CHINA_TED and GO_PARIS _TED occur as negative premises. The notion of stratification implies a hierarchy on the "definitions" of the propositions that depends on the program or database.

We just mention here without development that the problem of deciding whether a database is stratifiable, is polynomial. The algorithm proposed in [1] is easily generalizable to check whether a positivist default theory is stratifiable.

Remark: One should notice here that the notion of stratification is defined on the language and not on the set of default rules in D and clauses in W. This slightly different way of presenting the concept of stratification is one of the keys to a really simplified definition of perfect models[18] in the next section.

Notation : Given a stratified positivist default theory (D,W) and a stratification $S=L_1...L_s$ for (D,W), S induces a partitioning on D and W. In the following, we abuse notations by making no distinction between the sets of propositions L_i and the languages built on these sets. Also, when S is understood, we denote $D_1... D_s$ (respectively, $W_1... W_s$) the elements of the partitioning induced by S on D (respectively on W) and for i=1..s, $D_i=\{d \mid d\in D \text{ and } cons(d)\in L_i\}$ and $W_i=\{\alpha\to\beta \mid \alpha\to\beta\in W \text{ and } \beta\in L_i\}$. In the following, (D_i,W_i) is called the ith *stratum* induced by S on (D,W).When S is understood, CWA_i denotes the set of closed world default rules associated with the sub-language L_i of L. Note in particular, that for any stratification S for (D,W), $D_1=CWA_1$.

We will now use the hierarchy induced by the stratification of a positivist default theory in order to define the semantics of logic programs or databases. Given a stratification S of a stratifiable positivist default theory Δ, we successively consider each stratum induced by S on Δ and propagate the informations obtained at the ith level while examining the $(i+1)^{th}$ stratum. However, we show in the further discussion that this definition does not depend on the choosen stratification.

Definition 3.5: Let Δ be a positivist default theory over the language L such that Δ is stratifiable. Let $S=L_1..L_s$ be a stratification for Δ. A set E of sentences over L is an *extension of* Δ *with respect to* S iff there exists a sequence $E_1,...E_s$ such that:
i) $E=E_s$, and
ii) $\forall i\in[1..s]$, E_i is an extension of $\Delta_i=(D_i, W_i\cup E_{i-1})$, assuming $E_0=\varnothing$.

Example 3.1 (continued): Consider the already given stratification S. The first stratum (D_1,W_1) induced by S on (D,W) has two extensions, namely:

E_1 = Th({ VACATION_TED , ¬VACATION_ANN ,
GO_CHINA_TED , ¬GO_CHINA_ANN ,
¬GO_PARIS_TED , ¬GO_PARIS_ANN , }),

E'_1 = Th({ VACATION_TED , ¬VACATION_ANN ,
¬GO_CHINA_TED , ¬GO_CHINA_ANN ,
GO_PARIS_TED , ¬GO_PARIS_ANN , }),

If we propagate E_1 in the second stratum $(D_2,\varnothing)$ induced by S on (D,W), that is if we consider the default theory (D_2,E_1), it has one extension, namely:

E_2 = Th({ VACATION_TED , ¬VACATION_ANN ,
GO_CHINA_TED , ¬GO_CHINA_ANN ,
¬GO_PARIS_TED , ¬GO_PARIS_ANN ,
UNHAPPY_TED , ¬UNHAPPY_ANN }),

If we now propagate E'_1 in the second stratum $(D_2,\varnothing)$ induced by S on (D,W), that is if we consider the default theory (D_2,E'_1), it has one extension, namely:

E'_2 = Th({ VACATION_TED , ¬VACATION_ANN ,
¬GO_CHINA_TED ,¬GO_CHINA_ANN ,
GO_PARIS_TED , ¬GO_PARIS_ANN ,
UNHAPPY_TED , ¬UNHAPPY_ANN }).

Thus E_2 and E'_2 are two extensions of (D,W) with respect to the stratification S. Note that they respectively coincide with the already given extensions E and E'.

We now are going to show that a stratified positivist default theory has always at least one extension with respect to some stratification. Then we argue that for a stratified positivist default theory, the notion of extension (as defined by Reiter) and the notion of extension with respect to a stratification are strictly equivalent. From this, we easily deduce that the concept of extension with respect to a stratification is independent of the given stratification and moreover that the stratification property is sufficient to conclude the existence of canonical extensions for a positivist default theory.

In order to proceed with this study, we need some intermediate results. Roughly speaking, the next technical lemma states that given a positivist default theory (D,W), if justifications of non-CWA-default rules in D have their truth value determined by the contents of W, then these non-CWA-default rules can be turned into clauses that are added to W.

Lemma 3.3: Let Δ=(D,W) be a default theory over the language L such that D is a set of positivist default rules including CWA_L and W is a set of positive clauses and negative literals. Assume that $\forall(\neg Q)\in JUST(D-CWA_L)$, $Q\in W$ or $\neg Q\in W$. Then E is an extension of Δ iff E is an extension of $(CWA_L, W\cup W')$ where:

$W'=\{\alpha\to\gamma \mid d\in D, \alpha=prer(d), \gamma=cons(d), \text{ and } \forall(\neg Q)\in just(d), (\neg Q)\in W\}$.

Sketch of proof:
(⇒) Assume that E is an extension of Δ. Let T denote $Th(W\cup W'\cup\{\neg Q \mid \neg Q\in E\})$. To show that E is an extension of $\Delta'=(CWA_L,W\cup W')$, it suffices, by Theorem 3.2 b., to

show that E=T. By noticing that $W \subseteq E$ and by definition of W', we directly obtain that $T \subseteq E$. In order to prove that $E=\cup_{i=0..\infty} E_i \subseteq T$, we prove, by induction on i, that $E_i \subseteq T$ where $E_0=W$, and for $i \geq 0$, $E_{i+1}=Th(E_i) \cup F_i$ with
$F_i=\{cons(d) \mid d \in D, prer(d) \in E_i, \forall(\neg Q) \in just(d), (\neg Q) \in E\}$.
(⇐) Assume that E' is an extension of $\Delta'=(CWA_L, W \cup W')$. To prove that E' is an extension of $\Delta=(D,W)$, we show that $E'=\cup_{i=0..\infty} E_i$ where $E_0=W$, and for $i \geq 0$, $E_{i+1}=Th(E_i) \cup F_i$ with
$F_i=\{cons(d) \mid d \in D, prer(d) \in E_i, \forall(\neg Q) \in just(d), (\neg Q) \in E'\}$.
We note that $F_0=\{\neg Q \mid (\neg Q) \in W\} \cup \{\gamma \mid \alpha \to \gamma \in W', \alpha \in W\}$ and for $i \geq 1$, $F_i=\{\gamma \mid \alpha \to \gamma \in W', \alpha \in E_i\}$. On one hand, by induction on i, we show that $E_i \subseteq E'$. On the other hand, using Theorem 3.2 b., we show that
$E'=Th(W \cup W' \cup \{\neg Q \mid \neg Q \in E'\}) \subseteq \cup_{i=1..\infty} E_i$. □

Using previous Lemma, we propose an equivalent definition of an extension with respect to a stratification:

Corollary 3.4: Let Δ be a positivist default theory over the language L and assume that $S=L_1..L_s$ is a stratification for Δ. Then E is an extension of Δ with respect to S iff there exists a sequence $E_1,\ldots, E_s$ such that:
i) $E=E_s$ and
ii) $\forall i \in [1..s]$, E_i is an extension of $(CWA_{\to i}, V_i)$ with:
$V_i=\cup_{j=1..i}(W_j \cup W'_j)$ and, for j=1..s,
$W'_j=\{\alpha \to \gamma \mid d \in D_j, \alpha=prer(d), \gamma=cons(d)$ and, $\forall(\neg Q) \in just(d), \neg Q \in E_{j-1}\}$,
assuming $E_0=\varnothing$.

Sketch of proof:
We first show that:
(*) Given a sequence $E_1..E_s$, (+) E_i is an extension of $(D_i, W_i \cup E_{i-1})$, for i=1..s iff (++) E_i is an extension of $(CWA_{\to i}, V_i)$, for i=1..s. We prove (*) by induction on i, using Lemma 3.3 (E_i is an extension of $(D_i, W_i \cup E_{i-1})$ iff E_i is an extension of $(CWA_{\to i}, W_i \cup W'_i \cup E_{i-1})$) and Theorem 3.2 b. The proof of Corollary 3.4 is immediate from (*).

This result is of great interest because it gives a definition of an extension with respect to a stratification in terms of extensions of CWA-default theories. Then we know that the extensions of a CWA-default theory (D,W) can be identified with the minimal models of W. In fact, Corollary 3.4 together with Theorem 3.2 c. lead us to expect that minimalism is enough to define the semantics of stratifiable logic programs and databases (Theorem 4.1 and 4.2 of section 4).
We now simply invoke Corollary 3.4 to prove the two main results of this section: the first one shows that stratifiable programs or databases are consistent in the sense that, given a stratification S, an extension with respect to S can be exhibited for these programs or databases; the second one states the equivalence between Reiter's notion of extension and the notion of extension with respect to a stratification.

Theorem 3.5: Let Δ be a positivist default theory over the language L and assume that S is a stratification for Δ. Then Δ has an extension with respect to S.

Proof: Assuming $S=L_1...L_s$, it suffices to show that $\forall i \in [1..s]$, $(D_i, W_i \cup E_{i-1})$ has an extension or equivalently, that $\forall i \in [1..s]$, $(CWA_{\to i}, V_i)$ has an extension, where V_i is defined in Corollary 3.4. Note that $\forall i \in [1..s]$, $(CWA_{\to i}, V_i)$ is a closed normal default theory, therefore by Theorem 2.1, it has an extension. □

Again using Corollary 3.4, we have:

Theorem 3.6: Let Δ be a positivist default theory over the language L and assume that S is a stratification for Δ. Then E is an extension of Δ iff E is an extension of Δ with respect to S.

Sketch of proof:
(⇒) Let E be an extension of Δ with respect to $S=L_1...L_s$. By definition, there exists a sequence $E_1...E_s$ such that $E=E_s$ and for $i \in [1..s]$, E_i is an extension of $(CWA_{\to i}, V_i)$ (V_i is defined in Corollary 3.4). In order to show that E is an extension of Δ, we prove that $E=\cup_{i=0..\infty} G_i$ where $G_0=W$, and for $i \geq 0$ $G_{i+1}=Th(G_i) \cup T_i$ with
$T_i=\{cons(d) \mid d \in D, prer(d) \in G_i, \forall(\neg Q) \in just(d), \neg Q \in E\}$.
On one hand, we show, by induction on i, that $\forall i \in [0..\infty[$, $\exists j \in [1..s]$, $G_i \subseteq E_j$. On the other hand, we show, by induction on j, that $\forall j \in [1..s]$, $E_j \subseteq \cup_{i=0..\infty} G_i$.
(⇐) Assume now that E is an extension of Δ. Then $E=\cup_{i=0..\infty} G_i$ where $G_0=W$, and for $i \geq 0$ $G_{i+1}=Th(G_i) \cup T_i$ with
$T_i=\{cons(d) \mid d \in D, prer(d) \in G_i, \forall(\neg Q) \in just(d), \neg Q \in E\}$.
We first show that $\forall i,k \in [1...s]$, $Th(G_i)|L_{\to k}=Th(G_i|L_{\to k})$. Then, in order to prove that E is an extension of Δ with respect to S, we show, by induction on i that $\forall i \in [1..s]$, $E_i=E|L_{\to i}$ is an extension of $(D_i, W_i \cup E_{i-1})$. In the induction step, in order to prove that E_{k+1} is an extension of $(D_{k+1}, W_{k+1} \cup E_k)$ assuming for $i \leq k$, that E_i is an extension of $(D_i, W_i \cup E_{i-1})$, we show that $E_{k+1}=\cup_{j=0..\infty} H_j$ where $H_0=W_{k+1} \cup E_k$ and for $j \geq 0$ $H_{j+1}=Th(H_j) \cup S_j$ with
$S_j=\{cons(d) \mid d \in D_{k+1}, prer(d) \in H_j, \forall(\neg Q) \in just(d), \neg Q \in E_{k+1}\}$.
Thus, we show, in one hand by induction on j that $\forall j \in [0..\infty[$, $H_j \subseteq E_{k+1}$ and on the other hand by induction on i that $\forall i \in [0...\infty[$, $G_i|L_{\to k+1} \subseteq \cup_{j=0..\infty} H_j$. □

From Theorem 3.5 and 3.6, we immediately deduce that:

Corollary 3.7: Let Δ be a positivist default theory over the language L such that Δ is stratifiable. Assume that S and S' are two distinct stratifications for Δ. Then:

i) E is an extension of Δ with respect to S iff E is an extension of Δ with respect to S'.

ii) There exists a set E of formulas over L such that E is an extension of Δ.

Once again, we insist here on the fact that the stratification constraint on positivist default theory is a sufficient condition but is not necessary for the existence of an extension: Remind that the non-stratifiable default theory Δ_1 of Example 3.2 has two extensions.

As a matter of fact, we would like to lay stress on the significance of Corollary 3.7 ii) from the default logic point of view. Characterizing a class of default theories that have at least one extension is a problem that received a lot of attention but few and sometimes disappointing solutions. Reiter has only established the existence of extensions for normal theories (Theorem 2.1) whose semantics is given in [14]. Unfortunately, the class of normal theories has turned out to be insufficient for pratical applications like knowledge representation: semi-normal default theories whose default rules are of the form $\alpha : M(\beta \wedge \gamma) / \gamma$, have been introduced by Reiter and Criscuolo[20]. Although some semi-normal default theories (those corresponding to acyclic inheritance networks with exceptions) have an extension[10], in general they need not have extensions. In [11], a new class of default theories, called taxonomic default theories, is defined whose default rules are neither normal nor semi-normal. Roughly speaking, "taxonomy" rules out recursion completely and is not concerned with the CWA. In conclusion, the class of stratifiable positivist default theories for which the existence of extensions has been showed, extends the class of taxonomic default theories and is interesting from a practical point of view without a doubt.

In this section, we have defined the declarative semantics of logic programs and databases using default logic. For the class of stratifiable positivist default theories, we have provided a new definition of the concept of extension that uses the notion of stratification. We have shown that stratifiable programs or databases are consistent. We have not proved that they are non-ambiguous. However, via the equivalence between the default logic approach and the perfect model approach which is discussed in the next section, and since stratifiable logic programs have a unique perfect model, the non-ambiguosity can be established.

4.Comparative study of the Default Logic and the Perfect Model approaches

In this section we show the equivalence between the default logic approach and Przymunsinski's approach [18] based on prioritized circumscription. We first review the concept of perfect model introduced in [18] and show that the concept of minimal model is sufficient to characterize the concept of perfect model of a stratifiable set of P-clauses. After presenting a straightforward correspondence between positivist default theories and sets of P-clauses, we establish the associated semantic equivalence.

The notion of P-clause has been first introduced in [4] to syntactically distinguish deductive rules of the form $A \wedge \neg B \rightarrow C$ from deductive rules of the form $A \rightarrow B \vee C$ which are equivalent from the first order logic point of view but not from the database or logic programming points of view.

Definition 4.1: A *positivist clause (P-clause)* over L is an expression of the form :

$$P_1 \wedge ... \wedge P_p \wedge \neg Q_1 \wedge ... \wedge \neg Q_q \rightarrow R_1 \vee ... \vee R_r,$$

where $p \geq 0$, $q \geq 0$ and $r \geq 1$, $P_1,..., P_p, Q_1,...,Q_q, R_1,...R_r$ are propositions of L.

We will denote by $Prem(\sigma)=\{P_1,...,P_p,Q_1,...,Q_q\}$, $NPrem(\sigma)=\{Q_1,...,Q_q\}$, and $Cons(\sigma)=\{R_1, ..., R_r\}$.

Now, logic programs or databases are specified by sets of P-clauses and their semantics is given by certain (let say "good" for now) models of theses sets. Given a set Σ of P-clauses, Przymunsinski's approach[18] consists in deducing from the syntax of Σ a relation, called a *priority relation*, on the propositions of the language. Then, this relation is used to characterize the "good" models of Σ, called *preferable models*. Intuitively, the definition of the priority relation associated with Σ is based on the three following principles:

(a) consequents of a P-clause should have lower priority (for minimization) than negative premises of this P-clause,

(b) consequents of a P-clause should have priority not higher than positive premises of this P-clause, and

(c) propositions occuring in a consequence of a P-clause should have same priority.

Formally, a directed graph is associated with a set Σ of P-clauses[1]. The vertices of the graph are the propositions of the language L and the directed edges are pairs [X,Y] of propositions such that: $\exists \sigma \in \Sigma$, $X \in Prem(\sigma)$ and $Y \in Cons(\sigma)$. If $X \in NPrem(\sigma)$, then the edge is called a *negative edge* . Using this graph, the relation of *higher priority* [18], denoted $>_\Sigma$, induced by Σ, is defined on LxL as follows: $X >_\Sigma Y$ iff there exists a path in the directed graph associated with Σ from X to Y going through a negative edge. As previously indicated, this relation of higher priority $>_\Sigma$ is then used to "compare" the models of Σ. Among the possible minimal models of Σ, we prefer the ones which minimize higher priority propositions even at the price of enlarging the truth of propositions of lower priority. This leads to the following notion of preferability:

Definition 4.2 :[18] Let Σ be a set of P-clauses over the language L. Let M and N be two models of Σ . M is *preferable* to N, denoted $M \leq_{pref} N$, iff $\forall X \in M-N, \exists Y \in N-M / Y >_\Sigma X$.

M is a *perfect model* of Σ iff there exists no model distinct from M and preferable to M.

In [18], it is showed that:

Theorem 4.0 : Every perfect model is minimal .

Example 4.1: We specify below the logic database of Example 3.1 using a set of P-clauses.

Σ={VACATION_TED,

VACATION_TED → GO_CHINA_TED∨ GO_PARIS_TED,

VACATION_ANN → GO_CHINA_ANN ∨ GO_PARIS_ANN

¬GO_CHINA_TED → UNHAPPY_TED,

¬GO_PARIS_TED → UNHAPPY_TED }

This set of P-clauses gives rise to the following priority relation:

(i) GO_PARIS_TED $>_\Sigma$ UNHAPPY_TED,

(ii) GO_CHINA_TED $>_\Sigma$ UNHAPPY_TED.

Here are the three minimal models of Σ:

M ={ VACATION_TED, GO_CHINA_TED, UNHAPPY_TED }

M'={ VACATION_TED, GO_PARIS_TED, UNHAPPY_TED }

M"={ VACATION_TED, GO_CHINA_TED, GO_PARIS_TED }

From (i), we deduce that $M <_{pref} M"$ and from (ii) we deduce that $M' <_{pref} M"$. In conclusion, M and M' are the only perfect models of Σ.

Let us now consider the logic program $\Sigma=\{\neg A\rightarrow B, \neg B\rightarrow A\}$. It induces that $B>_\Sigma A$, $A>_\Sigma B$ and that the minimal models {A}, {B} of Σ are preferable one to each other ($\{A\}\leq_{pref}\{B\}\leq_{pref}\{A\}$). In other word, Σ is inconsistent in the sense that it has no preferable model. In fact, for sets of P-clauses, recursion on negation leads to problems similar to the ones discussed in section 3 for positivist default theories. Thus recursion on negation is eliminated by considering stratifiable sets of P-clauses. Because the notion of stratification for sets of P-clauses is the same as the notion of stratification defined for positivist default theories, we exhibit now a straightforward syntaxic correspondence between sets of P-clauses and positivist default theories. From this, we state that a set of P-clauses is stratifiable iff its associated positivist default theory is stratifiable.

Definition 4.3: Let Σ be a set of P-clauses. Let $\Delta=(D,W)$ be a positivist default theory.Then the default theory associated with Σ (resp. the set of P-clauses associated with Δ), denoted $\Delta_\Sigma=(D_\Sigma,W_\Sigma)$ (resp. denoted Σ_Δ) is defined by:

$D_\Sigma=CWA_L\cup\{\ \alpha:M\neg Q_1...M\neg Q_q/\beta\ |$

$\alpha\wedge\neg Q_1\wedge...\wedge\neg Q_q\rightarrow\beta\in\Sigma$ and $q>0\ \}$

and

$W_\Sigma=\{P_1\wedge...\wedge P_p\rightarrow\beta\ |\ P_1\wedge...\wedge P_p\rightarrow\beta\in\Sigma,\ P_i\in L,\ 1\leq i\leq p\}$,

(resp. $\Sigma_\Delta=W\cup\{\alpha\wedge\neg Q_1\wedge...\wedge\neg Q_q\rightarrow\beta\ |$

$\alpha:M\neg Q_1...M\neg Q_q/\beta\in D-CWA_L\}$).

Before stating the two main results of this section, we introduce them by comparing Example 3.1 and Example 4.1:

Example 4.2: Let Δ be the positivist default theory of Example 3.1 and Σ be the set of P-clauses of Example 4.1. Obviously $\Delta=\Delta_\Sigma$ and $\Sigma=\Sigma_\Delta$ and since Δ is stratifiable, so is Σ. Note that the perfect models M and M' of Σ are respectively the first order models of the extensions E and E' of Δ. In this case, the perfect model semantics and the default logic semantics coincide.

Consider the stratification S for Δ. We showed that S induces a partitioning on Δ. In the same way, S induces the following partitioning on Σ:

Σ_1={VACATION_TED,

VACATION_TED→GO_CHINA_TED∨ GO_PARIS_TED,

VACATION_ANN→GO_CHINA_ANN∨ GO_PARIS_ANN}

Σ_2={¬GO_CHINA_TED→UNHAPPY_TED,

¬GO_PARIS_TED→ UNHAPPY_TED }

Note that, on one hand:

$M_1=M|L_1$={VACATION_TED, GO_CHINA_TED} is a minimal model of Σ_1,

$M_2=M|(L_1\cup L_2)=M$ is a minimal model of $\Sigma_1\cup\Sigma_2=\Sigma$.

and on the other hand:

$M'_1=M'|L_1$={VACATION_TED, GO_PARIS_TED} is a minimal model of Σ_1,

$M'_2=M'|(L_1\cup L_2)=M'$ is a minimal model of $\Sigma_1\cup\Sigma_2=\Sigma$.

Furthermore, note that $M"|L_1=M"$ is not a minimal model of Σ_1.

This suggests a correspondence between the perfect model semantics and the (pure) minimal model semantics for stratified databases.

The purpose of our next result, besides it slightly facilitates the proof of the main result of this section (Theorem 4.2), is to hightlight the fact that the notion of minimal model is totaly sufficient to define the perfect model semantics for sets of P-clauses that are stratifiable. This result has been conjectured without proof in [5]. It permits a considerable simplification of the formalism used to define the declarative semantics of logic programs and deductive databases.

Theorem 4.1: Let Σ be a stratifiable set of P-clauses over the propositional language L. Let $S=L_1...L_s$ be a stratification for Σ. Then M is a perfect model of Σ iff $\forall i\in[1..s]$, $M_i=M|L_{\rightarrow i}$ is a minimal model of $\Sigma_{\rightarrow i}$ where:

$M|L_{\rightarrow i}$ denotes the restriction of M to the language $L_{\rightarrow i}$ and $\Sigma_i=\{\sigma\ |\ \sigma\in\Sigma$ and $Cons(\sigma)\in L_i\}$.

Sketch of proof:

(⇒) Let M be a model of Σ such that for $i\in[1..s]$, $M_i=M|L_{\rightarrow i}$ is a minimal model of $\Sigma_{\rightarrow i}$. To show that M is a perfect model of Σ, we prove by induction on i that M_i is a perfect model of $\Sigma_{\rightarrow i}$. In the induction step, given that for $i\leq p$, M_i is a perfect model of $\Sigma_{\rightarrow i}$, assuming that there exists a model N of $\Sigma_{\rightarrow p+1}$ such that $N<_{pref}M_{p+1}$ leads to a contradiction.

(⇐)Let M be a perfect model of Σ. To show that for $i\in[1..s]$, $M_i=M|L_{\rightarrow i}$ is a minimal model of $\Sigma_{\rightarrow i}$, we proceed by induction on the number s of strata of the stratification S.

Induction Step: We assume that each stratifiable set Σ of P-clauses whose stratification S has s strata, $s\leq p$, satisfies: (*) M is a perfect model of Σ implies that for $i\in[1..s]$, $M_i=M|L_{\rightarrow i}$ is a minimal model of $\Sigma_{\rightarrow i}$.

Let consider a set Σ of P-clauses with a stratification $S=L_1...L_{p+1}$. To show that Σ satisfies (*), note that, given M a perfect model of Σ, by Theorem 4.0, $M=M_{P+1}$ is a minimal model of $\Sigma=\Sigma_{\rightarrow P+1}$. Thus, by induction hypothesis, it remains to show that $M|L_{\rightarrow p}=M_P$ is a perfect model of $\Sigma_{\rightarrow P}$. At that point, we assume that there exists N' model of $\Sigma_{\rightarrow P}$ such that $N'<_{pref}M_P$ and we construct a model N of $\Sigma_{\rightarrow P+1}$ such that $N'=N|L_{\rightarrow p}$ (the construction starts with N', model of $\Sigma_{\rightarrow P}$, which is "augmented" with propositions of L_{p+1} in order to obtain a model that satisfies $\Sigma_{\rightarrow P+1}=\Sigma_{\rightarrow P}\cup\Sigma_{P+1}$) and such that $N<_{pref}M$ (the propositions added to N' are carefully choosen). This leads to a contradiction. □

In the following, we use the above characterization as a definition of a perfect model.

The purpose of our next result is to show the equivalence of the default logic approach with the already studied approaches used to define the declarative semantics of logic programs and databases. In [18], the declarative semantics of logic programs and databases is defined through the notion of perfect models. It is shown that:

- stratifiable logic programs, that is non-disjunctive sets of P-clauses, have a unique perfect model;
- this unique perfect model coincides with the model obtained by the iterative fixed point method[1] and by Van Gelder's method[21].
- perfect models can also be characterized using the concept of prioritized circumscription.

In [13], the equivalence between circumscription and iterative fixed points is emphasized. The following result establishes the semantic equivalence of the default logic approach with the perfect model approach and therefore with the above mentioned approaches.

<u>Theorem 4.2:</u> Let Σ be a stratifiable set of P-clauses. Then M is a perfect model of Σ iff M is the model of an extension E of the default theory Δ_Σ.

Note that this equivalence is modular in the sense of [12].

<u>Sketch of proof:</u> Let $\Delta_\Sigma=(D,W)$ and $S=L_1...L_s$ a stratification for Δ_Σ. We first show that:

(*) Given a sequence $M_1...M_s$ such that $\forall i\in[1..s]$, M_i is a model of $L_{\rightarrow i}$, (+) $\forall i\in[1..s]$, M_i is a minimal model of $\Sigma_{\rightarrow i}$ iff (++) $\forall i\in[1..s]$, M_i is a minimal model of U_i where: $U_1=W_1$ and $\forall i\in[1..s-1]$, $U_{i+1}=U_i\cup W_{i+1}\cup U'_{i+1}$ with $U'_j=\{\ \alpha\rightarrow\gamma \mid d\in D_j,\ prer(d)=\alpha,\ cons(d)=\gamma,\ \forall\neg Q\in just(d),\ Q\notin M_{j-1}\ \}$.

We prove (*) by induction on i, and given that for $i\leq k$, (+) iff (++) is satisfied, the proof that minimal models of $\Sigma_{\rightarrow k+1}$ coincide with minimal models of U_{k+1} mainly consists in showing that a model M' of $L_{\rightarrow k+1}$ such that $M'|L_{\rightarrow k}=M_k$ is a model of $\Sigma_{\rightarrow k+1}$ iff it is a model of U_{k+1}.

($\Rightarrow$) Given a perfect model M of Σ, $\forall i\in[1..s]$, $M_i=M|L_{\rightarrow i}$ is a minimal model of $\Sigma_{\rightarrow i}$ and by (*) $\forall i\in[1..s]$, M_i is a minimal model of U_i. Let $E=Th(\{\ \sigma \mid \sigma\in L \text{ and } M \models \sigma\ \})$. To show that E is an extension of $\Delta_\Sigma=(D,W)$, it suffices to show (Theorem 3.5) that E is an extension of $\Delta_\Sigma=(D,W)$ with respect to S (i.e.) to prove that $E_i=E|L_{\rightarrow i}=Th(\{\ \sigma \mid \sigma\in L_{\rightarrow i}$ and $M_i \models \sigma\ \})$ is an extension of $(CWA_{\rightarrow i}, V_i)$ where V_i is defined in Corollary 3.4. To conclude, it suffices to note that, by Theorem 3.2, the first order models of extensions of $(CWA_{\rightarrow i}, V_i)$ over $L_{\rightarrow i}$ coincide with minimal models of V_i and that $\forall i\in[1..s], V_i=U_i$.

($\Leftarrow$) is done in a similar manner. □

In conclusion, during the past few years, logic programing and deductive databases have recieved a great and active interest from the "non-monotonic logics" community. Neglected until now, default logic has been investigated here as a natural tool to define the declarative semantics of logic programs and databases. Using default logic, in this context, is motivated by a modular simple structure and a well-defined semantics. The state of researches in this area did entail a comparative study: we have shown that in the context of stratifiable logic programming and databases, default logic is equivalent to the other non-monotonic logic approaches. Finally, studying logic programing and deductive databases from the point of view of default logic has led us to exhibit a very elegant definition of the semantics of stratifiable programs and databases that uses exclusively the notion of minimal model.

However, interesting problems related to default logic in a general manner (see conclusion of Section 3) and to logic programing and deductive databases more specifically, remain to be explored. The generalization of the concept of stratification to encompass full first order languages, if made in a straightforward way, is too restrictive. This problem is partially adressed in [18] by introducing the notion of local stratification; it turns out that checking local stratifiability requires a complete instantiation of the program or database examined which seems unreasonnable. Also we believe that this problem ranges among those raised by the dynamic aspects[2] and thus the non-monotonic behavior[4] of logic programing and deductive databases which are not yet solved to the general satisfaction.

Acknowledgements: The authors are grateful to Jean-Pierre Jouannaud and Nicolas Spyratos for helpful discussions and comments.

References

[1] Apt, R. K., H. Blair, A. Walker, Towards a Theory of Declarative Knowlegde, Workshop on Foundations of Deductive Databases and Logic Programming, 1986, pp 546-628.

[2] Apt, R. K., J-M. Pugin, Maintenance of Stratified Databases Viewed as a Belief Revision System, to appear in Proc. ACM SIGACT-SIGMOD Symposium on Principles of Database System, 1987.

[3] Bidoit N., C. Froidevaux, Minimalism subsumes Default Logic and Circumscription in Stratified Logic Programming and Databases, L.R.I. Research Report, to appear.

[4] Bidoit N., R. Hull, Positivism vs Minimalism in Deductive Databases, Proc. ACM SIGACT-SIGMOD Symposium on Principles of Database System, 1986, pp 123-132.

[5] Bidoit N., R. Hull, Minimalism, Justification and Non-Monotonicity in Deductive Databases, L.R.I. Research Report 304, 1986.

[6] Bossu G., P. Siegel, Saturation, Nonmonotonic Reasoning and the Closed World Assumption, AI 25 (1985), pp 13-63.

[7] Clark K. L., Negation as Failure, In H. Gallaire and J. Minker, Ed., Logic and Databases, Plenum Press, New-York, 1978, pp 293-322.

[8] Chandra A.K., D. Harrel, Horn Clause Queries and Generalizations, Journal of Logic Programming, vol. 2, 1, 1985, pp 1-15.

[9] Clark K. L., S. A. Tarnlund (Ed.), Logic Programming, Academic Press, New-York, 1982.

[10] Etherington D. W., R. Reiter, On Inheritance Hierarchies with Exceptions, Proc. of AAAI-1983, pp 104-108.

[11] Froidevaux C., Taxonomic Default Theory, Proceedings European Conference on Artificial Intelligence, Brighton, 1986, pp 123-129.

[12] Imielinski T., Results on Translating Defaults to Circumscription, Proceedings IJCAI, 1985, pp 114-120.

[13] Lifschitz V., On the Declarative Semantics of Logic Programs with Negation, Workshop on Foundations of Deductive Databases and Logic Programming, 1986, pp 420-432.

[14] Lukaszewicz W., Two results on Default Logic, Proc. IJCAI, 1985, pp 459-461.

[15] Mc Carthy J., Circumscription - A form of Nonmonotonic Reasoning, AI 13:1, 1980, pp 27-39.

[16] Mc Dermott D., J. Doyle, Nonmonotonic Logic I, AI 13:1, 1980, pp 41-72.

[17] Naqvi S. A., A Logic for Negation in Database Systems, Workshop on Foundations of Deductive Databases and Logic Programming, 1986, pp 378-387.

[18] Przymunsinski T. C., On the Semantics of Stratified Deductive Databases,Workshop on Foundations of Deductive Databases and Logic Programming, 1986, pp 433-443.

[19] Reiter R., A Logic for Default Reasoning, AI 13:1, 1980, pp 81-132.

[20] Reiter R., G. Criscuolo, On iteracting defaults, Proc. IJCAI, 1981, pp 270-276.

[21] Van Gelder A., Negation as Failure using Tight Derivations for General Logic Programs, to appear in the Proceedings of the third IEEE Symposium on Logic Programming, Sept. 86.

HEREDITARY HARROP FORMULAS AND UNIFORM PROOF SYSTEMS

Dale Miller Computer and Information Science Department
University of Pennsylvania, Philadelphia, PA 19104
Gopalan Nadathur Computer Science Department
Duke University, Durham, NC 27706
Andre Scedrov Mathematics Department
University of Pennsylvania, Philadelphia, PA 19104

Abstract: In this paper, we are concerned with strengthening the logical foundations of the logic programming paradigm. In particular, we are interested in those logical systems whose provability predicate preserves a simple and natural search-related interpretation of the logical connectives. Proof systems which are sound and complete for this interpretation will be called *uniform proof systems.* For the purposes of this paper, we will identify a logic programming language with any logical system whose proof predicate is uniform. We present three logic programming languages which extend the positive Horn clause logic programming language. Our most expressive language is based on *hereditary Harrop formulas* and uses higher-order intuitionistic logic as its proof system. We also present several metatheoretic properties of hereditary Harrop formulas.

1. Introduction.

The Prolog programming language [18] can be thought of as implementing the classical logic theory of positive Horn clauses. Although this programming language has many interesting features, it lacks many other features commonly found in most modern programming languages. For example, Horn clauses are not capable of representing block structures, modules, abstract data types, or higher-order functions.

There are essentially three broad approaches to extending the logic programming paradigm to contain these and other features. The first approach takes programming constructs from other languages and mixes them into Horn clauses. For example, some of the higher-order mechanisms of Lisp can be mixed with Horn clauses to make Prolog more higher-order. The second approach attempts to take existing interpreters and modify them in simple ways so that the resulting interpreter has a behavior which could be utilized to provide aspects of these missing features. Although both of these approaches generally provide quick and usable extensions, they also clutter up the language's semantics and declarative meaning.

The third approach to extending logic programming is to consider extending the underlying logical foundations of the language. While this approach does not always provide the immediate and tangible solutions of the other two approaches, it often has the advantage that the extended language continues to have a clear semantics and a declarative reading. There are, however, great extremes to how logic could be used to define a logic programming language. The classical logic theory of Horn clauses is a weak extreme, while full and unrestricted quantificational logic is a strong extreme. At such an extreme, general purpose theorem provers would need to be employed to implement the declarative meaning for programs. Our present paper was motivated by trying to find a criterion to help determine where a good boundary between these two extremes might lie.

The central feature of logic programming which we wish to maintain in any extension of the logic on which it is built is that a logic program should be considered as the specification of a search. Given this approach to the abstract character of logic programming, we view logical connectives as having certain natural and nondeterministic operational meanings. In particular, we shall fix the success/failure semantics of the the five connectives, $\wedge$, $\vee$, $\supset$, $\exists$, and $\forall$, in a very natural way. For example, the binary connectives $\wedge$ and $\vee$ will be considered as operational specifications for AND and OR nodes in a search tree. Our criterion for judging a logical system as being appropriate for specifying a logic programming language will be based on whether or not it supports this operational meaning of the connectives. Derivational systems which are sound and complete with respect to this operational meaning of connectives will be called *uniform proof systems.* It is such systems which we consider to be appropriate as logic programming languages.

After defining these notions of uniform proofs and logic programs, we shall describe four logic programming languages. The first logic programming language we present is the familiar one, that is, the one based on first-order positive Horn clauses. The other three are more expressive languages. For each of these new programming languages, we briefly describe how it can be used to specify programs not directly expressible in Horn clauses. The last half of this paper discusses the metatheoretical properties of our final and most expressive logic programming language.

2. Uniform Proof Systems.

Let $\mathcal{L}$ be some formulation of logic which contains the logical connectives $\wedge$, $\vee$, $\supset$, $\forall$, and $\exists$. Let $\mathcal{D}$ and $\mathcal{G}$ be sets of $\mathcal{L}$-formulas and let $\vdash_R$ be a provability predicate for the language $\mathcal{L}$. We write $\mathcal{P} \vdash_R^* G$ to denote that $\mathcal{P} \vdash_R G$ and $G \in \mathcal{G}$ and $\mathcal{P}$ is a finite subset of $\mathcal{D}$. We say that $\vdash_R$ is *uniform* over the pair $\langle \mathcal{D}, \mathcal{G} \rangle$ if for every $\mathcal{P}$ and G such that $\mathcal{P} \vdash_R^* G$, the following conditions hold:

(1) If G is $A \wedge B$ then $\mathcal{P} \vdash_R^* A$ and $\mathcal{P} \vdash_R^* B$.

(2) If G is $A \vee B$ then $\mathcal{P} \vdash_R^* A$ or $\mathcal{P} \vdash_R^* B$.

(3) If G is $A \supset B$ then $A, \mathcal{P} \vdash_R^* B$.

(4) If G is $\exists x\, B$ then there exists a term t such that $\mathcal{P} \vdash_R^* [x/t]B$.

(5) If G is $\forall x\, B$ then $\mathcal{P} \vdash_R^* [x/y]B$ for all parameters y not free in $\mathcal{P}$ or G.

Furthermore, we assume the following additional property on $\vdash_R$:

(6) The converse of (1) – (5) holds for $\vdash_R$.

Condition (6) provides a very simple declarative reading of the logical connectives which is common to many different logical systems. Conditions (1) – (5), however, substantially restrict which logical systems are uniform.

The formulas in the set $\mathcal{G}$ are considered queries or *goals*, while finite subsets of $\mathcal{D}$ are considered logic programs. When conditions (1) – (5) hold, a very simple, nondeterministic search procedure can be designed to try and satisfy non-atomic goals. That is, to determine if $\mathcal{P} \vdash_R A \wedge B$, one can try to determine both $\mathcal{P} \vdash_R A$ and $\mathcal{P} \vdash_R B$. Hence, $\wedge$ becomes an AND node in the search process; similarly, $\vee$ becomes an OR node. The quantifiers $\forall$ and $\exists$ become infinite versions of AND and OR nodes. Finally, implication directs the search procedure to change its context by extending its program. The actual program $\mathcal{P}$ is used only to determine the meaning of the atomic goals. All the logical systems we shall examine have an inference rule of the form: if $\mathcal{P} \vdash_R G$ then $G \supset A, \mathcal{P} \vdash_R A$. Hence, proving an atomic goal will generally mean attempting to prove a non-atomic goal.

We define a *logic programming language* as a quadruple $\langle \mathcal{L}, \mathcal{D}, \mathcal{G}, \vdash_R \rangle$ where $\mathcal{D}$ and $\mathcal{G}$ are sets of formulas of $\mathcal{L}$ such that $\vdash_R$ is uniform over $\langle \mathcal{D}, \mathcal{G} \rangle$.

In order to present examples of logic programming languages, consider the following definitions. Let $\mathcal{F}$ be a formulation of first-order logic, and let $\mathcal{T}$ be a formulation of higher-order logic based on Church's simple theory of types [1]. In both formulations, we assume that the five logical connectives $\wedge$, $\vee$, $\supset$, $\forall$, and $\exists$ are primitive. Let $\vdash_I$ denote intuitionistic provability in both of these logic formulations. Similarly, let $\vdash_C$ denote classical provability. Provability in $\mathcal{T}$ will be assumed to be purely logical in the sense that the axioms of description, choice, extensionality, and infinity are not assumed.

When we deal with the classical and intuitionistic theories of $\mathcal{F}$ and $\mathcal{T}$ we shall assume that provability is defined by the sequential calculus in Appendix A of [16]. Using the sequential calculus makes it possible to give another characterization of uniform provability. We say that a sequential proof is a *uniform proof* (over $\langle \mathcal{D}, \mathcal{G} \rangle$) if for every sequent occurrence $\mathcal{P} \rightarrow \Delta$ in the proof, $\mathcal{P} \subseteq \mathcal{D}$, Δ is a singleton set $\{G\}$ with $G \in \mathcal{G}$, and if G is non-atomic, that sequent occurrence is the conclusion of an introduction rule which introduces its top-level connective. One way to prove that $\vdash_C$ (resp. $\vdash_I$) is uniform for some pair $\langle \mathcal{D}, \mathcal{G} \rangle$ is to show that if $\mathcal{P} \vdash_C G$ (resp. $\mathcal{P} \vdash_I G$) then $\mathcal{P} \rightarrow G$ has a uniform, classical (resp. intuitionistic) sequential proof.

Let $\mathcal{G}_1$ be the set of all first-order formulas which are the existential closure of formulas of the form $A_1 \wedge \ldots \wedge A_n$, where $n > 0$ and the A's are atomic. Let $\mathcal{D}_1$ be the set of all first-order formulas which are the universal closure of formulas of either the form $[A_1 \wedge \ldots \wedge A_n] \supset A_0$ or the form A_0 where $n > 0$ and again the A's are atomic. Members of the $\mathcal{D}_1$ are commonly called *positive Horn clauses*. It is easy to show that $LP_1 = \langle \mathcal{F}, \mathcal{D}_1, \mathcal{G}_1, \vdash_C \rangle$ is a logic programming language: a simple inductive argument shows that any cut-free proof can be converted to a uniform proof. This conclusion is fortunate since this is the logical foundations for the programming language Prolog. Given that LP_1 is a logic programming language it is immediate that $\langle \mathcal{F}, \mathcal{D}_1, \mathcal{G}_1, \vdash_I \rangle$ is also (the same) logic programming language. It should be noted, however, that LP_1 is a weak logic programming languages in the sense that conditions (2), (3), and (5) are vacuously true for LP_1. We shall eventually present a logic programming language in which none of these conditions are vacuous.

Before presenting new logic programming languages, we present two logical systems which fail to be logic programming language. First consider the extension to the classical theory of Horn clauses which permit the body of clauses to contain negated literals (see for example [3]). This fails to be a logic programming language under our definition since

$$p \supset q(a),\ \neg p \supset q(b) \vdash_C \exists x\, q(x)$$

while there is no term t such that $q(t)$ follows from the same program. Another such case arises when the classical theory of Horn clauses is extended to permit negative Horn clauses (see [5]). This language fails to be a logic programming language since it permits the search problem

$$\neg p(a) \vee \neg p(b) \vdash_C \exists x\, \neg p(x)$$

while again, no particular instance of the existential goal can be proved. Both of these extensions to the syntax of Horn clauses are also tied to the use of classical logic to interpret them. As we shall see later, if intuitionistic logic is used instead, both of these languages can again be considered as logic programming languages.

3. Higher-Order Horn Formulas.

One way to strengthen the logic programming language LP_1 is to make its quantificational and term structure higher-order. Consider the following inductively defined set of simply typed λ-terms:

$$G := c \mid v \mid (G_1 G_2) \mid \lambda v\, G \mid \top \mid G_1 \vee G_2 \mid G_1 \wedge G_2 \mid \exists v\, G.$$

Here, c is any non-logical constant (parameter) and v is any variable. Notice that if G_1 and G_2 belong to this class of formulas then the result of substituting G_1 for a variable x in G_2 is also in this class. A higher-order formula which has a non-logical constant as its head will be called a *rigid* atom. Let $\mathcal{G}_2$ be the set of closed propositions G in the above inductively defined set. A *higher-order Horn clause* is any formula which is the universal closure of a formula of the form $G \supset A$ where A is a rigid atom and $G \in \mathcal{G}_2$. Let $\mathcal{D}_2$ be the set of higher-order Horn clauses. We then have the following theorem.

Theorem 1. *$LP_2 = \langle \mathcal{T}, \mathcal{D}_2, \mathcal{G}_2, \vdash_C \rangle$ is a logic programming language.*

This is not an immediate consequence of the cut-elimination theorem for higher-order logic. Cut-free proofs in LP_2 might be rather far from being uniform since connectives other than $\top$, $\vee$, $\wedge$, and $\exists$ can appear as succedents via higher-order instantiations of predicate variables. Nevertheless, a proof transformation can be described which can translate an arbitrary cut-free classical sequent proof in LP_2 into a uniform proof. In the resulting uniform proofs, the only terms used to introduce quantifiers are those formulas inductively defined above. For the full proof, see [14].

Notice that goal formulas in LP_2 may contain occurrences of $\vee$ and $\exists$ while this is not true of LP_1. These connectives could in fact be added to goals in LP_1 in a similar manner.

It is possible to specify many of the higher-order operations which are familiar to Lisp and ML programmers in LP_2. Such operations as mapping a function over a list or "reducing" one list using a binary function have very simple definitions. Although it is substantially more complex than LP_1, this logic programming language can be implemented in a fashion some what similar to Prolog. An abstract interpreter for LP_2 can be describe in terms of unification and SLD-resolution: in this case, of course, higher-order unification must be used. An experimental implementation of LP_2, called λProlog, is described in [11] and [14].

Since LP_2 uses λ-terms to represent objects, λProlog can be used to provide clean implementations of applications, such as program transformers and theorem provers, where reasoning about the intension of higher-order objects is important. Here higher-order unification can be used to probe the structure of such objects. See [7, 12, 15] for more illustrations of this approach.

Although the availability of higher-order terms in LP_2 makes this language more expressive, its use of logical connectives is not very strong. Any uniform proof in LP_2 vacuously satisfies conditions (3) and (5).

4. Hereditary Harrop Formulas.

To present a logic programming language which makes stronger use of logical connectives, we return for a moment to first-order logic $\mathcal{F}$. Consider the class of first-order formulas denoted by the following recursive definition of the syntactic variable D:

$$D := A \mid G \supset A \mid \forall x\, D \mid D_1 \wedge D_2.$$

Here we are assuming that A denotes atomic formulas and G denotes arbitrary first-order formulas. This class represents the set of all Harrop formulas [19], in the sense that for any Harrop formula, there is a formula D which is intuitionistically equivalent to it. Let $\mathcal{P}$ be a finite set of Harrop formula and let B be some non-atomic formula such that $\mathcal{P} \vdash_I B$. The well known property of Harrop formulas can be stated as: there is a sequential proof of $\mathcal{P} \longrightarrow B$ in which the last inference rule introduces the logical connective of B. Hence, proofs from Harrop formulas are uniform "at the root". In general, however, Harrop formulas do not necessarily possess uniform proofs. For example, let $\mathcal{P}$ be the empty set of Harrop formulas and let B be the formula $(p \vee q) \supset (q \vee p)$. There is no uniform proof of this latter formula.

There is, however, a very interesting subset of Harrop formulas which admits uniform proofs. We obtain this subset if we restrict G in the above definition so that immediate negative subformula occurrences are actually D formulas. More precisely, we introduce the following restricted definition of G:

$$G := A \mid G_1 \wedge G_2 \mid G_1 \vee G_2 \mid \forall v\ [c/v]G \mid \exists v\ G \mid D \supset G.$$

The definitions of G and D are now mutually recursive. The expression $\forall v\ [c/v]G$ is used to indicate that any constant can be universally generalized. Since only variables can appear as quantified, the expression $[c/v]G$ is used to replace the parameter c with the variable v prior to being quantified. We shall call any D formula a *hereditary Harrop* formula and any G formula a *goal formula*. Let $\mathcal{D}_3$ be the set of hereditary Harrop formulas and let $\mathcal{G}_3$ be the set of goal formulas.

Theorem 2. *$LP_3 = \langle \mathcal{F}, \mathcal{D}_3, \mathcal{G}_3, \vdash_I \rangle$ is a logic programming language.*

Again, the proof of this theorem follows from a simple inductive argument which shows that any cut-free sequential proof can be converted to a uniform proof. In the LP_3 case, none of the clauses defining uniform proofs are vacuously true. Notice also that this language properly includes the logic programming language LP_1 based on positive Horn formulas.

It is a common observation that if one wishes logic to have constructive content, then classical logic is too strong and forms of intuitionistic logic are required. A similar observation is true here also: if we wish to use logic to specify search with the five search primitives $\wedge$, $\vee$, $\supset$, $\forall$, and $\exists$, then classical logic is again too strong. Intuitionistic logic again helps to provide a suitable interpretation mechanism. The classical meaning of logical connectives undermines the intended search-related meaning of the logical connectives. For example, the formula $G_1 \vee (D \supset G_2)$ specifies a search which is successful if G_1 is successful or if G_2 is successful given D. However, classical logic contains all the following equivalences:

$$\begin{aligned} G_1 \vee (D \supset G_2) &\equiv G_1 \vee \neg D \vee G_2 \\ &\equiv (D \supset G_1) \vee G_2 \\ &\equiv (D \supset G_1) \vee (D \supset G_2). \end{aligned}$$

These clearly provide incompatible search specifications. Put another way, the quadruple $\langle \mathcal{F}, \mathcal{D}_3, \mathcal{G}_3, \vdash_C \rangle$ is not a logic programming language since $(p \supset q) \vee p$ has a classical proof but has no uniform proof.

The more expressive language LP_3 can express several programming features which are not available in its weaker first-order cousin LP_1. A weak notion of *program modules* can be supported by using implications within goal formulas. For example, consider proving the following goal in LP_3:

$$D_1 \supset (D_2 \supset G_1) \wedge (D_3 \supset G_2).$$

A search for a uniform proof of this formula would cause searches for uniform proofs to be made for the sequents

$$D_1, D_2 \longrightarrow G_1 \text{ and } D_1, D_3 \longrightarrow G_2.$$

These two search problems contain different programs. If D_1, D_2 and D_3 were bundles of code representing different program modules, then this use of implication can be used to partially control what code should be used in what context. This is contrary to the situation in LP_1 where the logic program stays constant throughout a computation.

Notice that an atom A can be both a goal formula and a hereditary Harrop formula, and furthermore that $A \wedge G$ is intuitionistically equivalent to $A \wedge (A \supset G)$. Hence, a query of the form $A \wedge G$ can be replaced by the one of the form $A \wedge (A \supset G)$. Proofs of the latter query could be shorter since the fact that A is provable is "stored" during the search for a proof of G. This use of implication makes it possible to implement memoizing techniques.

For more examples of how LP_3 can be used to write programs, see [4, 10].

5. Higher-Order Hereditary Harrop Formulas.

We now wish to merge the languages LP_2 and LP_3. To this end, consider the following two inductively defined sets of simply typed λ-terms.

$$\begin{aligned} G := c \mid v \mid (G_1 G_2) \mid \lambda v\ G \mid \top \mid G_1 \vee G_2 \mid G_1 \wedge G_2 \mid \\ D \supset G \mid \exists v\ G \mid \forall v\ [c/v]G \end{aligned}$$

$$D := c \mid \lambda v\ D \mid (DG) \mid \forall v\ D \mid D_1 \wedge D_2 \mid G \supset D$$

Here, c is any non-logical constant and v is a variable. Let $\mathcal{D}_4$ be the set of propositions satisfying the D-inductive definition. These formulas are called *higher-order hereditary Harrop formulas.* Let $\mathcal{H}^+$ denote the set of formulas satisfying the G inductive definition, and let $\mathcal{G}_4$ be the set of propositions in $\mathcal{H}^+$. Both $\mathcal{D}_4$ and $\mathcal{G}_4$ are closed under substitution with formulas in $\mathcal{H}^+$. Notice that $[c/v]G$ is not necessarily a member of $\mathcal{H}^+$ even if $G \in \mathcal{H}^+$. For example, if p is a parameter and x is a variable, then $p \supset p \in \mathcal{G}_4$, $x \supset x \notin \mathcal{G}_4$, and $\forall x\,(x \supset x) \in \mathcal{G}_4$.

The following theorem can be proved by extending the methods in [10, 14].

Theorem 3. *$LP_4 = \langle \mathcal{T}_4, \mathcal{D}_4, \mathcal{G}_4, \vdash_I \rangle$ is a logic programming language.*

Besides sharing the programming features discussed above for both LP_2 and LP_3, this logic programming language contains some additional programming features. One problem with traditional logic programming languages is that it is very hard to deny access to code or data structures. Thus it is not possible to implement abstract data types and support modular program construction in those languages. As was shown in [10] and was hinted at in the preceding section, using implications as goals can provide a partial solution to development of modular programming.

In LP_4, however, we can go further by showing how access to data type constructors can be denied logically. For example, let *Sort* be a set of Horn clauses which implements a binary tree sorting algorithm and assume that it internally builds a labeled binary tree using the ternary function symbol f and the constant symbol r: for example, $f(5, f(3,r,r), f(8,r,r))$ represents the three node tree with root labeled with 5 and with left and right siblings of 3 and 8, respectively. We now wish to ask a query which uses this sorting operation but we would like to guarantee that it is impossible for that query to access this internal representation of binary trees. In LP_4 this is possible. First, let D be the λ-term which results from abstracting out f and r from *Sort*, *i.e.* D does not contain occurrences of either f or r and $D(f,r)$ λ-converts to *Sort*. Consider the following λ-term which is a member of $\mathcal{H}^+$:

$$\lambda g\,(\forall f \forall r\,(D(f,r) \supset g)).$$

This term will take $G \in \mathcal{G}_4$ and yield another member of $\mathcal{G}_4$, namely

$$\forall f \forall r\,(D(f,r) \supset G))$$

where no free variable of G can be instantiated with a term containing f or r. G therefore can not access the constructors of *Sort*.

It is interesting to notice just how large the intersection between $\mathcal{D}_4$ and $\mathcal{G}_4$ actually is. This is important because this intersection contains exactly those formulas which can be "memoized" as described in the previous section. Let M be a syntactic variable which satisfies the following inductive definition:

$$M := c \mid (MG) \mid \lambda x\, M \mid M_1 \wedge M_2 \mid \forall x\, M \mid M_1 \supset M_2,$$

where G ranges over $\mathcal{H}^+$. The propositions in this class of formulas form a kind of first-order theory of $\mathcal{H}^+$ terms. This language does not contain LP_2 since its logical structure is invariant under higher-order substitution. Every atomic formula in one of these formulas is a rigid atom, a restriction not required of LP_2. This language does, however, contain LP_1. Thus LP_4 can be used to check the validity of LP_1 rules and then use them to augment its own programming to contract the length of future computations.

The fact that intuitionistic derivability is uniform over $\langle \mathcal{D}_4, \mathcal{G}_4 \rangle$ implies several other important proof theoretical conclusions. We now present three such conclusions: a slash semantics interpretation, a Herbrand Theorem, and an inductively defined Kripke model interpretation.

6. Slash Semantics and Sconing Construction.

An alternative method of establishing Theorems 2 and 3 is given by using the *slash* interpretation [2, 9, 17, 19]. Let $\vdash_O$ denote the uniform proof predicate, that is, $\mathcal{P} \vdash_O G$ means that the sequent $\mathcal{P} \rightarrow G$ has a uniform sequential proof. We now adapt the standard definition of the slash interpretation $\mathcal{P} \mid G$ by taking into consideration the uniform proof system. The symbol $\mathcal{P} \mid\vdash_O G$ will denote $\mathcal{P} \mid G$ and $\mathcal{P} \vdash_O G$.

- $\mathcal{P} \mid G_1 \wedge G_2$ if and only if $\mathcal{P} \mid G_1$ and $\mathcal{P} \mid G_2$.
- $\mathcal{P} \mid G_1 \vee G_2$ if and only if $\mathcal{P} \mid\vdash_O G_1$ or $\mathcal{P} \mid\vdash_O G_2$.
- $\mathcal{P} \mid D \supset G$ if and only if $\mathcal{P} \mid\vdash_O D$ implies $\mathcal{P} \mid G$.
- $\mathcal{P} \mid \exists x\, G$ if and only if $\mathcal{P} \mid\vdash_O [x/t]G$ for some $t \in \mathcal{H}^+$.
- $\mathcal{P} \mid \forall x\, G$ if and only if $\mathcal{P} \mid [x/t]G$ for all $t \in \mathcal{H}^+$.

The definition of the atomic case is obtained by an analogous adaptation of the standard atomic clauses in both first-order and higher-order cases [2, 9, 17, 19]. The following soundness lemma can be used to prove Theorems 2 and 3.

Lemma 4. *If $\mathcal{P} \vdash_I G$ then $\mathcal{P} \mid\vdash_O G$.*

In an algebraic framework, the corresponding embedding theorem for free categories may be obtained by the sconing construction (Freyd covers) [9, 17]. In particular, one shows that the full subcategory given by our fragment of intuitionistic proof system is a retract of the scone of the free category given by the *uniform* proof system. As in [8, 17], the interpretation in the scone may be shown to be equivalent to the slash interpretation considered above.

7. A Herbrand Theorem.

Full intuitionistic logic has not admitted a Herbrand Theorem. Because of the existence of uniform proofs, however, the fragment of intuitionistic logic based on LP_4 does admit such a theorem.

First augment the formulation of $\mathcal{T}$ with *Skolem functions*: that is, for all *arities* $p \geq 0$ and all types α of at least this functional arity, add denumerably many new constants, which we write as f^p_α. Using this augmented formulation of $\mathcal{T}$, define $\mathcal{H}^*$ similar to $\mathcal{H}^+$ in Section 5 except for the following restriction on forming abstractions over Skolem terms: if $A \in \mathcal{H}^*$ and if f^p is a Skolem function of arity p which has an occurrence in A then that occurrence has at least p arguments and any free variable occurrences in any of the first p arguments must also be free occurrences in A. For example, if h^1 is of type $\alpha \to \beta \to \gamma$, x and y are variables of type α and β respectively, then $h^1(x,y) \in \mathcal{H}^*$, $\lambda y\ h^1(x,y) \in \mathcal{H}^*$, and $\lambda x\ h^1(x,y) \notin \mathcal{H}^*$. This restriction on forming abstractions over Skolem functions is designed to make certain that Skolem functions do not play the role of choice functions. See [13] for a proof of the correctness of this use of Skolem functions.

To see that Skolem terms without this restriction can be unsound, consider the following formula in $\mathcal{H}^+$:

$$[\forall g\ P(a, g(a)] \supset \exists x \forall y\ P(x,y)).$$

It is easy to show that this formula has exactly one uniform proof in $\mathcal{T}$. The skolemize form, namely

$$[\forall g\ P(a, g(a))] \supset \exists x\ P(x, y^1(x)),$$

has two uniform proofs if the fact that y^1 is a Skolem function is ignored. These two proofs involve instantiating the $\forall g$ quantifier with $\lambda w\ y^1(a)$ and $\lambda w\ y^1(w)$. The second substitution term does not obey the restriction described above.

We define g-instances of skolemized forms of closed $\mathcal{G}_4$ propositions and d-instances of skolemized forms of closed $\mathcal{D}_4$ propositions as follows:

- If A is atomic, then A is both a g-instance and a d-instance of A.
- If E_1 and E_2 are d-instances of D_1 and D_2, then $E_1 \wedge E_2$ is a d-instance of $D_1 \wedge D_2$.
- If $t_1, \ldots, t_n$ $(n \geq 1)$ is a list of closed terms from $\mathcal{H}^*$ and if for all $i \in \{1, \ldots, n\}$, E_i is a d-instance of $[x/t_i]D$, then $E_1 \wedge \ldots \wedge E_n$ is a d-instance of $\forall x\ D$.
- If H_1 and H_2 are g-instances of G_1 and G_2, then $H_1 \wedge H_2$ is a g-instance of $G_1 \wedge G_2$ and $H_1 \vee H_2$ is a g-instance of $G_1 \vee G_2$.
- If $t \in \mathcal{H}^*$ is a closed term and H is a g-instance of $[x/t]G$ then H is a g-instance of $\exists x\ G$.
- If H is a g-instance of G then $H \supset A$ is a d-instance of $G \supset A$.
- If E is a d-instance of D and H is a g-instance of G then $E \supset H$ is a g-instance of $D \supset G$.

The following is a form of Herbrand's theorem for this fragment of intuitionistic logic. We shall write the skolemized form of B as B^*.

Theorem 5. *The closed formula $G \in \mathcal{G}_4$ is intuitionistically provable if and only if there is a g-instance of G^* which is an intuitionistic tautology.*

8. A Model Theory.

Given a set of higher-order hereditary Harrop formulas, it is interesting to consider how one can describe the set of all atomic formulas derivable from it. Below we present a Kripke-model structure built by a least fixed point construction which provides such a description.

In this section, we shall assume that higher-order hereditary Harrop formulas are universal closures of either atomic formulas or implications. This is no real restriction since any higher-order hereditary Harrop formula is intuitionistically equivalent to a set of such restricted formulas.

Let $\mathcal{W}$ be the set of all finite sets of closed, skolemized higher-order hereditary Harrop formulas. An *interpretation* is a function from $\mathcal{W}$ to sets of atomic $\mathcal{H}^*$ formulas which is internally monotone, that is, $\forall w_1, w_2 \in \mathcal{W}[w_1 \subseteq w_2 \supset I(w_1) \subseteq I(w_2)]$. We now define the following satisfiability notion: For any interpretation I, $w \in \mathcal{W}$, and G a proposition in $\mathcal{H}^*$, we write $I, w \models G$ if there is a sequence of pairs of members of $\mathcal{W}$ and closed $\mathcal{H}^*$ propositions, $(w_1, G_1), \ldots, (w_n, G_n)$ $(n \geq 1)$, such that for all $i \in \{1, \ldots, n\}$, the following condition is true:

- G_i is $\top$,
- G_i is atomic and $G_i \in I(w_i)$,
- G_i is $G' \wedge G''$ and both (w_i, G') and $(w_i,' G')$ appear earlier in the list,
- G_i is $G' \vee G''$ and either (w_i, G') or $(w_i,' G')$ appears earlier in the list,
- G_i is $\exists x\ G'$ and for some $t \in \mathcal{H}^*$, $(w_i, [x/t]G')$ appears earlier in the list, or

∘ G_i is $D \supset G$ and $(w_i \cup \{D\}, G)$ appears earlier in the list.

Notice that the set of all interpretations is a complete lattice under world-wise inclusion.

Let T be the function from interpretations to interpretations such that $T(I)(w)$ is the set of all closed atomic $\mathcal{H}^*$ formulas A such that there is a formula in w with either A or $G \supset A$ as a universal instance and, in the latter case, $I, w \models G$. Here, we are taking instances by using only $\mathcal{H}^*$ formulas. This operator is a continuous, order-preserving map from the lattice of interpretations to itself.

Theorem 6. *Let $w_0 \in \mathcal{W}$ be the empty set of formulas. The least fixed point of T is an interpretation J such that for all $G \in \mathcal{G}_4$, $J, w_0 \models G^*$ if and only if $\vdash_I G$. Put another way, if $\mathcal{P}$ is a set of higher-order hereditary Harrop formulas and A is an atomic $\mathcal{H}^+$ formula then $\mathcal{P} \vdash_I A$ if and only if $J, \mathcal{P}^* \models A^*$ (here, $\mathcal{P}^* = \{D* \mid D \in \mathcal{P}\}$).*

9. Conclusion.

In this paper we have surveyed our recent attempts to extend the logic programming paradigm by strengthening its logical foundations. In all these extensions, we strove to preserve the simple and natural success/failure semantics of the five logical connectives $\wedge$, $\vee$, $\supset$, $\forall$, and $\exists$ since this seems to be at the very heart of logic programming. Since these logical connectives possess these operational semantics, all four languages have simple, nondeterministic interpreters which can be shown to be sound and complete. The higher-order languages LP_2 and LP_4 require higher-order unification to actually implement such interpreters. As shown in [14], the usual backtracking mechanism of Prolog can be smoothly integrated with the higher-order unification search process described in [6] to provide interpreters for these languages. We have developed and tested an implementation of LP_2 in a system called λProlog. We are currently extending this language to encompass the full LP_4 language.

Interpreters for LP_3 and LP_4 must contain unification processes which extend the usual ones for both first-order and higher-order terms. An extension is necessary because the "new" parameters introduced during the interpretation of universally quantified goals must be treated in a special fashion. Their occurrences in substitution terms must at times be restricted properly. For example, the formula

$$\exists x \forall y\, (P(x) \supset P(y))$$

is a goal formula in both LP_3 and LP_4 which has no uniform proof. A naive interpreter for either of these languages would reduce this goal to the state $P(x) \rightarrow P(c)$ where x is a variable and c is a parameter. A simple unification algorithm would attempt to substitute x with c. But this violates the restriction of universal quantification which states that for c to be introduced into this problem, c did not occur free in $\forall y\, (P(x) \supset P(y))$. This restriction is not true if x were to be substituted with c. Obeying this restriction is central to the ability to deny access to data type constructors as was described in Section 5. An interpreter for LP_4 could use Skolem functions (Section 7) to implement this restriction correctly. Another approach which does not employ Skolem functions would instead require maintaining an additional graph structure among substitution terms and the parameters used to instantiate universally quantified goals (see [13, 15]). We have not yet experimented with this extension to unification.

10. Acknowledgements.

We are grateful to Frank Pfenning, Scott Weinstein and Rick Statman for helpful conversations. Miller and Nadathur are partially supported by NSF grant MCS-82-07294 and DARPA N000-14-85-K-0018. Scedrov is partially supported by NSF DMS85-01522.

11. References.

[1] A. Church, "A Formulation of the Simple Theory of Types", JSL **5** (1940), 56 – 68.

[2] H. Friedman, "Some Applications of Kleene's Methods for Intuitionistic Systems," in: "Cambridge Summer School in Mathematical Logic, Proceedings 1971" (ed. by A. R. D. Mathias and H. Rogers, Jr.), Springer LNM 337, Berlin, 1973, 113 – 170.

[3] M. Fitting, "A Kripke-Kleene Semantics for Logic Programming," Journal of Logic Programming, **4** (1985), 295 – 312.

[4] D. M. Gabbay, U. Reyle, "N-Prolog: An Extension of Prolog with Hypothetical Implications. I," Journal of Logic Programming **1** (1984), 319 – 355.

[5] J. Gallier, S. Raatz, "Logic Programming and Graph Rewriting," 1985 Sym. on Logic Programming, Boston, 208 – 219.

[6] G. P. Huet, "A Unification Algorithm for Typed λ-Calculus," Theoretical Computer Science 1, 1975, 27 – 57.

[7] G. P. Huet, B. Lang, "Proving and Applying Program Transformations Expressed with Second-Order Patterns," Acta Informatica 11, (1978), 31 – 55.

[8] J. Lambek, P. J. Scott, "New proofs of some intuitionistic principles," Zeitschrift für Math. Logik und Grundl.

Math. **29** (1983), 493 – 504.

[9] J. Lambek, P. J. Scott, *Introduction to Higher-order Categorical Logic*, Cambridge University Press, 1986.

[10] D. A. Miller, "A Theory of Modules for Logic Programming," Third Annual IEEE Symposium on Logic Programming, Salt Lake City, Utah, September 1986.

[11] D. A. Miller, G. Nadathur, "Higher-order logic programming," Proceedings of the Third Intern. Logic Programming Conference, London, June 1986, 448 – 462.

[12] D. A. Miller, G. Nadathur, "Some Uses of Higher-Order Logic in Computational Linguistics," Proceedings of the 24th Annual Meeting of the Association for Computational Linguistics, 1986, 247 – 255.

[13] D. A. Miller, "A Compact Representation of Proofs", to appear in *Studia Logica*.

[14] G. Nadathur, *A Higher-Order Logic as the Basis for Logic Programming*, Ph. D. dissertation, University of Pennsylvania, December 1986.

[15] L. C. Paulson, "Natural Deduction as Higher-Order Resolution," Journal of Logic Programming 3(3), 1986, 237 – 258.

[16] Dag Prawitz, *Natural Deduction,* Almqvist & Wiksell, Uppsala, 1965.

[17] A. Scedrov, P. J. Scott, "A note on the Friedman slash and Freyd covers," Proc. Brouwer Centenary Symposium, North Holland, 1982, 443 – 452.

[18] L. Sterling, E. Shapiro, *The Art of Prolog*, MIT Press, 1986.

[19] A. S. Troelstra, *Metamathematical Investigation of Intuitionistic Arithmetic and Analysis,* LNM 344, Springer-Verlag, 1973.

Undecidable Optimization Problems for Database Logic Programs

Preliminary Report

Haim Gaifman*
Hebrew University of Jerusalem
Yehoshua Sagiv ‡
Hebrew University of Jerusalem

Harry Mairson†
Oxford University
Moshe Y. Vardi§
IBM Almaden Research

Abstract

Datalog is the language of logic programs without function symbols. It is used as a database query language. If it is possible to eliminate recursion from a Datalog program P, then P is said to be *bounded*. We show that the problem of deciding whether a given Datalog program is bounded is undecidable, even for *linear* programs (i.e., programs where each rule contains at most one occurrence of a recursive predicate). We then show that every strongly nontrivial semantic property of Datalog programs that contain boundedness is undecidable.

1 Introduction

It has been recognized for some time that first-order database query languages are lacking in expressive power [AU79, GM78, Zl76]. Since then many higher-order query languages have been investigated [CH80, Ch81, CH82, Im86, Va82]. A language that has received considerable attention recently is *Datalog*, the language of logic programs (known also as Horn-clause programs) without function symbols [BR86, CH85, GM78, HN84, Ul85], which is essentially a fragment of fixpoint logic [CH85,Mo74]. The following program is "canonical" example of a Datalog query is to compute transitive closure, where we think of the "database" as a directed graph:

$$path(X,Y) \quad :-edge(X,Y).$$
$$path(X,Y) \quad :-path(X,Z), path(Z,Y).$$

In this example, we imagine *edge* is an *extensional database (EDB) predicate*, i.e., representing basic facts stored in the database. For example, $edge(1,5)$ is an EDB fact stating that there is an edge between vertices 1 and 5. The *intensional database (IDB) predicate path* represents facts deduced from the database via the logic program above: the first rule says every directed edge forms a path, and the second rule tells how paths can be joined together. We can now query, for instance, $path(1,7)$ or $path(2,V)$ to determine, respectively, whether there is a path from vertex 1 to vertex 7, or what vertices V are connected to vertex 2 by a path.

Recent works have addressed the problems of finding efficient evaluation methods for Datalog queries ([BR86] is a good survey on this topic) and developing optimization techniques for Datalog [CMG86, Io85, Na86b, JCV84]. A typical approach to the problem of efficient evaluation involves identifying "nice" properties of Datalog pro-

*Address: Inst. of Math. and Computer Science, Hebrew University, Jerusal 91904, Israel. This author is visiting the Computer Science Department of Stanford University during the academic year 86/87. The research reported here was done while this author was visiting the AI Center of SRI International, whose support he wishes to acknowledge.

†Address: Programming Research Group, Oxford University, 8-11 Keble Road, Oxford OX1 3QD, England. The research reported here was done while this author was at the Computer Science Department of Stanford University and was supported by ONR contract N00014-85-C-0731.

‡Address: Inst. of Math. and Computer Science, Hebrew University, Jerusalem 91904, Israel. The research reported here was done while this author was visiting the the Computer Science Department of Stanford University and was supported by a grant of AT&T Foundation, a grant of IBM Corp., and NSF grant IST-84-12791.

§Address: IBM Almaden Research K53-802, 650 Harry Rd., San Jose, CA 95120-6099, USA.

CH2464-6/87/0000/0106$01.00 © 1987 IEEE

gram that facilitate efficient computation of programs that have these properties. For example, Ullman and Van Gelder [UV86] have identified the *polynomial fringe property* of Datalog programs, where every proof involves a number of EDB facts (at the "fringe" of the proof tree) at most polynomial in the size of the database. While the complexity of evaluating arbitrary Datalog programs can be *PTIME*-complete [Im86,Va82], Ullman and Van Gelder have shown that the complexity of Datalog programs with the polynomial fringe property is in *NC*, i.e., all facts can be deduced in parallel time polynomial in the logarithm of the size of the database, given a number of processors polynomial in the size of the database.

At first, the problem of optimizing Datalog queries does not seem to be too difficult, since every rule in a Datalog program can be viewed as a *conjunctive query*. Conjunctive queries constitute a fragment of the class of first-order queries for which the optimization problem is completely solved [ASU79,CM77]. Unfortunately, it is the recursive application of the rules that make Datalog queries hard to evaluate. Let us consider some examples of how one might go about optimizing Datalog queries.

One might attempt to simplify a Datalog program by eliminating unnecessary variables or predicates. As an illustration, Jeff Naughton has given the following illuminating example [Na86b]:

$$\begin{array}{ll} buys(X,Y) & :-cheap(Y), likes(X,Y). \\ buys(X,Y) & :-cheap(Y), knows(X,Z), buys(Z,Y). \end{array}$$

In this Datalog program, $cheap(Y)$ can be eliminated from the second rule, and the resultant program can make the same deductions as the previous one. On the other hand, if $cheap(Y)$ were instead $rich(X)$ in the above example, then such an elimination could not be made.

Sometimes it is possible to change recursive predicates to nonrecursive ones. For example, in the above transitive closure program, $path(Z,Y)$ can be changed to $edge(Z,Y)$. Sometimes *all* recursions can be eliminated:

$$\begin{array}{ll} buys(X,Y) & :-likes(X,Y). \\ buys(X,Y) & :-trendy(X), buys(Z,Y). \end{array}$$

In this example, $buys(Z,Y)$ can be changed to $likes(Z,Y)$ [Na86a]. The reason is that every "proof" or deduction of a fact involving *buys* can be made where the number of EDB facts in the proof is independent of the number of facts in the database. A consequence of replacing a Datalog program P with recursions by a logically equivalent, recursion-free program P' is that for any database D, *all* facts deducible by P' from D can be proved in constant time, given a number of processors polynomial in the size of D, working together in parallel. If it is possible to eliminate recursion from a program P, then we say that P is *bounded*. This notion has been introduced in the context of the universal relation database model [MUV84], and has been studied since that time by several researchers [CK86, Io85, Na86a, NS87, Sa85].

The above examples give a glimmer of hope that a program of developing general optimization techniques along these lines might be fruitful, but the purpose of this paper is in part to quash such optimism. In particular, we show that the problem of deciding whether a Datalog program is bounded, i.e., whether it is possible to have all its recursions removed, is undecidable. We show boundedness to be undecidable, even for *linear* programs that have only one IDB predicate, i.e., all rules have at most one IDB subgoal. (We prove as well that a "strong" version of boundedness, where we view a Datalog program as an intensional database rather than a database query, is also undecidable. [1] As a consequence of the techniques used in the proof, we show that any nontrivial semantic property of logic programs that is always true for bounded programs must be undecidable. Our results show that the syntactical simplicity of Datalog can be quite misleading, in the sense that the problem of optimizing Datalog queries is just as hard as optimizing arbitrary first-order queries, or, for that matter, just as hard as optimizing any general-purpose programming language.

2 Undecidability of Boundedness

A Datalog program is a collection of function-free Horn clauses. We distinguish between the EDB predicates, which occur only in the body of the rules, and IDB predicates, which occur as heads of rules. One of the IDB predicates is the *goal predicate*. A database D is a collection of atomic sentences about the EDB predicates. Let $P^i(D)$ be

[1] It is interesting to note that for *typed* rules strong boundedness is known to be decidable [Sa85]. This is the first instance we are aware of where typedness marks the boundary between the decidable and the undecidable.

the collection of facts that can be deduced from D by at most i applications of the rules in P, and let

$$P^{\infty}(D) = \bigcup_{i \geq 0} P^{i}(D).$$

The result of applying the query P to the database D, denoted $P(D)$, is the set of atomic sentences about the goal predicate in $P^{\infty}(D)$. Since the Herbrand universe is finite, for each D there is some k such that $P^k(D) = P^{\infty}(D)$. That is, $P^k(D)$ is the *fixpoint* of P on D. P is *bounded* if there exists a constant k depending on P such that for any database D, $P^k(D) = P^{\infty}(D)$. In other words, P is bounded if every fact in the fixpoint can be deduced by a "proof tree" that has height of no more than some constant k.

To prove that boundedness is undecidable, we use a reduction from the halting problem for 2-counter machines. We spell the proof in detail, because later we will have to modify it to prove undecidability of "strong" boundedness.

A 2-counter machine (2CM) is a finite-state machine with two non-negative counters, where changes in machine configuration are determined from the finite state of the machine and whether or not the counters are zero or non-zero. If we think of the counters as stacks, we could characterize the transition function as

$$\delta : \Sigma \times \{=,>\} \times \{=,>\} \rightarrow \Sigma \times \{pop, push\} \times \{pop, push\},$$

where $\delta(a, >, =) = (b, pop, push)$ means "if in state a with counter 1 greater than zero and counter 2 equal to zero, then shift into state b, subtracting 1 from counter 1 and adding 1 to counter 2." We initialize the 2CM M in a distinguished *initial state* with counters 1 and 2 set to zero, and say M *halts* if it reaches a distinguished *halting state*, and otherwise *diverges* or *loops*. These counter machines can simulate machines with an arbitrary number of registers and Turing machines as well; for more details see [HU79]. The halting problem for 2-counter machines is, given a 2CM M, to decide whether M halts or diverges.

For every 2CM M, we construct a Datalog program P that simulates M, such that M halts if and only if P is bounded. Since the halting problem for 2-counter machines is undecidable, so then is boundedness of Datalog programs. The program P will have one IDB predicate $ID(T, S, C_1, C_2)$ that essentially represents a configuration of M at time T in state S, with C_1 and C_2 the contents of the counters. Since these four variables are integer valued, the constants of the database must serve in some sense as integers. We introduce two EDB predicates $zero(X)$ and $succ(X, Y)$: interpreting the first as "$X = 0$" and the second as "$Y = X+1$," the database represents a (possibly nonstandard) model of a finite subset of the integers.

The program P has three types of rules: one *initialization rule* that simulates the initial configuration of M, several *transition rules* that simulate δ, and a *halting rule* that says if M halts (that is, if a fact about ID can be proven attesting to a halting state), then $ID(X, Y, U, V)$ is in the fixpoint for *any* assignment to the variables X, Y, U, and V. Thus, if M halts in t steps, t is clearly dependent on P but independent of the database, and a deduction of any fact f will have a proof of height at most t. We now fill in some details of the construction of these types of rules:

Initialization. Without loss of generality, let the states of the 2CM be $\Sigma = \{0, 1, \ldots, h\}$ where 0 is the initial state and h is the halting state. We then wish to encode that M is initialized at time zero in state zero with counters set to zero, namely:

$$ID(Z, Z, Z, Z) :- zero(Z).$$

Transitions. For *each* transition, introduce a logic rule. To do so, the logic we are using must be expressive enough to say, "M is in state j" for any $j \in \Sigma$, or say "counter 1 is greater than zero," and so on. We write $S = j$ as an abbreviation for the Datalog expression

$$succ(Z, A_1), succ(A_1, A_2), \ldots, succ(A_{j-1}, S),$$

and encode, for example, the transition $\delta(a, >, =) = (b, pop, push)$ as

$$\begin{aligned} ID(T, S, C_1, C_2) :- \; & ID(T', S', C_1', C_2'), \\ & succ(T', T), \\ & zero(Z), S' = a, S = b, \\ & succ(X, C_1'), succ(C_1, C_1'), \\ & zero(C_2'), succ(C_2', C_2). \end{aligned}$$

In this example, the IDB subgoal $ID(T', S', C_1', C_2')$ represents the configuration $(a, >, =)$, and the rule head $ID(T, S, C_1, C_2)$ represents a reachable configuration from $(a, >, =)$; the second line of the rule asserts that $T = T' + 1$; the third line ensures that the states are properly represented; the fourth line ensures that counter 1 is greater than zero and then reduced by one and counter 2 is zero and then increased by one. Note that $succ(P, Q)$ is used both to express "$Q = P+1$" but also "$Q > 0$," namely that Q is the successor of something.

Halting. We add the single rule

$$ID(A, B, C, D) : -ID(T, S, C_1, C_2), zero(Z), S = h.$$

Since A, B, C, D do not appear in any subgoal of the rule, any fact about the predicate ID can be deduced using this rule *if* the subgoal can be satisfied.

Lemma 1 *If M diverges, then for any constant c there exists a database D of EDB facts such that the fixpoint of P on D includes a fact f, where all proofs of f have height greater than c.*

Proof. Let the database include the constants $\{0, 1, \ldots, c + 1\}$ with the standard interpretation, i.e., $zero(0)$ and $succ(i, i + 1)$ for $0 \leq i \leq c$. Since M diverges, the halting rule is never used, and $ID(c + 1, s, a, b)$ must be in the fixpoint for suitably chosen constants a, b and s, since M has a state and counter configuration at time $c + 1$. It should be clear that $ID(t, s, c_1, c_2)$ is in the fixpoint iff M is in state s at time t with c_1 and c_2 the contents of the counters. A straightforward induction argument shows the height of the proof of this fact must be of height $c + 1$, since the proof must include some fact $ID(c, s', a', b')$ as a child of $ID(c + 1, s, a, b)$ in the proof tree. ∎

Lemma 2 *If M halts in t steps, then for any database D of EDB facts, any fact f in the fixpoint of P on D has a proof of height no more than $t + 1$.*

Proof. Some examples of a possible D provide useful intuitions. If D_1 is the integers $\{0, 1, \ldots, c\}$ where $c \geq t$, with the standard *succ* and *zero*, the result is clear, when D is D_1: we prove $ID(t, h, a, b)$ in height t and then deduce f via the halting rule. The difficulty is dealing with "nonstandard" databases.

If D_2 has constants 0 and 1 with $zero(0)$, $succ(0, 1)$, and $succ(1, 0)$, the same is true: take the proof of f using D_1, and replace even and odd constants by 0 and 1 to get a proof using D_2 with the same height. Notice, however, that there may be a much shorter proof: for example, if the halting state h is even, then the initialization rule deduces $ID(0, 0, 0, 0)$ and the subgoals of the halting rule in P are satisfied by this predicate, since 0 "is" both zero and the halting state h; thus, all f in the fixpoint have proofs of height 2.

If the database D is empty or, say, has no facts about *zero*, then nothing can be deduced, and the fixpoint is already computed. Analogously, D may provide enough integers to simulate M for a few steps but not until halting, in which case we would like to argue that the fixpoint can still be computed in less than t steps. We intuitively can divide the facts in the fixpoint into those that simulate the configuration of M, and other "junk" that is generated by the nonstandardness of D and does not correspond to a "nice" simulation: we need to show that no such junk has unbounded proofs.

This can be proved in the following manner. Let F_{t+1} be the set of proofs constructible from P and D of height $t + 1$. If the halting rule is used in any of these proofs, then clearly all facts in the fixpoint have proofs of height at most $t+1$. If $F_{t+1} = \emptyset$ then all facts in the fixpoint have height at most t. Otherwise, let p be a proof in F_{t+1}. Now, p is a proof using only EDB facts, the initialization rule, and the transition rules, so that at height j in the proof p there is a fact of the form $ID(a_j, s_j, c_{1,j}, c_{2,j})$ for suitably chosen constants, in which case $zero(a_0), succ(a_0, a_1), \ldots, succ(a_{t-1}, a_t)$ are in D. Therefore, M can be simulated on these constants, producing a proof of $ID(t, h, a, b)$ in height t, so the fixpoint can be computed in one more step. ∎

From the above two lemmas we know M halts if and only if P is bounded.

Theorem 3 *Boundedness is r.e.-complete.*

Proof. The reduction above shows that boundedness is r.e.-hard. We now argue that boundedness is recursively enumerable. Consider a Datalog query P. It can be shown that P is equivalent to an infinite disjunction $\phi_1 \vee \phi_2 \vee \ldots$ of a recursive sequence of existential positive first-order formulas such that $\phi_i \supset \phi_{i+1}$ for all $i > 0$, and, furthermore, if for some $i > 0$ we have that $\phi_i \equiv \phi_{i+1}$, then $\phi_i \equiv \phi_j$ for all $j \geq i$. Thus, P is bounded iff there is some $i > 0$ such that $\phi_i \equiv \phi_{i+1}$. The claim follows, since for existential positive formulas finite equivalence (i.e., equivalence over all finite structures) is decidable [DG79,SY80]. ∎

Remarks.

1. The programs used in the above reduction are *linear*, i.e., at most one IDB predicate occurs on the right-hand side of the rules. Linear programs are in general more benign than arbitrary programs. For example, query evaluation for arbitrary program is complete for PTIME [Va82], while it is in *NC* for linear programs [UV86].

2. The reduction uses a 4-ary IDB predicate. Using the emptiness problem for two-headed automata [LPP70], we can sharpen our undecidabilty result to linear programs that use one 3-ary IDB predicate. It is possible to encode the 3-ary predicate by a binary predicate, but the resulting program is not linear.

3. By choosing a particular 2CM for which the halting program on various inputs is undecidable we get a particular program P_0 for which the following is undecidable: given an initialization rule r, decide whether P_0 is bounded with respect to r.

3 Undecidability of Strong Boundedness

So far we had a clear separation between EDB predicates, which we viewed as input, and IDB predicates, which we view as output. While this distinction is appropriate when we consider Datalog programs as queries, it is not quite appropriate when we consider Datalog programs as the intensional part of a ***deductive database*** [GM78]. In this application all predicates are in some sense both extensional and intensional. The facts that are explicitly represented in the database are extensional and the facts that can be derived from the database are intensional. Also, if we want to do *local* optimization, i.e., we want to consider programs that are part of bigger programs, then the distinction between IDB predicates and EDB predicates weakens.

In this section we study the boundedness of Datalog programs where we do not distinguish between EDB and IDB predicates. Thus, while in the previous section we assumed that the IDB predicates are initially empty, here we have to consider the case that all predicates have initially some arbitrary assignment. If a program is bounded in this model, then we say that it is ***strongly*** bounded. Clearly, strong boundedness implies boundedness. The reverse implication, however, does not necessarily hold.

If we study the reduction of the previous section, we see that it does not work for strong boundedness. Consider a machine M that begins in state 0 with empty counters, adds 1 to counter 1, and then halts. We add a state ℓ to M that is inaccessible from the initial state, and a transition rule $\delta(\ell,-,-) = (\ell, push, push)$, i.e., loop in state ℓ, increasing both counters whether or not they are zero.

Clearly M still halts, but observe the problem of computing the fixpoint with the following D: let the constants of D be $\{0, i-1, i, \ldots, i+n\}$, the EDB facts be $\{zero(0), succ(i-1, i), \ldots, succ(i+n-1, i+n)\}$, and let there be an initial IDB fact $ID(i,i,i,i)$ in D. This IDB fact represents a configuration of M in state i at time i, with i in both counters. The initialization rule puts $ID(0,0,0,0)$ in the fixpoint, but since 0 has no successor, the simulation of M cannot proceed beyond this point. However, the fixpoint will include $ID(i+n, i+n, i+n, i+n)$, which has exactly one proof, and this proof has height n. Since n depends on D but not M, we conclude that M halts but P is not bounded.

One immediately observes that were $zero(i)$ in the database, there would be no problem, since M could be simulated on the longer successor chain. Following this intuition, we could reconstruct the methods used so far, replacing the predicate *zero* by a variable, so that $ID(Z,S,T,C_1,C_2)$ denotes the fact that Z is the zero, T is the time, etc., and initialize the simulation of M by P as $ID(Z,Z,Z,Z,Z)$. The transition rules will ensure that $ID(Z,\ldots)$ cannot be used to prove $ID(Z',\ldots)$ if $Z \neq Z'$. For example, we could simulate $\delta(a,>,=) = (b, pop, push)$ as (again abbreviating $succ(Z,A_1), succ(A_1,A_2), \ldots, succ(A_{j-1},S)$ as $S=j$):

$$\begin{aligned} ID(Z,T,S,C_1,C_2) :- \quad & ID(Z,T',S',C_1',Z), \\ & succ(T',T), S'=a, S=b, \\ & succ(X,C_1') \\ & succ(C_1,C_1') \\ & succ(Z,C_2). \end{aligned}$$

In this rule, $C_1' > 0$ is represented as $succ(X,C_1')$, and $C_2' = 0$ by the Z in the ID predicate.

One final problem, though, remains: the proof of Lemma 1 breaks down. Suppose a machine M is initialized with zero in both counters, and diverges by continually adding 1 to counter 1. However, for every state $s \neq h$, it has a transition $\delta(s,>,>) = (h, push, push)$. These rules do not change the behavior of M because counter 2 is always zero. Since M diverges, P should not be bounded, but consider the database D like the one in Lemma 1, with constants $\{0,1,\ldots,n\}$, where $succ(i,i+1)$, $0 \leq i < n$. The initialization rule puts $ID(1,1,1,1,1)$ in the fixpoint, but since 1 is the successor of 0, the transition $\delta(0,>,>) = (h, push, push)$ lets us deduce $ID(1,2,h,2,2)$ in height 2 where h is the halting state; thus, by the halting rule any fact is deducible in height 3. Here M diverges, but we cannot prove P is unbounded by using previous methods.

To remedy this final anomaly, we introduce two more variables D_1 and D_2, and insist that there is a successor chain of length 1 or more from Z to D_i in any derived fact $ID(Z, D_1, D_2, T, S, C_1, C_2)$. Two new kinds of rules are introduced to "increase" the D_i and to "reset" them to 1, and we modify the initialization rule as well:

Initialization. $ID(Z, I, I, Z, Z, Z, Z) :- succ(Z, I)$.

D_1-increase.

$$ID(Z, D_1, D_2, T, S, C_1, C_2) :-$$
$$ID(Z, D_1', D_2, T', S, C_1, C_2), succ(D_1', D_1), succ(T', T).$$

D_1-reset.

$$ID(Z, I, D_2, T, S, C_1, C_2) :-$$
$$ID(Z, D_1, D_2, T', S, C_1, C_2), succ(Z, I), succ(T', T).$$

Two similar rules are introduced for D_2. Notice that the variable T no longer simulates the time M takes to run, since it is rather related to the height of the proof. More specifically, it ensures that if a proof of height k can be generated from P and D, then there is a chain of length k.

Transition.

The transition $\delta(a, >, =) = (b, pop, push)$, for example, can now be encoded as

$$ID(Z, D_1, D_2, T, S, C_1, C_2) :-$$
$$ID(Z, D_1, D_2, T', S', D_1, Z), succ(T', T), S' = a, S = b, succ(Z, C_2), succ(C_1, D_1).$$

and the rule $\delta(s, >, >) = (h, push, push)$ as

$$ID(Z, D_1, D_2, T, S, C_1, C_2) :-$$
$$ID(Z, D_1, D_2, T', S', D_1, D_2), succ(T', T), S' = s, S = h, succ(D_1, C_1), succ(D_2, C_2).$$

Note that two new variables are needed so the fact that both counters are nonzero can be expressed.

Halting.

$$ID(A, B, C, D, E, F, G) :-$$
$$ID(Z, D_1, D_2, T, S, C_1, C_2), S = h.$$

Lemma 4 *If M diverges, then for any constant c, there exists a data base D of EDB and IDB facts and a fact f in the fixpoint of P on D such that all proofs of f have height greater than c.*

Proof. As in the proof of undecidability of boundedness, let D have constants $\{0, 1, \ldots, c+1\}$ with the obvious *zero* and *succ*; $ID(0, d_1, d_2, c+1, s, c_1, c_2)$ must be in the fixpoint for suitably chosen d_1, d_2, s, c_1, c_2, and the halting rule cannot be used. Thus, height $c+1$ proofs are necessary. ∎

Lemma 5 *If M halts in t steps, then for any database D of EDB and IDB facts, any fact f in the fixpoint of P on D has a proof of height no more than $1 + t(2t+1)$.*

Proof. Let $r = 1 + t(2t+1)$. As in the proof of Lemma 2, let F_r denote the proofs constructible from P and D of height $r+1$. If F_r is empty or contains a proof using the halting rule, clearly the lemma is true. Otherwise, let p be a proof in F_r. Now, p is a proof using only EDB facts, the initialization rule, and the transition rules, where the lowest ID fact in the proof tree is either derived from the initialization rule, or was initially in the database. In either case, however, there is a long successor chain of the form $succ(a_0, a_1), \ldots, succ(a_{r-1}, a_r)$, since all rules in P except the initialization and halting rules have a subgoal of the form $succ(T', T)$ that enforces a *succ* relation among the constants instantiating variables in column T of the ID predicate. The machine can now be simulated on the constants a_i and the *succ* relation among them. In the simulation, a_0 is the zero, and each step of M is simulated by a proof subtree of height at most $2t+1$; we may have to "reset" the D_i to a_1 (representing 1) and increment them up to no more than t in order to generate a new ID fact representing the next configuration of M. Note that we need a successor chain of length r to ensure that the subgoal $succ(T', T)$ can always be satisfied. At most t such subtrees are needed to derive an IDB fact representing the halting state, and we can prove any IDB fact in one more step. ∎

It follows from the above lemmas that strong boundedness is undecidable.

Theorem 6 *Strong boundedness is r.e.-complete.*

We note that for *typed* rules, strong boundedness is decidable [Sa85]. This is the first example we are aware of where typedness makes the difference between the decidable and the undecidable.

4 Monadic Recursion

As we have remarked before, the undecidability proof uses 4-ary predicates. By a suitable encoding, the undecidability result can be shown to hold for binary predicates. This leaves open the question of boundedness for *monadic* Datalog programs, i.e., Datalog programs where all IDB predicates are monadic. While we do not know the answer to this question, we can show that the problem is undecidable for what seems to be a slight extension of Datalog.

The extension that we consider is the addition of a standard *inequality* EDB predicate, i.e, an binary predicate $\neq$ with the standard interpretation. (Notice that one can express equality in Datalog by repeated use of the same variable.) For example, we allow rules such as $A(X,Y) : -B(X,Y), X \neq Y$. We call the extended language Datalog+. It is known that Datalog+ is strictly more expressive than Datalog [Sh87]. From a practical point of view, however, Datalog+ queries do not seem to be any harder to evaluate than Datalog programs.

The idea of the previous reduction was to have the EDB consist of a prefix of the natural numbers, while the IDB represents the computation of a 2CM. The idea here is to have the EDB represent the computation of the 2CM. More specifically, we have three EDB predicates: $zero(X)$, $succ(x,y)$, and $ID(T,S,C_1,C_2)$, with the obvious intended interpretation. There is one monadic IDB predicate $B(X)$. The Datalog program now checks that the EDB is indeed standard. If there is any violation, then we can immediately deduce any fact about B. The first three rules check the *zero* and *succ* predicates.

Check Zero.

$$B(U) : -succ(X,Y), zero(Y)$$

Check Successor.

$$B(U) : -succ(X,Y), succ(X,Z), Y \neq Z$$
$$B(U) : -succ(Y,X), succ(Z,X), Y \neq Z$$

We now need rules to check the ID predicate.

Check Initialization.

$$B(U) \quad : -ID(T,S,C_1,C_2), zero(T), S \neq T$$
$$B(U) \quad : -ID(T,S,C_1,C_2), zero(T), C_1 \neq T$$
$$B(U) \quad : -ID(T,S,C_1,C_2), zero(T), C_2 \neq T$$

Check Transitions. Consider for example the transition $\delta(a,>,=) = (b, pop, push)$. Corresponding to it there are rules such as

$$\begin{aligned} T(U) : - \quad & ID(T,S,C_1,C_2), ID(T',S',C_1',C_2'), \\ & succ(T',T), \\ & zero(Z), S = a, \\ & succ(X, C_1), \\ & zero(C_2), \\ & S'' = b, S' \neq S'' \end{aligned}$$

The above rule checks whether a state transition is represented incorrectly in ID. Similar rules check that the counters are set correctly.

The next rule checks whether the halting state has been reached.

Halting.

$$B(U) : -ID(T,S,C_1,C_2), S = h$$

Finally, we have two rules that check whether the computation is bounded.

Boundedness.

$$\begin{aligned} B(T) : - \quad & ID(T,S,C_1,C_2), zero(T) \\ B(T') : - \quad & B(T), ID(T,S,C_1,C_2), \\ & ID(T',S',C_1',C_2'), \\ & succ(T,T'). \end{aligned}$$

Note that the above program is linear and contains only *one* recursive rule, which is somewhat surprising in view of the indications that boundedness for the class of Datalog programs with a single rule might be decidable (all the positive results in [Io85, Na86a, NS87] are for this class).

The proof of the analogs to Lemmas 1 and 2 is omitted from this preliminary version.

Theorem 7 *Boundedness is undecidable for monadic linear Datalog+ programs.*

We do not know whether strong boundedness is undecidable for monadic Datalog+ programs.

5 A General Undecidability Result

In the previous sections we have focused on the boundedness problem. There are several other properties of Datalog programs that are relevant to their evaluation. For example, we mentioned in the introduction the polynomial fringe property, which guarantees that the complexity of the program is in *NC*. We now mention several other properties of Datalog programs that are relevant to their evaluation.

A program P is ***first order*** if it is equivalent to a first-order query, that is, there is a first-order query Q such that $P(D) = Q(D)$ for every database D. First-order programs can be evaluated in *LOGSPACE*. A program P is ***essentially linear*** if it is equivalent to a linear program. Essentially linear programs can be evaluated in *NC*. Two other properies that are relevant to the complexity of evaluation are ***one-sidedness*** [Na87] and ***allowing propagation of selections*** [BKBR87].

Of course, the complexity of evaluation is also a property of a program. A program P is in *LOGSPACE* if the set $\{(f, D) : f \in P(D)\}$ is in *LOGSPACE*. Similarly, a program P is in *NC* if the set $\{(f, D) : f \in P(D)\}$ is in *NC*.

We now prove a Rice-style theorem for Datalog programs. As a result, it follows that none of the above properties is decidable. We first need some definitions.

A property π ***contains boundedness*** if every bounded program has the property π. All the properties mentioned above contain boundedness.

A property π is ***nontrivial*** if there is a program P that does not have the property π (clearly, all trivial properties are decidable). Suppose now that we restrict attention to ***ordered*** databases. In ordered databases, *zero*, and *succ* are considered to be standard EDB predicates. That is, *succ* is interpreted by some successor relation on the domain of the database, and *zero* is interpreted by the minimal element of *succ*. A property π is ***strongly nontrivial*** if there is program P that does not have the property π even when only ordered databases are considered. All the properties mentioned above are strongly nontrivial (assuming that *LOGSPACE* and *NC* are different from *PTIME*).

A property π is ***semantic*** if whenever P and Q are equivalent (i.e., $P(D) = Q(D)$ for any database D), then P has π iff Q has π. Among the properties mentioned above, only the polynomial fringe property and the one-sidedness property are not semantic.

Theorem 8 *Any semantic property that contains boundedness and is strongly nontrivial is undecidable.*

The proof of Theorem 8, which involves combining a program that simulates a 2CM with a program that does not have the considered property will be given in the full paper. A refinement of the proof shows that the polynomial fringe property and the one-sidedness property are also undecidable. The latter result was first proven in [Na87]. Papadimitriou and Van Gelder [PV86] observed that the undecidability of the polynomial fringe property and the *NC* property follow easily from Greibach's Theorem [HU79, Theorem 8.14]. Their proof requires, however, an unbounded number of predicates. Finally, we conjecture that Theorem 8 can be strengthened to hold for any nontrivial semantic property that contains boundedness.

Acknowledgements. We are grateful for the participants of the Stanford NAIL! Seminar for fruitful discussions. We'd also like to thank Ron Fagin and Phokion Kolaitis for their helpful comments on a previous draft of this paper.

6 References

[ASU79] Aho, V.H., Sagiv, Y., Ullman, J.D.: Efficient optimization of a class of relational expression. *ACM Trans. on Database Systems* 4(1979), pp. 435–454.

[AU79] Aho, V.H., Ullman, J.D.: Universality of data retrieval languages. *Proc. 6th ACM Symp. on Principles of Programming Languages*, 1979, pp. 110–117.

[BR86] Bancilhon, F., Ramakrishnan, R.: An amateur's introduction to recursive query processing strategies. *Proc. ACM Conf. on Management of Data*, Washington, 1986, pp. 16–52.

[BKBR87] Beeri, C., Kanellakis, P., Bancilhon, F., Ramakrishnan, R.: Bounds on the propagation of selection into logic programs. To appear in *Proc. 6th ACM Symp. on Principles of Database Systems*, San Diego, March 1987.

[Ch81] Chandra, A.K.,: Programming primitives for database languages. *Proc. 8th ACM Symp. on Principles of Programming Languages*, Williamsburg, 1981, pp. 50–62.

[CH80] Chandra, A.K., Harel, D.: Computable queries for relational databases. *J. Computer and Systems Sciences* 21(1980), pp. 156 178.

[CH82] Chandra, A.K., Harel, D.: Structure and Complexity of Relational Queries. *J. Computer and Systems Sciences* 25(1982), pp. 99 128.

[CH85] Chandra, A.K., Harel, D.: Horn-clause queries and generalizations. *J. Logic Programming* 1(1985), pp. 1 15.

[CK86] Cosmadakis, S.S., Kanellakis, P.: Parallel evaluation of recursive rule queries. *Proc. 5th ACM Symp. on Principles of Database Systems*, Cambridge, 1986, pp. 280 293.

[CM77] Chandra, A.K., Merlin, P.M.: Optimal implementation of conjunctive queries in relational databases. *Proc. 9th ACM Symp. on Theory of Computing*, Boulder, 1977, pp. 77 90.

[CMG86] Chakravarthy, U.S., Minker, J., Grant, J.: Semantic query optimization - additional constraints and control strategies. *Proc. 2nd Int'l Conf. on Expert Database Systems*, Charleston, 1986, pp. 259 169.

[DG79] Dreben, D., and Goldfarb, W.D.: *The Decision Problem: Solvable Classes of Quantificational Formulas*. Addison-Wesley,1979.

[GM78] Gallaire, H., Minker, J.: *Logic and Databases*. Plenum Press, 1978.

[HN84] Henschen, L.J., Naqvi, S.A.: On compiling queries in recursive first-order databases. *J. ACM* 31(1984), pp. 47 85.

[HU79] Hopcroft, J.E., Ullman, J.D.: *Introduction to Automata Theory, Languages, and Computation*. Addison-Wesley, 1979.

[Im86] Immerman, N.: Relational queries computable in polynomial time. *Information and Control* 68(1986), pp. 86 104.

[Io85] Ioannidis, Y.E.: A time bound on the materialization of some recursively defined views. *Proc. 11th Int'l Conf. on Very Large Data Bases*, Stockholm, 1985, pp. 219 226.

[JCV84] Jarke, M., Clifford, J., Vassiliou, Y.: An optimizing Prolog front-end to a relational query system. *Proc. ACM Conf. on Management of Data*, 1984, pp. 296 306.

[LPP70] Luckham, D.C., Park, D.M.R., Paterson, M.S.: On formalised computer programs. *J. Computer and System Sciences* 4(1970), pp. 220 249.

[Mo74] Moschovakis, Y.N.: *Elementary Induction on Abstract Structures*. North Holland, 1974.

[MUV84] Maier, D., Ullman, J.D., Vardi, M.Y.: On the foundations of the universal relation model. *ACM Trans. on Database Systems* 9(1984), pp. 283 308.

[Na86a] Naughton, J.F.: Data independent recursion in deductive databases. *Proc. 5th ACM Symp. on Principles of Database Systems*, Cambridge, 1986, pp. 267–279. Full version - Stanford University Technical Report STAN-CS-86-1102, to appear in J. Computer and System Sciences.

[Na86b] Naughton, J.F.: Redundancy in Function-free Horn clauses. *Proc. IEEE Symp. on Logic Programming*, Salt Lake Cisty, 1986, pp. 236 245.

[Na87] Naughton, J.F.: One-sided recursions. To appear in *Proc. 6th ACM Symp. on Principles of Database Systems*, San Diego, March 1987.

[NS87] Naughton, J.F., Sagiv, Y.: A decidable class of bounded recursions. To appear in *Proc. 6th ACM Symp. on Principles of Database Systems*, San Diego, March 1987.

[PV86] Papadimitriou, C., Van Gelder, A.: Private communication, 1986.

[Sa85] Sagiv, Y.: On computing restricted projections of representative instances. *Proc. 4th ACM Symp. on Principles of Database Systems*, Portland, 1985, pp. 171 180.

[Sh87] Shmueli, O.: Decidability and expressiveness aspects of logic queries. To appear in *Proc. 6th ACM Symp. on Principles of Database Systems*, San Diego, March 1987.

[SY80] Sagiv, Y., Yannakakis, M.: Equivalence among relational expressions with the union and difference operators. *J. ACM* 27(1980), pp. 633-655.

[Ul85] Ullman, J.D.: Implementation of logical query languages for databases. *ACM Trans. on Database Systems* 10(1985), pp. 289 321.

[UV86] Ullman, J.D., Van Gelder, A.: Parallel complexity of logical query programs. *Proc. 27th IEEE Symp. on Foundations of Computer Science*, Toronto, 1986, pp. 438–454.

[Va82] Vardi, M.Y.: The complexity of relational query languages. *Proc. 14th ACM Symp. on Theory of Computing*, San Francisco, 1982, pp. 137–146.

[Zl76] Zloof, M.; *Query-by-Example: Operations on the Transitive Closure.* IBM Research Report RC5526, 1976.

Invited Speaker

Chair

P. Scott

University of Ottawa

Speaker

J. Reynolds

Carnegie-Mellon University

Conjunctive Types and Algol-like Languages

(Abstract of Invited Lecture)

J. Reynolds
Computer Science Department
Carnegie Mellon University
Pittsburgh, PA 15213-3890

The idea of conjunctive types, i.e. that an identifier or phrase can simultaneously possess several types, originated in the work of Coppo and Dezani, who devised a conjunctive-type discipline for the un-typed lambda calculus. They showed that this discipline provides a model of the language and, as a corollary, that there is no algorithm for type inference.

This result seems to have discouraged the use of conjunctive types in practical programming languages; yet, it is no barrier to their use in explicitly typed languages. We will explore the application of conjunctive types to Algol-like languages and demonstrate that they can make such languages both simpler and more flexible.

Session 4

Chair

S. Brookes

Carnegie-Mellon University

THE POWER OF TEMPORAL PROOFS

Martín Abadi

Computer Science Department
Stanford University

Some methods to reason about concurrent programs and hardware devices have been based on proof systems for temporal logic. Unfortunately, all effective proof systems for temporal logic are incomplete for the standard semantics. We evaluate and compare the power of several proof systems for temporal logic. Specifically, we relate temporal systems to classical systems with explicit time parameters.

A usual temporal system turns out to be incomplete even for weak nonstandard semantics; we exhibit a short valid formula it fails to prove. We suggest the addition of new rules to define auxiliary predicates. With these rules, we obtain nonstandard completeness results. In particular, one of the simple temporal systems we describe is as powerful as Peano Arithmetic.

1. Introduction:

Temporal logic ([Pn]) has been extensively used to reason about concurrent systems (e.g., [MP3], [OL]). Some methods to verify concurrent programs and hardware devices have been based on proof systems for first-order temporal logic (FTL). Thus, the quality and specially the power of these verification methods depend directly on the power of the underlying FTL proof systems (e.g., [MP1]). Unfortunately, all effective FTL proof systems are incomplete for the standard semantics. The evaluation of the proposed proof systems and of the corresponding verification methods is therefore a nontrivial problem.

In this paper we start out by proving that all effective FTL proof systems are incomplete for the standard semantics and propose alternative notions of completeness. Specifically, we consider a translation of temporal formulas into classical formulas with explicit time parameters and ask questions such as "is the temporal formula u provable in (a given system for) temporal logic if and only if its translation is provable in (a given system for) classical logic?" We study three FTL proof systems. The first one, T_0, is an extension of the usual Hilbert system of [MP2] and equivalent to the resolution system of [AM]. This basic system is incomplete in a strong sense. We exhibit a short valid formula T_0 fails to prove. The other ones, T_1 and T_2, include T_0 with new natural rules to define auxiliary predicates. We give simple characterizations of T_1 and T_2. For instance, our main positive result is that T_2 is as powerful as Peano Arithmetic.

There has been much recent related work on nonstandard logics of programs (e.g., [N], [BS], [Sa1], [Sa2]), and it proposes notions of completeness similar to ours. However, the existing results, which we discuss in some more detail below, only consider provability of special classes of sentences, with restricted temporal formalisms, and in rather weak systems. In particular, they are of limited relevance to the verification of concurrent systems.

In the next section the syntax and semantics of FTL are reviewed; the semantics of FTL is formulated in two equivalent ways, in terms of possible worlds and through a correspondence with classical logic. In section 3 we show that the standard notion of validity is Π_1^1-complete (e.g., [R]) and suggest approximations based on provability in formal systems of arithmetic. In section 4 we describe the basic system T_0 and prove nonstandard completeness and incompleteness theorems. New additional rules to define auxiliary predicates and the systems T_1 and T_2 are presented in section 5. In section 6 we introduce the useful notions of "clock" and "arithmetical formula." Section 7 contains soundness and completeness results for T_1 and T_2. We compare our results with previous ones in section 8 and pose

This research was supported in part by the National Science Foundation under grant DCR-84-13230 and by the Defense Advanced Research Projects Agency under Contract N00039-84-C-0211.

The author's current address is: Digital Equipment Corporation, Systems Research Center, 130 Lytton Avenue, Palo Alto, CA 94301, USA.

some open problems in section 9. Details and analogous results for resolution systems appear in [A].

2. Syntax and semantics:

a. Informal syntax and semantics

Temporal formulas are formulas of the predicate calculus with equality, with additional modal operators. For simplicity, we assume that the only connectives are $\neg$, $\wedge$, $\vee$, and regard all other connectives as abbreviations. The modal operators we consider are the usual ones for discrete linear time: $\bigcirc$, $\Box$, $\Diamond$, and the more general $\mathcal{U}$ and $\mathcal{P}$. If u and v are formulas then

- $\bigcirc u$ means "u is true in the next state";
- $\Box u$ means "u is always true (from now on)";
- $\Diamond u$ means "u is eventually true";
- $u\mathcal{U}v$ means "u is true until v is true" (in particular, u is true forever if v is never true);
- $u\mathcal{P}v$ means "u precedes v" (in particular, u is true eventually even if v is always false).

A *language* is a countable collection of predicate and function symbols that may occur in formulas. Languages include *flexible* symbols, i.e., symbols that may change value with time. For practical reasons, languages also include *rigid* symbols with time-independent meanings.

b. Possible-world semantics

Formally, models and the satisfaction relation can be described in terms of possible worlds ([HC]). A *model* is a tuple $\langle D, W, w_0, R_1, R_2, \alpha, I\rangle$.

- The *domain* D is a non-empty set.
- The set W has a distinguished element w_0; intuitively W is the set of *worlds* and w_0 the *present world*. (Note that we require that there be just one domain D rather than one for each element of W.)
- The relations R_1 and R_2 are two binary *accessibility relations* on W; R_1 corresponds to "next" and R_2 to "eventually."
- The *assignment* α is a function from the set of variables to D.
- The *interpretation* I gives a meaning to predicate and function symbols; at each world, I maps each predicate symbol to a relation and each function symbol to a function; the meaning of rigid symbols must be the same at all worlds.

The *satisfaction* relation between models and formulas, $\models$, is defined inductively. The semantics of $\bigcirc$ is given by:

$$\langle D, W, w_0, R_1, R_2, \alpha, I\rangle \models \bigcirc u$$
$$\Leftrightarrow$$
$$\langle D, W, w_1, R_1, R_2, \alpha, I\rangle \models u \text{ for some } w_1 \text{ s.t. } w_0 R_1 w_1.$$

That of $\Diamond$ is given by:

$$\langle D, W, w_0, R_1, R_2, \alpha, I\rangle \models \Diamond u$$
$$\Leftrightarrow$$
$$\langle D, W, w_1, R_1, R_2, \alpha, I\rangle \models u \text{ for some } w_1 \text{ s.t. } w_0 R_2 w_1.$$

The meanings of $\Box$, $\mathcal{U}$, and $\mathcal{P}$ are also defined in terms of R_2.

The model M is *standard* if $\langle W, w_0, R_1, R_2\rangle$ is isomorphic to the structure $\langle N, 0, s, \leq\rangle$, that is, the natural numbers with the constant zero, the successor function, and the less-than relation. The formula u is *valid* (in the standard sense) if all standard models satisfy u; we denote this by $\models u$.

c. Arithmetical semantics

An alternative way to interpret FTL is to translate temporal formulas into classical formulas that contain some arithmetic symbols. This arithmetical semantics is actually equivalent to the possible-world semantics, but it leads to some insights on the complexity of FTL and on alternatives to the standard notion of completeness, typical of Correspondence Theory ([V]).

For each temporal language L, we define a countable two-sorted classical language L_O ("O" stands for "order"). The "number" sort S_N is equipped with the constant symbol 0, the function symbol s, the predicate symbol $\leq$, and the equality symbol $=$. It is technically practical to consider that in actuality 0 and s are just convenient, informal abbreviations for the unary predicate symbol 0_p and the binary predicate symbol s_p, respectively. A countable supply of variables of the number sort are denoted by letters like i; terms of this sort are denoted by letters like m. The equality symbol $=$ and all predicate and function symbols in L are also in L_O, to operate on the "data" sort S_D. The arity of rigid symbols in L_O is the same as in L. Terms of sort S_N cannot occur as arguments of these rigid symbols. The arity of flexible symbols in L_O is their arity in L incremented by one. Terms of sort S_N occur as last arguments of these flexible symbols, and in no other argument position.

By $M \models_O w$ we mean that the two-sorted classical model M satisfies the formula w, with no assumptions on the properties of M. We can give a standard semantics to L_O in the natural way, taking S_N to represent the natural numbers, $\leq$ the less-than relation between numbers, etc.; the interpretation of the symbols to operate on data is left open. The formula u is *valid* (in the standard sense) if all standard models satisfy u; we denote this by $\models_O u$.

Given L and L_O, the function P translates temporal formulas into classical formulas. For all u, let $P(u) = P^*(u, 0)$, where P^* is an auxiliary translation function defined by:

$$P^*\big(p(t_1, \ldots, t_k), m\big) = \begin{cases} p\big(P^*(t_1, m), \ldots, P^*(t_k, m)\big) \\ \quad \text{if } p \text{ is a rigid symbol} \\ p\big(P^*(t_1, m), \ldots, P^*(t_k, m), m\big) \\ \quad \text{if } p \text{ is a flexible symbol} \end{cases}$$

$$P^*(\bigcirc u, m) = P^*(u, s(m))$$

$$P^*(\Box u, m) = \forall i \geq m. P^*(u, i) \qquad (i \text{ and } j \text{ are fresh})$$

$$P^*(\Diamond u, m) = \exists i \geq m. P^*(u, i)$$

$$P^*(u \,\mathcal{U}\, v, m) = \forall i \geq m. (P^*(u, i) \vee \exists j. (m \leq j \leq i \wedge P^*(v, j)))$$

$$P^*(u \,\mathcal{P}\, v, m) = \exists i \geq m. (P^*(u, i) \wedge \forall j. (m \leq j \leq i \supset \neg P^*(v, j)))$$

and P^* preserves connectives, quantifiers, and variables. In a precise sense, if we redefine the meaning of an FTL formula u to be the meaning of $P(u)$, the semantics remains essentially the same. In particular, $\models u \Leftrightarrow \models_O P(u)$.

3. Standard incompleteness and new notions of completeness:

We prove that the standard concept of validity is highly intractable. In particular, no effective system for FTL can be complete in the standard sense. Then we propose more realistic and practical notions of completeness.

Proposition: $\models_O$ is in Π^1_1.

Corollary: $\models$ is in Π^1_1.

This upper bound is tight:

Theorem: $\models$ is Π^1_1-hard.

Proof sketch: We show how to reduce the truth problem for Π^1_1 formulas to the validity problem for FTL formulas. The key step is a temporal "definition" of the arithmetic operations.

If a is a flexible constant symbol then in any standard model that satisfies the formulas

$$\begin{aligned}
&(\forall x. \Diamond\, a = x), \\
&(\forall x. \Box(a = x \supset \bigcirc \Box\, a \neq x)), \\
&(a = 0), \\
&(\forall x \forall y. (s(x) = y \equiv \Diamond(a = x \wedge \bigcirc\, a = y)), \\
&(\forall x \forall y. (x \leq y \equiv \Diamond(a = x \wedge \Diamond\, a = y)), \\
&(\forall x. x + 0 = x), \\
&(\forall x \forall y. x + s(y) = s(x + y)), \\
&(\forall x. x \times 0 = 0), \\
&(\forall x \forall y. x \times s(y) = x \times y + x)
\end{aligned}$$

the domain is isomorphic to N and 0, s, $\leq$, $+$, and $\times$ are interpreted as the usual relations and functions on N. ∎

Remark: Parikh ([Pa1]) has also proved this theorem; we have given an independent proof.

It follows that $\models$ is Π^1_1-complete. In fact, $\models$ is Π^1_1-complete even if the temporal formalism is radically restricted (in particular, one flexible constant symbol and a few rigid symbols suffice in the proof). Thus, the standard concept of validity is overly demanding. Weaker, recursively enumerable alternatives to the standard concept of validity may be more appropriate and useful in the study of FTL proof systems. For instance, consider equipping L_O with a proof system. Take $\vdash_O$ to mean provability in first-order logic, with natural axioms about 0, s, and $\leq$ (including an induction schema). Given a proof concept $\vdash$ for FTL and a formula u, we may ask

$$\vdash u \text{ if and only if } \vdash_O P(u)?$$

The proof concept $\vdash_O$ is sound for a large class of nonstandard models. The equivalence "$\vdash u$ if and only if $\vdash_O P(u)$" is the least restrictive requirement we find acceptable: any FTL system incomplete with respect to $\vdash_O$ should probably be replaced with a system that translates temporal formulas into classical formulas and then uses $\vdash_O$.

Now suppose that the function symbols $+$ and $\times$ are added to L_O – again, it is practical to regard them as abbreviations for the ternary predicate symbols $+_p$ and $\times_p$, respectively. The new language is L_P ("P" stands for "Peano"). The usual Peano axioms for $+$ and $\times$ are added to $\vdash_O$. Also, the induction schema is extended to the language with $+$ and $\times$. We obtain $\vdash_P$. Note that $\vdash_P$ is not a conservative extension of $\vdash_O$ ([BS]). Given a proof concept $\vdash$ for FTL and a formula u, we may ask

$$\vdash u \text{ if and only if } \vdash_P P(u)?$$

Since Peano Arithmetic proves almost all valid sentences of practical interest, completeness with respect to $\vdash_P$ is an attractive requirement.

4. A basic proof system for FTL:

A few proof systems for FTL have been suggested (e.g., [MP2], [AM]). While they are very different in style, most of them have essentially the same power. For simplicity, we describe a basic Hilbert system T_0, an extension of the Hilbert system described in [MP2] for the class of languages we consider, equivalent to the resolution system of [AM].

- If $\vdash_{T_0} u$ and $\vdash_{T_0} (u \supset v)$ then $\vdash_{T_0} v$.
- If $\vdash_{T_0} u$ then $\vdash_{T_0} \Box u$.
- If $\vdash_{T_0} (u \supset v)$ and x does not occur free in u then $\vdash_{T_0} (u \supset \forall x.v)$.
- If u is an instance of a valid propositional-temporal schema then $\vdash_{T_0} u$.
- If u does not contain any flexible symbols then $\vdash_{T_0} u \equiv \bigcirc u$.
- If u is an equality axiom then $\vdash_{T_0} u$.
- $\vdash_{T_0} \exists x.\neg u \equiv \neg\forall x.u$.
- $\vdash_{T_0} (\forall x.w) \supset w\theta$ where the substitution θ does not create any new bound occurrences of variables or any new occurrences of flexible terms in the scope of modal operators.
- $\vdash_{T_0} (\forall x.\bigcirc u) \equiv (\bigcirc \forall x.u)$.
- $\vdash_{T_0} \left[\forall x.(u \,\mathcal{U}\, v)\right] \equiv \left[(\forall x.u) \,\mathcal{U}\, v\right]$, provided x does not occur free in v.

Systems similar to T_0 have been found empirically satisfactory. Furthermore, T_0 is complete in at least a very nonstandard sense, as we prove now. A *model of* T_0 is a model where all the axioms of T_0 hold at every world. A set of formulas Σ is T_0-*consistent* if $\not\vdash_{T_0} \neg(u_1 \wedge \ldots \wedge u_n)$ for all $u_1, \ldots, u_n \in \Sigma$. A new model construction technique – we make worlds out of saturated sets of formulas in a new way, to handle $\bigcirc$, $\mathcal{U}$, and $\mathcal{P}$ – yields:

Theorem: If the set of formulas Σ is T_0-consistent then Σ holds in some model of T_0.

However, $\vdash_{T_0}$ is incomplete even with respect to $\vdash_O$:

Theorem: There is a formula u such that $\vdash_O P(u)$ but $\not\vdash_{T_0} u$.

Proof sketch: Fix the language to contain only the flexible constant symbol a and the flexible predicate symbol p. Let u be

$$\begin{bmatrix} (\forall x.\Diamond\, a = x) \wedge p(a) \\ \wedge \\ (\forall x \forall y.(p(x) \wedge \Diamond(a = x \wedge \bigcirc\, a = y)) \supset p(y)) \end{bmatrix} \qquad (*)$$
$$\supset (\forall x.p(x)).$$

Intuitively, u says that if a enumerates the domain, p holds for the first element in the enumeration, and if it holds for an element it holds for its successor in the enumeration, then it must hold for all elements in the domain. In a sense, u connects induction on time and induction in a domain. We can show that u has the desired property. ∎

5. Auxiliary definitions:

As we showed, T_0 is surprisingly limited. An analysis of its incompleteness and of how actual temporal theorem proving is carried out gives rise to new rules. Similar rules can be added to other proposed FTL systems.

In practice, proofs often involve auxiliary symbols, both rigid and flexible. For instance, if we define the auxiliary rigid predicate q so that $q(x)$ holds if and only if $p(x)$ holds in the initial world, we can obtain a proof for the sentence u exhibited in the previous incompleteness theorem $(*)$. Also, Hailpern and Owicki ([HO]) have used inductive definitions for some auxiliary flexible objects (the "history variables") in informal proofs.

We propose to allow definitions for rigid and flexible auxiliary predicates in formal proofs – definitions for auxiliary functions can be formulated similarly. Rigid predicates are defined explicitly by formulas of the form

$$\forall x_1 \ldots \forall x_k.\left[p(x_1, \ldots, x_k) \equiv u\right],$$

where p is the new rigid predicate being defined and p does not occur in u. For flexible predicates, we are content with primitive recursive definitions of the form

$$\forall x_1 \ldots \forall x_n. \begin{bmatrix} p(x_1, \ldots, x_n) \equiv u \\ \wedge \\ \Box((\bigcirc\, p(x_1, \ldots, x_n)) \equiv v) \end{bmatrix},$$

where p is the new flexible predicate, p does not occur in u, and p does not occur in the scope of any modal operator in v. With no practical harm, we also require that p does not occur in the scope of $\forall$ or $\neg$ in v in order to keep low the logical complexity of definitions.

We allow the discharge of explicit definitions at the end of proofs to obtain T_1:

- If $\vdash_{T_0} w$ then $\vdash_{T_1} w$.
- If $\vdash_{T_1} (d \supset w)$ and d defines a rigid predicate not contained in w then $\vdash_{T_1} w$.

Similarly, we allow the discharge of all definitions at the end of proofs to obtain T_2:

- If $\vdash_{T_0} w$ then $\vdash_{T_2} w$.
- If $\vdash_{T_2} (d \supset w)$ and d defines a predicate not contained in w then $\vdash_{T_2} w$.

Remark: In some resolution systems, skolemization has a role similar to that of the rules to discharge definitions because, intuitively, skolemization introduces an auxiliary function (instead of an auxiliary predicate).

6. Clocks and arithmetical formulas:

In this section we define the class of arithmetical formulas. We have a completeness result for arithmetical formulas for T_1. Arithmetical formulas are also useful in the study of T_2, although our completeness theorem for T_2 is not restricted to arithmetical formulas.

Sometimes a clock is a useful device in proofs. For instance, a program counter may help us prove properties of a program even though the program never refers to the program counter. In some settings, clocks are actually not only useful but necessary ([Pa2]).

Informally, a *clock* is a formula c that distinguishes a set of tuples of elements of the domain at each point, without repetitions. The distinguished tuples in a world can be thought of as the "time" of that world. (E.g., $c(x)$ may be *program-counter* $= x$.) More precisely, c satisfies the *clock condition*

$$C(c): \ (\Box\, \exists \vec{x}.c(\vec{x})) \wedge (\Box\, \forall \vec{x}.(c(\vec{x}) \supset \bigcirc\, \Box \neg c(\vec{x}))).$$

The formula c is *a clock for u* if we can use $C(c)$ to show u, that is, if we can prove $C(c) \supset u$ then we can prove u. More precisely, consider a proof concept $\vdash$ (for instance, one of $\vdash_{T_0}$, $\vdash_{T_1}$, $\vdash_{T_2}$). The formula c is called a clock for u in $\vdash$ if $\vdash C(c) \supset u$ implies $\vdash u$. The formula u is *arithmetical* in $\vdash$ if there exists a clock for u in $\vdash$ (the name was chosen because arithmetical formulas have a natural interpretation in arithmetical universes ([H])).

Examples:

- Consider $\vdash_{T_1}$. Suppose we are interested in

$$\left[A \wedge \Box \forall z.(a = z \supset \bigcirc\, a > z)\right]$$
$$\supset (\forall y. \Diamond\, a > y),$$

where A is some basic collection of axioms about arithmetic and a is a flexible constant symbol. Since A and $\Box \forall z.(a = z \supset \bigcirc\, a > z)$ imply that a must take a different value at each instant, $a = x$ is a clock for this formula. ∎

- Consider $\vdash_{T_2}$. Suppose we are interested in

$$\left[\forall x.(s(x) \neq 0) \wedge \forall x \forall y.(s(x) = s(y) \supset x = y)\right]$$
$$\supset v$$

for some v. For instance, we may imagine that v expresses some temporal property of programs on numbers, and that is why some basic facts about 0 and s appear. In T_2, we can define a flexible predicate c

$$\forall x. \begin{bmatrix} c(x) \equiv (x = 0) \\ \wedge \\ \Box((\bigcirc\, c(x)) \equiv \exists y.(c(y) \wedge x = s(y))) \end{bmatrix}$$

to obtain a clock for the formula of interest. ∎

As the examples suggest, many of the formulas involved in reasoning about computations are arithmetical in T_1 and T_2. A most useful fact about arithmetical formulas is:

Theorem: If $\models u$ then u is arithmetical in $\vdash_{T_2}$.

Proof sketch: The completeness theorem of section 3 yields that if u is not arithmetical then some model of $\neg u$ cannot be expanded to satisfy $C(c)$, for any c. This enables us to prove that $\neg u$ must have some simple model where only propositional temporal facts and time-independent facts need to be taken into account. Then we can construct a standard model for $\neg u$. Therefore, u is not valid. ∎

7. Soundness and completeness:

The main results of this section are the soundness and completeness of $\vdash_{T_1}$ and $\vdash_{T_2}$ with respect to $\vdash_O$ and $\vdash_P$, respectively. The completeness theorem for $\vdash_{T_1}$

refers only to arithmetical formulas. The more important completeness theorem for $\vdash_{T_2}$ applies to all formulas.

Soundness Theorem:
For every formula u, $\vdash_{T_1} u \Rightarrow \vdash_O P(u)$.
For every formula u, $\vdash_{T_2} u \Rightarrow \vdash_P P(u)$.

Proof sketch: The proof is similar for both systems. We show how to transform a proof of v within T_0 into a classical proof of $P(\Box v)$ and how to avoid definitions for auxiliary predicates in classical proofs. ∎

Completeness Theorem:
For every arithmetical formula u, $\vdash_O P(u) \Rightarrow \vdash_{T_1} u$.
For every formula u, $\vdash_P P(u) \Rightarrow \vdash_{T_2} u$.

Proof sketch: Since the translation function P preserves standard validity and $\vdash_P$ is sound, $\vdash_P P(u)$ implies that $\models u$, and hence that u is arithmetical in $\vdash_{T_2}$. Therefore, it suffices to prove that for every arithmetical formula u (with clock c) $\vdash_O P(u) \Rightarrow \vdash_{T_1} u$ and $\vdash_P P(u) \Rightarrow \vdash_{T_2} u$. As a preliminary, we show that we may assume that there are no function symbols in the language – though we use some as abbreviations. Then the main steps of the proofs are:

Step 1: We use c to define 0, s, $\leq$, and $\simeq$ in T_1, and also $+$ and $\times$ in T_2:

First define the rigid numberhood predicate n by

$$\forall \vec{x}.\left[n(\vec{x}) \equiv \Diamond c(\vec{x})\right]$$

We may handle n as a sort, since n denotes a provably non-empty relation. In steps 2 and 3, we denote variables of this sort by letters like i, and terms of this sort by letters like m.

Define the rigid zero predicate 0_p by

$$\forall \vec{x}.\left[0_p(\vec{x}) \equiv c(\vec{x})\right]$$

Define the rigid successor predicate s_p by

$$\forall \vec{x}\forall \vec{y}.\left[s_p(\vec{x},\vec{y}) \equiv \Diamond(c(\vec{x}) \wedge \bigcirc c(\vec{y}))\right]$$

Similarly, $\leq$ can be defined by

$$\forall \vec{x}\forall \vec{y}.\left[\vec{x} \leq \vec{y} \equiv \Diamond(c(\vec{x}) \wedge \Diamond c(\vec{y}))\right]$$

and $\simeq$ can be defined by

$$\forall \vec{x}\forall \vec{y}.\left[\vec{x} \simeq \vec{y} \equiv \Diamond(c(\vec{x}) \wedge c(\vec{y}))\right]$$

In T_2, intermediate primitive-recursive definitions can be exploited to define the rigid predicates $+_p$ and $\times_p$. The defined symbols can be shown to satisfy enough of their usual properties within T_1. In particular, $C(c)$ implies that 0_p, s_p, $+_p$, and $\times_p$ are function-like in the sort n. Therefore, we use the abbreviations 0, s, $+$, $\times$.

Step 2: We translate u into a provably equivalent FTL formula $Q(u)$:

For all u, let $Q(u) = Q^*(u, 0)$, where Q^* is an auxiliary translation function such that:

$$Q^*(p(t_1, \ldots, t_k), m) = \begin{cases} p(t_1, \ldots, t_k) \\ \quad \text{if } p \text{ is a rigid predicate symbol} \\ \Diamond\left(c(m) \wedge p(t_1, \ldots, t_k)\right) \\ \quad \text{if } p \text{ is a flexible predicate symbol} \end{cases}$$

$$Q^*(\bigcirc u, m) = Q^*(u, s(m))$$

$$Q^*(\Box u, m) = \forall i \geq m.Q^*(u, i) \qquad (i \text{ and } j \text{ are fresh})$$

$$Q^*(\Diamond u, m) = \exists i \geq m.Q^*(u, i)$$

$$Q^*(u\, \mathcal{U}\, v, m) = \forall i \geq m.\left[Q^*(u, i) \vee \exists j.(m \leq j \leq i \wedge Q^*(v, j))\right]$$

$$Q^*(u\, \mathcal{P}\, v, m) = \exists i \geq m.\left[Q^*(u, i) \wedge \forall j.(m \leq j \leq i \supset \neg Q^*(v, j))\right]$$

and Q^* renames bound variables and preserves connectives and quantifiers.

Let D denote the definitions for n, 0_p, s_p, $\leq$, and $\simeq$. The function Q provably preserves meaning:

$$\vdash_{T_1} (C(c) \wedge D) \supset (u \equiv Q(u)) \quad \text{for all } u.$$

Thus, to prove u, it suffices to prove $Q(u)$ from $C(c)$ and the definitions for the appropriate auxiliary predicates.

Step 3: Any proof of $P(u)$ can be easily transformed into a proof of $Q(u)$ from $C(c)$ and the definitions for the appropriate auxiliary predicates:

The formulas $Q(u)$ and $P(u)$ have identical syntactic structures, except that when the atom $p(t_1, \ldots, t_k, m)$ occurs in $P(u)$, $\Diamond(c(m) \wedge p(t_1, \ldots, t_k))$ occurs in $Q(u)$. This difference is insignificant enough that any proof of $P(u)$ can be applied to $Q(u)$, with only minor modifications. ∎

Corollary: T_0 is strictly less powerful than T_1 and T_1 is strictly less powerful than T_2.

8. Related work:

In dynamic logic, the intractability theorems initially led to an interest in completeness results for arithmetical universes ([H]). We suspect these results do not carry over directly to temporal logic. On the other hand, literature on nonstandard logics of programs (e.g., [N], [BS], [Sa1], [Sa2]) discusses notions of completeness similar those we study.

Previous works on nonstandard temporal logics differ from ours in three major respects. First, the logics under consideration often include the modal operator *First*, but not $\mathcal{U}$ and $\mathcal{P}$, and the only flexible symbols are constant symbols. Second, the works focus on weak FTL proof systems, similar to T_0 or, at most, T_1. Third, the soundness and completeness theorems given are for special classes of sentences, such as partial correctness assertions for deterministic sequential programs. For instance, these theorems do not directly apply to reasoning about concurrent systems.

There have been results analogous to ours for other modal logics. In particular, Solovay ([So]) has proved an equivalence between the propositional logic of provability and Peano Arithmetic. Although our main positive result seems close in style and form to Solovay's, the constructions used in the proofs have little in common. Another fundamental difference is that the logic Solovay considers is axiomatizable, while temporal logic is highly intractable.

9. Open questions:

The system we are most interested in is T_2, because it corresponds well both to Peano Arithmetic and to informal proof methods, and because it is the most powerful one of those we have considered. Still, there are some intriguing open questions on T_0 and T_1:

- We have shown that $\vdash_{T_0}$ is incomplete with respect to $\vdash_O$. Is there any simple characterization of T_0?
- We would like to know whether $\vdash_{T_1}$ is complete with respect to $\vdash_O$ for all formulas (and not just for arithmetical formulas), or, in other words, whether a clock adds power to T_1.

Acknowledgments:

I am grateful to Gianluigi Bellin, Sol Feferman, Rob Goldblatt, Leo Harrington, and John Lamping for fruitful discussions on this work.

References:

[A] M. Abadi, *Temporal-Logic Theorem Proving*, PhD Thesis, Computer Science Department, Stanford University, 1987.

[AM] M. Abadi and Z. Manna, "A timely resolution," Symposium on Logic in Computer Science, 1986, pp. 176–186.

[BS] B. Biró and I. Sain, "Peano Arithmetic for the time scale of nonstandard logics of programs," unpublished manuscript, Mathematical Institute of the Hungarian Academy of Sciences, 1983.

[H] D. Harel, "Dynamic Logic," in *Handbook of Philosophical Logic, Vol. II* (D. Gabbay and F. Guenthner, eds.), D. Reidel Publishing Co., Dordrecht, 1984, pp. 497–604.

[HC] G.E. Hughes and M.J. Cresswell, *An Introduction to Modal Logic*, Methuen & Co., London, 1968.

[HO] B. Hailpern and S. Owicki, "Modular verification of computer communication protocols," *IEEE Trans. on Communications*, Vol. COM-31, No. 1, Jan. 1983, pp. 56–68.

[MP1] Z. Manna and A. Pnueli, "How to cook a temporal proof system for your pet language," Tenth ACM Symposium on Principles of Programming Languages, Jan. 1983, pp. 141–154.

[MP2] Z. Manna and A. Pnueli, "Verification of concurrent programs: A temporal proof system," Report No. STAN-CS-83-967, Computer Science Department, Stanford University, June 1983.

[MP3] Z. Manna and A. Pnueli, "Adequate proof principles for invariance and liveness properties of concurrent programs," *Science of Computer Programming*, Vol. 4, No. 3, Dec. 1984, pp. 257–289.

[N] I. Németi, "Nonstandard Dynamic Logic," in *Logics of Programs* (D. Kozen, ed.), Springer-Verlag LNCS 131, 1981, pp. 311-348.

[OL] S. Owicki and L. Lamport, "Proving liveness properties of concurrent programs," *ACM Transactions on Programming, Languages, and Systems*, Vol. 4, No. 3, July 1982, pp. 455–495.

[Pa1] R. Parikh, private communication.

[Pa2] R. Parikh, "A decidability result for Second Order Process Logic," 19th Annual Symposium on Foundations of Computer Science, 1978, pp. 177–183.

[Pn] A. Pnueli, "The temporal logic of programs," 18th Annual Symposium on Foundations of Computer Science, 1977, pp. 46–57.

[R] H. Rogers, *Theory of Recursive Functions and Effective Computability*, McGraw-Hill Book Co., New York, 1967.

[Sa1] I. Sain, "The reasoning powers of Burstall's (modal logic) and Pnueli's (temporal logic) program verification methods," in *Logics of Programs* (R. Parikh, ed.), Springer-Verlag LNCS 193, 1985, pp. 302–320.

[Sa2] I. Sain, "Relative program verifying powers of the various temporal logics," unpublished manuscript, Mathematical Institute of the Hungarian Academy of Sciences, 1985.

[So] R. Solovay, "Provability interpretations of modal logic," *Israel Journal of Mathematics*, Vol. 25, 1976, pp. 287–304.

[V] J. Van Benthem, "Correspondence Theory," in *Handbook of Philosophical Logic, Vol. II* (D. Gabbay and F. Guenthner, eds.), D. Reidel Publishing Co., Dordrecht, 1984, pp. 167–247.

Proving Boolean Combinations of Deterministic Properties

Bowen Alpern

Watson Research Center
Box 218
Yorktown Heights, NY 10598

Fred B. Schneider*

Department of Computer Science
Cornell University
Ithaca, NY 14853

Abstract This paper gives a method for proving that a program satisfies a temporal property that has been specified in terms of Buchi automata. The method permits extraction of proof obligations for a property formulated as the Boolean combination of properties, each of which is specified by a deterministic Buchi automaton, directly from the individual automata. The proof obligations can be formulated as Hoare triples. The method is proved sound and relatively complete. A simple example illustrates application of the method.

1. Introduction

Over the past 20 years, there has been increasing interest in ways to deduce properties of program behavior from the program text itself. One technique that is attracting attention is based on specifying a temporal property P with a Buchi automata that accepts every sequence of program states satisfying P.[1] Proof obligations are then extracted from this automaton. These obligations are generalizations of the invariant and variant function used to prove partial correctness and termination of a **while** loop. They define verification conditions that must hold for any program satisfying P. Since the verification conditions themselves are formulated as Hoare triples [Hoare 69], all reasoning can be done in first-order predicate logic, and temporal logic is not required.

Extraction of proof obligations from Buchi automata was first proposed in [Alpern & Schneider 85] for *deterministic properties*—those properties that can be specified by deterministic Buchi automata. Subsequently, [Manna & Pnueli 87] generalized the approach to handle properties that can be specified by non-deterministic Buchi automata.[2] Both [Alpern & Schneider 85] and [Manna & Pnueli 87], however, treat a property as a monolithic entity. Doing so has some practical disadvantages. First, the Buchi automaton specifying a property that is the Boolean combination of simpler properties can be exponentially bigger than the combined size of the automata specifying its components [Sistla et al 85]. Since the amount of work required to prove correctness is linear in the size of the automata specifying the property being proved, working with the combined automata can be impractical. Second, combining properties requires complex automata constructions and simplifying properties requires automata transformations, both of which are error prone processes. By contrast, when, for example, temporal logic is used to specify properties, logical connectives permit properties to be combined and the laws of logic allow properties to be simplified.

This paper shows how to avoid these disadvantages by giving a way that proof obligations for a property formulated as the Boolean combination of deterministic properties can be extracted directly from the automata specifying those components. The method also unifies the approaches in [Alpern & Schneider 85] and [Manna & Pnueli 87]. The method of [Alpern & Schneider 85] extracts obligations for P from a deterministic Buchi automata that accepts P; the method of [Manna & Pnueli 87] is equivalent to extracting obligations for $\neg P$ from a Buchi automata that accepts P.

In our new approach, a property is presented as a conjunction of *clauses*, each of which is proved separately and is formulated as the disjunction of deterministic properties and negations of deterministic properties. To prove that a program satisfies a clause, three *proof instruments* must be exhibited. An invariant handles the safety aspects of the proof; a variant function handles the liveness aspects; and a *candidate function*, arbitrates among the automata specifying the disjuncts of a clause to ensure that any program execution will be accepted by at least one automata representing a deterministic property or rejected by at least one automata representing the negation of a deterministic property. The three instruments define verification conditions, which can be formulated as Hoare triples.

In section 2, a simple concurrent programming language and its semantics is defined. Section 3 reviews Buchi automata for specifying properties. Proof instruments for a single clause are discussed in section 4; sound-

*Supported, in part, by NSF Grant DCR-8320274 and Office of Naval Research contract N00014-86-K-0092.

[1]Buchi automata are expressive enough for use in proving all linear-time temporal properties described in [Manna & Pnueli 81], [Owicki & Lamport 82], etc.

[2]Non-deterministic Buchi automata can specify properties that cannot be specified using deterministic Buchi automata [Eilenberg 74].

ness and completeness proofs are also given there. The method is illustrated in section 5 by proving that assuming weak fairness, Peterson's protocol for mutual exclusion [Peterson 81] satisfies a non-starvation property. Section 6 relates our approach to other techniques for proving properties of concurrent programs.

2. Programs

A program π is specified by a predicate $Init_\pi$ describing possible initial states and a set of atomic actions A_π. An execution of π is modeled by an infinite sequence of program states, called a *history*, in which the first state satisfies $Init_\pi$ and every subsequent state results from executing an element of A_π in the preceding state. In a concurrent or distributed program, a history is the sequence of states that results from interleaving the atomic actions of processes as they are executed.

An atomic action α defines a set of pairs of program states. Execution of α is *enabled* in a state s, denoted $enabled(\alpha, s)$, provided $(\exists\ t\colon \langle s, t\rangle \in \alpha)$. The statement

$$\langle \mathbf{if}\ b \rightarrow S\ \mathbf{fi}\rangle$$

specifies an atomic action containing those elements $\langle s, t\rangle$ such that b holds on s and t is the state produced by executing S starting in state s.

Rather than enumerating the atomic actions of a program directly, it is frequently convenient to annotate a program with control points that delimit its atomic actions. We will denote control points by marking and numbering them. For example, program fragment of process π

$$\ldots\ \{3{:}\}\ \ S\ \ \{4{:}\}\ \ldots$$

defines a single atomic action

$$\langle \mathbf{if}\ pc_\pi = 3 \rightarrow pc_\pi := 4;\ S\ \mathbf{fi}\rangle$$

where pc_π simulates the program counter.

All histories are assumed to be infinite. One way to achieve this is by including in A_π an atomic action that has no effect on the program state and is enabled when no other atomic action is. Thus, terminating executions are extended to infinite histories by repeating the final state.

An example program *MEP* is shown in Figure 2.1. It is a solution to the two-process critical section problem described in [Peterson 81]. Based on the control point annotations, we obtain set of atomic actions A_{MEP} of Figure 2.2. In those atomic actions, variable pc_A simulates the program counter for process A and variable pc_B simulates the program counter for process B. Finally, we have

$$Init_{MEP}\colon\ pc_A = 1 \wedge pc_B = 1$$

because when execution is begun, both processes start at the the beginning of their loops.

```
MEP: cobegin
  A :: do true → {1: } ncs_A;
                 {2: } active_A := true;
                 {3: } turn := B;
                 {4: } do active_B ∧ turn=B → {5: } skip
                       od;
                 {6: } cs_A;
                 {7: } active_A := false
       od
  //
  B :: do true → {1: } ncs_B;
                 {2: } active_B := true;
                 {3: } turn := A;
                 {4: } do active_A ∧ turn=A → {5: } skip
                       od;
                 {6: } cs_B;
                 {7: } active_B := false
       od
  coend
```

Figure 2.1. Peterson's Mutual Exclusion Protocol

$$
\begin{aligned}
A_{MEP} = \{ & \alpha_1^A\colon \langle \mathbf{if}\ pc_A = 1 \rightarrow pc_A := 2;\ ncs_A\ \mathbf{fi}\rangle,\\
& \alpha_2^A\colon \langle \mathbf{if}\ pc_A = 2 \rightarrow pc_A,\ active_A := 3,\ true\ \mathbf{fi}\rangle,\\
& \alpha_3^A\colon \langle \mathbf{if}\ pc_A = 3 \rightarrow pc_A,\ turn := 4,\ B\ \mathbf{fi}\rangle,\\
& \alpha_4^A\colon \langle \mathbf{if}\ pc_A = 4 \wedge active_B \wedge turn = B\\
& \qquad \rightarrow pc_A := 5\ \mathbf{fi}\rangle,\\
& \alpha_5^A\colon \langle \mathbf{if}\ pc_A = 4 \wedge \neg(active_B \wedge turn = B)\\
& \qquad \rightarrow pc_A := 6\ \mathbf{fi}\rangle,\\
& \alpha_6^A\colon \langle \mathbf{if}\ pc_A = 5 \rightarrow pc_A := 4\ \mathbf{fi}\rangle,\\
& \alpha_7^A\colon \langle \mathbf{if}\ pc_A = 6 \rightarrow pc_A := 7;\ cs_A\ \mathbf{fi}\rangle,\\
& \alpha_8^A\colon \langle \mathbf{if}\ pc_A = 7 \rightarrow pc_A,\ active_A := 1,\ false\ \mathbf{fi}\rangle,\\
& \alpha_1^B\colon \langle \mathbf{if}\ pc_B = 1 \rightarrow pc_B := 2;\ ncs_B\ \mathbf{fi}\rangle,\\
& \alpha_2^B\colon \langle \mathbf{if}\ pc_B = 2 \rightarrow pc_B,\ active_B := 3,\ true\ \mathbf{fi}\rangle,\\
& \alpha_3^B\colon \langle \mathbf{if}\ pc_B = 3 \rightarrow pc_B,\ turn := 4,\ A\ \mathbf{fi}\rangle,\\
& \alpha_4^B\colon \langle \mathbf{if}\ pc_B = 4 \wedge active_A \wedge turn = A\\
& \qquad \rightarrow pc_B := 5\ \mathbf{fi}\rangle,\\
& \alpha_5^B\colon \langle \mathbf{if}\ pc_B = 4 \wedge \neg(active_A \wedge turn = A)\\
& \qquad \rightarrow pc_B := 6\ \mathbf{fi}\rangle,\\
& \alpha_6^B\colon \langle \mathbf{if}\ pc_B = 5 \rightarrow pc_B := 4\ \mathbf{fi}\rangle,\\
& \alpha_7^B\colon \langle \mathbf{if}\ pc_B = 6 \rightarrow pc_B := 7;\ cs_B\ \mathbf{fi}\rangle,\\
& \alpha_8^B\colon \langle \mathbf{if}\ pc_B = 7 \rightarrow pc_B,\ active_B := 1,\ false\ \mathbf{fi}\rangle\}
\end{aligned}
$$

Figure 2.1. Atomic Actions A_{MEP}

3. Specifying Properties using Buchi Automata

A Buchi automaton is a finite state machine that accepts infinite sequences. Since a property of a program can be viewed as defining a set of infinite sequences of program states, a Buchi automaton m can be used to specify the property containing exactly those sequences accepted by m. Mechanical procedures exist to translate linear-time first-order temporal formulas into Buchi automata where state transitions are defined in terms of first-order program state predicates [Wolper et al 83] [Alpern 86]. Moreover, Buchi automata have natural diagrammatic representations and this is sometimes convenient.

Figure 3.1 is an example of a Buchi automaton m_{ae}. It accepts an infinite sequence in which after a finite prefix each state satisfies the program state predicate P. In temporal logic, this property is given by $\Diamond\Box P$. Automaton m_{ae} contains three *automaton states* labeled q_0, q_1, and q_2. The *start state*, q_0, is denoted by an edge with no origin, and *accepting state*, q_1, is denoted by two concentric circles. A Buchi automaton accepts a sequence σ if and only if it enters an accepting state infinitely often while reading σ. Notice, there is no way in m_{ae} to get from q_2 to an accepting state. Such states are called *dead states*. If an automaton is in a dead state, it cannot accept its input.

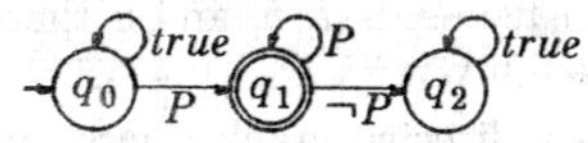

Figure 3.1. m_{ae}

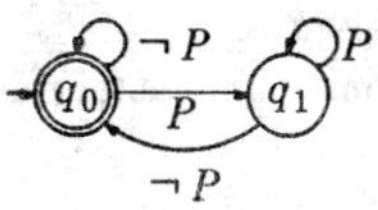

Figure 3.2. m_{io}

Edges between automaton states are labeled by program-state predicates that are called *transition predicates* and define transitions between automaton states. If a program state satisfies the transition predicate on an edge then that edge is defined for that program state. For example, because there is an edge labeled P from q_0 to q_1 in m_{ae}, whenever m_{ae} is in q_0 and the next symbol read is a program state satisfying P, then a transition to q_1 can be made. We adopt the convention that there be an edge defined from each automaton state for each input symbol.

In order to define Buchi automata formally, the following notation will be useful. For any sequence $\sigma = s_0 s_1 \ldots$,

$\sigma[i] \equiv s_i$,
$\sigma[..i] \equiv s_0 s_1 \ldots s_{i-1}$,
$\sigma[i..] \equiv s_i s_{i+1} \ldots$,
$|\sigma| \equiv$ the length of σ (ω if σ is infinite),
$INF(\sigma) \equiv \{s | s$ appears infinitely often in $\sigma\}$.

A Buchi automaton m for a property of a program π is a five-tuple $\langle S_\pi, Q, Q_0, A, \delta \rangle$, where

S_π is the (countable) set of program states of π,
Q is the (finite) set of automaton states of m,
$Q_0 \subseteq Q$ is the set of start states of m,
$A \subseteq Q$ is the set of accepting states of m,
$\delta \in (Q \times S) \rightarrow 2^Q - \varnothing$ is the *transition function* of m.

Transition predicate T_{ij} associated with the edge from automaton state q_i to q_j, holds for a program state s if and only if $q_j \in \delta(q_i, s)$. (Although S_π may be infinite, we only consider properties for which the transition predicates have finite description as a first-order formula involving program variables.) Transition function δ can be extended to handle finite sequences of program states in the usual way:

$$\delta^*(q, \sigma) \equiv \begin{cases} \{q\} & \text{if } |\sigma| = 0 \\ \{q' \mid \exists q'': q'' \in \delta^*(q, \sigma[..|\sigma|-1]): \\ \quad q' \in \delta(q'', \sigma[|\sigma|-1])\} & \text{if } 0 < |\sigma| < \omega \end{cases}$$

A sequence of automaton states that m might occupy while reading σ is called a *run*. Thus, ρ is a run of m on σ if and only if

$$\rho[0] \in Q_0 \text{ and } (\forall i: 0 < i < |\sigma|: \rho[i] \in \delta(\rho[i-1], \sigma[i-1])).$$

A Buchi automaton m accepts a sequence σ if and only if there is a run ρ of m on σ for which $INF(\rho) \cap A \neq \varnothing$.

Notice in m_{ae} (Figure 3.1) that two transitions are possible from q_0 for a program state satisfying P, because any program state that satisfies P also satisfies *true*. When there is more than one start state or more than one transition is possible from some automaton state for a given input symbol, the automaton is *non-deterministic*; otherwise, it is *deterministic*. Thus, m_{ae} is non-deterministic. However, $L(m_{ae})$ the language accepted by m_{ae} is the negation of the deterministic property $\Box\Diamond\neg P$ accepted by m_{io} of Figure 3.2.

4. Proof Instruments from Buchi Automata

Let property P be the conjunction of clauses $P_1, P_2, \ldots P_m$. To prove that a program π satisfies P, we prove separately that π satisfies each of the clauses. Thus, it suffices to derive proof instruments for a single clause P_i of the form

$$D_1 \vee \ldots \vee D_p \vee \neg D_{p+1} \vee \ldots \vee \neg D_{p+n},$$

where each D_k is specified by m_k, a deterministic Buchi automaton. Any property that can be specified by a non-deterministic Buchi automaton can be put in this form [Eilenberg 74]. We call m_1 through m_p the *positive automata* of P_i and m_{p+1} through m_{p+n} the *negative automata*. Let m_k be defined by $\langle S_\pi, Q_k, \{q_{k0}\}, A_k, \delta_k \rangle$.

To formulate proof instruments for π and P_i, define a *joint state* x to be an element of $JS(P_i, \pi)$ the *joint state space*, $Q_1 \times \cdots \times Q_{p+n} \times S_\pi$. Let $x^{(k)}$ denote the kth element of a joint state x and let $x^{(\pi)}$ abbreviate $x^{(p+n+1)}$. A joint state x is *positive*, denoted $Pos(x)$, iff for some positive automata m_j, $x^{(j)} \in A_j$. Thus, x is positive if one of m_1 through m_p is in an accepting state. The set of negative automata that are in an accepting state in a joint state x is $neg(x) = \{k \mid p < k \leq p+n \wedge x^{(k)} \in A_k\}$. For ρ a sequence of joint states, define $\rho^{(k)}$ to be the projection of ρ onto its kth element; i.e. $\rho^{(k)} = \rho[0]^{(k)} \rho[1]^{(k)} \ldots$. A sequence of joint states ρ is a *joint history* of π and P iff $\rho^{(\pi)}$ is a history of π and for all $1 \leq k \leq p+n$, $\rho^{(k)}$ is a run of m_k on $\rho^{(\pi)}$.

A program π satisfies the property specified by a clause P_i iff each history σ of π is either accepted by one of the positive automata—and therefore satisfies one of the properties D_1 through D_p—or is rejected by one of the negative automata—and therefore satisfies one of $\neg D_{p+1}$ through $\neg D_{p+n}$. Thus, π satisfies P_i iff for every history σ there is a joint history ρ such that $\sigma = \rho^{(\pi)}$ and either (i) there is a positive automata m_j, such that $INF(\rho^{(j)}) \cap A_j \neq \varnothing$ or (ii) there is a negative automata m_k such that $INF(\rho^{(k)}) \cap A_k = \varnothing$.

To prove that π satisfies the property specified by a clause P_i, three proof instruments must be exhibited:

- an *invariant* $I \subseteq JS(P_i, \pi)$,
- a *candidate function* $u: JS(P_i, \pi) \rightarrow 2^{[p+1..p+n]}$, and
- a *variant function* $v: JS(P_i, \pi) \rightarrow W$, where W is a well-founded set.

The invariant relates program states in a history to automaton states occupied while reading that history. The candidate function identifies negative automata that might never again enter an accepting state. And, the variant function bounds the number of times that the candidate function can become empty before one of the positive automata enters an accepting state.

If the invariant, candidate function, and variant function satisfy the following obligations, then π will satisfy P_i. In these obligations, x and x' denote elements of $JS(P_i, \pi)$.

The first two obligations ensure that I holds throughout any joint history.

O1: If $x = \rho[0]$ for some joint history of π and P_i then $x \in I$.

O2: If $x \in I$ and $\langle x^{(\pi)}, x'^{(\pi)} \rangle \in \alpha$ then $x' \in I$.

O1 constitutes the base case and O2 an induction step for an argument that execution of each atomic action produces a joint state in I. Choosing an invariant I permits unreachable joint states to be ignored in the obligations that follow.

The next obligation requires that a variant function v increase only in or immediately after processing a joint state in which a positive automata is in an accepting state.

O3: If $x \in I$ and $\langle x^{(\pi)}, x'^{(\pi)} \rangle \in \alpha$ then $Pos(x) \vee Pos(x') \vee v(x) \leq v(x')$.

Thus, O3 ensures that either (i) some positive automaton enters an accepting state infinitely often (and the history is accepted) or (ii) after some point v never increases and no positive automaton subsequently enters an accepting state.

Since the range of v is a well-founded set, if v never increases then eventually its value must become constant. The next obligation implies that under these circumstances, throughout the rest of the history, the candidate function is a non-empty set and contains the index of some negative automaton m_k.

O4: If $x \in I$ and $\langle x^{(\pi)}, x'^{(\pi)} \rangle \in \alpha$ then $Pos(x) \vee Pos(x') \vee v(x) < v(x') \vee \emptyset \subset u(x') \subseteq u(x)$.

The final obligation ensures that a negative automata that enters an accepting state cannot be a candidate unless a positive state is entered or the variant function decreases. Thus, if no positive state is entered and the variant function does not decrease then m_k does not enter an accepting state for the remainder of the history, hence it rejects the history.

O5: If $x \in I$ and $\langle x^{(\pi)}, x'^{(\pi)} \rangle \in \alpha$ then $Pos(x) \vee Pos(x') \vee neg(x') \cap u(x') = \emptyset$.

Since m_k rejects the history, the history satisfies $\neg D_k$ and therefore satisfies P_i.

We can now prove:

Soundness Theorem: If there are proof instruments I, v, and u that satisfy obligations O1 through O5 then π satisfies P_i.

Proof: Let ρ be a joint history of π and P_i. $\rho[0] \in I$ by O1. By O2 and induction, $\rho[j] \in I$ for all $j \geq 0$. We must show that ρ causes some positive automaton to be in an accepting state infinitely often or some negative automaton to be in an accepting state only finitely often. Assume that no positive automaton is in an accepting state infinitely often. Thus, there is an index l_1 such that $\rho[l_1..]$ contains no positive states. By O3, the variant function is non-increasing on $\rho[l_1..]$. Since its range is well-founded, there must be an index l_2 such that $l_1 \leq l_2$ and the variant function is constant on $\rho[l_2..]$. By O4, there is a negated automaton m_k such that $k \in u(\rho[l_2])$. Also by O4, for all $l_2 < j$, $k \in u(\rho[j])$. Therefore, by O5, m_k does not enter an accepting state after l_2. This means that m_k rejects ρ, so π satisfies P_i.

We now show that our technique is relatively complete.

Completeness Theorem: If π satisfies P then there exist proof instruments I, v, and u that satisfy obligations O1 through O5.

Proof: Form a directed graph where the nodes are the joint states appearing in joint histories and there is an edge from node x to y iff y is not a positive accepting state and x immediately precedes y in some joint history. Define partial order $\gg$ on the nodes of this graph such that $x \gg y$ iff there is a path with non-zero length from x to y and somewhere on this path appears an accepting state for each negative automaton.

Partial order $\gg$ is well-founded, as is shown by the following proof by contradiction. If $\gg$ were not well-founded then there would be an infinite descending chain $x_1 \gg x_2 ....$ By construction of the graph, this implies the existence of a joint history that includes x_1. Let σ_0 be a prefix of such a joint history that ends with x_1. For each x_i in the infinite descending chain, let σ_i be the path from x_i to x_{i+1} that includes an accepting state for every negative automaton. Such a path exists by definition, because $x_i \gg x_{i+1}$. Finally, let σ be $\sigma_0 \sigma_1 ....$ Notice that σ is a joint history, that σ contains no positive accepting states after σ_0, and that there are infinitely many accepting states for each negative automaton in σ. Thus, σ does not satisfy P. This is a contradiction, and we conclude that $\gg$ is well-founded.

Since $\gg$ is well-founded, the following recursive function is well defined:

$$H(x) = \sup_{x \gg y} \{H(y)+1\}.$$

H is a function from the joint state space to the ordinals. If there is no y such that $x \gg y$ then $H(x)=0$ by definition of *sup*, so the function is total. Notice that if $x \gg y$ then $H(x) > H(y)$. Moreover, if there is any path from x to y in the graph then $H(x) \geq H(y)$.

The variant function will be constructed using H and the *level* $l(x)$ of a node x, defined as follows. Level $l(x) = i$ iff for any collection of i and no more than i negative automata, there exists some node w with $H(w)=H(x)$ such that there is a path to x to w and there is an accepting state for each automaton in the collection somewhere on the path. Note that by definition of H, the level of a node will be less than n.

The three proof instruments can now be defined. Choose I to be the characteristic predicate for the set of joint states that appear in joint histories of π and P_i. Choose $v(x)$ to be $\langle H(x), n-l(x) \rangle$. The range of v with lexicographic ordering of pairs as the ordering relation is well-founded because the ordinals are. Finally, choose $u(x)$ to be the set of negative automata that do not have accepting states on any path from w to x for any $w \neq x$ such that $v(w)=v(x)$.

Proof obligations O1 and O2 follow immediately from the definition of I.

To see that O3 holds, notice that if neither x nor x' is positive then there is a path (of length 1) from x to x' in the graph. Thus, $H(x) \geq H(x')$. Suppose $H(x)=H(x')$. Since any path to x can be extended to x', $l(x) \leq l(x')$. Therefore, $v(x) \geq v(x')$.

To see that O4 holds, suppose that neither x nor x' is positive and that $v(x)=v(x')$. By construction of v, both x and x' must be at the same level. By the construction of u, $u(x') \subset u(x)$, since there is a path (of length 1) from x to x'. Also by construction of u, $u(x') \neq \varnothing$.

If there exists a node w such that $v(w)=v(x')$ and there is a path from w to x' then $neg(x') \cap u(x') = \varnothing$ since x' is (trivially) included on the path to x'. If there is no such w then $v(x) > v(x')$. So, O5 holds. This completes the proof.

Obligations O1 through O5 can be translated into verification conditions formulated as Hoare triples and first-order predicate logic formulas. A Hoare triple $\{P\}\ \alpha\ \{Q\}$ for an atomic action α asserts that any execution of α started in a state satisfying P terminates in a state satisfying Q.[3] Thus, $\{P\}\ \alpha\ \{Q\}$ is valid iff $(\forall \langle s,t \rangle: \langle s,t \rangle \in \alpha: P(s) \Rightarrow Q(t))$.

To reformulate O1 through O5 in terms of Hoare triples, we define slight variations of the three proof instruments. Define $PJS(P_i)$ the projection of $JS(P_i, \pi)$ with respect to program states as $PJS(P_i) = Q_1 \times \cdots \times Q_{p+n}$. Elements of $PJS(P_i)$ are called *projected joint states*. The projected joint state in which every automaton is in its start state is called the *projected joint start state*. A projected joint state y is considered *positive* if it is the projection of a positive state. (Similarly, if y is a projection of joint state x then define $neg(y) = neg(x)$.) We now define projections of the three proof instruments with respect to projected joint states. For an invariant I, I_y is the projection of I with respect to a projected joint state y; i.e., $I_y = \{s \mid s \in S_\pi \wedge y \times s \in I\}$. For a variant function v, projection v_y is a function from S_π to W such that $v(y, s) = v_y(s)$ for $s \in S_\pi$. And, for a candidate function u, define u_y such that $u(y, s) = u_y(s)$ for $s \in S_\pi$.

Finally, we define a *projected joint state transition predicate* T_{yz} to be a predicate that holds for any program state causing a transition from a projected joint state y to a projected joint state z. T_{yz} can be formed by taking the conjunction for all m_i of the transition predicates labeling the edge from $y^{(i)}$ to $z^{(i)}$. T_{0z} is the projected joint state transition predicate from the joint start state to z.

Verifying each of the following formulas implies that O1 through O5 hold. The first verification condition implies O1.

VC1: $(Init_\pi \wedge T_{0z}) \Rightarrow I_z$

The next implies O2 through O5.

VC2: For all projected joint states y and z and atomic actions $\alpha \in A_\pi$:

(i) If y or z is positive then $\{I_y\}\ \alpha\ \{T_{yz} \Rightarrow I_z\}$.

(ii) Otherwise,

$$\{I_y \wedge v_y = \mathrm{V} \wedge u_y = \mathrm{U}\}$$
$$\alpha$$
$$\{T_{yz} \Rightarrow (I_z \wedge (v_z < \mathrm{V} \vee (v_z = \mathrm{V} \wedge \varnothing \subset u_z \subseteq \mathrm{U} - neg(z))))\}$$

O2 is implied by $T_{yz} \Rightarrow I_z$ in the postcondition of VC2(i) and VC2(ii). To see that O3, O4, and O5 follow from VC1 and VC2, choose

$$x = \langle y, s \rangle \text{ and } x' = \langle z, s' \rangle$$

and assume $x \in I$ and $\langle s, s' \rangle \in \alpha$. It follows immediately from O2 that $x' \in I$. We conclude that s' satisfies T_{yz} directly from the definition of T_{yz}. If y or z is positive, then O3, O4, and O5 are trivially satisfied. Suppose neither y nor z is positive and let $v(x) = \mathrm{V}$ and $u(x) = \mathrm{U}$. From the postcondition of VC2(ii), it follows that either $v(x') < \mathrm{V}$ or $v(x') = \mathrm{V}$. Thus, O3 holds. If $v(x') < \mathrm{V}$ does not hold then, from the postcondition of VC2(ii), $\varnothing \subset u(x') \subseteq \mathrm{U}$ and $u(x') \subseteq \mathrm{U} - neg(x')$. Thus, O4 and O5 hold.

Conversely, assume O1 through O5 hold. VC1 follows from O1. From O2 we get

$$\{I_y\}\ \alpha\ \{T_{yz} \Rightarrow I_z\}.$$

Thus, VC2(i) holds. Assume that neither y nor z is positive. From O3 we get

$$\{I_y \wedge v_y = \mathrm{V}\}\ \alpha\ \{T_{yz} \Rightarrow v_z \leq \mathrm{V}\}.$$

From O4 we get

$$\{I_y \wedge v_y = \mathrm{V} \wedge u_y = \mathrm{U}\}\ \alpha\ \{T_{yz} \Rightarrow (v_z < \mathrm{V} \vee \varnothing \subset u_z \subseteq \mathrm{U})\}.$$

Finally, from O5 we get

$$\{I_y \wedge v_y = \mathrm{V} \wedge u_y = \mathrm{U}\}\ \alpha\ \{T_{yz} \Rightarrow (v_z < \mathrm{V} \vee u_z \subseteq \mathrm{U} - neg(z)\}.$$

Together, these four Hoare triples imply VC2(ii).

We have shown that obligations O1 through O5 are equivalent to verifivation conditions VC1 and VC2. If the underlying first-order predicate logic is expressive enough to capture the preconditions and postconditions of the Hoare triples of VC2 then the verification conditions can be expressed in this logic. Since Hoare Logic is semantically complete relative to the completeness of the underlying first-order predicate logic [Apt 81], our proof technique is complete relative to the semantic and expressive completeness of this logic.

5. Example: Proving Non-Starvation Assuming Fairness

In addition to mutual exclusion, a solution to the critical section problem should ensure that processes attempting entry to critical sections actually do enter eventually. A process of *MEP* (Figure 2.1) is said to *starve* if it trys to enter its critical section but never succeeds. To formalize this, let pc_A (pc_B) be a variable containing the value of the program counter for process A (B). Process A of *MEP* should eventually enter cs_A whenever

$$TRY_A:\ pc_A = 4 \vee pc_A = 5$$

holds, and similarly process B should eventually enter cs_B whenever

$$TRY_B:\ pc_B = 4 \vee pc_B = 5$$

holds. The Non-Starvation Property NS_{MEP} asserts that neither process starves. This can be formalized in temporal logic as

$$NS_{MEP}:\ (\Box\Diamond\neg TRY_A) \wedge (\Box\Diamond\neg TRY_B).$$

It is easy to see that *MEP* does not satisfy NS_{MEP} for histories in which one or the other process is not given sufficient opportunity to execute. A *fairness assumption* asserts that an atomic action that is enabled "often enough" will be executed eventually. Let F_α be a fairness assumption for atomic action α.[4] A fairness assumption for a program π is the conjunction of fairness assumptions—one for each atomic action in A_π. Thus, F_{MEP} the fairness assumption for *MEP* is defined by

[3]Since α is an atomic action, it *must* terminate once execution commences.

[4]See [Francez 86] for various types of fairness assumptions.

F_{MEP}: $\bigwedge_{\alpha \in A_{MEP}} F_\alpha$.

To show that *MEP* satisfies NS_{MEP} for all histories satisfying F_{MEP}, we must prove that *MEP* satisfies $F_{MEP} \Rightarrow NS_{MEP}$. Putting this property into conjunctive normal form, we get

$$FNS_{MEP}: \ (\bigvee_{\alpha \in A_{MEP}} \neg F_\alpha \ \vee \ \Box\Diamond\neg TRY_A) \wedge (\bigvee_{\alpha \in A_{MEP}} \neg F_\alpha \ \vee \ \Box\Diamond\neg TRY_B)$$

Each of the two clauses (conjuncts) in FNS_{MEP} is proved separately. However, since the two clauses are symmetric, only the first one is proved here; the proof of the second is similar.

As a fairness assumption for atomic actions, we choose *weak fairness*, which asserts that an atomic action that becomes enabled is eventually executed. This is expressed in temporal logic as

$$WF_\alpha: \ \Box\Diamond\neg Before_\alpha.$$

where $Before_\alpha(s)$ is the predicate $(\exists\ t{:}\ \langle s, t\rangle \in \alpha)$. Thus, the first conjunct of FNS_{MEP} property to be proven is

$$FNS^A_{MEP}: \ \bigvee_{\alpha \in A_{MEP}} \neg WF_\alpha \ \vee \ \Box\Diamond\neg TRY_A$$

$$= \ \bigvee_{\alpha \in A_{MEP}} \neg\Box\Diamond\neg Before_\alpha \ \vee \ \Box\Diamond\neg TRY_A$$

This clause contains seventeen disjuncts because $|A_{MEP}| = 16$; all but one of these disjuncts is negated. Each disjunct is of the form $\Box\Diamond\neg P$, so the Buchi automaton specification for each literal is m_{io} of Figure 3.2.

To prove that FNS^A_{MEP} holds we use the following proof instruments.

$$I \ = \ JS(FNS^A_{MEP}, MEP)$$

$$v \ = \ \begin{cases} 0 & \neg TRY_A \\ pc_A - 3 & TRY_A \wedge TRY_B \wedge turn{=}A \\ 2+(4-pc_B) \bmod 7 & TRY_A \wedge \neg TRY_B \\ 7+pc_B-3 & TRY_A \wedge TRY_B \wedge turn{=}B \end{cases}$$

$$u \ = \ \begin{cases} \varnothing & \neg TRY_A \\ \{i \mid enbl(\alpha^A_i)\} & TRY_A \wedge TRY_B \wedge turn{=}A \\ \{i \mid enbl(\alpha^B_i)\} & TRY_A \wedge \neg TRY_B \\ \{i \mid enbl(\alpha^B_i)\} & TRY_A \wedge TRY_B \wedge turn{=}B \end{cases}$$

where $enbl(\alpha)$ holds in any program state s where atomic action α is enalbed (i.e., $enabled(\alpha, s)$).

Rather than checking that verification conditions VC1 and VC2 hold, we argue (informally) that obligations O1–O5 are satisfied by this choice of proof instruments.

Clearly, O1 and O2 are satisfied by the choice of invariant, since the invariant rules out no joint state.

O3 follows from the construction of the variant function, as follows. When $\neg TRY_A$, $v{=}0$, but an automaton for a positive disjunct is in an accepting state, so O3 is satisfied in that case. If $TRY_A \wedge TRY_B \wedge turn{=}A$, then v is the number of atomic actions that A must execute before entering cs_A. Since $turn{=}A$, subsequent execution by B does not alter this value. If $TRY_A \wedge \neg TRY_B$ then v includes the number of atomic actions B must execute to establish the previous case $(TRY_A \wedge TRY_B \wedge turn{=}A)$. Clearly, execution by A does not alter this value. Finally, when $TRY_A \wedge TRY_B \wedge turn{=}B$, then v is the maximum value of v in the preceding case $(TRY_A \wedge \neg TRY_B)$ plus the number of atomic actions that B must execute to make $TRY_A \wedge \neg TRY_B$ hold.

O4 follows from the construction of the candidate function, which always contains the index of the automaton corresponding the fairness assumption for the atomic action that will reduce v.

O5 holds because m_{io} for an enabled atomic action is not in an accepting state.

Note that this proof is an instance of the method of helpful directions for weak fairness [Francez 86]. Each process corresponds to a direction. Execution of an enabled atomic action in the helpful direction decreases the variant function. Execution of an enabled atomic action in some other direction does not increase the variant function nor does it disable a helpful atomic action. Thus, when $TRY_A \wedge TRY_B \wedge turn{=}A$, the helpful direction is process A; when $TRY_A \wedge \neg TRY_B$ or $TRY_A \wedge TRY_B \wedge turn{=}B$ the helpful direction is process B. The weak fairness assumption guarantees that the variant function decreases eventually.

The method of helpful directions is a special case (for proving properties that assume weak fairness) of the technique developed in this paper. To see this observe that the candidate function identifies the helpful directions. The stipulation that execution of a helpful atomic action decrease the variant function guarantees O5. The stipulation that a non-helpful atomic action not increase the variant function guarantees O3. And, the stipulation that a non-helpful atomic action leave a helpful one enabled guarantees O4.

6. Discussion

Formulated in the terminology of this paper, our previous method ([Alpern & Schneider 85]) for extracting proof obligations from a deterministic Buchi automaton requires the program prover to exhibit an invariant I and a variant function v satisfying:

AS1: If x is the first state of a joint history then $x \in I$.

AS2: If $x \in I$ and $\langle x^{(\pi)}, x'^{(\pi)}\rangle \in \alpha$ then $x' \in I$.

AS3: If $x \in I$ and $\langle x^{(\pi)}, x'^{(\pi)}\rangle \in \alpha$ then $Pos(x) \vee Pos(x') \vee v(x') < v(x)$.

AS1 and AS2 are obligations O1 and O2 of the approach outlined in Section 4. Consider the remaining obligations (O3 through O5) of that approach. The deterministic property is a single clause that consists of a single, non-negated property, so there are no negative automata. Thus, $u(x) = \varnothing$ for every joint state x and O5 is trivially satisfied because its final disjunct is. Moreover, the final disjunct of O4 must be false. AS3 and O4 are therefore equivalent, and each implies O3. Thus, the two techniques yield essentially the same proof obligations when applied to a deterministic property.

The method in [Alpern & Schneider 85] is unsatisfactory for properties specified by non-deterministic Buchi automata. To use it to prove that a program π satisfies such a property P, a deterministic property D that is contained in P is found. Proof obligations are then extracted from the deterministic Buchi automata for D. If a (finite-state) program π satisfies P, an appropriate D always exists but may be big and difficult to find. Furthermore, the proof obligations for a non-deterministic property now depend on the program as well as on the Buchi automata for the property to be proved. The approach of Section 4 does not suffer from these difficulties. Since every property that can be specified using a non-deterministic Buchi automata can be specified as a Boolean combination of deterministic properties [Eilenberg 74] and we can now handle such Boolean combinations, our new technique is general enough to prove non-deterministic as well as deterministic properties.

In [Manna & Pnueli 87], a different technique is given for obtaining proof obligations for non-deterministic properties. The approach is based upon a ∀-automaton for a property. Simplifying slightly,[5] a ∀-automaton is a Buchi automaton that accepts its input iff every run on that input eventually is restricted to accepting states. Using the parlance of Section 4, to show that every history of a program will be accepted by a ∀-automaton M, one must exhibit an invariant I that satisfies obligations O1 and O2 and a variant function v satisfying:

MP1: If $x \in I$, $\langle x^{(\pi)}, x'^{(\pi)} \rangle \in \alpha$, and $x'^{(1)}$ is an accepting state of M then $v(x') \leq v(x)$.

MP2: If $x \in I$, $\langle x^{(\pi)}, x'^{(\pi)} \rangle \in \alpha$, and $x'^{(1)}$ is a non-accepting state of M then $v(x') < v(x)$.

The ∀-automaton for a property is isomorphic to the Buchi automaton for the negation of that property.[6] This suggests there might be a connection between the proof obligations that are obtained from a ∀-automaton for the negation of a deterministic property and the proof obligations we obtain for a clause with a single negated property. And, there is. Since there are no positive joint states with a single negated property, O3 implies MP1, and MP1 and MP2 imply O3. O5 requires that the candidate function be empty whenever the Buchi automaton (∀-automaton) enters an accepting (non-accepting) state. Thus, we can choose the candidate function such that O4 and MP2 are equivalent—define u to be empty whenever the Buchi automata is in an accepting state and to be $\{1\}$ when it is not. Therefore, the two techniques yield the same proof obligations for a property whose negation is deterministic.

The key insight underlying the approach of [Manna & Pnueli 87] is that proof obligations for the negation of a property can be extracted directly from a Buchi automaton for the property—whether or not this automaton is deterministic. Given a property specified by a Buchi automata, to extract proof obligations using the approach of [Manna & Pnueli 87], the Buchi automata for the negation of the property is constructed. With the technique presented in this paper, the property is decomposed into a Boolean combination of properties where the non-negated terms must be specified by deterministic Buchi automata. Depending on the property, one or the other approach may be easier.

[5]We are ignoring the behavior of ∀-automata on finite sequences, the placement of transition predicates in states rather than on edges, and ∀-automata with recurrant states (which are shown to be equivalent ∀-automaton without such states in [Manna & Pnueli 87]).

[6]To obtain a ∀-automaton for P from a Buchi automaton for $\neg P$, exchange the accepting and non-accepting states.

An added advantage of the Boolean decomposition approach is that parts of the proof may be reusable since other properties might be constructed from these parts.

Acknowledgments

Discussions with Starvos Cosmadakis and Sheryl Brady were helpful, especially in formulating the completeness proof.

References

[Alpern 86] Alpern, B. Proving Temporal Properties of Concurrent Programs: A Non-Temporal Approach. Ph.D. Thesis. Department of Computer Science, Cornell University. January 1986.

[Alpern & Schneider 85] Alpern, B. and F.B. Schneider. Verifying Temporal Properties without using Temporal Logic. Submitted for publication. Also available as Technical Report TR 85-723, Department of Computer Science, Cornell University, Dec. 1985.

[Apt 81] Apt, K.R. Ten years of Hoare's logic: A survey. *ACM TOPLAS 3*, 4 (Oct. 1981), 431-483.

[Eilenberg 74] Eilenberg, S. *Automata, Languages and Machines, Vol A.* Academic Press, New York, 1974.

[Francez 86] Francez, N. *Fairness.* Lecture Notes in Computer Science, Springer-Verlag, Berlin, 1986.

[Hoare 69] Hoare, C.A.R. An axiomatic basis for computer programming. *Commun. ACM 12*, 10 (Oct. 1969) 576-580.

[Manna & Pnueli 81] Manna, Z. and A. Pnueli. Verification of concurrent programs: The temporal framework. *The Correctness Problem in Computer Science* (R.S. Boyer and J.S. Moore, eds.), International Lecture Series in Computer Science, Academic Press, London, 1981, 141-154.

[Manna & Pnueli 84] Manna, Z. and A. Pnueli. Adequate proof principles for invariance and liveness properties of concurrent programs. *Science of Computer Programming 4* (1984), 257-289.

[Manna & Pnueli 87] Manna, Z. and A. Pnueli. Specification and Verification of Concurrent Programs by ∀-Automata. *Proc. 14th Sym. Principles of Programming Languages*, ACM, Munich, Jan. 1987, 1-12.

[Owicki & Lamport 82] Owicki, S.S. and L. Lamport. Proving liveness properties of concurrent programs. *ACM TOPLAS 4*, 3 (July 1982), 455-496.

[Peterson 81] Peterson, G.L. Myths about the mutual exclusion problem. *Information Processing Letters 12*, 3 (June 1981), 115-116.

[Sistla et al 85] Sistla A.P., M.Y. Vardi, and P. Wolper. The Complementation Problem for Buchi Automata with Applications to Temporal Logic. *Proc. ICALP 85*, Nafplion, Greece, July 1985.

[Wolper et al 83] Wolper, P., M. Vardi, and A.P. Sistla. Reasoning about infinite computation paths. (Extended abstract). *Proc. Twenty-fourth Annual Symposium on Foundations of Computer Science.* (Tucson, Arizona, Nov. 1983), ACM, New York, 185-194.

Reasoning with Many Processes

A.P.Sistla,
S.M.German

GTE Laboratories Inc., Waltham, Massachusetts

Abstract: We consider the problem of automatically verifying temporal properties of concurrent systems with an arbitrary number of identical finite state CCS processes. We consider two models of concurrent systems. In the first model all processes are identical. For this model we present an efficient decision procedure that checks if every execution of a process satisfies a given specification. This algorithm runs in time polynomial in the size of a process. The second model consists of a unique control process and an arbitrary number of identical user processes. For this model we give a decision procedure to check if all the executions of a process satisfy the given specification. This algorithm runs in time double exponential in the sizes of the control process and the user process. We also prove that the problem of checking if all the fair executions of a process satisfy a given specification, is decidable. Finally, we show how these decision procedures can be used to reason about certain algorithms on networks of processes.

1. Introduction

Automatic verification of finite state concurrent programs has been an active area of research recently. Many different algorithms for checking if a finite state concurrent system meets a specification given in a Temporal Logic have been proposed in literature ([SC],[CES],[LP],[EL],[VW],[MP]). Some of these algorithms have been implemented and have been successfully used to automatically verify concurrent programs and hardware designs. All these algorithms assume that the global behavior of the concurrent system can be modelled by a finite state graph. They first construct the global state graph and verify that it satisfies the given specification. However, there are many concurrent and distributed systems that are designed to operate with an arbitrary number of processes. Clearly, the previous techniques can not be applied to these systems. The problem of extending the previous techniques to networks of many identical processes has been addressed in [CGB]. In this work the authors argue that under certain conditions and for some properties, the correctness of a network with many processes can be inferred from the correctness of the network with two processes. This approach is only partly automatic. In this paper we present, for the first time, fully automatic methods for verifying certain properties of concurrent systems with an arbitrary number of communicating processes. Our methods are complete for verifying a well defined class of properties in certain natural models of computation.

Our specification language is *Propositional Linear Temporal Logic* (PTL). We assume that the concurrent system has an arbitrary number of finite state CCS(or CSP) processes. Given such a system we investigate the problem of checking if all the executions of a process satisfy a specification given in PTL (or given by a finite state automaton on infinite strings). We consider two different models. In the first model we assume that the system contains an arbitrary finite number of identical processes. For this system we show that the set of executions of a single process induced by a computation of the system is exactly the set of strings accepted by a certain finite state automaton on infinite strings. The size of this automaton is linear in the size of the process. We present an algorithm to construct this automaton. This algorithm takes time polynomial in the size of the process. For the given PTL specification f, we construct the automaton $A_{\neg f}$ which accepts exactly the set of strings that satisfy $\neg$f, and check that the intersection of this and the automaton for the process is empty. The whole algorithm runs in time $O(p(n) \cdot 2^{|f|})$ where p(n) is a polynomial in n which is the size of a process. The above procedure can also be used for systems with a fixed number of classes, each class containing an arbitrary number identical processes.

The second model is a generalization of the first one and is computationally stronger. We assume that there is a unique *controller* process and an arbitrary number of *user* processes. The addition of the unique controller process permits some resource allocation methods and network protocols to be defined in this model at certain level of abstraction. For example, the mutual exclusion algorithm on rings considered in [CGB] can be handled in this model. For this model we present an algorithm that checks if the executions of any of the processes satisfy a given specification. The algorithm first constructs a *Vector Addition System with States* (VASS) that captures the behavior of the concurrent system and then checks if the VASS has an infinite path that contains a *final* state occurring infinitely often. This algorithm runs in time double exponential in the size of the processes, triple exponential in the size of the temporal specification. It uses space exponential in the size of the process and double exponential in the size of the specification.

In concurrent systems, many times we are only interested in verifying that the correctness specification is satisfied by all the *fair* computations. This is especially the case for *liveness* properties. For this reason, we consider the problem of checking if all the executions of a process induced by fair computations in the second model satisfy a given specification. We present an algorithm for this problem which uses the decision procedure for the ***reachability problem*** of vector addition systems. We also show that this problem is as hard as the reachability problem for vector addition systems. Another use of the fairness property is to model systems of processes that are connected on a network. For example, we show in section 6 how to model a token passing algorithm on rings. In this algorithm, the only purpose served by the ring is to circulate the token in a fair manner, and so we can formulate this algorithm in our model of computation using a fairness assumption.

Although we consider systems of many processes, the logic we use, PTL, only specifies the properties of the executions of single processes in a system. However, some of the important properties, such as ***mutual exclusion***, are ***global properties*** of the computations. We show that there is a straight-forward way to verify the mutual exclusion property, by verifying certain properties of a single process in a modified system. Thus the algorithms in the paper can also be used to verify certain important global properties.

Finally, we extend PTL by allowing quantifiers over processes. This is a very natural extension of PTL and allows us to specify a wider class of properties of concurrent systems with many processes. This logic is similar to ICTL* considered in [CGB] except that we use linear time logic instead of branching time logic. We show that the validity problem for this extended PTL is EXSPACE-complete. We also show that the the problem of verifying if a system of processes containing a control process satisfies a given specification in the above logic is undecidable.

There has been other work on checking for certain properties in a system of CCS processes. The complexity of checking for lockouts, absence of deadlocks and related properties in systems of finite state CCS processes has been analyzed in ([La],[KS]). It is assumed in these works that the number of processes is fixed.

The paper is organized as follows: Section 2 gives the definitions and the notation used in the paper. Section 3 presents the algorithms for analyzing a system containing many identical processes. Section 4 presents the results for a system containing a control process and many user processes. Section 5 presents the results on the extended logic IPTL. Section 6 shows how we can reason about certain algorithms on networks of identical processes. Section 7 contains the conclusions.

2. Definitions and Notation.

The specification language we use is the Propositional Linear Temporal Logic (PTL). The language of PTL uses a finite set P of atomic propositions, the connectives $\wedge, \vee, \supset, \neg$, the temporal modalities **U**(*until*), **F**(*some time in future*), **G**(*always in the future*). A ***model*** is a pair (t,Φ) where t is an infinite sequence of states drawn from a state set S, and $\Phi: S \rightarrow 2^P$ is a mapping which associates with each state a set of atomic propositions true in that state. An interpretation is a pair (M,i) where M is a model and $i \geq 0$ is an integer. In the usual way, we inductively define when an interpretation satisfies a PTL formula. In some places, we say that an ω-sequence of states t satisfies f if the interpretation (M,0) satisfies f, where $M=(t,\Phi)$ and Φ is understood from the context. Let $t = (t_0,t_1,...)$ be a ω-sequence of states. A segment in t is a finite sequence $(t_i,t_{i+1},...,t_j)$ of identical states such that t_j is distinct from t_{j+1}, and (if $i>0$ then t_{i-1} is distinct from t_i). Let h(t) be the ω-sequence obtained by replacing each segment in t by a single occurrence of the state in the segment. Note that, if t has a suffix which is a repetition of a single state, then this suffix will be retained in h(t) because it is not a segment according to the previous definition. We say that two sequences t,t′ are *equivalent under stuttering* if $h(t)=h(t')$. Let t,t′ be two sequences which are equivalent under stuttering and let $M=(t,\Phi)$, $M'=(t',\Phi)$. Since we are not using the *nexttime* operator, for any formula f in PTL, (M,0) satisfies f iff (M′,0) satisfies f.

A finite state automaton A on infinite strings is 5-tuple (Q,Δ,δ,I,F) where Q is a finite set of automaton states; Δ is a finite set of input symbols; $\delta: Q \times \Delta \rightarrow 2^Q$ is the transition function which given a state and an input symbol specifies the set of possible next states; $I \subseteq Q$ is the set of *initial* states; $F \subseteq Q$ is the set of *final* states. Let $t=(t_0,t_1, ...) \in \Delta^\omega$ be an ω-sequence of input symbols. A *run* of A on t is an ω-sequence $(s_0,s_1,...)$ of the automaton states such that $s_0 \in I$, for $i \geq 0, s_{i+1} \in \delta(t_i)$. A run is said to be an *accepting* run if it has a final state appearing infinitely often. The automaton A is said to *accept* t if there is an accepting run of A on t. For every PTL formula f, there exists an automaton A_f such that the set of sequences accepted by A_f is exactly the set of sequences that satisfy f.

The processes we consider are finite state CCS processes. The communication alphabet Σ is a finite set of symbols with the following property. There is a partition of Σ into the sets Σ^+, Σ^-, $\{\epsilon\}$ where Σ^+ is the set of actions, Σ^- is the set of complements of actions i.e. $\Sigma^- = \{\bar{c}: c \in \Sigma^+\}$, and ϵ indicates an internal move of a process. A process P is triple (S,R,I) where S is a finite set of process states, $R \subseteq S \times S \times \Sigma$ is the set of possible transitions, and $I \subseteq S$ is the set of initial states. If $(s,s',\epsilon) \in R$, then a process in state s can make an internal transition to the state s′ without external communication. If both (s,s',c), $(t,t',\bar{c})$ are in R, then two processes in states s,t can *synchronize* and make transitions simultaneously to states s′,t′ respectively. We assume that for each process P, there is a function $\Phi: S \rightarrow 2^P$ that associates with each state of P a set of atomic propositions true in that state. The size of a process is the sum of the number states and number of transitions.

Consider a system with n processes. A global state σ is an n-tuple $(s_1,s_2,...,s_n)$ where $s_i \in S$ $(1 \leq i \leq n)$. We say that a process p is *enabled* in σ if either there is a possible internal move for the process in its current state, or there exists another process q with which it can synchronize in the global state σ. A computation is a sequence of global states $\sigma_0,\sigma_1,...$ where $\sigma_i = (s_{i,1}, s_{i,2},...,s_{i,n})$ is a global state, $s_{0,1},s_{0,2},...,s_{0,n}$ are all initial states, and σ_{i+1} is obtained from σ_i by either the internal transition of exactly one process or by synchronization of exactly one pair of processes on a common action, and either the sequence is infinite or it is a finite sequence such that no process is enabled in the final state. We call all finite computations as ***deadlocked*** **computations. For most part of the paper, we only consider infinite computations and choose to ignore deadlocked computations. Unless otherwise** stated, a computation always refers to an infinite computations. We say that a computation is ***fair*** if every process that is enabled infinitely often makes transitions infinitely often in the computation.

The execution of a process p induced by the global computation $\sigma_0,\sigma_1,...$ is the ω-sequence $s_{0,p},s_{1,p},...,s_{i,p},...$. Now consider a system of identical processes. Let EXEC = {t : t is an execution of a process induced by a global computation of a system with a finite number of processes.}. Given a formula f in PTL and the description of the process P, the *model-checking* problem is to determine if every element in EXEC satisfies f, i.e. to determine if for all t in EXEC, the interpretation (M,0) satisfies f where $M=(t,\Phi)$. Note that Φ is the function that associates with each state of P a set of atomic propositions which are true in that state. Let EX = {t : there exists a t′ in EXEC such that t is equivalent under stuttering to t′}. We call EX as the expanded set of executions of a process. Since we are not using the nexttime operator in PTL, it is to be noted that every sequence in EXEC satisfies f iff every sequence in EX satisfies f. Let FEXEC = {t: t is an execution of a process induced by a fair infinite global computation in a system with a finite number of processes}. The *model-checking problem under fairness* is the problem of determining if every sequence in FEXEC satisfies f, i.e. to determine if for all t in FEXEC, the interpretation (M,0) satisfies f, where $M = (t, \Phi)$. Let EF = {t: there exists a t′ in FEXEC such that t is equivalent under stuttering to t′ }. It is to be noted that every element of FEXEC satisfies f iff every element of EF satisfies f. The above definitions can be extended to systems with a control process and many user processes.

3. Model Checking for a Family of Identical Processes.

In this section we describe the algorithm for model checking in a system containing an arbitrary number of identical processes. The same algorithm with some modifications can be used for systems with families of identical processes. Consider a system with many identical copies of a CCS process P as defined in the previous section. For technical convenience, we make the following two assumptions about P: there are no self loops in R, i.e. there are no transitions of the form (s,s,c); for any pair of states (s,s′) there is at most one transition of the form (s,s′,c) in R. If P does not meet these assumptions, we can obtain a new process P′ that meets the assumptions, and such that for any formula f, all the executions of P satisfy f iff all the executions of P′ satisfy f. We can obtain P′ as follows: For each transition t = (s,s′,b) of P where $b \in \Sigma$, we add a new state q_t, and introduce an internal transition from s to q_t and the transition (q_t, s', c); We make q_t satisfy the same atomic propositions as s. Clearly, the number states in $P' = n + m$, the number of transitions in $P' = 2m$ where n,m respectively are the number of states, number of transitions of P.

Our strategy is to infer EX, the expanded set of executions of a process without constructing a global state graph. We construct a Buchi automaton A which accepts EX. Then we check that there is no string that satisfies ¬f and that is also accepted by A. The major steps of the model-checking algorithm are as follows:

1. Determine the set of *reachable* states of a process which we call S′. The reachable states are those states which can be reached by a process in some computation of a system with n processes for some $n > 0$.

2. Construct a *Kripke Structure* K from S′ and P. Roughly speaking, K is the restriction of P to the set of reachable states S′. EX, the expanded set of executions of a process is contained in the set of infinite paths of K starting from the initial states. However, every such path need not be an execution of a process.

3. We show that there exists a set E of edges of K such that EX is exactly the set of infinite paths of K that start from an initial state and in which every edge not in E appears only a finite number of times. In this step, the edge set E is determined.

4. Using K and E, construct the Buchi automaton A that accepts the set EX.

5. Build the automaton $A_{\neg f}$ which accepts the set of strings that satisfy ¬f.

6. In the final step, check that there is no string accepted both by A and $A_{\neg f}$.

We will describe the steps of the algorithm in more detail. In the first step the following algorithm is used to compute S′, the set of reachable states of a process: Initially S′ is set to I,the set of initial states of P. Add a new state t to S′ if the following condition is satisfied: Either there is a state $s \in S'$ having an internal transition to t, or there exist $s, s' \in S'$ such that two processes in these states can synchronize causing one of them to make a transition to t.

The above step is repeated until no more new states can be added to S′. Clearly, this procedure takes time proportional to |S|. The following lemma can be proved by induction on the number of iterations of the main step in the above procedure.

LEMMA 3.1: A state s is in S′ iff there is a process which reaches the state s in some computation of a system with n copies of P for some $n>0$. □

Now we briefly sketch the second step of the algorithm which constructs the Kripke structure K. The structure K consists of the set of states S′, a binary relation $R' \subseteq S' \times S'$ which is the set of edges and the function Φ′ that assigns atomic propositions to states. S′ is the set of reachable states obtained in step 1. Φ′ is the restriction of Φ to S′. R′ contains exactly the following set of edges: for each state s in S′, the self loop $(s,s) \in R'$; for $s,t \in S'$, if there is an internal transition from s to t in the process P then the edge (s,t) is in R′; for the states s,s′,t,t′ in S′, if two processes in states s,t can synchronize and make transitions to s′,t′ respectively then the edges (s,s′), (t,t′) are in R′. Since we are not considering fairness, it is possible for a process to remain in a particular state forever. The self loops in R′ model this possibility. They also model the possibility of stuttering in each state.

Let the states in S′ be $q_1,q_2,\ldots,q_m$. A path in K is a sequence of states $(s_0,s_1,\ldots)$ such that for all $i \geq 0$, (s_i,s_{i+1}) is an edge in K. An infinite path is a path which is an infinite sequence of states.

The first part of the following lemma relates the finite executions of a process to the finite paths in K. The second part of the lemma states that there can be an arbitrary large number of processes in each reachable state.

LEMMA 3.2: (a) The set of finite paths in K starting from an initial state is exactly the set of prefixes of elements in EX;

(b) For any given positive integers $n_1,n_2,\ldots,n_m$ there exist integers $N_1,N_2,\ldots,N_m$ such that $N_i \geq n_i$ (for $1 \leq i \leq m$) and there exists a finite global computation at the end of which there are N_i number of processes in state q_i (for $1 \leq i \leq m$).

Proof: Consider any finite execution of a process. From our construction of K, every state in the above execution is in S′ and there is an edge in R′ corresponding to every transition taken by the process. Hence the above execution is a path in K. Again from the construction of K, it can easily be proved that every finite path in K is a finite execution of a process. The second part of the above lemma is easily seen from the fact that we allow any number of processes in any start state. □

Let α be an infinite path in K. We say that an edge (s,s′) appears infinitely often in α if there are infinitely many values of i such that $s_i = s$ and $s_{i+1} = s'$. Let inf(α) be the set of edges that appear infinitely often in α. Let ω-paths(K) be the set of infinite paths in K starting from an initial state. The following lemma states that the expanded set of executions EX of a process is a subset of ω-paths(K). It can easily be proved using lemma 3.2.

LEMMA 3.3: EX ⊆ ω-paths(K). □

There can be sequences in ω-paths(K) which are not in EX. Consider the following example of a process. States s_1,s_5 are the start states.

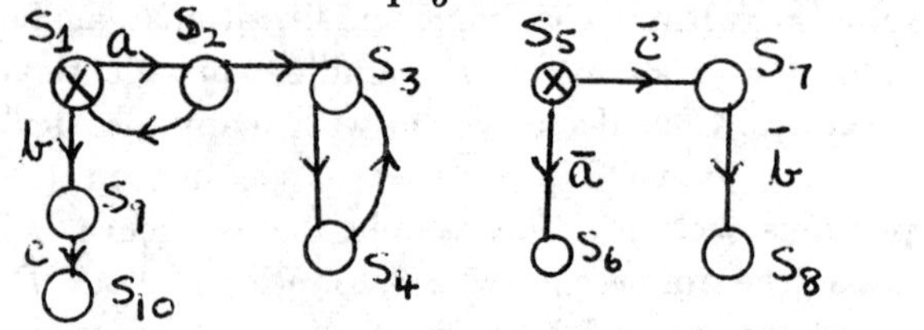

In the above example, it is easily seen that there exists a computation with (n + 2) processes in which $(s_1s_2)^n(s_3s_4)^\omega$ is an execution of a process starting in the initial state s_1. The state graph corresponding to K is shown below. It is to be noted that the path $(s_1s_2)^\omega$ is not an execution of a process.

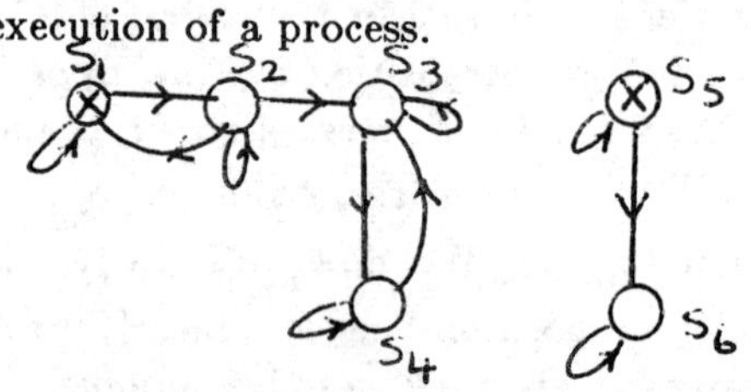

In step 3 of the algorithm, we show that there exists an edge set $E \subseteq R'$ such that $EX = \{\alpha : \alpha \in \omega\text{-paths}(K) \text{ and } \inf(\alpha) \subseteq E\}$.

Now we briefly sketch the algorithm that determines E in the next two paragraphs. This algorithm uses Linear Programming to determine if an edge e is in E. Roughly speaking, we will use Linear Programming to determine if there is a finite global computation that starts and ends in the same global state, and that uses the transition corresponding to the edge e at least once. If there exists such computation then it can be repeated infinitely to get a computation that contains the transition corresponding to e infinitely often.

For any state i in K, let in(i) be the set of edges incident on i, and out(i) be the set of edges leaving i. For any action c, let edges(c) be the set of edges (s,s′) in R′ which are labelled with c in the original process P, that is (s,s′,c) is in R. Similarly, edges($\bar{c}$) be the set of edges labelled with $\bar{c}$. Corresponding to each edge e in K, we have an integer variable n_e. Intuitively, n_e is the number of times the transition corresponding to e is used. We will now set up a a set of linear constraints that ensure the existence of a global computation with the required property.

(A) For each node i, $\sum_{e \in in(i)} n_e = \sum_{e \in out(i)} n_e$. These equations ensure that the total number of transitions entering a node is equal to the total number of transitions leaving a node.

(B) For each action c, $\sum_{e \in edges(c)} n_e = \sum_{e \in edges(\bar{c})} n_e$. These equations ensure that the total number of transitions along edges labelled with c is equal to the total number of transitions along edges labelled with $\bar{c}$.

(C) For each edge e, $n_e \geq 0$.

Let E be the set of all edges e with the property that the above system of equations together with the constraint $n_e > 0$ has a solution. Since this system is a homogeneous system of inequalities, it has an integer solution iff it has a rational solution. Using the polynomial time algorithm for Linear Programming we can determine the set E in time polynomial in the size of K and hence in the size of P.

Next, we will show in theorem 3.5 that EX, the expanded set of executions of a process is exactly the set of infinite paths p in K such that p starts from an initial state and every edge that appears infinitely often in p is in E. We need the following technical lemma in the proof of theorem 3.5.

LEMMA 3.4: For any $s \in S'$, the self loop (s,s) is in E.

Proof: Let f be the edge (s,s) for any $s \in S'$. Let $n_f = 1$ and $n_e = 0$ for $e \neq f$. Clearly, these values satisfy the equations given by (A),(C). Since there are no self loops in the original process P, the above values also satisfy the equations given by (B). Thus every self loop is in E. □

THEOREM 3.5: $EX = \{\alpha : \alpha \in \omega\text{-paths}(K)$ and $inf(\alpha) \subseteq E\}$.

Proof: Let $t = (t_0, t_1, ...) \in EX$. As shown in lemma 3.3, $t \in \omega$-paths(K). We prove below that $inf(t) \subseteq E$. From the definition of EX, it is the case that there exists an $s \in EX$ such that t is equivalent to s under stuttering and s is an execution of a process induced by a global computation. For any edge e which is not a self loop, $e \in inf(t)$ iff $e \in inf(s)$. Now consider a global computation $\sigma_0, \sigma_1, ...$ with n processes which induces the execution s. Let E′ be the set of all edges along which a transition is taken infinitely often in the above global computation. Clearly, certain global states appear infinitely often in the above computation. Let i,j be integers such that $j > i$, $\sigma_i = \sigma_j$, a transition along along every edge in E′ is taken at least once between the instances i,j and these are the only transitions taken between these instances. Clearly such i,j exist. Let n_e be the number of transitions that are taken along e between the instances i,j. Clearly, for $e \in E'$, $n_e > 0$, and for $e \notin E'$, $n_e = 0$. Since, for each node q in K the number of processes in state q in the global state σ_i is same as the number of processes in state q in the global state σ_j the following holds: for each node q in K, the number of transitions between i,j that enter the node q is same as the number of transitions that leave node q. Hence equation (A) is satisfied. For each action c, between i,j, the number of transitions taken along edges labelled with c is same as the number of transitions taken along edges labelled with $\bar{c}$. Hence equation (B) is satisfied. From the above argument, it is clearly seen that

$E' \subseteq E$. Hence $inf(s) \subseteq E$. Since every self loop of K is in E, it follows that $inf(t) \subseteq E$, as required.

Now we would like to prove that if $\alpha \in \omega$-paths(K) and $inf(a) \subseteq E$ then $\alpha \in EX$. We do this by constructing an infinite global computation in which one process, say process 0 has an execution that is equivalent under stuttering to α. Since the system of equations given by (A),(B),(C) is a homogeneous system, and since E is the set of edges e such that there is a solution for (A),(B),(C) with the constraint $n_e > 0$, we see that there is a solution for the system of inequalities given by (A),(B),(C) that simultaneously satisfies the constraints $n_e > 0$ for all $e \in E$. For each node i in K, let $N_i = \sum_{e \in in(i)} n_e$. Consider any global state σ in which there are at least N_i processes in state i. We show that there is a finite global computation β which starts in σ, ends in σ, uses at least one transition along each edge in E, and uses only the transitions along the edges in E. By repeating this finite computation β, we will be able to get a global computation that induces an execution on process 0 which is equivalent under stuttering to α. We start β in the global state σ and in β we make n_e processes make a transition along e for each $e \in E$. We can do so because from equations given by (B), the number of transitions labelled with c is equal to the number of transitions labelled with $\bar{c}$. After the computation β, we will have the same number of processes in each state and it can be repeated infinitely many times.

In the path α, let i be the earliest instance with the property that every edge that is taken beyond the instance i in α is taken infinitely often. We can have a finite global computation γ with the following properties: all processes start in an initial state; at the end of γ there are at least N_i processes in state i; process 0 has an execution in γ which is equivalent under stuttering to $(\alpha_0, \alpha_1, \ldots, \alpha_i)$. Since $inf(\alpha) \subseteq E$ and the computation β has at least one transition along every edge in E, in the global computation obtained by repeating β forever we can make process 0 take an execution that is equivalent under stuttering to $(\alpha_i, \alpha_{i+1}, \ldots)$. Now consider the computation $\gamma\beta^{\omega}$. Clearly, in this computation we can make process 0 take a computation which is equivalent under stuttering to α. From the definition of EX, it follows that $\alpha \in EX$. □

Step 4 of the algorithm uses K and E to construct a finite state Buchi automaton A that operates on infinite strings. The automaton accepts exactly EX. To construct A, another Kripke structure K'' is constructed as follows. K'' consists of K together with another copy of K which is denoted by K'. All those edges not in E are deleted from K', and an edge is introduced from each node of K to the copy of the same node appearing in K'. The construction of A from K'' is fairly straight-forward. The size of A is linear in the size of K and hence is linear in the size of P.

Let f be a PTL formula which is the given correctness specification. In step 5, the Buchi automaton $A_{\neg f}$ which accepts exactly the set of strings that satisfy $\neg f$ is constructed. Now to verify that every execution of a process satisfies f, it is enough to check that there is no string that is accepted by both A and $A_{\neg f}$. In step 6, the techniques of [VW] are used to check for the above condition. This algorithm runs in time $O(|A| \cdot |A_{\neg f}|)$. This completes the entire verification algorithm.

Let n be the size of P. Steps 1 and 2 take time linear in n. In step 3, we have to solve certain Linear Programming Problems. For this we use the polynomial time algorithm for Linear Programming. After a more detailed analysis, it can be shown that this step takes time $O(p(n))$ for certain polynomial $p(n)$. Steps 4 through 6, take time $O(|A| \cdot |A_{\neg f}|)$. Since $|A|$ is proportional to n, and $|A_{\neg f}|$ is proportional to $2^{|f|}$, it can be shown that the above algorithm takes time $O(p(n) + n \cdot 2^{|f|})$ where n is the size of P and p is a polynomial in n.

4. Systems with a Control Process and many User Processes

In this section we consider a generalization of the model analyzed in the previous section. In this model, there is a unique control process and many identical user processes. The addition of the unique control process makes this a more powerful model. We believe that many resource allocation algorithms, network protocols and mutual exclusion algorithms can be handled in this system at a certain level of abstraction. In section 6, we show that the algorithm for mutual exclusion on rings considered in [CGB] can be handled in this model.

4.1 Model-checking without Fairness

We will now describe the decision procedure which is complete for this model. As mentioned in section 2, let Σ be the communication alphabet containing actions, complements of actions, and the special symbol ϵ. Let $C = (S_C, R_C, I_C)$ be the description of the control process and $U = (S_U, R_U, I_U)$ be the description of a user process. Let Φ_C be the function that gives the set of atomic propositions that are true in each state of C. Let Φ_U be the corresponding function for the user process. In this section we give algorithms to determine if the executions of the control process and those of the user processes satisfy a given PTL specification f. First we present the algorithm for the control process C. The same method with a slight modification can be applied to the user processes.

Now we describe the various steps of our algorithm. Let f be the given PTL specification. First, we construct the automaton $A_{\neg f}$ which accepts exactly the set of strings that satisfy $\neg$f. The input symbols for $A_{\neg f}$ are subsets of $\mathcal{P}$ (the set of atomic propositions). Each input symbol of $A_{\neg f}$ specifies which atomic propositions are true at the next instant. Now we construct another process $C'' = (S'', R'', I'')$ which is a *cross product* of C and $A_{\neg f}$. This process acts like C and at the same time it also simulates $A_{\neg f}$ on the executions of C. The state set S'' is the set of pairs (s,q) where s,q are the states of C,$A_{\neg f}$ respectively. For b in the communication alphabet Σ, the transition ((s,q),(s',q'),b) is in R'' iff (s,s',b) is a transition of C and the automaton $A_{\neg f}$ has a transition from q to q' on the input $\Phi_C(s')$. The set of initial states $I'' = \{$ (s,q) : s is an initial state of C and there exists a transition of $A_{\neg f}$ from its initial state to state q on the input $\Phi_C(s)$ $\}$. A pair (s,q) is is called a *final state* of C'' iff q is a final state of $A_{\neg f}$.

Now, we construct a system of processes containing C'' and the user processes. We model the executions of C'' by a *Vector Addition System with States* (VASS). A *Vector Addition System with States* (VASS) of dimension m is a finite labelled directed graph in which the label of each edge is a vector of m integers. Let **Z**,**N** be the set of integers and the set of non-negative integers respectively. Formally, a VASS G of dimension m is a pair (V,E) where V is a finite set of states and $E \subseteq V \times V \times \mathbf{Z}^m$ is a finite set of transitions. We can consider G to be a labelled directed graph in which there is an edge from s to s' with label $\vec{a}$ iff $(s,s',\vec{a}) \in E$. A configuration of G is a pair $(s,\vec{a})$ where $s \in V$ and $\vec{a} \in \mathbf{N}^m$. We call $\vec{a}$ the configuration vector of c. Note that all the components of a configuration vector are non-negative. If $(s,\vec{a}),(s',\vec{c})$ are configurations of G and $(s,s',\vec{e})$ is a transition of G such that $\vec{c} = \vec{a}+\vec{e}$ then we say that the configuration $(s', \vec{c})$ can be reached from $(s,\vec{a})$ by the above transition. A *path* of G is a sequence of configurations $c_0, c_1, \ldots, c_i, \ldots$ such that for $i \geq 0$ c_{i+1} can be reached from c_i by some transition of G. A configuration d is said to be reachable from c in G if there is a path of G starting from c and ending in d.

We model the executions of C'' by the VASS G = (V,E). V is the set of nodes of the VASS which contains all the states from S'' including an additional state s_0 which is the initial state of G. E is the set of transitions of G. We briefly describe the construction of the VASS G = (V,E) which models the execution of the process C''. Let $\{t_1, t_2, \ldots, t_m\}$ be the set of states of a user process. As far as the control process is concerned, at any instant of a computation the information regarding the user processes can be represented by a vector of integers $(n_1, n_2, \ldots, n_m)$ where n_i is the number of user processes in state t_i for $1 \leq i \leq m$. The reason we can use this representation is that the behavior of a user process depends only on its state but not on its name. E contains exactly the following types of transitions:

(i) For each initial state t_i of the user process, there is a transition in E to generate an arbitrary number of user processes starting in the state t_i. The transition that does this is $(s_0, s_0, \vec{a})$ where $a_i = 1$, $a_j = 0$ for $j \neq i$;

(ii) These transitions model the move from s_0

to the initial state of C″. For each $s \in I''$, $(s_0,s,\mathbf{0})$ is in E where $\mathbf{0}$ denotes the zero vector;

(iii) These transitions model the synchronization between the user processes. Let (t_i,t_j,c), $(t_k,t_l,\bar{c})$ be any two complementing transitions of a user process. Let $\vec{u},\vec{v} \in \mathbf{Z}^m$ be vectors such that $u_i = -1$, $u_j = 1$, $u_r = 0$ for $r \neq i,j$ and $v_k = -1$, $v_l = 1$, $v_r = 0$ for $r \neq k,l$. Corresponding to the above transitions of the user process, for each $s \in V$ such that $s \neq s_0$, the transition $(s,s,\vec{u}+\vec{v})$ is in E;

(iv) These transitions model the communication between the control process and the user processes. For each action c, for each $(s,s',c) \in R''$ and $(t_i,t_j,\bar{c}) \in R_U$, the transition $(s,s',\vec{a})$ is in E where $a_i = -1$, $a_j = 1$, $a_k = 0$ for $k \neq i,j$;

(v) These transitions model the internal moves of the control process. For each $(s,s',\epsilon) \in R''$, $(s,s',\mathbf{0})$ is in E;

(vi) These transitions model the internal move of the user processes. For each (t_i,t_j,ϵ) in R_U and for each $s \in V$ such that $s \neq s_0$, the transition $(s,s,\vec{a})$ is in E where $a_i = -1$, $a_j = 1$, $a_r = 0$ for $r \neq i,j$.

The configuration $(s_0,\mathbf{0})$ is the *initial* configuration. A configuration $(s,\vec{a})$ is called a *final* configuration if s is a final state of C″. It can easily be shown that every infinite path of G starting from the initial configuration and containing s_0 only a finite number of times models an execution of C″ and hence an execution of C and the run of $A_{\neg f}$ on this execution.

The following lemma establishes the relationship between the executions of C that satisfy ¬f and the infinite paths in G.

LEMMA 4.1: The following are equivalent.

(a) There is an execution of C in a system with a finite number of user processes that satisfies ¬f.

(b) G has an infinite path starting from the initial configuration and containing infinitely many final configurations. □

Using the techniques of ([Ra]) we show that there is an infinite path of G containing a final configuration infinitely often iff G has an infinite path of the form $\alpha\beta^\omega$ where α,β are finite paths of G of length double exponential in the size of G and β contains a final configuration. Using this result we give an algorithm that checks for the condition of the above lemma. This algorithm runs in time double exponential in $(|C|+|U|)|A_{\neg f}|$. Since $|A_{\neg f}|$ is exponential in $|f|$, the above algorithm runs in time triple exponential in $|f|$.

We can also use a procedure similar to the above to check if all the possible executions of a user process satisfy a given specification. This procedure will be presented in the full paper. This completes the algorithms for model checking in a system with a control process and many user processes without fairness.

4.2 Model-checking Under Fairness

In concurrent systems, many times we are interested in verifying that a correctness property holds on all fair computations. This is especially the case for liveness properties. In certain problems we can also use fairness to model the network behavior and get rid of the network. This is true in many token passing algorithms where the only purpose served by the network is to circulate the token in a fair manner.

In this subsection, we consider the model-checking problem for fair computations of a system with a control process and many user processes. Specifically, we consider the problem of verifying that every execution of the process C induced by fair computations with a finite number of user processes satisfies the given specification f. As in the previous section, from C,U, $A_{\neg f}$ we construct the VASS G = (V,E). Consider a configuration $(s,\vec{a})$ of G where $\vec{a} \in \mathbf{N}^m$, and $s = (s',q)$ where s′,q are the states of C, $A_{\neg f}$ respectively. Each component a_i of $\vec{a}$ specifies the number of user processes in state t_i. We say that the state t_i is *enabled* in the configuration c if $a_i > 0$ and one of the following holds: (1) there is a possible internal transition from state t_i; (2) there is a state t_j such that $a_j > 0$ and a user process in t_i can synchronize with the one in t_j; (3) a user process in state t_i can synchronize with C″ which is in state s. We say that the process C'' is enabled in the above configuration if either there is a possible internal transition for C'' in the state s , or if there exists j such that $a_j > 0$ and the process C'' in state s can synchronize with a user process in state t_j. An infinite path α of G is *fair* if the following condition is satisfied: If the process C'' is enabled infinitely often in α then a transition of C'' is taken infinitely often in α, and for any user state t_i, if t_i is enabled infinitely often in α then a transition from t_i is taken infinitely often in α. Fair infinite paths of G correspond to fair computations. Now, we give a complete decision procedure for model-checking under fairness.

The following lemma gives a necessary and sufficient condition for the existence of an execution of C that satisfies $\neg f$ and that is induced by a fair global computation.

LEMMA 4.2: The following are equivalent.

(a)There exists an execution of C which satisfies $\neg f$ and which is induced by a fair global computation.

(b) G has an infinite fair path starting from the initial configuration and containing infinitely many final configurations.

Proof: Assume (a). Let $\sigma = \sigma_0, \sigma_1, \ldots$ be a fair global computation of a system with n user processes such that the execution of C in this computation satisfies $\neg f$. Let $u_0, u_1, \ldots$ be the execution of C in the above computation and $q_0, q_1, \ldots$ be an accepting run of $A_{\neg f}$ on this execution. Since the above run of $A_{\neg f}$ is an accepting run, this run contains a final state of $A_{\neg f}$ infinitely often. Let $\vec{a}_i$ be the vector indicating the number of user processes in each user state in the global state σ_i. Let $c = c_0, c_1, \ldots$ be a path of G where for $i \geq 0$, c_i is the configuration of G given by $((u_i, q_i), \vec{a}_i)$. It is easily seen that the configuration c_{i+1} can be reached from c_i by a transition of G. Hence, the sequence c is a path of G. Since σ is a fair computation, it can be shown that c is a fair path. Also, c contains infinitely many final configurations. We can attach a prefix to c with the following property: the prefix starts with the initial configuration $(s_0, \mathbf{0})$ and generates enough number of user processes in the various start states using the transitions of type (i) given in the definition of G. The resulting path satisfies (b).

Now assume (b). Let $c = c_0, c_1, \ldots$ be an infinite fair path of G starting from the initial configuration $(s_0, \mathbf{0})$ and containing infinitely many final configurations. Let c_i be the earliest configuration in the above path such that the state of G in c_i is different from s_0. The transitions in c up to c_i generate a finite number n of processes in various user states, and the transitions beyond c_i correspond to internal moves of processes or synchronizations between processes. Now we can obtain a global computation of a system consisting of the process C'' and of n user processes that corresponds to the path $c_i, c_{i+1}, \ldots$ Since c is a fair path, we can make the above computation satisfy the fairness property. In the resulting computation, the execution of C'' consists of the execution of C and the run of $A_{\neg f}$ on this execution. Clearly, in the above run of $A_{\neg f}$ a final state of $A_{\neg f}$ appears infinitely often. From this it follows that the execution of C induced by the above global computation satisfies $\neg f$. □

LEMMA 4.3: G has an infinite fair path starting from the initial configuration and containing infinitely many final configurations iff G has a finite path $c_0, c_1, \ldots, c_i, \ldots, c_{i+k}$ such that c_0 is the initial configuration, and the following properties are satisfied:

(a) $c_i = c_{i+k}$;

(b) A final configuration appears in between c_i and c_{i+k};

(c) If a user state is enabled in some configuration between c_i and c_{i+k} then a transition from this user state is taken some where between c_i and c_{i+k};

(d) If C'' is enabled in some configuration between c_i and c_{i+k}, then a transition of C'' is taken some where between c_i, c_{i+k}.

Proof: Assume that G has an infinite fair path starting from an initial configuration and containing infinitely many final configurations. Let $c = c_0, c_1, \ldots$ be such a path. For $j \geq 0$, let $c_j = (s_j, \vec{a}_j)$ and $\text{weight}(c_j) = $ sum of the components of $\vec{a}_j$. Let c_p be the earliest configuration such that s_p is not the initial state of G. Beyond c_p, no transition of type (i) is taken in the above path. Hence for $k \geq p$, weight(c_k) = weight(c_p). Clearly, the total number of distinct configurations appearing in c is finite. Thus there exists an instance j, with the following properties: the only configurations that appear beyond c_j are those that appear infinitely often in c; every user state that is enabled only a finite number of times is never enabled beyond c_j; if C″ is enabled only a finite number of times then it is never enabled beyond c_j. From the above observations, it can be shown that there exist integers $i,k \geq 0$ such that properties (a),(b),(c),(d) are satisfied.

Now assume that there is a finite path $(c_0,\ldots,c_i,\ldots,c_{i+k})$ that satisfies the conditions (a) thru (d) of the lemma. By repeating the path $(c_{i+1},c_{i+2},\ldots,c_{i+k})$ infinitely many times we get an infinite path with the required property. □

THEOREM 4.4: The problem of model checking under fairness is decidable.

Proof Sketch: We will use the decidability of the reachability problem for a VASS ([Ma],[Ko]) to determine whether there is a finite path of G that satisfies (a) thru (d) of lemma 4.3. Given a VASS and two configurations, the reachability problem is to decide whether there is a finite path starting from the first configuration and ending in the second configuration. In order to express the problem of determining whether there is a finite path of G that satisfies conditions (a) thru (d) as a reachability problem, we construct a new VASS G* which has all the dimensions of G together with three additional coordinates for each user state. For each user state, one of the additional coordinates is used to record whether a transition from this state is used between c_i and c_{i+k}. Another coordinate is used to record if the user state is ever enabled between c_i and c_{i+k}. The third additional coordinate is used to record whether there is a process in the user state between c_i,c_{i+k}. Using these additional three coordinates for each user state, we can convert the problem of determining whether there is a finite path of G satsying (a) thru (d) of lemma 4.3 to the problem of determining whether there is a path between two particular configurations in G*. The details of the construction of G* will appear in the full paper. □

The following theorem indicates that it is difficult to find computationally efficient procedures for model checking under fairness. The proof of the following theorem will be given in the full paper.

THEOREM 4.5: There is a polynomial time reduction from the reachability problem for Vector Addition Systems to the complement of the problem of model-checking under fairness. □

4.3 Deadlocked Computations

So far, we have only considered infinite computations of a system. We have not included in the set of computations for modelchecking those computations which end in deadlock. Now, we extend the deadlocked computations to infinite computations by repeating the final global state forever and include these in the set of computations for model checking. The following theorem shows that it is difficult to find efficient algorithms for the model checking problem without fairness for this set of computations.

THEOREM 4.6: There is a polynomial time reduction from the reachability problem for VASS to the complement of the model checking problem (with deadlock) without fairness. □

THEOREM 4.7: Both the model checking problems (with deadlocks) with fairness and without fairness are decidable. □

The proofs of the above theorems will be given in the full paper.

5. Global Properties and Extended Logics

So far we have only considered the problem of verifying if all the executions of a single process satisfy a PTL specification. However, some of the important properties such as mutual exclusion are global properties. In this section, we show how the techniques developed in the previous sections can be used to verify certain global properties such as mutual exclusion. We also introduce a new logic IPTL which allows us to specify global properties of systems with many processes.

Consider a system with many identical processes. Let P be the description of a typical process, and C be a subset of the set of states which is the *critical region*. We want to prove that in any global state of a computation there can be at most one process in the critical region. This is the mutual exclusion property for the system of processes. We modify the process as follows: We add two new states e1,e2, and introduce edges from each state in C to e1 and e2 labelled with the action c,$\bar{c}$ respectively, where c is a new action name. We also use a new atomic proposition E1 which is true only in the state e1. The new process P′ is shown below.

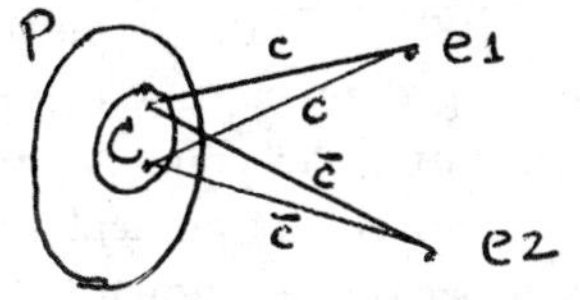

Now consider a new system with many identical copies of the process P′. In this system, in all the possible executions of a process the state e1 is never reached iff the original system satisfies the mutual exclusion property. Hence, the specification G(¬ E1) is true in all the executions of a process in the new system iff the original system satisfies the mutual exclusion property. This trick can also be extended to verify the property that "there are at most k processes in the critical region".

Transformations similar to the previous one can also be used to prove mutual exclusion in systems with a control process and many identical user processes.

So far, we have used the logic PTL to specify the properties of the executions of a single process. Now we introduce a new logic IPTL which is an extension of PTL. This logic allows us to specify a wider class of properties with ease. It uses the additional modality $\sqcap$. This modality is a universal quantifier over processes. We add the following rule for forming well formed formulas. If f is an IPTL formula then $\sqcap(f)$ is also a formula in IPTL. We use the following abbreviation: $\sqcup \equiv \neg \sqcap \neg$.

A model of IPTL is a 4-tuple (I,S,Ψ,Φ) where I is a finite set of processes or indices, S is a set of states, Ψ: $I \rightarrow S^{\omega}$ associates with each process an ω-sequence of states, Φ: $S \rightarrow 2^{P}$ associates with each state the set of atomic propositions true in that state. For $p \in I$, we denote $\Psi(p)$ by $s_p = (s_{p,0}, s_{p,1}, \ldots)$. An *interpretation* is a triple (M,p,i) where M is a model as given above, $p \in I$, $i \geq 0$ is an integer. Intuitively, a model is a set of executions indexed by process names, and an interpretation specifies a model, a process name and an instant on the execution of the process. We inductively define by the relation $|=$ when a formula is true in an interpretation:

$(M,p,i) |= P$, where P is an atomic formula iff $P \in \Phi(s_{p,i})$;

$(M,p,i) |= \sqcap(f)$ iff $\forall q \in I$, $(M,q,i) |= f$;

$(M,p,i) |= (f \ \mathbf{U} \ g)$ iff $\exists j \geq i$ such that $(M,p,j) |= g$ and $\forall k$ such that $i \leq k < j$ $(M,p,k) |= f$.

A formula is said to be satisfiable if there exists an interpretation in which the formula is true, and a formula is said to be valid if it is true in all interpretations. IPTL is special case of the muti-process network logic of [RS], it is also a special case of one person logic of knowledge and time of [Le]. We can express many interesting properties in this logic. The following formula expresses the property that if a process requests for resource then eventually some process is granted the resource.

$(\sqcup\ \textit{request} \supset \mathbf{F}\sqcup\ \textit{granted})$

In the above formula *request*, *granted* are atomic propositions.

The following theorem shows that the deciding the validity of an IPTL formula can be done in time double exponential in the length of the formula and in space exponential in the length of the formula.

THEOREM 5.1: The set of valid formula in IPTL is EXSPACE-complete. □

The following theorem shows that the model-checking problem for a system with a control process and many identical user processes is undecidable when the correctness specification is given in IPTL. The theorem will be proved in the full paper.

THEOREM 5.2: The set of triples (C,U,f) satisfying the following property is π_1^0-complete:

C,U are finite state CCS processes, f is an IPTL formula and for all $n \geq 0$, in the system containing the control process C and n user processes whose description is given by U, all the computations satisfy the specification f. □

6. Reasoning about Networks of Processes

We believe that our algorithms of the previous sections can also be used to verify certain distributed algorithms on networks of identical finite state CSP processes where the size of the network can be arbitrary. Consider a system M of processes connected on a network. Each process is only allowed to communicate with its neighbours. Each action of a process is of the form p:c or p:$\bar{c}$, where p is the name of a process and c is an element of a message alphabet. Here the rules for synchronization are as for CSP,i.e. if process p is in a state from which there is a transition labelled with q:c and process q is in a state from which there is a transition labelled with p:$\bar{c}$ then they can simultaneously make the above transitions.

We transform the system M of processes as follows. In each process, we replace each action of the form p:c by c, and each action of the form p:$\bar{c}$ by $\bar{c}$,i.e. in each communication action we erase the process names. Let M* be the resulting system of CCS processes. Clearly, any process in M* is allowed to communicate with any other process. It is also the case that every computation of M is also a computation of M*. Now we can prove that every computation of M satisfies a property by proving that every computation of M* satisfies the property.

Many times we are only interested in proving that every fair computation of M satisfies a given property. Even though every computation of M is a computation of M*, it need not be the case that every fair computation of M is a fair computation of M*. For example, there can be a computation of M in which a process is disabled forever after a certain instant and hence is executed only a finite number of times, while in the same computation of M* the same process may be enabled infinitely often. Thus this computation is not fair in M*. If we can establish by other means that every fair computation of M is also a fair computation of M* ,then we can prove that every fair computation of M satisfies a given property by proving that every fair computation of M* satisfies the given property. One way of establishing the above condition is to show that in every fair computation of M, all the processes are enabled infinitely often. Thus we can split the proof method into the following two steps: (1) prove that in every fair execution of M all the processes are enabled infinitely often; (2) prove that every fair computation of M* satisfies the given property. In the full paper, we give an easily checked property which guarantees that the computations of n processes on a ring satisfy condition (1).

We illustrate the above method by the example of the mutual exclusion on rings considered in [CGB]. Here many identical processes are arranged on a ring. The processes circulate a token along the ring. A process that has the token can enter the critical region. The description of a process is as shown below:

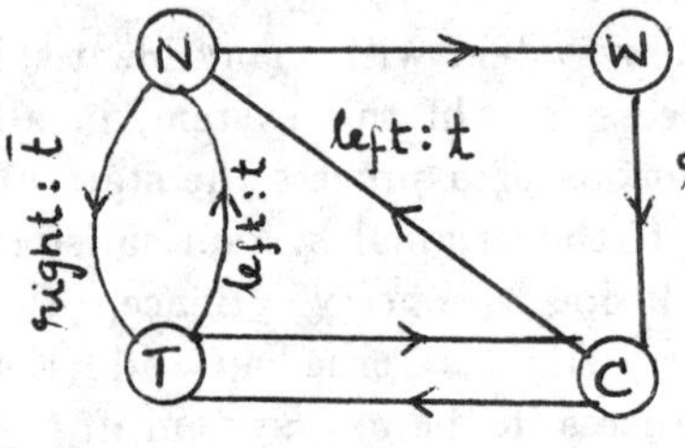

Each process has two types of actions left:t, right:$\bar{t}$. Here "left" is the name of its left neighbour and "right" is the name of its right neighbour. Each process can be in any of the following states: C,T,N,W. Intuitively, a process is in state C if it has the token and is in critical section, it is in T if it has the token but is not in the critical section, it is in W if it is waiting to enter the critical section, it is in N in all other cases. Exactly one process starts in state T and all other processes start in state N. It can be shown that in all the fair executions of M the token is circulated in the clockwise direction, and hence condition (1) is satisfied. It is not difficult to establish this property through other means. The description of a process in M* is obtained by replacing left:$\bar{t}$ by $\bar{t}$, right:t by t in the previous figure.

Now M* is a system in our second model of processes. The control process is the process that starts in the state T and the user processes are all the other processes which start in state N. Now we can use the algorithms of the previous sections to prove that if a process wants to enter the critical section it does so eventually. Clearly, this can be expressed in PTL. We can also establish mutual exclusion as given in the beginning of this section. Although this is a simple example, it illustrates the use of our algorithms. We feel that many token passing algorithms on rings can be verified using this approach. In the final version of this paper, we also extend this approach to more general network topologies.

Assume that the set of computations are extended so as to include deadlocked computations as in sub-section 4.3. The following lemma shows that fairness is irrelevant for proving *safety* properties. See [AS] for a definition of safety properties.

LEMMA 6.1: If all fair computations of a system satisfy a safety property then all the computations of the system satisfy the same property. □

Now consider the problem of verifying that every fair computation of M satisfies a safety property. From the above lemma, it follows that it is enough if we establish (2).

7. Conclusion

In this paper, we have for the first time considered the model-checking problem for two models of concurrent systems with an arbitrary number of finite-state CCS processes. For these models, we have presented algorithms to check if the executions of a process satisfy a given PTL specification. We have also shown that these algorithms can also be used to verify certain global properties such as mutual exclusion. We have illustrated the application of theses algorithms by considering an example. We believe that many other token passing algorithms on rings and other networks, some resource allocation problems can be handled in this model at some level of abstraction. The algorithms we have given for the second model have high complexity. We feel that it may be possible to place sufficient realistic restrictions on processes and obtain more efficient model-checking algorithms for these classes of problems. In [CG] the problem of avoiding *state explosion* for concurrent systems with many processes is considered.

Instead of PTL, we can also use finite state Buchi automata on infinite strings to specify the properties of the executions of a single process. In this case the specification automaton B should satisfy the following property: if B accepts a string "t" then it should accept all the strings that are equivalent to "t" under stuttering. Since all our algorithms check for the existence of an execution that does not satisfy the given specification, we have to construct the complement B′ of B, i.e. we have to construct an automaton that accepts the set of strings that are not accepted by B. We modify the present algorithms by using B′ in place of the automaton $A_{\neg f}$. Using the algorithm of [SVW] we can obtain B′ in time $O(2^{|B|})$, and such that $|B'| \leq 2^{|B|}$. In this case the algorithm of section 3, will have complexity $O(n2^{|B|} + p(n))$ and the algorithm in section 4 for the second model of processes without fairness will have complexity triple exponential in $|B|$.

We can extend the algorithms to the case when there is a lower bound k on the number of processes. Since we are not considering fairness in the first model of processes, we do not have to modify the algorithm given in section 3. In case of the second model, the VASS G constructed in the algorithm has to be modified so that it generates at least k number of user processes. It is straight-foraward to make this modification. We can also modify the algorithms to the case where the user processes are divided into a fixed number of classes such that there are arbitrary number of processes in each class.

The algorithm that is given in section 3 takes time polynomial in the size of the process. This algorithm does not consider fairness. It will be interesting to investigate if there are algorithms of complexity polynomial in the size of the process and which also take fairness into consideration. It will also be interesting to consider other examples that can be verified using these algorithms.

REFERENCES:

[AK] K.R.Apt, D.Kozen, Limits to Automatic Program Verification, Information Processing Letters, 1986.

[AS] B.Alper, F.Schneider, Defining Liveness, Information Processing Letters, 21,

Oct. 1985.

[CES] E.M.Clarke, E.A.Emerson, A.P.Sistla, Automatic Verification of Finite State Concurrent Programs from Temporal Specifications, ACM Transactions on Programming Languages and Systems, Vol.8, No.2, April 86, pp 244-263.

[CGB] E.M.Clarke, O.Grumberg, M.Browne, Reasoning About Networks with many Finite State Processes, Proceedings of 5th ACM Symposium on Principles of Distributed Computing, August 86, Calgary, Canada pp 240-248.

[EL] E.A.Emerson, C.L.Lei, Modalities for Model Checking: Branching Time Strikes Back, Proceedings of 12th ACM Symposium on Principles of Programming Languages, 1985, pp 84-96.

[CG] E.M.Clarke, O.Grumburg, Avoiding the State Explosion Problem in the Temporal Logic Model Checking Algorithms, Carnegie-Mellon University, Pittsburgh.

[KS] P.C.Kanellakis, S.A.Smolka, On the Analysis of Cooperation and Antagonism in Networks of Communicating Processes, 4th ACM Symposium on Principles of Distributed Computing, Minaki, Canada, August 1985.

[KO] S.R.Kosaraju, Decidability of Reachability in VAS, Proc. of 14th ACM Symposium on Theory of Computing, pp 267-281.

[Le] D.Lehman, Knowledge, Common Knowledge, and Related Puzzles, Proceedings of the Third Annual ACM Symposium on Principles of Distributed Computing, 1984, pp 62-67.

[La] R.Ladner, The Complexity of Problems in Systems of Communicating Sequential Processes, Proc. of 11th ACM Symposium on Theory of Computing, 1979, pp 214-222.

[LP] O.Lichenstein, A.Pnueli, Checking that Finite State Concurrent Programs Satisfy their Linear Specification, Proc. of 12th ACM Symposium on Principles of Programming Languages, 1985, pp 97-107.

[Ma] E.W.Mayr, An Algorithm for general Petrinet Reachability Problem, Proc. of 13th ACM Symposium on Theory of Computing, 1981, pp 238-246.

[MP] Z.Manna, A.Pnueli, Specification and Verification of Concurrent Programs by ∀-automata, To appear in 13th ACM Symp on Principles of Programming Languages, 1987.

[Ra] C.Rackoff, The Covering and Boundedness Problem for VAS, Theoretical Computer Science. 6, 1978, pp 223-231.

[RS] J.Reif, A.P.Sistla, A Multiprocess Network Logic with Temporal and Spatial Modalities, Journal of Computer and System Sciences, Vol. 30, No.1, Feb 1985, pp 41-53.

[RY] L.Rosier, H.Yen, A Multi-parameter Analysis of the Boundedness Problem for VAS, Journal of Computer and System Sciences, 32, 1986, pp 105-135.

[SVW] A.P.Sistla, M.Vardi, P.Wolper, Complementation Problem for Buchi Automaton and its Applications to Temporal Logic, Proceedings of International Conference on Automata,Languages and Programming, August,1985.

[VW] M.Vardi, P.Wolper, An Automata Theoretic Approach to Automatic Program verification, Proc. of IEEE Symposium on Logic in Computer Science, Boston, 1986.

On the Eventuality Operator in Temporal Logic

A. Prasad Sistla
GTE Laboratories Inc., Waltham, Mass.

Lenore D. Zuck*
Department of Computer Science, Yale University

Abstract

We consider RTL, a linear time propositional temporal logic whose only modalities are the $\Diamond$ (*eventually*) operator and its dual— $\Box$ (*always*). Although less expressive than the full temporal logic, RTL is the fragment of temporal logic that is used most often and in many verification systems. Indeed, most properties of distributed systems discussed in the literature are RTL properties. Another advantage of RTL over the full temporal logic is in the decidability procedure; while deciding satisfiability of a formula in full temporal logic is a PSPACE complete procedure, doing that for an RTL formula is in co-NP. We characterize the class of ω-regular languages that are definable in RTL and show simple translations between ω-regular sets and RTL formulae that define them. We explore the applications of RTL in reasoning about communication systems and the relationship between RTL and several fragments of Interval Modal Logic.

1 Introduction

Propositional Linear Time Temporal Logic (TL) was introduced in [Pnu77] as a formal system for reasoning about concurrent programs. Recent trends in program verification (e.g., [Var85], [VW86], and [AS85]) suggest using automata-theoretic approaches in program verification, i.e., applying techniques developed in automata-theory in the temporal framework. The classical finite-state automata (see [RS59]) were used to define regular languages. Later works (see [Buc62,McN66]) showed how they can be used to define classes of infinite sequences. The resulting languages are termed *ω-regular*. TL was shown to be (expressibility-wise) a strict subset of the class of ω-regular languages. (This was first implied by a combination of several works, for example [GPSS80] or [Kam68] with [MP71] or [Tho81].)

The "strict subclass" of the ω-regular languages which is equivalent to TL is the language definable by *ω-star free* regular expressions, which, in turn, are equivalent to the *ω-non-counting* languages. (Definitions and discussions of these ω-regular languages appear in [Tho81,LPZ85,Zuc86].)

In most formal systems that allow temporal-like reasoning, the $\Diamond$ (eventually) operator is used as the main modal operator. It is therefore natural to consider a temporal logic that uses $\Diamond$ as the only temporal operator. We call the restricted temporal logic obtained RTL. At first glance RTL seems to be a very limited language. Yet, if we are concerned with properties of concurrent programs, there are convincing indications that the RTL language is adequate:

It was shown in [Sis85] that RTL is sufficient to define the set of *strong safety* properties. Chandy and Misra conjectured that there is essentially one class of interesting liveness properties of concurrent programs, namely, the class of *progress* properties ([CM86]). In their propositional version, progress properties are easily definable by RTL. Owicki and Lamport, when giving proof rules for liveness properties, considered only formulae of the form $\Box(p \rightarrow \Diamond q)$ ([OL82]), which provides another indication that RTL is an adequate temporal language.

Indeed, most temporal properties of distributed programs discussed in the literature are given in RTL. As shown in [SC85], the satisfiability problem for RTL formulae is NP complete, while the problem for general TL formulae is PSPACE complete. Hence, using RTL instead of TL provides a consid-

*Research of this author was partly supported by the National Science Foundation under grant DCR-84-05478 erable advantage.

We characterize below the class of ω-regular languages that are definable in RTL. In particular, we show that every RTL formula is equivalent to a finite union of some simply defined ω-regular sets which we call *temporal sets*, and that every union of such temporal sets is definable by some RTL formula.

We then consider problems concerning theories of message buffers in RTL. For example, we show that the theory of unbounded fifo buffers in RTL is in co-NP; the corresponding theory in the full TL is Π_1^1-complete (cf.[SCFM84]).

Finally, we consider the relationships between several simple extensions of RTL and fragments of Interval Modal Logic (see [HS86]). For example, we show that RTL, when interpreted over points in the (continuous) interval $[0,1]$, is equivalent to the fragment of Interval Modal Logic that uses only the modality $\langle E \rangle$. We show that the satisfiability problem for RTL that is interpreted over the continuous line $[0,1]$ is NP-complete.

2 Notations and Definitions

2.1 Restricted Regular Sets and Temporal Sets

Let S be a finite set of *states*, Π be a finite set of propositions, $\Sigma = 2^{\Pi}$ be an *alphabet*, and $I: S \to \Sigma$ be an *evaluation* mapping each state $s \in S$ to the set of propositions $I(s) \in \Sigma$ that are true in s. We assume that I is an isomorphism. We hold S, Π, Σ, and I fixed for the subsequent discussion.

We shall consider both finite and infinite sequences of states, i.e., sequences over S. Every sequence σ over S can be mapped into a *string* $I(\sigma)$ which is a sequence over Σ. Similarly, a string σ over Σ can be mapped to a set of sequences $I^{-1}(\sigma)$ over S. When there is no danger of confusion, we shall interchange strings and sequences over S.

Let $\sigma = s_0, \ldots, s_k$ be a *finite* sequence over S and let $\sigma' = s'_0, \ldots$ be a (possibly infinite) sequence over S. The concatenation of σ and σ' is the (possibly infinite) sequence $\sigma;\sigma' = s_0, \ldots, s_k, s'_0, \ldots$.

Let A be a subset of S. We define the following *restricted regular sets* over S:

- A is a restricted regular set.
- A^*, the set of all (possibly empty) *finite* sequences over A, is a restricted regular set.
- A^+, the set of all *non-empty* finite sequences over A, is a restricted regular set.
- A^ω, the set of all *infinite* sequences over A, is a restricted regular set.
- $A^\infty = A^* \cup A^\omega$, the set of all sequences over A, is a restricted regular set.
- Let L_1 and L_2 be restricted regular sets. We denote by $L_1 \circ L_2$ the *concatenation* of the two sets, defined by: $L_1 \circ L_2 = \{\sigma;\sigma' \mid \sigma \in L_1 \cap S^*$ and $\sigma' \in L_2\} \cup \{\sigma \mid \sigma \in L_1 \cap S^\omega\}$. The set $L_1 \circ L_2$ is a restricted regular set.

If a set A is a singleton, e.g., $A = \{a\}$, we omit the braces and write, for example, a^* instead of $\{a\}^*$.

Let $s \in S$ be an element of S. We denote by $\mathrm{inf}(s)$ the set of infinite sequences where s appears infinitely many times. Similarly, for a subset $S' \subseteq S$, we denote

$$\mathrm{inf}(S') = \bigcap_{s \in S'} \mathrm{inf}(s)$$

Let $L \subseteq S^\omega$ be a restricted regular set over S and assume $S' \subseteq S$. We define $L_{\mathrm{inf}(S')} = L \cap \mathrm{inf}(S')$, i.e., $L_{\mathrm{inf}(S')}$ is the set of (infinite) sequences of L where every element of S' occurs infinitely many times.

Note that the set of restricted regular sets defined above is a subset of the set of ω-regular sets, i.e., the sets of infinite strings languages accepted by regular automata that accept infinite strings (for more elaborate definitions see, e.g., [McN66,Buc62,SVW85,Zuc86]).

A restricted regular set L is called a Λ-*set* if

$$L = s_0 \circ S_1^* \circ s_1 \circ S_2^* \circ s_2 \circ \cdots \circ S_{m-1}^* \circ s_{m-1} \circ S_m^\omega$$

for some $S_1, \ldots, S_m \subseteq S$ and $s_1, \ldots, s_{m-1} \in S$ such that $s_0 \in S_1$ and for every i, $1 \le i < m$, $s_i \in S_i - S_{i+1}$.

A restricted regular set L is called a *temporal set* if

$$L = \bigcup_{i=1}^{n} L^i_{\mathrm{inf}(S'_i)}$$

for some Λ-sets $L^1, \ldots, L^n$ and some $S'_1, \ldots, S'_n \subseteq S$.

2.2 Restricted Temporal Logic—RTL

A *model* for RTL is an infinite sequence of states $\sigma \in S^\omega$, i.e.,

$$\sigma : s_0, s_1, \ldots \qquad s_i \in S$$

Usually, a model is generated by an underlying program; however, in our discussions we shall not use this fact directly.

Given a model σ and a position $i \geq 0$, we denote by $\sigma^{(i)}$ the suffix of σ from the i'th position, i.e., $\sigma^{(i)} = s_i, s_{i+1}, \ldots$. Similarly, we denote by $\sigma_{\rightarrow i}$ the prefix of σ until the i'th position, i.e., $\sigma_{\rightarrow i} = s_0, \ldots, s_i$. We introduce a temporal language over the propositional formulae in Π using the boolean connectives $\neg$ and $\vee$, and the *temporal* operator $\Diamond$ (*eventually*).

Temporal formulae are constructed by the following:

- T and F are RTL formulae..
- Every proposition $Q \in \Pi$ is an RTL formula.
- If φ is an RTL formula, then so are $\neg\varphi$ and $\Diamond\varphi$.
- If φ_1 and φ_2 are RTL formulae, then so is $\varphi_1 \vee \varphi_2$.

We define a satisfiability relation $\models$ between a model σ and an RTL formula. The satisfiability relation is defined inductively as follows:

$\sigma \models T$ and $\sigma \not\models F$ for every $\sigma \in S^\omega$.

For a proposition $Q \in \Pi$, $\sigma \models Q$ *iff* $Q \in I(s_j)$.

$$\begin{array}{ll} \sigma \models \neg\varphi & \textit{iff } \sigma \not\models \varphi. \\ \sigma \models \varphi_1 \vee \varphi_2 & \textit{iff } \sigma \models \varphi_1 \textbf{ or } \sigma \models \varphi_2. \\ \sigma \models \Diamond\varphi & \textit{iff } \text{For some } i \geq 0,\ \sigma^{(i)} \models \varphi. \end{array}$$

Additional boolean connectives (such as $\wedge$, $\rightarrow$, $\equiv$) can be defined in the usual way. We define an additional temporal operator, $\Box$ (*always*), by:

$$\Box\varphi \equiv \neg\Diamond\neg\varphi$$

Let φ be an RTL formula. If for some $\sigma \in S^\omega$, $\sigma \models \varphi$, we say that σ ***satisfies*** φ. If there is a model σ that satisfies φ, we say that φ is ***satisfiable***. If all $\sigma \in S^\omega$ satisfy φ, we say that φ is ***valid***.

For a given RTL formula φ, we denote by $\mathcal{L}(\varphi)$ the set of models that satisfy φ, i.e.,

$$\mathcal{L}(\varphi) = \{\sigma \in S^\omega \mid \sigma \models \varphi\}.$$

3 From Temporal Sets to RTL

As mentioned above, for every TL formula there exists a regular set whose members are exactly those sequences satisfying the formula. As RTL formulae are special cases of TL formulae, it follows that for every RTL formula φ, $\mathcal{L}(\varphi)$ is a regular set. In this section we show that every temporal set is equivalent to $\mathcal{L}(\varphi)$ for some $\varphi \in$RTL, or, as we term it, every temporal set is *RTL-definable*.

We first show that every Λ-set is RTL-definable. Let LS be a Λ-set defined by:

$$LS = s_0 \circ S_1^* \circ s_1 \circ S_2^* \circ s_2 \circ \cdots \circ S_{m-1}^* \circ s_{m-1} \circ S_m^\omega$$

for some $S_1, \ldots, S_m \subseteq S$ and $s_1, \ldots, s_{m-1} \in S$ such that $s_0 \in S_1$ and for every i, $1 \leq i < m$, $s_i \in S_i - S_{i+1}$.

We define the following RTL formulae inductively:

$$\psi_m = \Box S_m$$

and for every i, $1 \leq i < m$,

$$\psi_i = \Box(S_i \vee \psi_{i+1}).$$

Note that we use S_i to denote $\bigvee_{s \in S_i}(\bigwedge_{Q \in I(s)} Q \wedge \bigwedge_{Q \in \Pi - I(s)} \neg Q)$.

We next define a sequence $\{E_i\}_{i=1}^{m-1}$ of restricted regular sets, and a sequence $\{\varphi_i\}_{i=1}^{m-1}$ of RTL formulae. The two sequences are defined inductively by:

$$\begin{array}{rcl} E_{m-1} & = & s_{m-1}^+ \circ S_m^\omega \\ \varphi_{m-1} & = & s_{m-1} \wedge \Box(s_{m-1} \vee \Box S_m) \wedge \Diamond(\neg s_{m-1}) \end{array}$$

For every i, $1 \leq i < m-1$:

$$\begin{array}{rcl} E_i & = & s_i^+ \circ S_{i+1}^* \circ E_{i+1} \\ \varphi_i & = & s_i \wedge \Box(s_i \vee \psi_{i+1}) \wedge \Diamond(\varphi_{i+1}). \end{array}$$

Our goal here is to show that for every $i = 1, \ldots, m-1$:

$$E_i = \mathcal{L}(\varphi_i) \tag{1}$$

from which we derive that $LS = \mathcal{L}(s_0 \wedge \psi_1 \wedge \Diamond\varphi_1)$, i.e., that the Λ-set LS is equivalent to the set of sequences that satisfy $s_0 \wedge \psi_1 \wedge \Diamond\varphi_1$.

The following observations and claims are used to establish (1):

Observation 3.1 *Let $p \in \Sigma$ and let χ be an RTL formula. Then the following holds:*

1. $\mathcal{L}(p) = p \circ S^\omega$.
2. $\mathcal{L}(\Diamond\chi) = S^* \circ \mathcal{L}(\chi)$.
3. *If $\chi = \Box\varphi$ for some RTL formula φ, then $\mathcal{L}(\Box(p \vee \chi)) = p^\infty \circ \mathcal{L}(\chi)$.*

Proof We prove only part (3) of the Observation. In one direction, assume $\sigma \in (\Box(p \vee \chi))$, i.e., $\sigma \models \Box(p \vee \chi)$. There are two cases to consider: The first case is when $\sigma \models \Box p$, and then $\sigma \in p^\omega$ and the claim is established. The second case is when $\sigma \models \Diamond\neg p$. Let $j \geq 0$ be the minimal such that $\sigma^{(j)} \models \neg p$, i.e., $\sigma^{(j)} \models \chi$. It follows that $\sigma = \sigma_1;\sigma_2$, where σ_1 (which consists of the first j elements of σ) is in p^* and $\sigma_2 \in \mathcal{L}(\Box\chi) = \mathcal{L}(\chi)$.

In the other directions assume that $\sigma \in p^\infty \circ \mathcal{L}(\chi)$. If $\sigma \in p^\omega$ then clearly $\sigma \models \Box p$. Otherwise, $\sigma \in p^* \circ \mathcal{L}(\chi)$. Let i be the minimal such that $\sigma^{(i)} \in \mathcal{L}(\chi)$. It follows that for all j, $0 \leq j < i$, $\sigma^{(j)} \models p$. As $\sigma^{(i)} \models \chi$ and $\chi \rightarrow \Box\chi$, for all $j \geq i$, $\sigma^{(j)} \models \chi$. Hence, for all $i \geq 0$, $\sigma^{(i)} \models p \vee \chi$, and therefore $\sigma \models \Box(p \vee \chi)$. ⋈

Claim 3.1 *For every i, $1 \leq i \leq m$,*

$$\mathcal{L}(\psi_i) = S_i^\infty \circ \cdots \circ S_{m-1}^\infty \circ S_m^\omega.$$

Proof The proof is by (decreasing) induction on i. The base case ($i = m$) is trivial as S_m is a singleton and therefore $\mathcal{L}(\Box S_m)$ equals S_m^ω.

Assume that the claim is true for $i = k+1 \leq m$, i.e., assume:

$$\mathcal{L}(\psi_{k+1}) = S_{k+1}^\infty \circ \cdots \circ S_{m-1}^\infty \circ S_m^\omega.$$

By definition, $\psi_k = \Box(S_k \vee \psi_{k+1})$, hence, by Observation 3.1 (as $\psi_k = \Box\chi$ for some χ and S_k is a singleton),

$$\mathcal{L}(\Box(S_k \vee \psi_{k+1})) = S_k^\infty \circ \mathcal{L}(\psi_{k+1})$$

From the induction hypothesis it follows that:

$$\mathcal{L}(\psi_k) = S_k^\infty \circ \cdots \circ S_{m-1}^\infty \circ S_m^\omega.$$

⋈

Observation 3.2 *For every i, $1 \leq i < m$ the following holds:*

1. $\varphi_i \rightarrow \psi_i$.
2. $\varphi_i \rightarrow \neg\psi_{i+1}$.
3. $\psi_{i+1} \rightarrow \neg\Diamond\varphi_i$.

Proof

1. By definition, for every i, $1 \leq i < m$, φ_i implies $\Box(s_i \vee \psi_{i+1})$. As $s_i \in S_i$ (i.e., $s_i \rightarrow S_i$) and as $\psi_i = \Box(S_i \vee \psi_{i+1})$, the claim follows.
2. The proof is by (decreasing) induction on i:

   Base case ($i = m-1$): By definition, $\varphi_{m-1} \rightarrow s_{m-1}$ and $s_{m-1} \rightarrow \neg S_m$, hence $\varphi_{m-1} \rightarrow \neg\Box S_m$. As $\psi_m = \Box S_m$, it follows that

   $$\varphi_{m-1} \rightarrow \neg\psi_m.$$

   Inductive step: Assume that for some k, $1 \leq k < m-1$, $\varphi_{k+1} \rightarrow \neg\psi_{k+2}$. Assume to the contrary that there exists a model $\sigma \in S^\omega$ such that $\sigma \models \varphi_k \wedge \psi_{k+1}$. As $\varphi_k \rightarrow s_k$ $s_k \notin S_{k+1}$, $\psi_{k+1} \rightarrow \Box(S_{k+1} \vee \psi_{k+2})$, and ψ_{k+2} is a $\Box$-formula it follows that $\sigma \models \Box\psi_{k+2}$. By definition, $\varphi_k \rightarrow \Diamond\varphi_{k+1}$, hence $\sigma \models \Diamond(\varphi_{k+1} \wedge \psi_{k+2})$, which contradicts the induction hypothesis. Hence there exists no model σ such that $\sigma \models \varphi_k \wedge \psi_{k+1}$. We can therefore conclude that:

   $$\varphi_k \rightarrow \neg\psi_{k+1}.$$

3. Assume to the contrary that for some k, $1 \leq k < m$, there exists a model $\sigma \in S^\omega$ such that $\sigma \models \psi_{k+1} \wedge \Diamond\varphi_k$. As ψ_{k+1} is a $\Box$-formula, it follows that for some $i \geq 0$, $\sigma^{(i)} \models \psi_{k+1} \wedge \varphi_k$, contradicting part (2) of the claim. ⋈

Claim 3.2 *For every $i = 1, \ldots, m-1$, $\mathcal{L}(\varphi_i) \subseteq E_i$.*

Proof The proof is by (decreasing) induction on i.

Base case ($i = m-1$): Assume that $\sigma \in \varphi_{m-1}$. Recall that:

$$\varphi_{m-1} = s_{m-1} \wedge \Box(s_{m-1} \vee \Box S_m) \wedge \Diamond(\neg s_{m-1})$$

By Observation 3.1, it follows that:

(a) $\sigma \in s_{m-1} \circ S^\omega$.

(b) $\sigma \in s_{m-1}^\infty \circ S_m^\omega$.

(c) $\sigma \in S^* \circ (\neg s_{m-1}) \circ S^\omega$.

(c) implies that $\sigma \notin s_{m-1}^{\omega}$, and together with (a) and (b) it follows that $\sigma \in s_{m-1}^{+} \circ S_m^{\omega}$. Hence $\sigma \in E_{m-1}$.

Inductive step: Assume that the claim is true for $i = k+1 < m$, i.e., assume:

$$\mathcal{L}(\varphi_{k+1}) \subseteq E_{k+1}$$

Let σ be a sequence such that $\sigma \models \varphi_k$, i.e.,

$$\sigma \models s_k \wedge \Box(s_k \vee \psi_{k+1}) \wedge \Diamond(\varphi_{k+1}).$$

By definition, $\varphi_{k+1} \rightarrow s_{k+1}$. As $s_{k+1} \neq s_k$ (since $s_k \notin S_{k+1}$ and $s_{k+1} \in S_{k+1}$) it follows that $\sigma \in S^{+} \circ \mathcal{L}(\varphi_{k+1})$. Using similar reasoning to the base case, we derive that:

(a) $\sigma \in s_k^{+} \circ \mathcal{L}(\psi_{k+1})$.

(b) $\sigma \in s_k^{+} \circ S^{*} \circ \mathcal{L}(\varphi_{k+1})$.

The induction hypothesis implies that $\mathcal{L}(\varphi_{k+1}) \subseteq E_{k+1}$. Claim 3.1 implies that $\mathcal{L}(\psi_{k+1}) = S_{k+1}^{\infty} \circ \mathcal{L}(\psi_{k+2})$. Putting it all together, we derive that:

(a) $\sigma \in s_k^{+} \circ S_{k+1}^{\infty} \circ \mathcal{L}(\psi_{k+2})$.

(b) $\sigma \in s_k^{+} \circ S^{*} \circ E_{k+1}$.

We can distinguish between the following two cases:

case 1: $\sigma \in s_k^{+} \circ S_{k+1}^{*} \circ E_{k+1}$. Then trivially $\sigma \in E_k$.

case 2: $\sigma = \sigma_1;\sigma_2$, where

$$\begin{aligned}\sigma_1 &\in s_k^{+} \circ S_{k+1}^{*} \\ \sigma_2 &\in \mathcal{L}(\psi_{k+2}) \cap S^{*} \circ E_{k+1}.\end{aligned}$$

By Observation 3.1, this implies that

$$\sigma_2 \models \psi_{k+2} \wedge \Diamond\varphi_{k+1},$$

which contradicts Observation 3.2 (part 3).

We may therefore conclude that $\sigma \in E_k$. ⋈

Claim 3.3 *For every* $i = 1, \ldots, m-1$, $E_i \subseteq \mathcal{L}(\varphi_i)$.

Proof The proof is by (decreasing) induction on i.

Base case ($i = m-1$): Let σ be a model such that $\sigma \in E_{m-1}$, i.e., $\sigma \in s_{m-1}^{+} \circ S_m^{\omega}$. Observe that:

1. $\sigma \in s_{m-1} \circ S^{\omega}$ and hence, by Observation 3.1 (part 1), $\sigma \models s_{m-1}$.
2. $\sigma \in S^{*} \circ S_m \circ S^{\omega}$, and since $s_{m-1} \notin S_m$, Observation 3.1 (parts 1 and 2) implies that $\sigma \models \Diamond(\neg s_m)$.
3. $\sigma \in s_{m-1}^{\infty} \circ S_m^{\omega}$ and hence, by Observation 3.1 (part 3), $\sigma \models \Box(s_{m-1} \vee \Box S_m)$.

It follows that $\sigma \models s_{m-1} \wedge \Box(s_{m-1} \vee \Box S_m) \wedge \Diamond(\neg s_{m-1})$, i.e., $\sigma \models \varphi_{m-1}$. We may therefore conclude that:

$$E_{m-1} \subseteq \mathcal{L}(\varphi_{m-1}).$$

Inductive step Assume that for all i, $k+1 \leq i < m$, $E_i \subseteq \mathcal{L}(\varphi_i)$. Let σ be such that $\sigma \in E_k$, i.e., $\sigma \in s_k^{+} \circ S_{k+1}^{*} \circ E_{k+1}$. Similar reasoning to that of the base case establishes that:

1. $\sigma \models s_k$.
2. $\sigma \models \Diamond(\neg s_k)$.
3. By the induction hypothesis, $\sigma \in s_k^{+} \circ S_{k+1}^{*} \circ \mathcal{L}(\varphi_{k+1})$. From Observation 3.2 it follows that $\sigma \in s_k^{+} \circ S_{k+1}^{*} \circ \mathcal{L}(\psi_{k+1})$. From Claim 3.1 it follows that

$$S_{k+1}^{*} \circ \mathcal{L}(\psi_{k+1}) \subseteq \mathcal{L}(\psi_{k+1}),$$

and therefore $\sigma \in s_k^{+} \circ \mathcal{L}(\psi_{k+1})$. Since ψ_{k+1} is a $\Box$-formula, we can apply Observation 3.1 and derive that $\sigma \models \Box(s_k \vee \psi_{k+1})$.

Putting it all together, it follows that $\sigma \in \varphi_k$, hence:

$$E_k \subseteq \mathcal{L}(\varphi_k).$$

⋈

The above two claims establish:

Corollary 3.1 *For every* $i = 1, \ldots, m-1$, $E_i = \mathcal{L}(\varphi_i)$.

The following lemma establishes that LS is RTL-definable:

Lemma 3.1

$$LS \;=\; \mathcal{L}(s_0 \wedge \psi_1 \wedge \Diamond\varphi_1)$$

Proof In one direction, let σ be such that $\sigma \in LS$, i.e., $\sigma \in s_0 \circ S_1^* \circ E_1$. From Claim 3.1 it follows that $\sigma \models s_0 \wedge \psi_1$. From Corollary 3.1 and Observation 3.1 it follows that $\sigma \models \Diamond\varphi_1$, hence $\sigma \in \mathcal{L}(s_0 \wedge \psi_1 \wedge \Diamond\varphi_1)$.

In the other direction, let σ be such that $\sigma \models (s_0 \wedge \psi_1 \wedge \Diamond\varphi_1)$. From Corollary 3.1 and Observation 3.1, it follows that we can distinguish between the following two cases:

case: $\sigma \in s_0 \circ S_1^* \circ E_1$. Obviously, $\sigma \in LS$.
case: $\sigma = \sigma_1;\sigma_2$ where $\sigma_1 \in s_0 \circ S_1^*$, $\sigma_2 \in \mathcal{L}(\psi_2)$, and $\sigma_2 \in S^* \circ E_1$. It follows that $\sigma_2 \models \psi_2 \wedge \Diamond\varphi_1$, contradicting Claim 3.2 which established that $\psi_2 \rightarrow \neg\Diamond\varphi_1$.

We may therefore conclude that $\sigma \in s_0 \circ S_1^* \circ E_1$ and hence $\sigma \in LS$. ⋈

The following theorem establishes that every temporal set is RTL-definable:

Theorem 3.1 *Let L be a temporal set, i.e., let*

$$L = \bigcup_{i=1}^{n} L^i_{\mathrm{inf}(S_i)}$$

such that for every $i = 1, \ldots, n$, L^i *is a* Λ*-set and* $S_i \subseteq S$. *Then L is RTL-definable.*

Proof It suffices to prove the theorem for the case $n = 1$. Let L be defined by $L = LS_{\mathrm{inf}(S')}$ where LS is a Λ-set and $S' \subseteq S$. Let χ be the RTL-formula defining LS (whose construction is described above). Let θ be the RTL-formula defined by:

$$\theta = \chi \wedge \bigwedge_{s \in S'} \Box\Diamond s.$$

Obviously, $L = \mathcal{L}(\theta)$. Thus L is RTL-definable. ⋈

4 From RTL to Temporal Sets

Let φ be an RTL formula. Following Fischer and Ladner ([FL79]), we define the *closure* of φ, $CL(\varphi)$, to be the smallest set of formulae containing φ and satisfying:

$T, F \in CL(\varphi)$		
$\neg\psi \in CL(\varphi)$	$\Leftrightarrow$	$\psi \in CL(\varphi)$ (we identify $\neg\neg\psi$ with ψ)
$\psi_1 \vee \psi_2 \in CL(\varphi)$	$\Rightarrow$	$\psi_1, \psi_2 \in CL(\varphi)$
$\Diamond\psi \in CL(\varphi)$	$\Rightarrow$	$\psi \in CL(\varphi)$

An *atom* is a set of formulae $A \subseteq CL(\varphi)$ such that:

- $T \in A$.
- For every $\psi \in CL(\varphi)$, $\psi \in A \Leftrightarrow \neg\psi \notin A$.
- For every $\psi_1 \vee \psi_2 \in CL(\varphi)$, $\psi_1 \vee \psi_2 \in A \Leftrightarrow (\psi_1 \in A$ **or** $\psi_2 \in A)$.
- For every $\Diamond\psi \in CL(\varphi)$, $\psi \in A \Rightarrow \Diamond\psi \in A$.

The set of all atoms is denoted by At. An atom A that contains φ is called *initial*. The procedure for checking satisfiability attempts to construct a structure of atoms, interpreted as states, which contains a path satisfying φ. When interpreting atoms as states we take the natural evaluation I defined by $I(A) = A \cap \Pi$, i.e., the propositions taken to be true in A are all the propositions contained in A. Similarly, for a subset $At' \subseteq At$ of atoms, we denote $I(At') = \cup_{A \in At'}\{I(A)\}$. We assume that the set of propositional variables in φ is exactly Π.

We construct a structure $\mathcal{A} = (At, R)$ which is a graph whose nodes are all the atoms and whose edges are defined by the relation R:

$$(A, B) \in R$$
iff
For every $\Diamond\psi \in CL(\varphi)$,
$\Diamond\psi \in A \Leftrightarrow \psi \in A$ or $\Diamond\psi \in B$.

The following claims establish properties of paths and (maximally) strongly connected components (SCC's) in the structure $\mathcal{A}$. These claims shall be used when we describe how to construct the temporal set that equals to $\mathcal{L}(\varphi)$.

Observation 4.1 *Let* $\pi = A_0, \ldots$ *be a (possibly infinite) path in* $\mathcal{A}$ *and assume* $\Diamond\psi \in CL(\varphi)$. *Then:*

1. *If* $\Diamond\psi \notin A_0$ *then for every* $i \geq 0$, $\Diamond\psi \notin A_i$.
2. *If for some* $i \geq 0$, $\Diamond\psi \in A_i$, *then for all* j, $0 \leq j \leq i$, $\Diamond\psi \in A_j$.

Proof

1. By definition, for every $i \geq 0$, $\Diamond\psi \notin A_i$ and $(A_i, A_{i+1}) \in R$ imply that $\Diamond\psi \notin A_{i+1}$. The claim trivially follows.
2. Follows immediately from (1). ⋈

The following corollary establishes that all the atoms in a SCC of $\mathcal{A}$ have the same future subformulae.

Corollary 4.1 *Let C be a SCC of $\mathcal{A}$, and let A and B be atoms in C. Then for every $\Diamond\psi \in CL(\varphi)$:*

$$\Diamond\psi \in A \iff \Diamond\psi \in B.$$

Proof Follows immediately from Observation 4.1 as $A, B \in C$ imply that there exists a path from A to B and a path from B to A. ⋈

The following corollary establishes that every SCC is a clique.

Corollary 4.2 *Let C be a SCC of $\mathcal{A}$, and let A and B be atoms in C. Then $(A, B) \in R$.*

Proof By Corollary 4.1, for every $\Diamond\psi \in CL(\varphi)$, $\Diamond\psi \in A$ iff $\Diamond\psi \in B$. From the definition of R it follows that $\Diamond\psi \in A \equiv \Diamond\psi \in B$ implies that $(A, B) \in R$. ⋈

The following corollary establishes if an atom is R-connected to an atom in a SCC, then it is R-connected to all the atoms in the SCC.

Corollary 4.3 *Let C be a SCC of $\mathcal{A}$, let A_1 and A_2 be atoms in C, and let B be an atom in At. Then*

$$(B, A_1) \in R \iff (B, A_2) \in R.$$

Proof As (by Corollary 4.1) A_1 and A_2 contain the same future formulae, the claim follows immediately from the definition of R. ⋈

The following observation establishes that if an edge connects two disjoint atoms then these atoms differ in some propositional formula.

Observation 4.2 *Let A and B be two atoms such that $(A, B) \in R$. Then:*

$$A \neq B \implies I(A) \neq I(B).$$

Proof Let $A, B \in At$ be such that $(A, B) \in R$ and $A \neq B$. Hence, there exists a formula $\psi \in CL(\varphi)$ such that $\psi \in A$ and $\psi \notin B$. Let χ be such a formula whose length is minimal. We distinguish between the following cases:

case: χ is propositional. Then $I(A) \neq I(B)$ follows.

case: $\chi = \theta_1 \vee \theta_2$. Then either $\theta_1 \in A$ or $\theta_2 \in A$ and $\theta_1, \theta_2 \notin B$. Hence at least one of θ_1 and θ_2 is both shorter than χ and distinguishes between A and B, contradicting the minimality of $|\chi|$.

case: $\chi = \neg\theta$ where χ is not propositional. We distinguish between the following subcases:

subcase: $\theta = \theta_1 \vee \theta_2$. This subcase is symmetric to the previous case (i.e., $\chi = \theta_1 \vee \theta_2$) and hence contradicts the minimality of $|\chi|$.

subcase: $\theta = \Diamond\theta_1$. Then $\neg\Diamond\theta_1 \in A$ and $\Diamond\theta_1 \in B$. This contradicts Observation 4.1.

case: $\chi = \Diamond\theta$. i.e., $\Diamond\theta \in A$ and $\Diamond\theta \notin B$. From the definition of R it follows that $\theta \in A$. From the definition of atoms, it follows that $\theta \notin B$. Hence at θ is both shorter than χ and distinguishes between A and B, contradicting the minimality of $|\chi|$.

It follows that ψ is propositional and therefore $I(A) \neq I(B)$. ⋈

Corollary 4.4 *Let C be a SCC of $\mathcal{A}$, and let A and B be such that $(A, B) \in R$, $A \notin C$ and $B \in C$. Then for every $B' \in C$, $I(A) \neq I(B')$.*

Proof Follows immediately from Corollary 4.3 and Observation 4.2. ⋈

Let C be a set of atoms. C defined to be *self-fulfilling* if for every formula $\Diamond\psi \in A \in C$ there exists an atom $B \in C$ such that $\psi \in B$.

Let C be a self-fulfilling set of atoms. We define $\mathcal{F}(C)$ to be the set of C's subsets such that for every $F \in \mathcal{F}(C)$, F is self-fulfilling and no proper subset $F' \subset F$ is self-fulfilling.

Observation 4.3 *Let $C \in \mathcal{A}$ be a self-fulfulling SCC. Then for every $F \in \mathcal{F}(C)$, $|F| = O(|\varphi|)$.*

Proof Let F be an element of $\mathcal{F}(C)$. Then for every $A \in F$ there exists some $\Diamond\psi \in CL(\varphi)$ such that $\psi \in A$ and for every $A' \in F - \{A\}$, $\psi \notin A'$. The claim immediately follows. ⋈

The following observation establishes that every self-fulfilling SCC $C \in \mathcal{A}$ can be uniquely identified by its set of propositions.

Observation 4.4 *Let $C_1, C_2 \in \mathcal{A}$ be self-fulfilling SCC's. Then:*

$$I(C_1) = I(C_2) \implies C_1 = C_2.$$

Proof Assume to the contrary that $I(C_1) = I(C_2)$ and that $C_1 \neq C_2$. Let $A_1, \ldots, A_n \in At$ and $B_1, \ldots, B_n \in At$ be C_1's and C_2's atoms respectively. As $I(C_1) = I(C_2)$, we can choose the A_i's and B_i's such that for every i, $1 \leq i \leq n$, $I(A_i) = I(B_i)$. As $C_1 \neq C_2$, there exists some j, $1 \leq j \leq n$, such that $A_j \neq B_j$. For each such j, let $\psi_j \in CL(\varphi)$ be the minimal length formula such that $\psi_j \in A_j$ and $\psi_j \notin B_j$. Let $\psi = \psi_l$ be the shortest among the ψ_j formulae. As $I(A_l) = I(B_l)$, ψ is not propositional. It is obvious that ψ is not a disjunction. Therefore, we can assume that $\psi = \Diamond\chi$ for some $\chi \in CL(\varphi)$. As C_1 is self-fulfilling and $\Diamond\chi \in A_l \in C_1$, it follows that for some $A_k \in C_1$, $\chi \in A_k$. As C_2 is a SCC, it follows (from Corollary 4.1) that $\chi \notin B_k$. Hence $\chi \in CL(\varphi)$ is a formula which both distinguishes between A_k and B_k and is shorter than ψ, contradicting the minimality of ψ. ⋈

Let $\pi = A_0, A_1, \ldots$ be an infinite path in $\mathcal{A}$, i.e., for every $i \geq 0$, $(A_i, A_{i+1}) \in R$. Denote by $\inf(\pi)$ the set of atoms which appear in π infinitely many times. Note that the set $\inf(\pi)$ defines a SCC $C \in \mathcal{A}$.

The following proposition establishes the relation between $\mathcal{L}(\varphi)$ and paths in $\mathcal{A}$. It is a collection of results that were originally established in [SC85] and extended in [VW86] and in [Zuc86].

Proposition 4.1 *For every model* $\sigma = s_0, \ldots$, $\sigma \models \varphi$ iff *there exists a path* $\pi = A_0, \ldots$ *in* $\mathcal{A}$ *such that the following holds:*

1. A_0 *is an intial atom.*
2. $\inf(\pi)$ *is self-fulfilling.*
3. $I(\pi) = \sigma$*, i.e., for every* $i \geq 0$, $I(A_i) = I(s_i)$.

Let $\{C_i\}_{0=1}^{m-1}$ and $\{C_i\}_{i=1}^{m}$ be sequences of atoms and of SCC's respectively. We say that $\mathbf{C} = \langle\{C_i\}_{i=0}^{m-1}, \{C_i\}_{i=1}^{m}\rangle$ is a Λ-*structure* if the following holds:

1. $C_0 \in C_1$ is an initial atom.
2. C_m is self-fulfilling.
3. For every i, $1 \leq i < m$, $C_i \in C_i - C_{i+1}$ and C_i is R-connected to some node $A \in C_{i+1}$.

From Observation 4.1 and Corollary 4.1 it follows that if $\mathbf{C} = \langle\{C_i\}_{i=0}^{m-1}, \{C_i\}_{i=1}^{m}\rangle$ is a Λ-structure, then for every $i = 1, \ldots, m-1$, the set of $\Diamond$-formulae in C_i (i.e., $\{\psi \mid \Diamond\psi \in CL(\varphi)$ and $\Diamond\psi \in A \in C_i\}$) is a strict superset of the set of $\Diamond$-formulae in C_{i+1}. As the number of $\Diamond$-formulae is linear in φ, we conclude:

Observation 4.5 *Let* $\mathbf{C} = \langle\{C_i\}_{i=0}^{m-1}, \{C_i\}_{i=1}^{m}\rangle$ *be a* Λ*-structure. Then* $m = O(|\varphi|)$.

Let $\mathbf{C}$ be a Λ-structure as above. We associate with $\mathbf{C}$ a restricted regular set $L(\mathbf{C})$ defined by:

$$L(\mathbf{C}) = I(C_0) \circ I(C_1)^* \circ I(C_1) \circ \cdots \circ I(C_{m-1}) \circ I(C_m)^\omega.$$

Observation 4.6 *Let* $\mathbf{C}$ *and* $L(\mathbf{C})$ *be defined as above. Then* $L(\mathbf{C})$ *is a* Λ*-set.*

Proof It suffices to show that for every i, $1 \leq i < m$, $I(C_i) \notin I(C_{i+1})$, i.e., that for every $A \in C_{i+1}$, $I(C_i) \neq I(A)$. By definition, C_i is R-connected to C_{i+1}. As $C_i \notin C_{i+1}$, the claim follows immediately from Corollary 4.4. ⋈

Let $\mathbf{C}$ be a Λ-structure as above. We define $L_{\mathbf{C}} = \bigcup_{F \in \mathcal{F}(C_m)} L(\mathbf{C})_{\inf(I(F))}$. From Observation 4.6 it follows that $L_{\mathbf{C}}$ is a temporal set. As $\mathcal{A}$ is a finite structure, there are finitely many disjoint Λ-structures that $\mathcal{A}$ defines. Let $\mathbf{C}(\mathcal{A})$ denote the set of all these Λ-structures. We show below that $\mathcal{L}(\varphi)$ equals to the union of the temporal sets defined by $\mathbf{C}(\mathcal{A})$'s elements. From this we derive that $\mathcal{L}(\varphi)$ is a temporal set.

Theorem 4.1

$$\mathcal{L}(\varphi) = \bigcup_{\mathbf{C} \in \mathbf{C}(\mathcal{A})} L_{\mathbf{C}}$$

Proof In one direction, let σ be such that $\sigma \models \varphi$. From Proposition 4.1 it follows that there exists a path $\pi = A_0, \ldots$ in $\mathcal{A}$ such that A_0 is an initial atom, $\inf(\pi)$ is self-fulfilling, and $I(\pi) = \sigma$. The path π can be partitioned into fragments $\pi_1, \ldots, \pi_m$ such that $\pi = \pi_1; \ldots; \pi_m$ and for some SCC's $\mathcal{A}_1, \ldots, \mathcal{A}_m$ the following holds:

1. For every i, $1 \leq i < m$, $\mathcal{A}_i \neq \mathcal{A}_{i+1}$.
2. For every i, $1 \leq i < m$, π_i includes only atoms from $\mathcal{A}_i$, and ends in an atom $A^i \in \mathcal{A}_i - \mathcal{A}_{i+1}$.
3. $\inf(\pi)$ defines a self-fulfling SCC $\mathcal{A}_m \in \mathcal{A}$.

Define $A^0 = A_0$. The structure $\mathbf{C} = \langle\{A^i\}_{i=0}^{m-1}, \{\mathcal{A}_i\}_{i=1}^{m}\rangle$ is a obviously a Λ-structure which is in $\mathbf{C}(\mathcal{A})$. By construction, $I(\pi) \in L(\mathbf{C})$.

Moreover, since $\mathcal{A}_m \supseteq \inf(\pi)$, it follows that $I(\pi) \in L_{\mathbf{C}}$. As $I(\pi) = \sigma$, the claim follows.

In the other direction, assume that $\mathbf{C} = \langle \{C_i\}_{i=0}^{m-1}, \{C_i\}_{i=1}^{m} \rangle \in \mathbf{C}(\mathcal{A})$. Let $\sigma = s_0, \ldots$ be a sequence such that $\sigma \in L_{\mathbf{C}}$. From Corollaries 4.2 and 4.3, and Observations 4.2 and 4.4, it follows that σ identifies a unique path $\pi = A_0, \ldots$ in $\mathcal{A}$ such that $I(\pi) = \sigma$ and A_0 is an initial atom. Moreover, from the definition of σ it follows that $\inf(\pi)$ is self-fulfilling. Consequently, by Proposition 4.1, $\sigma \models \varphi$. ⋈

The corollary below will play a major role in the section discussing message buffers:

Corollary 4.5 *Let σ be such that $\sigma \models \varphi$. Then there exists a Λ-set LS defined by:*

$$L = s_0 \circ S_1^* \circ s_1 \circ S_2^* \circ s_2 \circ \cdots \circ S_{m-1}^* \circ s_{m-1} \circ S_m^\omega$$

such that for some $S' \subseteq S$, $\sigma \in LS_{\inf(S')}$ and $m, |S'| = O(|\varphi|)$

Proof Follows immediately from Observations 4.3 and 4.5, and Theorem 4.1.

5 Fairness in RTL

A concurrent (or distributed) program is usually associated with a set of *fairness properties*. This set corresponds to the properties which every computation of the program is assumed to satisfy. Verifying that all executions of a program P satisfy a property φ usually means verifying that all *fair* executions of P satisfy φ. Fairness properties play a major role in verification of liveness properties, where very often the property would not hold over computations which are not fair. An example of a fairness property is *impartiality* which asserts that every process which is permanently enabled is eventually activated. Impartiality thus requires that every process which has not terminated eventually perform some action. In this section we present a normal-form for fairness properties that are RTL-definable.

A set $L \subseteq S^\omega$ is defined to be a *Fairness-set* (or simply *F-set*) if for every $\sigma \in L$ the following holds:

1. For every $i \geq 0$, $\sigma^{(i)} \in L$, i.e., every suffix of σ is also in L.
2. For every $\sigma' \in S^*$, $\sigma'; \sigma \in L$, i.e., the string obtained by attaching any finite string as a prefix to σ is also in L.

Claim 5.1 *Let L be an F-set which is definable by $LS_{\inf(S')}$ for some Λ-set LS and $S' \subseteq S$. Then there exists $p_1, \ldots, p_n, q_1, \ldots, q_n \in \Sigma$ such that:*

$$L = \mathcal{L}\Big(\bigwedge_{i=1}^{n} (\Diamond\Box p_i \wedge \Box\Diamond q_i)\Big).$$

Proof As LS is a Λ-set it is definable by

$$L = s_0 \circ S_1^* \circ s_1 \circ S_2^* \circ s_2 \circ \cdots \circ S_{m-1}^* \circ s_{m-1} \circ S_m^\omega$$

for some $S_1, \ldots, S_m \subseteq S$ and $s_0, \ldots, s_{m-1} \in S$.

Let φ_L be the RTL formula defined by:

$$\varphi_L = \Diamond\Box I(S_m) \wedge \bigwedge_{s \in S'} \Box\Diamond I(s).$$

We establish the claim by showing that $\mathcal{L}(\varphi_L) = L$. In one direction, if $\sigma \in L$ then obviously $\sigma \models \varphi_L$. In the other direction, assume that $\sigma \models \varphi_L$. σ has a suffix σ'' such that $\sigma'' \models \Box I(S_m) \wedge \bigwedge_{s \in S'} \Diamond I(s)$. Hence, there exists some finite sequence $\sigma' \in S^*$ such that $\sigma'; \sigma'' \in L$. As L is an F-set, every suffix of $\sigma'; \sigma''$ is in L, in particular, $\sigma'' \in L$. Similarly, since L is an F-set, any finite string attached as a prefix to σ'' is also in L; in particular, it follows that $\sigma \in L$, which establishes the claim. ⋈

The equivalence between temporal sets and RTL-definability together with the above claim yield:

Corollary 5.1 *Let φ be an RTL formula such that $\mathcal{L}(\varphi)$ is an F-set. Then φ is equivalent to some RTL formula of the form:*

$$\bigvee_{i=1}^{n} \Big(\bigwedge_{j=1}^{n_i} (\Diamond\Box p_i^j \wedge \Box\Diamond q_i^j)\Big)$$

for some $p_i^j, q_i^j \in \Sigma$ $(i = 1, \ldots n,\ j = 1, \ldots, n_i)$.

6 Reasoning about message buffers in RTL

In this section we consider the problem of axiomatizing different message buffers in RTL. Message buffers model communication between processes through message passing and are of special importance to distributed computing. The problem of characterizing message buffers in TL was studied in [SCFM84]. It is shown there that the theory of bounded buffers is axiomatizable in TL, while the theory of unbounded fifo buffers is Π_1^1-complete (and hence not axiomatizable). We consider the theory of unbounded message buffers in RTL and show that for both the fifo and the unordered case these theories are in co-NP (and hence axiomatizable in RTL). This is of practical significance as fifo buffers is the most widely used model of communication. The results in this section provide more evidence that reasoning in RTL is both easier and more plausible than reasoning in the full TL.

A message buffer is characterized by the set of *read/write* operations allowed on it. A *write* operation writes a message onto the buffer. A *read* operation reads a message and deletes it from the buffer. Reading from an empty buffer is not allowed. We consider both unbounded *fifo* buffers where a read operation reads the last message written, and unbounded *unordered* buffers where a read operation can read any message that was written (and is still in the buffer).

Let $\Delta = \{0, 1\}$ be the message alphabet. We extend Π to include the set $\Pi_\Delta = \{R_0, W_0, R_1, W_1\}$. We similarly extend the evaluation such that for every $s \in S$ there exists exactly one operation $P \in \Pi_\Delta$ such that $P \in I(s)$, i.e., with each $s \in S$ we associate one read/write operation.

Let $\sigma = s_0, s_1, \ldots$ be a (possibly finite) sequence of states. We define $W(\sigma)$ to be the sequence of messages written in σ and $R(\sigma)$ to be the sequence message read in σ. For every $\delta \in \Delta$ and $X \in \{R, W\}$, let $\sharp X_\delta(\sigma)$ denote the number of X_δ operations in σ.

Let *FIFO* denote the set of sequences over S that consist of valid operations in a fifo buffer, and *UNOR* denote those that consist of valid operations in an unordered buffer. Formally:

$$\text{FIFO} = \{\sigma \in S^\omega \mid \text{For every } i \geq 0,\ R(\sigma_{\rightarrow i}) \preceq W(\sigma_{\rightarrow i})\}$$

and

$$\text{UNOR} = \{\sigma \in S^\omega \mid \text{For every } i \geq 0 \text{ and } \delta \in \Delta,\ \sharp R_\delta(\sigma_{\rightarrow i}) \leq \sharp W_\delta(\sigma_{\rightarrow i})\}$$

The *theory of fifo buffers in RTL*, $\mathcal{T}$(fifo), is the set of all RTL formulae φ such that for every model $\sigma \in$FIFO, $\sigma \models \varphi$. Similarly, the *theory of unordered buffers in RTL*, $\mathcal{T}$(unor), is the set of all RTL formulae φ such that for every model $\sigma \in$UNOR, $\sigma \models \varphi$.

Let $\overline{\mathcal{T}}$ be the complement of $\mathcal{T}$(fifo), i.e.,

$$\overline{\mathcal{T}} = \{\varphi \in RTL \mid \text{For some } \sigma \in \text{FIFO}, \sigma \not\models \varphi\}.$$

The following claim enables us to show that the $\overline{\mathcal{T}}$ is in NP.

Claim 6.1 *Let $\varphi \in \overline{\mathcal{T}}$ be such that $|\varphi| = n - 1$ for some $n > 1$. Then there exists a sequence $\sigma \in$FIFO such that $\sigma = \sigma_1; \sigma_2^\omega$ where $|\sigma_1|, |\sigma_2| = O(n)$ and $\sigma \models \neg\varphi$.*

Proof As $\varphi \in \overline{\mathcal{T}}$, there exists a sequence $\alpha = s^0, s^1, \ldots \in$FIFO such that $\alpha \models \neg\varphi$. From Corollary 4.5, it follows that there exists a Λ-set LS defined by:

$$LS = s_0 \circ S_1^* \circ s_1 \circ S_2^* \circ s_2 \circ \cdots \circ S_{m-1}^* \circ s_{m-1} \circ S_m^\omega$$

such that $\alpha \in LS_{\text{inf}(S')}$ for some $S' \subseteq S$ where $m, |S'| = O(n)$.

Let $0 = i_0 < i_1 < \ldots < i_{m-1}$ be such that for every j, $0 \leq j < m$, $s^{i_j} = s_j$ and for every j, $0 \leq j < m-1$, for every k, $i_j < k < i_{j+1}$, $s^k \in S_j$. (As $\alpha \in LS$, the existence of such i_j's is guaranteed.) The sequence σ_1 is constructed by taking the sequence $s^{i_0}, \ldots, s^{i_{m-1}}$, and adding states to it such that the resulting sequence preserves the fifo properties and is a prefix of some model that satisfies $\neg\varphi$. The states are added as follows:

For every j, $0 \leq j < m$, if for some $x \in \{0, 1\}$, $R_x \in I(s^{i_j})$ then, as $\alpha \in$ FIFO, there exists some $k < i_j$ such that $W_x \in I(s^k)$ and $R(\alpha_{\rightarrow i_j}) = W(\alpha_{\rightarrow k})$. Moreover, since $\alpha \in LS$, there exists some $l < j$ such that $i_l \leq k < i_{l+1}$. If $k \neq i_l$, then we add the state s^k to the sequence and place it arbitrarily between s^{i_l} and $s^{i_{l+1}}$.

Similarly, for every j, $0 \leq j < m$, if for some $x \in \{0, 1\}$, $W_x \in I(s^{i_j})$ and there exsits a $k > i_j$, $k \neq i_{j+1}, \ldots, i_{m-1}$, such that $R_x \in I(s^k)$ and $R(\alpha_{\rightarrow k}) = W(\alpha_{\rightarrow i_j})$, we add the state s^k to the sequence and place in the appropriate location.

We define σ_1 to be the resulting sequence. Clearly, $|\sigma_1| \leq 2 \cdot m$. We construct σ_2 as follows: We first construct as set $S'' \subseteq S$ such that $|S''| \leq 4$ by choosing one representative for each operation that is performed by some state that is in $\text{inf}(\alpha)$. Note that if both writes (i.e., W_0 and W_1) are represented in S'' then either none or both of the reads are represented. We construct a sequence σ_2 such that:

- If S'' has no read states (i.e., states representing read operations), we take σ_2 to be any sequence that contains one occurrence of each of S'''s elements.
- If S'' has one read state, then we take σ_2 to be a concatenation of two sequences, σ_2^1 and σ_2^2, such that σ_2^1 contains one or more occurrence of each write state that is in $S' \cup S''$, and σ_2^2 contains all the read states that are in $s \in S' \cup S''$. Note that $|\sigma_2^1| \geq |\sigma_2^2|$.
- If S'' contains both read operations, then we take σ_2 to be a concatenation of two sequences, σ_2^1 and σ_2^2, such that σ_2^1 contains one or more occurrence of each write state that is in $S' \cup S''$, σ_2^2 contains one or more occurrence of each read state that is in $s \in S' \cup S''$, and if $\sigma_2^1 = W_{x_1}, \ldots, W_{x_m}$ then $\sigma_2^2 = R_{x_1}, \ldots, R_{x_m}$.

Note that $|\sigma_2| = O(n)$ and that σ_2^ω is a fifo sequence.

Let $\sigma = \sigma_1; \sigma_2^\omega$. Obviously, $|\sigma_1|, \sigma_2| = O(n)$. From the construction it follows that $\sigma \in$ FIFO and that $\sigma \in LS_{\text{inf}(S')}$. Consequently, $\sigma \models \neg\varphi$. ⋈

From Claim 6.1 we establish:

Theorem 6.1 *$\mathcal{T}$(fifo) is in co-NP.*

Proof It suffices to show that there exists a procedure in NP that decides whether a given formula φ ∈RTL where $|\varphi| = n$ is in $\mathcal{T}$(fifo). The procedure guesses two sequences of states σ_1 and σ_2 such that $|\sigma_1|, |\sigma_2| = O(n)$, checks whether $\sigma_1; \sigma_2^\omega$ is in FIFO, and checks whether $\sigma \models \neg\varphi$. The latter can be done in time which is polynomial in n. (This is established in [SC85].) ⋈

Similar arguments establish:

Theorem 6.2 *$\mathcal{T}$(unor) is in co-NP.*

7 Relationship between IML and RTL

Propositional Modal Logic of Intervals, or, Interval Modal Logic (IML) was introduced in [HS86], where it has been proposed to reason about the behavior of dynamic systems over intervals of time. While satisfiability of TL formulae is defined over discrete time models, satisfiability of IML formulae is defined over *time intervals*. In this section we define several Continuous-time RTL's and show how each corresponds to some subset of IML.

7.1 IML

The work in [HS86] considered different time structures that have "linear intervals". We, however, consider only the time structure $T = ([0,1], \leq)$ where $[0,1]$ is the closed interval included between the points 0 and 1 on the real line, and $\leq$ is the usual total ordering relation on these points. A *model M* for IML is a pair (J, I) where J is the set of all closed intervals in $[0,1]$ (i.e., $J = \{[t_1, t_2] \mid 0 \leq t_1 \leq t_2 \leq 1\}$), and $I: J \rightarrow 2^{\Pi}$ is an evaluation that associates with each interval $j \in J$ the set of atomic propositions that are true in it.

We introduce an IML language over the propositional formulae in Π using the boolean connectives $\neg$ and $\vee$, and the IML operators $\langle B \rangle$, $\langle E \rangle$, $\langle \overline{B} \rangle$, and $\langle \overline{E} \rangle$. IML formulae are constructed by the following:

- Every proposition $Q \in \Pi$ is an IML formula.
- If φ is an IML formula, then so are $\neg\varphi$, $\langle B \rangle\varphi$, $\langle E \rangle\varphi$, $\langle \overline{B} \rangle\varphi$, and $\langle \overline{E} \rangle\varphi$.
- If φ_1 and φ_2 are IML formulae, then so is $\varphi_1 \vee \varphi_2$.

We define a satisfiability relation $\models_i$ between a model M, an interval $j = [t_1, t_2] \in J$ and an IML formlua. We omit the model M whenever it is understood from the context. The satisfiability relation is defined as follows:

For a proposition $Q \in \Pi$,

$[t_1, t_2] \models_i Q$ *iff* $Q \in I([t_1, t_2])$.

$[t_1, t_2] \models_i \neg\varphi$ *iff* $[t_1, t_2] \not\models_i \varphi$.

$[t_1, t_2] \models_i \varphi_1 \vee \varphi_2$ *iff* $[t_1, t_2] \models_i \varphi_1$ **or** $[t_1, t_2] \models_i \varphi_2$.

$[t_1, t_2] \models_i \langle B \rangle\varphi$ *iff* For some t_3, $t_1 \leq t_3 \leq t_2$, $[t_1, t_3] \models_i \varphi$.

$[t_1, t_2] \models_i \langle \overline{B} \rangle\varphi$ *iff* For some $t_3 \geq t_2$, $[t_1, t_3] \models_i \varphi$.

$[t_1, t_2] \models_i \langle E \rangle\varphi$ *iff* For some t_3, $t_1 \leq t_3 \leq t_2$, $[t_3, t_2] \models_i \varphi$.

$[t_1, t_2] \models_i \langle \overline{E} \rangle\varphi$ *iff* For some $t_3 \leq t_1$, $[t_3, t_2] \models_i \varphi$.

Note that the semantics above does not coincide with that of [HS86].

For $X \subseteq \{\langle E \rangle, \langle B \rangle, \langle \overline{E} \rangle, \langle \overline{B} \rangle\}$ let $IML(X)$ denote the fragment of IML that uses only the modal operators that are in X.

7.2 Continuous Time RTL

Cosider a Continuous-time RTL (CRTL) which is similar to RTL. CRTL formulae are interpreted over points in time structure $T = ([0,1], \leq)$, where we assume an evaluation $I': [0,1] \rightarrow 2^{\Pi}$ that maps each point $t \in [0,1]$ to $I'(t)$, the set of propositions true in it. The satisfiability relation between a point $t \in [0,1]$ and an CRTL formula is denoted by $\models_c$ and defined in the obvious way.

Assume $\varphi \in IML(\langle E \rangle)$, and let R_φ be the RTL formula obtained by replacing every occurrence of $\langle E \rangle$ in φ by $\diamond$. Let M be a model of IML such that for every $t \in [0,1]$, $I([t,1]) = I'(t)$.

Lemma 7.1 *For every $t \in [0,1]$, $[t,1] \models_i \varphi$ iff $t \models_c R_\varphi$.*

Proof The proof is by induction on the structure of φ. The base case is when φ is propositional, and then, as $I([t,1]) = I'(t)$, the claim is trivially true. Assume the claim is true for φ' such that $|\varphi'| < |\varphi|$. We distinguish between the following cases:

case: $\varphi = \neg\varphi'$, i.e., $R_\varphi = \neg R_{\varphi'}$. This case is trivial.

case: $\varphi = \varphi' \vee \varphi''$,i.e., $R_\varphi = R_{\varphi'} \vee R_{\varphi''}$. This case is trivial.

case: $\varphi = \langle E \rangle \varphi'$, i.e., $R_\varphi = \diamond R_{\varphi'}$. By definition , $[t,1] \models_i \langle E \rangle \varphi'$ iff for some t', $t \leq t' \leq 1$, $[t',1] \models_i \varphi'$, and $t \models_c \diamond R_{\varphi'}$ iff for some t', $t \leq t' \leq 1$, $t' \models_c R_{\varphi'}$. By the induction hypothesis, for every t', $t \leq t' \leq 1$, $[t',1] \models_i \varphi'$ iff $t' \models_c R_{\varphi'}$. Consequently, $[t,1] \models_i \varphi$ iff $t \models_c R_\varphi$.

⋈

Let CRTLP be CRTL enriched with the past operator $\diamond^-$. The semantics of CRTLP is similar to that of CRTL, where we define for every $t \in [0,1]$:

$t \models_{cp} \diamond^- \varphi$ iff For some t', $0 \leq t' \leq t$, $t' \models_{cp} \varphi$.

Assume $\varphi \in IML(\langle E \rangle, \langle \overline{E} \rangle)$. Let R_φ be the RTLP formula obtained by replacing every occurrence of $\langle E \rangle$ in φ by $\diamond$, and every occurrence of $\langle \overline{E} \rangle$—by $\diamond^-$. Let M be a model of IML such that for every $t \in [0,1]$, $I([t,1]) = I'(t)$. By a similar proof to that of Lemma 7.1 we obtain:

Lemma 7.2 *For every $t \in [0,1]$, $[t,1] \models_i \varphi$ iff $t \models_{cp} R_\varphi$.*

In the full version of the paper we prove:

Theorem 7.1 *The satisfiability (resp. validity) problems for CRTL, CRTLP, $IML(\langle E \rangle)$, and $IML(\langle E \rangle, \langle \overline{E} \rangle)$ are NP complete (resp. Co-NP complete).*

7.3 Two dimensional RTL

A model for the *two dimensional restricted temporal logic* (2d-RTL) consits of Δ—the set of points in the triangle enclosed between the points $(0,0)$, $(0,1)$ and $(1,1)$, (i.e., $\Delta = \{(x,y) \mid 0 \leq x \leq 1, 0 \leq y \leq 1$, and $y \leq 1-x\}$), and an evaluation $I': \Delta \rightarrow 2^{\Pi}$ that maps to each point $\delta \in \Delta$ the set of atomic propositions true in δ.

We introduce a *2d-RTL language* over the propositional formulae in Π using the boolean connectives $\neg$ and $\vee$, and the 2d-temporal operators $\diamond_x$ (*eventually in the x direction*) and $\diamond_y$ (*eventually in the y direction*). 2d-RTL formulae are constructed in the obvious way.

We define a satisfiability relation $\models_{2d}$ between a model M, a point $\delta = (x,y) \in \Delta$ and a 2d-RTL formlua. The satisfiability relation is defined as follows: (As usual, we omit the model M whenever possible.)

For a proposition $Q \in \Pi$,

$(x,y) \models_{2d} Q$ *iff* $Q \in I'((x,y))$.

$(x,y) \models_{2d} \neg\varphi$ *iff* $(x,y) \not\models_{2d} \varphi$.

$(x,y) \models_{2d} \varphi_1 \vee \varphi_2$ *iff* $(x,y) \models_{2d} \varphi_1$ or $(x,y) \models_{2d} \varphi_2$.

$(x,y) \models_{2d} \diamond_x \varphi$ *iff* For some $x' \geq x$, $(x',y) \in \Delta$ and $(x',y) \models_{2d} \varphi$.

$(x,y) \models_{2d} \diamond_y \varphi$ *iff* For some $y' \geq y$, $(x,y') \in \Delta$ and $(x,y') \models_{2d} \varphi$.

Let $M_i = (I,J)$ and $M_{2d} = (I',\Delta)$ be models for IML and 2d-RTL respectively such that for every $0 \leq x \leq y \leq 1$ and $Q \in \Pi$, $I'((x,1-y)) = I([x,y])$. Let φ be an $IML(\langle B \rangle, \langle E \rangle)$ formula. We define a 2d-RTL formula D_φ by replacing each occurrence of $\langle E \rangle$ in φ be $\diamond_x$, and each occurrence of $\langle B \rangle$—by $\diamond_y$.

Lemma 7.3 *For every x and y such that $0 \leq x \leq y \leq 1$,*

$$(M_i,[x,y]) \models_i \varphi \quad \textit{iff} \quad (M_{2d},(x,1-y)) \models_{2d} D_\varphi.$$

Proof The proof is by induction on the structure of φ. The base case is when φ is propositional, and then, as $I([x,y]) = I'((x,1-y))$, the claim is trivially true. Assume the claim is true for all φ', φ'' such that $|\varphi'|, |\varphi''| < |\varphi|$. We distinguish between the following cases:

case: $\varphi = \neg\varphi'$, i.e., $D_\varphi = \neg D_{\varphi'}$. This case is trivial.

case: $\varphi = \varphi' \vee \varphi''$,i.e., $D_\varphi = D_{\varphi'} \vee D_{\varphi''}$. This case is trivial.

case: $\varphi = \langle E \rangle \varphi'$, i.e., $D_\varphi = \Diamond_x D_{\varphi'}$. By definition , $[x, y] \models_i \langle E \rangle \varphi'$ iff for some x', $x \le x' \le y$, $(M_i, [x', y]) \models_i \varphi'$. From the induction hypothesis it follows that the above is true iff for some x', $x \le x' \le y$, $(M_{2d}, (x', 1-y)) \models_{2d} D_{\varphi'}$, which, by the semantics of 2d-RTL, is true iff $(M_{2d}, (x, 1-y)) \models_{2d} \Diamond_x D_\varphi$. We may therefore conclude that $(M_i, [x, y]) \models_i \varphi$ iff $(M_{2d}, (x, 1-y)) \models_{2d} D_\varphi$.

case: $\varphi = \langle B \rangle \varphi'$, i.e., $D_\varphi = \Diamond_y D_{\varphi'}$. This case is similar to the previous case. ⋈

Let 2d-RTLP be 2d-RTL enriched with the past operators $\Diamond_x^-$ and $\Diamond_y^-$. The semantics of 2d-RTLP is similar to this of 2d-RTL, where we define:

$(x, y) \models_{2dp} \Diamond_x^- \varphi$ *iff*
For some $x' \le x$,$(x', y) \in \Delta$ and $(x', y) \models_{2d} \varphi$
$(x, y) \models_{2dp} \Diamond_y^- \varphi$ *iff*
For some $y' \le y$, $(x, y') \in \Delta$ and $(x, y') \models_{2d} \varphi$

Assume $\varphi \in IML(\langle E \rangle, \langle B \rangle, \langle \overline{E} \rangle \langle \overline{B} \rangle)$. Let D_φ be the 2d-RTLP formula obtained by replacing every occurrence of $\langle E \rangle$ in φ by $\Diamond_x$, every occurrence of $\langle B \rangle$—by $\Diamond_y$, every occurrence of $\langle \overline{E} \rangle$—by $\Diamond_x^-$, and every occurrence of $\langle \overline{B} \rangle$—by $\Diamond_y^-$.

A similar proof to that of Lemma 7.3 establishes:

Lemma 7.4 *Let* $\varphi \in IML(\langle E \rangle, \langle B \rangle, \langle \overline{E} \rangle, \langle \overline{B} \rangle)$. *Then for every* x *and* y *such that* $0 \le x \le y \le 1$,

$$(M_i, [x, y]) \models_i \varphi \quad \textit{iff} \quad (M_{2d}, (x, 1-y)) \models_{2dp} D_\varphi.$$

The lemma above implies that any decision procedure for $IML(\langle E \rangle, \langle B \rangle, \langle \overline{E} \rangle, \langle \overline{B} \rangle)$ can be used as a decision procedure for 2d-RTLP and vice versa.

8 Conclusions and Future Work

We showed the equivalence between RTL and a subclass of the ω-regular languages. The translations from one language into the other are simple. We demonsrated some of the usefulness of RTL for verification systems. In particular, we showed that if we restrict ourselves to RTL, then there are properties (e.g., fairness) that can be easily expressed and normal formed. We also showed that axiomatizing message buffers in RTL is easier than doing that in the full TL.

We defined a Real Time RTL which is interpreted over real intervals, and compared it to fragments of IML. We also defined a two dimensional RTL, which we also compared to fragments of IML.

We are currently working on finding a sound and complete deductive system for establishing validity of RTL formulae. We are also looking for a decision procedure for 2d-RTL.

In order to compare RTL to the version of IML presented in [HS86], we need to define the eventually operator as a *strict* operator. This seems advetagoeus also for other purposes. We would like to investigate how the work reported above can be adjusted so as to accommodate the strict eventually operator.

References

[AS85] B. Alpern and F. B. Schneider. Defining liveness. *Information Processing Letters*, **21**:10, 1985.

[Buc62] J. R. Büchi. On decision methods in restricted second order arithmetic. In *Proc. Int'l Congr. Logic, Methods, and Philos.*, pp. 1–12, Stanford University Press, 1962.

[CM86] K. M. Chandy and J. Misra. *Parallel Program Design: A Fundation.* (A draft), 1986.

[FL79] M. J. Fischer and R. E. Ladner. Propositional Dynamic Logic of regular programs. *Journal of Computer and System Science*, **18**, pp. 194–211, 1979.

[GPSS80] D. Gabbay, A. Pnueli, S. Shelah, and J. Stavi. The temporal analysis of fairness. In *Proc. 7th ACM Symp. on Principles of Programming Languages*, pp. 163–173, 1980.

[HS86] J. Y. Halpern and Y. Shoham. A propositional modal logic for time intervals. In *Proc. 1st IEEE Symp. on Logics in Computer Science*, 1986.

[Kam68] J. A. Kamp. *Tense Logic and the Theory of Linear Order.* PhD thesis, University of California, Los Angeles, 1968.

[LPZ85] O. Lichtenstein, A. Pnueli, and L. Zuck. The glory of the past. In *Proc. of the Workshop on Logics of Programs*, pp. 196–218, 1985.

[McN66] R. McNaughton. Testing and generating infinite sequences by a finite automaton. *Information and Control*, **9**, pp. 521–530, 1966.

[MP71] R. McNaughton and S. Papert. *Counter Free Automata.* MIT Press, Cambridge, Mass, 1971.

[OL82] S. Owicki and L. Lamport. Proving liveness properties of concurrent programs. *TOPLAS*, **4**:3, pp. 455–495, 1982.

[Pnu77] A. Pnueli. The Temporal Logic of programs. In *Proc. 18th IEEE Symp. on Foundation of Computer Science*, pp. 46–57, 1977.

[RS59] M. O. Rabin and D. Scott. Finite automata and their decision problems. *IBM J. Res.*, **3**:2, pp. 115–125, 1959.

[SC85] A. P. Sistla and E. M. Clarke. The complexity of Propositional Linear Temporal Logic. *Journal of the ACM*, **32**, pp. 733–749, 1985.

[SCFM84] A. P. Sistla, E. M. Clarke, N. Francez, and A. R. Meyer. Can message buffers be axiomatized in linear temporal logic? *Information and Control*, **63**:1/2, pp. 88–112, 1984.

[Sis85] A. P. Sistla. On characterization of safety and liveness properties in Temporal Logic. In *Proc. 4th ACM Symp. on Principles of Distributed Computing*, pp. 39–48, 1985.

[SVW85] A. P. Sistla, M. Y. Vardi, and P. Wolper. The complementation problem for Büchi automata with applications to Temporal Logic. In *Proc. 12th International Colloq. on Automata, Languages, and Programming*, pp. 465–474, LNCS, Springer Verlag, 1985.

[Tho81] W. Thomas. A combinatorial approach to the theory of ω-automata. *Information and Control*, **48**, pp. 261–283, 1981.

[Var85] M. Y. Vardi. Automatic verification of concurrent probabilistic finite state programs. In *Proc. 26th IEEE Symp. on Foundation of Computer Science*, pp. 327–338, 1985.

[VW86] M. Y. Vardi and P. Wolper. An automata-theoretic approach to automatic program verification (preliminary report). In *Proc. 1st IEEE Symp. on Logics in Computer Science*, 1986.

[Zuc86] L. Zuck. *Past Temporal Logic.* PhD thesis, The Weizmann Institute of Science, 1986.

Verification of Concurrent Programs: The Automata-Theoretic Framework

Preliminary Report

Moshe Y. Vardi*
IBM Almaden Research Center

Abstract

We present an automata-theoretic framework to the verification of concurrent and nondeterministic programs. The basic idea is that to verify that a program P is correct one writes a program A that receives the computation of P as input and diverges only on incorrect computations of P. Now P is correct if and only if the program P_A, which is obtained by combining P and A, terminates. This unifies previous works on verification of fair termination and verification of temporal properties.

1 Introduction

In this paper we present an automata-theoretic framework that unifies work that has taken place in the area of concurrent program verification over the last decade. Let us start with a survey of that work.

In 1977 Pnueli suggested the use of *temporal logic* in the verification of concurrent programs [Pn77]. The basic motivation is that in the verification of concurrent programs it is easier to reason about computation sequences than about input-output relations. Temporal logic is a modal logic that enables one to describe how a situation changes over time [RU71]. Hence, it is appropriate for reasoning about concurrent programs.

Since 1977, there has been significant progress in the development of techniques and methodologies for proving temporal properties of concurrent programs [HO83, MP81, MP83a, MP83b, MP84, OL82, Pn81]. The developed methods reduce program correctness to truth of sentences in first-order temporal logic. Thus, these methods require *temporal reasoning*, and do not provide a reduction of a proof of a temporal property into a sequence of proofs of *nontemporal verification conditions* in the underlying assertion languages. This should be contrasted with proof systems for sequential programs, one of whose main features is precisely such a reduction (cf. [Ap81,Ap84]). We call this *proof by reduction*. For some isolated classes of properties such reductions have been found [MP83b,MP84], but the general case remained open.

At the same time, a lot of attention has been given to the development of methods for proving *fair* termination of nondeterministic programs ([Fr86] is a good survey of the area). (Since nondeterministic programs are often used to model concurrent programs, this research is also applicable to the latter ones.) A program is fairly terminating if it admits no infinite computation, provided the scheduling of nondeterministic choices is "fair". There are many different notions of fairness, and each one requires a different proof rule for termination.

One approach to fair termination is the method of *explicit schedulers* [AO83, APS84, Bo82, Pa81a]. The main idea of this approach is to reduce fair termination to ordinary termination by augmenting the program with random assignments. A unifying treatment of this method was given by Harel in [Ha86] and pursued in [DH86]. Harel introduced an infinitary language L in which one can express

*Address: IBM Almaden Research K53-802, 650 Harry Rd., San Jose, CA 95120-6099. Part of this research was done while the author was visiting the Weizmann Institute of Science.

CH2464-6/87/0000/0167$01.00 © 1987 IEEE

almost all notions of fairness that have appeared in the literature. He then showed how fair termination can be reduced to termination. More precisely, given a program P and a fairness assertion ϕ, a program P' is constructed such that P admits no infinite computation that obeys ϕ if and only if P' admits no infinite computation [DH86,Ha86]. Since we know how to prove termination by reduction to an underlying assertion language [AP86], Harel's method provide a reduction technique for fair termination. It still leaves open the general problem of verifying arbitrary temporal properties.

Another approach to fair termination is the method of *helpful directions* [GFMR85, LPS81]. The main idea of this approach is to define some ranking of program states by means of elements of some well-founded sets. This ranking has to decrease along a computation according to rules that depends on the notion of fairness under consideration. A uniform treatment of this method was given by Rinat et al. [RFG85]. They introduced a proof rule for arbitrary fairness properties expressed in a fragment L^- of Harel's L.

A concurrent development is the development of proof techniques for *finite-state* programs. It was already shown by Pnueli [Pn77], that verifying arbitrary temporal properties of finite-state programs is decidable. More efficient algorithms were developed in [CES86, LP85, QS83] and lower bounds were proven in [SC85]. An automata-theoretic approach to the verification of finite-state programs was described by Vardi and Wolper [Va85,VW86]. They use the fact that one can effectively translate a temporal specification into an equivalent specification by a finite-state automaton over infinite execution sequences [WVS83]. Vardi and Wolper have shown how by combining the finite-state program and the finite-state specification, the verification problem can be reduced to an automata-theoretic problem. Essentially, their method is to "get away" from temporal logic, since it seems difficult to directly verify properties specified in temporal logic.

The relevance of automata theory to the verification of concurrent programs was first recognized by Park [Pa79,Pa81b]. The trend of "getting away" from temporal logic was started by Wolper [Wo83], who argued the temporal logic lacks expressive power, and introduced *extended temporal logic* (*ETL*), which uses finite-state automata as a specification language. This trend was continued by Alpern and Schneider [AS85], who describe a proof by reduction method for properties specified by finite-state automata. The weakness of their method is that it can deal only with *deterministic* automata.[1]

The automata-theoretic framework that we present here unifies the above mentioned works on fair termination, Vardi and Wolper's approach to the verification of finite-state programs, and Alpern and Schneider's approach to deterministic properties. As in [Va85,VW86], the basic idea is to combine the specification with the program. We still deal with specification by automata, but not necessarily finite-state automata. This requires a development of a theory of *recursive automata*. Just as temporal logic formulas can be expressed by finite-state automata, formulas in *recursive temporal logic*, which is an infinitary version of temporal logic, can be expressed by recursive automata. It turns out that all methods for proving fair termination have at their foundations reductions between automata with different acceptance conditions. Thus, the theory gives a simple method of proving by reduction any property specified by recursive automata, and in particular any temporal property.

The outline of the paper is as follows. In Section 2 we develop a theory of automata on infinite words, which can have infinitely many states. We describe three types of acceptance conditions: called *looping* acceptance, *Büchi* acceptance, and *Streett* acceptance. These acceptance conditions generalize in the natural way corresponding conditions for finite-state automata. We then prove that these conditions all have the same power. Our proofs use and have to deal with the fact that the automata have infinitely many states. We then show that recursive automata can capture properties expressed in recursive temporal logic. In Section 3 we show how our automata-theoretic results can be used to transform infinite trees in the spirit of [Ha86]. Our results extend Harel's results, with what we believe are conceptually simpler proofs. The interest in infinite trees stems for the correspondence between nondeterministic programs and their computation trees. We show in Section 4 how our results on tree transformation can be used to verify temporal properties of programs. We develop proof methods that follow the two major approaches to fair termination: the method of explicit schedulers and the method of helpful directions.

[1] The more recent [AS87] shows how to deal with Boolean combinations of deterministic Büchi automata, which turns out to be sufficient to enable one to deal with arbitrary finite-state automata.

2 Recursive Automata on Infinite Words

2.1 Basic Definitions

An *infinite word* w is a function $w : \omega \rightarrow \omega$. (One can view w as an infinite word over the alphabet $\{i : \exists j \text{ s.t. } w(j) = i\}$.) Given $i \geq 0$, we denote by $\overline{w}(i)$ the the sequence $w(0) \cdots w(i)$. A *language* is a set of words, i.e., a subset of ω^ω. A language L is Σ_1^1 if there is an arithmetical relation $R \subseteq \omega^\omega \times \omega^\omega$ such that $L = \{w : \exists u R(w, u)\}$ [Ro67].

A *table* T is a tuple (S, S_0, α), where S is a (possibly infinite) set of *states*, $S_0 \subseteq S$ is the set of *starting* states, and $\alpha \subseteq S \times \omega \times S$ is the *transition relation*. T is said to be *recursive* in case S, S_0, and α are recursive. A *run* r of T *on* the word w is a sequence $r : \omega \rightarrow S$ such that $r(0) \in S_0$ and $(r(i), w(i), r(i+1)) \in \alpha$ for all $i \geq 0$.

A *looping automaton* is a table $T = (S, S_0, \alpha)$. It *accepts* a word w if it has a run on w. A *Büchi automaton* A is a pair (T, F), where $F \subseteq S$. A accepts a word w if there is a run r of T on w such that for infinitely many i's we have $r(i) \in F$. A is recursive if T and F are recursive. A *Streett automaton* A is a pair (T, I, L, U), where I is some index set, $L \subseteq I \times S$, and $U \subseteq I \times S$. Intuitively, L and U can be viewed as collections of sets indexed by I, i.e., for every $i \in I$, there are sets of states $L_i = \{s : (i, s) \in L\}$ and $U_i = \{s : (i, s) \in U\}$. A is recursive if T is recursive and also I, L, and U are recursive. A accepts a word w if T has a run r on w such that for every $i \in I$, if there are infinitely many j's such that $r(j) \in L_i$, then there are infinitely many j's such that $r(j) \in U_i$. The language accepted by an automaton A is denoted $L_\omega(A)$. For recursive Streett automata, we can assume without loss of generality that $I < \omega + 1$, i.e., either $I = \omega$ or I is finite. Two automata A and A' are *equivalent* when $L_\omega(A) = L_\omega(A')$.

The above definitions generalize the definitions in [WVS83] of finite looping automata, in [Bu62] of finite Büchi automata, and in [St82] of finite Streett automata.

Clearly, a looping automaton $T = (S, S_0, \alpha)$ is equivalent to the Büchi automaton (T, S). Also, a Büchi automaton (T, F) is equivalent to the Streett automaton $(T, \{(S, F)\})$. It is well known that finite Büchi automata and finite Streett automata have the same expressive power, which is stronger than the expressive power of looping automata [Ch74]. Both facts, the inequivalence of finite looping and Büchi automata and the equivalence of finite Büchi and Streets automata, depend on the finiteness of the state set. In what follows we show that if we allow infinitely many states, then the three classes of automata have the same expressive power. That is, Büchi and Streett automata are equivalent even if we allow infinitely many states, and looping and Büchi automata become equivalent once we allow infinitely many states.

2.2 Automata-Theoretic Reductions

We first show that every Σ_1^1 language is definable by a looping automaton. (This theorem was observed by G. Plotkin. It is closely related to the results in [WS77].)

Theorem 1 *Let L be a Σ_1^1 language. Then there is a looping automaton T such that $L = L_\omega(A)$.*

Proof. We use the Normal Form Theorem for Σ_1^1: A language L is Σ_1^1 if there is a recursive relation $R \subseteq \omega^* \times \omega^*$ such that $L = \{w : \exists u \forall n R(\overline{w}(n), \overline{u}(n))\}$ [Ro67].

Let $T = (S, S_0, \alpha)$, where $S = \omega^* \times \omega^*$, $S_0 = \{(\lambda, \lambda)\}$ (λ denotes the null sequence), and α is defined as follows: for $\sigma_1, \sigma_2, \tau_1, \tau_2 \in \omega^*$ and $n \geq 0$, we have that $((\sigma_1, \sigma_2), n, (\tau_1, \tau_2)) \in \alpha$ iff $R(\tau_1, \tau_2)$, $\tau_1 = \sigma_1 n$, and there exists some $m \geq 0$ such that $\tau_1 = \sigma_2 m$. The reader can check that $L = L_\omega(T)$. ∎

We now show that, unlike the case for finite automata, Büchi automata are not more expressive than looping automata.

Theorem 2 *There is an effective transformation that maps every recursive Büchi automaton to an equivalent recursive looping automaton.*

Proof. Let $A = (S, S_0, \alpha, F)$ be a recursive Büchi automaton. Then a word w is in $L_\omega(A)$ if there exists a run $r : \omega \rightarrow S$ such that $r(0) \in S_0$, $(r(i), w(i), r(i+1)) \in \alpha$ for all $i \geq 0$, and for all $n \geq 0$ there exists some $m > n$ such that $r(m) \in F$. Clearly, $L_\omega(A)$ is Σ_1^1, and the proof of Theorem 1 gives us an effective transformation of A to an equivalent recursive looping automaton automaton.

We now describe a simpler transformation that does not require using Theorem 1. Let $B = (\Sigma, T, T_0, \beta)$ be defined as follows. The state set T is $S \times \omega$. The starting state set T_0 is $S_0 \times \omega$. Finally, the transition relation satisfies $((p, i), a, (q, j)) \in \beta$ if and only if $(p, a, q) \in \alpha$ and either $j = i - 1$ or $q \in F$. Clearly, if A is recursive then so is B, and so is the transformation from A to B. Also, it can be shown that $L_\omega(A) = L_\omega(B)$. ∎

Notice that the above proof uses in a strong way the fact that B has infinitely many states. The theorem does not hold if we restrict ourselves to finite-state automata.

We now show that Büchi automata and Streett automata have the same expressive power even for infinite state set.

Theorem 3 *There is an effective transformation that maps every recursive Streett automaton to an equivalent recursive Büchi automaton.*

Proof. Let $A = (S, S_0, \alpha, I, L, U)$ be a Streett automaton. Again, it is easy to see that $L_\omega(A)$ is Σ_1^1, so the proof of Theorem 1 yields the desired transformation.

We give here a direct construction that has the advantage that it yields a finite Büchi automaton when given a finite Streett automaton. We describe the construction of an equivalent Büchi automaton in two steps.

Let $B = (T, T_0, \beta)$ be a table defined as follows. The state set T is $S \times 3^{<I}$.[2] The starting state set is $T_0 = S_0 \times \{\lambda\}$, where λ is the null sequence. The transition relation β satisfies: $((p, \mathbf{x}), a, (q, \mathbf{y})) \in \beta$ if and only the following holds for all $i < I$:

- $(p, a, q) \in \alpha$,
- If $|\mathbf{x}| < I$, then $|\mathbf{y}| = |\mathbf{x}| + 1$, otherwise $|\mathbf{y}| = |\mathbf{x}|$,
- if $x_i = 2$, then $y_i = 2$,
- if $x_i = 1$, then $y_i \leq 1$, and
- if $x_i = 0$, then $y_i = 0$ and $q \notin L_i$.

Intuitively, the second component of a state carries a "prediction" about how many times some L_i will be encountered. A "2" in the i-th place denotes a prediction that L_i will be encountered infinitely many times. A "1" in the i-th place denotes a prediction that L_i will be encountered only finitely many times. A "0" in the i-th place denotes a prediction that L_i will not be encountered any more.

[2] For a set X and an ordinal ν, we use $X^{<\nu}$ to denote $\bigcup_{\mu<\nu} X^\mu$. In particular $X^{<\omega} = X^*$.

Consider now a run $(p^0, \mathbf{x}^0), (p^1, \mathbf{x}^1), \ldots$ of B on a word w. The run $p^0, p^1, \ldots$ of A on w is accepting, if for all $j < I$, either $x_j^k = 2$ for all $k \geq j$ and there are infinitely many i's such that $p^i \in U_j$, or the sequence $x_j^j, x_j^{j+1}, x_j^{j+2}, \ldots$ contain a 0.

Let $C = (U, T_0 \times \{(0,0)\}, \gamma)$ be a table defined as follows. The state set U is $T \times I^2$. The transition relation γ satisfies the following condition: $((p, \mathbf{x}, i, j), a, (q, \mathbf{y}, k, l)) \in \gamma$ if

- $((p, \mathbf{x}), a, (q, \mathbf{y}) \in \beta$,
- if $i < j$, then $l = j$,
- if $i < j$, then either $y_i > 0$ and $q \notin U_i$, in which case $k = i$, or otherwise, $y_i = 0$ or $q \in U_i$, in which case $k = i + 1$, and
- if $i = j$ then $k = 0$ and either $j = I$ and $l = j$ or $j < I$ and $l = j + 1$.

Intuitively, the third component of a state verifies that all predictions are satisfied.

Consider now a run $(p^0, \mathbf{x}^0, 0, 0), \ldots (p^i, \mathbf{x}^i, k^i, l^i), \ldots$ of B on a word w. The run $p^0, p^1, \ldots$ of A on w is accepting, if for infinitely many i's we have $k^i = l^i$. Thus, A is equivalent to the Büchi automaton (C, F), where $F = T \times \{(i, i) : i \in I\}$. ∎

We note that C is infinite only because A is infinite. If A is finite, then C is also finite. This should be contrasted with the earlier transformation from Büchi automata to looping automata.

It is known that the classes of finite Büchi and Streett automata are closed under finite unions, finite intersections, and complementation. We now state some closure results for recursive automata.

Theorem 4 *There is an effective transformation that given a recursive sequence $A_0, A_1, \ldots$ of recursive Streett automata gives a recursive Streett automaton A such that $L_\omega(A) = \bigcup_{i\in\omega} L_\omega(A_i)$. Similarly, there is an effective transformation that given a recursive sequence $A_0, A_1, \ldots$ of recursive Streett automata gives a recursive Streett automaton A such that $L_\omega(A) = \bigcap_{i\in\omega} L_\omega(A_i)$.*

As in the previous theorems, the claim of the above theorem follows by Theorem 1. In the full paper we will describe direct transformations that have the feature that when given a finite sequence of finite automata they yield finite automata.

One should note that not all results from finite automata theory carry over to recursive automata.

For example, it follows immediately from Theorem 1 that recursive automata are not closed under complement and are not determinizable.

2.3 Recursive Temporal Logic

Wolper introduced an infinitary version of temporal logic, which he called *IPTL* [Wo86]. We define here ***recursive infinitary temporal logic*** *RITL*, which is the effective fragment of *IPTL*.

Let $\theta_0, \theta_1, \ldots$ be an recursive sequence of predicates on ω. (That is, $\theta_i \in 2^\omega$ and the relation $\{i, j) : j \in \theta_i\}$ is recursive.) The θ_i's are the atomic formulas of *RITL*. The closure of the atomic formulas under negations, under the $\bigcirc$ connective, and finite or recursively infinite conjunctions and disjunctions constitutes *RITL*. Satisfaction of formulas by a word w is defined as follows:

- $w \models \theta_i$ if $\theta_i(w(0)) = 1$.
- $w \models \neg\phi$ if it is not the case that $w \models \phi$.
- $w \models \bigcirc\phi$ if $w' \models \phi$, where $w'(i) = w(i+1)$ for all $i \geq 0$.
- $w \models \bigwedge_{i \in I} \phi_i$ if $w \models \phi_i$ for all $i \in I$.

The language *RITL* is a very powerful language. Note that all the standard temporal connective, such as the "until", can be expressed in *RITL*. Also, *RITL* can express very rich notions of fairness. For example, *RITL* can express ***equifairness*** [Fr86] without auxiliary variables. Harel's infinitary assertion language L [Ha86], which is constructed by finite and recursively infinite conjunctions and disjunctions from the atomic formulas $\exists\theta_i$ ("θ_i is true at some point"), $\forall\theta_i$ ("θ_i is true at all points"), $\exists^\infty\theta_i$ ("θ_i is true at infinitely many points"), and $\forall^\infty\theta_i$ ("θ_i is true at all but finitely many points"), is a fragment of recursive infinitary temporal logic. Essentially, *RITL* is obtained from L by augmenting it with the ability to talk about the "present moment" and the "next moment".

Given a formula ϕ of *RITL*, let $L_\omega(\phi)$ be the set of words satisfied by ϕ.

Theorem 5 *There is an effective transformation that maps very formula ϕ of RITL to a recursive Streett automaton A such that $L_\omega(\phi) = L_\omega(A)$.*

Proof. It is not hard to see that $L_\omega(\phi)$ is Σ_1^1. Thus, the claim follows by Theorem 1.[3] In the full paper we will show a direct transformation that does not use Theoerem 1. ∎

[3] In fact, the claim also holds for *arithmetical infinitary temporal logic*, which is the arithmetical analogue of *RITL*

Wolper et al. [WVS83] have shown that every temporal logic formula can be effectively translated to an equivalent finite-state automaton. Theorem 5 is the natural generalization to *RITL*. Note that the theorem holds in spite of the fact that *RITL* is closed under negation and recursive automata are not. The reason is that negation can be pushed down to atomic formulas.

3 Infinite Trees

We associated computation trees with nondeterministic programs in the natural way. Conditions about the correctness of the program can then be expressed as conditions on the paths of the computation tree. The main technical result in [Ha86] is a transformation of trees with complicated correctness conditions to trees with simple correctness conditions. In this section we apply the results of Section 2 to derive certain transformation on trees in the spirit of [Ha86]. In the next section we show how to apply these transformations to program verification.

A ***node*** is an element of ω^*. A ***tree*** is a set of nodes closed under the prefix operation. The ***root*** of the tree is λ, and a ***path*** is a maximal increasing sequence of successive nodes (by the prefix ordering) starting at λ. Thus, a path is a sequence of elements in ω^*. A tree is ***well-founded*** if all its paths are finite. We adopt some standard encoding e of ω^*, so we can view an infinite path $x_0, x_1, \ldots$ as the infinite word $e(x_0)e(x_1)\cdots$. A tree is ***recursive*** if its characteristic function is recursive.

A ***recurrence-free*** tree is a pair (τ, M), consisting of a tree τ and a set $M \subseteq \omega$ such that no path in τ has an infinite intersection with M. (A path that has an infinite intersection with M is called ***recurrent***.) It is recursive if both τ and M are recursive. An ***avoiding*** tree is a pair (τ, A), consisting of a tree τ and an automaton A such that no infinite path in τ is accepted by A. (Paths accepted by A are called ***A-abiding***.) It is recursive if both τ and A are recursive. Clearly, recurrence-free trees can be seen as subclass of the avoiding trees. Note that by Theorem 5, the notion of avoiding trees is a generalization of Harel's notion of ϕ-avoiding trees for assertions ϕ in L.

Intuitively, a well-founded tree is the computation tree of a terminating program. An avoiding tree (τ, A) is the computation tree of a fairly terminating program, where A accepts precisely the fair computations. Our goal is to establish a transformation between recursive avoiding trees and recursive well-founded trees. Now, it is known that the set of (notations for) recursive well-founded trees is Π_1^1-complete [Ro67]. Also, it follows from results in [HPS83] that the sets of recursive recurrence-free trees and recursive avoiding trees are Π_1^1-complete. Thus, by definition, the sets of recursive well-founded trees, the set of recursive recurrence-free trees, and the set of recursive avoiding trees are pairwise recursively isomorphic. Our interest, however, is in *simple* transformations from avoiding trees to recurrence-free trees and to well-founded trees that preserve structure as much as possible. In particular, we would like the transformations to preserve the structure of paths (which represent computations).

We first describe a transformation from avoiding trees to recurrence-free trees.

Theorem 6 *There is a recursive one-to-one transformation from the set of avoiding trees to the set of recurrence-free trees.*

Proof. Let τ be a tree, and let A be a recursive Streett automaton. By Theorem 3, we can assume that A is a Büchi automaton (S, S_0, α, F). We define a tree τ_A as a subset of $\omega^* \times S^*$. (Strictly speaking, a tree has to be a subset of ω^*, but we will ignore this technicality here). The root of the tree is $\langle\lambda, \lambda\rangle$. A pair (i, pq) is a child of $\langle\lambda, \lambda\rangle$. if $(p, e(i), q) \in \alpha$ and $p \in S_0$, and (ui, ypq), where $u \in \omega^+$ and $y \in S^*$, is a child of (u, yp) if $(p, e(ui), q) \in \alpha$.

The sequence $(u_1, p_0p_1), (u_2, p_0p_1p_2), \ldots$ is a path in τ_A if and only if $u_1, u_2, \ldots$ is a path in τ, $p_0 \in S_0$, and the sequence $p_0, p_1, p_2, \ldots$ is a run of A on $e(u_1), e(u_2), \ldots$. Thus, $u_1, u_2, \ldots$ is A-abiding iff $(u_1, p_0p_1), (u_2, p_0p_1p_2), \ldots$ is a recurrent with respect to $\omega^* \times S^*F$. If (τ, A) is avoiding, then $(\tau_A, \omega^* \times S^*F)$ is recurrence-free. ∎

We now describe the transformation from avoiding trees to well-founded trees.

Theorem 7 *There is a recursive one-to-one transformation from the set avoiding trees to the set of well-founded trees.*

Proof. Let τ be a tree, and let A be a recursive Streett automaton. By Theorem 2, we can assume that A is a looping automaton (S, S_0, α). The construction in the proof of the previous theorem yields a well-founded tree. ∎

Theorems 6 and 7 extends Harel's result [Ha86], and with much simpler proofs (cf. the proof of Theorem 8.1 in [Ha86]). So where is the catch? The direct proof in [Ha86] essentially combines the automata-theoretic and the tree-theoretic transformations. Our approach is to separate the automata-theoretic part from the tree-theoretic part. Once we have the automata-theoretic results, the tree-theoretic results are straightforward.

4 Program Verification

4.1 The Basic Approach

Rather than restrict ourselves to a particular programming language, we use here an abstract model for nondeterministic programs (we model concurrency by nondeterminism). A *program* P is a triple (W, R, I), where W is a set of *program states*, R is a binary *transition relation* on W, and I is a set of initial states. Given that programs are supposed to be effective, and assuming that the programs run over an arithmetical domain, we require that W, R, and I are recursive sets. A computation is a sequence σ in W^ω such that $\sigma(0) \in I$ and $(\sigma(i), \sigma(i+1)) \in R$ for all $i \geq 0$. (For simplicity we assume that the program has only infinite computations. A terminating computation is assumed to stay forever in its last state.)

We assume some underlying *assertion language*, say a first-order logic, in which one can express assertions about program states. The assertion language gives the building blocks to the *fairness language* and the *specification language*. The fairness language is used to specify what computations are considered to be "fair", i.e., when is the scheduling of nondeterministic choices not too pathological (we assume that the assertion language can express statements about the scheduling). Thus, only computations that satisfy the fairness condition need be considered when the program is verified. The specification language is used to express the correctness required of the computation, in other words, this is what the user demands of the computation.

Given a fairness condition Φ and a correctness condition Ψ, the program P is *correct* with respect to (Φ, Ψ) if every computation of P that satisfies Φ also satisfies Ψ. The crux of our approach is to prove that the program is not *incorrect*, i.e., there is no computation of P that satisfies $\Phi \wedge \neg\Psi$. Or, to put it in the automata-theoretic framework, if τ_P is the computation tree of the program (defined in the obvious way) and A is an automaton that accepts precisely the words satisfying $\Phi \wedge \neg\Psi$, then we have to show that (τ_P, A) is avoiding.

We have to decide now in what languages are Φ and Ψ specified. If we use *RITL* as both the fairness language and specification language, then, since *RITL* is closed under negation, we can apply Theorem 5 and *voilà*. Also, if Ψ is a finite-state automaton, then it can be complemented [SVW85]. If, however, we want to directly use the power of recursive automata in the specification, then we have to directly specify incorrectness, since we cannot complement recursive automata. (Indeed, Manna and Pnueli's decision to use $\forall$-automata [MP87], which are essentially Büchi automata that specify incorrectness, was influenced by an early exposition of the ideas in this paper.)

We now assume that we already have a Streett automaton $A_{\Phi,\Psi}$ that expresses $\Phi \wedge \neg\Psi$. In what follows we describe two approaches to verification, in the spirit of the method of explicit schedulers and the method of helpful directions.

4.2 Explicit Schedulers

The idea is to transform P to a program $P_{\Phi,\Psi}$ such that P is correct with respect to (Φ, Ψ) iff $P_{\Phi,\Psi}$ terminates. (Thus, we reduce correctness to termination, while previous works that use the explicit schedulers approach [AO83, APS84, Bo82, DH86, Ha86, Pa81a] reduce fair termination to termination.) The transformation is essentially the transformation in the proof of Theorem 7. That is, first we apply Theorems 3 and 2, so we can assume that $A = (S, S_0, \alpha)$ is a looping automaton. Now, $P_{\Phi,\Psi}$ is obtained by combining P with $A_{\Phi,\Psi}$. More precisely, $P_{\Phi,\Psi} = (W \times S, I \times S_0, R_\alpha)$, where $((u,p),(v,q)) \in R_\alpha$ iff $(u,v) \in R$ and $(p,u,q) \in \alpha$. Note that while P has only infinite computations, that is not necessarily the case for $P_{\Phi,\Psi}$. The nondeterministic choices in P are now directed by $A_{\Phi,\Psi}$. Thus, $A_{\Phi,\Psi}$ can be viewed as a scheduler for P.

Theorem 8 *P is correct with respect to (Φ, Ψ) iff $P_{\Phi,\Psi}$ terminates.*

In practice, a program is not an abstract set of states, but an actual syntactical object. Theorem 8 gives a method of syntactically transforming the program P to the program $P_{\Phi,\Psi}$. The combining of P and $A_{\Phi,\Psi}$ is done by adding to P *auxiliary variables* that keep the information about the automaton states. In general, $P_{\Phi,\Psi}$ can be a very complicated program, since $A_{\Phi,\Psi}$ can be a very complicated automaton. But in most cases we expect $A_{\Phi,\Psi}$ to be a finite-state automaton, so the transformation from P to $P_{\Phi,\Psi}$ is not too complicated.

To prove termination of $P_{\Phi,\Psi}$, we use the proof by reduction technique of [AP86]. (Note, however, that the proof requires intermediate assertions in fixpoint logic.) If P and A are finite state, then so is $P_{\Phi,\Psi}$. Checking termination of $P_{\Phi,\Psi}$ can now be done algorithmically. This is the essence of Vardi and Wolper's approach to the verification of finite-state programs [Va85,VW86].

4.3 Helpful Directions

The standard approach to prove termination is is to associate rank in a well-founded set with every state of the program and to show that every transition decrease the rank. When dealing with fair termination, we cannot require that every transition decrease the rank; rather we require that transitions cannot increase the rank, and "helpful" transitions decrease it. To prove fair termination it suffices then to show that in fair computations the "helpful" transitions are taken infinitely often [GFMR85,LPS81] To prove correctness we show that in "bad" computations, i.e., computations that satisfies $\Phi \wedge \neg\Psi$, the "helpful" transitions are taken infinitely often, which is impossible. Here we apply first Theorem 3, so we can assume that $A_{\Phi,\Psi}$ is a Büchi automaton. We now let $A_{\Phi,\Psi}$ decide what are the "helpful" directions.

Theorem 9 *$P = (W, R, I)$ is correct with respect to (Φ, Ψ), where $A_{\Phi,\Psi} = (S, S_0, \alpha, F)$, iff there exists an ordinal κ and a rank predicate $\rho : 2^{W \times S \times \kappa}$ such that the following holds:*

- *for all $u \in I$ and $p \in S_0$, we have that $\rho(u, p, \kappa)$ holds,*
- *for all $u, v \in W$ and $p, q \in S$, if $\rho(u, p, \mu)$ holds, $(u, v) \in R$, and $(p, u, q) \in \alpha$, then $\rho(v, q, \nu)$ holds for some $\nu \leq \mu$,*
- *for all $u, v \in W$ and $p, q \in S$, if $\rho(u, p, \mu)$ holds, $(u, v) \in R$, $(p, u, q) \in \alpha$, and $q \in F$, then $\rho(v, q, \nu)$ holds for some $\nu < \mu$.*

Note that we have assigned ranks to to programs states, but rather to pairs consisting of a program state and an automaton state as in [AS85]. Alternatively, one can associate a rank predicate with each state of $A_{\Phi,\Psi}$. Another alternative is to combine P and $A_{\Phi,\Psi}$ as in the method of explicit schedulers, and then associate rank with each state of the combined program.

Theorem 9 extends the results in [RFG85]. In that paper, the method of helpful directions was applied to derive a proof rule for fair termination for arbitrary fairness properties expressed in a fragment L^- of Harel's L. L^- is obtained from L by allowing only finite conjunctions and disjunctions. The automata-theoretic approach enables us to deal also with recursively infinite conjunctions and disjunctions.

Theorem 9 gives a "generic" proof rule. By substituting automata that correspond to certain fairness and correctness condition, one can derive explicit proof rules for such conditions. For example, one can obtain a proof rule for *just* termination [LPS81] or a proof rule for *precedence* properties [MP83b]. In the full paper we will show that for specification given by a Streett automaton $A = (T, I, L, U)$ where $I < \omega$, we can obtain a proof rule directly, without transforming A to a Büchi automaton.

5 Concluding Remarks

We have presented an automata-theoretic framework to the verification of of concurrent and nondeterministic programs. The basic idea is that to verify that a program P is correct one writes a program A that receives the computation of P as input and diverges only on incorrect computation of P. Now P is correct if and only if the program P_A, which is obtained by combining P and A, terminates. This unifies previous works on verification of fair termination and verification of temporal properties.

We do not claim that our approach makes verification easy. After all, termination itself is a Π_1^1-complete problem. Rather, the point is that our approach enables one to deal with very complicated correctness conditions by reducing the problem to the most basic one: proving termination.

Acknowledgements. I am grateful to David Harel, Gordon Plotkin, and Amir Pnueli for fruitful discussions. In particular, Gordon Plotkin observed that every Σ_1^1 language is definable by a recursive automaton. I'd also like to thank David Harel and Joe Halpern for helpful comments on a previous draft of this paper.

6 References

[Ap81] Apt, K.R.: Ten years of Hoare's logic: a survey - Part I. *ACM Trans. on Programming Languages and Systems* 3(1981), pp. 431-483.

[Ap84] Apt, K.R.: Ten years of Hoare's logic: a survey - Part II. *Theoretical Computer Science* 28(1984), pp. 83-109.

[AO83] Apt, K.R., Olderog, E.R.: Proof rules and transformation dealing with fairness. *Science of Computer Programming* 3(1983), pp. 65-100.

[AP86] Apt, K.R., Plotkin, G.D.: Countable nondeterminism and random assignment. *J. ACM* 33(1986), pp. 724-767.

[APS84] Apt, K.R., Pnueli, A., Stavi, J.: Fair termination revisited - with delay. *Theoretical Computer Science* 33 (1984), pp. 65-84.

[AS85] Alpern, B., Schneider, F.B.: *Verifying temporal properties without using temporal logic.* Technical Report TR-85-723, Cornell University, Dec. 1985.

[AS87] Alpern, B., Schneider, F.B.: Proving Boolean combinations of deterministic properties. *This volume.*

[Bo82] Boom, H.J.: A weaker precondition for loops. *ACM Trans. on Programming Languages and Systems* 4(1982), pp. 668-677.

[Bu62] Büchi, J.R.: On a decision method in restricted second-order arithmetics. *Proc. Int'l Congr. on Logic, Method. and Phil. of Sci. 1960*, Stanford University Press, 1962, pp. 1-12.

[Ch74] Choueka, Y.: Theories of automata on ω-tapes - a simplified approach. *J. Computer and System Science* 8(1974), pp. 117-141.

[CES86] Clarke, E.M., Emerson, E.A., Sistla, A.P.: Automatic verification of finite-state concurrent systems using temporal logic specification. *ACM Trans. on Programming Languages and Systems* 8(1986), pp. 244-263.

[DH86] Dayan, I., Harel, D.: Fair termination with cruel schedulers. *Fundamenta Informatica* 9(1986), pp. 1-12.

[Fr86] Francez, N.: *Fairness*. Text and Monographs in Computer Science, Springer-Verlag, 1986.

[GFMR85]
Grumberg, O., Francez, N., Makowsky, J.A., de Roever, W.P.: A proof rule for fair termination of guarded command. *Information and Control* 66(1985), pp. 83-102.

[Ha86] Harel, D.: Effective transformations on infinite trees, with applications to high undecidability, dominoes, and fairness. *J. ACM* 33(1986), pp. 225-248.

[HO83] Hailpern, B.T., Owicki, S.S.: Modular verification of computer communication protocols. *IEEE Trans. on Comm.* COM 31(1983), pp. 56-68.

[HPS83] Harel, D., Pnueli, A., Stavi, J.: Propositional dynamic logic of non-regular programs. *J. Computer and System Sciences* 26(1983) 222-243.

[LP85] Lichtenstein, O., Pnueli, A.: Checking that finite-state concurrent programs satisfy their linear specification. *Proc. 12th ACM Symp. on Principles of programming Languages*, 1985, pp. 97-107.

[LPS81] Lehman, D., Pnueli, A., Stavi, J.: Impartiality, justice, and fairness - the ethic of concurrent termination. *Proc. 8th Int'l Colloq. on Automata, Language, and Programming*, LNCS 115, Springer Verlag, 1981, pp. 264-277.

[MP81] Z. Manna , A. Pnueli - Verification of concurrent programs: the temporal framework. In *The Correctness Problem in Computer Science*, (R.S. Boyer , J.S. Moore, eds.) International Lecture Series in Computer Science, Academic Press, London, 1981, 215-273.

[MP83a] Manna, Z., Pnueli, A.: How to cook a temporal proof system for your pet language. *Proc. 10th Symposium on Principles of Programming Languages*, Austin, Texas, 1983, pp. 141-154.

[MP83b] Manna, Z., Pnueli, A.: Proving precedence properties: The temporal way. *Proc. 10 Int'l Colloq.on Automata Languages and Programming*, LNCS 154 , Springer Verlag, 1983, pp. 491-512.

[MP84] Manna, Z., Pnueli, A.: Adequte proof principles for invariance and liveness of concurrent programs. *Science of Computer Programming* 4(1984), pp. 257-289.

[MP87] Manna, Z., Pnueli, A.: Specification and verification of concurrent programs by ∀-automata. *Proc. 14 ACM Symp. on Principles of Programming Languages*, Munich, Jan. 1987, pp. 1-12.

[OL82] Owicki, S.S., Lamport, L.: Proving liveness properties of concurrent programs. *ACM Trans. on Programming Languages and Systems* 4(1982), pp. 455-495.

[Pa79] Park, D.: On the semantics of fair parallelism. *Proc. Copenhagen Winter School on Abstract Software Specification*, 1979, LNCS 86, Springer-Verlag.

[Pa81a] Park, D.: A predicate transformer for weak fair termination. *Proc. 6th IBM Symp. on Math. Foundations of Computer Science*, Hakone, Japan, 1981.

[Pa81a] Park, D.: Concurrency and automata on infinite sequences. *Proc. 5th GI Conf. on Theoretical Computer Science*, 1981, Springer-Verlag, LNCS 104, pp. 167-183.

[Pn77] Pnueli, A.: The temporal logic of programs. *Proc. 18th Symp. on Foundations of Computer Science*, 1977, pp. 46-57.

[Pn81] Pnueli, A: The temporal semantics of concurrent programs. *Theoretical Computer Science* 13 (1981), pp. 45-60.

[QS83] Queille, J.P., Sifakis, J.: Fairness and related properties in transition systems - a temporal logic to deal with fairness. *Acta Informatica* 19(1983), pp. 195-220.

[Ro67] Rogers, H.: *Theory of recursive functions and effective computability*. McGraw-Hill, 1967.

[RFG86] Rinat, R., Francez, N., Grumberg, O.: Infinite trees, markings, and well-foundedness. *Proc. 11th Colloq. on Trees in Algebra and Programming (CAAP 86)*, LNCS 214, Springer Verlag, pp. 238-253.

[RU71] Rescher, N, Urquhart, A.: *Temporal Logic.* Springer–Verlag, 1971.

[St82] Streett, R.S.: *Propositional dynamic logic of looping and converse.* Information and Control 54(1982), pp. 121–141.

[SC85] Sistla, A.P., Clarke, E.M.: The complexity of propositional linear temporal logics. *J. ACM* 32(1985), pp. 733–749.

[SVW85] Sistla, A.P., Vardi, M.Y., Wolper, P.: The complementation problem for Büchi automata with applications to temporal logic. *Proc. 12th Int'l Colloq. on Automata, Languages, and Programming,* LNCS 194, Springer–Verlag, 1985, pp. 465–474. To appear in Theoretical Computer Science.

[Va85] Vardi, M.Y.: Automatic verification of probabilistic concurrent finite-state programs. *Proc. 26th IEEE Symp. on Foundations of Computer Science,* Portland, 1985, pp. 327–338.

[VW86] Vardi, M.Y., Wolper, P.: An automata-theoretic approach to automatic program verification. *Proc. IEEE Symp. on Logic in Computer Science,* Cambridge, 1986, pp. 332–344.

[Wo83] Wolper, P.: Temporal logic can be more expressive. *Information and Control* 56(1983), pp. 72–99.

[Wo86] Wolper, P.: Expressing interesting properties of programs in propositional temporal logic. *Proc. 13th ACM Symp. on Principles of programming Languages.* St. Petersburg Beach, Florida, 1986, pp. 184–193.

[WS77] Wagner, K., Staiger, L.: Recursive ω-languages. *Proc. Symp. on Foundation of Computation Theory,* LNCS 56, Springer–Verlag, 1977, pp. 532–537.

[WVS83] Wolper, P.L., Vardi, M.Y., Sistla, A.P.: Reasoning about infinite computation paths. *Proc. 24th IEEE Symp. on Foundation of Computer Science,* Tuscon, 1983, pp. 185–194.

Invited Speaker

Chair

J. Goguen

SRI International

Speaker

W.H. van Emden

University of Waterloo

First-order Predicate Logic as a Common Basis for Relational and Functional Programming

(Abstract of Invited Lecture)

W.H. van Emden
University of Waterloo
Computer Science Department
University of Waterloo
Waterloo, Ontario
Canada N2L 3G1

This lecture will report on joint work with K. Yukawa and M.H.M. Cheng aiming at the amalgamation of relational and functional programming. The starting point is the thesis that logic programming can be used to proceed systematically from definitions of relations expressed in logic to computer programs expressed in Prolog.

Our goal is to free logic programming of some of its limitations --to allow

* functions to be defined as functions;
* functional expressions to be evaluated; and
* functions to be considered as "first-class citizens" by the use of lambda notation.

However, programs should still be first-order theories, semantics should be determined by least Herbrand models, and prolog implementation techniques should be sufficient.

Our methods of proceeding require that

* Expression evaluation be an inference about an equality relation, using the same resolution as in Prolog;
* The definition of equality relation be a first-order theory consisting of equality axioms and equations; and
* Lambda notation have the status of syntactic sugar for first-order equations.

Session 5

Chair

M. Fitting

Herbert H. Lehman College

Partial Objects In Constructive Type Theory

Robert L. Constable Scott Fraser Smith
Department of Computer Science, Cornell University, Ithaca, NY 14853

Abstract

Constructive type theories generally treat only total functions; partial functions present serious difficulties. In this paper, a theory of partial objects is given which puts partial functions in a general context. Semantic foundations for the theory are given in terms of a theory of inductive relations. The domain of convergence of a partial function is exactly characterized by a predicate within the theory, allowing for abstract reasoning about termination. Induction principles are given for reasoning about these functions, and comparisons are made to the domain theoretic account of LCF. Finally, an undecidability result is presented to suggest connections to a subset of recursive function theory.

1 Introduction

1.1 Background

It has become widely accepted in the past few years that constructive type theory is relevant to many of the concerns of computer science. Such theories have become the core of functional programming languages [10,27] and have influenced the design of procedural languages as well [8,9,14,16]. They have served to organize the study of type disciplines generally [17,22,29], leading to new insights into polymorphism, modularity, and abstractions. Type theory has also played a significant role in proof checking and automated theorem proving [3,7,10,12,15,18,26], and it serves as a knowledge representation language for AI [10,35]. The theory has become central in the study of semantics [11,24,25,32], and it is influencing categorical and domain theoretic approaches to computing theory [21,24,28].

There are however important computing concepts that type theory does not presently treat in a satisfactory manner, in particular *partial functions*. Four of the most completely presented constructive type theories illustrate this point; they are Martin-Löf's Intuitionistic Type Theory [23], the Cornell type theory in the Nuprl system [10], and the Girard–Reynolds second order type theory [17,29] and its generalizations to the Theory of Constructions [15] and the Theory of Species [34]. Neither Martin-Löf's theory, call it ITT, nor the Theory of Constructions, say TC, nor the Theory of Species, say TS, treat the collection of partial functions from a type A to a type B as a distinct type. Nuprl does have a primitive type constructor $\sim>$ which given types A and B builds a type of partial computable functions from A to B, $A \sim> B$. This type constructor has shortcomings, however, that are described below.

In the next section we will examine some of the ways that partial functions can be treated in these theories. The lack of a partial function space constructor inhibits comparison of domain theory and type theory because the primitive function space constructor on domains builds just the space of all *partial* computable functions. The absence of a partial function space in type theory also inhibits comparing a type–theoretic computability theory with the classical theory developed by Turing, Kleene, Church, etc., which has become known as *Basic Recursive Function Theory*, BRFT. The novel treatment of partial functions presented here leads to results in both of these directions: we can show that the fixpoint induction rule from LCF, a domain-theoretic formalism, is meaningful and valid in type theory, and we show that there are unsolvable problems in the computability theory inside Nuprl.

Partial functions are also important because they arise naturally in practical programming languages. Even if one is interested exclusively in computing total functions, there are nevertheless compact notations which use constructors such as unbounded iteration and general recursion that in certain combinations define diverging computations, and these com-

CH2464-6/87/0000/0183$01.00 © 1987 IEEE

binations cannot be computably separated from those which define total functions. Indeed, there are theoretical results which show that notation for partial functions is essential in any formalism which gives a compact interpretation of any r.e. class of total computable functions[5]. Theories such as ITT, TC, and TS do not permit these notations and so are significantly impoverished.

Partial functions play an especially interesting role in logics which allow programs as proofs, so-called *programming logics.* Type theories based on the propositions-as-types principle are examples of such logics (PL/CV[13] is another example). In these logics, partial functions represent proof attempts or *partial proofs.* It is possible to factor a problem into a partial proof and a demonstration that the partial proof is total. We give an induction rule below which produces partial proofs. This type of argument is interesting not only in programming but in mathematics generally.

Partial functions also pose a nontrivial challenge to logic designers. We will see shortly that there are many possible formalizations of the basic concept of partial functions, some easily accommodated in type theory and some not. In the remainder of this introduction, we will discuss four approaches which are sensible and progress toward the approach taken in this paper.

1.2 Approaches to Partial Functions

1.2.1 Total Functions on Subsets

In algebra a partial function f from a set A to a set B is often construed as a total function $f{:}D \to B$ where $D \subseteq A$ (D is the *domain* of f). This is the approach taken in Bourbaki[6], for example. This concept can be approximated in ITT by taking the type of partial functions from A to B, call it $\mathcal{P}(A \to B)$, as $\Sigma D \in (A \to U_1).\ \Pi x \in (\Sigma y \in A.\ D(y)).\ B$. A partial function is a pair $<D,f>$, where D is the domain of convergence of the algorithm f, and f maps pairs $<a,p>$ to elements of B, where $a \in A$ and $p \in D(a)$. This is awkward, especially since we want f to operate on elements of A. In Nuprl this rendering is somewhat less clumsy because the set type can be used, e.g. $\mathcal{P}(A\text{->}B)$ is $D\texttt{:(}A\texttt{->U1)\#\{}x\texttt{:}A\,|\,D(x)\texttt{\}->}B^1$. Partial functions are still pairs, $<D,f>$, but f maps elements of A into B.

[1]The set type hides the witness to $D(x)$, so for example $0 \in \{x\texttt{:int}\,|\,x\texttt{<5}\}$.

1.2.2 Untyped Algorithms

A further refinement of the above idea is possible in Nuprl. All of the terms of the untyped lambda calculus are available in the computation system, including terms untypable directly in the theory such as the Y-combinator. The Nuprl term $\texttt{fix(}f\texttt{,}x\texttt{.}b\texttt{)}$ is computationally equivalent to $Y(\lambda f.\lambda x.b)$, and is more concise. Terms built from the `fix` term can be typed in Nuprl (but not in ITT) because there are so-called *direct computation* rules which permit computation on terms as part of an argument to show that they are well-typed. The point is illustrated by a simple example:

$$F \equiv \texttt{fix(f,x.if x=0 then } \lambda\texttt{y.1 else f(x-1))}$$

is of type $N\text{->}(N\text{->}N)$, where N is the natural numbers. This can be proved by induction on N. In the induction case, assume that $F\texttt{(x-1)}$ is in $N\text{->}N$. To show $F\texttt{(x)} \in N\text{->}N$, perform a step of direct computation, which reduces the term to $F\texttt{(x-1)}$, whereupon we may apply the induction hypothesis. In a system like ITT without direct computation rules, the reductions must be treated as equalities $a = b \in A$, and this requires that $a \in A$ and $b \in A$ are known. But in this case, $a \in A$ is not known until a is reduced to b.

1.2.3 Inductive Functions

The combination of untyped algorithms (λ-terms) and subtypes provides a flexible mechanism for defining partial functions, but this is not the only possibility. For example, in set-theoretic terms we can speak of defining a partial function and its domain of convergence by simultaneous induction. This will allow us to prove properties of the function by induction on the structure of the domain. For example, the function `fix(f,x.if even(x) then x/2 else f(f(3*x+1)))` can be treated as a graph, say $F(x,y)$, and defined inductively, or it can be treated as a function from D to N, where f and D are defined recursively. Examples of the two approaches are given below.

Functions-as-graphs:

$$F(x,y) = (\text{even}(x)\ \&\ y = x/2) \text{ or } (\text{odd}(x)\ \&\ \exists z.F(3*x+1,z)\ \&\ F(z,y))$$
$$D(x) = \exists y{:}N.F(x,y)$$

Functions-as-recursion:

$$f(x) = \text{if even}(x) \text{ then } f(x/2) \text{ else } f(f(3*x+1))$$
$$D = \{x{:}N|\text{even}(x) \text{ or } (\text{odd}(x)\ \&\ (3*x+1) \in D\ \&\ f(3*x+1) \in D)\}$$

In constructive type theory, functions cannot be identified with the graphs of their relations, and only the second style of mutual recursive definition is possible. This is expressible in theories such as Nuprl which permit the simultaneous definition of a type and a function over that type. The "$3x+1$" function and its graph are mutually defined in Nuprl as:

The function f:

```
fix(f,x.if x=1 then 0 else if even(x)
      then x/2 else f(3*x+1))
```

The graph D:

```
λx'.rec(F,x.if x=1 then true else
   if even(x) then F(x/2) else F(3*x+1);x')
```

We know that $f \in \{x{:}N|D(x)\}$->N. Although it is not known that this function is total, we can prove by induction on D that $\forall x{:}N.(D(x) \Rightarrow f(x) = 0 \in N)$. Such inductive arguments are not available in any of the treatments of partial functions discussed above.

This inductive approach to partial functions is discussed in [10]. In the case of partial functions from A to B, denoted A~>B, which do not use higher order functions, this theory appears adequate. For this restricted class of types, there is a procedure for automatically computing from the algorithm f a recursive predicate dom which defines exactly the subtype $\{x{:}A|$dom$(f)(x)\}$ on which the algorithm converges. However, these exact domains are not computable in general. For example, a function such as

```
fix(f,x.if x=0 then λy.1 else λy.f(x+1)(y))
```

presents difficulties. `λy.f(x+1)(y)` is a canonical value, so it appears that the exact domain would be given by `λy.rec(F,x.if x=0 then true else true;y)`. However, the function clearly does not return a total function as its value.

1.2.4 Total Functionals

In an attempt to characterize the domain of a partial function exactly, we would like to introduce a relation such as $f(x)$ `in!` B to mean that $f(x)$ converges and the result lies in B. With this predicate defined, the *exact* domain of a partial function from A to B would be $\{x{:}A|f(x)$ `in!` $B\}$. But in order for the relationship to make sense, f must be assigned a type, say as a partial function. In order for that type to make sense, there must be an equality relation defined on it. But equality should mean that the functions are equal where they converge, and to speak of convergence, $f(x)$ `in!` B must be defined. One way to break the circularity is to only consider partial functions from A to B of the form fix$(f,x.b)$, where $\lambda f, x.b$ is a total functional mapping A->B to A->B, and to define fix$(f,x.b)$=fix$(f,x.b')$ iff $\lambda f, x.b = \lambda f, x.b' \in$ $(A$->$B)$->$(A$->$B)$. Such a theory is sound, but it does not allow unrestricted nesting of partial functions in the bodies of other partial functions. However, it does show that a theory of partial functions with exact domains is possible. We offer the theory described below as a better alternative.

2 The Theory

2.1 Overview

Our goal is to define a general theory of partial objects with a wide range of applications. One of the key requirements is that it compare favorably with PPλ from LCF [18]. In the theories discussed here, we in fact have a class of types richer than those in LCF. It is also important to be able to exactly characterize termination within the theory and for there to be induction principles comparable to those of PPλ. It remains an open question to compare these function classes with higher type function classes studied by recursion theorists [19,31].

The key idea in solving this problem is to allow possibly nonterminating objects to inhabit some types; such a theory may be called a ***partial type theory.*** Corresponding to every type T in the underlying total theory there is a type $\overline{T}$ consisting of computations of elements of T. From a metalevel, the elements of $\overline{T}$ are terms in the underlying computation system which if they converge denote elements of T. Diverging terms are thus members of any type $\overline{T}$. From the object level, elements of $\overline{T}$ denote partial recursive computations, but the theory does not address the structure of the computation beyond giving a type to its final value. These computations are nevertheless mathematical objects. Given a type T of Nuprl, the *bar* type operator allows the type $\overline{T}$, which may contain diverging terms, to be formed. Types such as $T\#\overline{T'}$ may also be formed, allowing nontermination to be localized. We also define a termination predicate t `in!` T which asserts that t is a term that in fact terminates. This will allow us to abstractly reason about termination in the theory.

In this section, we will present the basic mathematical notions underlying the concept of partial types. We first will review the relational semantics of Stuart Allen [1,2] which serve as a foundation for predicative type theories. A simple theory will be defined which illustrates the essential ideas of this semantics. Then we will show how partial types may be added to this theory. Among the metatheorems proved are those which validate basic inference rules, including some forms of fixed point induction. This provides a comparison with LCF. We also illustrate a method of doing recursion theory in this context by proving a version of the unsolvability of the halting problem for functions in int->$\overline{\texttt{int}}$.

2.2 Relational Semantics for Type Theories

Elsewhere in this volume[2], Stuart Allen defines semantics for Martin-Löf's ITT[23]; this semantics will also serve as the foundation for the partial type theory that is the object of this study. The types and their inhabitants (i.e. members) are defined inductively, so for example if A and B[2] are known to be types and the inhabitants and equalities thereupon are also known, the function space A->B may be defined to be a type and its inhabitants and equality relation in turn defined. The situation is less obvious for dependent types, for it may not be clear that our definition is inductive. For this purpose we need to explicitly define the order in which the types of the theory are to be constructed. A type theory may be said to be a two–place relation Θ with $\Theta\ T\ \epsilon$ meaning T is a type in the theory Θ and has equality and membership relation ϵ. Allen defines a monotone mapping $\mathcal{M}$ which given a type theory Θ defines a new theory Θ' which extends Θ. The least fixpoint of this mapping $\Psi = \mathcal{M}\Psi$ defines the complete type theory Ψ. By adding partial type constructors to the mapping, semantics for a partial type theory will be obtained. Here less formal semantics, which are not obviously inductive yet which are much more readable, will be used to define a Simple Type Theory, STT, which is a manageable subtheory of Nuprl. In section 2.3, STT will then be extended to a Simple Partial Type Theory, SPTT. The STT types are the type of integers int, the product constructor A#B, and the dependent function space constructor x:A->B (x may occur free in the type B), also known as a Π–type.

Beneath the type theory lies an untyped computation system which, in the case of STT, is simply the untyped λ–calculus with integers and pairing. The terms are listed in figure 1.

The reduction strategy used is lazy– or head–reduction, and many features of the theory hinge on this fact; other reduction strategies yield different theories. Terms are divided into two classes, *canonical* and *noncanonical* terms, as delineated in figure 1. Canonical terms are reduced no further in lazy evaluation, for the outermost form is not a computation. Types may themselves be objects of computation in this theory (int_eq(5;7;int;int#int) is a type.), so the type constructors are included in the class of canonical terms. We write $a \leftarrow t$ to indicate that term t head–reduces to a canonical term a. This relation is formally defined in figure 2. Note that $t \leftarrow t$ for all canonical t, and that there is no a where $a \leftarrow$ <a,b>+3 or $a \leftarrow$ (\x.x(x))(\x.x(x)).

To define STT, we define relations for what our types are (T type), when objects inhabit a type ($t \in T$), and when objects are equal elements in a type ($t = t' \in T$). We can in fact combine the last two to simplify things: $t \in T$ means $t = t \in T$. It suffices to define these relations for closed terms only, for an open term has a meaning given by the meaning of a class of closed terms.

[2] In this discussion, x,y, and q range over variables, n and k range over integers, a, b, f, and t range over terms, and A, B, and T range over types. Types are actually just terms, and different variables are used for clarity only.

Canonical terms:
integers 0,1,-1,2,-2,...
λ–abstraction \x.b, pairing <a,b>
type expressions int, A#B, x:A->B

Noncanonical terms:
a *int_op* b (*int_op* $\equiv$ + - * mod)
decision terms int_eq(a;b;t;f), less(a;b;t;f)
application $a(b)$, projections a.1 and a.2

Figure 1: The Terms of STT

$a \leftarrow t$ iff eval(t)=a, where eval is defined as:

eval(t), where t is any canonical term $\equiv t$
eval(a *int_op* b)$\equiv$eval(a) int_op eval(b)
eval(int_eq(a;b;t;f))$\equiv$ if eval(a)$=_{int}$eval(b)
then eval(t) else eval(f)
eval(less(a;b;t;f))$\equiv$ if eval(a)$<_{int}$eval(b)
then eval(t) else eval(f)
eval($a(c)$)$\equiv$ if eval(a)=\x.b
then eval($b[c/x]$) else error
eval(a.1)$\equiv$ if eval(a)=<b,c> then eval(b) else error
eval(a.2)$\equiv$ if eval(a)=<b,c> then eval(c) else error

Figure 2: The Evaluation Strategy of STT

Definition 1 *STT is defined as follows:*

T type iff int$\leftarrow T$
or $\exists A, B.\ A\#B \leftarrow T$ & A type & B type
or $\exists A, x, B.\ x{:}A\text{->}B \leftarrow T$ & A type &
$\forall a.\ B[a/x]$ type if $a \in A$

$t = t' \in T$ iff int$\leftarrow T$ & $\exists n.\ n \leftarrow t$ & $n \leftarrow t'$

or $A\#B \leftarrow T$ & $A\#B$ type
  & $\exists a, a', b, b'$. $<a,b> \leftarrow t$ & $<a',b'> \leftarrow t'$ &
  $a = a' \in A$ & $b = b' \in B$
or x:A->$B \leftarrow T$ & x:A->B type
  & $\exists y, y', b, b'$. \\$y.b \leftarrow t$ & \\$y'.b' \leftarrow t'$
  & $\forall a, a'$. $b[a/y] = b'[a'/y'] \in B[a/x]$
    if $a = a' \in A$

$t \in T$ iff $t = t \in T$

The following facts are true in STT:

Fact 1 `(3+(5*2))=13` $\in$ `(\x.x)(int)`
The type expression reduces to `int`; `13`$\leftarrow$`(3+(5*2))`, and `13` is an integer.

Fact 2 `(\x.<x.2,x.1>)(<7,6>)` $\in$`int#int`
`<<7,6>.2,<7,6>.1>`$\leftarrow$`(\x.<x.2,x.1>)(<7,6>)`, so for this term to be in `int#int` it must be the case that `<7,6>.2`$\in$`int` and `<7,6>.1`$\in$`int`, facts that follow trivially once we compute these terms to canonical form.

Fact 3 Y[3]`(\q,x.`
`int_eq(x;0;0;<x,q(x-1)>))` $\in$
`x:int->Y(\q,x.int_eq(x;0;int;int#q(x-1)))(x)`

Our type is well-formed because for every integer x, we get on the right hand side of the arrow an x-ary product of `int` types, each of which is a type. To prove membership, we must show that for an arbitrary integer n that the function applied to n is in the range type. This fact follows by induction on the integers.

We may use this semantics to justify rules for a logic. There will be a class of rules by which types are defined, and for each kind of type there are introduction and elimination rules. We also have a computation rule which allows terms to be reduced. If we wished to use the Y-combinator in the manner of the example above, rules for this would also be needed.

2.3 Partial Types

We wish to define a new class of types, *partial* types, embodied in the *bar* operator $\overline{T}$ on type T. The type $\overline{T}$ is inhabited by terms which may not converge under head-reduction. If a term $t \in \overline{T}$ does converge, however, it must inhabit T. The inhabitants of the types $\overline{T}$ are thus defined in terms of the inhabitants of T. This is the reverse of domain theory, where total objects are understood in terms of partial entities. As will be seen below, this approach fits in nicely with our semantic definitions.

[3]Y is the Y-combinator

The bar operator allows us to capture precisely the points in computation where divergence is accepted. For example, the type `int#`$\overline{\texttt{int}}$ is inhabited by terms which all must converge to pairs `<a,b>` (such is the meaning of `#` types). The first element of the pair converges to an integer while the second element, *if* it converges, is an integer. The type $\overline{\texttt{int\#int}}$, however, contains terms which may diverge. Yet once a term in this type converges, the result must be a pair of `int`'s. The domain-theoretic partial objects amount to putting bars over all subtypes in an expression, as with $\overline{\overline{\texttt{int}}\#\overline{\texttt{int}}}$: diverging terms, pairs with one or two diverging elements, and pairs of integers all inhabit this type. A partial type theory thus has a more refined notion of convergence than domain theory.

It is not precise to say a function is a partial function, for there are many possibilities: $\overline{A\text{->}B}$, $A\text{->}\overline{B}$, $\overline{A}\text{->}\overline{B}$, and $\overline{\overline{A}\text{->}\overline{B}}$ could all be said to be partial functions, and each type has a slightly different meaning. However, the type which most closely corresponds to the programming language notion of partial function is $A\text{->}\overline{B}$: all inhabitants of the type converge to λ-terms \\$x.b$, but upon applying elements $a \in A$, (\\$x.b)(a)$ inhabits the type $\overline{B}$, admitting the possibility of divergence. This is the type we will hereafter refer to as a partial function space.

Definition 2 *The following equations extend STT to a Simple Partial Type Theory, SPTT:*

$t\downarrow$[4]iff $\exists a.\ a \leftarrow t$

$t \asymp t'$ iff $(t \downarrow \Leftrightarrow t' \downarrow)$

$\overline{T}$ type iff $T \downarrow \Rightarrow T$ type

$t = t' \in \overline{T}$ iff $\overline{T}$ type & $t \asymp t'$ & $(t, t' \downarrow$ [5]$\Rightarrow t = t' \in T)$

These equations are in fact very similar to those used to extend Nuprl to be a partial type theory; the semantic equations for Nuprl are discussed in section 2.5. $t \in \overline{T}$ means $t = t \in \overline{T}$, which can be seen to mean $t \downarrow \Rightarrow t \in T$. Two terms are said to be equal members in a bar type if when we know one converges, the other does, and if they both do converge, they are equal members of the (base) type T. One fact that follows from this is that any two diverging terms are equal members of any bar type. This corresponds to our intuition that one diverging term is as good as another, and hereafter they will all be represented by the generic symbol $\perp$.

[4]This relation is the formal definition of what is informally meant when we state that t terminates, converges, or halts.

[5]$t, t' \downarrow$ means $t \downarrow$ & $t' \downarrow$

Typehood for partial types should at least allow $\overline{T}$ to be a type when T is, but is this sufficient? Consider the possible type `x:int->int_eq(x;0;int;int#int)`: if `x` diverges the int_eq computation will diverge as well, and the resulting expression will not be a type. It would be better to extend our notion of typehood for bar types: for $\overline{T}$ to be a type, T must be a type *provided* it converges. The above expression is then a type; so $\overline{(\bot)}$ is also a type.

Observe the following fact about the semantics: the meaning of type $\overline{T}$ is clearly defined in terms of the type T only. Thus, we will be able to formulate an inductively defined partial type theory in the spirit of Allen[2].

2.3.1 Facts About Partial Types

The following elementary facts about partial types give insights into the theory and also correspond to basic rules likely to be found in an implementation of a partial type logic.

Fact 1 *$t \in T$ implies $t \in \overline{T}$*

Fact 2 *$t \in \overline{T}$ and t is a canonical term implies $t \in T$*

Fact 3 *$\forall T.\ T$ Type implies $\bot \in \overline{T}$*

Fact 4 *$t = t' \in \overline{T}$ and $t \in T$ implies $t = t' \in T$*

Fact 5 *$f \in \overline{A\text{->}\overline{B}}$ and $a \in A$ implies $f(a) \in \overline{B}$*
Recall from the definition of -> types that $f' \in A\text{->}\overline{B}$ means $\forall a.\ a \in A$ implies $f'(a) \in \overline{B}$, which means $f'(a)\downarrow$ implies $f'(a) \in B$. To prove the fact above, suppose $f(a)\downarrow$; this means $f\downarrow$ because the first step of the reduction algorithm is to reduce f, so $f \in A\text{->}\overline{B}$; by the above, $f(a) \in B$ would hold.

Fact 6 *$f \in A\text{->}\overline{B}$ and $a \in \overline{A}$ does not necessarily imply that $f(a) \in \overline{B}$*
For example, take f =`\x.<x,1>`$\in$ `int->int#int`: $\bot \in \overline{\texttt{int}}$, but $f(\bot)$=`<`$\bot$`,1>` $\in$ $\overline{\texttt{int\#int}}$ is a contradiction.

2.4 Inhabiting $\overline{T}$ Types

The interest in a partial type theory centers on the ability to define partial functions like `Y(\f.\x. if x=0 then 1 else f(x-1)*x)`$\in$`int->`$\overline{\texttt{int}}$. We need a principle which allows such functions to be formed freely in the logic. To express recursive computation concisely we introduce a new canonical term, `fix(q,x.b)`, which has computational behavior identical to `Y(\f.\x.b)`: `fix(q,x.b)(a)` reduces to b[`fix(q,x.b)`$,a/q,x$].

In programming languages, recursive functions are typed by assuming all recursive calls are of the proper type:

$$\frac{q \in A\text{->}\overline{B} \Rightarrow \backslash x.b \in A\text{->}\overline{B}}{\texttt{fix}(q,x.b) \in A\text{->}\overline{B}}$$

We would like to have such a principle in type theory, but it does not follow trivially from the semantics.

To get started, we may observe the following: we know $\backslash x.\bot \in A\text{->}\overline{B}$, so given the assumptions above the line and letting q be $\backslash x.\bot$, we have $\backslash x.b[\backslash x.\bot/q] \in A\text{->}\overline{B}$; this function may in turn be q in the above, etcetera. Thus all of the unrollings of the function inhabit $A\text{->}\overline{B}$. These finite approximations for a functional f are often written as $f^k(\bot)$; we will notate unrollings over a `fix` body b with q and x free in it as b^k. By induction, we may show $\forall k.\ b^k \in A\text{->}\overline{B}$, so all finite approximations of a `fix` term are properly typed.

Consider the case where the type $A\text{->}\overline{B}$ is `int->`$\overline{\texttt{int}}$. For arbitrary $q \in$`int->`$\overline{\texttt{int}}$ and $x \in$ `int`, it is known that $b \in \overline{\texttt{int}}$; we wish to show `fix(q,x.b)` $\in$ `int->`$\overline{\texttt{int}}$. By the definition of ->, this means showing $\forall n \in$ `int`. `fix(q,x.b)(n)` $\in$ $\overline{\texttt{int}}$, which by the definition of the bar operator means `fix(q,x.b)(n)`$\downarrow$ implies `fix(q,x.b)(n)` $\in$ `int`. In programming language terms, if our recursive program terminates, the stack size must have had some maximum depth k over the computation. Analogously, given the fact that the `fix` term terminates, $b^k(n)$ must also terminate for some k, giving the same value as `fix(q,x.b)(n)`. $b^k(n) \in$ `int`, so `fix(q,x.b)(n)` $\in$ `int` as well.

If the codomain type $\overline{B}$ is more complex, this approach falls short because there could be free occurrences of the `fix` term in the resulting canonical form. Consider showing `fix(q,x.<q(x).2,7>)` $\in$ `int->`$\overline{\texttt{(int\#}\overline{\texttt{int}}\texttt{)}}$: this means that for arbitrary integer n, `<fix(q,x.b)(n).2,7>` $\in$ `int#`$\overline{\texttt{int}}$. However, all we have for the approximations is $\forall k, n$. `<`b^k`(n).2,7>` $\in$ $\overline{\texttt{int\#int}}$. In the case for the simple type $\overline{\texttt{int}}$ above, for large enough k the values of $b^k(n)$ and `fix(q,x.b)(n)` were *identical*. Here, however, the two terms will never be identical for any k. What we need to do is to apply the argument used above on each element of the pair: we know $\forall k$. $b^k(n) \in \overline{\texttt{int}}$ by the definition of #, and we would like to show `fix(q,x.b)(n).2` $\in$ $\overline{\texttt{int}}$. Assume the `fix` computation terminates: the reasoning then parallels the above, for $b^k(n)$ must terminate for some k. Thus, `fix(q,x.b)(n).2` $\in$ $\overline{\texttt{int}}$, which after putting the pair back together gives the result.

In general, the following principle can be proven valid in SPTT:

Theorem 1 (fix introduction)

$$\frac{\forall q{:}A\text{->}\overline{B}.\ \backslash x.b \in \overline{B}}{\texttt{fix}(q,x.b) \in A\text{->}\overline{B}}$$

The proof proceeds by induction on the semantic type structure. The int and $A\#B$ cases are sketched above, and the $x : A\text{->}B$ case proves no more difficult.

2.5 The Nuprl Type Theory

Ultimately, partial types should be a component of a powerful logic such as Nuprl, so after briefly describing some of the features of Nuprl not found in STT, we will explain how Nuprl may be extended to be a partial type theory.

The principle of treating types as propositions allows us to reason in the Nuprl theory. Empty types are false propositions, and inhabited types are true ones. Equality is extended to types as well; type equality is intensional in Nuprl as opposed to the extensional equality of ITT.

Some of the new types not found in STT are:

equality types t=t' in T are types which reflect the equalities $t = t' \in T$ back into the type theory. These types are well-formed when t and t' inhabit T and are inhabited only when $t = t' \in T$.

dependent products $x{:}A\#B$ (with x free in B), also known as dependent sums or sigma types, are useful as type constructors and also allow existential propositions to be represented.

empty type void , which is uninhabited and represents the unprovable proposition false.

other types $A|B$, $\{x{:}A|B\}$ and list A are disjoint unions which represent disjunction, set types which hide information, and list types.

universes Uk are a hierarchy of type universes which allow predicates and other higher-order objects to be treated abstractly. U1 is a type which is inhabited by all "base" types; types inhabiting U2 may treat U1 itself as a type, so abstract predicates inhabit A->U1, which in turn inhabits U2. To be a type is to inhabit some universe Uk. Equality on universe types is the intensional type equality mentioned previously.

The semantics for partial types in Nuprl are the same as the definitions for SPTT with in addition definitions of type equality and universe inhabitation for bar types:

$\overline{T} = \overline{T'} \in \mathtt{U}k$ iff $T = T' \in \overline{\mathtt{U}k}$

$T = T' \in \overline{\mathtt{U}k}$ iff $T \asymp T'$ & $(T, T' \downarrow \Rightarrow T = T' \in \mathtt{U}k)$

Rules for bar types have been formulated to extend Nuprl, although they have yet to be implemented. The Nuprl partial type theory will be the theory the rest of this paper refers to.

2.6 Abstract Reasoning About Termination

It is desirable to make abstract statements concerning the termination of a particular term, for example: "$f(7)$=5 provided f terminates everywhere". The first attempt at writing this in Nuprl is (∀x:int.f(x) in int)->f(7)=5 in int. For this term to be admitted as a proposition, it must be shown to be a type; this requires f(n) in int to be a type for all integers n; by definition, (f(n) in int) Type iff f(n) $\in$ int. Writing this statement thus asserts its truth, so another form of expression must be found. Attempts to directly reflect termination f(x)$\downarrow$ into the theory will fail because there is no way we can admit such expressions as types and keep the theory sound. The solution is to define a typed termination predicate.

Definition 3 *The termination predicate* in! *is defined as follows:*
$(a$ in! $A) \in \mathtt{U}k$ iff $a \in \overline{A}$

$t \in (a$ in! $A)$ iff $(a$ in! $A) \in \mathtt{U}k$ & axiom$\leftarrow t$ & $a \downarrow$

(t in! T) is a type when t inhabits $\overline{T}$ and is true when t converges; this allows us to sensibly hypothesize termination, writing the above example as (∀x:int.f(x) in! int)->f(7)=5 in int, assuming that we know $f \in$ int->$\overline{\text{int}}$. There are a multitude of uses for this predicate, some of which will be seen in the next section.

2.7 Induction Principles

There is a wide assortment of induction principles applicable to partial types. All of the principles discussed here will be for partial functions $A\text{->}\overline{B}$, and although principles for other types may be derived, what we do come up with is in fact quite general.

2.7.1 Computational Induction

If a recursive function fix(q,x.b) is known to terminate upon application of a, the trace of the recursive calls will form a finite-depth, finitely-branching tree. This structure is well-founded, so induction principles may be formulated for it: if fix(q,x.b)(a)

terminates and we wish to show some property $P[\mathtt{fix}(q,x.b)(a)]$[6], it suffices to show $P[b]$ holds for arbitrary q and x, under the assumption that P is true for all values of the function called recursively in b. Since all recursive calls eventually terminate, our induction is well-founded. More formally[7],

$$\frac{\begin{array}{l}\mathtt{fix}(q,x.b)(a)\ \mathtt{in!}\ B\\ \forall q{:}A\text{->}\overline{B}.\ \forall x{:}A.\\ (\forall x'{:}A.\ \text{“}q(x')\text{ called in }b\text{”} \Rightarrow P[q(x')])\Rightarrow P[b]\end{array}}{P[\mathtt{fix}(q,x.b)(a)]}$$

The induction hypothesis is valid only for those $q(x')$ which are known to be on the computation path. If $q(x'')$ diverged, $P[q(x'')]$ could be false.

This principle may be proven sound by induction on the structure of the computation $\mathtt{fix}(q,x.b)(a)$, known to terminate by hypothesis.

For this rule to be implemented we need to be able to recognize when a particular $q(x')$ is on the computation path, and there is no mechanism in the logic which could perform such a task: intensional term analysis is required. But it is not difficult to recognize the class of terms which must recursively call $q(x')$ at the meta-level; for example, if b computes to $q(x')$ or $q(x')$+5 or $\mathtt{int\_eq}(q(x');b;t;f)$, $q(x')$ must be computed. However, not all terms with $q(x')$ free must compute it, for example <$q(x')$,b>: this computation has already terminated. In general, if b computes to any term t specified by the following grammar, we know $q(x')$ lies on the computation path, and the induction hypothesis is valid at that point:

$$\begin{array}{l}
t \rightarrow q(x')\\
X \rightarrow\text{(any term)}\\
t \rightarrow t\ \texttt{+ * - mod}\ X\\
t \rightarrow X\ \texttt{+ * - mod}\ t\\
t \rightarrow -t\\
t \rightarrow \mathtt{int_eq}(t;X;X;X)\\
t \rightarrow \mathtt{int_eq}(X;t;X;X)\\
t \rightarrow \mathtt{less}(t;X;X;X)\\
t \rightarrow \mathtt{less}(X;t;X;X)\\
t \rightarrow \mathtt{ind}(t;u,v.X;X;u,v.X)\\
t \rightarrow \mathtt{decide}(t;x.X;y.X)\\
t \rightarrow \mathtt{spread}(t;x,y.X)\\
t \rightarrow t(X)
\end{array}$$

Because this language is decidable, our rule may check that t is of this form before allowing the induction hypothesis to be applied.

An interesting consequence of this approach is that the refinement-style sequent judgement >> of Nuprl needs to be reinterpreted to allow for such a rule. In the subtrees below the induction rule invocation, the judgement form is $>>^{P[b]}$, which has a new rule that allows for the induction hypothesis to be applied to terms t that meet the above criterion. Our sequents thus become dependent sequents. Perhaps there are other interesting dependent-sequent rules.

There is a classical computational induction rule worth mentioning:

$$\frac{\begin{array}{l}\mathtt{fix}(q,x.b)(a)\ \mathtt{in}\ \overline{B} \quad P[\bot]\\ \forall q{:}A\text{->}\overline{B},x{:}A.(\forall x'{:}A.P[q(x')])\Rightarrow P[b]\end{array}}{P[\mathtt{fix}(q,x.b)(a)]}$$

Because we know classically that our fix term either converges or diverges, we do not need to require that all applications of the induction hypothesis terminate; we merely prove $P[\bot]$, so our predicate is true even when the function diverges.

There is a novel form of induction for partial type theory, partial computational induction:

$$\frac{\begin{array}{l}\mathtt{fix}(q,x.b)(a)\ \mathtt{in}\ \overline{B}\\ \forall q{:}A\text{->}\overline{B},x{:}A.(\forall x'{:}A.\overline{P[q(x')]})\Rightarrow \overline{P[b]}\end{array}}{\overline{P[\mathtt{fix}(q,x.b)(a)]}}$$

This rule is similar to the classical rule in that it is not necessary to restrict attention to calls that terminate. We can justify this because our predicate $\overline{P}$ is a bar type, and its inhabiting object may not converge. In fact, if we apply the induction hypothesis to some $q(x'')$ that diverges, the object inhabiting $\overline{P}$ will diverge as well. Why bother to inhabit $\overline{P}$ when this type has no logical meaning as it is always inhabited? This is because if the inhabitant of $\overline{P}$ *does* converge, we will have a proof of the proposition P. Such a proof may be called a *partial proof*, for it is only a real proof if the inhabiting object converges. Such proofs give a different characterization of partial correctness, and deserve further study.

2.7.2 Fixpoint Induction

The most widely used induction principle in theories such as PPλ is fixpoint induction:

$$\frac{P[\lambda x.\bot] \quad \forall q.P[q] \Rightarrow P[\lambda x.b]}{P[\mathtt{fix}(q,x.b)]}$$

This rule is very concise and powerful, but it is only valid for a restricted subclass of the predicates P, the *admissable* P's. If P is continuous with respect to the limit of the finite approximations b^k, the rule is valid for that P. Because many predicates are continuous, this is a useful rule.

There is an analogue of fixpoint induction in partial type theory, although the class of admissable predicates is different. Because the type structure of Nuprl is so rich, even simple predicates may not be admissable if the type of the function is complicated. The types of PPλ are simple enough that this is not

[6] P is a one-place predicate with the argument in braces

[7] Under the propositions-as-types principle, $\forall x{:}A.B$ is represented by the type $x{:}A\text{->}B$, and the proposition $A \Rightarrow B$ is represented by the type $A\text{->}B$.

an issue, but it makes admissability conditions more baroque in Nuprl. Also, the term extracted to justify this rule would not be expressible in the current type theory because some intensional term analysis is required. Thus the proposition P could not be treated as a type if a fixpoint rule were to be implemented. Such problems illustrate disadvantages with the propositions–as–types paradigm.

3 Computability Theory

3.1 A Comparison to BRFT

Basic recursive function theory is a theory of partial computable functions on the natural numbers N; it is well-known and highly developed[30]. Our theory can be understood by comparison because facts about the type $N\text{->}\overline{N}$ constitute a theory of partial computable functions on N. First it is interesting to know that our theory is talking about the same objects. We can prove

Theorem 2 *If ϕ is a partial recursive function from N to N, then there is a term f of Nuprl such that $f \in N\text{->}\overline{N}$ and for all n, m in N, $\phi(n) = m$ iff $f(n) = m \in \overline{N}$.*

In BRFT we proceed by defining an indexing of the partial recursive functions, $\{\phi_i\}$. This would correspond to defining a function $e\text{:}(n\text{:}N\text{->}N\text{->}(N^n\text{->}\overline{N}))$ which is onto and which satisfies the S–m–n theorem and the universal machine theorem. It is possible to add axioms to Nuprl which approximate this concept. We may postulate an enumeration axiom:

$$\exists e\text{:}(n\text{:}N\text{->}N\text{->}(N^n\text{->}\overline{N})).\forall f\text{:}N^n\text{->}\overline{N}.\ \downarrow(\exists i\text{:}N.e(n)(i) = f \text{ in } N^n\text{->}\overline{N})$$

where the operation $\downarrow$ is called the *squash operator*. This operation uses the set type to hide the witness to $\exists i\text{:}N$ (see [10] for details of this operator), for the witness is not directly expressible in Nuprl. We then can also axiomatize the S–m–n relation. This realizable axiom leads to one version of recursive function theory, a theory which is similar to BRFT.

It is also possible to consider a theory in which $N\text{->}\overline{N}$ is not enumerable by postulating the negation of the enumeration axiom. This theory would be more like the classical theory of *all* partial functions.

3.2 Primitive Unsolvability

We may also approach some of the results of recursion theory directly without reference to enumerations. For example, the undecidability of the halting problem for terms in `int` may be proven inside the Nuprl partial type theory.

Theorem 3 (undecidability)

$$\neg(\forall \mathtt{t}\text{:}\overline{\mathtt{int}}.(\mathtt{t\ in!\ int})\,|\,\neg(\mathtt{t\ in!\ int}))^8$$

If the symbols are given their computational meanings, this statement means that there is no algorithm that can decide whether a term in type $\overline{\mathtt{int}}$ halts.

Proof. Assume that we could prove the body, i.e.

$$\uparrow\downarrow\in\forall \mathtt{t}\text{:}\overline{\mathtt{int}}.(\mathtt{t\ in!\ int})\,|\,\neg(\mathtt{t\ in!\ int})$$

Consider the function

$$f \equiv \mathtt{fix(q,x.decide(}\uparrow\downarrow\mathtt{(q(x));a.}\bot\mathtt{;b.1))}^9$$

$f \in \mathtt{int\text{->}}\overline{\mathtt{int}}$ follows because the result of the `decide` is either $\bot$ or 1.

By application of f to any integer (say 2) and computing, we have

$$f\mathtt{(2)=decide(}\uparrow\downarrow(f\mathtt{(2));x.}\bot\mathtt{;y.1)\ in\ }\overline{\mathtt{int}}$$

we know by hypothesis that

$$\uparrow\downarrow(f\mathtt{(2))\ in\ (}f\mathtt{(2)\ in!\ int)}\,|\,\neg(f\mathtt{(2)\ in!\ int)}$$

and can show that each case of this disjunction yields a contradiction.

case f`(2) in! int`: computing the `decide` term then gives f`(2)=`$\bot$ `in` $\overline{\mathtt{int}}$; this contradicts the fact that f`(2)` terminates.

case $\neg$(f`(2) in! int`): computing the `decide` term then gives f`(2)=1 in` $\overline{\mathtt{int}}$; this contradicts the fact that f`(2)` diverges.

Acknowledgements

This work owes much to Stuart Allen's approach to type theory. We also thank Stuart, Doug Howe and Nax Mendler for helpful discussions.

References

[1] Stuart F. Allen, *The Semantics of Type Theoretic Languages.* Doctoral Dissertation, Computer Science Department, Cornell University, June 1987 (expected).

[2] Stuart F. Allen, A Non–Type–Theoretic Definition of Martin-Löf's types. (This volume).

---

[8] $\neg A$ is represented as A`->void`, and $\forall x\text{:}A.B$ is represented as $x\text{:}A\text{->}B$ in Nuprl

[9] `decide` is the name of the decision procedure for disjoint unions; if $\uparrow\downarrow$`(q(x))` inhabits the left half of the union (meaning `t` terminates), the `decide` term evaluates to $\bot$; in the other case it evaluates to 1.

[3] P. B. Andrews, Resolution in Type Theory. *J. Symbolic Logic*, v. 36 (1971), pages 414–432.

[4] Errett Bishop, *Foundations of Constructive Analysis.* McGraw–Hill, New York, 1967.

[5] M. Blum, On the Size of Machines. *Information and Control*,v. 11 (1967), pages 257–265.

[6] N. Bourbaki, *Elements of Mathematics.* Addison–Wesley, Reading, 1968.

[7] N. G. deBruijn, A Survey of the Project AUTOMATH. In *Essays in Combinatory Logic, Lambda Calculus, and Formalism*, J. P. Seldin and J. R. Hindley, eds. Academic Press, New York, 1980, pages 589–606.

[8] R. M. Burstall and B. Lampson, A Kernel Language for Abstract Data Types and Modules. In *Semantics of Data Types, Lecture Notes in Computer Science,* Vol. 173. Springer–Verlag, New York, 1984 pages 1–50.

[9] L. Cardelli, The Functional Abstract Machine. *Polymorphism: The ML/LCF/Hope Newsletter I* (1983).

[10] Robert L. Constable et. al., *Implementing Mathematics with the Nuprl Proof Development System.* Prentice–Hall, 1986.

[11] Robert L. Constable and N. P. Mendler, Recursive Definitions in Type Theory. In *Proceedings of Logics of Programs Conference, Lecture Notes in Computer Science*, Springer–Verlag, New York, 1985, pages 61–78.

[12] Robert L. Constable, Todd B. Knoblock, and Joseph L. Bates, Writing Programs That Construct Proofs. *J. Automated Reasoning,* v. 1 n. 3, (1984), pages 285–326.

[13] Robert L. Constable and Michael J. O'Donnell, *A Programming Logic.* Winthrop, Cambridge, MA, 1978.

[14] Robert L. Constable and Daniel R. Zlatin, The Type Theory of PL/CV3. ACM Trans. Prog. Lang. Sys., v. 7, n. 1 (1984), pages 72–93.

[15] Thierry Coquand and Gerard Huet, Constructions: A Higher Order Proof System for Mechanizing Mathematics. EUROCAL 85, Linz, Austria, April 1985.

[16] J. E. Donahue and A. J. Demers, Revised Report on Russell. *Computer Science Department Technical Report*, TR 79–389. Cornell University, Ithaca, NY, September 1979.

[17] J. Y. Girard, Une extension de l'interpretation de Godel a l'analyse, et son application a l'elimination des coupures dans l'analyse et la theorie des types. In *2nd Scandinavian Logic Symposium*, J. E. Fenstad, ed. North–Holland, Amsterdam, 1971, pages 63–92.

[18] Michael Gordon, Robin Milner, and Christopher Wadsworth, Edinburgh LCF: A Mechanized Logic of Computation. *Lecture Notes in Computer Science,* Vol. 78 Springer–Verlag, New York, 1979.

[19] Stephen C. Kleene, Recursive Functionals and Quantifiers of Finite Type. *Trans. Amer. Math. Soc.* v. 91 (1959), pages 1–52.

[20] Todd B. Knoblock and Robert L. Constable, Formalized Metareasoning in Type Theory. In *Proceedings of Symposium on Logic in Computer Science,* 1986, pages 237–248.

[21] J. Lambek and P. J. Scott, *Introduction to Higher Order Categorical Logic.* Cambridge University Press, 1986.

[22] D. B. MacQueen, Using Dependent Types to Express Modular Structure. In *13th ACM Symposium on Principles of Programming Languages,* 1986.

[23] Per Martin-Löf, Constructive Mathematics and Computer Programming. In *Sixth International Congress for Logic, Methodology, and Philosophy of Science.* North–Holland, Amsterdam, 1982, pages 153–175.

[24] N. P. Mendler, P. Panangaden, and R. L. Constable, Infinite Objects in Type Theory. In *Proceedings of Symposium on Logic in Computer Science,* 1986, pages 249–255.

[25] Meyer and Reinhold, 'Type' is not a Type. In *13th ACM Symposium on Principles of Programming Languages,* 1986.

[26] Dale Miller, *Automating Higher Order Logic.* PhD Thesis, Carnegie–Mellon University, 1984.

[27] Bengt Nordstrom, Programming in Constructive Set Theory: Some Examples. In *Proceedings 1981 Conference on Functional Programming Languages and Computer Architecture.* Portsmouth, England, 1981, pages 141–153.

[28] P. Panangaden and M. I. Schwartzbach, Categorical Type Thoery. *Computer Science Department Technical Report,* TR 85–716. Cornell University, Ithaca, NY, 1985.

[29] John C. Reynolds, Towards a Theory of Type Structure. In *Proceedings Colloque sur la Programmation, Lecture Notes in Computer Science* Vol. 19. Springer–Verlag, New York, 1974, pages 408–423.

[30] H. Rogers, Jr., *Theory of Recursive Functions and Effective Computability*. McGraw–Hill, 1967.

[31] Andre Scedrov, Kleene Computable Functionals and the Higher Order Existence Property. preprint, 1986.

[32] Dana Scott, Constructive Validity. In *Symposium on Automatic Demonstration, Lecture Notes in Mathematics*, Vol. 125. Springer–Verlag, New York, 1970, pages 237–275.

[33] Dana Scott, Data Types as Lattices. *SIAM J. Computing*, v. 5 (1976), pages 522–587.

[34] Sören Stenlund, *Combinators, λ-terms, and Proof Theory*. D. Reidel, Dordrecht, The Netherlands, 1972.

[35] Raymond Turner, *Logics for Artificial Intelligence*. Halsted Press (John Wiley & Sons), New York, 1984.

A Framework for Defining Logics

Robert Harper Furio Honsell Gordon Plotkin
Laboratory for Foundations of Computer Science
University of Edinburgh

Abstract

The Logical Framework (LF) is a system for defining a wide class of logics. It is based on a general treatment of syntax, rules, and proofs in terms of a typed λ-calculus with dependent types. Syntax is treated in a style similar to, but more general than, Martin-Löf's system of arities. The treatment of rules and proofs focuses on the notion of a *judgement*. Logics are encoded in the LF via a new principle, the *judgements as types* principle, whereby each judgement is identified with the type of its proofs. This allows for a smooth treatment of discharge and variable occurrence conditions and leads to a uniform treatment of rules and proofs whereby rules are viewed as proofs of higher-order judgements and proof checking is reduced to type checking. An important benefit of our treatment of formal systems is that logic-independent tools such as proof editors and proof checkers can be constructed.

1 Introduction

Much work has been devoted to building systems for checking and building formal proofs in various logical systems. The AUTOMATH project of deBruijn [4] considered first proof checking. The problem of interactive proof construction was first considered by Milner, *et. al.* in the LCF system [11]. The LCF system was adapted to type theory by Petersson [19]. The work of Huet and Coquand on the Calculus of Constructions [7,8] extends the AUTOMATH and LCF work to a more powerful logic. Paulson's work on Isabelle [18] is a general approach to proof construction based on higher-order resolution. The NuPRL system of Constable [6] is a display-based interactive proof development environment for type theory that includes facilities for notation extension, library management, and automated proof search.

There are a great many logics of interest (equational, first-order, higher-order, temporal, type and set theories, type assigment systems and operational semantics for programming languages). Implementing an interactive proof development environment for any style of presentation of any of these logics is a daunting task. For example, one must implement a parser, term manipulation operations (such as substitution and α-conversion), definitions and notation extension, inference rules, proofs, tactics, and tacticals. Thus it is desirable to find a general theory of inference systems that captures the uniformities of a large class of logics so that much of this effort can be expended once and for all.

The Logical Framework is an attempt to provide such a general theory of logics. It is based on a weak type theory that is closely related to AUT-PI and AUT-QE [9], to Martin-Löf's early type theory [14], to Huet and Coquand's Calculus of Constructions [8], and to Meyer and Reinhold's λ^{π} [16]. It is able to specify both the language of a logic, its axiom and rule schemes, and its proofs. The language of a logic is defined in a general theory of expressions that exploits the λ-calculus structure to provide binding operators, substitution, capture, α-conversion, and schematic abstraction and instantiation.

The treatment of rules and proofs is based on the notion of a *judgement* [15], the unit of assertion in a logical system. (See also Schroeder-Heister [22] for a related point of view.) Each logic is a system for asserting basic judgements. The set of judgements is then closed under two higher-order judgement forms that are used to specify inference rule schemes and to model discharge and variable occurrence conditions such as arise in Hilbert systems or systems of natural deduction. Rules are viewed as the proofs of (possibly higher-order) judgements that specify them. There is no distinction between primitive and derived rules. The extension to higher-order judgements allows for a natural presentation of many logical systems that avoids side conditions on rules. Judgements, rules, and proofs are represented in the LF type theory by applying what we call the *judgements as types* principle whereby each judgement is identified with the type of its proofs. Each basic judgement is represented by a base type of the LF type theory and the higher-order judgements are represented in a logic-independent way by functional types. Proofs, and hence rules, are represented as terms of the LF type theory, thereby reducing proof checking to type checking.

In Section 2 we present the type theory of the LF, along with some of its important proof-theoretic properties. In Section 3, we introduce the LF's theory of expressions, and consider predicate calculus and Church's higher-order logic as examples. In Section 4 we consider the treatment of judgements, rules, and proofs in the LF. The method is illustrated for predicate calculus and higher-order logic. In Section 5 we compare our work with other systems for defining logics, and in Section 6 we suggest directions for future research.

We gratefully acknowlege the influence of Per Martin-Löf, particularly the lectures delivered in Edinburgh in the spring of 1986. We are grateful to Tim Griffin of Cornell University for his efforts in building a prototype implementation of the LF. We also thank the other members of the Computer Assisted Formal Reasoning project at Edinburgh, especially Arnon Avron and Ian Mason, for their comments and criticisms. Support for this research was provided by the Science and Engineering Research Council.

2 The LF Type Theory

The type theory of the LF is closely related to the Π-fragment of AUT-PI, a language belonging to the AUTOMATH family. The LF type theory is a language with entities of three levels: (1) objects, (2) types and families of types, and (3) kinds. Objects are classified by types, types and families of types by kinds. The kind Type classifies the types; the other kinds classify functions f which yield a type $f(x_1)\dots(x_n)$ when applied to objects $x_1,\dots,x_n$ of certain types determined by the kind of f. Any function definable in the system has a type as domain, while its range can either be a type, if it is an object, or a kind, if it is a family of types. The LF type theory is therefore predicative.

A number of different presentations of this system can be given. We shall describe a version which trades off conciseness against readability. The theory we shall deal with is a formal system for deriving assertions of one of the following shapes:

$\vdash \Sigma$ sig	Σ is a signature
$\vdash_\Sigma \Gamma$ context	Γ is a context
$\Gamma \vdash_\Sigma K$ kind	K is a kind
$\Gamma \vdash_\Sigma A : K$	A has kind K
$\Gamma \vdash_\Sigma M : A$	M has type A

where the syntax is specified by the following grammar:

$$\begin{array}{lcl} \Sigma & ::= & \langle\rangle \mid \Sigma, c{:}\,K \mid \Sigma, c{:}\,A \\ \Gamma & ::= & \langle\rangle \mid \Gamma, x{:}\,A \\ K & ::= & \mathrm{Type} \mid \Pi x{:}\,A.K \\ A & ::= & c \mid \Pi x{:}\,A.B \mid \lambda x{:}\,A.B \mid AM \\ M & ::= & c \mid x \mid \lambda x{:}\,A.M \mid MN \end{array}$$

We let M and N range over expressions for objects, A and B for types and families of types, K for kinds, x and y over variables, and c over constants. We write $A \to B$ for $\Pi x{:}\,A.B$ when x does not occur free in B.

The inference rules of the LF type theory appear in Table 1. A term is said to be *well-typed in a signature and context* if it can be shown to either be a kind, have a kind, or have a type in that signature and context. A term is *well-typed* if it is well-typed in some signature and context. The notion of $\beta\eta$-contraction, written $\to_{\beta\eta}$, can be defined both at the level of objects and at the level of types and families of types in the obvious way. Rules (12) and (17) make use of a relation $=_{\beta\eta}$ between terms which is defined as follows: $M =_{\beta\eta} N$ iff $M \to^*_{\beta\eta} P$ and $N \to^*_{\beta\eta} P$ for some term P. We conjecture that variants of rules (12) and (17) obtained by taking $=_{\beta\eta}$ to be $\beta\eta$-conversion are admissible rules of the theory.

Since the notion of $\beta\eta$ conversion over $K \cup A \cup M$ is not Church-Rosser, the order of technical priority in which the basic metatheoretical results are proved is essential. The following theorem summarizes these results in a convenient order (here α ranges over the basic assertions of the type theory):

Theorem 2.1

1. *Thinning is an admissible rule: if* $\Gamma \vdash_\Sigma \alpha$ *and* $\vdash_{\Sigma,\Sigma'} \Gamma, \Gamma'$ context, *then* $\Gamma, \Gamma' \vdash_{\Sigma,\Sigma'} \alpha$.
2. *Transitivity is an admissible rule: if* $\Gamma \vdash_\Sigma M : A$ *and* $\Gamma, x{:}\,A, \Delta \vdash_\Sigma \alpha$, *then* $\Gamma, [M/x]\Delta \vdash_\Sigma [M/x]\alpha$.
3. *Uniqueness of types and kinds: if* $\Gamma \vdash_\Sigma M : A$ *and* $\Gamma \vdash_\Sigma M : A'$, *then* $A =_{\beta\eta} A'$, *and similarly for types.*
4. *Subject reduction: if* $\Gamma \vdash_\Sigma M : A$ *and* $M \to^*_{\beta\eta} M'$, *then* $\Gamma \vdash_\Sigma M' : A$, *and similarly for types.*
5. *All well-typed terms are strongly normalizing.*
6. *All well-typed terms are Church-Rosser.*

Valid Signature

$$\frac{}{\vdash \langle\rangle \text{ sig}} \tag{1}$$

$$\frac{\vdash \Sigma \text{ sig} \quad \vdash_\Sigma K \text{ kind} \quad c \notin \mathrm{Dom}(\Sigma)}{\vdash \Sigma, c{:}\, K \text{ sig}} \tag{2}$$

$$\frac{\vdash \Sigma \text{ sig} \quad \vdash_\Sigma A : \mathrm{Type} \quad c \notin \mathrm{Dom}(\Sigma)}{\vdash \Sigma, c{:}\, A \text{ sig}} \tag{3}$$

Valid Context

$$\frac{\vdash \Sigma \text{ sig}}{\vdash_\Sigma \langle\rangle \text{ context}} \tag{4}$$

$$\frac{\vdash_\Sigma \Gamma \text{ context} \quad \Gamma \vdash_\Sigma A : \mathrm{Type} \quad x \notin \mathrm{Dom}(\Gamma)}{\vdash_\Sigma \Gamma, x{:}\, A \text{ context}} \tag{5}$$

Valid Kinds

$$\frac{\vdash_\Sigma \Gamma \text{ context}}{\Gamma \vdash_\Sigma \mathrm{Type} \text{ kind}} \tag{6}$$

$$\frac{\Gamma \vdash_\Sigma A : \mathrm{Type} \quad \Gamma, x{:}\, A \vdash_\Sigma K \text{ kind}}{\Gamma \vdash_\Sigma \Pi x{:}\, A.K \text{ kind}} \tag{7}$$

Valid Elements of a Kind

$$\frac{\vdash_\Sigma \Gamma \text{ context} \quad c{:}\, K \in \Sigma}{\Gamma \vdash_\Sigma c : K} \tag{8}$$

$$\frac{\Gamma \vdash_\Sigma A : \mathrm{Type} \quad \Gamma, x{:}\, A \vdash_\Sigma B : \mathrm{Type}}{\Gamma \vdash_\Sigma \Pi x{:}\, A.B : \mathrm{Type}} \tag{9}$$

$$\frac{\Gamma \vdash_\Sigma A : \mathrm{Type} \quad \Gamma, x{:}\, A \vdash_\Sigma B : K}{\Gamma \vdash_\Sigma \lambda x{:}\, A.B : \Pi x{:}\, A.K} \tag{10}$$

$$\frac{\Gamma \vdash_\Sigma B : \Pi x{:}\, A.K \quad \Gamma \vdash_\Sigma N : A}{\Gamma \vdash_\Sigma BN : [N/x]K} \tag{11}$$

$$\frac{\Gamma \vdash_\Sigma A : K \quad \Gamma \vdash_\Sigma K' \text{ kind} \quad K =_{\beta\eta} K'}{\Gamma \vdash_\Sigma A : K'} \tag{12}$$

Valid Elements of a Type

$$\frac{\vdash_\Sigma \Gamma \text{ context} \quad c{:}\, A \in \Sigma}{\Gamma \vdash_\Sigma c : A} \tag{13}$$

$$\frac{\vdash_\Sigma \Gamma \text{ context} \quad x{:}\, A \in \Gamma}{\Gamma \vdash_\Sigma x : A} \tag{14}$$

$$\frac{\Gamma \vdash_\Sigma A : \mathrm{Type} \quad \Gamma, x{:}\, A \vdash_\Sigma M : B}{\Gamma \vdash_\Sigma \lambda x{:}\, A.M : \Pi x{:}\, A.B} \tag{15}$$

$$\frac{\Gamma \vdash_\Sigma M : \Pi x{:}\, A.B \quad \Gamma \vdash_\Sigma N : A}{\Gamma \vdash_\Sigma MN : [N/x]B} \tag{16}$$

$$\frac{\Gamma \vdash_\Sigma M : A \quad \Gamma \vdash_\Sigma A' : \mathrm{Type} \quad A =_{\beta\eta} A'}{\Gamma \vdash_\Sigma M : A'} \tag{17}$$

Table 1: The LF Type System

7. *Each of the five relations defined by the inference system of Table 1 is decidable, as is the property of being well-typed.*

The proof of this theorem is surprisingly complicated. However, the methods developed by van Daalen in his thesis [9] can be adapted to this type theory. It is important to note that the Church–Rosser property, strong normalization, and the presence of type labels are essential in the proof of decidability of the type theory. In particular, given a signature and a context and any object (type) expression, it is decidable if the object (type) expression is well-typed; if so, a type (kind) can be computed for it.

We shall outline only the proof of strong normalization, since, unlike the systems dealt with by van Daalen, it can be proved independently of the other metatheoretic results. Moreover, it yields a corollary that is useful for characterizing the terms that are definable in the LF type theory:

Corollary 2.2 *If* $\Gamma \vdash_\Sigma M : A$, *then* Erase($M$) *can be typed in Curry's type assignment system, where* Erase(M) *denotes the term obtained from* M *by removing the type labels from the* λ *abstractions.*

We start by defining a translation τ of the LF types and kinds into simple types with a base type α, and a translation $\tilde{}$ of LF objects and types into the untyped λ terms with a constant π. These translations are extended to signatures and contexts in the obvious way.

Definition 2.3

$$
\begin{aligned}
\tau(\text{Type}) &= \alpha \\
\tau(\Pi x{:}\,A.K) &= \tau(A) \to \tau(K) \\
\tau(c) &= \alpha \\
\tau(\lambda x{:}\,A.B) &= \tau(B) \\
\tau(AM) &= \tau(A) \\
\tau(\Pi x{:}\,A.B) &= \tau(A) \to \tau(B) \\
\tilde{c} &= c \\
\tilde{x} &= x \\
\widetilde{AM} &= \tilde{A}\tilde{M} \\
\widetilde{MN} &= \tilde{M}\tilde{N} \\
\widetilde{\Pi x{:}\,A.B} &= \pi\tilde{A}\tilde{B} \\
\widetilde{\lambda x{:}\,A.M} &= (\lambda y.\lambda x.\tilde{M})\tilde{A} \quad (y \notin \text{FV}(\lambda x.\tilde{M})) \\
\widetilde{\lambda x{:}\,A.B} &= (\lambda y.\lambda x.\tilde{B})\tilde{A} \quad (y \notin \text{FV}(\lambda x.\tilde{M}))
\end{aligned}
$$

The precise sense in which this definition is consistent is stated in the following lemma:

Lemma 2.4

1. *If* $\Gamma \vdash_\Sigma A : K$, *then* $\tau(\Gamma) \vdash_{\tau(\Sigma)} \tilde{A} : \tau(K)$;
2. *If* $\Gamma \vdash_\Sigma M : A$, *then* $\tau(\Gamma) \vdash_{\tau(\Sigma),\pi:\alpha\to\alpha\to\alpha} \tilde{M} : \tau(A)$.

Proof. *By induction on the structure of the proof of* $\Gamma \vdash_\Sigma A : K$ *and* $\Gamma \vdash_\Sigma M : A$. *We have only to notice that any derivation of* $\vdash_\Sigma \Gamma, x : A$ context *contains as a subderivation a derivation of* $\Gamma \vdash_\Sigma A :$ Type. □

The translation has been carried out in such a way that the extra combinatorial complexity in the LF terms due to the presence of type labels is not lost. We then have the following result:

Theorem 2.5

1. *If* $A \to_{\beta\eta} A'$, *then* $\tilde{A} \to^*_{\beta\eta} \tilde{A}'$;
2. *If* $M \to_{\beta\eta} M'$, *then* $\tilde{M} \to^*_{\beta\eta} \tilde{M}'$.

Proof. *By induction on the derivation of* $A \to A'$ *and* $M \to M'$. □

Now since the Curry typable terms are strongly normalizing, so too are the terms of the LF. Moreover, it can be easily seen that $\tilde{A} \to^*_{\beta\eta}$ Erase(A), and $\tilde{M} \to^*_{\beta\eta}$ Erase(M).

A few remarks about the choice of the type theory are in order. It is essential that the type theory be decidable, at least theoretically, for, as we shall see below, proof checking is reduced to type checking. The use of conversion as the only counterpart of definitional equality is due to the fact that at this stage the LF does not deal with the issue of proof reduction and equality in the sense of Prawitz. We use η–conversion in order to make the encoding of syntax more transparent.

3 Theory of Expressions

The approach to formalizing the syntax of a language is inspired by Church [5] and Martin-Löf system of arities [17]. Each syntactic category of the logic is represented by a type. The expressions of each category are built up using expression–forming constructors, which are formalized by suitable constants of the LF. Variable binding operators are represented by constants whose domain is a function type, so that binding is handled by the λ–calculus of the LF. The type theory of the LF being richer than simple type theory, our approach to syntax is more general than Martin-Löf's. Explicit use of this extra generality is made in the formalization of Church's higher–order logic.

To illustrate the formalization of syntax within the LF, we consider two examples: the language of Peano arithmetic (as defined in Schoenfield [21]) and the language of higher–order logic [5]. The presentation of the syntax of Peano arithmetic will form a part of its signature, Σ_{PA}, and similarly for the signature of higher-order logic, Σ_{HOL}.

In a first-order language there are two syntactic categories: the *individual expressions*, which stand for individuals (objects in the domain of quantification), and the *formulas*, which stand for propositions. These are represented in the LF by the type ι of individuals, and the type o of propositions. Thus Σ_{PA} begins with:

$$\begin{aligned} \iota &: \text{Type} \\ o &: \text{Type} \end{aligned}$$

The individual expression constructors of Peano arithmetic are formalized in Σ_{PA} by:

$$\begin{aligned} 0 \quad &: \iota \\ \text{succ} &: \iota \to \iota \\ + \quad &: \iota \to \iota \to \iota \\ \times \quad &: \iota \to \iota \to \iota \end{aligned}$$

Terms of type ι in Σ_{PA} represent the individual expressions of Peano arithmetic. There are no declarations for the variables of first-order logic. The variables of the object langauge are identified with the variables of the LF, so that an open term of type ι in Σ_{PA}, all of whose free variables are of type ι, represents an open individual expression. For example, in a context containing $x{:}\,\iota$, the term $\text{succ}(x)$ has type ι as well. This representation is defined compositionally by: $x^\circ = x$, $0^\circ = 0$, $\text{succ}(t)^\circ = \text{succ}(t^\circ)$, $t + u^\circ = +(t^\circ)(u^\circ)$, and $t \times u^\circ = \times(t^\circ)(u^\circ)$,

Theorem 3.1 (Adequacy for Syntax, I) *The correspondence $^\circ$ is a bijection between the expressions of Peano arithmetic and the normal forms of type ι in Σ_{PA} with all free variables of type ι.*

Proof sketch. *The translation is evidently well-defined and one-one. Surjectivity is proved by induction on the structure of the normal forms.* □

The following are the other constant declarations for the formulas of Peano arithmetic:

$$\begin{aligned} = &: \iota \to \iota \to o & < &: \iota \to \iota \to o \\ \neg &: o \to o & \wedge &: o \to o \to o \\ \vee &: o \to o \to o & \supset &: o \to o \to o \\ \forall &: (\iota \to o) \to o & \exists &: (\iota \to o) \to o \end{aligned}$$

The formula $\psi = \forall x.\phi[x]$ is represented by the term $\psi^\circ = \forall(\lambda x{:}\,\iota.\phi^\circ)$. This approach allows α-conversion and capture-avoiding substitution to be factored out of the definition of each individual logic, leaving it to be implemented once and for all by the framework. This treatment of binding operators relies on the variables of the first-order language being identified with the variables of the LF type theory. For example, if x is a variable of type ι, then $x = x$ is a term of type o.[1] We can bind x by λ-abstraction, obtaining $\lambda x{:}\,\iota.x = x$, and universally quantify it by applying it to the constant $\forall$, obtaining $\forall(\lambda x{:}\,\iota.x = x)$, which represents the first-order formula $\forall x.x = x$.

In this way, each formula ϕ of Peano arithmetic is represented by a term ϕ° of type o in Σ_{PA}, all of whose free variables are of type ι; sentences are represented by the closed terms of type o. An open term M of type o is an *incomplete formula.* Its λ-abstraction is a *formula scheme.* For example, the formula scheme

$$M = \lambda\phi{:}\,o.\lambda\Phi{:}\,\iota \to o.\phi \supset \exists(\Phi)$$

can be instantiated by application to a formula ϕ and a matrix Φ, so that

$$M(\forall(\lambda x{:}\,\iota.x = x))(\lambda x{:}\,\iota.x = x)$$

represents the first-order formula

$$\forall x.x = x \supset \exists x.x = x.$$

Theorem 3.2 (Adequacy for Syntax, II) *The compositional translation $^\circ$ is a bijection between the formulas of Peano arithmetic and the long $\beta\eta$ normal forms of type o in Σ_{PA} with all free variables of type ι.*

Proof sketch. *Similar to Theorem 3.1.* □

The role of η-conversion in the above proof is mainly to ensure that the well-typed terms of type o in Σ_{PA} are exactly the formulas of Peano arithmetic, up to the notion of definitional equality built in to the system. There is no intrinsic difference between $\forall(<(0))$ and $\forall(\lambda x{:}\,\iota.<(0)(x))$.

The formalization of the syntax of higher-order logic makes use of the dependent function type of the LF. Quantification in higher-order logic is over a type drawn from the hierarchy of simple functional types with two base types ι (of individuals) and o (of propositions). In order to avoid confusion with the types of the LF, we call the types of higher-order logic "sorts," and we shall write $\sigma \Rightarrow \tau$ for the sort of functions from sort σ to sort τ. In the formalization of higher-order logic the collection of sorts is represented as a type with members ι and o, closed under $\Rightarrow$. The signature Σ_{HOL} thus begins as follows:

$$\begin{aligned} \text{sorts} &: \text{Type} \\ \iota \quad &: \text{sorts} \\ o \quad &: \text{sorts} \\ \Rightarrow \quad &: \text{sorts} \to \text{sorts} \to \text{sorts} \end{aligned}$$

[1] We freely use infix and postfix application in accordance with custom and readability considerations.

To each sort is associated the type of objects of that sort. The objects of sort ι are, for the present purposes, the natural numbers. The objects of sort o are the propositions of higher–order logic. The quantifiers range over an abitrary sort, rather than the fixed sort of individuals as in first–order logic. The objects of functional sort are given by typed λ terms (which we write with a capital Λ to avoid confusion), and there is a form for expressing application.

$$
\begin{array}{lll}
\mathrm{obj} & : & \mathrm{sorts} \rightarrow \mathrm{Type} \\
0 & : & \mathrm{obj}(\iota) \\
\mathrm{succ} & : & \mathrm{obj}(\iota \Rightarrow \iota) \\
= & : & \Pi\sigma\!: \mathrm{sorts}.\ \mathrm{obj}(\sigma \Rightarrow \sigma \Rightarrow o) \\
\neg & : & \mathrm{obj}(o \Rightarrow o) \\
\wedge & : & \mathrm{obj}(o \Rightarrow o \Rightarrow o) \\
\vee & : & \mathrm{obj}(o \Rightarrow o \Rightarrow o) \\
\supset & : & \mathrm{obj}(o \Rightarrow o \Rightarrow o) \\
\forall & : & \Pi\sigma\!: \mathrm{sorts}.\ \mathrm{obj}((\sigma \Rightarrow o) \Rightarrow o) \\
\exists & : & \Pi\sigma\!: \mathrm{sorts}.\ \mathrm{obj}((\sigma \Rightarrow o) \Rightarrow o) \\
\Lambda & : & \Pi\sigma\!: \mathrm{sorts}.\Pi\tau\!: \mathrm{sorts}. \\
 & & (\mathrm{obj}(\sigma) \rightarrow \mathrm{obj}(\tau)) \rightarrow \mathrm{obj}(\sigma \Rightarrow \tau) \\
\mathrm{ap} & : & \Pi\sigma\!: \mathrm{sorts}.\Pi\tau\!: \mathrm{sorts}. \\
 & & \mathrm{obj}(\sigma \Rightarrow \tau) \rightarrow \mathrm{obj}(\sigma) \rightarrow \mathrm{obj}(\tau)
\end{array}
$$

The representation of equality and the quantifiers makes use of the dependent function types of the LF. For each sort σ, the equality relation for objects of sort σ is written $=_\sigma$; it is an object of sort $\sigma \Rightarrow \sigma \Rightarrow o$. Similarly, the quantifiers ranging over sort σ are written $\forall_\sigma$ and $\exists_\sigma$; they are objects of sort $(\sigma \Rightarrow o) \Rightarrow o$, just as in Church's formulation. The Λ and ap forms must similarly be tagged with types, which we write as subscripts. It is unfortunate that the Λ form must be tagged with both the domain and range types, unlike in Church's definition. The difference is minor, and we expect that analogs of Theorems 3.1 and 3.2 can be proved.

4 Theory of Rules and Proofs

The treatment of inference rules and proofs lies at the heart of the LF. The approach is organized around the notion of a *judgement* [15], the unit of inference of a logic. Each logic comes with a set of *basic* judgements. In first–order logic there is only one form of basic judgement, the assertion ϕ true that a formula ϕ is (logically) true (usually written as $\vdash \phi$ or just ϕ). Sequent calculi also have one basic judgement, written $\Gamma \Rightarrow \Delta$, the assertion that some formula in Δ is a logical consequence of all the formulas in Γ. In Martin-Löf's system of type theory, there are four basic judgements, A type, $A = B$, $a \in A$, and $a = b \in A$.

In traditional logical systems the inference rules determine the set of proofs of basic judgements, and thereby also determine the set of "correct" or "evident" [15] basic judgements, namely those that have proofs. There are several approaches to the definition of a proof in a formal system. [21,20] Proofs are sometimes viewed as sequences of formulas that satisfy the condition that each formula is obtained from previous formulas by application of a rule. Another view is that proofs are trees satisfying certain conditions. In any case the *notion* of a proof is independent of the particular rules of inference.

We extend the notion of proof to include our view of rules as proofs of *higher–order judgements.* There are two forms: the *hypothetical* and the *schematic* (or *general*). The hypothetical judgement $J_1 \vdash J_2$ is the assertion that J_2 is a logical consequence of J_1, according to the rules of the logic. It is proved by a function mapping proofs of J_1 to proofs of J_2. The schematic judgement $\bigwedge_{x:A} J(x)$ represents the idea of generality: the judgement $J(x)$ is evident for any object x of type A. It is proved by a function mapping objects x of type A to proofs of $J(x)$.

Rules and proofs are represented as terms of the LF type theory. The basic rules are presented as constants in the signature of the logic, and the derived rules are complex proofs that are λ–abstracted with respect to their premises. Since rules are functions, complex proofs are built by applying (in the sense of the λ–calculus) rules to the proof(s) of their premise(s). Rule schemes are represented as proofs of schematic judgements. Schematic variables are identified with the variables of the LF, so that schematization is achieved by λ abstraction, and schematic instantiation by application.

If rules and proofs are terms, what are to be their types? Since a proof is viewed as evidence for a judgement, it seems natural to identify judgements with the type of their proofs: a judgement is evident iff it has a proof iff there is a term of that type (in the signature of the logic). We call this the *judgements as types* principle, by analogy with the propositions as types principle of Curry, deBruijn, and Howard. Here we are making no commitment to the semantics of a logic. Instead we are merely formalizing the idea that to make an assertion in a logical system, one must have a proof of it.

The type of proofs of a basic judgement is determined by the inference rules of the logic. The types of proofs of the higher–order judgement forms are defined by the LF. We define $J_1 \vdash J_2$ to be $J_1 \rightarrow J_2$, the type of functions mapping J_1 to J_2. This definition is motivated by the meaning of the hypothetical judgement and the judgements as types principle. Similarly, we define $\bigwedge_{x:A} J(x)$ to be $\Pi x{:}\,A.J(x)$, the type of functions mapping objects x of type A to $J(x)$. We write $J_1, \ldots, J_m \vdash_{x_1:A_1,\ldots,x_n:A_n} J$ for $\bigwedge_{x_1:A_1} \cdots \bigwedge_{x_n:A_n} J_1 \vdash \cdots (J_m \vdash J)$. This incorporates and generalizes Martin-Löf's hypothetico–general judgements [15].

We take incomplete proofs to be open terms of judgement type J. They can be completed by substitution or by λ–abstraction, yielding proofs of schematic judgements. Abstraction on judgement type variables not occurring in J yields proofs of hypothetical judgements.

An important consequence of the judgements as types principle is that we are able to reduce proof checking to type checking. A term M is a proof of a judgement J iff M has type J in the signature of the logic. This reduction is the most important reason for insisting that the type theory of the LF be decidable, for otherwise one could not construct a mechanical proof checker for a logic.

To illustrate these ideas, we formalize an illustrative selection of rules from first–order and higher–order logic formalized as systems of natural deduction. Returning to $\Sigma_{\rm PA}$, we represent the single judgement form ϕ true by introducing a family of types indexed by the propositions:

$$\text{true} : o \rightarrow \text{Type}$$

We write "ϕ true" for "true(ϕ)." For any formula ϕ (*i.e.*, any term of type o in $\Sigma_{\rm PA}$), the type ϕ true is the type of proofs of ϕ.

Each rule in Table 2 is represented by a constant whose type is the specification of the rule, a higher–order judgement. For instance, the double negation elimination rule is given by:

$$\neg\neg\text{E} : \neg\neg\phi \text{ true} \vdash_{\phi:o} \phi \text{ true}$$

The judgement is schematic over formulas and hypothetical in proofs of $\neg\neg\phi$, so if ϕ is a formula and M is a proof of $\neg\neg\phi$ true, then $\neg\neg\text{E}(\phi)(M)$ is a proof of ϕ true.

The implication introduction rule makes use of the hypothetical judgement form to model discharge. The formulation of $\supset$I in Table 2 takes a *hypothetical proof of* ϕ as premise, and discharges the hypothesis. We instead treat $\supset$I as taking a *proof of a hypothetical judgement.* The general intention is that a sufficient condition for establishing the truth of $\phi \supset \psi$ is to establish that ψ is a logical consequence of ϕ. The formalization of $\supset$I, which is schematic in ϕ and ψ, is:

$$\supset\text{I} : (\phi \text{ true} \vdash \psi \text{ true}) \vdash_{\phi:o,\psi:o} \phi \supset \psi \text{ true}$$

So, for example, $\supset\text{I}(\phi)(\phi)(\lambda x{:}\,\phi \text{ true}.x)$ is a proof of $\phi \supset \phi$ true.

Universal elimination is given by:

$$\forall\text{E} : \forall(\Phi) \text{ true} \vdash_{\Phi:\iota\rightarrow o, a:\iota} \Phi(a) \text{ true}$$

The rule is schematic in Φ, the matrix of the universally quantified formula, and a, the instance. Given such and a proof M of $\forall(\Phi)$ true, $\forall\text{E}(\Phi)(a)(M)$ is a proof of $\Phi(a)$ true. Substitution is modelled by applying the matrix to the instance.

Universal introduction is formalized like implication introduction. A condition for the truth of $\forall(\Phi)$ is that $\Phi(x)$ is true for arbitrary x. In Table 2 variable occurrence conditions are used for a *schematic proof of the judgement* $\Phi(x)$. We instead use a *proof of the schematic judgement* $\bigwedge_x{:}\,\iota.\Phi(x)$. The rule is given by:

$$\forall\text{I} : (\textstyle\bigwedge_{x:\iota} \Phi(x) \text{ true}) \vdash_{\Phi:\iota\rightarrow o} \forall(\Phi) \text{ true}$$

Existential elimination uses both hypothetical and schematic judgements, and makes use of scoping to avoid side conditions:

$$\begin{array}{rl}\exists\text{E} : & \exists(\Phi) \text{ true}, (\Phi(x) \text{ true} \vdash_{x:\iota} \psi \text{ true}) \\ & \vdash_{\Phi:\iota\rightarrow o,\psi:o} \psi \text{ true}\end{array}$$

Since ψ is bound outermost, there is no possibility that the x of the schematic judgement form occur free in an instance.

Induction makes use of scoping and higher–order judgements:

$$\begin{array}{rl}\text{IND} : & \Phi(0) \text{ true}, \\ & (\Phi(x) \text{ true} \vdash_{x:\iota} \Phi(\text{succ}(x)) \text{ true}) \\ & \vdash_{\Phi:\iota\rightarrow o, x:\iota} \Phi(x) \text{ true}\end{array}$$

The correctness of the formalization is expressed by the following theorem:

Theorem 4.1 (Adequacy for Theorems) *There is a (compositionally-defined) bijection between first-order natural deduction proofs of a formula ϕ of Peano arithmetic from assumptions $\phi_1, \ldots, \phi_n$ and normal forms M of type ϕ°* true *in $\Sigma_{\rm PA}$, all of whose free variables are of type ι and ϕ_i°* true *$(1 \le i \le n)$.*

Proof. *It is straightforward to prove by induction on the length of derivations, that if $A_1, \ldots, A_n \vdash_{\rm PA} A$ is derivable, then*

$$\Gamma, x_1{:}\,A_1 \text{ true}, \ldots, x_n{:}\,A_n \text{ true} \vdash_{\Sigma_{\rm PA}} M : A_{n+1} \text{ true}$$

$$(\neg\neg\text{E})\quad \frac{\neg\neg\phi}{\phi} \qquad\qquad (\supset\text{I})\quad \frac{\begin{matrix}(\phi)\\ \psi\end{matrix}}{\phi\supset\psi}$$

$$(\forall\text{I}^*)\quad \frac{\phi[x]}{\forall x.\phi[x]} \qquad\qquad (\forall\text{E})\quad \frac{\forall x.\phi[x]}{\phi[t/x]}$$

(x not free in any assumption on which ϕ depends.)*

$$(\exists\text{E}^*)\quad \frac{\exists x.\phi[x] \quad \begin{matrix}(\phi)\\ \psi\end{matrix}}{\psi}$$

(x not free in ψ or any assumptions on which ψ depends.)*

$$(\text{IND}^*)\quad \frac{\phi(0) \quad \begin{matrix}(\phi(x))\\ \phi(\text{succ}(x))\end{matrix}}{\phi(x)}$$

(x not free in any assumption, other than $\phi(x)$, in which $\phi(\text{succ}(x))$ depends.)*

Table 2: Some Rules of Peano Arithmetic

is derivable, where Γ contains assignments of the form $x{:}\,\iota$ for the free object variables x occurring in the A_i's and in M, and where M faithfully encodes instantiation and application of rules. Surjectivity can be proved by induction on the structure of the normal forms of type ϕ true *(for $\phi{:}\,o$), keeping in mind the uniqueness of types and the Church–Rosser property.* □

Note that it is possible for M in the above proof to have free variables of type ι, even when $n = 0$ (*i.e.*, when there are no assumptions) and when ϕ has no free variables. This is true, for example, in a proof of

$$\forall x.\phi \supset \exists x.\phi(x).$$

It is a peculiarity of first–order logic that the assumption that the domain of quantification is non–empty is not made explicit in proofs.

The above proof illustrates the fact that judgements in the LF actually encode consequence relations that satisfy, in view of Theorem 2.1, weak forms of thinning, transitivity, and contraction.

We shall give two examples. In the first we present a proof of $\phi \supset (\psi \supset \phi)$ true as a well–typed term in the signature Σ_{PA}. Let x have type ϕ true, and let y have type ψ true. Abstracting the incomplete proof x with respect to y, we obtain a proof $\lambda y{:}\,\psi$ true.x of ψ true $\vdash \phi$ true. Applying $\supset$I to this proof, we obtain the (incomplete) proof $\supset\text{I}(\psi)(\phi)(\lambda y{:}\,\psi \text{ true}.x)$ of $\psi \supset \phi$ true. Abstracting with respect to x, and applying $\supset$I again, we obtain the complete proof

$$\supset\text{I}(\phi)(\psi\supset\psi)(\lambda x{:}\,\phi \text{ true}.\supset\text{I}(\psi)(\phi)(\lambda y{:}\,\psi \text{ true}.x))$$

of $\phi \supset (\psi \supset \phi)$ true.

In the second example we give evidence for the claim that the traditional notion of a derivable rule has a formal counterpart in the LF. We show that in the signature Σ_{PA} the elimination rule for the universal quantifier in Schroeder–Heister's style can be derived. The Schroeder–Heister rule is specified by the following type:

$$\forall(\Phi) \text{ true}, ((\bigwedge_{x:\iota} \Phi(x) \text{ true}) \vdash \psi \text{ true}) \vdash_{\Phi:\iota\to o,\psi:o} \psi \text{ true}.$$

It can be easily verified that the term

$$\begin{array}{l}\lambda\Phi{:}\,\iota\to o.\lambda\psi{:}\,o.\lambda p{:}\,\forall(\Phi) \text{ true}.\\ \lambda q{:}\,((\bigwedge_{x:\iota}\Phi(x) \text{ true}) \vdash \phi \text{ true}).\\ q(\lambda x{:}\,\iota.\forall\text{E}(\Phi)(p)(x))\end{array}$$

has the above type.

With regard to derived rules, it is interesting to point out that in view of the fact that thinning is an admissible rule of the LF type theory, judgements are "open" concepts. This precludes an induction principle on proofs. Therefore typical admissible rules for a given logic $\mathcal{L}$, or meta rules such as the deduction theorem for a Hilbert–style presentation of first–order logic, are not directly derivable in certain adequate signatures for $\mathcal{L}$.

Turning to the formalization of higher–order logic, we formalize the inference rules in a manner quite similar to that of first–order logic. There is one judgement form, the assertion that ϕ is true, for ϕ an object of sort o.

$$\mathsf{true} : \mathsf{obj}(o) \rightarrow \mathsf{Type}$$

The rules of β and η–conversion for the λ–calculus appear as axioms about equality. They are schematic in the domain and range sorts of the functions, and in the terms themselves:

$$\begin{aligned} \beta : \; & \textstyle\bigwedge_{\sigma:\mathrm{sorts},\tau:\mathrm{sorts},f:\mathrm{obj}(\sigma)\rightarrow\mathrm{obj}(\tau),a:\mathrm{obj}(\sigma)} \\ & \mathrm{ap}_{\sigma,\tau}(\Lambda_{\sigma,\tau}(f), a) =_{\tau} f(a) \text{ true} \\ \eta : \; & \textstyle\bigwedge_{\sigma:\mathrm{sorts},\tau:\mathrm{sorts},f:\mathrm{obj}(\sigma\Rightarrow\tau)} \\ & \Lambda_{\sigma,\tau}(\lambda x{:}\,\mathrm{obj}(\sigma).\,\mathrm{ap}_{\sigma,\tau}(f, x)) =_{\sigma\Rightarrow\tau} f \text{ true} \end{aligned}$$

The formalization of the logical rules is similar to that of first–order logic. The universal introduction and elimination rules are formalized as follows:

$$\begin{aligned} \forall\mathrm{I} : \; & (\textstyle\bigwedge_{x:\mathrm{obj}(\sigma)} \mathrm{ap}(f, x) \text{ true}) \\ & \vdash_{\sigma:\mathrm{sorts},f:\mathrm{obj}(\sigma\Rightarrow o)} \forall_{\sigma}(f) \text{ true} \\ \forall\mathrm{E} : \; & \forall_{\sigma}(f) \text{ true} \vdash_{\sigma:\mathrm{sorts},f:\mathrm{obj}(\sigma\Rightarrow o),a:\mathrm{obj}(\sigma)} \\ & \mathrm{ap}(f, a) \text{ true} \end{aligned}$$

The adequacy of this representation of higher–order logic can be established by means similar to that for Peano arithmetic.

5 Comparison with Related Work

Work in the area of proof checking began with the AUTOMATH project [4]. They sought to build a framework for expressing arbitrary mathematical texts in a formal way, and developed many examples, notably the formalization of Landau's textbook on Analysis by Jutting [12]. In contrast to the LF approach they work directly within the type theory, using the propositions as types principle. They do not seem to have isolated any general principles about the formalization of logic. Our work can be seen as a development of the AUTOMATH ideas by providing a framework that keeps the meta– and object level clearly separated. We are also concerned with supporting interactive proof development, particularly automated proof assistance, an area that was never considered by the AUTOMATH project.

Paulson's Isabelle system, as presented in [18], is a generalization of LCF to an arbitrary logic. He is primarily concerned with theorem proving, rather than proof checking and proof editing. Consequently his approach is quite different from ours, particularly in the treatment of rules and proofs. Isabelle avoids the construction of proof trees by viewing proof search as a process of building derived rules of inference. His representation of rules is based on a direct encoding of rules and their side conditions, using a clever algorithm to enforce variable occurrence conditions.

6 Directions for Future Research

The LF system is a first step towards developing a general theory of interactive proof checking and proof construction. Much more work remains to be done. At present we do not treat definitions and abbreviations for an object logic. There appear to be at least two ways in which the LF type theory might be extended to include a more comprehensive account of definitional equality. One way is to add axioms for δ reductions [4,23]. We have not yet conducted a thorough analysis of such an extension. Another approach is to formalize LF type theory as an equational theory, with a set of equations representing definitions being included as part of the signature of the logic. These equations may be directed to obtain a reduction relation suitable for use by the type checker, but in general this relation will not be Church–Rosser or normalizing, and so decidability of type checking is lost.

It would be interesting to develop a characterization of the class of logics that can be formalized within the LF. It is clear from recent results of Avron and Mason [1,2] that one can exploit multiple judgement forms to encode logics that ordinarily have complex side conditions on their rules. While it appears that almost any formal system can be represented in the LF, some representations seem more natural than others. Is there a precise characterization of naturality in this sense? If so, what logics admit natural representations?

In a natural representation of a logic, the variables of the object language are represented by variables of the metalanguage. This means that, for the case of first–order logic, that the type ι can be viewed as the domain of quantification in a given model. Thus a satisfactory account of our treatment of variables seems to involve a notion of model for the LF. We have defined a class of models for which the type theory is complete.

It is interesting to consider the possibility of connections between the LF and Burstall and Goguen's institutions [10] and Barwise's abstract model theory [3].

A general treatment of tactics is clearly desirable. The terms representing proofs in an LF encoding of a logic can be viewed as validations (in the sense of LCF [11].) Since the proof terms are total functions, a tactic that is validated by a proof term has the property that any proofs of the subgoals are guaranteed to lead to a proof of the goal (such tactics are called *valid* by Milner). Griffin's implementation of the LF demonstrates that this property can be checked automatically for a small class of tactics called *refinement rules*. The work of Constable and Knoblock [13] carries this idea even further by considering the possibility of proving the validity of tactics for type theory in the type theory itself. It would be interesting to adapt these ideas to the more general setting of the LF. In another direction we have defined a logic-independent search space that generalizes Paulson's higher-order resolution [18].

References

[1] Arnon Avron. *Simple Consequence Relations.* Technical Report, Laboratory for the Foundations of Computer Science, Edinburgh University, 1987. In preparation.

[2] Arnon Avron and Ian Mason. *Case Studies in the Edinburgh Logical Framework.* Technical Report, Laboratory for the Foundations of Computer Science, Edinburgh University, 1987. In preparation.

[3] J. Barwise and S. Feferman, editors. *Model-Theoretic Logics. Perspectives in Mathematical Logic*, Springer-Verlag, 1985.

[4] Nicolas G. de Bruijn. A survey of the project AUTOMATH. In J. P. Seldin and J. R. Hindley, editors, *To H. B. Curry: Essays in Combinatory Logic, Lambda Calculus, and Formalism*, pages 589–606, Academic Press, 1980.

[5] Alonzo Church. A formulation of the simple theory of types. *Journal of Symbolic Logic*, 5:56–68, 1940.

[6] Robert L. Constable, *et. al. Implementing Mathematics with the NuPRL Proof Development System.* Prentice–Hall, Englewood Cliffs, NJ, 1986.

[7] Thierry Coquand. *Une théorie des constructions.* Thèse de Troisième Cycle, Université Paris VII, January 1985.

[8] Thierry Coquand and Gérard Huet. Constructions: a higher-order proof system for mechanizing mathematics. In B. Buchberger, editor, *EUROCAL '85: European Conference on Computer Algebra*, pages 151–184, Springer-Verlag, 1985.

[9] Diedrik T. van Daalen. *The Language Theory of AUTOMATH.* PhD thesis, Technical University of Eindhoven, Eindhoven, Netherlands, 1980.

[10] Joseph Goguen and Rod Burstall. Introducing Institutions. In E. Clarke and D. Kozen, editors, *Logics of Programs*, pages 221–256, Springer-Verlag, 1984.

[11] Michael Gordon, Robin Milner, and Christopher Wadsworth. *Edinburgh LCF: A Mechanized Logic of Computation.* Volume 78 of *Lecture Notes in Computer Science*, Springer-Verlag, Heidelberg, 1979.

[12] L. S. Jutting. *Checking Landau's Grundlagen in the AUTOMATH System.* PhD thesis, Eindhoven University, The Netherlands, 1977.

[13] Todd B. Knoblock and Robert L. Constable. Formalized metareasoning in type theory. In *Proceedings of the Symposium on Logic in Computer Science*, pages 237–248, 1986.

[14] Per Martin-Löf. An intuitionistic theory of types: predicative part. In H. E. Rose and J. C. Shepherdson, editors, *Logic Colloquium, '73*, pages 73–118, North-Holland, Amsterdam, 1973.

[15] Per Martin-Löf. *On the Meanings of the Logical Constants and the Justifications of the Logical Laws.* Technical Report 2, Scuola di Specializzazione in Logica Matematica, Dipartimento di Matematica, Università di Siena, 1985.

[16] Albert Meyer and Mark Reinhold. 'Type' is not a type: preliminary report. In *Proceedings of the 13th ACM Symposium on the Principles of Programming Languages*, 1986.

[17] Bengt Nordström, Kent Petersson, and Jan Smith. *An Introduction to Martin-Löf's Type Theory.* University of Göteborg, Göteborg, Sweden, 1986. Preprint.

[18] Lawrence Paulson. Natural deduction proof as higher-order resolution. *Journal of Logic Programming*, 3:237–258, 1986.

[19] Kent Petersson. *A Programming System for Type Theory.* Technical Report 21, Programming Methodology Group, University of Göteborg/Chalmers Institute of Technology, March 1982.

[20] Dag Prawitz. *Natural Deduction: A Proof-Theoretical Study.* Almquist & Wiksell, Stockholm, 1965.

[21] Joseph R. Schoenfield. *Mathematical Logic.* Addison–Wesley, Reading, Massachusetts, 1967.

[22] Peter Schroeder–Heister. A natural extension of natural deduction. *Journal of Symbolic Logic*, 49(4), December 1984.

[23] Sören Stenlund. *Combinators, λ-terms, and Proof Theory.* D. Reidel, Dordrecht, Holland, 1972.

The Computational Behaviour of Girard's Paradox*

Douglas J. Howe
Department of Computer Science
Cornell University

Abstract

In their paper *"Type" Is Not a Type*, Meyer and Reinhold argued that serious pathologies can result when a type of all types is added to a programming language with dependent types. Central to their argument is the claim that by following the proof of Girard's paradox it is possible to construct in their calculus $\lambda^{\tau\tau}$ a term having a fixed-point property. Because of the tremendous amount of formal detail involved, they were unable to establish this claim. We have made use of the Nuprl proof development system in constructing a formal proof of Girard's paradox and analysing the resulting term. We can show that the term does not have the desired fixed-point property, but does have a weaker form of it that is sufficient to establish some of the results of Meyer and Reinhold. We believe that the method used here is in itself of some interest, representing a new kind of application of a computer to a problem in symbolic logic.

1 Introduction

For the purpose of studying the effect of the type-of-all-types assumption on programming languages with dependent types, Meyer and Reinhold defined λ^{Π}, a polymorphically typed λ-calculus with dependent types, and $\lambda^{\tau\tau}$, the calculus obtained from λ^{Π} by adding the axiom $\tau \in \tau$ (where τ represents the type of all types). They asserted that by following the proof of Girard's paradox [4] they could construct in $\lambda^{\tau\tau}$ a polymorphic fixed-point combinator

$$Y \in \Pi\ T{:}\tau\,.\,(T \to T) \to T$$

such that for any type T and any $F \in T \to T$

$$YTF = F(YTF).$$

*This work was supported, in part, by NSF grant no. MCS-81-04018.

They then showed that the existence of such a Y had some important implications for $\lambda^{\tau\tau}$:

- A non-normalizing term is derivable.
- Equality of terms is undecidable.
- $\lambda^{\tau\tau}$ does not conservatively extend base-type theories, so that classical reasoning about base-type objects is not valid in the programming language formed by $\lambda^{\tau\tau}$ together with base-types.

However, they were not able to establish the existence of Y. It appears that the problem may involve so much formal detail that a solution without mechanical assistance is infeasible. A non-trivial proof must be carried out in a formal system in which even the basic notions of logic need to be encoded, and the behaviour under reduction of a very large term must be characterized. (A printout, with no spaces, of the term constructed in our effort is about 40 pages long.)

In [8], Reinhold considered an extension of $\lambda^{\tau\tau}$ that included the natural numbers (together with a recursion combinator) and a dependent sum (or sigma) type constructor. He outlined a proof that by following Martin-Löf's simplification of the proof of the paradox [6], it was possible to obtain in the extension a term Y, of the proper type, such that there exist terms Y_n for $n \geq 0$ with $Y_0 \equiv Y$ and for all n

$$Y_n TF = F(Y_{n+1} TF).$$

He called a term satisfying this property a *looping combinator*, and conjectured that an analogous construction in $\lambda^{\tau\tau}$ would give a fixed-point combinator.

In this paper, we show that at least one particular proof of Girard's paradox yields a term which is a looping combinator and *not* a fixed-point combinator. The computer plays an essential role in the argument. The Nuprl proof development system [2] was used to deal with the vast amounts of syntactic detail that an analysis of the computational behaviour of the paradox seems to entail. It was straightforward (taking less than two days) to formalize a proof of the paradox in a subset of the Nuprl type-theory that is similar to $\lambda^{\tau\tau}$, using the proof-development tools provided by the system. We show how the proof that the resulting term is a looping but not a fixed-point combinator can be reduced to the verification of a (small) finite number of machine-checkable assertions about reduction. These verifications were carried out using Nuprl's term-manipulation facilities. What we present, then, is not a complete proof, in that the argument depends on the correctness of the Nuprl implementation. More specifically, we prove that if the formal argument carried out in the system constitutes a valid proof in the Nuprl type theory, and if the implementation of the programming language ML [5] is correct insofar as it was used to perform certain reduction sequences and to verify certain simple properties of some Nuprl proofs, then the resulting term has the properties we claim.

Several features of Nuprl played an important role in the construction of the term by allowing us to formalize the paradox at a high level of abstraction. Nuprl's *definition* mechanism permits highly readable notations for basic concepts. The *tactic* mechanism provides for the sound addition of derived inference rules and for the construction of proof-finding programs. Finally, the *extractor* makes it possible to construct terms implicitly; one can represent a mathematical proposition P by a Nuprl type T, construct a proof which resembles a conventional proof of P, and then have the system *extract* from the proof a term $t \in T$ that embodies the computational content of the proposition. Because of these features, the formal proof we constructed, although providing the construction of a massive term, bears a strong resemblance to the conventional proof on which it is based.

Of course, the negative half of our result is based on one particular proof of the paradox. Although it is possible that some other approach would give a different result, it seems that the failure of the fixed-point property results from the essential content of the paradox. It should be straightforward, though, to apply our techniques to alternate proofs. If the fixed-point property cannot be obtained, then the argument in [7] establishing the failure of conservative extension for $\lambda^{\tau\tau}$ is no longer valid. However, the looping property is enough to prove both the undecidability of equality and the existence of a non-normalizing term.

In Section 2 we present the variant of $\lambda^{\tau\tau}$ that corresponds to the subset of the Nuprl type theory we used. In Section 3, we discuss Girard's paradox and its formalization. In Section 4 we analyze the computational behaviour of the resulting term. At end we make a few concluding remarks.

2 $\nu^{\tau\tau}$

In this section we present a polymorphic λ-calculus $\nu^{\tau\tau}$ that has dependent types and a type of all of types. It is a simple matter to check that the actual Nuprl proof of Girard's paradox that we constructed yields a proof in $\nu^{\tau\tau}$; it seems certain it also yields a proof in $\lambda^{\tau\tau}$ but this has not been verified. Details are contained in an appendix that we have not included here. The chief difference between $\lambda^{\tau\tau}$ and $\nu^{\tau\tau}$ is that λ-abstractions in $\lambda^{\tau\tau}$ contain the type for the bound variable.

The set of terms of $\nu^{\tau\tau}$ is the smallest set containing an infinite set of variables, the constant τ, $a(b)$ whenever a and b are terms, and $\lambda x.\, B$ and $\Pi\, x\!:\!A\,.\,B$ whenever x is a variable and A and B are terms. We will write $t[a/x]$ to denote the result of substituting a for x in t. The rules of $\nu^{\tau\tau}$ deal with *sequents*, of the form:

$$x_1 : A_1, \ldots, x_n : A_n \vdash t \in T,$$

where the variables x_i are all distinct, for each i the set of free variables of A_i is contained in $\{x_1, \ldots, x_{i-1}\}$, and the set of free variables of $t \in T$ is contained in $\{x_1, \ldots, x_n\}$. We will call the portion of a sequent to the left of the turnstile a *context*. The extension of a context $\mathcal{A}$ by an assumption $x : A$ or by another context $\mathcal{A}'$ will be denoted by $\mathcal{A}, x : A$ and $\mathcal{A}, \mathcal{A}'$ respectively. We will write $t \to t'$ if t' can be obtained from t by a sequence of β-reductions.

Following are the the rules of $\nu^{\tau\tau}$. We omit an axiomatization of a theory of equality.

τ-formation $\qquad \mathcal{A} \vdash \tau \in \tau$

Π-formation $$\frac{\mathcal{A} \vdash A \in \tau \qquad \mathcal{A},\, x : A \vdash B \in \tau}{\mathcal{A} \vdash \Pi\, x : A\,.\, B \in \tau}$$

λ-intro $$\frac{\mathcal{A} \vdash A \in \tau \qquad \mathcal{A},\, x : A \vdash b \in B}{\mathcal{A} \vdash \lambda x.\, b \in \Pi\, x : A\,.\, B}$$

function-elim $$\frac{\mathcal{A} \vdash f \in \Pi\, x : A\,.\, B \qquad \mathcal{A} \vdash a \in A}{\mathcal{A} \vdash f(a) \in B[a/x]}$$

assumption $\qquad \mathcal{A},\, x : A,\, \mathcal{A}' \vdash x \in A$

reduction-1 $$\frac{\mathcal{A} \vdash t \in T' \qquad \mathcal{A} \vdash T \in \tau \qquad T \to T'}{\mathcal{A} \vdash t \in T}$$

reduction-2 $$\frac{\mathcal{A},\, x : A',\, \mathcal{A}' \vdash t \in T \qquad A \to A'}{\mathcal{A},\, x : A,\, \mathcal{A}' \vdash t \in T}$$

3 Girard's Paradox

Girard's paradox is an adaptation by Girard [4] of the well-known Burali-Forti paradox. The proof of the paradox that we use is somewhat different from Girard's.

Informally, the argument proceeds as follows. Define an ordering (a type together with a transitive binary relation) to be well-founded if it has no infinite descending chains of elements. If the collection of all types is itself a type, then we can form the collection of all well-founded orderings. We make this collection into an ordering using the relation of embedding, and show that this ordering is well-founded. Any well-founded ordering can be embedded in the collection, and so the collection is embedded in itself. This gives an infinite descending chain, contradicting well-foundedness.

Formalizing this argument in $\nu^{\tau\tau}$ involves the *propositions-as-types* correspondence, whereby a proposition is associated with a type of $\nu^{\tau\tau}$ in such a way that the members of the type correspond to constructive proofs of the proposition. In this scheme, universal quantification corresponds to the Π type; most of the other concepts of logic must be coded. Falsity is represented by the type $\Pi\, t:\tau\,.\,t$; a member of this type would be a function taking any type and producing a member of that type. A formalization of the paradox in $\nu^{\tau\tau}$ yields a term that is a member of this type; the outermost reduction sequence starting with this term does not terminate.

What was noticed by Meyer and Reinhold was that given a type T and a function $F \in T \rightarrow T$, one could slightly modify the proof of the paradox so that F would be inserted into the looping process that gives the infinite reduction sequence. Using Nuprl [2], a computer system exploiting the propositions-as-types correspondence, we took a (modified) proof of the paradox, made formal definitions for the basic notions of logic and for the other concepts involved, and then used the reasoning facilities of Nuprl to construct a formal version of the informal argument. Nuprl is designed in such a way that the system could then *extract* from the formal derivation the required term, which can be shown in $\nu^{\tau\tau}$ to have the type T. We then analysed this term with the help of Nuprl's symbolic computation facilities. An important point here is that Nuprl made it possible to quickly construct, in a natural way, a formal argument that looks very much like a detailed version of the informal one and that produces, via extraction, the term to be analysed. The complete Nuprl proof comprises eleven lemmas, with an average of about ten steps per lemma. (An example of a step is given later.)

We now give a detailed version of the informal argument above, which can be rather directly translated into Nuprl. We point out the two modifications that are made to the proof of the paradox in order to obtain the looping combinator. After presenting this detailed version, we will very briefly discuss its translation into Nuprl. This translation into Nuprl is sufficiently direct that the interested reader should be able to determine the correspondence between the detailed argument below and the terms discussed in the next section. We assume at the outset that we are given a type `T` and a function `F` $\in$ `T` $\rightarrow$ `T`; in the Nuprl proof, the function and its type are represented by variables, and it is assumed as an axiom that `F` $\in$ `T` $\rightarrow$ `T`. Also taken as an axiom in the Nuprl proof is the $\tau \in \tau$ assumption.

The definitions of embedding, U, and $<_U$ given below are variants of those given by Coquand [3]. We will not present the (well-known) encodings for logic; as an example, existential quantification is defined by

$$\exists\, x \in A\,.\,B \;\equiv\; \Pi\, C:\tau\,.\,(\Pi\, x:A\,.\,B \rightarrow C) \rightarrow C$$

where we use $A \rightarrow B$ to abbreviate $\Pi\, x : A\,.\,B$ when x does not occur free in B.

An *ordering* is a type A together with propositional functions $r \in A \rightarrow A \rightarrow \mathit{Prop}$ and $d \in A \rightarrow \mathit{Prop}$. (We use *Prop* and *Type* as synonyms for τ.) r is to be understood as a relation over A, and d as a subset of A. Typical names for orderings will be (A, r, d) and (B, s, e). We will be somewhat sloppy about notation for function application, writing, e.g., $f(x, y)$ for $f(x)(y)$. We will also abbreviate by writing R for (A, r, d) and S for (B, s, e).

If $f \in A \rightarrow B$ and $b \in B$, and

$$\begin{aligned} & e(b) \;\&\; \forall\, x \in A\,.\,d(x) \Rightarrow e(f(x)) \\ & \&\; \forall\, x, y \in A\,.\,d(x) \Rightarrow d(y) \\ & \qquad \Rightarrow r(x, y) \Rightarrow s(f(x), f(y)) \\ & \&\; \forall\, x \in A\,.\,d(x) \Rightarrow s(f(x), b) \end{aligned}$$

then we will say that (f, b) *embeds* R in S. We will say that the first ordering is *embedded* in the second, and write $R < S$, if such an f and b exist. We will refer to f and b as the *order-preserving map* and the *bound* of the embedding, respectively.

Define transitivity, $\mathit{trans}(R)$, in the obvious way. R is *well-founded* if there are no non-empty subsets P of A such that for every y in P there is an x in P with $r(x, y)$. We call such subsets *chains*. More formally, $P \in A \rightarrow \mathit{Prop}$ is a chain in R if

$$\begin{aligned} & \exists\, x \in A\,.\,P(x) \;\&\; d(x) \\ & \&\; \forall\, y \in A\,.\,P(y) \Rightarrow \exists\, x \in A\,.\,P(x) \;\&\; r(x, y). \end{aligned}$$

Well-foundedness is defined by:

$$wf(R) \equiv \forall\, P \in A \to Prop\,.\,(P \textit{ chain in } R \to \textit{false}).$$

The definition of $wf(R)$ is the only one that needs to be changed in order to obtain the looping combinator; we replace *false* by the assumed type T.

We now define *Uord*, the collection of all well-founded orderings. Define the type U to be

$$(\Pi\, B\colon Type\,.\,(B \to B \to Prop) \to (B \to Prop) \to Prop) \to Prop$$

and the injection i by $i(R) \equiv \lambda\, x\,.\, x(R)$. U can be viewed as the collection of all sets of sets of orderings, and i as the function which associates to each ordering the set of all sets of orderings that contain it. The mapping i is injective with respect to intensional equality, defined by

$$a = b \equiv \forall\, P \in U \to Prop\,.\, P(a) \Rightarrow P(b).$$

If $i(R) = i(S)$ then we can prove that the two orderings have the same properties. The ordering on U is defined by: $u <_U v$ *iff* there are R and S such that $u = i(R)$, $v = i(S)$, and $R < S$. Finally, define: $d_U(u)$ *iff* there is an R such that $u = i(R)$, *trans*(R), and $wf(R)$. We will refer to the ordering $(U, <_U, d_U)$ as *Uord.*

Our proof of the paradox consists of eight lemmas, to each of which except the first corresponds a lemma in the Nuprl formalization. The parenthesized numbers in lemma statements below give the number of steps in the corresponding Nuprl proof. There are three additional lemmas in the Nuprl development; they contain a total of ten steps. We will abuse notation by writing R (possibly with subscripts) for (A, r, d). We will also omit type information when it is clear from the context. The proofs of the lemmas below are for the most part straightforward, and so they are omitted or sketched.

Lemma 1 *If* $i(R_1) = i(R_2) \in U$ *and* P *is such that* $P(R_1)$*, then* $P(R_2)$.

Lemma 2 *(9). If* $R_1 < R_2$ *and* (f_1, b_1) *embeds* R_2 *in* R_3 *then there are* f_2 *and* b_2 *which embed* R_1 *in* R_3 *and such that* $r_3(b_2, b_1)$.

Lemma 3 *(4). If* $d_U(i(R))$ *then trans*(R) *(4) and* $wf(R)$.

Lemma 4 *(8). trans(Uord).*

Lemma 5 *(31). wf(Uord).*

Proof. Suppose P is a chain in *Uord.* Then there is an R_0 such that $P(i(R_0))$ and $d_U(i(R_0))$. Let Q be

$$\lambda\, a\,.\, \exists\, R\,.\, \exists\, f\,.\, P(i(R))\ \&\ (f, a) \textit{ embeds } R \textit{ in } R_0.$$

Q is a chain in R_0. □

The previous two lemmas, together with the assumption $\tau \in \tau$, imply that $d_U(i(Uord))$.

It is the proof of Lemma 5 that is modified for the construction of the looping combinator. The basic idea of this proof is to assume that there is a chain in *Uord* and obtain from it a chain in a *member* of *Uord* (this member is the element asserted to exist in the definition of chain). With the *modified* definition of well-foundedness, to prove this lemma we must give a function which takes chains in *Uord* to members of T. Given a chain P in *Uord,* we can obtain a chain Q in some R as in the unmodified proof. Since $wf(R)$, we can get a member x of T. Instead of using x directly, we first apply F to it.

Denote by R_a the ordering

$$(A, r, \lambda\, x\,.\, d(x)\ \&\ r(x, a))$$

Lemma 6 *(9). If* $d_U(i(R))$ *and* $a \in A$ *is such that* $d(a)$*, then* $d_U(i(R_a))$.

Lemma 7 *(16). If* $d_U(i(R))$ *then* $R <$ *Uord.*

Proof. $\lambda\, a\,.\, i(R_a)$ and $i(R)$ give an embedding. □

Lemma 8 *(13). Contradiction.*

Proof. $\lambda\, u\,.\,(u = i(Uord))$ is a chain in *Uord,* contradicting 5. □

In the Nuprl version of Lemma 8, instead of obtaining a contradiction, we obtain a member of the type T. That is, the complete Nuprl proof of the lemma yields a term t and a proof in $\nu^{\tau\tau}$ that $\vdash t \in$ T. We have space here only for a few examples that illustrate the Nuprl version of the preceding argument. For more information on Nuprl, see the Nuprl book [2].

The definitions given above can be directly transcribed into Nuprl. For example, the (modified) well-foundedness predicate is the term

```
λ A r d. ∀P:A->Type. P chain in (A,r,d) => T
```

(which uses other definitions). Also defined is a display form for applications of this predicate. For example, the term which consists of the above lambda-term applied to three arguments `A`, `r`, and `d` appears on the computer screen as `wf(A,r,d)`.

In Figure 1 is a step from the Nuprl proof of Lemma 7. From top to bottom, the components are: a vertically presented sequent (using >> as a turnstile)

```
1. A: Type
2. q: A->A->Type
3. c: A->Type
4. dU(i(A, q, c))
5. a1: A
6. c(a1)
>> (A,q,(λa. c(a) & q(a,a1))) < (A,q,c)

BY (DIntro ['λw. w'; 'a1'] [] [] ...)
   THEN (DIntro [][][] ...)
   THEN (Reduce ...)

1* 7. x: A
   8. c(x) & q(x,a1)
   >> c(x)

2* 7. x: A
   8. c(x) & q(x,a1)
   >> (q(x))(a1)
```

Figure 1: A step from Lemma 7.

with numbered hypotheses; an ML program, called a *tactic*, (the text following the BY) that was entered by the author; and two *subgoal* sequents that were generated by the system as the result of the tactic execution (the subgoals inherit all the hypotheses of the first sequent). We will not explain the operation of the tactic shown in the figure except to note that the effect is roughly to make progress toward proving the asserted embedding by supplying an order-preserving map and an embedding bound.

4 Analysis of the Extracted Term

The Nuprl formalization of lemma 8 yields a term t such that $\vdash t \in \mathtt{T}$. The term we will examine, call it L, is a reduced (via β-reductions) form of t. The term L actually contains constants which denote extractions from other Nuprl theorems. Since there is a linear ordering of theorem dependencies, these constants can be eliminated by successively replacing them by the terms they denote. The actual Nuprl terms to which we apply symbolic computation will retain these constants, since they provide convenient labels for certain subterms of interest, although they are replaced by their denotations when necessary for computation.

We will write $t \xrightarrow{h} t'$ if t reduces to t' via a sequence of *head* β-reductions, and $t \rightarrow t'$ if t reduces to t' via *some* sequence of β-reductions. We write $t \equiv t'$ if t and t' are the same except for the names of bound variables. Two terms are equal if they are identical up to β-conversion.

In what follows, we will be interested in the results of computations in which certain subterms are irrelevant. We will therefore consider terms which contain a special variable ι. We will say that t is an *instance* of t', and write $t \leq t'$, if t can be obtained from t' by replacing some occurrences of ι by another term (possibly different terms for different occurrences). A term will be called *ground* if it does not contain ι. We also generalize the notion of reduction (but equality will only apply to ground terms). When we say that t reduces to t' in a certain way, we mean that for any instance of t there is an instance of t' such that the statement is true in the sense previously defined. To verify $t \rightarrow t'$ using Nuprl's computation facilities, we can proceed as follows. Replace by some distinct Nuprl variable all occurrences of ι in t, apply some Nuprl reduction steps to obtain t'', and check that t'' is an instance of t'.

The Looping Property

The basic idea, due to Meyer and Reinhold, behind the proof that L has the looping property is as follows. The proof of the paradox involves constructing a chain in *Uord* and deriving a contradiction (member of T) from *Uord*'s well-foundedness. This is reflected in the form of L, which is

$$wf(P^0)(pf^0)$$

where wf is the term extracted from the Nuprl proof of Lemma 5, P^0 is the chain in *Uord* from the proof of Lemma 8, and pf^0 is the term which constitutes a proof that P^0 is a chain. *Uord*'s well-foundedness gives a procedure which when applied to P^0 (together with pf^0), produces a chain P^1 (with proof pf^1) in a *member* of the chain P^0, which, by construction of P^0, is again *Uord*, and then applies this member's well-foundedness proof. This is reflected in the reduction sequence

$$wf(P^0)(pf^0) \rightarrow \mathtt{F}(wf(P^1)(pf^1)).$$

P^1 and pf^1 are similar to P^0 and pf^0, so we can repeat the above, obtaining P^k and pf^k for $k > 1$, and thus obtaining the required L_k.

The problem in turning the above idea into a proof is that one must characterize the reduction behaviour of a massive term. It is likely that the task is not feasible for a human without the aid of a computer.

We have solved the problem by reducing it to a small set of machine-checkable assertions.

The proof we give below involves verifying certain properties of certain terms via symbolic computation. Whenever we state that a computation has a certain result, then unless stated otherwise the computation was carried out using utilities of the Nuprl system. We will not completely describe the strategies for reduction that were used; the two main strategies were head reduction, and normalization while holding constant a small number of terms that were extractions from theorems. (A transcript of the session in which these computations were done is available from the author.) In what follows, when confusion might otherwise arise, object variables, i.e., Nuprl variables that are part of the terms being discussed, will have typewriter typeface (e.g., n instead of n).

Theorem 1 *For each k there is a ground term L_k such that $L_0 \equiv L$ and for all k, $L_k \rightarrow \mathtt{F}(L_{k+1})$.*

Proof. We first make some simple definitions. The first definitions are for pairing and projection: for terms a and b, let $\langle a, b\rangle$ denote $\lambda tf.\, f(a)(b)$, and let $\pi_1(a)$ and $\pi_2(a)$ denote $a(\iota)(\lambda xy.\, x)$ and $a(\iota)(\lambda xy.\, y)$, respectively. We assume that the variables in the pairing definition are always named so as to avoid capturing free variables of a and b. We extend the pairing notation to n-tuples by right-associating. Next, denote by eq, id, pf_1, pf_2, and pf_3 the terms $\lambda P.\, \lambda x.\, x$, $\lambda x.\, x$, $\lambda xy.\, \pi_1(y)$, $\lambda uvwxy.\, y$, and $\lambda xy.\, \pi_2(y)$, respectively. Finally, let d and wf denote the terms extracted from the Nuprl proof that $i(Uord)$ is in d_U, and from the Nuprl proof of Lemma 5 (that $Uord$ is well-founded), respectively (actually, these terms are just Nuprl constants denoting other terms, as discussed earlier).

We inductively define (non-ground) terms f^k, p^k_n and s_n such that the following three properties hold for all $k \geq 1$ and $n \geq 0$:

$$wf(\iota)(\langle\langle \iota, p^k_0, d\rangle, f^k\rangle) \rightarrow \mathtt{F}(wf(\iota)(\langle\langle \iota, p^{k+1}_0, d\rangle, f^{k+1}\rangle)),$$

$$f^k(\iota)(p^k_n) \rightarrow \langle \iota, p^k_{n+1}, s_n\rangle,$$

and

$$L \rightarrow \mathtt{F}(wf(\iota)(\langle\langle \iota, p^1_0, d\rangle, f^1\rangle)).$$

Intuitively, the tuple $\langle \iota, p^k_0, d\rangle$ corresponds to the proof that the chain P^k is non-empty (with ι taking the place of $Uord$ and with p^k_0 corresponding to the proof that $Uord$ is in P^k), and f^k is a function which takes a member of P^k and returns another member which is smaller in the embedding ordering. In the tuple $\langle \iota, p^k_{n+1}, s_n\rangle$, ι takes the place of this other member, p^k_{n+1} corresponds to the proof that this member is a member of P^k, and s_n corresponds to a proof that this member is smaller than the first member. The three properties above suffice to prove the theorem, since we can apply the third property, and then repeatedly apply the first to obtain L_k, for $k \geq 1$, as a ground instance of

$$wf(\iota)(\langle\langle \iota, p^k_0, d\rangle, f^k\rangle).$$

Define, for t a term,

$$\begin{aligned} \mathcal{S}_0[t] &\equiv \langle \iota, \iota, \iota, \iota, \iota, \iota, eq, eq, id, \iota, t, pf_1, pf_2, pf_3\rangle \\ \mathcal{S}[t] &\equiv \langle \iota, \iota, \iota, \iota, \iota, \iota, eq, eq, id, \iota, \langle \iota, t\rangle, \\ &\qquad \lambda xp.\, \langle \pi_1(p), \iota\rangle, pf_2, pf_3\rangle \end{aligned}$$

Define the terms s_n inductively by $s_0 = \mathcal{S}_0[d]$, $s_{n+1} = \mathcal{S}[s_n]$. Next, for t, t' terms, denote by $\mathcal{P}_1[t, t']$ the term

$$\langle \iota, \iota, \iota, \iota, eq, \iota, \iota, t, t'\rangle.$$

We define by induction on $k \geq 1$ the terms f^k and p^k_n, and simultaneously show that they satisfy the required properties. For the case $k = 1$, we define by induction on $n \geq 0$ terms

$$p^1_n \equiv \mathcal{P}_1[op_n, bpf_n],$$

where op_n and bpf_n are terms such that for each $j \geq 0$

$$op_n(\iota)(\iota)(\iota)(\iota)(s_j) \rightarrow s_{n+j+1}$$

and

$$bpf_n(\iota)(d) \rightarrow s_n.$$

Computing, we get

$$L \rightarrow \mathtt{F}(wf(\iota)(t))$$

where t is ground and

$$t \rightarrow \langle\langle \iota, \mathcal{P}_1[op_0, bpf_0], d\rangle, f\rangle$$

for some op_0 bpf_0, and f. Take p^1_0 to be $\mathcal{P}_1[op_0, bpf_0]$, and f^1 to be f. We now verify the required properties of op_0 and bpf_0 with two computations (sj is a single Nuprl variable):

$$op_0(\iota)(\iota)(\iota)(\iota)(\mathtt{sj}) \rightarrow \mathcal{S}[\mathtt{sj}]$$

and

$$bpf_0(\iota)(\mathtt{d}) \rightarrow \mathcal{S}_0(\mathtt{d}).$$

Suppose that we have defined p^1_n, and that op_n and bpf_n have the required properties. We have

$$\begin{aligned} &f^1(\iota)(\mathcal{P}_1[\mathtt{opn}, \mathtt{bpfn}]) \\ &\rightarrow \langle \iota, \mathcal{P}_1[op'_{n+1}, bpf'_{n+1}], \mathtt{bpfn}(\iota)(d)\rangle \end{aligned}$$

for some terms op'_{n+1} and bpf'_{n+1}. Define p^1_{n+1} to be $\mathcal{P}_1[op'_{n+1}, bpf'_{n+1}]$ with op_n and bpf_n substituted for opn and bpfn respectively. By the induction hypothesis, $bpf_n(\iota)(d)$ reduces to s_n, so if we can verify the required properties for p_{n+1} then we will have completed the construction of the terms p^1_n and shown that for all $n \geq 0$

$$f^1(\iota)(p^1_n) \rightarrow \langle \iota, p^1_{n+1}, s_n \rangle.$$

The properties for p^1_{n+1} are verified by computing

$$op'_{n+1}(\iota)(\iota)(\iota)(\iota)(\mathtt{sj}) \rightarrow (\mathtt{opn})(\iota)(\iota)(\iota)(\iota)(\mathcal{S}[\mathtt{sj}])$$

and

$$bpf'_{n+1}(\iota)(\mathrm{d}) \rightarrow (\mathtt{opn})(\iota)(\iota)(\iota)(\iota)(\mathcal{S}_0[\mathrm{d}])$$

and applying the induction hypothesis.

Suppose now that $k \geq 1$ and that the terms f^k and p^k_n have been defined and satisfy

$$f^k(\iota)(p^k_n) \rightarrow \langle \iota, p^k_{n+1}, s_n \rangle. \quad (*)$$

For t, t' terms, denote by $\mathcal{P}[t, t']$ the term

$$\langle \iota, \iota, \iota, id, t, t', pf_1, pf_2, pf_3 \rangle.$$

Define, for all $n \geq 0$, p^{k+1}_n to be

$$\mathcal{P}[p^k_{n+1}, u],$$

where u is d if $n = 0$, and ι otherwise. For any term t denote by $\sigma(t)$ the term

$$t[p^k_0, f^k / \mathtt{pk0}, \mathtt{fk}]$$

Now

$$wf(\iota)(\langle\langle \iota, \mathtt{pk0}, d \rangle, \mathtt{fk} \rangle) \xrightarrow{h} \mathtt{F}(w(\iota)(u))$$

where $w \xrightarrow{h} wf$ and $u \xrightarrow{h} \langle t, f \rangle$. Define f^{k+1} to be $\sigma(f)$. t is

$$\mathtt{fk}(\iota)(\mathtt{pk0})(v)(v').$$

This term, under σ, contains a subterm to which, by induction, $(*)$ can be applied. We have

$$(\langle \iota, \mathtt{pk1}, s_0 \rangle)(v)(v') \rightarrow \langle \iota, \mathcal{P}[\mathtt{pk1}, d], d \rangle.$$

This proves that

$$\sigma(t) \rightarrow \langle \iota, p^{k+1}_0, d \rangle.$$

We must now show that f^{k+1} has the required property. Suppose $n \geq 0$. Let r be $\mathcal{P}[\mathrm{p}, u]$ where u is d if $n = 0$ or ι if $n > 0$, and let r' be $\mathcal{S}[\mathrm{sn}]$. For t a term, let $\tau(t)$ be

$$t[p^k_0, f^k, p^k_{n+1}, s_n / \mathtt{pk0}, \mathtt{fk}, \mathrm{p}, \mathrm{sn}].$$

We must show that

$$\tau(f(\iota)(r)) \rightarrow \langle \iota, p^{k+1}_{n+1}, s_n \rangle.$$

Computing, we get

$$f(\iota)(r) \rightarrow \mathtt{fk}(\iota)(\mathrm{p})(a)(a')$$

for some a and a'. Now by induction

$$\tau(\mathtt{fk}(\iota)(\mathrm{p})) \rightarrow \langle \iota, p^k_{n+2}, s_{n+1} \rangle.$$

By computation,

$$(\langle \iota, \mathrm{q}, r' \rangle)(a)(a') \rightarrow \langle \iota, \mathcal{P}[\mathrm{q}, d], \mathrm{sn} \rangle.$$

□

Not a Fixed-Point

We will now show that L is not an application of a fixed-point combinator. In doing so, we only make one use of Nuprl symbolic computation to establish a fact about reduction; this use will be indicated explicitly. Let L_k, for $k \geq 0$, be the terms constructed as the proof of Theorem 1. Define u^k to be

$$\langle\langle \iota, p^k_0, d \rangle, f^k \rangle.$$

For $k \geq 1$, L_k is an instance of $wf(\iota)(u^k)$. We consider T and F to be constants in what follows.

Figure 2 contains part of a printout of the term wf with some subterms elided, and containing names of theorems (which refer to the corresponding extractions). From it we obtain the term wf' by replacing the (unique) subterm of the form $\lambda \mathtt{y}.\mathtt{F}(t)$ by $\mathtt{X}(\lambda \mathtt{y}.\mathtt{F}(t))$, ($\mathtt{X}$ is a fresh variable). Note that t is headed by y. The idea here is to block certain reductions in order to show that all reductions from L must repeatedly satisfy a certain property. We will call a term t F-*reducible* if it has no subterm of the form $\mathtt{F}(t')$ such that $t \xrightarrow{h} \mathtt{F}(t')$. We will write $\mathtt{F}^{(n)}(t)$ for the term which is the n-fold application of F to t. In the remainder of this section, *all* terms will be *ground* unless indicated otherwise.

Lemma 9 *If* $w \xrightarrow{h} wf$, $u \rightarrow u^k$, $k \geq 1$, *and for some terms* c *and* t, $w(c)(u) \rightarrow \mathtt{F}^{(i)}(t)$, *where* $i \geq 0$ *and* t *is* F-*reducible, then* $t \xrightarrow{h} \mathtt{F}((\iota)(\iota)(u'))$ *for some* u' *equal to an instance of* u^{k+i+1} *(i.e., where there exists* $u'' \leq u^{k+i+1}$ *with* $u' = u''$*).*

```
(λ P v0.
  (v0
    . . .
    (λ x v9.
      (v9
        . . .
              . . .
                (λ d0 y.
                  (F
                    (y
                      (and (trans A0 r0 d0)
                           (wf A0 r0 d0))
                      (λ v3 v4. v4)
                      (wf A0 r0 d0)
                      (λ v3 v4. v4)
                      . . .
                      . . .)))))))))))
```

Figure 2: *wf* with some subterms elided.

Proof. The proof is by induction on i. We will do the induction step first. Suppose, then, that $i > 0$. By standardization[1] we have

$$w(c)(u) \xrightarrow{h} wf(c)(u) \xrightarrow{h} \mathtt{F}(t')$$

for some t' with $t' \to \mathtt{F}^{(i-1)}(t)$. Therefore, to prove the induction step it suffices to show that t' has the form $w'(c')(u')$ where $w' \xrightarrow{h} wf$ and $u' \to u^{k+1}$.

Nuprl's symbolic computation gives

$$wf'(\iota)(\langle\langle\langle\iota, \text{pk0}, d\rangle, \iota\rangle) \xrightarrow{h} \mathtt{X}(\lambda \mathtt{y}.\, \mathtt{F}(w_0(c_0)(u_0)))(v_0)$$

for some terms w_0, c_0, u_0, and v_0 that are not ground terms, are minimal with respect to $\leq$ (i.e., are obtained by treating ι as a variable, doing the computation, and not making any replacements, in the reduct, of subterms by ι), and do not contain X. It follows that

$$wf'(\iota)(u^k) \xrightarrow{h} \mathtt{X}(\lambda \mathtt{y}.\, \mathtt{F}(w_1(\iota)(u_1)))(v_1)$$

for some terms w_1, u_1, and v_1 that are not ground terms, do not contain X, and are minimal with respect to $\leq$. Note that, since w_1, u_1, and v_1 do not contain X, for any c', w', u', v' and any $u \leq u^k$ such that

$$wf'(c')(u) \xrightarrow{h} \mathtt{X}(\lambda \mathtt{y}.\, \mathtt{F}(w'(\iota)(u')))(v'),$$

w', u' and v' do not contain X. Removing the X and doing the final β-conversion in the reduction defining w_1, etc., we get

$$wf(\iota)(u^k) \xrightarrow{h} \mathtt{F}(w_1[v_1/\mathtt{y}](\iota)(u_1[v_1/\mathtt{y}])).$$

[1]Roughly, for every reduction sequence, there is a left-to-right reduction sequence with the same initial and final terms. For details, see [1].

In the proof of Theorem 1, we showed that

$$wf(\iota)(u^k) \xrightarrow{h} \mathtt{F}(w_2(\iota)(u_2))$$

where w_2 and u_2 are not ground, $w_2 \xrightarrow{h} wf$ and $u_2 \to u^{k+1}$. By the minimality of w_1, u_1, and v_1, we have

$$w_1[v_1/\mathtt{y}] \leq w_2 \quad \textit{and} \quad u_1[v_1/\mathtt{y}] \leq u_2.$$

Now,

$$wf'(c)(u) \to wf'(c)(u_0^k) \xrightarrow{h} \mathtt{X}(\lambda \mathtt{y}.\, \mathtt{F}(w_3(\iota)(u_3)))(v_3)$$

where u_0^k, w_3, u_3, and v_3 are instances of u^k, w_1, u_1, and v_1, respectively. Standardizing, we get

$$wf'(c)(u) \xrightarrow{h} \mathtt{X}(\lambda \mathtt{y}.\, \mathtt{F}(w_4(\iota)(u_4)))(v_4) \quad (*)$$

where, since w_4 must be in head normal form by the construction of wf', $w_4 \to w_3$, $u_4 \to u_3$, and $v_4 \to v_3$. Therefore,

$$w_4[v_4/\mathtt{y}] \to w_3[v_3/\mathtt{y}] \leq w_1[v_1/\mathtt{y}] \leq w_2 \xrightarrow{h} wf.$$

Note that wf was actually defined to be a constant denoting an extraction, so we must have

$$w_4[v_4/\mathtt{y}] \xrightarrow{h} wf.$$

Also,

$$u_4[v_4/\mathtt{y}] \to u_3[v_3/\mathtt{y}] \leq u_1[v_1/\mathtt{y}] \leq u_2 \to u^{k+1},$$

so $u_4[v_4/\mathtt{y}] \to u^{k+1}$. Removing the X in $(*)$, then, we have

$$w(c)(u) \xrightarrow{h} wf(c)(u) \xrightarrow{h} (\lambda \mathtt{y}.\, \mathtt{F}(w_4(\iota)(u_4)))(v_4)$$
$$\xrightarrow{h} \mathtt{F}(w_4[v_4/\mathtt{y}](\iota)(u_4[v_4/\mathtt{y}])).$$

This completes the proof of the induction case.

To prove the base case, we must show that if $w \xrightarrow{h} wf$, $u \to u^k$, and $w(c)(u) \to t$ where t is F-reducible, then $t \xrightarrow{h} \mathtt{F}((\iota)(\iota)(u'))$, where u' is equal to an instance of u^{k+1}. For v a term, let $\varepsilon(v)$ be the term obtained by repeatedly replacing subterms of the form $\mathtt{X}(a)$ by a.

Figure 3 contains a diagram which summarizes the reductions discussed in the following. Let w' be w with all occurrences of wf replaced by wf'. Using the argument in the induction case, we have

$$w'(c)(u) \xrightarrow{h} wf'(c)(u) \xrightarrow{h} \mathtt{X}(\lambda \mathtt{y}.\, \mathtt{F}((s_1)(s_2)(u')))(v)$$

where

$$u'[v/\mathtt{y}] \to u^{k+1},$$

$$
\begin{array}{ccccc}
w'(c)(u) & \xrightarrow{h} & wf'(c)(u) & \xrightarrow{h} & \mathtt{X}(\lambda \mathtt{y}.\, \mathtt{F}((s_1)(s_2)(u')))(v) \\
\downarrow & & & & \downarrow \\
t' & & \xrightarrow{h} & & r \equiv \mathtt{X}(\lambda \mathtt{y}.\, \mathtt{F}((s_3)(s_4)(u'')))(v') \\
\Downarrow & & & & \Downarrow \\
t & & \xrightarrow{h} & & r' \equiv (\lambda \mathtt{y}.\, \mathtt{F}((\iota)(\iota)(u''')))(v'')
\end{array}
$$

Figure 3: Reductions in the base case argument.

and u' and v do not contain X. Now consider the reduction sequence from $w(c)(u)$ to t. Note that if b is such that $w'(c)(u) \rightarrow b$, and if for some a and a' $\mathtt{X}(a)(a')$ is a subterm of b, then $a(a')$ is a redex and has no free variables, and if this redex is contracted, the resulting term is head normal (see Figure 2). It follows that we can obtain a reduction sequence from $w'(c)(u)$ to some t' where t can be obtained from t' by replacing maximal subterms of the form $\mathtt{X}(a_1)(a_2)$ or $\mathtt{X}(a_1)$ by some term a_3 where $\varepsilon(a_1(a_2)) \rightarrow a_3$ or $\varepsilon(a_1) \rightarrow a_3$, respectively. (Such a set of replacements is indicated in the diagram in Figure 3 by a double arrow.) We must also have

$$t' \xrightarrow{h} \mathtt{X}(\lambda \mathtt{y}.\, \mathtt{F}((s_3)(s_4)(u'')))(v')$$

for some u'' and v' where, using standardization and the fact that s_1 is head-normal, $u' \rightarrow u''$ and $v \rightarrow v'$. Call the reduct above r. The head reduction sequence from t' to r gives, step for step, a sequence $t \xrightarrow{h} r'$ for some r'. The replacements taking t' to t give rise to a replacement taking r to r'. Suppose that the replacement involves contracting the topmost redex

$$\lambda \mathtt{y}.\, \mathtt{F}((s_3)(s_4)(u''))(v').$$

Then, since also any subterm of t' of the form $\mathtt{X}(a)(a')$ must be closed, we must have that

$$\mathtt{X}(\lambda \mathtt{y}.\, \mathtt{F}((s_3)(s_4)(u'')))(v')$$

is a subterm of t', and that the replacements which take t' to t involve replacing this subterm by r'. This contradicts the assumption that t is F-reducible. Therefore the term r' is of the form

$$(\lambda \mathtt{y}.\, \mathtt{F}((\iota)(\iota)(u''')))(v'')$$

for some u''' and v''. Since u'' and v' do not contain X, and since s_3 is head-normal, we have $u'' \rightarrow u'''$ and $v' \rightarrow v''$. Now

$$u'[v/\mathtt{y}] \rightarrow u''[v'/\mathtt{y}] \rightarrow u'''[v''/\mathtt{y}].$$

Since also $u'[v/\mathtt{y}]$ reduces to an instance of u^{k+1}, we are done. □

Lemma 10 *Any term t can be reduced to a term $\mathtt{F}^{(i)}(t')$ where t' is* F*-reducible.*

Proof. The proof is a simple induction on the size of terms. Write t as $\mathtt{F}^{(i)}(t')$ with i maximal, and suppose t' is not F-reducible. Then t' reduces to a term $\mathtt{F}(t'')$ which appears in t'. This term is smaller than t'. □

Theorem 2 *If $1 \leq k < k'$, then $L_k \neq L_{k'}$.*

Proof. Suppose not. Then L_k and $L_{k'}$ have a common reduct t. By Lemma 10 we may assume that t is of the form $F^{(i)}(t')$ where t' is F-reducible. Applying Lemma 9, we get

$$t' \xrightarrow{h} \mathtt{F}((\iota)(\iota)(u)),$$

where u is equal to an instance of u^{k+i+1} and equal to an instance of $u^{k'+i+1}$. This means that there are instances of u^{k+i+1} and $u^{k'+i+1}$ that have a common reduct, which implies that there are instances of p_0^{k+i+1} and $p_0^{k'+i+1}$ that have a common reduct. From the definition of these latter two terms, it follows that there are instances of p^1_{k+i} and $p^{k'-k+1}_{k+i}$ that have a common reduct. But this is impossible, since the first of these terms is a nine-tuple whose fifth component is *eq*, while the second is a nine-tuple whose fifth component is also a nine-tuple. □

The following is immediate.

Theorem 3 *There is no Z such that $Z = L$ and $Z = \mathtt{F}(Z)$.*

5 Conclusion

We formalized one particular proof of Girard's paradox. It is possible that another proof would yield a term which is a fixed-point combinator, but it seems unlikely. The focus of the looping structure of the paradox seems to be in the proof that *Uord* is well-founded, where, to show that a particular entity does not exist (a chain in our case, a proof that some member is less than itself in the case of Girard's proof), one assumes that it does, transforms it into an analogous entity in a *member* of *Uord*, and applies that member's well-foundedness property. It seems certain that if the transformation adds any structure, then the fixed-point cannot be obtained.

Nuprl was used in an essential way in this effort. The formal proof of Girard's paradox was carried out at a fairly high level and in a reasonably short time (about two working days), and involved very little explicit reasoning about the components of the term that was being constructed. Nuprl's collection of tools for term manipulation were then used to verify certain properties of the huge resulting term. Nuprl also played a valuable role in the discovery of parts of the argument presented in this paper, since the straightforward formalization of the informal proof yielded a term in whose correctness one could have confidence, and on which one could quickly test certain kinds of conjectures using the various tools provided by the system.

The result of this effort indicates a possible role for mechanized formal problem solving environments such as Nuprl in mathematical research. There may arise other problems such as the one addressed in this paper, where the computer plays an indispensable role in the solution. If this is the case, then systems like Nuprl, that can support high-level formal reasoning in a variety of problem domains, and that provide a large set of facilities for manipulation and analysis of proofs and terms, will prove to be valuable tools.

Acknowledgements

The author is grateful to Bob Constable, Todd Knoblock, and Scott Smith for their suggestions concerning the presentation of this work.

References

[1] H. P. Barendregt. *The Lambda Calculus: Its Syntax and Semantics.* Volume 103 of *Studies in Logic and the Foundations of Mathematics*, North-Holland, Amsterdam, revised edition, 1984.

[2] R. L. Constable, et al. *Implementing Mathematics with the Nuprl Proof Development System.* Prentice-Hall, Englewood Cliffs, New Jersey, 1986.

[3] T. Coquand. An analysis of Girard's paradox. In *First Annual Symposium on Logic in Computer Science*, IEEE, 1986.

[4] J. Girard. Interprétation fonctionelle et élimination des coupures dans l'arithmétique d'ordre supérieur. 1972. Thèse de Doctorat d'Etat, University of Paris, France.

[5] M. J. Gordon, R. Milner, and C. P. Wadsworth. *Edinburgh LCF: A Mechanized Logic of Computation.* Volume 78 of *Lecture Notes in Computer Science*, Springer-Verlag, 1979.

[6] P. Martin-Löf. An intuitionistic theory of types. 1972. Mimeographed manuscript.

[7] A. R. Meyer and M. B. Reinhold. 'Type' is not a type. In *Conference Record of the Thirteenth Annual ACM Symposium on Principles of Programming Languages*, Association for Computing Machinery, SIGACT, SIGPLAN, 1986.

[8] M. Reinhold. Looping with Girard's paradox. 1986. Unpublished manuscript.

A Non-Type-Theoretic Definition of Martin-Löf's Types

Stuart Allen
Computer Science Dept.
Cornell University

Abstract

It is possible to make a natural non-type-theoretic reinterpretation of Martin-Löf's type theory. This paper presents an inductive definition of the types explicitly defined in Martin-Löf's paper, *Constructive Mathematics and Computer Programming.* The definition is set-theoretically valid, and probably will be convincing to intuitionists as well. When this definition is used with methods set out in the author's thesis, the inference rules presented in Martin-Löf's paper can be shown to be valid under the non-type-theoretic interpretation. This interpretation is non-trivial, that is, there are both inhabited types and empty types, and so, validity entails simple consistency. Finally, Michael Beeson has defined some recursive realizability models which we shall compare with the term model presented here, and we shall compare the methods of definition.

Introduction

There is some interest among computer scientists in using the formal language of Martin-Löf's intuitionistic theory of types [Martin-Löf] as a basis for programming. The work presented in this paper is a piece of a larger effort (see [Allen]) to provide a non-type-theoretic semantics for the expressive machinery of Martin-Löf's theory. The primary goal of this reinterpretation is to make most of the practice of mathematics that is based on intuitionistic type theory available to those who do not subscribe to the theory itself.

The reinterpretation of the theory of [Martin-Löf] proceeds in three phases. First, instead of using terms constructed from an open-ended body of term constructors, we use a fixed class of terms and an evaluation relation. In [Martin-Löf], a term constructor is introduced by specifying its argument places and variable binding structure, and also how one evaluates the terms with that constructor outermost. Second, instead of an open-ended body of type definitions, we use a property of terms T type, which we may call *typehood*, and a three-place relation on terms $t = s \in T$, which we may call *member equality*. In [Martin-Löf], a type is *defined* by choosing a canonical term T, the type, then specifying which canonical terms are to be *members* of T, and then specifying an equivalence relation on the canonical members of T as the *equality* on T. Finally, we reinterpret the judgements of [Martin-Löf] purely in terms of the property typehood, the relation member equality, and the syntax of the forms of judgement. The syntax of the judgement forms may be inductively defined from terms.

Is this reinterpretation possible for a "real" system of types, such as is defined in [Martin-Löf]? Clearly, we can define by induction the terms built using the term constructors actually introduced in [Martin-Löf], and we can define by induction the evaluation relation between those terms. It should also be easy for those familiar with [Martin-Löf] to believe that, given the property T type and the relation $t = s \in T$, the judgements of [Martin-Löf] may be reinterpreted appropriately. The issue then is whether the property T type and the relation $t = s \in T$ can be defined so that they capture the types defined in [Martin-Löf][1].

Anatomy of the Type Constructors

The canonical type constructors that are defined in [Martin-Löf] are conveniently divisible into three groups. The constituent types of a type are those upon whose definition the type construction depends.

- N_n N $I(A, a, b)$ $A + B$. Each of these defines a type from finitely many, explicitly given, con-

[1] or rather, the types that are definable using only the type constructors defined in [Martin-Löf]. I think we may consider a type constructor definition to be a procedure for defining a type from its constituent types, the procedure being applicable to types not yet defined.

stituent types.

- $(\Sigma x \in A)B$ $(\Pi x \in A)B$ $(\mathrm{W} x \in A)B$. Each of these defines a type from an explicitly given family of constituent types that is indexed by an explicitly given constituent type.

- U_n. The equal members of universe U_n are the extensionally equal types[2] that are definable from the type constructors other than U_{n+i}. Although we might have included universes in the first group as having no constituent types, it seems clearer to conceive of them as resulting from a second order type constructor that builds a universe from a level number and a collection of ordinary first order type constructors.

Suppose we were to define T type and $t = s \in T$ by mutual recursion of some sort. What might the clauses defining the canonical types be? Let $s \leftarrow t$ mean that t is a closed term that evaluates to s. The defining clauses for the first group of constructors are simple, those for $A+B$ being

$A+B$ type iff A type & B type

and

$$\begin{aligned} &t = t' \in A+B \\ &\text{iff } A+B \text{ type} \\ &\quad \& \ \exists\, a\, a'.\ \mathrm{i}(a) \leftarrow t \ \&\ \mathrm{i}(a') \leftarrow t' \ \&\ a = a' \in A \\ &\quad\quad \text{or } \exists\, b\, b'.\ \mathrm{j}(b) \leftarrow t \ \&\ \mathrm{j}(b') \leftarrow t' \ \&\ b = b' \in B, \end{aligned}$$

where $\mathrm{i}(t)$ and $\mathrm{j}(t)$ are canonical term constructors used for injection.

The second group of type constructors requires a certain kind of specification for families of types, namely, a term B_x and a type A over which B_x is *type functional*. We may say that a term B is *type functional over A in x* when substitution of equal members of A for x in B results in extensionally equal types. Suppose we included a clause defining $T = S$ as extensional type equality.

$$\begin{aligned} &T = S \\ &\text{iff } T \text{ type} \ \&\ S \text{ type} \ \&\ \forall\, t\, s.\ t = s \in T \text{ iff } t = s \in S. \end{aligned}$$

Then the clauses defining $(\Pi x \in A)B$, typical of the second group, might be

$$\begin{aligned} &(\Pi x \in A)B \text{ type} \\ &\text{iff } A \text{ type} \ \&\ \forall\, a\, a'.\ B[a/x] = B[a'/x] \text{ if } a = a' \in A \end{aligned}$$

and

$$\begin{aligned} &t = t' \in (\Pi x \in A)B \\ &\text{iff } (\Pi x \in A)B \text{ type} \\ &\quad \& \ \exists\, u\, b\, u'\, b'.\ (\lambda u)b \leftarrow t \ \&\ (\lambda u')b' \leftarrow t' \\ &\quad\quad \& \ \forall\, a\, a'.\ b[a/u] = \\ &\quad\quad\quad b'[a'/u'] \in B[a'/x] \\ &\quad\quad\quad \text{if } a = a' \in A. \end{aligned}$$

The clause admitting U_n as a type would be simply

U_n type.

To define equality on U_n, we need only define the membership of U_n, and then define the equality to be extensional type equality on the members.

$t \in T$ iff $t = t \in T$.

$T = S \in \mathrm{U}_n$ iff $T \in \mathrm{U}_n$ & $S \in \mathrm{U}_n$ & $T = S$.

To define the membership of U_n, we might duplicate the clauses defining typehood, except that instead of the clause U_n type we would use

$\mathrm{U}_m \in \mathrm{U}_n$ iff $m < n$,

and in the other typehood defining clauses we would replace T type by $T \in \mathrm{U}_n$.

Finally, in addition to the clauses defining the other canonical types, we would include clauses defining the non-canonical types.

T type iff $\exists S \leftarrow T.\ S$ type.
$t = s \in T$ iff $\exists S \leftarrow T.\ t = s \in S$.

While a putative definition of T type and $t = s \in T$ having the form just outlined may well serve as a convincing definition when properly read, the reading is not as straightforward as possible. If one inspects the right-hand sides of the clauses, one finds various negative, as well as positive, occurrences of the three-place relation $t = s \in T$;[3] there are no strongest T type and $t = s \in T$ satisfying those clauses. Our aim will be to express more explicitly, by means of an appropriate monotonic operator, what would be meant by the recursive definition sketched above.

Extensional Type Systems

The method we shall use for defining type systems is more easily applied to type systems with extensional type equality than to those with intensional equality. Since the only type systems to be defined here

[2]Types are extensionally equal when they have the same membership and the same equality between members.

[3]For example, the right-hand sides of the Π type formation and equality clauses contain explicitly negative occurrences of $() = () \in ()$. Wherever $() = ()$ occurs, we may say that $() = () \in ()$ implicitly occurs both positively and negatively. Occurrences of $() = ()$ are to be found in the clauses for Π type formation and U_n equality.

are extensional, we shall restrict our consideration to such.

By $s \leftarrow t$, let us mean that term t evaluates to term s. For our purposes, what is important about evaluation is that

if $s \leftarrow t$ then t is closed & $s \leftarrow s$

and

if $s \leftarrow t$ & $s' \leftarrow t$ then s is s',

that is, $s \leftarrow t$ defines a partial function in t. A *canonical* term is one that is its own value.

Let us say that a *possible type system* is (or is represented by) a relation $\tau T \phi$ between terms (T) and two-place relations on terms (ϕ). The intention is that when τ is a type system, $\tau T \phi$ is true just when T is a type and ϕ is the equality between members of T.[4] Let us define four relations which should make clear the intended use of type systems.

$T =_\tau S$ iff $\exists \phi.\, \tau T \phi$ & $\tau S \phi$.

T type$_\tau$ iff $T =_\tau T$.

$t = s \in_\tau T$ iff $\exists \phi.\, \tau T \phi$ & $t \phi s$.

$t \in_\tau T$ iff $t = t \in_\tau T$.

A(n extensional) *type system* has certain properties which we now define.

Fun(τ) iff $\forall\, T\, \phi\, \phi'.\, \phi$ is ϕ' if $\tau T \phi$ & $\tau T \phi'$,

that is, $\tau T \phi$ defines a partial (relation valued) function in T.

TyVal(τ) iff $\forall\, T\, \phi.\, \tau T \phi$ iff $\exists T' \leftarrow T.\, \tau T' \phi$,

that is, to be a type is to evaluate to a(n equal) type.

TrSy(τ)
iff $\forall\, T\, \phi.\, \phi$ is transitive and symmetric if $\tau T \phi$,

thus, member equality is an equivalence relation on members.

Val(τ)
iff $\forall\, T\, \phi.$ if $\tau T \phi$ then $\forall\, t\, s.\, t \phi s$ iff $\exists t' \leftarrow t.\, t' \phi s$,

and so, in view of TrSy(τ), to be a member is to evaluate to a(n equal) member. A possible type system τ is a type system, or ETS(τ), just when it has these four properties.

This characterization of type systems has been chosen because our central method of definition will be inductive definition of particular relations of the kind we have called possible type systems.

[4]If we wanted to include type systems with intensional type equality, we would characterize type systems by three-place relations $\tau T T' \phi$, such that $\tau T T' \phi$ holds when T and T' are equal types with member equality ϕ.

The Inductive Definition

We shall define our principal type system as the strongest possible type system closed under the type constructors. Defining a universe U_n requires selecting the strongest possible type system closed under the type constructors other than U_{n+i}. These definitions might be treated uniformly if we had a method for defining the strongest possible type system closed under a given collection of universe constructors as well as under the non-universe type constructors.

Defined below is a function TyF which is a two-place operator on possible type systems. For possible type systems σ and τ, TyF$(\sigma;\tau)T\phi$ holds when type T (with equality ϕ) is a type of σ (with equality ϕ) or else it is constructed from the types of τ by a non-universe constructor. The parameter σ provides a means of including base types, and by this means we will introduce universes.

We will define a one-place possible type system operator $\mu(\sigma)$ such that $\mu(\sigma)$ is the strongest possible type system closed under TyF(σ;). But is such a definition valid? That depends upon TyF and upon the reader's understanding of inductive definition. There are three kinds of readers whom I would address. Those who subscribe to set theory, those whose ontology includes extensional properties and relations, and intuitionists or other constructivists.

Set theoretically, the definition is valid if TyF(σ;) may be construed as a monotonic operator on the subsets of some set. Clearly, the terms can be represented as members of a set $\mathcal{T}$. If TyF(σ;) is monotonic on the subsets of $\mathcal{T} \times Pow(\mathcal{T} \times \mathcal{T})$ then

$\mu(\sigma)$ is $\bigcap \{\tau \subseteq \mathcal{T} \times Pow(\mathcal{T} \times \mathcal{T}) \mid \mathrm{TyF}(\sigma;\tau) \subseteq \tau\}$.

If relations are essentially extensional,[5] and if they are ontologically real,[6] then the definition is valid if TyF$(\sigma;\tau)T\phi$ is monotonic in τ, since μ is explicitly definable by

$\mu(\sigma)T\phi$ iff $\forall \tau.\, \tau T \phi$ if $\forall\, S\, \psi.\, \tau S \psi$ if TyF$(\sigma;\tau)S\psi$.

Standard intuitionistic theory of inductive definition directly licenses inductive definitions of

the strongest P such that $\forall \overline{x}.\, P\overline{x}$ if $\theta(\overline{x}; P)$,

where $\theta(\overline{x}; P)$ is a relation between individuals and properties of individuals that is (strictly) positive in P. The definition of $\mu(\sigma)$ does not quite conform to this standard since it is not a relation between individuals, but rather, for each σ, $\mu(\sigma)$ is a relation between individuals and two-place relations between individuals. Still, the intuitionist might be convinced of

[5]as opposed to extensional equality between relations being a relation between intensional relations,
[6]rather than *façons de parler*,

the validity of our definition if $\mathrm{TyF}(\sigma;\tau)T\phi$ is strictly positive in τ.

It will be seen that TyF does indeed meet these various criteria for the validity of the definition of μ.

We begin the definition by setting out the type formation methods. This is done by defining the relations $\widehat{\mathrm{N}}_?$, $\widehat{\mathrm{N}}$, $\widehat{\mathrm{I}}$, $\widehat{+}$, $\widehat{\Sigma}$, $\widehat{\Pi}$ and $\widehat{\mathrm{W}}$. Each of these is an operator on possible type systems,[7] whose value (a possible type system) has only the types that evaluate to a certain form.

The types N_n and N have no constituent types.

$\widehat{\mathrm{N}}_? T\phi$
iff $\exists n.\ \mathrm{N}_n \leftarrow T \ \&\ \forall\, a\, b.\ a\phi b$ iff $\exists m < n.\ m_n \leftarrow a, b$.

Define N-equality by

$$\begin{aligned}&\text{Neq is the strongest } \phi \text{ such that}\\ &\forall\, a\, b.\ a\phi b \text{ if } 0\leftarrow a, b \text{ or } \exists\, a'\, b'.\ a'\phi b'\\ &\qquad\qquad\&\ \mathrm{suc}(a')\leftarrow a\\ &\qquad\qquad\&\ \mathrm{suc}(b')\leftarrow b.\end{aligned}$$

$\widehat{\mathrm{N}} T\phi$ iff $\mathrm{N}\leftarrow T \ \&\ \phi$ is Neq.

The rest of the non-universe type constructors have constituent types, and so the type formation operators need, as a parameter, a possible type system from which to get these constituent types. In the definitions that follow, α and β range over two-place relations on terms.

$$\begin{aligned}&\widehat{\mathrm{I}}(\tau)T\phi\\ &\text{iff } \exists\, A\, \alpha\, a\, b.\ \mathrm{I}(A,a,b)\leftarrow T \ \&\ \tau A\alpha \ \&\ a\alpha a \ \&\ b\alpha b\\ &\qquad \&\ \forall\, t\, t'.\ t\phi t' \text{ iff } \mathrm{r}\leftarrow t, t' \ \&\ a\alpha b.\end{aligned}$$

$$\begin{aligned}&t +\!\mathrm{eq}(\alpha;\beta)\ t'\\ &\text{iff } \exists\, a\, a'.\ \mathrm{i}(a)\leftarrow t \ \&\ \mathrm{i}(a')\leftarrow t' \ \&\ a\alpha a'\\ &\quad \text{or } \exists\, b\, b'.\ \mathrm{j}(b)\leftarrow t \ \&\ \mathrm{j}(b')\leftarrow t' \ \&\ b\beta b'.\end{aligned}$$

$$\begin{aligned}&\widehat{+}(\tau)T\phi \text{ iff } \exists\, A\, \alpha\, B\, \beta.\ A+B\leftarrow T \ \&\ \tau A\alpha \ \&\ \tau B\beta\\ &\qquad\qquad \&\ \phi \text{ is } +\!\mathrm{eq}(\alpha;\beta).\end{aligned}$$

Now we proceed with the second group of type constructors, those having families of constituent types. In the definitions below, α ranges over two-place relations between terms and γ ranges over three-place relations between terms. The application of γ to terms is indicated by $t\gamma_a s$.

$$\begin{aligned}&\mathrm{Fam}(\tau;A;\alpha;x;B;\gamma)\\ &\text{iff } \tau A\alpha \ \&\ \forall\, a\, a'.\ \text{if } a\alpha a' \text{ then } \gamma_a \text{ is } \gamma_{a'}\\ &\qquad\qquad \&\ \tau\, B[a/x]\,\gamma_a\\ &\qquad\qquad \&\ \tau\, B[a'/x]\,\gamma_{a'}.\end{aligned}$$

[7]We may consider possible type systems to be zero-place operators.

When τ is a type system, i.e., when $\mathrm{ETS}(\tau)$, then B is type functional over A in x if and only if there are α and γ such that $\mathrm{Fam}(\tau;A;\alpha;x;B;\gamma)$. The definition of the type functionality in the previous section is easily seen to identify the type functionality of B over A in x with

$$\begin{aligned}&\mathrm{Fam}(\tau;\, A;\, a, a'.\,(a = a' \in_\tau A)\,;\\ &\qquad x;\, B;\, a, b, b'.\,(b = b' \in_\tau B[a/x])\,).\end{aligned}$$

In a type system, the type determines a unique member equality, so, we can eliminate the occurrences of member equality by dropping all reference to it, thus:

$$\exists\, \alpha\, \gamma.\ \mathrm{Fam}(\tau;A;\alpha;x;B;\gamma).$$

Note that $\mathrm{Fam}(\tau;A;\alpha;x;B;\gamma)$ is strictly positive in τ.

Using the same method, we eliminate the occurrences of member equality that would occur on the right-hand sides of the clauses defining the second group of type constructors.

$$\begin{aligned}&t\ \Sigma\mathrm{eq}(\alpha;\gamma)\ t' \text{ iff } \exists\, a\, b\, a'\, b'.\ (a,b)\leftarrow t \ \&\ (a',b')\leftarrow t'\\ &\qquad\qquad \&\ a\alpha a' \ \&\ b\,\gamma_a b'.\end{aligned}$$

$$\begin{aligned}&\widehat{\Sigma}(\tau)T\phi \text{ iff } \exists\, A\, \alpha\, x\, B\, \gamma.\ (\Sigma x\in A)B\leftarrow T\\ &\qquad\qquad \&\ \mathrm{Fam}(\tau;A;\alpha;x;B;\gamma)\\ &\qquad\qquad \&\ \phi \text{ is } \Sigma\mathrm{eq}(\alpha;\gamma).\end{aligned}$$

$$\begin{aligned}&t\ \Pi\mathrm{eq}(\alpha;\gamma)\ t'\\ &\text{iff } \exists\, u\, b\, u'\, b'.\ (\lambda u)b\leftarrow t \ \&\ (\lambda u')b'\leftarrow t'\\ &\qquad \&\ \forall\, a\, a'.b[a/u]\,\gamma_a\, b'[a'/u'] \text{ if } a\alpha a'.\end{aligned}$$

$$\begin{aligned}&\widehat{\Pi}(\tau)T\phi \text{ iff } \exists\, A\, \alpha\, x\, B\, \gamma.\ (\Pi x\in A)B\leftarrow T\\ &\qquad\qquad \&\ \mathrm{Fam}(\tau;A;\alpha;x;B;\gamma)\\ &\qquad\qquad \&\ \phi \text{ is } \Pi\mathrm{eq}(\alpha;\gamma).\end{aligned}$$

$$\begin{aligned}&\mathrm{Weq}(\alpha;\gamma) \text{ is the strongest } \phi \text{ such that}\\ &\forall\, t\, t'.\ t\phi t' \text{ if } \exists\, a\, f\, u\, s\, a'\, f'\, u'\, s'.\\ &\qquad \mathrm{sup}(a,f)\leftarrow t \ \&\ (\lambda u)s\leftarrow f\\ &\qquad \&\ \mathrm{sup}(a',f')\leftarrow t' \ \&\ (\lambda u')s'\leftarrow f'\\ &\qquad \&\ a\alpha a' \ \&\ \forall\, b\, b'.\ s[b/u]\,\phi\, s'[b'/u']\\ &\qquad\qquad \text{if } b\,\gamma_a b'.\end{aligned}$$

$$\begin{aligned}&\widehat{\mathrm{W}}(\tau)T\phi \text{ iff } \exists\, A\, \alpha\, x\, B\, \gamma.\ (\mathrm{W}x\in A)B\leftarrow T\\ &\qquad\qquad \&\ \mathrm{Fam}(\tau;A;\alpha;x;B;\gamma)\\ &\qquad\qquad \&\ \phi \text{ is } \mathrm{Weq}(\alpha;\gamma).\end{aligned}$$

It may be of interest that in each of these definitions of type formation, the definition of the member equality of a type depends only on the member equalities of its constituent types.

We may now define type formation under these constructors plus any base types.

$$\mathrm{TyF}(\sigma;\tau)T\phi \text{ iff } \sigma T\phi \text{ or } \widehat{\mathrm{N}}_?T\phi \text{ or } \widehat{\mathrm{N}}T\phi \text{ or } \widehat{\mathrm{I}}(\tau)T\phi \text{ or } \widehat{+}(\tau)T\phi \text{ or } \widehat{\Sigma}(\tau)T\phi \text{ or } \widehat{\Pi}(\tau)T\phi \text{ or } \widehat{\mathrm{W}}(\tau)T\phi.$$

The relation $\mathrm{TyF}(\sigma;\tau)T\phi$ is strictly positive, hence monotonic, in τ. Clearly, the relation $s{\leftarrow}t$ can be graphed as a subset of $\mathcal{T} \times \mathcal{T}$, and therefore, $\mathrm{TyF}(\sigma;\tau)$ is a two-place operator on the subsets of $\mathcal{T} \times Pow(\mathcal{T} \times \mathcal{T})$, which are the graphable possible type systems. Hence, the definition of $\mu(\sigma)$ will be valid for graphable σ. Let us introduce a convenient notation for closure under $\mathrm{TyF}(\sigma;)$.

$$\mathrm{CTyF}(\sigma;\tau) \text{ iff } \forall T\ \phi.\ \tau T\phi \text{ if } \mathrm{TyF}(\sigma;\tau)T\phi.$$

Now we define μ.

$\mu(\sigma)$ is the strongest τ such that $\mathrm{CTyF}(\sigma;\tau)$.[8]

To complete the definition, we need only define the universes and add them as base types. We shall define the hierarchy HAN_n of type systems that are reflected in universes. The types of the type system spine_n are the universes of HAN_n.[9]

HAN_n is $\mu(\mathrm{spine}_n)$.

$$\mathrm{spine}_n T\phi \text{ iff } \exists m < n.\ \mathrm{U}_m{\leftarrow}T \ \&\ \phi \text{ is } =_{\mathrm{HAN}_m}.$$

We now define the principal type system via the union of spines.[10]

HAN_ω is $\mu(\mathrm{spine}_\omega)$.

$$\mathrm{spine}_\omega T\phi \text{ iff } \exists m.\ \mathrm{U}_m{\leftarrow}T \ \&\ \phi \text{ is } =_{\mathrm{HAN}_m}.$$

It remains to be seen that these possible type systems are indeed type systems.

Adequacy of the Definition

Is HAN_ω a reasonable reinterpretation of the type constructors defined in [Martin-Löf]? It seems to me that the definition is posed in a way that would make the adequacy of HAN_ω obvious if only we should ascertain that

- HAN_ω and each HAN_n are extensional type systems, and
- each type of HAN_n is also a type of HAN_{n+i} and of HAN_ω, with the same member equality.

If the theorems that follow are to be read set theoretically, the variables σ and τ should be restricted to graphable possible type systems.

[8] This is set theoretically valid when σ is graphable, and this is sufficient for our purpose.

[9] HAN_n and spine_n are graphable.

[10] HAN_ω and spine_ω are graphable.

Theorem $\mu(\sigma)$ is $\mathrm{TyF}(\sigma;\mu(\sigma))$.

Since $\mathrm{CTyF}(\sigma;\mathrm{TyF}(\sigma;\mu(\sigma)))$,
since $\mathrm{TyF}(\sigma;\tau)$ is monotonic in τ,
and $\mathrm{CTyF}(\sigma;\mu(\sigma))$.

In fact, $\mu(\sigma)$ is the strongest fixed point of $\mathrm{TyF}(\sigma;)$.

It will be convenient to make the following crude abstraction from the spines.

$$\mathrm{Uonly}(\sigma) \text{ iff } \forall T\ \phi.\ \text{if } \sigma T\phi \text{ then } \exists n.\ \mathrm{U}_n{\leftarrow}T.$$

Lemma $\mathrm{Fun}(\mu(\sigma))$ if $\mathrm{Fun}(\sigma)$ & $\mathrm{Uonly}(\sigma)$.

Since $\mathrm{Fun}(\mu(\sigma))$ iff $\forall T\ \phi.$ if $\mu(\sigma)T\phi$ then $\forall\phi'.\ \phi$ is ϕ' if $\mu(\sigma)T\phi'$,
and if $\mathrm{Fun}(\sigma)$ & $\mathrm{Uonly}(\sigma)$ then
$\mathrm{CTyF}(\ \sigma\ ;\ T,\phi.\ \forall\phi'.\ \phi$ is ϕ' if $\mu(\sigma)T\phi'\ )$.

Lemma $\mathrm{TyVal}(\mu(\sigma))$ if $\mathrm{TyVal}(\sigma)$.

Since $\forall\tau.\ \mathrm{TyVal}(\mathrm{TyF}(\sigma;\tau))$ if $\mathrm{TyVal}(\sigma)$.

Lemma $\mathrm{TrSy}(\mu(\sigma))$ if $\mathrm{TrSy}(\sigma)$.

Since if $\mathrm{TrSy}(\sigma)$ then
$\mathrm{CTyF}(\sigma;T,\phi.\ \phi$ is transitive and symmetric$)$.

Lemma $\mathrm{Val}(\mu(\sigma))$ if $\mathrm{Val}(\sigma)$.

Since if $\mathrm{Val}(\sigma)$ then
$\mathrm{CTyF}(\ \sigma\ ;\ T,\phi.\ \forall\ t\ s.\ t\phi s \text{ iff } \exists t'{\leftarrow}t.\ t'\phi\, s\ )$.

Lemma $\mathrm{ETS}(\mu(\sigma))$ if $\mathrm{ETS}(\sigma)$ & $\mathrm{Uonly}(\sigma)$.

Lemma If $\mathrm{Fun}(\tau)$
then $=_\tau$ is transitive and symmetric.

Lemma If $\mathrm{TyVal}(\tau)$ then
$\forall\ t\ s.\ t =_\tau s$ iff $\exists t'{\leftarrow}t.\ t' =_\tau s$.

Theorem $\mathrm{ETS}(\mathrm{HAN}_n)$ & $\mathrm{ETS}(\mathrm{spine}_n)$,
by induction on n.

Since $\forall n.\ \mathrm{Uonly}(\mathrm{spine}_n)$.

Theorem $\mathrm{ETS}(\mathrm{HAN}_\omega)$.

Since $\mathrm{ETS}(\mathrm{spine}_\omega)$ & $\mathrm{Uonly}(\mathrm{spine}_\omega)$.

Lemma $\mu(\sigma)$ is monotonic in σ.

Since assuming σ to be as strong as σ',
$\mathrm{CTyF}(\sigma;\mu(\sigma'))$, since $\mathrm{CTyF}(\tau;\tau')$ is antimonotonic in τ, and $\mathrm{CTyF}(\sigma';\mu(\sigma'))$.

Theorem HAN_n is a subrelation of HAN_{n+i} and HAN_ω.

Since μ is monotonic and spine_n is a subrelation of spine_{n+i} and spine_ω.

Formal Proof — Consistency

Let us call the signs expressing the judgements of [Martin-Löf] *sequents.* Sequents can be defined by induction from the terms.[11] In [Allen], the reinterpretation of the judgements of [Martin-Löf] is rather directly effected by defining a property, Fn, of sequents in terms of the property T type and the relation $t = s \in T$. There are methods set out in [Allen] by means of which one can prove all the inference rules of [Martin-Löf] to be valid under the reinterpretation, that is, the conclusion of each rule is a sequent that satisfies Fn if the premises do.[12] Thus, every sequent provable using only those rules satisfies Fn.

For any terms T and t, there is a sequent, let us write $t \in T$, that satisfies Fn just when $t \in_{\mathrm{HAN}_\omega} T$. If T is an empty type of HAN_ω then the sequent $t \in T$ is not derivable, for any t, using the rules of [Martin-Löf]. We may consider this as a form of simple consistency when propositions are represented by types the representation being such that a proposition is true just when the type representing it is inhabited.

Comparison with Beeson's Recursive Models

We shall compare the type systems defined in this paper with Beeson's models for type theory, and we shall also compare the methods of definition. The difference between Beeson's models and the type systems presented here are of some practical interest, and there is some theoretical significance to the difference between the definitions. In [Beeson], Beeson presents a sequence $M_n W$ of models for the sequence $\mathrm{ML}_n\mathrm{W}$ of formal systems. The system $\mathrm{ML}_n\mathrm{W}$ consists of the inference rules given in [Martin-Löf], excluding those about universes U_{n+i}.[13] The model $M_n W$, which may be viewed as a recursive realizability interpretation, corresponds to the type system HAN_n, which may be viewed as a term model.

The basic difference between HAN_n and $M_n W$ is that HAN_n is a term model based upon the so-called lazy evaluation procedure described in [Martin-Löf], whereas $M_n W$ uses numbers instead of terms, and uses call-by-value computation semantics. Beeson codes the canonical term constructors, except for lambda, and uses $\{m\}(n)$ instead of the application of one term to another.

By means of a recursive definition, to be discussed below, Beeson defines some relations between numbers, including $M_n W \models i = j$ and $M_n W \models i = j \in k$. The terms of [Martin-Löf] are made to correspond to numbers by an effective *partial* function on closed terms, $\hat{t}$, also written $t\hat{}$. The connection with [Martin-Löf] is made by the following facts.

If $\mathrm{ML}_n\mathrm{W}$ proves $A = B$
then $M_n W \models \hat{A} = \hat{B}$

and

if $\mathrm{ML}_n\mathrm{W}$ proves $a = b \in A$
then $M_n W \models \hat{a} = \hat{b} \in \hat{A}$.

This model deviates immediately from the semantics even when restricted to the terms and type constructors explicitly given in [Martin-Löf]. For example, if t is $(\lambda z)(\,z(z), 0\,)$ then $t(t)$ evaluates to $(t(t), 0)$, hence $(\mathrm{E}\,x, y)(\,t(t), 0\,)$ evaluates to 0, and so the judgement $(\mathrm{E}\,x, y)(\,t(t), 0\,) = 0 \in \mathrm{N}$ is valid. But, $t(t)\hat{}$ is undefined, hence $(\mathrm{E}\,x, y)(\,t(t), 0\,)\hat{}$ is also undefined, and so it is false that $M_n W \models (\mathrm{E}\,x, y)(\,t(t), 0\,)\hat{} = \hat{0} \in \hat{\mathrm{N}}$. But, $t(t)\hat{}$ is undefined, hence, $(\mathrm{E}\,x, y)(\,t(t), 0\,)\hat{}$ is also undefined, and so, it is false that $M_n W \models (\mathrm{E}\,x, y)(\,t(t), 0\,)\hat{} = \hat{0} \in \hat{\mathrm{N}}$.

While there may be no theoretically significant difference between the realizability model $M_n W$ and the term model HAN_n, the latter is a more direct reinterpretation of the semantics of type definition given in [Martin-Löf]. Also, HAN_n is more convenient to use when one is concerned directly with the terms.

Now we turn to the definitions. In [Beeson], $M_n W$ is defined, given $M_m W$ for $m < n$, by mutual recursion between five properties and relations on numbers:

$M_n W \models i$ type,
$M_n W \models i = j \in k$,
$M_n W \models i \in j$,
i is a family of types in $M_n W$ over j,
$M_n W \models i = j$.

The definition could have been accomplished by defining $M_n W \models i$ type and $M_n W \models i = j \in k$ by mutual recursion, and then explicitly defining each of the others in terms of these. To simplify our discussion we shall suppose the definition to have been given in this way.

---

[11] Here we include only the terms built using a fixed collection of term constructors.

[12] Martin-Löf intentionally elides some premises from the presentation of some inference rules in [Martin-Löf], so these must be made explicit in order to show these rules to be valid.

[13] Actually, Beeson adds the rule

$$\frac{x \in \mathrm{N}}{\mathrm{I}(\mathrm{N}, \mathrm{suc}(x), 0) = \mathrm{N}_0}$$

which is derivable, but the derivation uses a universe. Beeson needs this rule to establish certain facts about $\mathrm{ML}_0\mathrm{W}$, but these are of no importance to us.

This definition is of essentially the same form as the one sketched in this paper in the section headed *Anatomy of the Type Constructors*. The form is not the standard one for inductive definitions because of negative occurrences of $M_n W \models i = j \in k$ on the right-hand sides of some clauses of the definition. Nevertheless, Beeson explains, the definition is valid because all the members of a type are added at the same time as the type is introduced as such. Beeson then indicates how to define the model by standard means of induction. He applies the following *device* (*trick*). Define, by mutual recursion, not only $M_n W \models i$ type and $M_n W \models i = j \in k$, but also a relation $M_n W \not\models i = j \in k$. When $M_n W \models k$ type, $M_n W \not\models i = j \in k$ is to be defined to be the negation of $M_n W \models i = j \in k$. Wherever, in the clauses of the earlier definition, $M_n W \models i = j \in k$ occurs negatively on the right-hand side, replace that occurrence by the negation of $M_n W \not\models i = j \in k$. The defining clauses for $M_n W \not\models i = j \in k$ are made by imitating those for $M_n W \models i = j \in k$ except that the right-hand sides are negated (classically) in such a way that occurrences of $M_n W \models k$ type are positive, and then negative occurrences of $M_n W \models i = j \in k$ are eliminated as earlier suggested. The resulting definition consists of clauses whose right-hand sides are positive, though not strictly positive, in the definienda. Beeson says that, classically, it can be shown that $M_n W \models i = j \in k$ and $M_n W \not\models i = j \in k$ are complementary when $M_n W \models k$ type.

The similar definition of T type and $t = s \in T$ which was sketched in this paper has the same negative occurrences of the definienda on the right-hand sides of some clauses. However, here we proceeded to improve the definition by making explicit Beeson's explanation for the validity of the original definition, namely that the membership (and equality) of a type is defined when the type is. The validity of the definition does not depend upon defining the complement of $t = s \in T$ and so no appeal to non-intuitionistic principles is needed to justify the reformulation of the definition. More significantly, the resulting definition is, in this author's opinion, far more perspicuous than either the original one or the one achieved by the device utilized in [Beeson], as is evidenced by the immediate availability of induction over types.

References

[Martin-Löf] Per Martin-Löf. Constructive Mathematics and Computer Programming. *Sixth International Congress for Logic, Methodology, and Philosophy of Science.* North-Holland, Amsterdam, 1982.

[Allen] Stuart F. Allen. Doctoral Dissertation, Computer Science Department, Cornell University, 1987 (expected).

[Beeson] Michael Beeson. Recursive Models for Constructive Set Theories. *Annals of Mathematical Logic,* v. 23 (1982).

Session 6

Chair

G. Plotkin

University of Edinburgh

THE HIERARCHY OF FINITELY TYPED FUNCTIONAL PROGRAMS [1]

(Short Version)

A.J. Kfoury
Boston University
Computer Science Dept [2]

J. Tiuryn
University of Warsaw
Institute of Mathematics [3]

P. Urzyczyn
University of Warsaw
Institute of Mathematics [3]

Abstract

Finitely typed functional programs are naturally classified by their levels. We prove that this syntactic classification of functional programs corresponds to a semantical classification: the higher the level of functional programs, the more functions they can compute. We achieve this result by a detour through imperative languages that operate on higher-order pushdown stores and higher-order arrays.

A lower bound on the computational power of functional programs of a finite level k is obtained by translating into them the class of flowcharts equipped each with a level-k pushdown store; this translation is based on a call-by-name operational semantics.

An upper bound on the computational power of functional programs of level k is obtained by reducing their spectral complexity to the spectral complexity of flowcharts equipped with level-k arrays; this reduction uses the denotational semantics of our functional language.

1. Introduction

Many modern programming languages allow their programs to use higher-order objects in their computations. The role of such objects is purely auxiliary in that, semantically, a program is seen as transforming ground values into ground values, i.e., higher-order values are not mentioned in the input-output relation of the program.

We take as a functional programming language the finitely typed λ-calculus, with first-order constants, and with recursion introduced by means of mutually recursive function definitions. The main function definition in a functional program is always first-order, i.e., the function is applied to input values of ground type and returns an output value (if any) of ground type, but it can call intermediary defined functions of arbitrary finite orders. This is essentially the language PCF described in [P1], except that we do not interpret programs in arithmetic, and leave them as "program schemes" that are compared over all possible interpretations. Relative to a single interpretation we use a call-by-name operational semantics, which we may define by structured rules in the style of [P1,P2].

The finitely typed functional programs are naturally classified by their order or "level". The level of a functional program is a syntactic measure of the highest-order function definition in the program.

The aim of this paper is to study the impact of restricting the maximal level of higher-order objects used by programs on the computational power of such a class of programs. The expression *computational power of a class $\mathcal{P}$ of programs* should be understood as the collection

$$COMP(\mathcal{P}) = \{COMP(\mathcal{P},\mathcal{A}) \mid \text{arbitrary } \mathcal{A}\}$$

where $\mathcal{A}$ ranges over all structures in the same first-order signature (the universe of each being a set of ground values) and $COMP(\mathcal{P},\mathcal{A})$ is the set of all input-output relations computed in $\mathcal{A}$ by programs of $\mathcal{P}$.

Let us note that this notion of computational power is closely related to the natural notion of *semantical equivalence* of programs, and therefore it captures the "real" computational power of programs in all abstract structures. It should not be confused with other, usually stronger, notions of program equivalence, e.g., *formal equivalence* (cf. [L]). Two programs are said to be *formally equivalent* if their reduced formal computation

---

[1] This research was partly supported by NSF grant CCR-8601592 and by a grant of the Polish Ministry of Science and Higher Education, no. RP.I.09.

[2] 111 Cummington Street, Boston, Mass. 02215, USA

[3] PKiN, 00-901 Warszawa, Poland

lattices are the same; program equivalence in this sense leads to the comparison of certain formal languages associated with program schemes. With respect to this latter notion of program equivalence, the study of recursion on higher types as a control structure for programming languages (both imperative and functional) is not new. It can be traced at least as far back as [M], [P1], and [I]. With an interest more in formal languages than in programming languages, Damm, Engelfriet, and several of their colleagues, studied various hierarchies which appear related to ours (see [DFI], [DGo], [E], [ES], among others). An important paper of Damm ([D]) establishes the strictness of the hierarchy of (finite mode) ALGOL-68 program schemes with respect to the maximal level of types (i.e., modes) of procedures; however, this strictness result is merely related to the notion of formal equivalence of programs. Thus, the question of whether the hierarchy is strict with respect to the usual notion of program equivalence was left open.

We illustrate the difference between the results of [D] and the questions we ask in this paper: there are two distinct senses in which one can justify the statement "recursive procedures (with ground type parameters) are more powerful than iterative programs". In the first sense, corresponding to formal equivalence, one justifies the statement by observing that the context-free languages form a richer family than the regular languages. In the second sense, related to the usual notion of program equivalence, one justifies the statement by using a "pebble-game" argument ([F], [PH]) to show that there exists an interpretation in which recursive procedures compute *more functions* than iterative programs. Since the formal equivalence of programs is a stronger notion than the semantical equivalence, it follows that strictness of the hierarchy with respect to the latter notion implies strictness with respect to the former notion.

In the present paper we prove that increasing the level of functional programs results in a gain of computational power. We achieve this result by a detour through imperative languages, but the detour itself is also of independent interest, and is thus the second goal of our study. We address the question of how higher-order datatypes affect the computational power of an imperative language. Specifically, we extend the basic language of flowcharts to operate on higher-level pushdown stores and higher-level arrays. Using the method of "spectral complexities" developed in [TU1], a precise complexity-theoretic characterization of flowcharts operating on various higher-level datatypes is given in [T], which shows in particular that the datatype "pushdown store" corresponds to *deterministic time* and the datatype "array" to *deterministic space* (in a sense to be made precise). From this characterization it follows, for all $k \geq 1$, that "level-k pushdown store" $<$ "level-$(k+1)$ pushdown store" and likewise for "arrays", and that "level-k pushdown store" $\leq$ "level-k arrays" $\leq$ "level-$(k+1)$ pushdown store".

Using the method of spectral complexities again, we prove that level-k functional programs are reducible to flowcharts augmented with level-k arrays, i.e., for every level-k functional program there is an equivalent flowchart augmented with level-k arrays. This result illustrates the thesis that an enriched programming language can be represented by a suitably enriched datatype (in the sense argued in [W]), and our proof for it demonstrates the power and versatility of the spectral method. A proof of this result by direct translation or simulation, if at all possible, appears to be very difficult. The difficulty here is similar to that encountered in earlier attempts to simulate on higher-level pushdown stores the run-time behavior of programs with higher-level procedures. These attempts could only be completed in the sense of a translation of a higher-order grammar into a higher-order pushdown automaton (see [DGo], [DGu], [K]), provided also certain restrictions were imposed on the grammar. This sense of program equivalence is again different from the sense anticipated in our paper. Translations in the opposite direction, from higher-level datatypes to higher-level procedures or higher-level functional programs, appear to be more manageable.

By an intermediary translation to an imperative language with higher level procedures (related but not identical to L4 of [C]), we also show that flowcharts each augmented with a level-k pushdown store are reducible to level-k functional programs. (The translation in the opposite direction remains an open problem.) These results put together imply the following hierarchy result: level-$(k+2)$ functional programs are not reducible to level-k functional programs, for all $k \geq 1$.

2. Definitions and preliminary results

We start with the fundamental notion of a *type*. The set of all finite types is the least set containing $\mathbf{0}$ (the ground type of individuals) and BOOL (the ground type of truth-values), and containing $(\sigma \to \tau)$ whenever it contains σ and τ. We use the abbreviation $(\sigma_1, \ldots, \sigma_n, \tau)$ for $(\sigma_1 \to (\cdots(\sigma_n \to \tau)\cdots))$, $n \geq 1$. The *level* of a type σ is:

$$\ell(\sigma) = \begin{cases} 0, & \text{if } \sigma = \mathbf{0} \text{ or BOOL;} \\ max\{\ell(\tau_1)+1, \ell(\tau_2)\}, & \text{if } \sigma = (\tau_1 \to \tau_2). \end{cases}$$

Every type σ may be expanded into the form $\sigma = (\sigma_1, \ldots, \sigma_n, \tau)$ where $\tau \in \{\mathbf{0}, \text{BOOL}\}$, and an equivalent definition of the level of σ is:

$$\ell(\sigma) = 1 + max\{\ell(\sigma_1), \ldots, \ell(\sigma_n)\}$$

In what follows, every constant symbol, variable symbol, and term will have a type — and its level will be the level of its type.

Our classes of program schemes are defined relative to a first-order *signature* Σ, which is a finite sequence of *primitive relation, function and individual symbols*:

$$\Sigma = (r_1, \ldots, r_m; f_1, \ldots, f_n; c_1, \ldots, c_k) .$$

Every primitive function symbol f (respectively relation symbol r) has a fixed arity ≥ 1; if it has arity k, then its type is

$$\underbrace{(\mathbf{0}, \ldots, \mathbf{0}, \sigma)}_{k+1}$$

where $\sigma = \mathbf{0}$ (respectively BOOL). The level of a primitive function or relation symbol is therefore always 1. Individual constants are of type $\mathbf{0}$ and level 0.

The syntax of our functional programs is equivalent to that of the finitely typed λ-calculus with recursion, and with constants in $\Sigma \cup \{\mathbf{cond_0}, \mathbf{cond_{BOOL}}\}$ where $\mathbf{cond}_\sigma$ is the (sequential) conditional of type (BOOL,σ,σ,σ) with $\sigma \in \{\mathbf{0}, \text{BOOL}\}$. For the purposes of this paper, however, it is convenient to use a slightly different representation which does not use λ-abstractions. It can be shown that these variations in the syntax do not affect the computational power of the language. Let us then assume that for every type τ, there is a countably infinite set of variables of type τ, and we define the set of (purely applicative) *terms* to be the smallest set satisfying:

- every symbol in Σ of type τ is a term of type τ, the symbols *true* and *false* are terms of type BOOL, every variable of type τ is a term of type τ,
- if T is a term of type $(\sigma \to \tau)$ and U a term of type σ, then $(T\ U)$ is a term of type τ.

The level of a term is the level of its type. A *function definition* is an equation of the form

$$\mathcal{F} F_1 \ldots F_n \ \Leftarrow\ \textbf{if } B \textbf{ then } T \textbf{ else } U$$

where $\mathcal{F}$ (a defined function symbol) is a variable of type $(\tau_1, \ldots, \tau_n, \sigma)$, every F_i is a variable of type τ_i, and B, T, U, are terms of types BOOL, σ, σ, respectively, where $\sigma \in \{\mathbf{0}, \text{BOOL}\}$. We call n the *arity* of the defined function $\mathcal{F}$. A *functional program* is a finite sequence of function definitions, together with a distinguished defined function symbol $\mathcal{F}$ such that:

- the type of $\mathcal{F}$ is $(\mathbf{0}, \ldots, \mathbf{0}, \mathbf{0})$, with $k+1$ entries for some $k \geq 0$;
- the variables occurring on the right-hand side of any function definition must either occur on the left-hand side of that definition, or must be defined function symbols;
- there is exactly one function definition for every defined function symbol.

A functional program P is said to be of level n if n is the maximum of levels of the defined function symbols of P. The arity of the distinguished defined function $\mathcal{F}$ of P is also the arity of P. The language of all functional programs will be denoted by $\mathcal{L}^f$, while $\mathcal{L}^f_n$ will stand for the sublanguage consisting of all functional programs of level $\leq n$.

A *Σ-structure* is an algebraic structure $\mathcal{A}$ whose underlying functions, relations, and constants, provide meanings to the symbols in Σ. Elements of the universe of $\mathcal{A}$, also denoted $\mathcal{A}$, are of type $\mathbf{0}$, while every underlying function and relation of $\mathcal{A}$ has the type of the corresponding symbol in Σ. The association of types to semantic objects is generalized in the obvious way: functions which take arguments of type σ and give results of type τ are of type $(\sigma \to \tau)$.

Given a functional program P of arity k, and a Σ-structure $\mathcal{A}$, we may define the meaning of P in $\mathcal{A}$ as a k-ary function $P^{\mathcal{A}}$ of level 1. The details of a call-by-name operational semantics are not difficult to supply [KU1]. Although this semantics can be exactly formulated in the style of [P1, Sect 2], we depart slightly from the organization of that paper for convenience. Briefly, we need *reduction rules* which are applied to variable-free terms, the *redexes*:

- An $\mathcal{F}$-redex, for a defined function symbol $\mathcal{F}$ of P of type $(\tau_1, \ldots, \tau_n, \sigma)$ with $\sigma \in \{0, \text{BOOL}\}$ is any term of the form $\mathcal{F} U_1 \cdots U_n$. The reduction of $\mathcal{F} U_1 \cdots U_n$ consists in replacing it by the term $T[X_1 := U_1, \ldots, X_n := U_n]$ where T is the right-hand side of the definition of $\mathcal{F}$ in P.
- An if-redex has the form **if** b **then** T **else** U, where $b \in \{true, false\}$. If $b = true$, it reduces to T, otherwise to U.
- A Σ-redex is an expression of the form $f b_1 \cdots b_n$, where f is a k-ary function (or relation) symbol in Σ and $b_1, \ldots, b_n$ are constants in $\mathcal{A}$. The reduction is performed by evaluating this expression in $\mathcal{A}$ and results in a value in $\mathcal{A}$ (or in $\{true, false\}$).

A (variable-free) term M reduces to a term M' iff M' is obtained from M by reducing the *leftmost* redex of M, in which case we write $M \longrightarrow M'$. The transitive reflexive closure of $\longrightarrow$ is denoted $\twoheadrightarrow$. A term with no redex is said to be in *normal form*. Let the distinguished defined function of P be $\mathcal{F}$ of arity k. A *computation* of P in $\mathcal{A}$, with input $a_1, \ldots, a_k \in \mathcal{A}$, is a reduction sequence $M_1 \longrightarrow M_2 \longrightarrow \cdots$ where M_1 is $\mathcal{F} a_1 \cdots a_k$. The computation converges if $M_1 \twoheadrightarrow M_n$ for some $n \geq 1$ and M_n is in normal form; in this case, it is easy to verify that M_n is unique and always in $\mathcal{A}$.

In order to investigate the computational power of the language $\mathcal{L}^f$, we consider two extensions of the classical language of flowcharts. Our flowcharts are built up from basic instructions and tests, together with the constructs **while-do**, **if-then-else**, and **begin-end**. Tests are terms of type BOOL constructed from variables of ground type and symbols in Σ (note that tests are not arbitrary terms of type BOOL). The class of basic instructions allowed will be different in different classes.

Higher level pushdown stores

We use the abbreviation "pds" for the expression "pushdown store". A *level-1 pds* (or a *1-pds*) over a set $\mathcal{A}$ is an arbitrary sequence $(a_1, \ldots, a_m)$ of elements of $\mathcal{A}$, with $m \geq 0$. A *level-n pds* (or a *n-pds*), for $n \geq 2$, is a sequence $(s_1, \ldots, s_m)$ of $(n-1)$-pds's, where $m > 0$ (we assume that an "empty" n-pds contains an "empty" $(n-1)$-pds).

A *flowchart with a n-pds* is a flowchart allowing the following basic instructions:

(simple assignments)	$x := t;$
(1-pds operations)	$x := pop_1;$
	$push_1(x);$
(i-pds operations, for $1 < i \leq n$)	$pop_i;$
	$push_i;$

All symbols occurring in a flowchart with a n-pds are either ground type variables or symbols in Σ.

A *computation* of a flowchart with a n-pds in a Σ-structure $\mathcal{A}$ will be a sequence of *states*, each state consisting of a valuation of the ground type variables, a n-pds over $\mathcal{A}$, and the next instruction to be executed. At the outset of a computation, the pds is empty, and all the variables other than the input variables are initialized to a dummy value (denoting "not yet assigned a proper value"). The meaning of the pds instructions is the following:

pop_n executed on $(s_1, \ldots, s_m)$ results in $(s_1, \ldots, s_{m-1})$;

$push_n$ executed on $(s_1, \ldots, s_m)$ results in $(s_1, \ldots, s_m, s_m)$.

The operations pop_i, $push_i$, for $1 < i < n$ are defined similarly, but apply to the "top" pds of level i. (The "top" $(n-1)$-pds of $s = (s_1, \ldots, s_m)$ is of course s_m, while the "top" i-pds of s, for $i < n-1$ is defined to be the "top" i-pds of s_m.) Level-1 operations have their usual meaning, and are of course applied to the "top" 1-pds. Clearly, the notion of a flowchart with a n-pds is a direct generalization of the notion of a "flowchart with a pds", as considered for example in [TU1]. The language of flowcharts each with a n-pds is denoted $\mathcal{L}^s_n$, while $\mathcal{L}^s$ is the union of $\mathcal{L}^s_n$, for all $n \geq 1$. If k input variables and one output variable are specified for a $P \in \mathcal{L}^s$, the operational semantics of P just outlined defines a (partial) function $P^{\mathcal{A}}$ in a given Σ-structure $\mathcal{A}$.

Let us recall some standard definitions (used in the statement of the next theorem and in the next section). Two programs P_1 and P_2 are *equivalent* ($P_1 \equiv P_2$) iff, for every Σ-structure $\mathcal{A}$, $P_1^{\mathcal{A}} = P_2^{\mathcal{A}}$. A programming language $\mathcal{L}$ is *reducible* to another language $\mathcal{L}'$ ($\mathcal{L} \leq \mathcal{L}'$) iff for every $P \in \mathcal{L}$ there exists a $P' \in \mathcal{L}'$ such that $P \equiv P'$. $\mathcal{L}$ is *equivalent* to $\mathcal{L}'$ ($\mathcal{L} \equiv \mathcal{L}'$) iff $\mathcal{L} \leq \mathcal{L}'$ and $\mathcal{L}' \leq \mathcal{L}$. The inequality $\mathcal{L} < \mathcal{L}'$ stands for $\mathcal{L} \leq \mathcal{L}'$ and $\mathcal{L}' \not\leq \mathcal{L}$.

A "lower bound" for the computational power of $\mathcal{L}_k^f$ is obtained by comparing it with $\mathcal{L}_k^s$.

2.1 Theorem. *For every first-order signature, and for every* k, $\mathcal{L}_k^s \leq \mathcal{L}_k^f$.

Proof outline. It is shown in [KU1] and [KU2] that $\mathcal{L}^f$ is equivalent to an imperative language $\mathcal{L}$ with higher-type parameters. The language $\mathcal{L}$ is closely related, but not identical, to Clarke's L4 (see [C], or the more recent [GCH]). The main features of $\mathcal{L}$ are the following:

- nonlocal references of type **0** are allowed in procedures, but assignments to nonlocal variables are disallowed, except for assignments to "global" variables, i.e., those declared only in the main program;
- $\mathcal{L}$ exhibits a dynamic scope mechanism with "deep binding", i.e., a procedural parameter is always passed as a "closure", together with the environment of the *passing* procedure.

If $\mathcal{L}_k$ denotes the sublanguage of $\mathcal{L}$ allowing procedures of level at most k, then we have $\mathcal{L}_{k-1} \leq \mathcal{L}_k^f$, for all $k \geq 1$. (The cost in level in this translation is caused by the assignable globals of $\mathcal{L}$.) To show that $\mathcal{L}_k^s \leq \mathcal{L}_k^f$, we actually prove that $\mathcal{L}_k^s \leq \mathcal{L}_{k-1}$. We mention here the main idea of the proof. Let P be a program in $\mathcal{L}_k^s$. With no loss of generality, we may assume that P is of the form **while** α **do** S, where the program S has the following property:

- each execution of S involves exactly one instruction of the form $push_i$ or pop_i, which is also always the last instruction performed by S.

We describe a program Q in $\mathcal{L}_{k-1}$ which is equivalent to P. The procedures of Q will be the following:

- *Main*, the main program;
- *Push*, with formal parameters $Back_1, \ldots, Back_{k-1}$;
- Pop_i, for $i = 1, \ldots, k-1$, with formal parameters $Back_{i+1}, \ldots, Back_{k-1}$ (Pop_{k-1} does not have parameters);
- $Void_i$, for $i = 1, \ldots, k-1$, with the same formal parameters as Pop_i.

Let τ_k = BOOL, and $\tau_{i-1} = \tau_i \to \tau_i$ for $i = k-1, \ldots, 1$. Assume that variable $Back_i$ is of type τ_i. It follows that the type of both Pop_i and $Void_i$ is τ_i, and that of *Push* is τ_0. Clearly, $\ell(\tau_0) = k-1$, which is also the level of Q.

The original variables of P are all global in Q. Variables $Back_1, \ldots, Back_i$ are nonlocal in Pop_i. The procedure *Push* has a distinguished local variable *top*: **0**, which is nonlocally referenced by procedure Pop_i.

We now describe the bodies of the procedures. The simplest case is that of $Void_i$, which serves as a "dummy parameter". A call to $Void_i$ results in entering an infinite loop, thus causing program divergence. The main program consists of a call

$$b := Push\ Void_1\ \cdots\ Void_{k-1}$$

followed by a test on the local variable b, which in case of *false* results in entering an infinite loop. Otherwise, the program terminates with the value of the (global) output variable of P.

The simulation of the behavior of P is mainly performed in different activations of the procedure *Push*. The main idea is that each modification of the pds is simulated by a call creating a new activation of *Push*. The current configuration of the pds is simulated by the bindings of the parameters $Back_1, \ldots, Back_{k-1}$. For $i = 1, \ldots, k-1$, $Back_i$ represents the topmost i-pds. Starting with $i = 1$, the current value of *top* (if defined) is the topmost value on the topmost 1-pds. $Back_1$ is then bound to Pop_1 in some environment E, where *top* is the next value on the topmost 1-pds. Further, $Back_1$ is bound in another environment E' and so on. Note that, initially, $Back_1$ is bound to $Void_1$ which reflects the convention that an attempt to "pop" an empty pds is considered faulty. For $i > 1$, a similar chain of references is used to represent the topmost i-pds. The parameter $Back_i$ is again bound to Pop_i in some environment E, and the meaning of $Back_1, \ldots, Back_i$ in E represents the contents of the next i-pds.

The body of *Push* will essentially have the form:

begin while α **do** S'; return(*true*) **end**

where S' is obtained from S by replacing $push_1(x)$, $push_i$ for $1 < i < k$, $push_k$, pop_k, and pop_i for $i < k$, by the following program fragments. $push_1(x)$ is replaced by:

begin $top := x$;
$b := (Push\ Pop_1\ Back_2\ \cdots\ Back_{k-1})$;
$return(b)$ **end**

$push_i$ for $1 < i < k$ is replaced by:

begin
$b := (Push\ Back_1\ \cdots\ Back_{i-1}$
$Pop_i\ Back_{i+1}\ \cdots\ Back_{k-1})$;
$return(b)$ **end**

$push_k$ is replaced by:

begin
$b := (Push\ Back_1\ \cdots\ Back_{k-1})$;
if b **then** $return(b)$ **end**

Thus, whenever a $push_i$ for $i < k$ is executed, a new activation of *Push* is started. Now, however, $Back_i$ is bound to Pop_i in the environment of the caller, while the meaning of every other parameter remains the same as in the caller procedure. The instruction $push_k$ is handled differently: b is returned only if it is *true*, otherwise the simulation is continued in the current *Push*. pop_k is replaced by:

begin *return(false)* **end**

pop_i for $i < k$ is replaced by:

begin
$b := (Back_i\ Back_{i+1}\ \cdots\ Back_{k-1})$;
$return(b)$ **end**

Thus, pop_i for $i < k$ is simulated by calling $Back_i$, which is bound to Pop_i in some environment. The body of Pop_1 has the form:

begin $x := top$;
$b := (Push\ Back_1\ \cdots\ Back_{k-1})$;
$return(b)$ **end**

The body of Pop_i for $i > 1$ is simpler:

begin
$b := (Push\ Back_1\ \cdots\ Back_{k-1})$;
$return(b)$ **end**

Let us consider what happens: a call to $Back_i$ results in running Pop_i in the environment E representing a "previous" i-pds. Thus, the meaning of (nonlocal) $Back_1, \ldots, Back_i$ in the newly activated Pop_i is the same as in E while $Back_{i+1}, \ldots, Back_{k-1}$ are passed from the caller. This meaning of parameters is then passed to the next *Push* (the next phase of the simulation). This implies the following: a pop_i causes a return to the "old" i-pds, which in turn restores the "old" j-pds's, for $j < i$. On the other hand, the length of all topmost j'-pds's, for $j' > i$, remains unchanged.

The "pop" and "push" mechanism of a topmost k-pds is different. A pop_k is simulated by a sequence of returns rather by a call to a new *Push*. This brings back the environment of the "previous" k-pds, much in the same way as in the ordinary recursive simulation of a pds of level 1. This exception allows us to "save" one level in procedure types, as we do not need an additional parameter for *Push* to pass information about the top level. ∎

Higher level arrays

A *flowchart with arrays* allows assignments of the form

$$t_1 := t_2$$

as basic instructions, where t_1 and t_2 are arbitrary terms of the same ground type (except that t_1 is neither a ground constant nor of the form $(f\ t\ \cdots)$, where f is a symbol in Σ). In contrast to a flowchart with a higher level pds, however, the variables occurring in a flowchart with higher level arrays may be of arbitrary types. The semantics of flowcharts with arrays is defined by means of computations, each state of a computation being a valuation of the variables occurring in the program, together with the next instruction to be executed. Higher level variables are assigned higher level functions over $\mathcal{A}$; at every instant of a computation, the value assigned to a variable of type τ is a finite-support function of type τ. The class of flowcharts with arrays is denoted $\mathcal{L}^a$, while $\mathcal{L}^a_n$ denotes the subclass of $\mathcal{L}^a$ consisting of all programs P such that the maximum level of variables occurring in P is n. Of course, $\mathcal{L}^a_1$ is exactly the class *FDA* of "flowcharts with arrays" considered in [TU1] . Specifying input variables and an output variable, all of type **0**, a program $P \in \mathcal{L}^a$ defines in a Σ-structure $\mathcal{A}$ a function $P^{\mathcal{A}}$.

Throughout the remainder of the paper we will be using the notion of an *acceptable programming language.* Roughly speaking, $\mathcal{L}$ is an acceptable programming language if the meaning of every program in $\mathcal{L}$ can be described by an "informal algorithm" which is deterministic and whose computational power is less than, or equal to, that of a flowchart with two pushdown stores (of level 1). Moreover $\mathcal{L}$ should be semantically closed under several natural syntactic constructs: renaming and adding variables, composition, **if-then-else**, **while-do**, and the possibility of running a given program after each step of another program. The details of this definition can be found in [Li], [CGH], and [TU2].

It is not difficult to check that the languages $\mathcal{L}_n^s$ and $\mathcal{L}_n^a$ are acceptable for every n; the acceptability of $\mathcal{L}_n^f$ follows from the equivalence of $\mathcal{L}_n^f$ and a certain imperative language ([KU1]), the latter being acceptable.

3. Programs over finite interpretations

For us, an *interpretation* is a pair $\mathcal{I} = (\mathcal{A}, \mathbf{a})$, where $\mathcal{A}$ is a Σ-structure and $\mathbf{a}$ is a vector of its elements which generates $\mathcal{A}$. This definition is motivated by the following fact: let $\mathcal{L}$ be an acceptable programming language, the behaviour of a program $P \in \mathcal{L}$ for an input $\mathbf{a}$ in a Σ-structure $\mathcal{B}$ is fully determined by the substructure $\mathcal{A}$ generated by $\mathbf{a}$. Whenever we talk about the behaviour of a program P in an interpretation $(\mathcal{A}, \mathbf{a})$, we always mean its behaviour in $\mathcal{A}$ with input $\mathbf{a}$.

If $\mathbf{a} \in \mathcal{A}^k$, we also say that $\mathcal{I} = (\mathcal{A}, \mathbf{a})$ is a *k-interpretation*. The interpretation $\mathcal{I}$ is *finite* if $\mathcal{A}$ (i.e., its universe) is finite, otherwise it is *infinite*. From our assumption that $\mathbf{a}$ generates $\mathcal{A}$, the cardinality of $\mathcal{A}$ is at most countable, and we think of $\mathcal{A}$ as being effectively generated (strictly speaking: provided we have oracles for the primitive functions of $\mathcal{A}$).

Henceforth, we assume that the equality relation $=$ is available on ground values. We choose to treat $=$ as a symbol outside the signature Σ. We need the equality relation on ground values in order to properly define the concepts of "semi-universality" and "spectral complexity" (below). Note that there is no loss of generality in our results, because if $\mathcal{L} < \mathcal{L}'$ in the presence of equality on ground values then it is certainly the case that $\mathcal{L} < \mathcal{L}'$ without this assumption.

A programming language $\mathcal{L}$ is said to be *semi-universal* (see [TU1]) iff, for every integer $m \geq 0$, there exists $P \in \mathcal{L}$ such that, for every m-interpretation $(\mathcal{A}, \mathbf{a})$,

$$P \text{ converges in } (\mathcal{A}, \mathbf{a}) \quad \text{iff} \quad \mathcal{A} \text{ is finite.}$$

One of the main properties of semi-universal acceptable languages is the following:

3.1 Proposition ([TU2]). *All semi-universal acceptable programming languages are equivalent over infinite interpretations.*

It follows from results in [TU1] and [TU2] that the languages $\mathcal{L}_1^s$ and $\mathcal{L}_1^a$ are semi-universal. Therefore, by Theorem 2.1, $\mathcal{L}_1^f$ is semi-universal too. Obviously, $\mathcal{L}_n^f$, $\mathcal{L}_n^s$, and $\mathcal{L}_n^a$, must then be semi-universal for every n, and thus the analysis of their computational power naturally leads to investigating behaviour of programs over finite interpretations.

The signature Σ is fixed throughout. Let us assume that there is a given coding c which assigns to each finite interpretation $\mathcal{I} = (\mathcal{A}, \mathbf{a})$, a string $c(\mathcal{I}) \in \{0,1\}^*$, such that: *for k-interpretations $\mathcal{I}$ and $\mathcal{I}'$, $c(\mathcal{I}) = c(\mathcal{I}')$ iff $\mathcal{I}$ and $\mathcal{I}'$ are isomorphic.* The *spectrum* of the language $\mathcal{L}$ (see [TU1]) is the set

$$sp(\mathcal{L}) = \{sp_k(P) | k \geq 0 \text{ and } P \text{ is a } k\text{-ary program in } \mathcal{L}\}$$

where $sp_k(P)$ is the *spectrum* of P, i.e., the set of all codes of finite k-interpretations $\mathcal{I}$ such that P converges in $\mathcal{I}$.

Let now $\mathcal{C}$ be a complexity class. We say that the *spectral complexity of $\mathcal{L}$ is in $\mathcal{C}$* if $sp(\mathcal{L}) \subseteq \mathcal{C}$. An acceptable language $\mathcal{L}$ is said to be *$\mathcal{C}$-universal* (see [T]) iff its spectral complexity is in $\mathcal{C}$ and $\mathcal{L}' \leq \mathcal{L}$ for every acceptable language $\mathcal{L}'$ whose spectral complexity is in $\mathcal{C}$.

Let us notice that the notion of $\mathcal{C}$-universality and that of spectral complexity of a given acceptable programming language depend on a coding function c. The choice of c may also depend on the signature Σ. Σ is said to be *nontrivial* if it contains an operation symbol of positive arity. Nontrivial signatures are further classified into two categories. A nontrivial signature Σ is said to be *poor* if the sum of all arities of function and relation symbols in Σ is equal to 1. A nontrivial signature Σ is said to be *rich* if it is not poor. The essential difference between rich and poor signatures, whose impact will be seen in the next theorem, is that the coding function for rich signatures can be defined so that the length of a code of $\mathcal{I}$ is polynomial in the cardinality of the universe of I, while for poor signatures this length can be made logarithmic.

Let $exp_0(n) = n$ and $exp_{k+1}(n) = 2^{exp_k(n)}$. The following theorem characterizes the spectral complexity of the languages $\mathcal{L}_k^s$ and $\mathcal{L}_k^a$.

3.2 Theorem ([T, Thm. 4.1.8]).

(i) *For every rich signature Σ, there exists a coding function c such that for every $k \geq 1$, $\mathcal{L}_k^s$ is DTIME($exp_k(O(\log n))$)-universal and the language $\mathcal{L}_k^a$ is DSPACE($exp_k(O(\log n))$)-universal.*

(ii) *For every poor signature Σ, there exists a coding function c such that for every $k \geq 1$, $\mathcal{L}_k^s$ is DTIME($exp_k(O(n))$)-universal and the language $\mathcal{L}_k^a$ is DSPACE($exp_k(O(n))$)-universal.*

The proof of the theorem involves the methods developed in [TU1], where a special case ($k = 1$) was considered. For $k > 1$, the analysis for $\mathcal{L}_k^s$ uses a result of [KNT] which provides a complexity-theoretic characterization of formal languages recognized by "auxiliary push-down automata of level k". The latter is a generalization of the notion of an "APDA" introduced by Cook (see [HU]). The coding functions mentioned in the above theorem are constructed in [T] explicitly. We shall refer to them in the proof of Theorem 3.5.

It also follows from the results of [T, Thm. 4.1.5] that the languages $\mathcal{L}_k^s$ and $\mathcal{L}_k^a$ form infinite hierarchies

$$\mathcal{L}_1^s < \mathcal{L}_2^s < \cdots$$

$$\mathcal{L}_1^a < \mathcal{L}_2^a < \cdots$$

which are connected by the inequalities

$$\mathcal{L}_k^s \leq \mathcal{L}_k^a \leq \mathcal{L}_{k+1}^s$$

for every $k \geq 1$ and for every nontrivial signature. We next determine the relationships between the languages $\mathcal{L}_k^f$ and the above hierarchies. First we consider an "upper bound" for the computational power of $\mathcal{L}_k^f$.

For the proof of the next theorem we need to consider the denotational semantics of $\mathcal{L}_k^f$. We briefly recall some of the basic concepts. A subset S of a set X partially ordered by $\sqsubseteq$ is *directed* if it is non-empty and every pair of elements in S have an upper bound in S. A partial order $\langle X, \sqsubseteq\rangle$ is a *complete partial order* (or a *cpo*) if it has a bottom element $\perp$ and every directed subset S of X has a least upper bound $\sqcup S$. A function $\theta : X \to Y$ from a cpo X to a cpo Y is *continuous* if $\theta(\sqcup S) = \sqcup\{\theta(x) | x \in S\}$ for every directed subset S of X. The set of all continuous functions from X to Y is itself a cpo under the induced pointwise ordering.

Let $\mathcal{A}$ be an arbitrary Σ-structure. We turn $\mathcal{A}$ and $\{true, false\}$ into flat cpo's $\mathcal{A}_0 = \mathcal{A} \cup \{\perp_0\}$ and $\mathcal{A}_{BOOL} = \{true, false, \perp_{BOOL}\}$, respectively. Consider the full continuous type frame on the ground domains $\mathcal{A}_0$ and $\mathcal{A}_{BOOL}$. Then, for all types σ and τ,

$$\mathcal{A}_{(\sigma\to\tau)} = \{\text{all continuous functions from } \mathcal{A}_\sigma \text{ to } \mathcal{A}_\tau\}$$

$\mathcal{A}_{(\sigma\to\tau)}$ is a cpo with bottom element $\perp_{(\sigma\to\tau)}$, which is the function that maps every element of $\mathcal{A}_\sigma$ to $\perp_\tau$. As usual, for every closed term M of type τ, $[\![M]\!] \in \mathcal{A}_\tau$ denotes the function defined by M. We omit a formal definition for the "meaning" function $[\![\ ]\!]$, by induction on the formation rules for terms, which also requires the additional concept of *environment*, and refer instead the reader to Section 2 of [P1]. This induction starts by setting $[\![a]\!] = a$ for every constant symbol a of ground type, and by letting $[\![f]\!]$ denote the meaning of the primitive function f on $\mathcal{A}$, for every f in the signature. If f has arity $k \geq 1$, we agree that $[\![f]\!]$ returns $\perp_0$ if any of its k arguments is $\perp_0$, thus making $[\![f]\!]$ a continuous function. The sequential interpretation of the conditional makes $[\![\mathbf{if} - \mathbf{then} - \mathbf{else}_\sigma]\!]$ continuous also, for $\sigma \in \{\mathbf{0}, \text{BOOL}\}$. The following result establishes the equivalence of the call-by-name operational semantics and the denotational semantics of our functional programming language.

3.3 Lemma. *Let P be a functional program with defined function symbols $\mathcal{F}_1, \ldots, \mathcal{F}_n$, where $\mathcal{F}_1$ is the distinguished one of arity $m \geq 0$. Let $I = (\mathcal{A}, a_1, \ldots, a_m)$ be a m-interpretation for P. Then for any $b \in \mathcal{A}$,*

$$(\mathcal{F}_1\ a_1 \cdots a_m) \twoheadrightarrow b \ \textit{ iff } \ [\![(\mathcal{F}_1\ a_1 \cdots a_m)]\!] = b$$

In particular, $(\mathcal{F}_1\ a_1 \cdots a_m)$ diverges iff $[\![(\mathcal{F}_1\ a_1 \cdots a_m)]\!] = \perp_0$.

Proof. This is easily extracted from the material of Section 3 in [P1]. In [P1] the operational semantics of functional programs is part of a provability relation relative to axioms for arithmetic, and the denotational semantics is defined over the ground domain $\{\perp, 0, 1, 2, \ldots\}$. Although Theorem 3.1 in that paper is stated and proved for the special case of arithmetic, it is not difficult to check that it remains valid for the general case of any effectively given Σ-structure $\mathcal{A}$. ∎

If the ground domain $\mathcal{A}_0$ is finite then every function in the full continuous (or monotone) type frame can be described by, say, a finite list of ordered pairs. Assume that we have already generated all the functions in $\mathcal{A}_\sigma$ and $\mathcal{A}_\tau$:

$$\mathcal{A}_\sigma = \{\alpha_1, \ldots, \alpha_m\}$$
$$\mathcal{A}_\tau = \{\beta_1, \ldots, \beta_n\}$$

where each function α_i and each function β_j is given in the form of a finite list that fully describes it. Each $\gamma \in \mathcal{A}_{(\sigma\to\tau)}$ may be specified by a finite list of the form[4]

$$\gamma = \begin{pmatrix} \alpha_1 & \alpha_2 & \ldots & \alpha_m \\ \beta_{j_1} & \beta_{j_2} & \ldots & \beta_{j_m} \end{pmatrix}$$

i.e., α_i is mapped to β_{j_i} for $i = 1, \ldots, m$. Exactly one of the α_i's is $\perp_\sigma$, and zero or more of the β_j's are $\perp_\tau$. We can thus effectively generate all the functions in the full continuous type hierarchy, each being specified by a finite list. It is also easy to set up type-respecting rules of application for these finitely presented functions:

$$\left(\begin{pmatrix} \alpha_1 & \alpha_2 & \ldots & \alpha_m \\ \beta_{j_1} & \beta_{j_2} & \ldots & \beta_{j_m} \end{pmatrix} \alpha_i \right) = \beta_{j_i}$$

These finitely presented functions will be substituted for the "unknowns" (the defined function symbols) in functional equations. In doing so, we shall treat the bottom elements as formal symbols, which may thus appear in terms as a result of such a substitution (recall that the original syntax of terms does not include $\perp$ as a symbol).

3.4 Lemma. *Let P be a functional program as in Lemma 3.3, and let $\mathcal{I} = (\mathcal{A}, a_1, \ldots, a_m)$ be a finite m-interpretation for P. It is decidable whether the resulting computation of P converges.*

Proof. We set up the n definitions of P as n simultaneous recursive equations, to be solved for the unknowns $\mathcal{F}_1, \ldots, \mathcal{F}_n$:

$$\mathcal{F}_1 = M_1 \ , \ \ldots \ , \ \mathcal{F}_n = M_n$$

We have temporarily reverted here to a syntax involving λ-abstractions: if the definition for $\mathcal{F}_i$ is

$$\mathcal{F}_i X_1 \cdots X_j \Leftarrow \textbf{if } B \textbf{ then } T \textbf{ else } U$$

then M_i above is $\lambda X_1 \cdots X_j.\textbf{if } B \textbf{ then } T \textbf{ else } U$. Suppose the types of $\mathcal{F}_1, \ldots, \mathcal{F}_n$, are $\tau_1, \ldots, \tau_n$, respectively. $\mathcal{A}_{\tau_1} \times \cdots \times \mathcal{A}_{\tau_n}$ is itself a finite cpo with bottom element $\langle \perp_{\tau_1}, \ldots, \perp_{\tau_n} \rangle$. The system of n simultaneous equations defines a continuous map

$$\Psi : \mathcal{A}_{\tau_1} \times \cdots \times \mathcal{A}_{\tau_n} \longrightarrow \mathcal{A}_{\tau_1} \times \cdots \times \mathcal{A}_{\tau_n}$$

The denotation $[\![\mathcal{F}_1]\!]$ of the distinguished function symbol $\mathcal{F}_1$ of P, i.e., the function $P^{\mathcal{A}}$, is the first coordinate of the the minimal fixed-point of Ψ, namely,

$$\bigsqcup_{i \geq 0} \Psi^{(i)} \langle \perp_{\tau_1}, \ldots, \perp_{\tau_n} \rangle$$

which can be effectively determined, all domains under consideration being finite. $[\![\mathcal{F}_1]\!]$ is given in the form of a finite list, and $(\mathcal{F}_1 a_1 \cdots a_m)$ converges iff $([\![\mathcal{F}_1]\!]\ a_1 \cdots a_m) \neq \perp$, by the preceding lemma. ∎

3.5 Theorem. *For every $k \geq 1$, $\mathcal{L}_k^f \leq \mathcal{L}_k^a$.*

Proof outline. Let P be a functional program as in Lemmas 3.3 and 3.4. We construct a deterministic Turing machine $\mathcal{M}$ for each such P which will be the formal counterpart of the algorithm described in the proof of Lemma 3.4. An input tape for $\mathcal{M}$ is an appropriately coded finite m-interpretation $(\mathcal{A}, a_1, \ldots, a_m)$. Starting from (the code of) the vector $\langle \perp_{\tau_1}, \ldots, \perp_{\tau_n} \rangle$, $\mathcal{M}$ repeatedly constructs a new vector α' in $\mathcal{A}_{\tau_1} \times \cdots \times \mathcal{A}_{\tau_n}$ from a preceding vector α using the equations defining Ψ: $\alpha' = \Psi(\alpha)$. $\mathcal{M}$ stops this process when it finds the minimal fixed-point $\alpha = \Psi(\alpha)$. After it completes the construction of the new α' and finds that α' is *not* a fixed-point, $\mathcal{M}$ erases the old α from its working tapes before continuing the process. When it finds the minimal fixed-point α, $\mathcal{M}$ checks whether $(\alpha_1 a_1 \cdots a_m) \neq \perp$, where α_1 is the first component of α, and accepts or rejects its input tape accordingly. This process is coded in the control mechanism of $\mathcal{M}$ (coding details of the operation of $\mathcal{M}$ omitted). The space complexity of $\mathcal{M}$ is essentially determined by the space required to represent a bounded number of vectors in $\mathcal{A}_{\tau_1} \times \cdots \times \mathcal{A}_{\tau_n}$ (this bounded number depends on the n equations defining Ψ, and not on the size of the input tape).

[4] This is a "higher-order" list of lists of lists of ....

Let $k = max\{\ell(\tau_1), \ldots, \ell(\tau_n)\}$; k is also the level of P. If $|\mathcal{A}| = u \geq 1$, a little calculation shows that there are at most $exp_k(\mathcal{O}(u\ log\ u))$ vectors in $\mathcal{A}_{\tau_1} \times \cdots \times \mathcal{A}_{\tau_n}$, and therefore the space required to store a bounded number of such vectors is $exp_{k-1}(\mathcal{O}(u\ log\ u)) = exp_k(\mathcal{O}(log\ u))$.

Consider the case when Σ is a poor signature (the case of a rich signature is treated similarly). In this case, the space required to code the input $(\mathcal{A}, a_1, \ldots, a_m)$ is logarithmic in u. The space complexity of $\mathcal{M}$ is therefore in $DSPACE(exp_k(\mathcal{O}(n)))$. P being an arbitrary member of $\mathcal{L}^f_k$, it also follows that $sp(\mathcal{L}^f_k) \subseteq DSPACE(exp_k(\mathcal{O}(n)))$. Since $\mathcal{L}^a_k$ is $DSPACE(exp_k(\mathcal{O}(n)))$-universal, by Theorem 3.2, we conclude that $\mathcal{L}^f_k \leq \mathcal{L}^a_k$. ∎

As an immediate consequence of Theorems 2.1 and 3.5 we obtain:

3.6 Theorem. *For every k, $\mathcal{L}^s_k \leq \mathcal{L}^f_k \leq \mathcal{L}^a_k$.*

The above, together with the hierarchy result of Theorem 3.2, enables us to establish the following hierarchy result:

3.7 Theorem. *The hierarchy of higher-level functional programs $\mathcal{L}^f_1 \leq \mathcal{L}^f_2 \leq \cdots$ is infinite, and it is "almost strict" in the sense that $\mathcal{L}^f_k < \mathcal{L}^f_{k+2}$,* for all k.

It also follows from all that precedes that the union $\mathcal{L}^f$ of the hierarchy is equivalent to both $\mathcal{L}^a$ and $\mathcal{L}^s$, and thus is $\mathcal{E}$-universal, where $\mathcal{E}$ is the class of all elementarily recursive languages.

Let us note that the question of whether $\mathcal{L}^f_k \equiv \mathcal{L}^s_k$ is open. A direct proof of $\mathcal{L}^f_k \leq \mathcal{L}^s_k$ by direct translation or simulation, if at all possible, will be difficult, as suggested in the Introduction. A more promising approach will be to relate $sp(\mathcal{L}^f_k)$ to $DTIME(exp_k(\mathcal{O}(T(n))))$, where $T(n) = log(n)$ or $T(n) = n$ depending on whether the signature is rich or poor, and then use the fact that $\mathcal{L}^s_k$ is $DTIME(exp_k(\mathcal{O}(T(n))))$-universal.

References

[C] Clarke, E.M., "Programming language constructs for which it is impossible to obtain good Hoare-like axioms", *Journal of the ACM*, Vol. 26, pp 129-147, 1979.

[CGH] Clarke, E.M., German, S.M., Halpern, J.Y., "Effective axiomatizations of Hoare logics", Research Report, Harvard University, 1982.

[D] Damm, W., "The IO- and OI-hierarchies", *Theoret. Comput. Sci.*, Vol. 20, pp 95-207, May 1982.

[DFI] Damm, W., Fehr, E., Indermark, K., "Higher type recursion and self-application as control structures", in *Formal Description of Programming Concepts*, ed. by Neuhold, pp 461-487, North Holland, 1978.

[DGo] Damm, W., Goerdt, A., "An automata-theoretic characterization of the OI-hierarchy", *Information and Control*, Vol. 71, pp 1-32, Oct/Nov 1986.

[DGu] Damm, W., Guessarian, I., "Implementation techniques for recursive tree transducers on higher order datatypes", LITP report, Université Paris VII, Paris, 1983.

[E] Engelfriet, J., "Iterated push-down automata and complexity classes", Proc. 15th STOC, pp 365-373, 1983.

[ES] Engelfriet, J., Schmidt, E.M., "IO and OI", *J. Computer and System Sciences*, Vol. 15, pp 328-353, 1977, and Vol. 16, pp 67-99, 1978.

[F] Friedman, H., "Algorithmic procedures, generalized Turing algorithms, and elementary recursion theory", in: *Logic Colloquium '69*, North Holland, Amsterdam, pp 361-389, 1971.

[GCH] German, S.M., Clarke, E.M., Halpern, J.Y., "True relative completeness of an axiom system for the language L4", Proc. of LICS 1986.

[HU] Hopcroft, J.E., Ullman, J.D., *Introduction to Automata Theory, Languages and Computation*, Addison-Wesley, 1979.

[I] Indermark, K., "Schemes with recursion on higher types", Proc. of 5th MFCS, LNCS 45, Springer Verlag, Berlin, pp 352-358, 1976

[K] Klein, H.-J., "Zur Charakterisierung von Programmen mit endlichen Arten", dissertation, Univ of Kiel, 1980.

[KNT] Kowalczyk, W., Niwiński, D., Tiuryn, J., "A generalization of of Cook's Auxiliary-Pushdown-Automata Theorem", Research report, Institute of Math, Univ of Warsaw, 1986.

[KU1] Kfoury, A.J., Urzyczyn, P., "Finitely typed functional programs, Part I: syntax, semantics and implementation", Research report, Boston University 1986.

[KU2] Kfoury, A.J., Urzyczyn, P., "Finitely typed functional programs, Part II", Research report, Boston Univ, under preparation.

[L] Langmaack, H., "On procedures as open subroutines", *Acta Informatica*, Vol 2, pp 311-333, 1973, and Vol. 3, pp 227-241, 1974.

[Li] Lipton, R.J., "A necessary and sufficient condition for the existence of Hoare logics", Proc. 18th FOCS, 1977.

[M] Milner, R., "Models of LCF", Memo AIM-186, Stanford Univ, 1973.

[P1] Plotkin, G., "LCF considered as a programming language", *Theoret. Comput. Sci.*, Vol. 5, pp 223-255, 1977.

[P2] Plotkin, G., "A structural approach to operational semantics", Report DAIMI FN-19, Computer Science Dept, Aarhus Univ, 1981.

[PH] Paterson, M.S., Hewitt, C.E., "Comparative schematology", in: *Record on Project MAC Conference on Concurrent Systems and Parallel Computation*, ACM, New York, pp 119-128, 1970.

[T] Tiuryn, J., "Higher-order arrays and stacks in programming: An application of complexity theory to logics of programs", Proc. 12th MFCS, LNCS 233, Springer Verlag, Berlin, pp 177-198, 1986.

[TU1] Tiuryn, J., Urzyczyn, P., "Some connections between logics of programs and complexity theory", in: Proc. 24th FOCS, pp 180-184, 1983.

[TU2] Tiuryn, J., Urzyczyn, P., "Remarks on comparing expressive power of logics of programs", in: Proc. MFCS 1984, LNCS 176 Springer, Berlin, pp 535-543, 1984.

[W] Wand, M., "First-order identities as a defining language", *Acta Informatica*, Vol. 14, pp 337-357, Oct 1980.

DEFINABILITY WITH BOUNDED NUMBER OF BOUND VARIABLES

Neil Immerman[1]

Department of Computer Science
Yale University
New Haven, Connecticut 06520

Dexter Kozen[2]

Department of Computer Science
Cornell University
Ithaca, New York 14853

Abstract. A theory satisfies the *k-variable property* if every first-order formula is equivalent to a formula with at most k bound variables (possibly reused). Gabbay has shown that a fixed time structure satisfies the k-variable property for some k if and only if there exists a finite basis for the temporal connectives over that structure. We give a model-theoretic method for establishing the k-variable property, involving a restricted Ehrenfeucht-Fraisse game in which each player has only k pebbles. We use the method to unify and simplify results in the literature for linear orders. We also establish new k-variable properties for various theories of bounded-degree trees, and in each case obtain tight upper and lower bounds on k. This gives the first finite basis theorems for branching-time models.

1. Introduction

A first-order theory Σ satisfies the *k-variable property* if every first-order formula is equivalent under Σ to a formula with at most k bound variables (possibly reused). For example, in an arbitrary partial order, five bound variables are needed to express the statement "there are at least five elements below x," but in a linear order, two variables suffice:

$$(1.1)\quad \exists y\ y<x \wedge (\exists x\ x<y \wedge (\exists y\ y<x \wedge (\exists x\ x<y \wedge (\exists y\ y<x)))).$$

The k-variable property is important in temporal logic: Gabbay [G] has shown that a fixed time structure satisfies the k-variable property for some k if and only if there exists a finite basis for the temporal connectives over that structure, in the same sense that $\vee$ and $\neg$ form a basis for the propositional connectives.

Kamp [K] showed that any Dedekind-complete linear order with arbitrary monadic predicates admits a finite basis for the temporal connectives. This result was extended to other linear time structures by Stavi [S]. Amir and Gabbay [AG] showed that any definable lexicographic product of time structures admitting a finite basis also admits a finite basis. This result gave the first infinite non-linear structures admitting a finite basis, although up to now no results have been established for trees.

The methods used by these researchers were largely syntactic. In this paper we give a model-theoretic method for establishing the k-variable property uniformly for all models of certain first-order theories. The method uses a variant of the Ehrenfeucht-Fraisse game [E,F] which allows each player only k pebbles [I]. Applying this method to the theory of linear order, we are able to unify the results of [K,S]. We also establish new k-variable expressiveness results for various theories of bounded-degree trees, and in each case obtain tight upper and lower bounds on k. We thus have, by Gabbay's result [G], the existence of a finite basis for the first-order-expressible branching-time temporal connectives over tree models of bounded degree.

2. A model-theoretic lemma

Let L be a first-order language with individual variables $\{x_1, x_2, \ldots\}$. A *partial valuation* over a structure A for L is a partial function $u:\{x_1, \ldots\} \to A$. The domain of u is denoted ∂u. The cardinality of ∂u is denoted $|u|$. A *(k-)configuration* over A, B is a pair (u, v), where u is a partial valuation over A and v is a partial valuation

[1]Supported by NSF grants DCR-8603346 and DCR-8301766.
[2]Supported by NSF grant DCR-8602663.

over B such that $\partial u = \partial v \subseteq \{x_1, \ldots, x_k\}$. If (u, v) is a k-configuration and if $L' \subseteq L$, then u and v are said to be L'-*equivalent* if they have the same L'-type; i.e., if for all formulas $\varphi \in L'$ with free variables in ∂u,

$$A, u \models \varphi \text{ iff } B, v \models \varphi.$$

Lemma 2.1. Let Σ be a set of sentences in L. Let L', $L'' \subseteq L$ such that L' is closed under the propositional operators. The following two conditions are equivalent:

(i) For all A, B models of Σ and k-configurations (u, v) over A, B, if u and v are L'-equivalent, then they are L''-equivalent.

(ii) For all $\varphi \in L''$ with free variables among $\{x_1, \ldots, x_k\}$, there exists a $\psi \in L'$ such that $\Sigma \models \varphi \leftrightarrow \psi$.

Proof. $(ii) \rightarrow (i)$ is immediate. $(i) \rightarrow (ii)$: If $\Sigma \cup \{\varphi\}$ is inconsistent, take $\psi = false$ and we are done. Otherwise, let Γ be an arbitrary complete L'-type in the variables $\{x_1, \ldots, x_k\}$ extending $\Sigma \cup \{\varphi\}$. Then $\Sigma \cup \Gamma \cup \{\neg \varphi\}$ is inconsistent, otherwise models A, u and B, v of $\Sigma \cup \Gamma$ could be constructed with $\partial u = \partial v = \{x_1, \ldots, x_k\}$ such that $A, u \models \varphi$ and $B, v \models \neg \varphi$, violating (i). Therefore $\Sigma \cup \Gamma \models \varphi$. By compactness, there exists a $\psi_\Gamma \in \Gamma$ such that $\Sigma \models \psi_\Gamma \rightarrow \varphi$. Now φ is covered by all such ψ_Γ, in the sense that

$$\Sigma \models (\bigvee_{\Gamma} \psi_\Gamma) \leftrightarrow \varphi$$

where the infinitary join is taken over all L'-types Γ consistent with Σ. Again by compactness, there is a finite set F of such Γ such that

$$\Sigma \models (\bigvee_{\Gamma \in F} \psi_\Gamma) \leftrightarrow \varphi$$

so we may take $\psi = \bigvee_{\Gamma \in F} \psi_\Gamma$. □

We are interested in a special case of the above lemma which applies to the k-variable property.

Define the *quantifier depth* of a formula φ to be the depth of the deepest nesting of quantifiers in φ. For example, a formula has quantifier depth 0 if it is quantifier-free, and the quantifier depth of the formula (1.1) is 5.

Let $n, k \geq 0$. Define $L_{k,n}$ to be the sublanguage of L consisting of all formulas φ of quantifier depth at most n containing only variables $\{x_1, \ldots, x_k\}$. For example, the formula (1.1) is in $L_{2,5}$. Define

$$L_k = \bigcup_n L_{k,n}.$$

Thus $L = \bigcup_k L_k$.

Definition 2.2. A first-order theory Σ is said to satisfy the k-*variable property* if for all formulas $\varphi \in L$ with free variables among $\{x_1, \ldots, x_k\}$, there exists a $\psi \in L_k$ such that $\Sigma \models \varphi \leftrightarrow \psi$. □

In this special case, Lemma 2.1 gives

Corollary 2.3. The following two conditions are equivalent:

(i) For all A, B models of Σ and k-configurations (u, v) over A, B, if u and v are L_k-equivalent, then they are L-equivalent.

(ii) Σ satisfies the k-variable property. □

3. An Ehrenfeucht-Fraisse game with bounded number of pebbles

Let Σ be a theory in a first-order language L with equality. Assume further that in every model of Σ, every finitely generated substructure is finite. We have reduced the problem of establishing the k-variable property for Σ to checking the condition of Corollary 2.3(i). This will done using a modification of the standard Ehrenfeucht-Fraisse game [E,F,FR] which uses only a bounded number of pebbles [I].

Definition 3.1 (the game $G(u, v, k, n)$). Let A, B be structures for L, $n, k \geq 0$, and (u, v) a k-configuration. The game $G(u, v, k, n)$ is played by two players, I and II, who take turns placing pebbles on elements of A and B. Player I tries to demonstrate that A and B are nonisomorphic, and player II tries to make A and B appear isomorphic. There are $2k$ pebbles, each colored with one of k distinct colors $x_1, \ldots, x_k$, with exactly two pebbles of each color.

The configuration (u, v) denotes that the two pebbles colored x_i are currently occupying $u(x_i) \in A$ and $v(x_i) \in B$, for $x_i \in \partial u$, and that the pebbles colored $x_i \notin \partial u$ are not currently in play. The initial configuration is $(u_0, v_0) = (u, v)$. The players alternate, with player I first. Each round consists of a move of player I followed by a move of player II. Player I can select any pebble and place it on an element of either A or B. Player II then has to place the other pebble of the same color on an element of the other structure. Play proceeds for n rounds, generating a sequence of configurations (u_t, v_t), $0 \le t \le n$. Let

$$R(u_t, v_t) = \{(\tau^{A,u_t}, \tau^{B,v_t}) \mid \tau \text{ is a term over } \partial u_t\} \subseteq A \times B.$$

Player II wins the game if all the relations $R(u_t, v_t)$, $0 \le t \le n$, are local isomorphisms, i.e., if the map $u_t(x) \to v_t(x)$, $x \in \partial u$, is well-defined and extends to an isomorphism of the substructures of A and B generated by $\{u_t(x) \mid x \in \partial u\}$ and $\{v_t(x) \mid x \in \partial v\}$, respectively. Otherwise player I wins. □

Definition 3.2. A *forced win* for player II is defined by induction on n. Player II has a forced win in $G(u,v,k,0)$ if $R(u,v)$ is a local isomorphism. Player II has a forced win in $G(u,v,k,n+1)$ if $R(u,v)$ is a local isomorphism, and for all legal moves of player I from configuration (u,v), there exists a legal move of player II resulting in a configuration (u',v') such that player II has a forced win in $G(u',v',k,n)$. Player I has a forced win if player II does not. □

Intuitively, a player has a forced win if there is always a choice of moves for that player leading to a win, no matter how well his opponent plays.

Remark. It is always to player I's advantage to play a pebble not currently on the board, if possible, and to place a pebble on an element not currently covered by another pebble, if possible; from player I's point of view, the more elements of A and B that are covered, the better. Any winning strategy for player I that does not satisfy these conditions can be mapped into a winning strategy that does.

Lemma 3.3. If player II has a forced win in the game $G(u,v,k,n)$, then player II has a forced win in the game $G(u',v',k',n')$, for any $n' \le n$, $k' \le k$, and u' and v' restrictions of u and v, respectively, to a smaller domain. □

We now establish the relationship between the games $G(u,v,k,n)$ and the k-variable property. The following is a generalization of [I], Theorem C.1, to structures allowing function symbols, provided that all finitely generated substructures are finite.

Lemma 3.4. Let A and B be models of Σ. Let (u,v) be a k-configuration. Then player II has a forced win in the game $G(u,v,k,n)$ if and only if u and v are $L_{k,n}$-equivalent.

Proof. We prove the lemma by induction on n. For the basis, player II has a forced win in $G(u,v,k,0)$ iff $R(u,v)$ is a local isomorphism iff u and v agree on all quantifier-free formulas of L_k with variables among ∂u, i.e., u and v are $L_{k,0}$-equivalent. Now suppose $n > 0$.

($\rightarrow$) Suppose player II has a forced win in the game $G(u,v,k,n)$. It suffices to show that u and v agree on all formulas of $L_{k,n}$ of the form $\exists x_i\, \psi$. Suppose $A, u \models \exists x_i\, \psi$. Let $a \in A$ such that $A, u[x_i/a] \models \psi$. If player I should move the pebble colored x_i to a, then player II has a response $b \in B$ such that player II has a forced win in $G(u[x_i/a], v[x_i/b], k, n-1)$, by Definition 3.2. Since $\psi \in L_{k,n-1}$, by the induction hypothesis, $B, v[x_i/b] \models \psi$, thus $B, v \models \exists x_i\, \psi$. A symmetric argument shows that if $B, v \models \exists x_i\, \psi$ then $A, u \models \exists x_i\, \psi$.

($\leftarrow$) If player II does not have a forced win in $G(u,v,k,n)$, then player I does. Thus there is a move for player I, say the pebble colored x_i to $a \in A$, such that for any move for player II, say to $b \in B$, player I has a forced win in the game $G(u[x_i/a], v[x_i/b], k, n-1)$. By the induction hypothesis, there is a formula $\psi_b \in L_{k,n-1}$ such that $A, u[x_i/a] \models \psi_b$ but $B, v[x_i/b] \models \neg\psi_b$.

Using the assumption that all finitely generated substructures are finite, a compactness argument gives a uniform bound on the size of substructures generated by k elements in any model of Σ. This in turn implies that there are only finitely many inequivalent formulas of $L_{k,n-1}$. Thus the infinitary formula

$$\bigwedge_{b \in B} \psi_b$$

is expressible by a formula of $L_{k,n-1}$, and

$$A, u \models \exists x_i \bigwedge_{b \in B} \psi_b, \qquad B, v \models \neg \exists x_i \bigwedge_{b \in B} \psi_b,$$

and $\exists x_i \bigwedge_{b \in B} \psi_b$ is expressible by a formula of $L_{k,n}$. Therefore u and v are not $L_{k,n}$-equivalent. □

The following lemma is an immediate consequence of Lemmas 2.3 and 3.4.

Lemma 3.5. Σ satisfies the k-variable property if and only if for all A, B models of Σ and k-configurations (u,v) over A, B, if player II has a forced win in every game $G(u, v, k, n)$, $n \geq 0$, then player II has a forced win in every game $G(u, v, m, n)$, $m \geq k$, $n \geq 0$. □

4. Three variables are necessary and sufficient for linear order

In this section we give a single proof that encompasses the results of [K,S], illustrating the Ehrenfeucht-Fraisse game of §3. We consider games played on linear orders with monadic predicates.

Theorem 4.1. Linear order satisfies the 3-variable property and does not satisfy the 2-variable property.

Proof. For the upper bound, by Lemma 3.5 it suffices to show that for any 3-configuration (u, v), if player II has a forced win in $G(u, v, 3, n)$, then player II has a forced win in $G(u, v, k, n)$, for all k. The result holds for any $k \leq 3$ by Lemma 3.3, so assume $k > 3$.

We will describe player II's best strategy in $G(u, v, k, n)$ and prove the theorem by simultaneous induction on n. For $n = 0$, the assertion that player II has a forced win in the game $G(u, v, k, 0)$ says that $R(u, v)$ is a local isomorphism, which follows immediately from the assumption that player II has a forced win in the game $G(u, v, 3, 0)$.

Suppose now that $n > 0$. If $|u| = |v| < 3$, then for any move that player I might make, let player II respond according to his best strategy in the game $G(u, v, 3, n)$. If the resulting configuration is (u', v'), then by Definition 3.2, player II has a forced win in the game $G(u', v', 3, n-1)$. By the induction hypothesis, player II has a forced win in every game $G(u', v', k, n-1)$, $k > 0$. Again by Definition 3.2, since the move of player I was arbitrary, player II has a forced win in $G(u, v, k, n)$, $k > 0$.

If $|u| = |v| = 3$, renumber the variables if necessary so that $u(x_1) < u(x_2) < u(x_3)$ and $v(x_1) < v(x_2) < v(x_3)$. (Note $R(u, v)$ is a local isomorphism, since player II has a forced win in $G(u, v, 3, 0)$. If some $u(x_i) = u(x_j)$, $i \neq j$, then a pair of pebbles can be removed, and we revert to the previous case.) Consider the pair of corresponding regions

$$\{a \in A \mid a < u(x_2)\}, \ \{b \in B \mid b < v(x_2)\}.$$

Associate with this pair of regions the game

$$G(u_<, v_<, 3, n),$$

where $u_<$ and $v_<$ are u and v, respectively, restricted to domain $\{x_1, x_2\}$. Similarly, associate with the pair of corresponding regions

$$\{a \in A \mid a \geq u(x_2)\}, \ \{b \in B \mid b \geq v(x_2)\}$$

the game

$$G(u_\geq, v_\geq, 3, n),$$

where $u_\geq$ and $v_\geq$ are u and v, respectively, restricted to domain $\{x_2, x_3\}$. By Lemma 3.3, player II has forced wins in both of these games. But $|u_<| = |u_\geq| < 3$, so by a case previously considered, player II has a forced win in the games $G(u_<, v_<, k, n)$ and $G(u_\geq, v_\geq, k, n)$, $k > 0$.

We now describe a strategy for player II in the game $G(u, v, k, n)$. Assume $k > n$, so that player I never needs to remove a pebble from the board. The result follows for smaller k by Lemma 3.3. Whenever player I moves in one of the designated regions of either A or B, player II responds with his best strategy in the game associated with that region. Player II will then move in the corresponding region in the other structure, since there is always a pebble on $u(x_2)$. If (u', v') is any subsequent (global) configuration, the restriction of (u', v') to either of the two pairs of regions is a local isomorphism, since player II has a forced win in the game associated with that region. Moreover, all points of the region $\{a \in A \mid a < u(x_2)\}$ are less than all points of the region $\{a \in A \mid a \geq u(x_2)\}$, and similarly for $\{b \in B \mid b < v(x_2)\}$ and $\{b \in B \mid b \geq v(x_2)\}$. Therefore (u', v') is a local isomorphism. This establishes the upper bound.

To show that two variables do not suffice, we observe that **Z** and **Q**, without monadic predicates, are L_2-equivalent but not L_3-equivalent. Player II's winning strategy in $G(\emptyset, \emptyset, 2, n)$ is as follows: in the first round, player II plays anywhere in response to player I's move. Subsequently, if player I plays a pebble to the left (right) of the pebble on the board, then player II does the same. The structures are not L_3-equivalent, because **Q** is dense and **Z** is not, and density is expressible with three variables:

$$\forall x \forall z \, (x < z \rightarrow \exists y \, x < y < z). \ \square$$

5. Theories of bounded-degree trees

In this section we define various theories of bounded-degree trees and establish tight upper and lower bounds on the number of bound variables needed to define any first-order definable formula.

Definition 5.1. Consider a language L with a binary relation symbol $\leq$ and equality $=$, possibly with extra monadic predicates. Let L^+ be L augmented with a binary function symbol $+$. The atomic formula $x \leq y$ is read, "x is a descendant of y" or "y is an ancestor of x". The function $+$ is intended to give the least common ancestor (LCA), or least upper bound with respect to $\leq$.

Consider the following axioms of L and L^+. The axioms (i)-(vd) are expressed in the language L, and (vi) is expressed in the language L^+.

(i) "$\leq$ is a partial order."
(ii) "$\leq$ is a linear order above any x."
(iii) "Every pair x, y has an LCA."
(iv$d$) "There is no set of $d+1$ proper descendants of x whose pairwise LCA is x."
(vd) "Every non-leaf x has a set of d proper descendants whose pairwise LCA is x."
(vi) "$x+y$ is the LCA of x and y."

The theories $S_d \subseteq L$ and $S_d^+ \subseteq L^+$ describe trees of degree d. S_d^+ consists of axioms (i)-(vi), and S_d is obtained from S_d^+ by omitting (vi). The theories $T_d \subseteq L$ and $T_d^+ \subseteq L^+$ describe trees of degree at most d. These theories are obtained from S_d and S_d^+, respectively, by omitting axiom (vd). □

For A a model of T_d, $a, a_1, a_2 \in A$, $a_1, a_2 < a$, define $a_1 \equiv_a a_2$ if $a_1 + a_2 < a$. It follows from the axioms of T_d that $\equiv_a$ is an equivalence relation with at most d equivalence classes, and exactly d if A is a model of S_d and a is not a leaf. These classes are called *subtrees of* a. For $a' < a$, denote the subtree of a containing a' by $T(a, a')$, and the $L_{k,n}$-type of the pair (a, a') by $\theta_{k,n}(a, a')$. The latter is a set of formulas of $L_{k,n}$ with free variables among x_1, x_2. For a subtree T of a, define

$$\Theta_{k,n}(T) = \{\theta_{k,n}(a, a') \mid a' \in T\}.$$

Lemma 5.2. Let Σ be one of the theories T_d, T_d^+, S_d, S_d^+. Let (u, v) be any k-configuration, and let a and b be the suprema of $\{u(x) \mid x \in \partial u\}$ and $\{v(x) \mid x \in \partial v\}$, respectively. Let $f(n)$ be any sufficiently fast-growing function of n, and let

$$k = \begin{cases} \max(4, d) & \text{if } \Sigma = T_d \text{ or } T_d^+, \\ \max(4, \lceil d/2 \rceil) & \text{if } \Sigma = S_d \text{ or } S_d^+. \end{cases}$$

If player II has a forced win in $G(u, v, k, f(n))$, then there is a one-one correspondence between subtrees $A_1, \ldots, A_l$ of a and subtrees $B_1, \ldots, B_l$ of b such that

(i) $\Theta_{k,n}(A_i) = \Theta_{k,n}(B_i)$, $1 \leq i \leq l$,
(ii) $u(x) \in A_j$ iff $v(x) \in B_j$.

Proof. For the case of T_d or T_d^+, we show first that a and b have the same number of subtrees. If not, suppose a has more than b. We will describe a winning strategy for player I, contradicting the assumption that player II has a forced win in $G(u, v, k, f(n))$. Let player I play a pebble on a, if a is not already covered. Then player II must play b, otherwise player I wins in at most one move. (It follows from T_d that $a = u(x) + u(y)$ for some $x, y \in \partial u$, and $b = v(x) + v(y)$.) Now let player I successively play pebbles in as many distinct subtrees of a as possible, leaving a pebble on a. Player II must respond by pebbling in separate subtrees of b, otherwise player I wins in at most one move. Thus, if the number of subtrees of a is less than d, or if $d < 4$, we are done. Otherwise, since there are d pebbles, there must be d subtrees of a, of which $d-1$ have pebbles, and $d-1$ subtrees of b, all of which have pebbles. Now player I removes the pebble from a and places it somewhere in the last subtree of a. Player II must play the corresponding pebble on a point in one of the subtrees of b, otherwise player I wins immediately. Now there exist pebbled points b_0, b_1, b_2 such that $b_0 + b_1 < b_1 + b_2$, whereas for the corresponding points a_0, a_1, a_2, $a_0 + a_1 = a_1 + a_2$. Thus player I wins in one more move by pebbling $b_0 + b_1$ with the fourth pebble. Note that $k = max(4, d)$ pebbles are required for this argument.

The remainder of the argument uses only $\max(4, \lceil d/2 \rceil)$ pebbles and works for all four theories under consideration. By the preceding paragraph, we may assume that a and b have the same number of subtrees. We show (i) first. Suppose there is a Θ such that the number of subtrees T of a with $\Theta_{k,n}(T) = \Theta$ is different from the number of subtrees of b satisfying this property. We will again describe a winning strategy for player I. Note that there must be some $r < \lceil d/2 \rceil$ and Θ such that exactly r subtrees T of b have $\Theta_{k,n}(T) = \Theta$ and the number of subtrees of a satisfying this property is strictly greater than r, or vice-versa (without loss of generality, assume the former). As above, player I will pebble in $r+1$ subtrees of a of type Θ, and player II will be forced to play in a subtree of b of type different from Θ. Now there are pebbles on a', b' and at least two other points a'', b'' such that $a'+a''=a$ and $b'+b''=b$, and

$$\Theta_{k,n}(T(a,a')) \neq \Theta_{k,n}(T(b,b')).$$

let $a'' \in T(a,a')$ such that for no $b'' \in T(b,b')$ is $\theta_{k,n}(a,a'')=\theta_{k,n}(b,b'')$. Player I plays a if not already played. Player II must respond with b, otherwise player I wins in 1 move. Player I now plays a''. Player II must respond with some $b''<b$, but whatever b'' is played,

$$\theta_{k,n}(a,a'') \neq \theta_{k,n}(b,b'').$$

By Lemma 3.4, player I has a forced win in $G((a,a''),(b,b''),k,n)$ and therefore also in $G(u,v,k,f(n))$, by Lemma 3.3. This is a contradiction.

Finally we show that $\Theta_{k,n}(T(a,u(x))) = \Theta_{k,n}(T(b,v(x)))$. If not, let $a' \in T(a,u(x_i))$ such that $\theta_{k,n}(a,a') \notin \Theta_{k,n}(T(b,v(x_i)))$. (The opposite case is symmetric.) Player I pebbles a' with a pebble of color other than x_i, and the argument now proceeds as in the preceding paragraph. □

Definition 5.3. For a theory Σ, define $var(\Sigma)$ to be the minimum k such that Σ has the k-variable property, if such a k exists, or ∞ otherwise. □

The following results determine $var(\Sigma)$ exactly for T_d, T_d^+, S_d, and S_d^+.

Theorem 5.4.

$$var(T_d)=var(T_d^+)=3 \text{ if } d=1, \quad max(4,d) \text{ if } d>1.$$

$$var(S_d)=var(S_d^+)=3 \text{ if } d=1, \quad max(4,\lceil d/2\rceil) \text{ if } d>1.$$

Proof. The bounds for $d=1$ were proved in Theorem 4.1. For $d>1$ and for Σ any of the four theories we are considering, define

$$k=\max(4,d) \text{ if } \Sigma=T_d \text{ or } T_d^+,$$
$$k=\max(4,\lceil d/2\rceil) \text{ if } \Sigma=S_d \text{ or } S_d^+.$$

Let g and h be sufficiently fast-growing functions of n such that $g(n)>>f(h(n))$ and $h(n)>>g(n-1)$, where f is the function of Lemma 5.2.

We must show that for all A and B satisfying Σ, and for all k-configurations (u,v) over A and B, if player II has a forced win in the games $G(u,v,k,n)$ for all n, then player II has a forced win in the games $G(u,v,m,n)$ for all m and n. We actually show by induction on n that if player II has a forced win in the game $G(u,v,k,g(n))$, then player II has a forced win in the games $G(u,v,m,n)$ for all m.

As in Theorem 4.1, the basis $n=0$ is immediate. Suppose now that the theorem holds for $n-1$. Assume $m>n$, so that player I will never have to remove a pebble from the board. The result will follow for smaller values of m by Lemma 3.3. If $|u|=|v|<k$, let player II respond to any move of player I with an optimal move according to player II's winning strategy in $G(u,v,k,g(n))$. By Definition 3.2, if the resulting configuration is (u',v'), then player II has a forced win in $G(u',v',k,g(n)-1)$, and $g(n)-1>g(n-1)$. By Lemma 3.3 and the induction hypothesis, player II has a forced win in $G(u',v',m,n-1)$ for all m. Since player I's move was arbitrary, this constitutes a forced win for player II in $G(u,v,m,n)$.

Now suppose $|u|=|v|=k$. As in the proof of Theorem 4.1, we will break the game $G(u,v,m,n)$ up into several smaller games on which player II has a forced win, and combine these strategies to produce a winning strategy for player II on $G(u,v,m,n)$.

Let $\langle u\rangle$ be the smallest subset of A containing all the $u(x)$ and closed under the operation $+$. Let $\langle v\rangle$ be the corresponding set in B. Let $a \in \langle u\rangle$, and let b be the corresponding element of $\langle v\rangle$. Let $A_1, \ldots, A_l$ be the subtrees of a, and let $B_1, \ldots, B_l$ be the subtrees of b, such that

$$\Theta_{k,h(n)}(A_i) = \Theta_{k,h(n)}(B_i), \quad 1\le i\le l,$$

and such that $u(x) \in A_i$ iff $v(x) \in B_i$. Such a correspondence between the subtrees of a and b exists, by Lemma 5.2.

If $\langle u\rangle \cap A_i \neq \emptyset$, let $a_i<a$ be its supremum. Let $b_i<b$ be the corresponding element of $\langle v\rangle \cap B_i$. In this case we associate the game

$$(5.5) \quad G((a,a_i),(b,b_i),k,h(n))$$

with the pair of regions

$$A_i-\{a' \mid a'<a_i\},$$
$$B_i-\{b' \mid b'<b_i\}.$$

If $\langle u \rangle \cap A_i = \varnothing$, let $a_i \in A_i$ and $b_i \in B_i$ such that

(5.6) $\theta_{k,h(n)}(a, a_i) = \theta_{k,h(n)}(b, b_i)$.

In this case we associate the game

(5.7) $G((a, a_i), (b, b_i), k, h(n))$

with the pair of corresponding regions A_i and B_i. Finally, if a and b are the suprema of $\langle u \rangle$ and $\langle v \rangle$, respectively, then we associate the game

(5.8) $G((a), (b), k, h(n))$

with the regions

$$A - \{a' \mid a' < a\},$$
$$B - \{b' \mid b' < b\}.$$

Observe that the designated regions of A partition A, and those of B partition B. We claim that player II has a forced win in each of the games

$$G(u', v', k, h(n))$$

associated with these regions. In case (5.7), this is because of the property (5.6) and Lemma 3.4; in cases (5.5) and (5.8), it is because with k pebbles and at most 2 moves, player I can force the configuration (u', v') from (u, v) as long as player II is playing optimally, thus player II has a forced win in $G(u', v', k, g(n)-2)$ and $g(n)-2 > h(n)$. (Here we are using the property that any uncovered $a \in \langle u \rangle$ is $u(x)+u(y)$ for some $x, y \in \partial u$.) Moreover, $|u'| = |v'| < k$. Therefore, by a previous case, player II has a forced win in the games

$$G(u', v', m, n), \text{ for all } m.$$

We now combine optimal strategies for player II in all these games, as in Theorem 4.1. Whenever player I plays in one of the designated regions, player II responds in the corresponding region of the other structure, according to his best strategy in the game associated with that region. Player II's play will always be in the correct region, since pebbles are never removed. Let (u_t, v_t) be the sequence of configurations. Since player II has a forced win in each of these games, each (u_t, v_t) restricted to each region is a local isomorphism; and by the choice of regions, if $u_t(x)$ and $u_t(y)$ are in different regions, then $u_t(x) \leq u_t(y)$ iff $v_t(x) \leq v_t(y)$.

The lower bounds follow from the lower bounds for linear order (Theorem 4.1), the lower bounds for finite trees (Theorem 6.1), and the following argument that all of $var(T_d)$, $var(T_d^+)$, $var(S_d)$, and $var(S_d^+)$ are at least 4 for $d > 1$.

Let $d > 1$ and let A be a full d-ary tree such that each path has order type $\mathbf{Z}+\mathbf{Z}$. Let a_3 and a_4 be two vertices in the lower part of A whose LCA is a_2 in the upper part of A. Thus the order type of the path from a_2 to a_3 and from a_2 to a_4 is $\omega + \omega^R$. Let a_1 be the parent of a_2, and let a_0 be the parent of a_1.

Let $B = A$ and consider the game

$$G((a_0, a_3, a_4), (a_1, a_3, a_4), 3, n).$$

Player II has a forced win, since the initial configuration $R(u, v)$ is a local isomorphism (even in the presence of $+$), and for subsequent moves, as soon as player I picks up a pebble, there is an automorphism of A sending the remaining two points on the left to the remaining two points on the right. From then on, player II can always play the image under that automorphism or its inverse of the point that player I plays.

However, player I has a forced win in

$$G((a_0, a_3, a_4), (a_1, a_3, a_4), 4, 2).$$

Player I first pebbles $a_2 = a_3 + a_4$ with the spare pebble on the left, to which player II must respond with a_2 with the spare pebble on the right; then player I removes the pebble on a_3 on the left and pebbles a_1, to which player II has no response. □

6. Finite models

It is interesting to note how the situation changes when we restrict our attention to finite models. Not only does $var()$ change, but the models are definable up to isomorphism. In this case we can give direct proofs of the upper bounds without using the Ehrenfeucht-Fraisse games of §3.

Define $Fin(\Sigma)$ to be the set of finite models of the theory Σ. For a set of structures S, define $var(S)$ to be the minimum k such that S satisfies Corollary 2.3(i).

Theorem 6.1.

(i) $var(Fin(T_d)) = 2$ if $d = 1$,
$max(3, d)$ if $d > 1$.

(ii) $var(Fin(S_d)) = 2$ if $d = 1$ or 2,
$max(3, \lceil d/2 \rceil)$ if $d > 2$.

Proof. We first establish the upper bounds. Given a finite tree A, we produce a formula $\varphi_A(x)$ such that, whenever B is a tree and $b \in B$, then $\varphi_A(b)$ holds in B iff the subtree of B with root b is isomorphic to A.

If A consists of a single node a, we assert that x satisfies the same monadic predicates that a does, and that x has no proper descendants. This takes two variables.

If A contains at least two nodes, let a be the root of A and let $A_1, \ldots, A_m$ be the maximal proper subtrees of A, with roots $a_1, \ldots, a_m$, respectively. Assume by induction on height that the formulas $\varphi_{A_1}(x), \ldots, \varphi_{A_m}(x)$ have been constructed. As above, we first assert that x satisfies the same monadic predicates that a does. We then assert that there exist proper subtrees satisfying each of the $\varphi_{A_i}(x)$:

$$\bigwedge_{i=1}^{m} \exists y < x \ \varphi_{A_i}(y)$$

and that every proper subtree has a supertree satisfying one of them:

$$\forall y < x \ \exists x \geq y \ \bigvee_{i=1}^{m} \varphi_{A_i}(x).$$

Each of these statements takes two variables. Together they establish the isomorphism types of the maximal proper subtrees. For the cases T_1 and S_1, we are done; for the other cases, it remains to show how to specify the number of maximal proper subtrees of each isomorphism type.

Consider the case T_d. Observe that the predicate "y is a child of z" is expressible with three variables:

$$y < z \wedge \forall x \ y < x \rightarrow z \leq x.$$

So is the predicate "y and z are siblings":

$$\forall x \ y \text{ is a child of } x \leftrightarrow z \text{ is a child of } x.$$

If there are $p < d$ children of a of isomorphism type A_i, we can express this with the formula

$$\begin{aligned} &\exists y_1 \cdots \exists y_p \text{ the } y_j \text{ are distinct children of } x \\ &\wedge \bigwedge_{j=1}^{p} \varphi_{A_i}(y_j) \\ &\wedge \forall x \ x \text{ and } y_1 \text{ are siblings} \wedge \varphi_{A_i}(x) \\ &\quad \rightarrow \bigvee_{j=1}^{p} y_j = x. \end{aligned}$$

This takes $max(3, p+1) \leq d$ variables. The only case of T_d not yet covered is when a has d maximal proper subtrees, all isomorphic to A_1. In this case we say that all children y of x satisfy $\varphi_{A_1}(y)$, and there is a child of x with $d-1$ distinct siblings. The variable x can be used to name one of the siblings. This takes $max(3, d)$ variables. This completes the argument for T_d.

Now consider the case S_d. Above, we specified all the isomorphism types of the maximal proper subtrees A_i of A. If all the A_i are isomorphic, or if all are of distinct isomorphism types, we are done. This exhausts the case $d = 2$, so let $d \geq 3$. We will show that $max(3, \lceil d/2 \rceil)$ variables are sufficient. If all isomorphism types are satisfied by at most $\lceil d/2 \rceil$ of the A_i, then as above we can use $\lceil d/2 \rceil$ variables y_j to name those a_i and assert $\varphi_{A_i}(y_j)$. This takes $max(3, \lceil d/2 \rceil)$ variables. If there are $m > \lceil d/2 \rceil$ A_i isomorphic to A_1, then all other isomorphism types are covered by the preceding case; we can then assert that there are $d - m < \lfloor d/2 \rfloor$ distinct children of x *not* satisfying φ_{A_1}, and then use one universally quantified variable to assert that all other siblings satisfy φ_{A_1}. In either case we have used $max(3, \lceil d/2 \rceil)$ variables.

We now establish the corresponding lower bounds. In each of the cases below, we produce two finite models A and B of one of our theories Σ such that A and B are not elementarily equivalent, but A and B are L_v equivalent, where $v = var(Fin(\Sigma)) - 1$. In each of the cases below, it is fairly straightforward to determine a winning strategy for player II for the game $G(\varnothing, \varnothing, v, n)$. We leave this to the reader.

(Case T_1, S_1, S_2, $v = 1$.) Let A and B be arbitrary nonempty nonisomorphic models with no monadic predicates.

(Case T_2, $v = 2$.) Let A be the complete binary tree of depth 2, and let B be the binary tree of depth 2 with two nodes of depth 1, three leaves of depth 2, and no monadic predicates.

(Case T_d, $v = d-1$.) Let A be the complete d-ary tree of depth 1, B the complete $(d-1)$-ary tree of depth 1, and no monadic predicates.

(Case S_3, S_4, $v=2$.) Let A and B be complete d-ary trees of depth 2. Let M be a monadic predicate such that one of each cluster of leaves satisfies M in A, and two of each cluster satisfy M in B.

(Case S_{2k}, $k>2$, $v=k-1$.) Let B and C be complete $2k$-ary trees of depth 1. Let M be a monadic predicate true of exactly $k-1$ leaves in A and k leaves in B.

(Case S_{2k+1}, $k>1$, $v=k$.) Let A and B be complete $(2k+1)$-ary trees of depth 1. Let M be a monadic predicate true of exactly k leaves in A and $k+1$ leaves in B. □

References

[AG] A. Amir and D. Gabbay, "Preservation of expressive completeness in temporal models," *Infor. and Comput.* 72:1 (1987), 66-83.

[E] A. Ehrenfeucht, "An application of games to the completeness problem for formalized theories," *Fund. Math.* 49 (1961), 129-141.

[F] R. Fraisse, "Sur les classifications des systems de relations," *Publ. Sci. Univ. Alger.* I (1954).

[FR] J. Ferrante and C. Rackoff, *The Computational Complexity of Logical Theories*, Springer-Verlag Lecture Notes in Mathematics 718, 1979.

[G] D. Gabbay, "Expressive functional completeness in tense logic," in: *Aspects of Philosophical Logic*, ed. Monnich, D. Reidel, Dordrecht, 1981, 91-117.

[I] N. Immerman, "Upper and lower bounds for first-order expressibility," *J. Comput. Syst. Sci.* 25:1 (1982), 76-98.

[K] H. Kamp, "Tense logic and the theory of linear order," Ph.D. thesis, Univ. of California at Los Angeles, 1968.

[S] J. Stavi, "Functional completeness over the rationals," unpublished manuscript, Bar-Ilan Univ., Ramat-Gan, Israel, 1979.

ON CHAIN LOGIC, PATH LOGIC, AND FIRST-ORDER LOGIC OVER INFINITE TREES

WOLFGANG THOMAS

Lehrstuhl für Informatik II, RWTH Aachen,
Büchel 29 - 31, D-5100 Aachen, W-Germany

Abstract

We study "chain logic" over infinite valued trees, a fragment of (Rabin's) monadic tree theory in which set quantification is restricted to chains, i.e. sets which are linearly ordered in the partial tree ordering. Chain logic suffices for many applications of Rabin's tree theory to modal logics or program logics. We characterize chain logic and subsystems of it (for example "path logic") in terms of regular-like expressions and connect them with algebraic language theory by introducing appropriate "tree monoids". As a consequence we obtain decidability results on expressiveness (e.g. for the problem whether a chain logic formula is equivalent to a path logic formula). An application in branching time logic is outlined.

1. Introduction

In the present paper we study systems of monadic second-order logic interpreted over infinite valued trees. These systems arise by restricting the range of set quantifiers in monadic second-order formulas to special sets of nodes in the (binary) tree. We deal with four kinds of such restrictions, each of which yields a proper subsystem of full monadic second-order logic over the binary tree (as investigated by Rabin [R 69]): We consider set quantification over chains, i.e. subsets of the tree which are linearly ordered by the partial tree ordering, quantification over finite chains, quantification over paths (i.e., maximal chains), and finally we study the case that set quantification is deleted completely and only first-order quantification remains. We call the resulting systems chain logic, finite chain logic, path logic and first-order logic over infinite trees, respectively.

Our main objective here is to develop some connections between these model theoretic notions and formal language theory, resp. semigroup theory. For this purpose, we introduce calculi of regular-like expressions for the definition of sets of trees which characterize the above mentioned four subsystems of monadic second-order logic. Also we associate with any monadic second-order definable set T of infinite trees a finite monoid M(T) (which consists of equivalence classes of trees that have a distinguished node for concatenation), from which information on definability of T in subsystems of chain logic can be deduced. In this framework we find analogues of some results of classical language theory, concerning the class of star-free regular languages, in the context of trees. In particular we show how McNaughton's characterization of star-free languages in terms of first-order logic and Schützenberger's characterization of these languages by group-free monoids can be carried over to sets of trees that are definable in chain logic. It turns out that path logic (resp. first-order logic) is related to chain logic (resp. to finite chain logic) in the same way as star-free expressions are related to (classical) regular expressions.

While chain logic is restricted enough to allow a satisfactory treatment in terms of language theoretical operations (like concatenation) and in terms of monoids, the system is still powerful enough for many interesting applications. It should be noted that chain logic suffices for the description of virtually all constructs appearing in modal logics or program logics (when we refer to interpretations over tree models). For instance, the known reductions of propositional dynamic logic PDL [FL 79], process logic PL [HKP 82], the μ-calculus Lμ [K 82] or computation tree logic CTL* [EH 86] to the monadic theory of the binary tree only involve set quantifiers ranging over chains. Moreover, it seems that the classification by the above four cases (chains, paths, finite chains, elements) yields a natural taxonomy for modal and program logics. For example, for PDL and Lμ only finite chains are required, for PL infinite chains, for CTL* paths; if CTL*-formulas are assumed to refer to finite paths only, first-order logic over trees suffices.

This paper relies on a model theoretic method which originates in work by Läuchli [L 66] and Shelah [Sh 75] on monadic second-order theories of linear orderings and has been generalized to trees by Gurevich and Shelah [GS 83] and in [T 84]. The technique allows to perform computations with finite fragments of the theory of a structure; in particular, it shows how to combine such theory-fragments of substructures to obtain the corresponding theory-fragment for the entire structure. We introduce these prerequisites in a special form here which suffices for the present purposes.

In section 2 we recall the results on star-free languages (of finite, resp. infinite words) that form the background of our results. Section 3 contains the definition of chain logic and its variants and compares the expressive power of these systems. In sections 4, 5 we introduce formalisms of path-oriented regular expressions for the description of sets of trees, define "tree monoids", and present the above mentioned charactization results. The final sections discuss an application in branching time logic and mention directions for further work.

2. Preliminaries from language theory

We shall use results of Büchi [B 60], [B 62] which characterize the regular sets of words and the ω-regular sets of infinite sequences in terms of monadic second-order logic. Given a finite alphabet Σ, a set $L \subset \Sigma^\omega$ of sequences (ω-words) is ω-regular if L is a finite union of sets $U \cdot V^\omega$ where $U, V \subset \Sigma^*$ are regular. The characterization in logic refers to an identification of words and ω-words with discrete linear orderings. Namely, if $\Sigma = \{a_1, \ldots, a_m\}$, a nonempty word $w = c_0 \ldots c_n$ is represented by a "word model" of the form $(\{0, \ldots, n\}, S, <, P_1, \ldots, P_m)$ where S is the successor relation and $<$ the usual order relation over $\{0, \ldots, n\}$, and $P_k = \{i \mid c_i = a_k\}$. Similarly, an ω-word is viewed as a "sequence model" (ω, S, $<$, $P_1, \ldots, P_m$) over the set ω of natural numbers. A language $L \subset \Sigma^+$ (resp. $L \subset \Sigma^\omega$) is called monadic second-order definable if for some sentence φ of the monadic second-order language in the signature $S, <, P_1, \ldots, P_m$, a word (resp. sequence) belongs to L iff the corresponding word model (resp. sequence model) satisfies φ. By [B 60] and [B 62], the monadic second-order definable languages $L \subset \Sigma^+$ (resp. $L \subset \Sigma^\omega$) are precisely the regular (resp. ω-regular) sets.

The starting point of the present paper is subsequent work on star-free regular sets. A set of words is <u>star-free</u> if it is constructible from finite sets of words by boolean operations and concatenation. McNaughton [McNP 71] and Schützenberger [S 65] established the following characterization of star-free sets:

<u>Theorem 2.1</u> [McNP 71], [S 65]

For a regular set $L \subset \Sigma^*$, the following conditions are equivalent:

(a) L is star-free,

(b) $L - \{\varepsilon\}$ is first-order definable (i.e., definable in the first-order fragment of the above mentioned monadic second-order language),

(c) the syntactic monoid $\Sigma^*/\sim_L$ is group-free (i.e. contains only singleton sets as groups).

Here the congruence $\sim_L$ over Σ^* is defined by

$$x \sim_L y \quad \text{iff} \quad \forall u,v \in \Sigma^* \quad (uxv \in L \Leftrightarrow uvy \in L).$$

Since the syntactic monoid is finite and effectively computable for regular L, it follows that for regular languages the property "star-free" is decidable.

More recently, similar results have been obtained for sets of ω-words. An ω-language L is called <u>ω-star-free</u> if it is a finite union of sets $U\cdot(V^*)^{\omega}$ where U and V^* are star-free. (There are also other equivalent language theoretical definitions.) We have

Theorem 2.2 [L 77], [T 79], [P 84]

For an ω-regular set $L \subset \Sigma^{\omega}$, the following conditions are equivalent:

(a) L is ω-star-free,

(b) L is first-order definable,

(c) the monoid $\Sigma^*/\approx_L$ is group-free.

Here a congruence $\approx_L$ over Σ^* is used which was suggested by Arnold in [A 85]:

$$x \approx_L y \text{ iff } \forall u,v,w \in \Sigma^* : (uxvw^{\omega} \in L \Leftrightarrow uyvw^{\omega} \in L) \text{ and } (u(xv)^{\omega} \in L \Leftrightarrow u(yv)^{\omega} \in L)$$

Again, by effective presentability of $\Sigma^*/\approx_L$, it is decidable whether an ω-regular sequence set is ω-star-free. - For later purposes, it is useful to give a different formulation of the condition that $\Sigma^*/\approx_L$ is group-free, in terms of the following "noncounting property": An ω-language $L \subset \Sigma^{\omega}$ is <u>noncounting</u> if for sufficiently large n and arbitrary $x,u,v,w \in \Sigma^*$ we have

$$ux^n vw^{\omega} \in L \Leftrightarrow ux^{n+1}vw^{\omega} \in L \quad \text{and}$$
$$u(x^n v)^{\omega} \in L \Leftrightarrow u(x^{n+1}v)^{\omega} \in L .$$

Otherwise we say L is "counting". It is easy to see (e.g. following the proof of [McNP71,p.52-53]) that a ω-regular set L is noncounting iff $\Sigma^*/\approx_L$ is group-free.

In the remainder of this paper, we show two analogues of Theorem 2.2 in the context of infinite trees. In one result we refer to chain definable sets of trees and characterize definability by path formulas, in the other we refer to finite chain definable sets of trees and characterize definability in first-order logic. As typical case we shall consider (except for section 6) only <u>binary</u> valued trees.

3. Chain logic over trees

A binary Σ-valued tree is a map $f:\{l,r\}^* \to \Sigma$, where the words over the alphabet $\{l,r\}$ ("left", "right") represent the nodes of the unlabelled binary tree. The set of all binary Σ-valued trees is denoted T_{Σ}. We identify a Σ-valued tree f with a relational structure of the form

$$(\{l,r\}^*, L, R, <, Root, (P_a)_{a\in\Sigma})$$

where L,R,< are binary relations and Root and P_a (for $a \in \Sigma$) are unary relations. We have, for $p,q \in \{l,r\}^*$, p L q (resp. p R q) iff pl = q (resp. pr = q), p < q iff p is a proper prefix of q, $p \in Root$ iff $p = \varepsilon$ (the empty word), and $p \in P_a$ iff f(p) = a. The corresponding monadic second-order language contains variables x,y,... ranging over nodes (from $\{l,r\}^*$) and variables X,Y,... ranging over sets of nodes. The formulas of the language are built up from atomic formulas of the form $x \in X$, $x \in P_a$, $x = y$, x L y, x R y, $x < y$, $x \in Root$ by means of the connectives $\neg$, $\vee$, $\wedge$, $\to$, $\leftrightarrow$ and the quantifiers $\exists$, $\forall$ acting on either kind of variable. (For technical reasons we use here a purely relational symbol set; however in some formalizations we shall write also function symbols for better readability. For example, $xll \in P_a$ is then a shortwriting for $\exists y\exists z(x\ L\ y \wedge y\ L\ z \wedge z \in P_a)$.)

If the interpretation of the quantified set variables is restricted to chains, finite chains, or paths of the tree (-model) under consideration, we speak of chain formulas, finite chain formulas, or path formulas, respectively. (Of course, these formulas are the same when considered as syntactical objects; we refer to them here together with their intended interpretation.) Given any of the above conventions for set quantification one obtains a corresponding satisfaction relation $t \models \varphi$ between trees and sentences; the set of trees ("tree language") defined by φ is $T(\varphi) := \{t \in T_{\Sigma} \mid t \models \varphi\}$. We say that a set $T \subset T_{\Sigma}$ is monadic second-order definable, chain definable, finite chain definable, path definable, first-order definable if a sentence φ of the respective logic exists with $T = T(\varphi)$.

In the sequel it will often be convenient to consider only alphabets of the form $\Sigma = \{0,1\}^n$. In this case we drop the 2^n symbols P_a for $a \in \Sigma$ and use n free set variables $X_1,\ldots,X_n$ instead; the atomic formulas $x \in P_a$ are then written as conjunctions of the form $(\neg)\ x \in X_1 \wedge \ldots \wedge (\neg)\ x \in X_n$; and a $\{0,1\}^n$-valued tree is given by a structure $(t,\bar{Q}) = (\{l,r\}^*, L, R, <, \mathrm{Root}, Q_1,\ldots,Q_n)$ where t stands for the unlabelled structure of the binary tree and $\bar{Q} = (Q_1,\ldots,Q_n)$ is an n-tuple of subsets of $\{l,r\}^*$. Node p belongs to Q_i iff the i-th component of the label of p (in $\{0,1\}^n$) is 1. Under this convention any formula $\varphi(X_1,\ldots,X_n)$ with free set variables $X_1,\ldots,X_n$ defines the set of trees $(t,\bar{Q})$ (over $\Sigma = \{0,1\}^n$) such that $(t,\bar{Q})$ satisfies $\varphi(\bar{X})$.

We need one further auxiliary notion. The <u>quantifier-depth</u> of a formula φ, written $qd(\varphi)$, is the maximum number of nested quantifiers in φ. (By inductive definition, we have $qd(\varphi) = 0$ for atomic φ, $qd(\neg\varphi) = qd(\varphi)$, $qd(\varphi \vee \psi) = \max(qd(\varphi), qd(\psi))$, similarly for $\wedge$, ->, <->, and $qd(\exists x\, \varphi) = qd(\exists X\, \varphi) = qd(\varphi) + 1$, similarly for $\forall$.)

We now relate the different versions of chain logic in expressive power:

<u>Theorem 3.1</u> For sets $T \subset T_\Sigma$ (over an alphabet Σ with at least two letters), the following implication diagram holds:

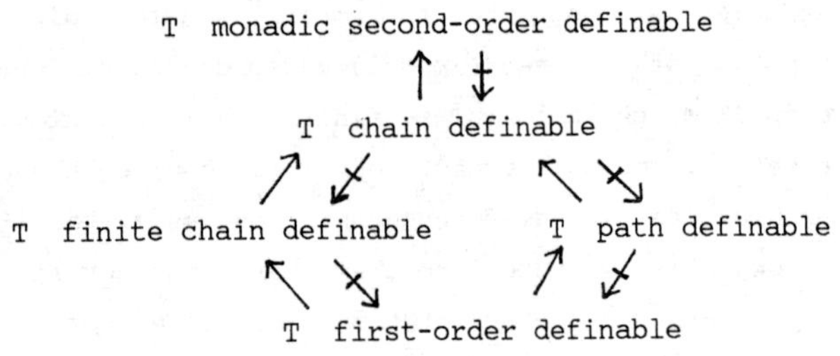

<u>Proof</u> It is easy to see that any of the upward implications is valid. For example, chain formulas can be expressed in monadic second-order logic since "X is a chain" is first-order formalizable in terms of <. Similarly, finiteness of chains and the property of being a path are expressible in chain logic.

A set of trees which is monadic second-order definable but not chain definable is, for example, the set of trees $f : \{l,r\}^* \to \{a,b\}$ for which the set $\{p \mid f(p) = b\}$ forms an antichain (i.e. a set of elements which are pairwise incomparable w.r.t. <) and has a (finite) even number of elements. For the proof we refer the reader to [T 84].

An example of a tree language that is definable both in chain logic and finite chain logic but neither in path logic nor in first- order logic is the set T of trees over $\Sigma = \{a,b\}$ having a single node $p = l^n$ labelled b, where n is even, and otherwise labelled a. T can be defined by a sentence saying that there is a unique node x labelled by b such that there is a (finite) chain which contains the root and then every second left successor until precisely node x is reached. The proof that T is neither definable in path logic nor in first-order logic is based on the notion of noncounting property for tree languages, introduced in section 5 below. It will turn out there that T does not share this property, and that any path definable and any first-order definable set of trees is noncounting.

Finally we verify the existence of a set of trees which is both path definable and chain definable but neither first-order definable nor finite chain definable. Consider the set of trees over $\{a,b\}$ that have on any path only a finite number of nodes labelled b. Rabin [R 70] showed that this set is not definable in the weak monadic second-order language, i.e. using quantifiers over arbitrary finite sets. Hence we have nondefinability in first-order logic and finite chain logic; on the other hand, this set is obviously definable in path logic and in chain logic.

4. <u>Regular-like expressions</u>

In this section we introduce "path-oriented" regular expressions defining sets of trees; they capture the expressive power of chain logic and its subsystems.

We generate sets of trees starting from T_Σ by using boolean operations and "tree concatenation along a path". Assume $T_1,\ldots,T_n$ are given sets of trees and $D_n = \{d_1,\ldots,d_n\}$ is a set of auxiliary symbols (not in Σ). An ω-sequence α from $(\Sigma \times \{l,r\} \times D_n)^\omega$ describes a set of trees in terms of the path defined by the first two components of α; label d_i at a position of this path indicates that a tree from T_i should be attached to the successor of this position that is not on the path.

Example $\alpha = (a,l,d_1)(a,l,d_2)(a,r,d_1))(b,l,d_1)\ldots$ describes the trees of the form

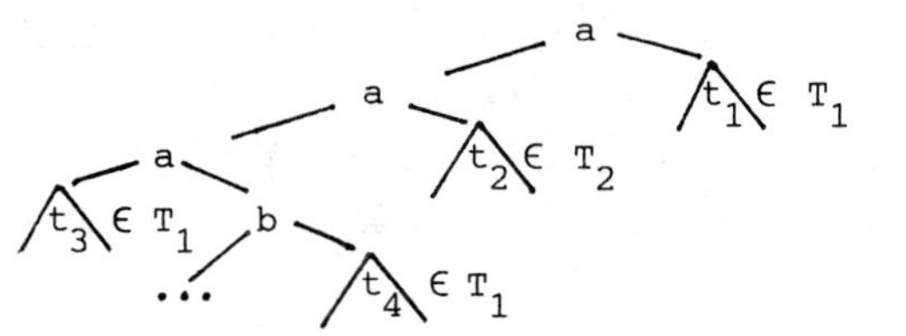

Now for any sequence set $L \subset (\Sigma \times \{l,r\} \times D_n)^\omega$ let $L\cdot(T_1,\ldots,T_n)$ be the set of trees obtainable in this way from the sequences $\alpha \in L$. Similarly we define sets of trees in terms of finite initial segments of paths. Then the sequences α are from $(\Sigma \times \{l,r\} \times D_n)^* \cdot (\Sigma \times D_n \times D_n)$, and their last element of the form (a,d_i,d_j) indicates that the last node, carrying label a, has two successors which are roots of trees in T_i and T_j.

Definition 4.1 We call $T \subset T_\Sigma$ p-regular (resp. p-star-free) if T is constructible from T_Σ using boolean operations $\sim$, $\cup$, $\cap$ and tree concatenations $L\cdot(T_1,\ldots,T_n)$ where $L \subset (\Sigma \times \{l,r\} \times D_n)^\omega$ is ω-regular (resp. ω-star-free). If only regular (resp. star-free) languages $L \subset (\Sigma \times \{l,r\} \times D_n)^* \cdot (\Sigma \times D_n \times D_n)$ are used, T is called fin-p-regular (resp. fin-p-star-free).

Following the inductive structure of this definition one obtains path-oriented expressions ("p-regular expressions") for sets of trees. As shown in the following theorem, they can be considered as a simple and transparent normal form for formulas in chain logic:

Theorem 4.2 For any $T \subset T_\Sigma$:

(a) T is chain definable iff T is p-regular,

(b) T is path definable iff T is p-star-free,

(c) T is finite chain definable iff T is fin-p-regular,

(d) T is first-order definable iff T is fin-p-star-free.

Remark When the definitions of "fin-p-regular" and "fin-p-star-free" are applied to sets of unary trees, i.e. to ω-languages, Theorem 4.2(c)(d) still holds and one obtains conditions which characterize the ω-regular and the ω-star-free sequence sets: An ω-language $L \subset \Sigma^\omega$ is ω-regular (resp. ω-star-free) iff L is constructible from Σ^ω by boolean operations w.r.t. Σ^ω and left concatenation with regular (resp. star-free) sets of finite words (cf. [T 79]). Expressions resulting from this inductive definition can be used to denote the ω-languages which appear in the construction of p-regular and p-star-free sets of trees.

Proof of 4.2 We treat only case (a) in greater detail and mention at selected places which modifications yield (b)-(d). For the implication from right to left proceed by induction over the construction of p-regular expressions. Definition of T_Σ and the induction steps for boolean operations are trivial. Consider $L\cdot(T_1,\ldots,T_n)$ where L is ω-regular and $T_1,\ldots,T_n$ are p-regular. By inductive hypothesis each T_i is defined by some chain sentence. It is easy to obtain from it a chain formula $\varphi_i(x)$ which is satisfied by a tree with node p as interpretation for x iff the subtree with root p belongs to T_i. Let ψ be a monadic second-order sentence which defines the ω-regular sequence set $L \subset (\Sigma \times \{l,r\} \times D_n)^\omega$. From ψ one constructs a formula $\bar{\psi}(X)$ which expresses that path X through the tree determines a sequence α from L : $\bar{\psi}(X)$ is obtained from ψ by relativizing all quantifiers to X and by substituting for an atomic formula like $x \in P_{(a,l,d_i)}$ the formula $x \in P_a \wedge xl \in X \wedge \psi_i(xr)$. Then $L\cdot(T_1,\ldots,T_n)$ is defined by $\exists X$("X is path" $\wedge$ $\bar{\psi}(X)$). The proofs for (b)-(d) are similar, using Theorem 2.2 for (b), [B 60] for (c), and 2.1 for (d) when $\bar{\psi}(X)$ is to be defined.

The converse directon of Theorem 4.2 is proved by induction over quantifier-depth of formulas. To facilitate the exposition we adopt a convention that eliminates problems arising with the treatment of individual variables: For the rest of this section we replace all individual variables by set variables and stipulate that the atomic formulas, now of form $X\ L\ Y$, $X\ R\ Y$, $X < Y$, $X \in \text{Root}$, and $X \in Z$, are true iff X and Y are interpreted by singleton sets whose unique elements belong to these relations in the usual sense. Note that under this convention $X \in X$ is true iff X is a singleton; thus first-order quantifiers $\exists x\ldots$, $\forall x\ldots$ can now be written as $\exists X(X \in X \wedge \ldots)$, $\forall X(X \in X \rightarrow \ldots)$.

The initial step for the inductive proof, concerning the quantifier-free formulas, will be clear from a typical case, the atomic formula $X_1 \in X_2$. This formula defines a set of trees over $\Sigma = \{0,1\}^2$ such that (a) there exists a node with value (1,1), and (b) not more than one node has a value with first component 1. To express (a), we define the set L_1 of sequences over the alphabet $\Sigma_1 = \Sigma \times \{l,r\} \times D_1$ coding paths with at least one occurrence of value (1,1):

$$L_1 = \Sigma_1^* \cdot (((1,1),l,d_1) \cup ((1,1),r,d_1)) \cdot \Sigma_1^\omega \quad .$$

Then $L_1 \cdot (T_\Sigma)$ is a p-regular expression defining the set of trees with property (a). Note that replacement of the central factor of L_1 by the union of the four elements $((1,\bullet),\bullet,d_1)$ yields a p-regular expression T_1 for the trees with at least one node carrying 1 in its first component and arbitrary second component. For property (b), we define an expression $\sim b_1 \cap \sim b_2$ where b_1 expresses the existence of two nodes with first component 1 on one path, and b_2 expresses the existence of two such nodes incomparable w.r.t. $<$. Expression b_1 is easily written down (following the pattern of L_1 above). For b_2 we use the alphabet $\Sigma_2 = \Sigma \times \{l,r\} \times \{d_1,d_2\}$; we guarantee a node such that one of its left and one of its right descendants carries 1 in its first component, by postulating the path through the left of these descendants and expressing that before reaching it there is a branch to the right into a subtree satisfing the expression T_1 mentioned above. So we write

$$L = \Sigma_1^* \cdot (\bullet,l,d_2) \cdot \Sigma_1^* \cdot ((1,\bullet),\bullet,d_1) \cdot \Sigma_1^\omega$$

where the elements with dots stand for the corresponding unions (both of four letters from Σ_2). We set $b_2 = L \cdot (T_\Sigma, T_1)$.

With this machinery for describing singletons it is easy to obtain p-regular expressions for the sets defined by other atomic formulas. Note that it is possible to write the above expressions also as p-star-free expressions. For instance, with respect to Σ_2, we have $\Sigma_1^* = \sim(\sim\emptyset \cdot (\bullet,\bullet,d_2) \cdot \sim\emptyset)$, which shows that the stars can be eliminated. Also it is obvious that the above definitions can be given in terms of finite paths, which yields fin-p-regular, resp. fin-p-star-free expressions as required in 4.2(c),(d).

Concerning the induction step, we consider the case of a chain formula $\exists Y\varphi(\bar{X},Y)$ of quantifier-depth $m+1$, assuming that the formulas of quantifier-depth m can be written as p-regular expressions. We suppose that $\exists Y$ is a chain quantifier; w.l.o.g. we may assume that it refers to infinite chains only. (If finite chains are to be included, one could rephrase this in terms of infinite ones by speaking about "complement chains".) The idea for obtaining a p-regular expression for $\exists Y\varphi$ is to "split" the condition $\varphi(\bar{X},Y)$ into two parts, one dealing with the path through Y (thus defining an ω-language L), the other dealing with the subtrees rooted along this path. This will enable us to write $\exists Y\varphi$ in the form $L \cdot (T_1,\ldots,T_n)$.

We need some auxiliary definitions from the model theory of monadic theories (emerging from [L 66], [Sh 75], [GS 83], [T 84]). We define the "m-type" (also called "m-theory") of a tree as a finite representation of the set of formulas of quantifier-depth m satisfied in the tree. We assume the variables are given a fixed indexing $X_1, X_2, \ldots$.

Definition 4.3 The chain-m-type $\tau_m(t,\bar{Q})$, of $(t,\bar{Q})$, where $\bar{Q} = (Q_1,\ldots,Q_n)$, is defined by induction as follows:

$$\tau_0(t,\bar{Q}) = \text{set of atomic formulas in the variables } X_1,\ldots,X_n \text{ that hold in } (t,\bar{Q}),$$

$$\tau_{m+1}(t,\bar{Q}) = \{\tau_m(t,\bar{Q},P) \mid P \subset \{l,r\}^*,\ P \text{ chain}\}.$$

Similarly, if P ranges over finite chains, paths and singletons, only singletons, or arbitrary sets instead, one obtains finite chain-, path-, first-order-, monadic second-order-m-types, respectively.

The following facts can be proved by induction on m:

Lemma 4.4

(a) The chain m-type $\tau_m(t,\bar{Q})$ is a finite object, which effectively determines for any chain formula $\varphi(\bar{X})$ of quantifier-depth m whether $(t,\bar{Q}) \models \varphi(\bar{X})$.

(b) Any chain m-type (in the variables $X_1,\ldots,X_n$) is defined by a chain formula $\varphi_\tau(\bar{X})$ of quantifier-depth m (i.e. we have $(t,\bar{R}) \models \varphi_\tau(\bar{X})$ iff $\tau_m(t,\bar{R}) = \tau$).

(c) Any chain formula of quantifier-depth m is equivalent to a disjunction of such "type descriptions" φ_τ where the τ are chain m-types.

(d) Analogous statements hold for finite chain-, path-, first-oder-, and monadic second-order-m-types.

Definition 4.3 and the Lemma 4.4 are easily adapted to other kinds of structures (besides trees); in the sequel we shall refer also to sequence models over $(\omega,<)$ (where of course chain-m-types and monadic second order m-types coincide).

We return to the proof of the induction step concerning the formula $\exists Y\varphi(\bar{X},Y)$. By 4.4(c) we may assume that $\varphi(\bar{X},Y)$ is a chain m-type description $\varphi_\tau(\bar{X},Y)$.

Suppose all possible chain m-types (in the variables $X_1,\ldots,X_n$) are given in some fixed sequence $\sigma_1,\ldots,\sigma_s$. Let T_i be the set of trees $(t,\bar{Q})$ of chain m-type σ_i. By 4.4(b) and the inductive hypothesis, T_i is p-regular.

Consider a tree $(t,\bar{Q},P)$ where P is an infinite chain. P determines a path which itself is coded by a sequence α over the alphabet $\{0,1\}^{n+1} \times \{l,r\} \times D_s$, referring to the sets $T_1,\ldots,T_s$ above. Denote by $(\alpha,\bar{Q},P,R_0,\ldots,R_s)$ the corresponding sequence model over $(\omega,<)$ with $i \in R_0$ iff $\alpha(i)$'s $\{l,r\}$-component is l, and for $k > 0$, $i \in R_k$ iff $\alpha(i)$'s last component is d_k. The following lemma shows how the m-type of $(t,\bar{Q},P)$ can be recovered from $(\alpha,\bar{Q},P,\bar{R})$. The lemma is similar to the "composition theorem" of [GS 83] and to the first "decomposition lemma" of [T 84].

Lemma 4.5

(a) The chain m-type τ of $(t,\bar{Q},P)$ is determined uniquely (and effectively) by the monadic second-order (2m+1)-type σ of $(\alpha,\bar{Q},P,\bar{R})$.

(b) Analogous statements hold for finite chain m-types of trees (using finite sequence models), path m-types (using first-order (2m+1)-types of sequence models) and first-order m-types (using finite sequence models and their first-order (2m+1)-types).

In the case described by Lemma 4.5(a) we say that the type σ induces τ. Since σ has a monadic second-order description (as in 4.4(b)), the sequences over $\{0,1\}^{n+1} \times \{l,r\} \times D_s$ of this type form an ω-regular sequence set L_σ. It follows that the chain formula $\exists Y\varphi_\tau(\bar{X},Y)$, to which our induction step was reduced, is equivalent to the p-regular expression $\bigcup_\sigma L_\sigma \cdot (T_1,\ldots,T_s)$ where σ ranges over those types which induce τ. This completes the proof of 4.2(a). The argument for 4.2(b)-(d) is similar, using 4.5(b).

Concerning the proof of Lemma 4.5, we give some remarks which indicate the main idea and explain the choice of 2m+1 as type level for σ. It turns out that in order to capture one further type level of t we need two further type levels of α. As an illustration consider the 0-type $\tau_0(t,Q_1,Q_2,P)$, where $Q_1 = \{q_1\}$, $Q_2 = \{q_2\}$, P is a chain with $q_1 \in P$, $q_2 \notin P$ and $q_1 < q_2$. How can we deduce that formula $X_1 < X_2$ (signalling $q_1 < q_2$) belongs to $\tau_0(t,Q_1,Q_2,P)$, given $\tau_1(\alpha,Q_1,Q_2,P,\bar{R})$? For readability assume that in the latter type the variable X_i refers to Q_i and variable Y_j refers to R_j. We have $q_1 < q_2$ in t iff there is some q_3 (namely the last element which is common to the path through P and to the path from q_1 to q_2) with $q_1 = q_3$ or $q_1 < q_3$ in α, and $q_3 \in R_j$ for an index j such that the j-th 0-type σ_j says that q_2 is present in subtrees of this type. Formally, $X_1 < X_2$ belongs to $\tau_0(t,Q_1,Q_2,P)$ iff for some type σ' $(= \tau_0(\alpha,Q_1,Q_2,P,\bar{R},Q_3))$ from $\tau_1(\alpha,Q_1,Q_2,P,\bar{R})$ we have in σ' the formula $X_3 \in Y_j$ (meaning $q_3 \in R_j$) for some j such that σ_j contains $X_2 \in X_2$. This condition can be checked by inspection of $\tau_1(\alpha, Q_1, Q_2, P, \bar{R})$ and the types σ_j.

If we consider the condition $q_1\ R\ q_2$ or $q_1\ L\ q_2$ instead of $q_1 < q_2$, the 0-type σ_j should not only offer the information that q_2 exists in the respective subtree but also that q_2 is its root. Since we have included the predicate Root in the signature of trees, this can be verified by searching for the formula $X_2 \in$ Root in σ_j.

5. Tree monoids

The introduction of tree monoids is based on the idea of a special tree (which has been described for finite trees e.g. in [T 84]). A special tree is obtained from a tree of T_Σ by deleting the subtree at some node and assigning to this node (now without successor) the special label c ($\notin \Sigma$). If the root of the given tree was chosen, we obtain the single symbol c. Let S_Σ be the set of special trees. For $s, s' \in S_\Sigma$, the product $s \cdot s'$ (short ss') is the special tree obtained from s by replacing its c by s'. Similarly, for $s \in S_\Sigma$ and $t \in T_\Sigma$, the product st is in T_Σ. The structure $(S_\Sigma, \cdot)$ is a monoid with identity c.

Referring to this concatenation product of special trees, we introduce congruence relations which correspond to the relations $\sim_L$ and $\approx_L$ of section 2 :

Definition 5.1 For $T \subset T_\Sigma$, $\sim_T$ and $\approx_T$ are defined over S_Σ by

$s \sim_T s'$ iff $\forall s_0 \in S_\Sigma\ \forall t \in T_\Sigma$
$(s_0 st \in T \iff s_0 s't \in T)$

$s \approx_T s'$ iff $\forall s_0, s_1, s_2 \in S_\Sigma$:
$s_0 ss_1 s_2^{\omega} \in T \iff s_0 s' s_1 s_2^{\omega} \in T$ and
$s_0(ss_1)^{\omega} \in T \iff s_0(s's_1)^{\omega} \in T$.

If T is monadic second-order definable then $\sim_T$ and $\approx_T$ are congruences of finite index and induce effectively constructible monoids $S_\Sigma/\sim_T$ and $S_\Sigma/\approx_T$. To verify this, we use Rabin's theorem that a set T is monadic second-order definable iff T is recognized by a Rabin tree automaton [R 69]. We assume familiarity with these automata. Let us show that a Rabin tree automaton A which recognizes T induces a finite congruence $\sim_A$ which refines both $\sim_T$ and $\approx_T$. We write, for states q and q' of A and for a subset Q of the state set Q_A of A, q -s-> q' (Q) iff there is a run of A on s which starts in q, reaches q' at the node labelled c, assumes the state set Q on the finite path from the root to this node, and satisfies the usual acceptance condition on the remaining infinite paths of s. Define $\sim_A$ by

$s \sim_A s'$ iff $\forall q, q' \in Q_A\ \ \forall Q \subset Q_A$
$(q$ -s-> q' $(Q) \iff q$-s'-> q' $(Q))$.

This relation is a congruence on S_Σ of finite index; the $\sim_A$-class of tree s is determined by a set of triples (q, q', Q), namely those triples with q -s -> q' (Q). It is easy to see that $\sim_A$ is a refinement of $\sim_T$ and $\approx_T$. Moreover, by decidability of the emptiness problem for Rabin automata, it can be decided effectively whether two $\sim_A$-classes belong to the same $\sim_T$-class (resp. $\approx_T$-class). Hence $S_\Sigma/\sim_T$ and $S_\Sigma/\approx_T$ are finite and effectively presentable monoids.

The relation $\sim_T$ is appropriate for the analysis of sets of finite trees. In the sequel we consider mainly infinite trees. As in section 2, it is useful to reformulate the condition that $S_\Sigma/\approx_T$ is group-free in terms of a noncounting property for trees. A set $T \subset T_\Sigma$ is noncounting if for sufficiently large n and all $s, s_0, s_1, s_2 \in S_\Sigma$:

(1) $s_0 s^n s_1 s_2^{\omega} \in T$ iff $s_0 s^{n+1} s_1 s_2^{\omega} \in T$, and
(2) $s_0(s^n s_1)^{\omega} \in T$ iff $s_0(s^{n+1} s_1)^{\omega} \in T$.

As an example consider the set of trees mentioned in 3.1 (with label b at node 1^n for some even n and label a elsewhere). This set violates part (1) of the noncounting condition: we set $s_0 = c$ and

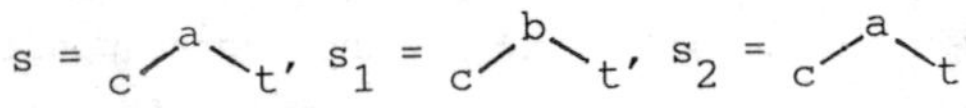

where t is the tree with label a everywhere. Another typical example of a "counting" set of trees, violating condition (2) above, contains those trees which have infinitely many value-segments $b\,a^n\,b$, with even n, on their leftmost path, and have label a everywhere else.

Lemma 5.2 Let T be p-regular. The monoid $S_\Sigma/\approx_T$ is group-free iff T is noncounting.

Theorem 5.3

(a) For p-regular $T \subset T_\Sigma$:
T is p-star-free iff $S_\Sigma/\approx_T$ is group-free.

(b) For fin-p-regular $T \subset T_\Sigma$:
T is fin-p-star-free iff $S_\Sigma/\approx_T$ is group-free.

Together with Theorem 4.2 this yields the two announced analogues of the characterization of ω-star-free sets as formulated in section 2:

Corollary 5.4 For p-regular (or equivalently: chain definable) sets $T \subset T_\Sigma$, the following conditions are equivalent:

(a) T is p-star-free,

(b) T is path definable

(c) the monoid $S_\Sigma/\approx_T$ is group-free.

Corollary 5.5 For fin-p-regular (or equivalently: finite chain definable) sets $T \subset T_\Sigma$, the following conditions are equivalent:

(a) T is fin-p-star-free,

(b) T is first-order definable,

(c) the monoid $S_\Sigma/\approx_T$ is group-free.

By effective presentability of $S_\Sigma/\approx_T$ we obtain:

Corollary 5.6 It is decidable whether a chain formula (resp. finite chain formula) is equivalent to a path formula (resp. first-order formula).

Without going into details, we mention that by a canonical restriction one gets from the above theorems a corresponding result for sets of finite trees. In this context there is no more distinction between p-regular and fin-p-regular sets, chain definable and finite chain definable sets etc., and one has to work with the relation $\sim_T$ instead of $\approx_T$. We skip a formal exposition of this case in the present paper.

Proof of 5.3 For the direction from left to right it suffices by Lemma 5.2 to show the noncounting property for (fin-)p-star-free sets. This is done by induction over (fin-) p-star-free expressions. In the induction step concerning $T = L \cdot (T_1,\dots,T_n)$, Theorem 2.2 (applied to L) and the induction hypothesis (applied to the T_i) yield the noncounting property for T.

The converse is shown here for (a). Essentially we use induction over p-regular expressions. However, these expressions need some preprocessing to make the induction work. Our aim is to generate a noncounting p-regular set in a way where solely noncounting sets are given by the subexpressions that appear as intermediate steps. Thus we want to exclude cases like the representation of the word-set a* as a product (ε ∪ a)•(aa)*, which contains a counting factor. In such a situation we enlarge the counting set to a noncounting one (in the example: change (aa)* to a*) without affecting the value of the entire expression. For this purpose we prepare a given p-regular expression by reformulating it in terms of monotone operations and restricting the use of complementation.

Two auxiliary notions are needed. First, we denote, for $L \subset \Sigma^\omega$, by L^{nc} the "noncounting closure" of L, i.e. the intersection of all noncounting sets L' with $L \subset L' \subset \Sigma^\omega$. L^{nc} exists because noncounting sets are closed under intersection. Similarly, T^{nc} denotes the noncounting closure of the tree language T. If L is ω-regular, say recognized by the Büchi automaton A (in the sense of [B 62]), one can construct from A a Büchi automaton A^{nc} which recognizes L^{nc} and thus show that also L^{nc} is ω-regular. (This process involves a modification of "counting loops" in A, in order to allow that these loops can be left not only at the end but also at intermediate states.) - Secondly we introduce a dual to the concatenation operation $L \cdot \langle T_1,\dots,T_n \rangle$, in a similar way as ∩ is a dual to ∪. Given an ω-language L and tree languages $T_1,\dots,T_n$, we say that a path through a tree t matches L if a sequence of values from D_n can be attached to the nodes of the path such that for the resulting sequence $\alpha \in (\Sigma \times \{l,r\} \times D_n)^\omega$ we have $t \in \{\alpha\} \cdot (T_1,\dots,T_n)$. Then $L \cdot \langle T_1,\dots,T_n \rangle$ contains all trees in which there exists a path matching L . Define now the set $L\circ(T_1,\ldots,T_n)$ to be the set of trees in which <u>all</u> paths match L . Note that tree concatenation $L\cdot(T_1,\ldots,T_n)$ and its dual $L\circ(T_1,\ldots,T_n)$ are monotone in all arguments $L,T_1,\ldots,T_n$. - We shall use the following lemma concerning the operations $\circ$ and ^{nc}:

Lemma 5.7

(a) If L is ω-regular (resp. ω-star-free) and $T_1,\ldots,T_n$ are p-regular (resp. p-star-free), then $L\circ(T_1,\ldots,T_n)$ is p-regular (resp. p-star-free).

(b) If $T_1,\ldots,T_n$ define a partition of T_Σ, then
$\sim(L\cdot(T_1,\ldots,T_n)) = (\sim L)\circ(T_1,\ldots,T_n)$ and
$\sim(L\circ(T_1,\ldots,T_n)) = (\sim L)\cdot(T_1,\ldots,T_n)$.

(c) For $\bar{T} = (T_1,\ldots,T_n)$:
$L^{nc}\cdot\bar{T} \subset (L\cdot\bar{T})^{nc}$,
$L\cdot(T_1,\ldots,T_i^{nc},\ldots,T_n) \subset (L\cdot\bar{T})^{nc}$,
$L^{nc}\circ\bar{T} \subset (L\circ\bar{T})^{nc}$,
$L\circ(T_1,\ldots,T_i^{nc},\ldots,T_n) \subset (L\circ\bar{T})^{nc}$,
$T_1^{nc} \cup T_2 \subset (T_1 \cup T_2)^{nc}$,
$T_1^{nc} \cap T_2 \subset (T_1 \cap T_2)^{nc}$.

Now the proof of 5.3 can be completed as follows. Consider a p-regular expression defining a noncounting set T_0. In a first-step, rewrite the expression such that essentially only the operations $\cup, \cap, \cdot, \circ$ are used. For this, replace (proceeding from outside) in every subexpression $L(T_1,\ldots,T_n)$ the sequence $(T_1,\ldots,T_n)$ by the sequence $(S_1,\ldots,S_k)$ with $k = 2^n$, where the S_j are the intersections $(\sim)\ T_1 \cap\ldots\cap (\sim)\ T_n$. It is easy to adjust the ω-language L to a new ω-language L' such that $L\cdot(T_1,\ldots,T_n) = L'\cdot(S_1,\ldots,S_k)$. Now push negations inside as far as possible (i.e. until applied to an ω-language), using the de Morgan laws and 5.7(b). We obtain an expression which is generated from T and ω-regular sets by the operations $\cup, \cap, \cdot, \circ$. - In a second step, replace (proceeding from inside) any subexpression which defines a counting language L by (an expression for) the set L^{nc}. By monotonicity of $\cup, \cap, \cdot, \circ$ and by 5.7(c) we have for the resulting tree language T' that $T_0 \subset T' \subset T_0^{nc}$. Since $T_0 = T_0^{nc}$ by assumption, we obtain $T_0 = T'$. After elimination of all counting ω-languages arising from subexpressions, we finally can transform the constructed expression, by successive application of Theorem 2.2 and 5.7(a), into an equivalent p-star-free expression.

6. An application to branching time logic

It is known that propositional linear time logic PTL [Pn 77] is expressively equivalent to first-order logic over $(\omega, <)$ [GPSS 80]. The extension ETL of PTL by "automaton operators" leads to the ω-regular sequence sets [W 83]. So Theorem 2.2 implies that for an ETL-formula it can be decided whether it is equivalent to a PTL-formula. We give a brief outline of a similar result in branching time logic, concerning the systems computation tree logic CTL* [EH 86] and extended computation tree logic ECTL* suggested in [VW 84]. If the interpretation of formulas is confined to <u>binary</u> trees only, i.e. to structures $(\{l,r\}^*, <, (P_a)_{a\in\Sigma})$, then CTL*, respectively ECTL*, has been shown to be equivalent to path logic, respectively chain logic [Ha 86, HT 87]. More generally, we consider (E)CTL*-formulas over R-generable models in the sense of [EH 86]. Such a model can be represented by a (countably branching) tree structure $(\omega^*, <, (P_a)_{a\in\Sigma})$ where S is the successor relation in the tree of finite sequences of natural numbers, $<$ the corresponding prefix relation, and $P_a \subset \omega^*$. Results similar to Theorems 4.2(a) and 5.3(a) are obtained when a formalism of regular-like expressions is used in which the ω-languages L appearing in concatenation steps $L\cdot(T_1,\ldots,T_n)$ are from a "coarser" alphabet. Namely, a path P through a tree is described by a sequence $\alpha \in (\Sigma \times P(D_n))^\omega$ (where $P(D_n)$ is the power set of D_n); $\alpha(i) = (a,D)$ indicates that the i-th node p of P has label a and that D is the set of those d_j such that some subtree, rooted at a successor of p, belongs to T_j. This reflects the fact that the successors of a node are not ordered and that successors with a given property cannot be counted beyond cardinality 1. From the analogue to 5.3(a) it follows that for ECTL*-formulas the equivalence to CTL*-formulas can be decided effectively.

7. Problems

We end the paper by listing some directions for further work.

(1) Find applications to further systems of modal logic or program logic.

(2) Connect other properties of monoids (than "group-free") with definability notions in chain logic. Take, for instance, those monoids which are known to characterize the locally testable languages; for the step from finite words to infinite words the results of [Pec 86] can be used.

(3) Characterize chain- (path - etc.) definability by tree automata.

(4) Show that chain-, path-, finite chain-, and first-order definability are all decidable properties relative to the full monadic second-order language over the binary tree.

References

[A 85] A. Arnold, A syntactic congruence for rational ω-languages, Theor. Comput. Sci. 39 (1985), 333-335.

[B 60] J.R. Büchi, Weak second-order arithmetic and finite automata, Z. math Logik u. Grundl. Math. 6 (1960), 66-92.

[B 62] J.R. Büchi, On a desision method in restricted second-order arithmetic, in: Proc. Int. Congr. Logic, Meth. and Phil. of Sci. 1960, Stanford Univ. Press, Stanford, Calif. 1962, 1-11.

[EH 86] E.A. Emerson, J.Y. Halpern, "Sometimes" and "Not Never" Revisited: On branching versus linear time temporal logic, J. Ass. Comput. Mach. 33 (1986), 151-178.

[FL 79] M. Fischer, R. Ladner, Propositional Dynamic Logic of Regular Programs, J. of Comp. and System Sci. 18(2) (1979), 194-211.

[GPSS 80] D. Gabbay, A. Pnueli, S. Shelah, J. Stavi, On the temporal analysis of fairness, 7th ACM Symp. on Principles of Progr. Languages (1980), 163-173.

[GS 83] Y. Gurevich, S. Shelah, Rabin's uniformization problem, J. Symb. Logic 48 (1983), 1105-1119.

[HKP 82] D. Harel, D. Kozen, R. Parikh, Process Logic: Expressiveness, Decidability, Completeness, J.of Comput. and System Sci. 25 (1982), 144-170.

[Ha 86] T. Hafer, On the expressive completeness of CTL*, Schriften zur Informatik und Angewandten Mathematik Nr. 123, RWTH Aachen, Dez. 1986.

[HT 87] T. Hafer, W. Thomas, Computation Tree Logic CTL* and path quantifiers in the monadic theory of the binary tree, to appear in Proc. 14th ICALP.

[K 82] D. Kozen, Results on the propositional μ-calculus, in: Proc 9th ICALP, LNCS 140 (1982), 348-359.

[L 66] H. Läuchli, A decision procedure for the weak second order theory of linear order, in: "Contributions to Mathematical Logic, Proc. Logic Coll. Hannover 1966", (H.A. Schmidt et al, Eds), North-Holland, Amsterdam 1968, 189-197.

[La 77] R.E. Ladner, Application of model-theoretic games to discrete linear orders and finite automata, Inf. Contr. 33 (1977), 281-303.

[McNP 71] R. McNaughton, S. Papert, Counter-Free Automata, MIT-Press, Cambridge Mass. 1971.

[Pec 86] J.P. Pécuchet, Etude syntaxique des parties reconnaissables de mots infinis, in: Proc. 13th ICALP, LNCS 226 (1986), 294-303.

[P 84] D. Perrin, Recent results on automata and infinite words, in: Math. Found. of Comput. Sci. 1984, LNCS 176 (1984), 134-148.

[Pn 77] A. Pnueli, The temporal logic of programs, Proc. 18th IEEE Symp. Found. of Comput. Sci. (Providence, R.I.) 1977, 46-57.

[R 69] M.O. Rabin, Decidability of second-order theories and automata on infinite trees, Trans. Amer. Math. Soc. 141 (1969), 1-35.

[R 70] M.O. Rabin, Weakly definable relations and special automata, Proc. Symp. Math. Logic and Found. Set Theory (Y. Bar-Hillel, Ed.) North-Holland , 1970), 1-23.

[S 65] M.P. Schützenberger, On monoids having only trivial subgroups, Inf. Contr. 8 (1965), 190-194.

[Sh 75] S. Shelah, The monadic theory of order, Ann. of Math. 102 (1972), 379-419.

[T 79] W. Thomas, Star-free regular sets of ω-sequences, Inf. Contr. 42 (1979), 148-156.

[T 84] W. Thomas, Logical aspects in the study of tree languages, in: Ninth Coll. on Trees in Algebra and Programming (B. Courcelle, Ed.), Cambridge Univ. Press 1984, 31-49.

[VW 84] M.Y. Vardi, P. Wolper, Yet another process logic, in: "Logics of Programs", LNCS 164 (1984), 501-512.

[Wo 83] P. Wolper, Temporal logic can be more expressive, Inf. Contr. 56 (1983), 72-99.

Full Abstraction and Expressive Completeness for FP

Joseph Y. Halpern
Edward L. Wimmers

IBM Almaden Research Center
650 Harry Rd.
San Jose, CA 95120-6099
Email: Halpern@ibm.com, Wimmers@ibm.com (ARPANET)

Abstract: We consider issues related to the expressive power of FP. In particular, we consider whether a number of variants of FP are fully abstract and expressively complete. By considering these variants, we obtain a better understanding of what is required of a language and semantics in order to guarantee full abstraction and expressive completeness.

1. Introduction

In a sequence of previous papers [HW1,HW2,HW3] we considered the question: "What does it mean to have enough rewrite rules?" in the context of the functional programming language FP84 (henceforth called FP), which extends the FP originally defined by Backus [Ba]. We suggested a number of criteria by which to judge this question, and showed that with respect to all of these criteria, there indeed were enough rewrite rules in FP. The next obvious question, and the one we address in this paper, is "Do we have enough primitive functions?"

In one sense the answer is "yes". We do know that FP has enough primitive functions to allow us to *encode* all recursive functions on the integers (cf. [Wi]), but we want more, since we want to manipulate the objects in our domain, not just the integers. We consider here two other well-known criteria from the literature that deal with the question of having enough primitive functions. The first of these is called *full abstraction.* For a langugage defined by rewrite rules, we say that two terms are *behaviorally equivalent* if, roughly speaking, they rewrite to the same normal form in all contexts. A denotational semantics is called *fully abstract* with respect to a language if behavioral equivalence of terms in the language coincides with denotational equivalence. Full abstraction is of interest because it allows one to prove the operational equivalence (or inequivalence) of two expressions simply by proving the equality (or lack of it) of their meanings. Thus purely semantic reasoning allows us to deduce operational facts. The second (generally more powerful) criterion of language expressiveness is *expressive completeness.* A language is *expressively complete* if every "computable" element in the semantic domain is definable in the language.

In a seminal paper [Pl], Plotkin examines these criteria in the context of the programming language PCF (which is based on LCF, Scott's *logic of computable functions* [Mi]). Plotkin shows that what is perhaps the most natural denotational semantics for PCF is not fully abstract. However, he shows that if we add a parallel conditional to PCF, the semantic domain is fully abstract with respect to the resulting language. Moreover, he shows that by further augmenting PCF with a recursive "existential" operator, the resulting language is expressively complete with respect to the domain.

When we consider full abstraction and expressive completeness for FP, a number of issues arise that are not present in PCF. We hope that by understanding these issues better, we can eventually construct a general theory that

CH2464-6/87/0000/0257$01.00 © 1987 IEEE

relates the operational behavior of a programming language and its denotational semantics.

To understand the subtleties that arise in FP, we must review a little of its syntax and semantics. In FP we can define sequences of elements and manipulate them. We allow operations at both ends of a sequence. For example, we can append an element to the left-hand end of a sequence or to the right-hand end and remove the first element or last element of a sequence. FP is also powerful enough to allow us to define infinite sequences of elements. The fact that we can manipulate sequences from either end allows us to define sequences that are infinite to the right (such as $\langle a, a, a, \ldots \rangle$) and infinite to the left (such as $\langle \ldots, a, a, a \rangle$).

To deal with this semantically, we allow a * to appear in sequences. Intuitively, an expression like $\langle a, * \rangle$ is an *approximation* to any sequence whose first element is a (where we say that x approximates y if $x \leq_I y$ for some appropriate partial order $\leq_I$ on the elements of the domain). Thus $\langle a, * \rangle$ approximates all of the following: $\langle a \rangle$, $\langle a, \bot \rangle$, $\langle a, a, a \rangle$, $\langle a, *, a \rangle$ (where, as usual, $\bot$ is a bottom element which approximates all other elements). Similarly, $\langle *, a \rangle$ is an approximation to any sequence whose last element is a. It is easy to see that both $\langle a \rangle$ and $\langle a, *, a \rangle$ are upper bounds for the set $\{\langle a, * \rangle, \langle *, a \rangle\}$, and in fact they are minimal upper bounds for this set. However, this set has no *sup* (least upper bound), since $\langle a \rangle$ and $\langle a, *, a \rangle$ are incomparable. Thus, the semantic domain for FP is not *consistently complete*: it is not the case that two elements with an upper bound necessarily have a least upper bound. It can be shown that we lose consistent completeness exactly because the * may appear anywhere in a sequence.

This lack of consistent completeness has surprising implications for the expressive power of FP. For example, consider the apply-to-all function *apall*, which, when given a function f and a sequence $\langle a_1, \ldots, a_n \rangle$, applies the function f to all the elements in the sequence, producing $\langle f{:}a_1, \ldots, f{:}a_n \rangle$. (This is much like the LISP mapcar.) We can show that *apall* is not definable in FP. Intuitively, the problem is due to the fact that * may appear in the middle of a sequence in FP, so we do not know *a priori* when to apply f to the left-hand elements of the sequence, and when to apply it to the right-hand elements of the sequence.

On the other hand, consider FP1, the variant of FP which allows operations only on the left-hand elements of sequences. While the difference between FP and FP1 seems innocuous, it does have some surprising consequences. For one thing, since we can append only to the left-hand end of sequences, the * can occur only at the right-hand end of a sequence. It follows that the semantic domain for FP1 *is* consistently complete. Moreover, we can show that apply-to-all is definable in FP1; intuitively, this is because we just have to work from the left-hand end of the sequence.

These differences between FP1 and FP persist when we consider full abstraction and expressive completeness. For FP1 we can prove results analogous to those of Plotkin. We can show that FP1 is not fully abstract, but by adding a parallel conditional we get full abstraction, and by further adding an existential operator we also get expressive completeness. Our proofs are based on those of Plotkin, although the proof for FP1 presents new complexities since FP1 has greater structure than PCF, and, unlike PCF, is an untyped language. However, the straightforward analogue of these results for FP provably fails.

These results lead us to look for extensions to FP with four properties that we can express informally as: natural syntax, natural rewrite rules, enough rewrite rules, and reasonable expressive power. While it is hard to make precise exactly what natural syntax and semantics is, a minimal criterion is that the set of expressions be recursive and that the set of rewrite rules be recursively enumerable. We can judge whether the language has enough rewrite rules by seeing if we have *observable completeness* or *strong completeness* in the sense of [HW1,HW2,HW3] (these notions are reviewed in Section 2). Finally, reasonable expressive power for us will be either full abstraction or expressive completeness.

It seems that consistent completeness in the semantic domain together with a certain amount of parallelism in the language (such as a parallel conditional) is sufficient for full abstraction and expressive completeness. While we do not yet have a general theory in which to make this statement precise, we can offer evidence for the claim. Consider NFP, the nondeterministic variant of FP that results by adding **union** to FP, where **union**: $<x, y>$ rewrites (nondeterministically) to either **x** or **y**. We can easily modify our semantic domain to handle nondeterminism, and the resulting domain is consistently complete. Since elements in the domain are actually sets and the ordering relation is just the subset relation, the sup of any two elements is always their union. In NFP, the nondeterminism gives us almost enough parallelism to prove full abstraction and expressive completeness. However, there is a precise sense in which we still cannot distinguish between the elements $<\bot, *>$ and $<*, \bot>$. Once we add operators into the language that let us distinguish between these two elements, we can prove full abstraction and expressive completeness.

Proving full abstraction for NFP turns out to be much easier than proving full abstraction for FP1. The reason is that taking sups is so much easier in NFP. The sup of two elements is simply their union. Indeed, being able to take sups seems to be a more fundamental condition than consistent completeness when trying to prove full abstraction and expressive completeness. The insights gained in studying NFP enable us to construct extensions of FP that are fully abstract and expressively complete, and yet have the same domain as FP (and so, in particular, have a semantic domain which is not consistently complete). These extensions, however, make heavy use of a particular way of encoding finite elements in the semantic domain as *observable* elements (those obtained by starting with atoms and closing off under the sequence operator).

The rest of the paper is organized as follows. In the next section we review the syntax and semantics of FP and some results regarding completeness of rewrite rules from [HW1,HW2,HW3]. In Section 3 we prove that apply-to-all is not definable in FP, although it is definable in FP1. In Section 4 we define and discuss the notions of full abstraction and expressive completeness. In Section 5 we show that FP and FP1 are not fully abstract. In Section 6 we show how to extend FP1 to get a language that is fully abstract and expressively complete. In Section 7 we show that by adding a nondeterministic **union** construct to FP as well as constructs that distinguish $<\bot, *>$ and $<*, \bot>$, the resulting language is fully abstract and expressively complete. Adding **union** to FP forces us to extend the semantic domain to accomodate nondeterminism. In Section 8 we examine fully abstract and expressively complete extensions of FP that leave the semantic domain unchanged. We conclude in Section 9 with some discussion of the general issues involved in obtaining fully abstract and expressively complete languages and domains.

2. A review of FP: Syntax, Semantics, and Rewrite Rules

FP has a very simple syntax. We assume the existence of a finite set $\mathscr{A}$ of *atoms*,[1] which includes T and F (intuitively, *true* and *false*).

---

1 We take the set of atoms to be finite here for notational convenience. All of our results go through without change provided that the set of atoms is *finitely generated*; i.e. there is a finite set of atoms $\mathscr{A}'$ and a finite set of primitive functions $\mathscr{F}'$ such that all atoms can be obtained by repeatedly applying the primitive functions in $\mathscr{F}'$ to the atoms in $\mathscr{A}'$. For example, we could include the positive integers in our set of atoms as long as we had a successor function S, with the rewrite rule $S{:}n \rightarrow n+1$.

We also assume the existence of a set $\mathscr{F}$ of primitive function symbols which is disjoint from $\mathscr{A}$. For now we take the set $\mathscr{F}$ to be {**al, first, tl, ar, last, tr, null, cond, comp, cons, K, id, apply, eqatom, isatom, isseq, isfunc**}. Intuitively, **al** (which stands for *append left*), appends an element to the left end of a sequence; **tl** takes the tail of a sequence by removing the first element, and **first** returns the first element of a sequence; **ar, tr,** and **last** are the corresponding operators that work on the right-hand end of a sequence; **null** tests whether a sequence is empty; **cond** is a conditional; **comp** is the composition function; **cons** takes a sequence of functions $<f_1,...,f_n>$ as an argument and returns the function that, when applied to x, returns the sequence $<f_1:x,...,f_n:x>$; **K** is the familiar combinator from combinatory calculus that converts x to the constant function that always returns x; **id** is the identity function; **apply**, when given a pair of elements, applies the first to the second (so that we have the rewrite rule **apply:** $<f, x> \rightarrow f:x$); **eqatom** tests for equality between atoms (and is undefined if either of its arguments is not an atom); finally, **isatom** (resp. **isseq, isfunc**) tests whether its argument is an atom (resp., sequence, function). We remark that the FP used in [HW1,HW2,HW3] did not have **eqatom, isatom, isseq,** and **isfunc**, but there is no difficulty including them in the language and defining appropriate rewrite rules for them.

Definition 2.1. The *FP expressions* are the least set containing $\mathscr{A} \cup \mathscr{F}$ and closed under:

1. The formation of sequences: if $x_1, ..., x_n$ are FP expressions (for $n \geq 0$), then $<x_1, ..., x_n>$ is also an FP expression.
2. Application of expressions: if x_1 and x_2 are FP expressions, then $(x_1:x_2)$ is also an FP expression.

We get variants of FP by adding or removing elements from the set $\mathscr{F}$ of primitive function symbols. In particular, FP1 is obtained by removing **ar, tr** and **last.**

We provide a denotational semantics for FP as usual by defining a domain D^* and a mapping μ from FP expressions to D^*. In order to deal with infinite sequences in FP, we have elements of the form $\langle x_1, ..., x_m, *, x_{m+1}, ..., x_n \rangle$ in the domain. Intuitively, * is a placeholder for some (as yet unknown) sequence of items. An infinite sequence such as $\langle a, a, a, ... \rangle$ is the limit or sup of the set $\{\langle a, * \rangle, \langle a, a, * \rangle, ...\}$. Our domain D^* satisfies the domain equation $D = \mathscr{A} + Seqs(D) + (D \rightarrow D)$ where $Seqs(D)$ contains all sequences (including those potentially infinite from both the left and right) whose elements are all members of D. We would like to construct D^* using standard techniques of domain theory, but any domain that is the solution to a domain equation using the standard constructors $+$, $\times$, and $\rightarrow$ is consistently complete [SP]. Since, as we observed in the introduction, D^* is not consistently complete, we cannot construct it is this way. In order to describe our construction precisely, we need to recall a few standard technical definitions.

Definition 2.2. A *domain* $(D, \leq)$ consists of a set D and a reflexive, transitive ordering $\leq$. Intuitively, $x \leq y$ if y has at least as much "information" as x. A subset X of D is *directed* iff $x_1, x_2 \in X$ implies that there exists $x_3 \in X$ such that $x_1 \leq x_3$ and $x_2 \leq x_3$. $(D, \leq)$ is *complete* if every directed set in D has a sup in D. If X is a directed set with a sup x, we denote this by $x \in \sqcup X$. (Note that there may be more than one sup of X, since $\leq$ is not necessarily antisymmetric. However, if both x and x' are sups of X, then $x \equiv x'$, that is, $x \leq x'$ and $x' \leq x$.) A function $f:D \rightarrow D$ is *continuous* iff, whenever X is a directed subset of D with a sup x', then $\{f(x) \mid x \in X\}$ is a directed set and has $f(x')$ as a sup.

We construct D^* in stages. We first construct a sequence of domains $D_0, D_1, ...$, where D_0 consists of $\perp$ and, for each atom $a \in \mathscr{A}$, a corresponding *atomic item a*, and D_{n+1} consists of D_n together with all the continuous functions from

D_n to itself (these are called *function items*), and all sequences of the form $\langle x_1, ..., x_k \rangle$, where $x_i \in D_n \cup \{*\}$ and at most one $x_i = *$. An element of the latter form is called a *sequence item*, and if it contains no *, it is further called a *sequence of definite length.*

Let D be the union of the D_n's. We can define an ordering $\leq_I$ on D in a straightforward way. It turns out that D is not quite appropriate for our semantic domain, principally because it is not complete. For example, $\{\langle a, * \rangle, \langle a, a, * \rangle, \langle a, a, a, * \rangle, ...\}$ is a directed set in D which has no sup in D. Roughly speaking, D^* is the *completion* of D, that is, the domain that results by adding limits of sequences to D. The elements of D^* turn out to be subsets of D (just as we can view a real number as the set of rationals less than it). We can embed D into D^* by identifying an element d of D with the subset $\{d' \in D \mid d' \leq_I d\}$. The elements of D^* are ordered by the subset relation, which makes D^* into a complete partial order (thus every directed subset $\mathscr{X}$ of D^* has a unique sup, which we denote $\sqcup\mathscr{X}$). Further details of the domain construction can be found in [HW3]. The construction of the semantic domain for FP1, which we call $D1^*$, is identical except that we restrict sequence items so that the * can only occur at the right-hand end of a sequence. The semantic function mapping FP1 expressions to $D1^*$ is denoted μ_1.

Computation in FP proceeds by using rewrite rules to transform expressions. The rewrite rules are given in Appendix A. In the rules for **eqatom, isatom, isseq,** and **isfunc**, we say that x *looks like a sequence* if x is of the form $<x_1,...,x_n>$, **al:** $<y, z>$, or **ar:** $<y, z>$ and x *looks like a function* if x is either a primitive function symbol or of the form **K**:y, **comp:** $<f_1, f_2>$, or **cons**:z, where z looks like a sequence. Note that we use $x \rightarrow y$ to mean that "x can be rewritten to y in one step"; we take $\rightarrow^*$ to be the reflexive, transitive closure of the $\rightarrow$ relation. The set of rewrite rules for FP1 consists of all the rewrite rules for FP that do not mention **tr**, **ar**, or **last**.

We want the rewrite rules to preserve the meanings of expressions. Fortunately, we have carefully defined our semantics so that the rewrite rules are sound. We have:

Theorem 2.3. [HW3] *If* $x \rightarrow^* y$, *then* $\mu(x) = \mu(y)$.

Besides soundness, we also want to know that we have in some sense *enough* rewrite rules. This issue is investigated in detail in [HW1,HW2,HW3], so we just briefly review the results here that we need.

We call an FP expression *observable* if it is either an atom or a sequence $<x_1,...,x_n>$, where the x_i are observable. To each observable expression there corresponds an *observable item*, which is obtained by replacing <, >, and boldface wherever they occur by ≺, ≻, and italics. Given an observable item x, let x^e be the observable expression to which it corresponds. In [HW1,HW3] it is shown that

Theorem 2.4. [HW3] *If* x *is an expression such that* $\mu(x)$ *is an observable item, then* $x \rightarrow^* \mu(x)^e$.

For example, if we have an expression x such that $\mu(x) = \langle a, \langle b \rangle \rangle$, then it follows from Theorem 2.4 that $x \rightarrow^* <a, <b>>$. This result is extended in [HW3]. Intuitively, we want to show that if we have an expression whose meaning is an atom, then we can rewrite it to that atom, if its meaning is a sequence, then we can rewrite it to an expression that looks like a sequence, and if its meaning is a function, then we can rewrite it to an expression that looks like a function. These intuitions motivate the following definition.

Definition 2.5. An FP expression x is *transparent* iff

1. if $\mu(x) = a$ for some atomic item a, then $x = \mathbf{a}$,
2. if $\mu(x) = \langle w_1, ..., w_n \rangle$, then x looks like a sequence; if $\mu(x)$ is a sequence item of definite length, then x is of the form $<y_1,...,y_n>$, and

3. if $\mu(x)$ is a function item, then x looks like a function.

Note that if $\mu(x) = \perp$, then x is vacuously transparent and that once an expression is transparent, further rewriting cannot destroy transparency.

The proof of the following two results can be found in [HW3] (see also [HW2]). Recall a term is in *normal form* iff no rewrite rules apply.

Theorem 2.6. *If* x *is an FP expression in normal form then* x *is transparent.*

Definition 2.7. A set of rewrite rules is *strongly complete* if for all FP expressions x there is a transparent expression y such that $x \twoheadrightarrow^* y$.

Theorem 2.8. *The FP rewrite rules are strongly complete.*

3. The undefinability of apply-to-all

We begin our investigation of the question "Are there enough primitive functions in FP?" by considering apply-to-all. This is a function we would like to have in practice, and it is definable in the version of FP originally considered by Backus [Ba]. We show that apply-to-all is not definable in FP, but is definable in FP1. The proof will show the subtle difficulties caused by the presence of two-sided sequences in FP.

Let *apall* be the function on D^* such that

$$apall{:}f{:}\prec x_1, \dots, x_n \succ = \prec f{:}x_1, \dots, f{:}x_n \succ,$$

where we take $f{:}\ast = \ast$.

We take *apall1* to be the function in $D1^*$ with precisely the same definition. It is not hard to give an FP1 expression **apall1** such that $\mu_1(\mathbf{apall1}) = apall1$. We define **apall1** so that

$$\mathbf{apall1} = \lambda f, x.(\mathbf{cond}{:} < \mathbf{null}{:}x, < >, \mathbf{al}{:} < f{:}(\mathbf{first}{:}x), \mathbf{apall1}{:}f{:}(\mathbf{tl}{:}x) > >).$$

Using standard techniques for expressing lambda abstraction and fixpoints in FP, we can find an FP1 expression with this property.

Note that it is not the case that $\mu(\mathbf{apall1}) = apall$. Intuitively, since **apall1** works on a sequence starting with the left end, we can show, for example, that $\mu(\mathbf{apall1{:}id}){:}\prec \ast, a \succ = \prec \perp, \ast \succ$ rather than $\prec \ast, a \succ$. As we now show, this is in fact an unavoidable problem; there is no FP expression whose meaning is *apall*.

We proceed by first showing that FP has a more fundamental lack of expressive power. It is impossible to distinguish $\prec \perp, \ast \succ$ from $\prec \ast, \perp \succ$ in FP. More precisely, let *ef* and *el* (for "exists a first element" and "exists a last element") be functions on D^* such that:

$$ef{:}x = \begin{cases} T \text{ if } \prec \perp, \ast \succ \leq_I x \\ \perp \text{ otherwise} \end{cases}$$

$$el{:}x = \begin{cases} T \text{ if } \prec \ast, \perp \succ \leq_I x \\ \perp \text{ otherwise.} \end{cases}$$

Theorem 3.1. *There is no FP expression whose meaning is ef or el.*

Proof. Our first step is to define a relation $\mapsto$ between FP expressions. Intuitively, if $x \mapsto y$, then x and y are indistinguishable in their operational behavior.

Definition 3.2. $x \mapsto y$ is defined by induction on the structure of x:

1. If x is an atom or primitive function symbol, then $x \mapsto y$ iff $x = y$.
2. If $x = < x_1, \dots, x_n >$, then $x \mapsto y$ iff $y = < y_1, \dots, y_n >$ and $x_i \mapsto y_i$ for $i = 1, \dots, n$.
3. If $x = x_0{:}x_1$, then $x \mapsto y$ iff at least one of the following conditions holds:
   a. $\mu(x) = \mu(y) = \perp$
   b. $y = y_0{:}y_1$, $x_0 \mapsto y_0$, and $x_1 \mapsto y_1$
   c. $x = \mathbf{al}{:} < x_2, x_3 >$, $y = \mathbf{ar}{:} < y_2, y_3 >$, and $\mu(x_2) = \mu(x_3) = \mu(y_2) = \mu(y_3) = \perp$.

The interesting clause here is 3(c). To understand it, note that from the semantics of FP it follows that $\mu(\mathbf{al}){:}\prec \perp, \perp \succ = \prec \perp, \ast \succ$, while $\mu(\mathbf{ar}){:}\prec \perp, \perp \succ = \prec \ast, \perp \succ$. Intuitively, at a semantic level, clause 3(c) says at a term whose meaning is $\prec \ast, \perp \succ$ is operationally indistinguishable from one whose meaning is $\prec \perp, \ast \succ$. Of course, **ar** is not even part of the syntax of FP1, so clause 3(c) does not make sense for FP1.

The following lemma, whose proof proceeds by a relatively straightforward analysis of the FP rewrite rules, makes precise the intuition that if $x \mapsto y$, then x and y are indistinguishable with respect to their operational behavior:

Proposition 3.3. *If* $x \mapsto y$ *and* $x \to^* x'$, *then there exists an FP expression* y' *such that* $x' \mapsto y'$ *and* $y \to^* y'$.

Proof. It clearly suffices to prove the result in the case $x \to x'$; the result if $x \to^* x'$ follows by an easy induction on the length of the reduction sequence. It is easy to see by induction on the structure of x that it suffices to prove the result in the case that $x \to x'$ is an instance of an FP rewrite rule. So the result follows by checking it for each of the rewrite rules. The details are fairly straightforward and are left to the full paper. ■

Returning to the proof of Theorem 3.1, suppose there were an expression **ef** in FP such that $\mu(\mathbf{ef}) = ef$. Fix Ω to be an expression such that $\mu(\Omega) = \bot$ (for example, we can take Ω to be a:a). Recall that $\mu(\mathbf{al}:<\Omega,\Omega>) = \prec\bot,*\succ$ and $\mu(\mathbf{ar}:<\Omega,\Omega>) = \prec *,\bot\succ$. Thus we must have $\mu(\mathbf{ef}:(\mathbf{al}:<\Omega,\Omega>)) = T$ and $\mu(\mathbf{ef}:(\mathbf{ar}:<\Omega,\Omega>)) = \bot$. By definition of $\mapsto$, we have $\mathbf{ef}:(\mathbf{al}:<\Omega,\Omega>) \mapsto \mathbf{ef}:(\mathbf{ar}:<\Omega,\Omega>)$. By Theorem 2.8, we get that $\mathbf{ef}:(\mathbf{al}:<\Omega,\Omega>) \to^* \mathrm{T}$. Thus, by Proposition 3.3, $\mathbf{ef}:(\mathbf{ar}:<\Omega,\Omega>) \to^* \mathrm{T}$. But this contradicts the soundness of the FP rewrite rules. Thus **ef** is not definable in FP; a similar proof shows **el** is not definable either. ■

Corollary 3.4. *There is no FP expression whose meaning is apall.*

Proof. Suppose there were an FP expression **apall** with $\mu(\mathbf{apall}) = apall$. Then **ef** would be definable as λx.first:(**apall**:(**K**:**T**):x), contradicting Theorem 3.1. (Recall that μ(**K**:**T**) is the constant function which always returns *T*.) ■

The techniques of Theorem 3.1 go through to show that **ef** and **el** are not definable in a number of extensions of FP we consider. Thus it also follows that **apall** is not definable in these extensions. While this result is of technical interest (and will be used to show that it is necessary to add **ef** and **el** in order to obtain full abstraction and expressive completeness in some of the variants of FP that we consider), it does not seem to get at the essence of why **apall** is not definable. Intuitively, the real problem is that if we consider an expression such as **apall**:f:x, where μ(x) is a sequence item that may have a * somewhere in the middle, we do not know when to apply f to the left or the right end of x.

Let FP^+ be the result of augmenting FP with **ef** and **el**. Although the proof technique Theorem 3.1 now fails, the intuition that we cannot guess the location of the * can still be used to show that **apall** is not definable in FP^+.

Theorem 3.5. *There is no* FP^+ *expression whose meaning is* **apall**.

Proof. The idea is to show that there is no FP^+ expression g such that g:(**K**:**T**) acts like **apall**:(**K**:**T**). In particular, it must do the wrong thing when applied either an expression whose meaning is $\prec\bot,*\succ$ or to an expression whose meaning is $\prec *,\bot\succ$. (Note this is so even though we have both **ef** and **el** in the language.)

We capture this intuition by further extending FP^+ to EFP^+ by adding (among other things) a new symbol **oneof**. We then define two semantic functions μ' and μ'', both extending μ. We define $\mu'(\mathbf{oneof}) = \prec\bot,*\succ$ and $\mu''(\mathbf{oneof}) = \prec *,\bot\succ$. Finally, we show that in a precise sense, rewriting in EFP^+ is sound with respect to both μ' and μ''. However, this could not be the case if **apall** were definable in FP^+. We leave details to the full paper. ■

We remark that the techniques used to prove Theorem 3.5 can also be used to prove that other functions such as *cat* (the function that concatenates two sequences) and *parallel or* (see Section 5) are not FP definable.

4. Full abstraction and expressive completeness

In this section we formally define the notions of full abstraction and expressive completeness for FP and its variants.

As usual, we say a *context* is an expression with a "hole" in it. If C is a context, we write C[x] for the result of filling the hole in context C by x. For example, in FP, if C is the context al: <__, <a>>, then C[b] is al: <b, <a>>.

When we talk about full abstraction, it is really with respect to a given domain and language. In the standard definition of full abstraction (for example, the one given in [Pl]), the language is typed. In particular, there is a type prog that is the type of programs. In this case, we say two terms are *behaviorally equivalent*, and write x≈y, if in all contexts C of type prog the expressions C[x] and C[y] have the same operational behavior. (That is, C[x] rewrites to a normal form iff C[y] rewrites to a normal form, and if one rewrites to a normal form, they both rewrite to the same one.) A fully abstract language is one where x≈y iff $\nu(x) = \nu(y)$, where ν is the semantic function for the language. Thus, full abstraction says that two objects are semantically equal iff they are behaviorally equivalent.

Now FP and its variants are untyped, so there is no exact analogue to expressions of type prog. However, we can get an analogue by considering expressions whose meaning is an atom. More formally, we define full abstraction for any of the variants F of FP considered in this paper as follows.

Definition 4.1. Let F be a variant of FP, E its domain, and ν the semantic function that associates with each expression in F an element of E. Given a context C and an expression x, we say C is an *atomic context* for x if ν(C[x]) is an atomic item. We say two F expressions x and y are *behaviorally equivalent*, and again write x≈y, if (a) for all contexts C, C is an atomic context for x iff C is an atomic context for y, and (b) if C is an atomic context for x, then ν(C[x]) = ν(C[y]). Finally, we say that *F is fully abstract with respect to E* if for all F expressions x and y, we have x≈y iff $\nu(x) = \nu(y)$.

Note that by Theorem 2.4, for FP we have that if μ(C[x]) = a for some atomic item a, then C[x] $\to^*$ a. Thus, if x≈y, then in all atomic contexts both x and y rewrite to the same normal form. Analogues to Theorem 2.4 also hold for all the variants of FP we consider, so the same remark holds for them as well.

The intuition behind the notion of expressive completeness is that all computable elements are definable. But what is a computable element? Following Plotkin [Pl], we take the computable elements to be the sups of recursively enumerable sets of finite elements. To make this precise, we need a few more definitions.

Definition 4.2. An element x of a domain $(E, \leq)$ is finite if whenever $x \leq \sqcup Y$ for some directed subset Y of E, then $x \leq y$ for some $y \in Y$.

In [HW3], the finite elements of D^* are completely characterized. We briefly review this characterization here. The only difficulty comes in characterizing the finite function items. Roughly speaking, these are "step functions" of the form $[x_1 \to y_1, ..., x_k \to y_k]$. We define $[x \to y]{:}z = y$ if $x \leq_I z$, and $\perp$ otherwise. We extend this definition to the general case by taking $[x_1 \to y_1, ..., x_k \to y_k]{:}z = y_i$ if x_i is the "best approximation" to z among $x_1, ..., x_k$. The following definition makes this notion precise.

Definition 4.3. *$M \subseteq D_n$ has best approximations in D_n* if $M \cap \{x' \in D_n \mid x' \leq_I x\}$ is directed for all $x \in D_n$.

Note that if M is finite and has best approximations in D_n, then for all $x \in D_n$, if there is some $z \in M$ such that $z \leq_I x$, then there is a *best approximation* y to x in M, i.e., $y \in M$ and if $y' \in M$ and $y' \leq_I x$, then $y' \leq_I y$.

We now define Fin_m by induction on m, taking $Fin_0 = D_0$, and $Fin_{m+1} \subseteq D_{m+1}$ to consist of Fin_m together with all the items of the form:

1. $\langle y_1, \ldots, y_k \rangle$, where $y_i \in Fin_m \cup \{*\}$ for $i = 1, \ldots, k$
2. $[x_1 \to y_1, \ldots, x_k \to y_k]$ where
   a. $\{x_1, \ldots, x_k, y_1, \ldots, y_k\} \subseteq Fin_m$
   b. $\{x_1, \ldots, x_k\}$ has best approximations in D_m
   c. $x_{j'} \leq_I x_j$ implies $y_{j'} \leq_I y_j$
   d. $y_{j'} \equiv y_j$ implies $y_{j'} = y_j$,

   and for $z \in D_m$, we define

   $[x_1 \to y_1, \ldots, x_k \to y_k]{:}z =$

$$\begin{cases} \bot & \text{if there does not exist } j \text{ such that } x_j \leq_I z \\ y_j & \text{if } x_j \text{ is a best approximation in } \{x_1, \ldots, x_k\} \text{ to } z. \end{cases}$$

This completes the definition of Fin_{m+1}. Let $Fin = \cup_m Fin_m$.

Lemma 4.4. [HW3] *If y is a finite element of D^*, then $y \equiv y'$ for some $y' \in Fin$.*

Definition 4.5. A cpo is *algebraic* if every element is the sup of the finite elements less than it.

Theorem 4.6. [HW3] *D^* is algebraic.*

It is straightforward to extend these results to $D1^*$. Namely, we can characterize the finite elements of $D1^*$ in the same way (except that we restrict * to appearing only at the right-hand end of sequences in clause 1 of the definition of Fin_m) and show that $D1^*$ is algebraic.

In order to define the computable elements, we first need some way of encoding the finite elements as integers. We first show how to encode finite elements as observables (since we need this encoding later), and then show how to encode observables as integers.

Let *code* take finite elements in D^* (resp. $D1^*$) to observable items as follows:

$code(\bot) = \langle\rangle$,

$code(*) = \langle\langle\rangle\rangle$,

$code(a) = a$ for the atom a,

$code([x_1 \to y_1, \ldots, x_n \to y_n]) =$

$\langle T, code(x_1), code(y_1), \ldots, code(x_n), code(y_n)\rangle$,

$code(\langle x_1, \ldots, x_n\rangle) = \langle F, code(x_1), \ldots, code(x_n)\rangle$.

Note that we can easily write FP functions that test whether an element encodes bottom (i.e. we can write a function f such that $\mathbf{f{:}x} \to^* \mathbf{T}$ if $\mu(\mathbf{x}) = code(\bot)$ and $\mathbf{f{:}x} \to^* \mathbf{F}$ if $\mu(\mathbf{x}) \neq \bot$ and $\mu(\mathbf{x}) \neq code(\bot)$). Similarly, we can write FP functions to test whether an element encodes an atomic item, a finite sequence item of definite length, a finite sequence item of indefinite length, a function item, etc.

We next define a function taking observables to integers. Recall that we assumed that there were only finitely many atomic items. For convenience, suppose they are $a_1, \ldots, a_N$. Let p_i denote the ith prime. Let *enc* map observable items to integers as follows:

$enc(\mathbf{a}_i) = p_{i+1}$

$enc(\langle \mathbf{x}_1, \ldots, \mathbf{x}_n\rangle) = 2p_2^{enc(x_1)} \ldots p_{n+1}^{enc(x_n)}$.

Definition 4.7. A sequence $x_1, x_2, \ldots$ of finite elements is said to be *recursive* if there is a recursive function f on the integers such that $f(i) = enc(code(x_i))$. An element of D^* (resp. $D1^*$) is said to be *computable* if it is the sup of an increasing recursive sequence of finite elements of D^* (resp. $D1^*$).

Definition 4.8. Let F be a variant of FP, E its domain, and ν the semantic function that associates with each expression in F an element of E. We say that F is *expressively complete with respect to E* if for every computable element x in E, there is an expression $\mathbf{x}$ in F such that $\nu(\mathbf{x}) = x$. We say that F is *f.e. (finite element) complete with respect to E* if for every finite element of E, there is an expression $\mathbf{x}$ in F such that $\nu(\mathbf{x}) = x$.

Clearly expressive completeness implies f.e. completeness. F.e. completeness in turn implies full abstraction for algebraic domains. Since we have only defined full abstraction for variants of FP, we cannot make this statement formal, but we do prove it for variants of FP.

Proposition 4.9. *If F is a variant of FP with domain E and semantic function ν, E is algebraic, and F is f.e. complete with respect to E, then F is fully abstract with respect to E.*

Proof. Suppose the hypotheses of the proposition hold. If $\nu(x) \neq \nu(y)$, then since E is algebraic, without loss of generality there is some finite element x_0 such that $x_0 \leq_I \nu(x)$ and $x_0 \not\leq_I \nu(y)$. Now consider the finite function $f = [x_0 \rightarrow T]$. Since F is f.e. complete with respect to E, there is an F expression f such that $\nu(f) = f$. Consider the context C = f:__. We have $\nu(C[x]) = T$ and $\nu(C[y]) = \perp$. Thus $x \not\approx y$. ■

In general, we will prove full abstraction by showing f.e. completeness. We remark that Plotkin also proves f.e. completeness in the course of proving full abstraction for PCF.

5. FP and FP1 are not fully abstract

Our goal in this section is to prove that neither FP nor FP1 is fully abstract. As in [Pl], we proceed by showing *parallel or* is not definable in FP or FP1. However, the techniques we use to prove this are different from those of Plotkin.

Lemma 5.1. *If* x *is an FP expression in normal form such that* $\mu(x)$ *is a function item and* $\mu(x{:}y') = \perp$ *for all FP expressions* y′, *then* $x \approx K{:}\Omega$.

Proof. Define a new meaning function μ_x that acts just like μ except that $\mu_x(x) = \mu(K{:}\Omega)$. More formally, $\mu_x(f) = \mu(f)$ if f is an atom or primitive function symbol,

$$\mu_x(<y_1,...,y_n>) = \langle\mu_x(y_1), ..., \mu_x(y_n)\rangle,$$

$$\mu_x(y{:}z) = \begin{cases} \mu(K{:}\Omega) & \text{if } y{:}z = x \\ \mu_x(y){:}\mu_x(z) & \text{otherwise.} \end{cases}$$

The function μ_x has three important properties:

1. $\mu_x(y) \leq_I \mu(y)$ for all FP expressions y,
2. $\mu_x(C[x]) \leq_I \mu(C[K{:}\Omega])$ for all contexts C,
3. if $y \rightarrow^* z$, then $\mu_x(z) \leq_I \mu_x(y)$.

Properties (1) and (2) can be checked by a straightforward induction on the structure of y and the structure of C respectively. To see that property (3) holds, note that, as usual, straightforward inductions on the length of the reduction and the structure of y show that it suffices to consider the case where $y \rightarrow z$, and this is an instance of a rewrite rule. Again we must consider the rewrite rules on a case-by-case basis. For example, if y is of the form **apply**: $<f, y'>$ and z is of the form f:y′, then we know $y \neq x$ (since x is in normal form and y is not), so it is easy to see that $\mu_x(y) = \mu(\textbf{apply}){:}\langle\mu_x(f), \mu_x(y')\rangle = \mu_x(f){:}\mu_x(y')$. Thus $\mu_x(z) \leq_I \mu_x(y)$. (Note that if $x = z$ then we in fact have $\mu_x(z) <_I \mu_x(y)$.) Similar arguments work in all cases except when y is of the form f:y″:y′ and f is **comp**, **cons**, or **K**. We consider the case where y is of the form **comp**: $<f_1, f_2>$:y′ here; the other cases are similar and left to the reader. If $x \neq$ **comp**: $<f_1, f_2>$, then similar arguments to that used in the case of **apply** easily show that $\mu_x(z) \leq_I \mu_x(y)$. If $x =$ **comp**: $<f_1, f_2>$, then $\mu(y) = \perp$ by our assumption that $\mu(x{:}y') = \perp$ for all FP expressions y′. Thus, since FP rewriting is sound, we must have $\mu(z) = \perp$. Since $\mu_x(z) \leq_I \mu(z)$, we also have $\mu_x(z) = \perp$, so $\mu_x(z) \leq_I \mu_x(y)$.

We are now ready to prove that $x \approx K{:}\Omega$. If $\mu(C[K{:}\Omega]) = b$ for some atom b, then $\mu(C[x]) = b$ since $\mu(C[K{:}\Omega]) \leq_I \mu(C[x])$. Conversely, if $\mu(C[x]) = b$ for some atom b, then $C[x] \rightarrow^* b$. Thus, $b = \mu_x(b) \leq_I \mu_x(C[x]) \leq_I \mu(C[K{:}\Omega])$. Therefore, $\mu(C[K{:}\Omega]) = b = \mu(C[x])$. ■

Let *or* be the finite function item $[\langle T, \perp\rangle \rightarrow T, \langle\perp, T\rangle \rightarrow T, \langle F, F\rangle \rightarrow F]$.

Proposition 5.2. *There is no FP expression* g *such that or* $\leq_I \mu(g)$.

Proof. Similar in spirit to the proof of Theorem 3.5. We leave details to the full paper. ■

Theorem 5.3. *FP (resp. FP1) is not fully abstract with respect to D* (resp. D1*).*

Proof. We prove the result only for FP; the proof for FP1 is similar. Let f be an FP expression that tests to see if its argument is greater than *or*. That is, $f{:}g \rightarrow^* T$ iff $\mu(g){:}\langle T, \perp\rangle = T$, $\mu(g){:}\langle\perp, T\rangle = T$, and $\mu(g){:}\langle F, F\rangle = F$. We can take f to be the expression

λg.(cond: < g: < T, Ω > , cond: < g: < Ω, T > ,
cond: < g: < F, F > , Ω, T > , Ω > , Ω >).

By Proposition 5.2, there is no FP expression g such that $or \leq_I \mu(g)$, so we must have $\mu(f:g) = \perp$ for all FP expression g. Thus, by Lemma 5.1, f$\approx$K:Ω. Since $\mu(f) \neq \mu(K:\Omega)$, it follows that FP is not fully abstract with respect to D^*. ■

In the next few sections, we examine how we can extend FP and FP1 in order to get full abstraction.

6. Extending FP1 to get full abstraction and expressive completeness

In [Pl], Plotkin shows that by adding a parallel conditional facility to PCF we get full abstraction. PCF is typed, so Plotkin really has two parallel conditionals, one for each of his base types. Since FP is untyped, there is no notion of "base type". We generalize Plotkin's definition by adding a new primitive function symbol **pcond** to FP1, and defining μ_1(**pcond**) = *pcond*, where

$$pcond{:}\langle b,x,y\rangle = \begin{cases} x & \text{if } b=T \\ y & \text{if } b=F \\ glb(x,y) & \text{otherwise.} \end{cases}$$

Of course, $glb(x,y)$ is the greatest lower bound of x and y. This is well defined in $D1^*$, but not in D^*, since, for example, $glb(\langle a\rangle, \langle a, *, a\rangle)$ is not well defined. Plotkin's definition is similar, except that since b in Plotkin's definition is restricted to be of type Boolean, it can only take values $\perp$, T, and F, and x and y are restricted to be either both Booleans or both integers (the two base types in Plotkin's case). Plotkin defines $pcond(\perp,x,y)$ to be x if $x=y$ and $\perp$ otherwise. Since $glb(x,y) = \perp$ if x and y are unequal elements of base type, our definition generalizes Plotkin's.

Not surprisingly, we can capture the semantics of **pcond** with natural rewrite rules. Consider the rules:

pcond: < x, y, y > $\rightarrow$ y,

pcond: < x, y, z > $\rightarrow$
  al: < **pcond:** < x, first:y, first:z > ,
   pcond: < x, tl:y, tl:z > > if both
    y and z look like nonempty sequences,

(**pcond:** < x, y, z >):w $\rightarrow$ **pcond:** < x, y:w, z:w > .

Let FP1$^+$ be FP1 together with **pcond**; we take the rewrite rules for FP1$^+$ to be those for FP1 together with the rewrite rules for **pcond**, with the definition of "looks like a function" (as used in the rules for **eqatom**, **isatom**, **isseq**, and **isfunc**) extended so that expressions of the form **pcond:** < y, f, g > are also considered to look like functions if both f and g look like functions.

Theorem 6.1. *These rewrite rules are sound and strongly complete for FP1$^+$.*

Proof. The proof follows exactly the same lines as that of Theorem 2.8 given in [HW3], so we omit it here. ■

Given a finite element x in $D1^*$, let **code**(x) represent $code(x)^e$, the observable element corresponding to the observable item $code(x)$.

Theorem 6.2. *FP1$^+$ is f.e. complete with respect to $D1^*$. In fact, there is an FP1$^+$ expression* **E** *such that for all finite elements x in $D1^*$,* μ(**E**:**code**(x)) = x.

Proof. The proof follows along the lines of Plotkin's, but is more difficult since we are working in an untyped domain, so we cannot proceed by induction on types. We leave details to the full paper. ■

By applying Proposition 4.9, we immediately get

Corollary 6.3. *FP1$^+$ is fully abstract with respect to $D1^*$.*

In order to get expressive completeness for PCF, Plotkin adds a parallel conditional and an "existential" operator $\exists$ such that $\nu(\exists)(f) = F$ if $f(\perp) = F$ and $\nu(\exists)(f) = T$ if $f(n) = T$ for some natural number n. We use observable elements rather than natural numbers to get the same effect in our domain. Thus, we take FP1* to be FP1$^+$ augmented with the primitive function symbol **exists**, where

$$\mu_1(\textbf{exists}):f = \begin{cases} F & \text{if } f{:}\bot = F \\ T & \text{if } f{:}x = T \text{ for some} \\ & \text{observable item } x \\ \bot & \text{otherwise.} \end{cases}$$

Again, it is straightforward to add rewrite rules that capture the semantics of ∃. The following will do the trick:

exists:f → **pcond**: < f:t, T, **exists**:f > ,

where t is any observable expression,

exists:f → F if f:Ω →* F.

We take the rewrite rules for FP1* to be those for FP1$^+$ augmented with the rules for **exists**. The arguments of [HW3] can now be applied to show:

Theorem 6.4. *These rewrite rules are sound and strongly complete for FP1*.*

Note that the second rewrite rule for **exists** is r.e. rather than recursive; the instances of this rule form an r.e. (but not recursive) set, since the problem of deciding if f:Ω →* F is r.e. We could replace this rule by the recursive rule **exists**:f → **cond**: < f:Ω, T, F >. The latter rule is unsound (for example, if μ_1(f):⊥ = ⊥ but μ_1(f):*a* = *T*, then μ_1(**exists**:f) = *T* while μ_1(**cond**: < f:Ω, T, F >) = ⊥). However, it can only lower the meaning of an expression; adding this rule results in a set of rewrite rules that is *weakly sound*, in that if x →* y with respect to these rules, then $\mu_1(y) \le_I \mu_1(x)$. Moreover, we can still use the techniques of [HW3] to show that the resulting set of rewrite rules is strongly complete.

For either choice of rewrite rules we have:

Theorem 6.5. *FP1* is expressively complete with respect to D1*.*

Proof. Once again, the proof follows along the lines of Plotkin's. The key idea is to show that using **exists** we can encode the limit of an increasing recursive sequence of finite elements. We leave details to the full paper. ■

We cannot get immediate analogues to either Corollary 6.3 or Theorem 6.5 for FP. As we noted above, we cannot add **pcond** to FP because greatest lower bounds are not well defined in general. We could add a restricted form of **pcond** which only applies to, say, atoms. However, by combining techniques from the proofs of Theorem 3.1 and Theorem 5.3, we can show that the resulting language is not fully abstract. (The idea is to show that there is no expression g in the extended language such that [≺⊥, *≻ → ≺*a*, *≻, ≺*, ⊥≻ → ≺*, *a*≻] $\le_I$ g.) And if we add both the restricted form of **pcond** and **exists** to FP, we can extend the proof of Theorem 3.1 to show that **ef** (and hence **apall**) is still not definable, so that the language is not expressively complete.

7. Full abstraction and expressive completeness for nondeterministic FP

In the previous section we showed that by adding certain parallel facilities to FP1 we were able to get full abstraction and expressive completeness. However, the obvious analogues of these extensions for FP do not give full abstraction or expressive completeness. One major difference between FP and FP1 is that the domain for FP1 is consistently complete. In order to investigate the effect of consistent completeness, we extend FP to NFP by adding one more primitive function symbol **union**. The domain *ND** for NFP essentially consists of unions of elements of *D** We extend μ to μ_N by defining μ_N(**union**):≺$x_1, ..., x_n$≻ = $x_1 \cup ... \cup x_n$. *ND** is easily seen to be consistently complete; the sup of any two elements of *ND** is just their union.

NFP does allow a great deal of parallel evaluation. In particular, the *or* function described in Section 5 is definable in NFP. However, the proof of Theorem 3.1 can be extended to show that **ef** (and hence **apall**) is not definable in NFP. And again we can combine the ideas of Theorem 3.1 and Theorem 5.3 to show that NFP is not fully abstract. However, the inability to define **ef** and **el** is all that keeps NFP from being fully abstract and expressively complete. Let NFP$^+$ be the result of adding **ef** and **el** to NFP.

We can easily give rewrite rules to the new primitive functions of NFP$^+$. For ef we have:

ef: $<x_1, ..., x_n> \rightarrow$ T, $n \geq 1$

ef:(al: $<x, y>) \rightarrow$ T

ef:(ar: $<$ al: $<x, y>, z>) \rightarrow$ T

ef:(ar: $<$ ar: $<x, y>, z>) \rightarrow$ ef:(ar: $<x, y>$).

The rules for el are analogous. We omit them here.

The most obvious way of dealing with **union** is to have the rule:

union: $<x_1, ..., x_n> \rightarrow x_i$, $i = 1, ..., n$.

The last rule is not sound; for example $\mu(a) <_I \mu(\mathbf{union}: <a, b>)$. However, the rewrite rules given for NFP$^+$ are weakly sound. The techniques of [HW3] can be used to show strong completeness, so we get:

Theorem 7.1. *These rewrite rules are weakly sound and strongly complete for NFP.*

We could get sound and strongly complete rules for NFP by replacing the rule for **union** with a number of other rules such as **union**: $<f_1, ..., f_n>$:x $\rightarrow$ **union**: $<f_1$:x, ..., f_1:x$>$ and f:(**union**: $<x_1, ..., x_n>) \rightarrow$ **union**: $<$f:x_1, ..., f:$x_n>$. Our choice results in simpler rules. The results we now present hold with either choice of rewrite rules.

Theorem 7.2. *NFP$^+$ is f.e. complete with respect to ND*. In fact, there is an NFP expression* $\mathbf{E}_N$ *such that for all finite elements x in ND*, we have* $\mu_N(\mathbf{E}_N$:code$(x)) = x$.

Proof. We define $\mathbf{E}_N$ by induction on the structure of x, simultaneously defining an auxiliary expression $\mathbf{B}_N$ such that

$$\mu_N(\mathbf{B}_N):y:z = \begin{cases} T \text{ if } y = code(x) \text{ for some} \\ \quad \text{finite element } x \leq_I z \\ \bot \text{ otherwise.} \end{cases}$$

The definition $\mathbf{E}_N$ and $\mathbf{B}_N$ are quite straightforward (and indeed much easier than their counterparts in the proof of full abstraction for FP1). For example, we have

$\mathbf{E}_N$:code([$x \rightarrow y$]) =
  λg.(**cond**: $<$ **B**:code(x):g, $\mathbf{E}_N$:code(y), Ω $>$).

$\mathbf{E}_N$:code([$x_1 \rightarrow y_1$, ..., $x_n \rightarrow y_n$]) =
  union: $<$ $\mathbf{E}_N$:code([$x_1 \rightarrow y_1$]), ...,
   $\mathbf{E}_N$:code([$x_n \rightarrow y_n$]) $>$.

We leave the remaning clauses of the definition of $\mathbf{E}_N$ and $\mathbf{B}_N$ to the full paper. ∎

Corollary 7.3. *NFP$^+$ is fully abstract with respect to ND*.*

In order to extend the notion of expressive completeness to NFP, we must extend our encoding to encode all the finite elements of *ND** We can characterize the finite elements of *ND** by adding one more clause to the characterization of the finite elements of *D**. For example, we can define

$code(\{x_1, ..., x_n\}) = \langle\langle T\rangle, code(x_1), ..., code(x_n)\rangle$.

With this extension, the definition of expressive completeness goes through for NFP$^+$ and we have

Theorem 7.4. *NFP$^+$ is expressively complete with respect to ND*.*

Proof. As for FP1*, it suffices to be able to take the sup of an increasing recursive sequence of finite elements. Using **union**, we can do this in a straightforward way in NFP$^+$. We leave details to the full paper. ∎

We also note that if we extend FP1 by adding **union** and extend *D1** by allowing unions, the resulting language NFP1 is fully abstract and expressively complete with respect to the domain. The problem of distinguishing $\langle *, \bot\rangle$ from $\langle\bot, *\rangle$ does not arise since $\langle *, \bot\rangle$ is not in the domain.

8. Extending FP to get full abstraction and expressive completeness

In the previous section we showed that by extending FP with nondeterminism we could get a language that was fully abstract and expressively complete. However, in extending to nondeterminism, we also extended the domain *D** to *ND**, which is consistently complete. The reader may wonder at this point if we can get full abstraction or expressive completeness for an extension of FP that still has semantic domain D^*. Using the ideas from the proofs in the previous sections, we show that this can be done.

Our proofs of full abstraction for $FP1^+$ and NFP^+ both depend on constructing an expression **E** (resp. E_N) which maps $code(x)$ to x for a finite item x. The major difficulty in constructing such an expression lies in dealing with finite function items z of the form $[x_1 \to y_1, ..., x_n \to y_n]$. In this case we want $\mathbf{E}$:code(z) to be the sup of $\mathbf{E}$:code$([x_i \to y_i])$, $i = 1, ..., n$. In NFP it is easy to define the sup of any finite set of elements: it is just their union. In FP1 two elements may not have a sup (and indeed, sup is easily seen not to be a continuous function in FP1). Nevertheless, the fact that FP1 is consistently complete gives us a natural way of defining sups when they exist, by using **pcond**. We know of no natural construct in FP that allows us to construct an expression **E** with these properties. Nevertheless, we can simulate this construction by simply adding **E** as a primitive function symbol.

Let FPE be the result of augmenting FP with two primitive function symbols **E** and **B**. Extend μ so that

$$\mu(\mathbf{E}){:}y = \begin{cases} x \text{ if } y = code(x) \text{ for some} \\ \quad \text{finite element } x \\ \bot \text{ otherwise,} \end{cases}$$

$$\mu(\mathbf{B}){:}y{:}z = \begin{cases} T \text{ if } y = code(x) \text{ for some} \\ \quad \text{finite element } x \leq_I z \\ \bot \text{ otherwise.} \end{cases}$$

Let FPE^+ be FPE together with **ef** and **el** as defined in the previous section.

In the full paper we show that we can extend the FP rewrite rules to FPE^+ and still get strong completeness. Of course, the definition of **E** guarantees that FPE is f.e. complete, hence fully abstract.

The proofs of complete expressiveness for NFP* and FP1* show that the crucial factor in getting complete expressiveness is the ability to take sups of increasing recursive sequences of finite elements. Let FPE* be the result of extending FPE^+ with the primitive function symbol **sup**. Further extend μ so that $\mu(\mathbf{sup})$ is the least continuous function such that if $x_1, ..., x_m$ are finite elements with $x_1 \leq_I ... \leq_I x_m$, then

$$\mu(\mathbf{sup}){:}\langle code(x_1), ..., code(x_m), * \rangle = x_m.$$

In the full paper we provide r.e. rewrite rules for **sup** and show that FPE* is strongly complete with respect to these rewrite rules. Arguments similar to those used for NFP* can now be used to show that FPE* is expressively complete.

We do not want to claim that FPE^+ and FPE* are natural extensions of FP. However, they both have recursive syntax, r.e. rewrite rules, and a finite set of primitive functions. Moreover, these extensions do indicate exactly what is required of a language in order to get full abstraction and expressive completeness.

9. Conclusions

We have investigated the question of full abstraction and expressive completeness for FP and a number of its variants. By considering these issues for a number of related domains, we feel we have obtained a better understanding of what is required of a language and semantics in order to guarantee full abstraction and expressive completeness. We hope that the results of this paper will lead to a framework for a more general theory of constructing good programming languages, i.e. ones with natural syntax, natural rewrite rules, enough rewrite rules, and reasonable expressive power.

Acknowledgements: We would like to thank Albert Meyer for inspiring us to consider these questions and pointing out the relevance of the results in [Pl]. John Williams first conjectured that apply-to-all was not definable in FP, and David Chase encouraged us to prove it. John Backus, Ron Fagin, and John Williams provided useful comments on a draft of this paper.

References

[Ba] J.W. Backus, Can programming be liberated from the von Neumann style? A functional style and its algebra of programs, *CACM* **21:8** (August, 1978), pp. 613-641.

[HW1] J.Y. Halpern, J.H. Williams, E.L. Wimmers, and T.C. Winkler, Denotational semantics and rewrite rules for FP, *Proceedings of the 12th ACM Conference on Principles of Programming Languages* (1985), pp. 108-120.

[HW2] J.Y. Halpern, J.H. Williams, and E.L. Wimmers, Good rewrite strategies for FP, *Proceedings of the Symposium on Logic in Computer Science* (1986), pp. 149-162.

[HW3] J.Y. Halpern, J.H. Williams, and E.L. Wimmers, Completeness of rewrite rules and rewrite strategies for FP, IBM Research Report RJ5099 (1986)

[Mi] R. Milner, Models of LCF, Memo. AIM-186, Stanford Artificial Intelligence Laboratory, Stanford University, (1973).

[Pl] G.D. Plotkin, LCF considered as a programming language, *Theoretical Computer Science* **5** (1977), pp. 223-255.

[SP] M.B. Smyth and G.D. Plotkin, The category-theoretic solution of recursive domain equations, *SIAM Journal on Computing* **11**:4 (1982), pp. 761-783.

[Wi] J.H. Williams, Formal representations for recursively defined functional programs, in *Formalization of Programming Concepts*, Lecture Notes in Computer Science No. 107, Springer-Verlag (April, 1981), pp. 460-470.

Appendix A: The FP Rewrite Rules

$\text{al}: < x, < y_1, \ldots, y_n > > \to < x, y_1, \ldots, y_n >.$

$\text{ar}: < < y_1, \ldots, y_n >, x > \to < y_1, \ldots, y_n, x >.$

$\text{first}: < x_1, \ldots, x_n > \to x_1 \quad (n \geq 1).$

$\text{first}:(\text{al}: < x, y >) \to x.$

$\text{first}:(\text{ar}: < \text{al}: < x, y >, z >) \to x.$

$\text{first}:(\text{ar}: < \text{ar}: < x, y >, z >) \to \text{first}:(\text{ar}: < x, y >).$

$\text{last}: < x_1, \ldots, x_n > \to x_n \quad (n \geq 1).$

$\text{last}:(\text{ar}: < x, y >) \to y.$

$\text{last}:(\text{al}: < x, \text{ar}: < y, z > >) \to z.$

$\text{last}:(\text{al}: < x, \text{al}: < y, z > >) \to \text{last}:(\text{al}: < y, z >).$

$\text{tl}: < x_1, \ldots, x_n > \to < x_2, \ldots, x_n > \quad (n \geq 1).$

$\text{tl}:(\text{al}: < x, \text{al}: < y, z > >) \to \text{al}: < y, z >.$

$\text{tl}:(\text{al}: < x, \text{ar}: < y, z > >) \to \text{ar}: < y, z >.$

$\text{tl}:(\text{ar}: < \text{al}: < x, y >, z >) \to \text{ar}: < y, z >.$

$\text{tl}:(\text{ar}: < \text{ar}: < x, y >, z >) \to \text{ar}: < \text{tl}:(\text{ar}: < x, y >), z >.$

$\text{tr}: < x_1, \ldots, x_n > \to < x_1, \ldots, x_{n-1} > \quad (n \geq 1).$

$\text{tr}:(\text{ar}: < \text{ar}: < x, y >, z >) \to \text{ar}: < x, y >.$

$\text{tr}:(\text{ar}: < \text{al}: < x, y >, z >) \to \text{al}: < x, y >.$

$\text{tr}:(\text{al}: < x, \text{ar}: < y, z > >) \to \text{al}: < x, y >.$

$\text{tr}:(\text{al}: < x, \text{al}: < y, z > >) \to \text{al}: < x, \text{tr}:(\text{al}: < y, z >) >.$

$\text{null}: < \ > \to T.$

$\text{null}:a \to F$ (for any atom a).

$\text{null}: < x_1, \ldots, x_n > \to F \quad (n \geq 1).$

$\text{null}:(\text{al}: < x, y >) \to F.$

$\text{null}:(\text{ar}: < x, y >) \to F.$

$\text{cons}: < f_1, \ldots, f_n >:x \to < f_1:x, \ldots, f_n:x >.$

$\text{cons}:(\text{al}: < f, g >):x \to \text{al}: < f:x, \text{cons}:g:x >.$

$\text{cons}:(\text{ar}: < f, g >):x \to \text{ar}: < \text{cons}:f:x, g:x >.$

$\text{cond}: < T, x, y > \to x.$

$\text{cond}: < F, x, y > \to y.$

$\text{comp}: < f, g >:x \to f:(g:x).$

$\text{apply}: < f, x > \to f:x.$

$K:x:y \to x.$

$\text{id}:x \to x.$

$\text{eqatom}: < x, x > \to T$ if x looks like an atom.

$\text{eqatom}: < x, y > \to F$ if both x and y look like atoms and $x \neq y$.

$\text{isatom}:x \to T$ if x looks like an atom.

$\text{isatom}:x \to F$ if x looks like a sequence or function.

$\text{isseq}:x \to T$ if x looks like a sequence.

$\text{isseq}:x \to F$ if x looks like an atom or function.

$\text{isfunc}:x \to T$ if x looks like a function.

$\text{isfunc}:x \to F$ if x looks like an atom or sequence.

Session 7

Chair

A. Nerode

Cornell University

A Semantical Approach to Nonmonotonic Logics

(extended abstract)

Yoav Shoham
Stanford University
Computer Science Department[1]

Abstract

Recent years have seen a proliferation of so-called *nonmonotonic logics*, or formalisms that allow "jumping to conclusions," assigning formulas "default truth values," or making "defeasible inferences." The different systems that have been proposed have strong surface dissimilarities, and comparison between them has proven difficult.

In this paper we propose a uniform approach to constructing and understanding nonmonotonic logics. This framework subsumes existing nonmonotonic formalisms, and yet is remarkably simple, adding almost no extra baggage to traditional logic. In the new framework we redefine classical notions such as satisfiability and entailment, and look at what happens to some standard results from classical logic, such as the deduction theorem. We also briefly discuss how existing nonmonotonic logics are special cases of our general formulation, and how their new analysis serves to clarify them and relate them to one another.

1 Introduction

The last decade or so has seen many logical systems which support so-called *nonmonotonic inferences.* In these formalisms one is allowed not only traditional inferences of classical logic, but also more "speculative" ones. It is often said that in those systems one may "jump to a conclusion" in the absence of evidence to the contrary, or that one may assign formulas a "default value," or that one may make a "defeasible inference." The prototypical example is inferring that a particular individual can fly from the fact that it is a bird, but retracting that inference when an additional fact is added, that the individual is a penguin. This is why such formalisms are called nonmonotonic: a fact entailed by a theory might no longer be entailed by a larger theory. Of course, classical logic is monotonic.

The original and best-known nonmonotonic logics are McCarthy's *circumscription* [McC], Reiter's *default logic* [R], McDermott and Doyle's *nonmonotonic logic I* [McDD], McDermott's *nonmonotonic logic II* [McD], and Clark's *predicate completion* [C]. In recent years several other systems have been suggested, and the old ones were further explored. Lifschitz provided new results on circumscription [Li1]. Further investigations of default logic include Etherington's work [E] and Lukaszewicz' [Lu]. Moore's *autoepistemic logic* [M] is an adaptation of McDermott's NML II, and a version of it was further investigated by Halpern and Moses [HM].

These various formalisms are very different superficially. For example, circumscription amounts to adding a second-order axiom to a given first-order theory. A default theory, on the other hand, contains a collection of *default rules*, a notion quite outside classical logic, and its meaning is defined using a fixed-point construction which relies on those default rules. McDermott's and Moore's logics are still different, and formulas in those logics contain modal operators, which are meant to capture the notions of consistency and belief, respectively. The nonstandard nature of the various systems and their diversity has made it hard to gain a good understanding of them and to compare among them.

However, the main problem with existing nonmonotonic formalisms is not their overwhelming complexity, as much as it is their limited expressiveness. In particular, they were all shown to fail to capture nonmonotonic *temporal* inferences. The problems were first reported by Hanks and McDermott [HMcD], in response to which several solutions were offered. One such solution was proposed by Lifschitz, and it was to generalize circumscription to so-called *pointwise circumscription* [Li2]. My approach has been to construct the logic of *chronological ignorance* [S1], and in doing I defined a very general framework for nonmonotonic logics. The purpose of this paper is to present this general framework. The main contributions of this paper are twofold: On the one hand I offer a simple framework to which all existing nonmonotonic logics can be reduced (and thus easily understood and easily compared to one another), and on the other hand this general framework suggests radically new nonmonotonic logics.

[1]The paper describes work carried out when the author was a graduate student at the Computer Science Department of Yale University. The final manuscript was prepared at the Applied Mathematics Department of the Weizmann Institute in Israel, where the author was a postdoctoral fellow.

The basic idea behind the construction is the following. In traditional logic, the meaning of a formula is the set of interpretations that satisfy it, or its set of models (where "interpretation" means truth assignment for PC, a first-order interpretation for FOPC, and a ⟨Kripke interpretation, world⟩-pair for modal logic). One gets a nonmonotonic logic by changing the rules of the game, and focusing on only a subset of those models, those that are "preferable" in a certain respect (these preferred models are sometimes called "minimal models," a term introduced by McCarthy in connection with circumscription). The reason this transition makes the logic nonmonotonic is as follows. In classical logic $A \models C$ if C is true in all models of A. Since all models of $A \wedge B$ are also models of A, it follows that $A \wedge B \models C$, and hence that the logic is monotonic. In the new scheme we have that $A \models C$ if C is true in all *preferred* models of A, but $A \wedge B$ may have preferred models that are not preferred models of A. In fact, the class of preferred models of $A \wedge B$ and the class of preferred models of A may be completely disjoint.

Many different preference criteria are possible, all resulting in different nonmonotonic logics. In [S2] I look into particular preference criteria that are suitable for temporal reasoning. In this paper I look more closely at the general framework, and at the meaning in it of notions such as satisfiability and entailment.

2 Formal construction of nonmonotonic logics

The discussion here will be most general, and when I talk of a "standard logic" I allow in principle any logic with the usual compositional, model-theoretic semantics. Rather than give a precise definition of this condition, however, let me in the following assume that by a "standard logic" one means the propositional calculus or first-order predicate logic, either classical or modal (i.e., one of four logics); extension to other cases (such as higher-order logic) will be obvious.[2]

In order to have the following discussion apply uniformly to the classical and modal logics, let me misuse the terminology slightly by calling anything which goes to the left of the $\models$ an *interpretation.* In the classical cases this is what is indeed usually called an interpretation. In the modal cases it is a pair ⟨Kripke structure,world⟩.

The transition to nonmonotonic logic puts into question notions that are well understood in logic, such as satisfaction, entailment, satisfiability, validity, and proof theory. To see what these might mean in the context of nonmonotonic logic, it will be helpful to recall some definitions from the standard case.

Definition 1 (Reminder)
Let $\mathcal{L}$ be a standard logic, and A and B two sentences in $\mathcal{L}$. The fact that an interpretation M satisfies A is denoted by $M \models A$. In this case we say that M is a model of A. A is satisfiable if A has a model. A is valid if A is satisfied by all interpretations. Clearly A is satisfiable iff $\neg A$ is not valid. A entails B (written $A \models B$) if B is satisfied by all models of A, or equivalently, if all models of A are also models of B.

From these definitions, the deduction theorem follows very easily:

Theorem 1 (Reminder)
Let $\mathcal{L}$ be a standard logic, and A, B and C sentences in $\mathcal{L}$. Then $A \wedge B \models C$ iff $A \models B \supset C$.

Nonmonotonic logics are the result of associating with a standard logic a preference relation on models. More specifically, we make the following definitions. Let $\mathcal{L}$ be a standard logic and A a sentence in it, and let $<$ be a strict partial order on interpretations for $\mathcal{L}$. Intuitively, $M_1 < M_2$ will mean that the interpretation M_2 is *preferred over* the interpretation M_1. $\mathcal{L}$ and $<$ define a new logic $\mathcal{L}_<$. I will call such logics *preference logics.* The syntax of $\mathcal{L}_<$ is identical to that of $\mathcal{L}$. The semantics of $\mathcal{L}_<$ are as follows.

Definition 2 *An interpretation M preferentially satisfies A (written $M \models_< A$) if $M \models A$, and if there is no other interpretation M' such that $M < M'$ and $M' \models A$. In this case we say that M is a preferred model of A.*

Clearly, if $M \models_< A$ then also $M \models A$. Next I define the notions of satisfiability and validity in $\mathcal{L}_<$. These can be defined in more than one way, none of them entirely satisfactory. The definition of satisfiability is the more intuitive of the two.

Definition 3 *A is preferentially satisfiable if there exists an M such that $M \models_< A$.*

Clearly, all preferentially satisfiable formulas are also satisfiable, though the converse is not necessarily true. The definition of preferential validity is much less intuitive. In fact, I have no intuition at all on what preferential validity should mean. Since that is the case, I will define it simply as the dual relation to preferential satisfiability:

Definition 4 *A is preferentially valid (written $\models_< A$) iff $\neg A$ is not preferentially satisfiable.*

[2]When I say 'a modal logic' I deliberately do not commit myself to a particular modal system; that too is not essential here. Again, rather than define the class of all modal systems to which the following applies, let me in the following assume an S5 system whenever a modal logic is mentioned, and leave it to the reader to extend it to other systems.

Lemma 2 *A is preferentially valid if for any M, either*

1. *$M \models A$, or else*
2. *there is an M' such that $M < M'$ and $M' \not\models A$.*

Again, it is easy to see that all valid formulas are also preferentially valid, although the converse is not true. Indeed, preferential validity has some strange properties. For example, depending on $<$, both a formula and its negation can be preferentially valid. Or, as a more concrete example, for $<$ that is *unbounded* (that is, if for any M there is an M' such that $M < M'$), if φ is valid then, not only is φ preferentially valid, but so is $\neg\varphi$.

Perhaps it makes no sense to define the notion of validity in this general context. There are, however, restricted cases where the above definition of preferential validity is very well behaved:

Definition 5 *A partial order $<$ on models is said to be bounded if there does not exist an infinite sequence of models $M_1, M_2, M_3 \ldots$ such that $M_1 < M_2 < M_3 < \ldots$*

Proposition 3 *Let $\mathcal{L}$ be a preferential logic, $<$ a bounded partial order on its models, and A a formula in $\mathcal{L}$ (and therefore also in $\mathcal{L}_<$). Then A is satisfiable in $\mathcal{L}$ iff A is preferentially satisfiable in $\mathcal{L}_<$.*

Corollary 4 *Under the same conditions, A is valid in $\mathcal{L}$ iff A is preferentially valid in $\mathcal{L}_<$.*

Observation. $\mathcal{L}$ can be viewed as a special case of $\mathcal{L}_\phi$, where ϕ is the empty relation. Note that ϕ is bounded.

As was said before, despite these well-behaved properties, preferential satisfiability and validity are somewhat strange notions. Fortunately, neither is central to understanding nonmonotonic reasoning. What is crucial is the notion of preferential entailment, and that has a very intuitive definition:

Definition 6 *A preferentially entails B (written $A \models_< B$) if for any M, if $M \models_< A$ then $M \models B$, or equivalently, if the models of B (preferred and otherwise) are a superset of the preferred models of A.*

Observation. If $\mathcal{L}$ is a preferential logic, it may contain sentences A and B such that both $A \models_< B$ and $A \models_< \neg B$. Furthermore, A need not be inconsistent for this to be the case – it is sufficient that it have no preferred models. Indeed, in preferential logic the role played by preferential satisfiability is exactly analogous to that played by satisfiability in standard logics, witness the following obvious lemma:

Lemma 5 *Let $\mathcal{L}_<$ be a preferential logic, and A a sentence in it. Then A is preferentially satisfiable iff there does not exists a sentence B in $\mathcal{L}_<$ such that both $A \models_< B$ and $A \models_< \neg B$.*

Definition 7 *$\mathcal{L}_<$ is monotonic if for all A,B,C $\in \mathcal{L}$, if $A \models_< C$ then also $A \wedge B \models_< C$.*

Observation. The above definition is equivalent to saying that a logic is monotonic if all preferred models of $A \wedge B$ are also preferred models of A. Again viewing $\mathcal{L}$ as the special case $\mathcal{L}_\phi$, we note that $\mathcal{L}_\phi$ is monotonic.

It is interesting to see what happens to the deduction theorem in light of the new definition of entailment. It turns out that while the theorem is false in general, a weaker version of it still holds, in which the 'iff' is changed to an 'if':

Theorem 6 *Let $\mathcal{L}_<$ be a preferential logic, and A, B and C three sentences in it. Then, if $A \wedge B \models_< C$, then also $A \models_< B \supset C$.*

The converse to this theorem does not hold: if $A \models_< B \supset C$ then it does not necessarily follow that $A \wedge B \models_< C$. It is not hard to construct a counterexample, for example one in which C is identically false, $A \wedge B$ is *not* identically false, and B is false in all preferred models of A. In fact, it is easy to show that if the converse to the theorem holds then the logic is necessarily monotonic:

Theorem 7 *Let $\mathcal{L}_<$ be a preferential logic. Then the following two statements are equivalent:*

1. *For all A,B,C$\in\mathcal{L}_<$, if $A \models_< B \supset C$ then also $A \wedge B \models_< C$.*
2. *$\mathcal{L}_<$ is monotonic.*

3 Two special cases

Although very simple, the above framework is sufficiently expressive to capture all the nonmonotonic systems of which I am aware. In this section I show how two of these previous systems can be reduced to the general framework, McCarthy's circumscription and Halpern and Moses' logic of minimal knowledge. The result of this translation makes those logics very transparent, and in fact suggests a way of relating the seemingly disparate systems: It is shown that the first logic, at least in one of its forms, can be reduced to the latter one.

3.1 Circumscription

Circumscribing a formula amounts to adding a second order axiom to a theory. Different circumscription axioms exist, each leading to a different logic. McCarthy's original circumscription axiom (and I am using Lifschitz' recent reconstruction of it in [Li2]) was:

$$\texttt{CM(A,P)} =_{def} \texttt{A(P)} \wedge \forall \texttt{p}\ \neg(\texttt{A(p)} \wedge \texttt{p<P})$$

where A is a FO formula containing the predicate symbol P, p is a predicate variable, and p<P stands for

$$\forall \texttt{x}(\texttt{px} \supset \texttt{Px}) \wedge \neg\forall \texttt{x}(\texttt{Px} \supset \texttt{px})$$

(x are the free variables of both P and p.)

Proposition 8 *Let* A(P) *and* CM(A,P) *be as above, and* B *any FO formula.*
Then CM(A,P) $\models$ B *iff* A(P) $\models_<$ B, *where* $M_1 < M_2$ *iff*

1. *For all* x, M_1 *and* M_2 *agree on the interpretation of function symbols and all relation symbols other than* P,
2. *for all* x, *if* $M_2 \models$ P(x) *then also* $M_1 \models$ P(x), *and*
3. *there exists a* y *such that* $M_1 \models$ P(y) *but* $M_2 \not\models$ P(y).

To avoid giving the wrong impression, it must be said that the notion of preferred models was implicit in McCarthy's work from the start. In fact, in his original paper he gave a preference criterion similar to the one stated above, although in subsequent publications the model-theoretic discussion seemed to play a diminishing role. Other researchers too have addressed the model theory of circumscription, such as Lifschitz in [Li1] and Etherington in [E].

3.2 Minimal knowledge

In [HM], Halpern and Moses construct a nonmonotonic modal logic, which is a direct adaptation of Moore's autoepistmic logic (which in turn was the outgrowth of McDermott's NML II, and other work by Konolige and Stalnaker). Halpern and Moses ask what it means to say "I know α" and imply that that is *all* I know. For example, if my data base contains the assertions p and q, then all the base facts that I know are p, q, and their tautological consequences. In addition many nonbase facts are known, such as the fact $\neg\Box$r. Notice that this is a nonmonotonic property: if r is added to my data base then $\Box$r is true, and therefore $\neg\Box$r is no longer known.

Halpern and Moses conclude that the statement "all I know is α" is meaningful only for certain α's, and those are called *honest.* In the full paper I discuss Halpern and Moses' treatment in more detail. Here I will directly give the formulation in terms of preferred models, which is related to, but distinct from, one of their formulations.

Let us define a preference criterion on Kripke interpretations, according to which $M_1 < M_2$ iff

1. for all base wffs φ (i.e., those containing no occurrence of the modal operator), if $M_2 \models \Box\varphi$ then also $M_1 \models \Box\varphi$, and
2. there exists a base wff φ such that $M_1 \models \Box\varphi$ but $M_2 \not\models \Box\varphi$.

Let us also say that M_1 and M_2 are *equiignorant* if for all base wffs φ, $M_1 \models \Box\varphi$ iff $M_2 \models \Box\varphi$.

Proposition 9 *α is honest just in case all models of $\Box\alpha$ that are maximal w.r.t. < are equiignorant. Furthermore, if α is honest and "all I know is α," then "I know β" iff $\Box\alpha \models_< \Box\beta$.*

3.3 From circumscription to minimal knowledge

The above reformulations of the two nonmonotonic systems render each of them very transparent. In addition, the common framework of preferred models suggests a way of uniting these seemingly very different logics. In particular, the following new result states that the simple instance of circumscription discussed here can be easily be embeddded in the logic of minimal knowledge:

Proposition 10 *Let* A(P) *and* CM(A,P) *be as defined in the subsection on circumscription,* < *as defined in the subsection on minimal knowledge, and* B *any FO sentence. Then* CM(A,P) $\models$ B *iff* A(P) $\wedge$ $\forall$x (P(x) $\supset$ $\Box$P(x)) $\models_<$ B, *where* x *are the free variables of* P.

Indeed, in the full paper I argue that the seductive distinction between *default inferences* (such as those in circumscription) and *autoepistemic inferences* (such as those in the logic of minimal knowledge), proposed first in [M]and since then adopted quite widely, should be abolished.

4 Summary

I have presented a uniform approach to constructing and understanding nonmonotonic logics. The value of the formulation has not been its mathematical sophistication, but rather the opposite: the only notion added to traditional logic was that of a partial order on interpretations. The simplicity of the formulations makes transparent what in other systems is less immediate. The formulation is not only simple but also very general, and subsumes previous systems. I demonstrated that fact by defining two well-known nonmonotonic logics, those of circumscription and of minimal knowledge, in the new framework. The reformulations made it clear what was going on in the logics. They also suggested a connection between the two logics which until now have been unrelated to one another, and in particular it was shown that (one version of) circumscription can be reduced to the logic of minimal logic. In the full paper I discuss other nonmonotonic logics too: Reiter's default logic, a different version of it due to Lukaszewicz [Lu], and another system due to Bossu and Siegel [BS].

Several intriguing issues remain to be explored. One of them has to do with the relation to other nonstandard logical formulations. In particular, Johan van Benthem has drawn my attention to the close parallels between my formulations and formulations in Conditional Logic, as pioneered by D. Lewis [Le][vanB]. In CL one has, instead of a partial order on interpretations, a similarity measure on possible worlds, and the notion of counterfactual entailment is similar to my notion of preferential entailment. I would like to understand this connection better.

Another open question is which particular instances of the general framework I have outlined are interesting from the practical point of view. As I have said, the general treatment of nonmonotonic logics offered here grew out of limitations of existing systems. It is still the case, however, that very few concrete preference criteria on models have been investigated. The most common ones are those embodied in the various circumscription axioms and in some default theories. One preference criterion transcending those is that of chronological ignorance, presented in [S1]. Lifschitz too has investigated an instance of pointwise circumscription that does not collapse into "old" circumscription. All these, however, are still a drop in the bucket, and we have yet to understand which of the many possible partial orders on models are of practical importance.

Acknowledgements. Among the people who contributed to the form and content of this paper are Drew McDermott, Johan van Benthem, and Neil Immerman.

Bibliography

[vanB] J. F. A. K. van Benthem, Foundations of Conditional Logic, *Journal of Philosophical Logic* (13), January 1984, pp. 303-349.

[BS] G. Bossu & P. Siegel, Saturation, Nonmonotonic Reasoning, and the Closed-World Assumption, *Artificial Intelligence* 25(1), January 1985, pp. 13-65.

[C] K. L. Clark, Negation as Failure, in *Logic and Databases*, H. Gallaire & J. Minker (Eds.), Plenum Press, New York, 1978, pp. 293-322.

[E] D. Etherington, *Reasoning with Incomplete Information: Investigations of Non-Monotonic Reasoning*, Ph.D. dissertation, Computer Science Department, University of British Columbia, 1986.

[HM] J. Halpern & Y. Moses, *Towards a Theory of Knowledge and Ignorance: Preliminary Report*, IBM San Jose Research Laboratory RJ 4448 48136, October 1984.

[HMcD] S. Hanks and D. McDermott, *Temporal Reasoning and Default Logics*, Yale University, Computer Science Depratment YALEU/CSD/RR #430, October 1985.

[Le] D. Lewis, Counterfactuals and Comparative Possibility, in *Ifs*, Harper et al. (Eds.), Reidel, 1981, pp. 57-85.

[Li1] V. Lifschitz, Computing Circumscription, *Proc. IJCAI*, August, 1985.

[Li2] V. Lifschitz, Pointwise Circumscription, *Proc. AAAI*, August, 1986.

[Lu] V. Lukaszewicz, Considerations on Default Logic, *Proc. AAAI Workshop on Nonmonotonic Reasoning*, pp. 165-193, 1984.

[McC] J. M. McCarthy, Circumscription - A Form of Nonmonotonic Reasoning, *Artificial Intelligence* 13, 1980, pp. 27-39.

[McD] D. McDermott, Nonmonotonic Logic II: Nonmonotonic Modal Theories, *JACM* 29(1), 1982, pp. 33-57.

[McDD] D. McDermott & J. Doyle, Nonmonotonic Logic I, *Artificial Intelligence* 13, 1980, pp. 41-72.

[M] R. C. Moore, Semantical Considerations on Nonmonotonic Logic, *Proc. IJCAI*, 1983.

[R] R. Reiter, A Logic for Default Reasoning, *Artificial Intelligence* 13, 1980, pp. 81-132.

[S1] Y. Shoham, Chronological Ignorance, *Proc. AAAI*, August, 1986.

[S2] Y. Shoham, *Reasoning about Change: Time and Causation from the Standpoint of Artificial Intelligence*, Ph.D. Dissertation, Computer Science Department, Yale University, December 1986.

I'm OK if You're OK: On the Notion of Trusting Communication

Ronald Fagin
Joseph Y. Halpern

IBM Almaden Research Center
650 Harry Rd.
San Jose, CA 95120-6099
Email: Fagin@ibm.com, Halpern@ibm.com (ARPANET)

Abstract: We consider the issue of what an agent or a processor needs to know in order to know that its messages are true as a first step to a general theory of cooperative communication in distributed systems. An *honest* message is one that is known to be true when it is sent (or said). If every message that is sent is honest, then of course every message that is sent is true. Various weaker considitions than honesty are investigated with the property that provided every message sent satisfies the condition, then every message sent is true.

1. Introduction

In an analysis of communication between people or machines, a natural concept is that of an *honest* message. For a message m sent by machine (or said by person) p to be honest, it is not sufficient that m be true; it is also necessary for p to *know* that m is true at the time that p sends (or says) the message m. In the context of distributed computer systems, this notion of honesty was introduced by Halpern and Fagin [HF].

Although the notion of an honest message is quite natural, it is perhaps too strong a notion. In ordinary communication between people, what usually happens is that the information received via messages is combined with other information, and the resulting conclusion is passed on. For example, suppose that Alice knows that all managers at Acme Widget earn over $40,000, and then Charlie tells Alice that he has just been promoted to being a manager at Acme Widget. Alice then turns around and tells Bob that Charlie is now earning over $40,000.

Alice's message is not honest in the technical sense we have defined above. Alice does not *know* that Charlie earns over $40,000. After all, Charlie might be lying when he says that he is now a manager. By producing a more guarded statement (such as "Charlie told me that he has been promoted to manager, so I concluded that his salary is over $40,000"), Alice could have produced an honest message. If Alice believes quite strongly that Charlie is truthful, then it would be quite odd of her to make such a guarded statement; in fact, in practice, such a statement might convey implicitly that Alice has good reason to believe that Charlie is lying! Furthermore, in complex, real-life situations, there are many underlying assumptions, some of which the speaker may not even be aware of. So, in order to guarantee that her messages are honest, it would be necessary for Alice to produce extremely convoluted and unnatural messages. The theme of this paper is to consider less restrictive conditions than honesty, which still guarantee that provided every message satisfies the condition, then every message sent is true.

Our goal is to get a general theory of cooperative communication in distributed systems. Such a theory would lead to more efficient communication in systems of cooperating agents (such as distributed systems, where the "agents" are processors, or, in the context of AI, a group of communicating robots). It might also be useful in a general theory of natural language understanding. Our work is in somewhat the same spirit as that of the philosopher H.P. Grice (cf. [Gr]), who tries to characterize "helpful communication". Grice would say that although a guarded statement such as "Charlie told me that he has been promoted ..." might be honest, it would not be "helpful", exactly because it might give the wrong impression by darkly hinting that Charlie might be lying.

The idea we are trying to capture is essentially that of "I know that my message is true provided everyone else has been telling the truth." Formally, we say that a message m sent by p at time t is is *trusting* if p knows (at time t) that if every message sent up to time t is true, then m is true.[1] For example, Alice's message to Bob above that Charlie's salary is over $40,000 is trusting (although, as we observed, it is not honest).

We are really looking for an even less restrictive notion than trusting that, roughly speaking, corresponds to the idea "I'm OK if you're OK". Somewhat more formally, we want a notion *trusting** with the property that the message m sent by p is trusting* if p knows that if all previous messages are trusting*, then m is true. To understand the difference between trusting and trusting*, consider the following two situations. First suppose Charlie tells Alice "Richard loves Susan". If Alice now tells Bob "Richard loves Susan", then this would be a trusting message. It is true provided that Charlie's message is true. Suppose instead Alice tells Bob "Charlie knows that Richard loves Susan". Now this is no longer trusting. It is possible that Charlie's message is true without his knowing it (he might not know that Richard loves Susan and make a lucky guess). Thus Alice's message would be false although all previous messages are true. On the other hand, suppose that communication proceeds in rounds and Charlie's message was sent on the first round. Then for Charlie's message to be trusting*, Charlie would have to know it were true. Thus Alice's message would be trusting*.

Since trusting* is defined in terms of itself, it is not clear that it is well-defined. Indeed, we shall show that in general trusting* is *not* a well-defined notion. More formally, trusting* can be viewed as a fixed point of a certain equation. We say that there is a *complete consistent notion of trusting** in a system if there is a way of marking as "trusting*" some of the messages that are sent so as to satisfy this equation. A fixed point of this equation might not exist (and thus there are systems in which there is no complete consistent notion of trusting*), and even if one exists, it may not be unique. However, in systems where messages fulfill a certain well-foundedness property (such as systems with a global clock where messages proceed in rounds), we show that there is a unique complete consistent notion of trusting*. Moreover, we can show that whenever there is a complete consistent notion of trusting*, the messages labelled trusting* are a (not necessarily strict) superset of the trusting messages.

The rest of the paper is organized as follows. In the next section we briefly review ideas from [HM,HF] and other papers, describing how to ascribe knowledge to processors in a distributed system. In Section 3 we formally define the notions of honest and trusting, and give the intuition behind the notion of trusting*. We show that in a precise sense there is no notion

1 We could have taken a variant of this notion by defining a message sent by p at time t to be trusting if all messages previously received by p are true; i.e., instead of considering all messages sent, we could consider only the messages received by p. Everything we say in this paper goes through with this definition as well. The definition we actually use is slightly less restrictive, in that more messages will be considered trusting.

with the properties we want trusting* to have in a general system, but in well-founded systems, there is. In Section 4 we introduce the fixed point equation defining a complete consistent notion of trusting* and examine its solutions in more detail. In Section 5 we give our conclusions.

2. The model

Recently there have been a number of papers that ascribe knowledge to systems of communicating processors or agents ([HM,PR,CM, HF,DM,FI,LR,RK]; see [Ha] for a survey). All of the definitions have essentially the same features, which we briefly outline below. We phrase our definitions in terms of processors in a distributed system; we leave it to the reader to check that these definitions apply perfectly well to any group of communicating agents.

We assume that processors communicate by sending messages from some fixed set $\mathcal{M}$. A *run* r of a distributed system is a description of the execution of the system over time. We assume here for definiteness that "time" ranges over the natural numbers or the nonnegative reals here, although we could perfectly well have assumed that it ranged over any linearly ordered, unbounded set. The only facts about the run which will be relevant to us is the current state of a processor and the messages that it sends. Thus we take a run to be a function from time to *global states,* which are tuples of the form $<e,s_1,...,s_n>$, where s_i describes processor p_i's current *local state*, and e, the environment, describes which messages are currently being sent by each of the processors.[2] Thus, if r is a run and t is a time, then $r(t)$ is a global state. We also assume that only finitely many messages are sent up to any time t in a run r. As has been done in all the papers cited above, we will identify a system with a set R of runs.

We define a *point* in a system R to be a pair (r,t) consisting of a run $r \in R$ and time t. We say two points (r,t) and (r',t') in R are *indistinguishable* to processor p_i, and write $(r,t) \sim_i (r',t')$, if processor p_i has the same local state in $r(t)$ and $r'(t')$. That is, if $r(t) = <e, s_1, ..., s_n>$ and $r'(t') = <e', s'_1, ..., s'_n>$, then $s_i = s'_i$.

There are times when we want to restrict our attention to systems with certain properties. Of particular interest will be *synchronous phase systems.* These are systems where communication proceeds in rounds and there is a global clock, so that, intuitively, every processor knows what round it is. More formally, R is a synchronous phase system if time ranges over the natural numbers and for every two points (r,n) and (r',n') in R, we have $(r,n) \sim_i (r',n')$ only if $n = n'$.

In order to capture notions such as honesty, we need to be able to assign truth values to messages (which we are thinking of as formulas in some language). Given a set R of runs, a *semantic function* μ for R associates with each message m a set $\mu(m)$ of points in R. Intuitively, $\mu(m)$ is the set of points in R where m is true. In this paper we are viewing messages as black boxes, so there is no relationship between the sets $\mu(m)$ and $\mu(m')$ for distinct messages m and m'. In practice, there will be some fixed syntax for formulas (and thus for messages). We might

2 In a more detailed model of a distributed system, the global state would include more information and satisfy extra conditions. For example, we would expect the environment in the global state in run r at time t to describe all the messages that have been sent but not delivered up to that time. Moreover, we would expect a processor's local state to be a function of its *message history,* the sequence of messages it has sent and received in run r up to, but not including, time t, together with the times they were sent and received on the processor's local clock (if there are clocks in the system). However, the results and definitions of this paper are independent of these conditions, so we do not impose them here. We remark that all our impossibility results hold if we restrict attention to systems where a processor's state encodes its complete message history (this is the *total view* or *complete history* intepretation discussed in [HM]).

expect, for example, that if m and m' are messages, then there is a message $m \wedge m'$ and that $\mu(m \wedge m') = \mu(m) \cap \mu(m')$. We could easily extend μ to allow us to deal with conjunctions and negations of formulas as well as facts such as "all messages sent prior to this time are true". Although we do not do this formally here, we will informally assume that such more complicated statements also have truth values.

We call a pair (R, μ), consisting of a system R and a semantic function μ on R, an *interpreted system*. Finally we say m is *true at* (or *holds at*) the point (r,t) in the interpreted system $\mathcal{I} = (R, \mu)$ if $(r,t) \in \mu(m)$.

We want to extend the notion of truth at a point to assertions involving knowledge. This will allow us to talk about a processor *knowing* that a message is true, rather than the message just being true. Again, we follow the lines of all the papers previously cited. The intuition, which goes back to Hintikka [Hi], is that a processor knows a fact if it is true in all the worlds it considers possible. The worlds in an interpreted system will simply be the points, and the points that processor p_i considers possible at the point (r,t) are exactly those it cannot distinguish from (r,t), i.e. those worlds (r',t') such that $(r,t) \sim_i (r',t')$. Thus, for a message m, we say that $K_i m$ is *true at* or *holds at the point* (r,t) *in the interpreted system* $\mathcal{I} = (R, \mu)$ if $\{(r',t') \mid (r,t) \sim_i (r',t')\} \subseteq \mu(m)$. A formula such as $K_i m$ is read "processor p_i knows m".

As has been remarked before (eg. in [HM,HF,Ha]), this is an *external* notion of knowledge. We ascribe knowledge to a processor based on its local state. A processor cannot necessarily answer questions based on its knowledge, nor do we imagine it doing any computation in order to acquire its knowledge. This notion of knowledge has, however, been shown to be quite useful for analyzing distributed protocols [HM,CM,DM,MT,Ha]. Moreover, it is one way of giving a concrete interpretation to the standard S5 notion of knowledge discussed by Hintikka.

3. Honest, trusting, and trusting* messages

Following [HF], we say that a message is *honest* if it is known to be true. Formally, the message m sent by p_i at the point (r,t) in an interpreted system $\mathcal{I}$ is honest if $K_i m$ holds at (r,t). Note that it is not really a message that is honest or dishonest, it is a message sent by a particular processor at a particular point. The same message m may be honest at one point and not at another, or may be honest if sent by one processor but not by another. It will often be convenient for us to denote the message m sent by p_i at the point (r,t) by the tuple (m,i,r,t). We call such a tuple a *labelled message*. We say a labelled message (m,i,r,t) is true (resp. honest) if m is true (resp. honest) at the point (r,t).

As we mentioned in the introduction, we want to extend the notion of honesty to allow deductions based on previous messages under the assumption that the previous messages are true. As a first step towards capturing this intuition, we say that the labelled message (m,i,r,t) is *trusting* if p_i knows at the point (r,t) that if all previous messages are true, then m is true. More formally, the labelled message (m,i,r,t) in the interpreted system $\mathcal{I}$ is trusting if for all (r',t') such that $(r',t') \sim_i (r,t)$, either m is true at (r',t') (i.e. $(r',t') \in \mu(m)$) or for some $t'' < t'$, a message m' sent at time t'' in r' was not true when it was sent (i.e. $(r',t'') \notin \mu(m')$). It is easy to see that in the scenario described in the first example in the introduction, Alice's message is not honest, but it is trusting.

Recall that we are trying to capture the idea "I'm OK if you're OK." The notion of trusting intuitively captures the idea "I'm telling the truth provided you've been telling the truth", but does *not* capture the notion "I'm telling the truth provided all the statements you made were true provided all the statements I made were true provided ..." In order to capture this, we need a notion trusting* with the property that (m, i, r, t) is trusting* if p_i knows at the point (r, t) that if all previous messages are trusting*, then m is true. Given the circularity inherent in this notion, it is not clear that it is well-defined. Indeed, we shall show that in general it is not. We first provide a few formal definitions.

Suppose we have an interpreted system $\mathcal{I} = (R, \mu)$. A *consistent notion of trusting** in $\mathcal{I}$ is simply a function (called a *marking function*) that marks some labelled messages in $\mathcal{I}$ "trusting*" in such a way that if a labelled message (m, i, r, t) is marked "trusting*" then for all points (r', t') such that $(r', t') \sim_i (r, t)$, either m is true at (r', t') or some labelled message sent previously (before time t') in r' is not marked "trusting*". A *complete* consistent notion of trusting* is a consistent notion of trusting* where a message is marked "trusting*" *if and only if* for all points (r', t') such that $(r', t') \sim_i (r, t)$, either m is true at (r', t') or some labelled message sent previously (before time t') in r' is not marked "trusting*".[3] Note that here we have been somewhat lax and have talked about a "message" being marked "trusting*" rather than a labelled message. We are similarly lax throughout the paper; we hope that what is meant is clear from context.

We remark that a complete consistent notion of trusting* can be characterized as a solution to a fixed point equation. We do this in the next section. We first must check that the notion of trusting* has the properties that originally motivated its definition. Note that it is immediate from the definitions that a consistent notion of trusting* (resp. complete consistent notion of trusting*) has the property that a labelled message is marked "trusting*" only if (resp. iff) the sender knows that if all previous labelled messages are marked "trusting*", then l is true. It follows that a consistent notion of trusting* captures the intuition "I'm OK if you're OK." If every message in a run is OK (i.e. marked trusting*), then they are all true. The following proposition makes this precise.

Proposition 3.1. *Let $\mathcal{I}$ be an interpreted system and (r, t) a point in $\mathcal{I}$. For each consistent notion of trusting*, if every message that is sent in run r up to time t is marked trusting*, then every message sent in run r up to time t is true.*

Proof. Suppose we have a consistent notion of trusting* with a marking function f such that every message in run r up to time t is marked trusting* by f. Further suppose that p sends message m in run r at time t. It follows from the definition of a consistent notion of trusting* that p knows that if every previous message is

---

3 We could have considered a slight variant of the definition of consistent notion of trusting* by defining a consistent′ notion of trusting* to be a function that marks some (not necessarily all) labelled messages in $\mathcal{I}$ as either "trusting*" or "not trusting*" (but not both!) in such a way that (a) a labelled message (m, i, r, t) is marked "trusting*" only if for all points (r', t') such that $(r', t') \sim_i (r, t)$, either m is true at (r', t') or some labelled message sent previously is labelled "not trusting*" and (b) a labelled message (m, i, r, t) is marked "not trusting*" only if at some point (r', t') such that $(r', t') \sim_i (r, t)$ we have both that m is false and that all messages sent previously in r' are marked "trusting*". We could then define a *complete* consistent′ notion of trusting* to be one where all messages are marked either "trusting*" or "not trusting*". It is easy to see that a complete consistent′ notion of trusting* is simply a complete consistent notion of trusting* where all the messages not labelled "trusting*" are labelled "not trusting*". Thus, complete consistent and complete consistent′ notions of trusting* are essentially identical. Moreover, if we consider the messages marked "trusting*" by a consistent′ notion of trusting*, we get a consistent notion of trusting*. The converse, however, is not true in general. Consider an interpreted system $\mathcal{I}$ where a false message m is sent at the point (r, t) by p_1. Suppose that there are no other points in $\mathcal{I}$ where p_1 has the same local state as in (r, t), and further suppose that m is preceded in (r, t) by one message, which happens to be honest. The function that labels only m "trusting*" gives a consistent notion of trusting*, but it is easy to see that there is no consistent′ notion of trusting* that marks m "trusting*". All the theorems we state here hold if we replace consistent and complete by consistent′ and complete′, with essentially no change in proof. We gave the definitions we did simply because they are somewhat simpler and they make our proofs go through a little more smoothly. Both definitions agree on what we consider to be the most important properties.

marked "trusting*", then m is true. Since every previous message is indeed marked "trusting*", m is true. ■

We now examine the relationship between trusting* and the other notions we have defined. Clearly we can always get a trivial consistent notion of trusting* by simply not marking any messages "trusting*". It is also easy to see that we get a consistent notions of trusting* by marking the honest messages "trusting*" and we get another one by marking the trusting messages "trusting*". Thus a consistent notion of trusting* can be viewed as generalizing the notions of honest and trusting. However, it is clearly possible to have consistent notions of trusting* where some trusting messages are not marked trusting* (for example, the consistent notion of trusting* where no messages are marked "trusting*"). As the following result shows, this is not the case for a complete consistent notion of trusting*.

Proposition 3.2. *Every trusting message is marked "trusting*" by every complete consistent notion of trusting*.*

Proof. Suppose we have a complete consistent notion of trusting*. Let $l = (m, i, r, t)$ be a trusting labelled message. Then p_i knows when it sends m at the point (r, t) that if every previous message is marked trusting*, then (by Proposition 3.1) every previous message is true, so l is true (since l is trusting). So l must be marked "trusting*". ■

It is not hard to show that there are interpreted systems where the messages marked "trusting*" according to a complete consistent notion of trusting* form a strict superset of the trusting messages. (We gave an informal example in the introduction which can be easily formalized; another example is given at the end of this section.) Of course we still haven't shown that every interpreted system has a complete consistent notion of trusting*. Indeed, as we hinted above, this is not the case. We now prove this by example.

Given an interpreted system $\mathcal{I}$, let us say that the labelled messages (m, i, r, t) and (m, i, r', t') of $\mathcal{I}$ are *indistinguishable by the sender* (in this case p_i) if $(r, t) \sim_i (r', t')$. Note that in a complete consistent notion of trusting*, if two labelled messages are indistinguishable by the sender, then either both are marked "trusting*" or neither is marked "trusting*". This is as it should be, since we would expect that if two messages are indistinguishable by the sender, then they should be marked the same way.

Theorem 3.3. *There exists an interpreted system with no complete consistent notion of trusting*.*

Proof. Consider an interpreted system $\mathcal{I} = (R, \mu)$ where there are three processors p_1, p_2, and p_3, and where R consists of exactly three runs, say r_1, r_2, and r_3. The only message that is ever sent in any of these runs is the message m, which we can think of as saying "this is the first message in the run". In run r_1, processor p_1 sends m at time 1, and processor p_2 sends m at time 2. In run r_2, processor p_2 sends m at time 1, and processor p_3 sends m at time 2. In run r_3, processor p_3 sends m at time 1, and processor p_1 sends m at time 2. These are the only messages sent. We assume that each processor's local states are such that the processor is in the same state at the two points where it sends a message, and in a different state at the other points. Finally, we take μ to be such that m is true at time 1 in each of the runs, but false at time 2. The situation is described in Figure 1 (where we label a point T or F to indicate whether or not the message m is true at that point).

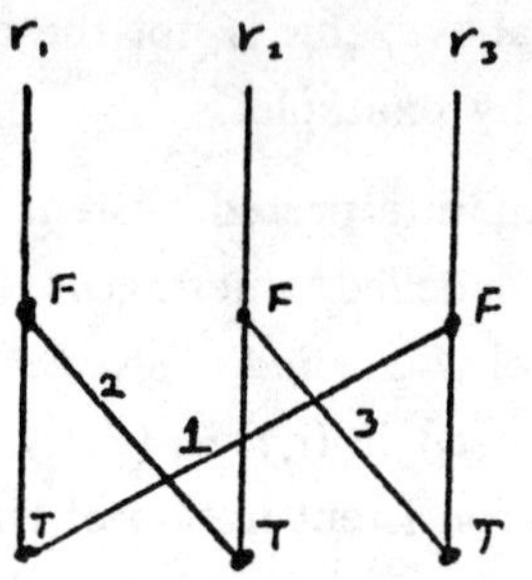

Figure 1

Suppose there were a complete consistent notion of trusting* in $\mathscr{I}$. Assume first that some message sent by p_1 is marked "trusting*". Since p_1 cannot distinguish the two points where it sent the message, each message sent by p_1 must be marked "trusting*". But then our definition forces us not to mark either message sent by p_2 "trusting*" (since, for example, $(m,2,r_1,2)$ is false and is preceded only by a message marked "trusting*"). We now leave it to the reader to check that this forces us to mark each message sent by p_3 "trusting*", which in turn forces us not to mark the message sent by p_1 "trusting*". We have shown that if some message sent by p_1 is marked "trusting*", then every message sent by p_1 should not be marked "trusting*", a contradiction. On the other hand, if no message sent by p_1 is marked "trusting*", then arguing as before, we see that this forces us to mark each message sent by p_2 "trusting*", which forces us not to mark any message sent by p_3 "trusting*", which forces us to mark every message sent by p_1 "trusting*", a contradiction. ■

Intuitively, the problem here is a certain lack of well-foundedness. We define a partial order $\prec$ on labelled messages in an interpreted system $\mathscr{I}$ by taking $\prec$ to be the least transitive relation such that (a) $(m,i,r,t)\prec(m',i',r,t')$ if $t<t'$ and (b) if l_1, l'_1 (resp. l_2, l'_2) are labelled messages that are indistinguishable by the sender and $l_1\prec l_2$, then $l'_1\prec l'_2$. We say that $\mathscr{I}$ is *well-founded* if $\prec$ is a well-founded partial order on labelled messages in $\mathscr{I}$; i.e., if there is no infinite descending chain $\ldots\prec l_3\prec l_2\prec l_1$ of labelled messages.

It is easy to see that the interpreted system described in Theorem 3.3 is not well-founded. On the other hand, synchronous phase systems are always well-founded. As we now show, well-foundedness is a sufficient condition for a system to have a *unique* complete consistent notion of trusting*. Intuitively, this is because in a well-founded system, we can define the notion of trusting* by induction.

Theorem 3.4. *In each well-founded interpreted system, there is a unique complete consistent notion of trusting*.*

Proof. Assume that the interpreted system $\mathscr{I}$ is well-founded. Let $\prec$ be as defined above. By transfinite induction on $\prec$, we can associate a *rank* with each labelled message l by letting $rank(l)$ be the least ordinal that is greater than every $rank(l')$ where $l'\prec l$. We now define, by transfinite induction, a marking function f.

If $rank(l)=0$, we mark l "trusting*" iff l is honest. Suppose $rank(l)>0$ and we have already decided which labelled messages with rank less than $rank(l)$ are marked "trusting*". If $l=(m,i,r,t)$, we mark l "trusting*" iff for all points (r',t') such that $(r',t')\sim_i(r,t)$, either m is true at (r',t') or some labelled message l' sent previously in r' is not marked "trusting*". This completes the definition of the marking function. A straightforward induction on rank can now be used to show that a labelled message $l=(m,i,r,t)$ is marked "trusting*" iff for all points (r',t') such that $(r',t')\sim_i(r,t)$, either m is true at (r',t') or some labelled message sent previously (before time t') in r' is not marked "trusting*". Thus f defines a complete consistent notion of trusting* in $\mathscr{I}$. If f' is another complete consistent notion of trusting*, we can show by induction on rank that l is marked "trusting*" by f iff it is marked "trusting*" by f'. Thus f defines the unique complete consistent notion of trusting* in $\mathscr{I}$. ■

It follows that in a well-founded system we can speak without ambiguity of a trusting* message. The following result says that in general we cannot. Even in a system where there is a complete consistent notion of trusting*, it might not be unique.

Theorem 3.5. *There are interpreted systems with more than one complete consistent notion of trusting*.*

Proof. We modify the system described in the proof of Theorem 3.3 so that there are now only two processors rather than three. Let $\mathcal{I} = (R, \mu)$ be an interpreted system with two processors, p_1 and p_2, where R consists of exactly two runs, say r_1 and r_2. Again there is only one message m. In run r_1, processor p_1 sends m at time 1, and processor p_2 sends m at time 2. In run r_2, processor p_2 sends m at time 1, and processor p_1 sends m at time 2. These are the only messages sent. We take the processors' local states to be such that each processor is in the same state at the two points where it sends a message, and in a different state at the other points. Finally, we take μ to be such that m is true at time 1 in both runs, but false at time 2. Thus, as in Theorem 3.3, we can think of m as saying "this is the first message in the run". It is straightforward to verify that it is we get a complete consistent notion of trusting* either (a) by marking only p_1's messages "trusting*", or (b) by marking only p_2's messages "trusting*". ∎

Theorem 3.3, Theorem 3.4, and Theorem 3.5 together show that in an interpreted system there may be no complete consistent notion of trusting*, exactly one such notion, or more than one.

Note that in the intepreted system constructed in the proof of Theorem 3.5, none of the messages are trusting. Thus we have an example of a complete consistent notion of trusting* where the messages marked "trusting*" form a strict superset of the trusting messages. We can also formalize the example given in the introduction to get a well-founded system with a unique complete consistent notion of trusting* where the messages marked "trusting*" form a strict superset of the trusting messages.

4. Viewing trusting* as a fixed point

We have seen that "trusting*" is not guaranteed to be a well-defined notion if the interpreted system is not well-founded. We can get a better understanding of the situation by viewing trusting* as a solution of a certain fixed point equation, and then constructing approximations to it.

Let $\mathcal{I}$ be an interpreted system. If X is a set of labelled messages of $\mathcal{I}$, define $F_1(X)$ to be the set of labelled messages (m, i, r, t) of $\mathcal{I}$ such that p_i knows at (r, t) that either m is true or some previous message is in X (i.e. $(m, i, r, t) \in F_1(X)$ if whenever $(r', t') \sim_i (r, t)$, either $(r', t') \in \mu(m)$, or some message sent before time t' in r' is in X). Similarly, define $F_2(X)$ to be the set of labelled messages (m, i, r, t) of $\mathcal{I}$ such that p_i considers it possible at (r, t) that all previous messages are in X and m is false (i.e. $(m, i, r, t) \in F_2(X)$ if there exists a point (r', t') such that (a) $(r', t') \sim_i (r, t)$, (b) $(r', t') \notin \mu(m)$, and (c) all messages sent before time t' in r' are in X). It is clear that F_1 and F_2 are monotone, in the sense that if $X \subseteq Y$, then $F_1(X) \subseteq F_1(Y)$ and $F_2(X) \subseteq F_2(Y)$.

The relation between these functions and the notion of trusting* is brought out in the following lemma (where X^c denotes the complement of X).

Lemma 4.1. *Let $\mathcal{I}$ be an interpreted system and let f be a function that marks the precisely the labelled messages in a set $\mathcal{T}$ "trusting*".*

1. *f is a consistent notion of trusting* iff $\mathcal{T} \subseteq F_1(\mathcal{T}^c)$.*
2. *f is a complete consistent notion of trusting* iff $\mathcal{T} = F_1(\mathcal{T}^c)$ and $\mathcal{T}^c = F_2(\mathcal{T})$.*

Proof. Straightforward. ∎

Define $F(X, Y) = (F_1(Y), F_2(X))$. By Lemma 4.1, it follows that f is a complete consistent notion of trusting* iff $F(\mathcal{T}, \mathcal{T}^c) = (\mathcal{T}, \mathcal{T}^c)$, where $\mathcal{T}$ is the set of labelled messages marked "trusting*" by f. We know from Theorem 3.3 that we will not always be able to find such a set $\mathcal{T}$. However, this fixed point equation suggests a way of approximating a complete consistent notion of trusting*. We define two hierarchies T_α and N_α of (labelled) messages of $\mathcal{I}$, where each hierarchy is indexed by ordinals α.

1. $T_0 = N_0 = \emptyset$.
2. $T_{\alpha+1} = F_1(N_\alpha)$.
3. $N_{\alpha+1} = F_2(T_\alpha)$.
4. If α is a limit ordinal, then $T_\alpha = \bigcup_{\delta<\alpha} T_\delta$ and $N_\alpha = \bigcup_{\delta<\alpha} N_\delta$.

Let $T^* = \bigcup_\alpha T_\alpha$ and let $N^* = \bigcup_\alpha N_\alpha$.[4]

It is easy to see that T_1 consists precisely of the honest messages, so the hierarchy extends the notion of honesty. We discuss how trusting messages relate to the hierarchy in the full paper.

Intuitively, T^* forms a lower bound on the labelled messages marked "trusting*" by any complete consistent notion of trusting*, while N^* forms a lower bound on the labelled messages not marked "trusting*". More formally we have

Proposition 4.2. *For each complete consistent notion of trusting*, every message in T^* is marked "trusting*" and every message in N^* is not marked "trusting*".*

Proof. If f is a complete consistent notion of trusting* in an interpreted system $\mathcal{I}$, we can show by a straightforward induction on α that every message in T_α is marked "trusting*" by f and every message in N_α is not marked "trusting*". ∎

Proposition 4.2 would lead us to expect that we get a unique complete consistent notion of trusting* when $T^* = (N^*)^c$. It is clear that if we have an interpreted system where $T^* = (N^*)^c$ and there is a complete consistent notion of trusting* in this system, then it must be unique. In order to show that there is a complete consistent notion of trusting* in such a system, we need an easy lemma, which shows that the T_α's and N_α's do indeed form a hierarchy. This observation will have a number of other interesting consequences.

Lemma 4.3.

1. *If $\alpha < \beta$, then $T_\alpha \subseteq T_\beta$ and $N_\alpha \subseteq N_\beta$.*
2. *T^* and N^* are disjoint.*

Proof. We prove (1) by induction on β. The result is clear if β is a limit ordinal. If β is a successor ordinal, suppose that $\beta = \beta' + 1$. Then

$$T_\beta = F_1(N_{\beta'}) \supseteq \bigcup_{\gamma<\beta'} F_1(N_\gamma) = \bigcup_{\gamma<\beta'} T_{\gamma+1} = T_{\beta'}.$$

Note that the inductive step is used in a number of these steps, as well as the fact that F_1 is monotonic. Finally, since $\alpha < \beta$, we have $\alpha \leq \beta'$, so from the inductive hypothesis it follows that $T_\alpha \subseteq T_{\beta'}$. Thus $T_\alpha \subseteq T_\beta$. Identically $N_\alpha \subseteq N_\beta$.

In order to prove (2), we show by induction on α that T_α and N_α are disjoint. There is no difficulty for limit ordinals. If α is a successor ordinal, suppose that $\alpha = \alpha' + 1$ and the labelled message $l = (m, i, r, t)$ is in N_α. By definition, there exists a point (r', t') such that (a) $(r', t') \sim_i (r, t)$, (b) $(r', t') \notin \mu(m)$, and (c) all messages sent before time t' in r' are in $T_{\alpha'}$. By the inductive hypothesis, no messages sent before time t' in r' are in $N_{\alpha'}$, so it is easy to see

[4] The reader familiar with the work of Kripke and other philosophers on defining a truth predicate [Kr,Gu] will immediately see the similarities between our approach and theirs. Kripke also defines a function analogous to our F and constructs its fixed point just as we have constructed T^* and N^*. Kripke is interested in all the fixed points of the function that he constructs. We only focus here on fixpoints of F of the form $(\mathcal{T}, \mathcal{T}^c)$ (which, as shown in Lemma 4.1, correspond to complete consistent notions of trusting*) and the fixed point (T^*, N^*). We remark that the labelled messages in $T^* \cup N^*$ are analogous to what Kripke called *grounded* formulas. It is interesting to note that whereas Kripke is interested in defining a notion of truth, we are working one level up. We need to assume a notion of truth in order to begin to make sense of notions such as honest, trusting, and trusting*.

that $l \notin F_1(N_{\alpha'}) = T_\alpha$. Thus T_α and N_α are disjoint. ∎

One easy consequence of Lemma 4.3 is that the T_α and N_α hierarchies must eventually collapse.

Theorem 4.4. *For each interpreted system, there exists γ such that $T_\gamma = T^*$ and $N_\gamma = N^*$.*

Proof. Let λ be the cardinality of the number of labelled messages. If the T_α hierarchy does not eventually collapse, then there are arbitrarily large values of β (and, in particular, more than λ distinct values of β) such that the difference $T_{\beta+1} - T_\beta$ is nonempty. But this gives us too many labelled messages. ∎

It follows easily from this proof that it is sufficient to take γ in the statement of Theorem 4.4 to be the least cardinal greater than the cardinality of the number of labelled messages. (We require the additional observation that if $T_\alpha = T_{\alpha+1} = T_{\alpha+2}$ then $T_\alpha = T^*$.)

Another consequence of the preceding results is that (T^*,N^*) is a fixed point of F; in fact, it is easy to see that the construction used guarantees that it is the least fixed point, although we do not bother to prove this here.

Theorem 4.5. $F(T^*,N^*) = (T^*,N^*)$.

Proof. We must show that $T^* = F_1(N^*)$ and $N^* = F_2(T^*)$. The argument is quite standard. We show that $T^* = F_1(N^*)$; the proof that $N^* = F_2(T^*)$ is similar and left to the reader.

Since F_1 is monotonic, we clearly have

$$F_1(N^*) \supseteq \cup_\alpha F_1(N_\alpha) = \cup_\alpha T_{\alpha+1} = T^*.$$

From Theorem 4.4, it follows that there exists γ such that $N^* = N_\gamma$, so that

$$F_1(N^*) = F_1(N_\gamma) \subseteq T_{\gamma+1} \subseteq T^*.$$

Thus $T^* = F_1(N^*)$. ∎

Theorem 4.6. *For all α, the function which marks all the labelled messages in T_α "trusting*" is a consistent notion of trusting*.*

Proof. Using Lemma 4.3, Theorem 4.5, and the fact that F_1 is monotonic, we get the following chain of containments:

$$T_\alpha \subseteq T^* = F_1(N^*) \subseteq F_1((T^*)^c) \subseteq F_1(T_\alpha^c).$$

Since $T_\alpha \subseteq F_1(T_\alpha^c)$, it follows from Lemma 4.1 that the function which marks all the labelled messages in T_α "trusting*" is a consistent notion of trusting*. ∎

We are now ready to prove:

Theorem 4.7. *If $T^* = (N^*)^c$, then there is a unique complete consistent notion of trusting* f, and the labelled messages marked "trusting*" by f are precisely the members of T^*.*

Proof. Let f be the function which marks the members of T^* as "trusting*". It follows immediately from Proposition 4.2 that the only possible complete consistent notion of trusting* is f. We now show that f is indeed a complete consistent notion of trusting*. We must show that a labelled message l is marked "trusting*" iff the sender knows that if all previous messages are marked "trusting*", then l is true. We shall simply show the "only if" direction, since the "if" direction is very similar. Let γ be so large that $T_\gamma = T_{\gamma+1} = T^*$ and $N_\gamma = N_{\gamma+1} = N^*$. Assume that a labelled message $l = (m, i, r, t)$ is marked "trusting*". Hence, $l \in T^*$. Therefore, $l \in T_{\gamma+1}$, and so p_i knows at (r, t) that either m is true or some previous message is in $N_\gamma = N^*$. Therefore, p_i knows that if all previous messages are marked "trusting*", then l is true. This was to be shown. ∎

We have already shown (Theorem 3.4) that for well-founded interpreted systems there is a unique complete consistent notion of trusting*. It will probably not surprise the reader to learn that the proof of this fact easily generalizes to show that in a well-founded interpreted system we also have $T^* = (N^*)^c$.

Theorem 4.8. *If the interpreted system is well-founded, then $T^* = (N^*)^c$.*

Proof. It is easy to modify the proof of Theorem 3.4 to show that T_α consists precisely of those labelled messages l with $rank(l) = \alpha$ that are marked "trusting*" while N_α consists of those labelled messages l with $rank(l) = \alpha$ that are not marked "trusting*". The result follows. ■

In the important special case of synchronous phase systems, we have the following result.

Corollary 4.9. *For synchronous phase systems,* $T_\omega = T^* = (N^*)^c = (N_\omega)^c$.

Proof. It follows immediately from the proof of Theorem 4.8 that if γ is larger than the rank of every labelled message in a well-founded system $\mathcal{I}$, then then $T^* = T_\gamma$ and $N^* = N_\gamma$. It is clear that the rank of a labelled message sent in the kth round of a synchronous phase system is at most $k-1$. Therefore, ω is larger than the rank of every labelled message in a synchronous phase system, so $T^* = T_\omega$ and $N^* = N_\omega$. This, together with Theorem 4.8, gives us the result desired. ■

Thus, for synchronous phase systems, we have

$$(*) \quad \begin{array}{l} T_0 \subseteq T_1 \subseteq \ldots \subseteq T_k \subseteq T_{k+1} \subseteq \ldots \subseteq T_\omega = T^*. \\ N_0 \subseteq N_1 \subseteq \ldots \subseteq N_k \subseteq N_{k+1} \subseteq \ldots \subseteq N_\omega = N^*. \end{array}$$

Does the T_α hierarchy (or the N_α hierarchy) collapse earlier than level ω in this case or are the inclusions in (*) strict? In general, the latter holds:

Theorem 4.10. *There is a synchronous phase system where all of the inclusions in (*) are strict.*

Proof. Consider a synchronous phase system $\mathcal{I} = (R, \mu)$ where there are two processors p_1 and p_2, and where R consists of countably many runs $r_1, r_2, r_3, \ldots$ and $r'_1, r'_2, r'_3, \ldots$. In each run, each processor sends exactly one message. In run r_k, message m_k is sent in round k and message m_{k+1} is sent in round $k+1$. In run r'_k, message m'_k is sent in round k and message m'_{k+1} is sent in round $k+1$. Processor p_1 sends the odd-numbered messages $(m_1, m'_1, m_3, m'_3, \ldots)$ while p_2 sends the even-numbered messages. We think of m_1 as being logically true, m'_1 as being logically false, and the messages m_{k+1} (resp. m'_{k+1}) for $k \geq 1$ as saying "if this is the point $(r_k, k+1)$ or $(r_{k+1}, k+1)$ (resp. $(r'_k, k+1)$ or $(r'_{k+1}, k+1)$), then this is the first message in the run". Thus, we take μ to be such that m_1 is true at all points, m'_1 is false at all points, and m_{k+1} (resp. m'_{k+1}) is false at the point (r_{k+1}, k) (resp. (r'_{k+1}, k)) but true at all other points. Finally, we assume that for all runs r, each of the processors is in distinct local states at every round of r (so that $\mathcal{I}$ really is a synchronous phase system) and that on odd-numbered rounds (resp. even-numbered rounds) processor p_1 (resp. p_2) is in the same state at the two points where it sends the message m_k and in the same state at the two points where it sends the message m'_k. This situation is described in Figure 2.

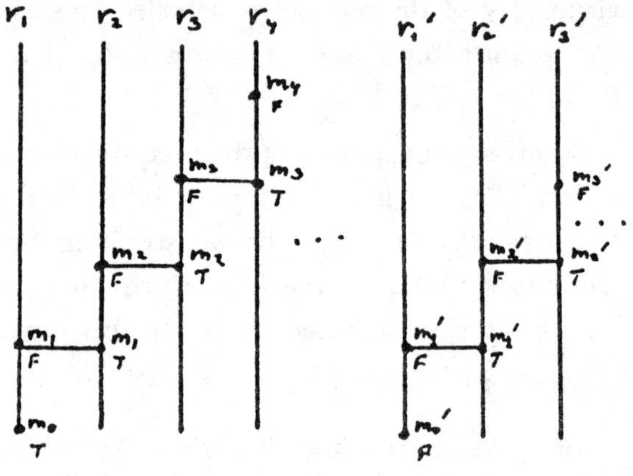

Figure 2

An easy induction on k now shows that for $k \geq 1$, if k is odd, then (the labelled version of) the message m_k is in T_k but not in T_{k-1}, and if k is even, then (the labelled version of) the message m_k is in N_k but not in N_{k-1}. A very similar argument shows that if k is odd, then (the labelled version of) the message m'_k is in N_k but not in N_{k-1}, and if k is even, then (the labelled version of) the message m'_k is in T_k but not in T_{k-1}. Taken together, of course, these results are sufficient to prove the theorem. We leave details to the reader. ■

We note that similarly, for each γ, we can find a well-founded interpreted system where $T_\alpha \neq T_\beta$ and $N_\alpha \neq N_\beta$ when α and β are distinct ordinals less than γ.

From Theorem 3.3 and Theorem 4.7 it follows that there will be interpreted systems where we do not have $T^* = (N^*)^c$. Techniques similar to those of Theorem 3.3 and Theorem 3.5 can be used to show that in interpreted systems where $T^* \neq (N^*)^c$, anything may happen. We may have no complete consistent notion of trusting*, a unique complete consistent notion of trusting*, and more than one complete consistent notion of trusting*. We omit details here.

5. Conclusions

We investigated the general issue of what an agent or processor needs to know in order to know that its messages are true. This led us to define the notion of trusting messages, where a message is trusting if it is known to be true provided that all previous messages are true. We tried to generalize this notion by defining trusting* messages, where intuitively a trusting* message is one that is known to be true provided that all previous messages are trusting*. We showed that trusting* messages are not well-defined in general. However, they are well-defined in many natural systems, such as synchronous phase systems, where communication proceeds in rounds and there is a global clock.

None of the results in this paper is difficult to prove. We believe that the major contribution of the paper lies not in the depth of the results, but in the ideas. We made a number of false starts in pursuing the ideas in this paper, and we now feel that we have the "right" definitions (although, as we indicated in a few places in the paper, there are some quite reasonable variants of the definitions we have chosen that lead to essentially the same results).

While we defined honest, trusting , and trusting* in the context of the S5 notion of knowledge used in distributed systems, they should make sense for other notions of knowledge as well. It would be interesting to pursue these issues in the context of other notions of knowledge, perhaps ones that better model resource-bounded human reasoners.

Acknowledgements: We would like to thank Gordon Plotkin, Moshe Vardi, and Ed Wimmers for their comments on a previous draft of this paper. Moshe also pointed out to us the connection between trusting* and the Kripke truth predicate.

References

[CM] M. Chandy and J. Misra, How processes learn, *Distributed Computing* **1**:1, 1986, pp. 40-52.

[DM] C. Dwork and Y. Moses, Knowledge and common knowledge in a Byzantine environment I: crash failures, *Theoretical Aspects of Reasoning About Knowledge: Proc. of the 1986 Conference* (ed. J.Y. Halpern), Morgan Kaufmann, 1986, pp. 149-169.

[FI] M.J. Fischer and N. Immerman, Foundations of knowledge for distributed systems, *Theoretical Aspects of Reasoning About Knowledge: Proceedings of the 1986 Conference* (ed. J.Y. Halpern), Morgan Kaufmann, 1986, pp. 171-185.

[Gr] H.P. Grice, Logic and conversation, in *Syntax and Semantics*, (eds. P. Cole and J.L. Morgan), Academic Press, 1975.

[Gu] A. Gupta, Truth and paradox, *Journal of Philosophical Logic* **11**, 1982, pp. 1-60. Reprinted in *Recent Essays on Truth and the Liar Paradox* (ed. R.L. Martin), Oxford University Press, 1984, pp. 175-235.

[Ha] J.Y. Halpern, Using reasoning about knowledge to analyze distributed systems, to appear in *Annual Review of Computer Science, Vol. 2* (ed. J. Traub et. al.), Annual Reviews Inc., 1987.

[HF] J.Y. Halpern and R. Fagin, A formal model of knowledge, action, and communication in distributed systems, *Proceedings of the 4th ACM Symposium on Principles of Distributed Computing*, 1985, pp. 224-236.

[HM] J.Y. Halpern and Y.O. Moses, Knowledge and common knowledge in a distributed environment, *Proceedings of the 3rd ACM Conference on Principles of Distributed Computing*, 1984, pp. 50-61; a revised version appears as IBM Research Report RJ 4421, 1986.

[Hi] J. Hintikka, *Knowledge and Belief*, Cornell University Press, 1962.

[Kr] S.A. Kripke, Outline of a theory of truth, in *Recent Essays on Truth and the Liar Paradox* (ed. R.L. Martin), 1984, Oxford University Press.

[LR] R. Ladner and J.H. Reif, The logic of distributed protocols, *Theoretical Aspects of Reasoning About Knowledge: Proc. of the 1986 Conference* (ed. J.Y. Halpern), Morgan Kaufmann, 1986, pp. 207-221.

[MT] Y. Moses and M. Tuttle, Programming simultaneous actions using common knowledge, *Proceedings of the 27th Annual Symposium on Foundations of Computer Science*, 1986, pp. 208-221.

[PR] R. Parikh and R. Ramanujam, Distributed processing and the logic of knowledge, *Proceedings of the Workshop on Logics of Programs* (ed. R. Parikh), 1985, pp. 256-268.

[RK] S. Rosenschein and L. Kaelbling, The synthesis of digital machines with provable epistemic properties, *Theoretical Aspects of Reasoning About Knowledge: Proceedings of the 1986 Conference* (ed. J.Y. Halpern), Morgan Kaufmann, 1986, pp. 83-97.

HOARE LOGIC FOR LAMBDA-TERMS AS BASIS OF HOARE LOGIC FOR IMPERATIVE LANGUAGES

Andreas Goerdt

Lehrstuhl für Informatik II, Technische Hochschule Aachen
Büchel 29 - 31, D-5100 Aachen, West-Germany

Abstract

Denotational semantics allows us to translate many imperative languages into the language of finitely typed λ-terms. Applying our[9, 10] Hoare Calculus for typed λ-terms, we get Hoare Calculi for such languages in a uniform way. Completeness results for these calculi follow from the completeness result proved by the author[9, 10].

We demonstrate our basic ideas for the language *While*, obtaining a calculus which is effectively equivalent to the classical Hoare Calculus for *While*. The same method as for *While* yields a Hoare Calculus for a language with higher type procedures and parameters standing for locations (reference parameters), the language L_4 from Clarke[2]. This calculus is for Herbrand definable interpretations complete in the sense of Cook. This shows the power of our method, for, though Hoare Logic for higher type concepts in programming languages raised some interest in the literature[4, 5, 6, 7, 8, 12, 13, 14], only the Hoare Calculus by German et al.[7, 8] has similar (in fact slightly stronger) completeness properties as our calculus.

The underlying idea

Let L be an imperative language which is translatable into the language of finitely typed λ-terms. That means, for any signature (made up from operation and relation symbols) for L there is a signature for λ-terms and a syntax-directed translation

$$\Lambda: \{S \mid S \text{ program of } L\} \rightarrow \{t \mid t \text{ typed } \lambda\text{-term over our signature}\}$$

such that for any interpretation $\mathcal{I}imp$ of the signature of L there is an interpretation $\mathcal{I}lam$ of our signature for λ-terms such that S and ΛS are semantically equivalent with respect to $\mathcal{I}imp$ and $\mathcal{I}lam$ (for an example see 2.1 (2)).

Let fixed signatures and interpretations $\mathcal{I}imp$, $\mathcal{I}lam$, and a translation Λ as above be given. We can define another effective and interpretation independent mapping Λ, translating partial correctness formulae {p} S {q} of L into formulae of the calculus for λ-terms, such that {p} S {q} and Λ{p} S {q} are semantically equivalent with respect to $\mathcal{I}imp$ and $\mathcal{I}lam$. We identify {p} S {q} and Λ{p} S {q} and the Hoare Calculus for typed λ-terms over the interpretation $\mathcal{I}lam$ *is* a syntax-directed calculus to derive valid (with respect to $\mathcal{I}imp$) formulae {p} S {q}, and hence a Hoare Calculus for L.

From the author's papers[9, 10] we know that the Hoare Calculus for typed λ-terms over $\mathcal{I}lam$ is complete relative to the oracle, the first-order theory of $\mathcal{I}lam$, for terms of first-order type (i. e. terms of type $\tau_1 \rightarrow \ldots \rightarrow \tau_n, \tau_k$ base type, subterms of arbitrary types are admitted), if $\mathcal{I}lam$ is Herbrand definable and finite or strongly arithmetic, cf. Clarke et al.[3]. As $\Lambda\{p\}$ S {q} = ΛS p_1 with p_1 being an assertion of the calculus for λ-terms depending on p and q, and ΛS a λ-term of the first-order type store → store (store is a base type), this completeness result applies to the calculus for λ-terms used to derive partial correctness formulae of L as above. But, a satisfactory Hoare Calculus for L should be complete relative to the first-order theory of $\mathcal{I}imp$ (not $\mathcal{I}lam$), if $\mathcal{I}imp$ (not $\mathcal{I}lam$) has certain properties. Therefore we introduce the following two conditions on $\mathcal{I}lam$:

(1) $\mathcal{I}imp$ strongly arithmetic or Herbrand definable finite implies $\mathcal{I}lam$ strongly arithmetic or Herbrand definable finite.

(2) There is an effective, interpretation independent translation

$$\rceil: \{p \mid p \text{ predicate over our signature for } \lambda\text{-terms}\} \rightarrow \{p \mid p \text{ predicate over the signature of } L\}$$

such that, p valid in $\mathcal{I}lam$ iff ⌉p valid in $\mathcal{I}imp$.

We assume, $\mathcal{I}lam$ as introduced above satisfies these two conditions (in this paper we construct such an $\mathcal{I}lam$ for languages up to the complexity of L_4) and identify p with ⌉p. Note that this identification is independent of the interpretation, hence admissable in a Hoare Calculus. Then the calculus for λ-terms over $\mathcal{I}lam$ is a calculus to derive formulae {p} S {q}, being complete relative to the first-order theory of $\mathcal{I}imp$ (because of the identification p = ⌉p) if $\mathcal{I}imp$ is strongly arithmetic or Herbrand definable finite, hence (cf. Urzyczyn[16]) complete in the sense of Cook for Herbrand definable interpretations.

Clarke[2] presents a language, for which no Hoare Calculus exists which is complete relative to the first-order theory of $\mathcal{I}imp$ for any finite $\mathcal{I}imp$ with at least two individuals. On the other hand this language is translatable into typed λ-terms. Why does our method not - as for the language L above - yield a Hoare Calculus for Clarke's language, which in particular is complete if $\mathcal{I}imp$ is Herbrand definable and finite, and thus lead to a contradiction? The calculus for λ-terms may induce a Hoare Calculus for Clarke's language, but the interpretation $\mathcal{I}lam$ used in this case will *not* satisfy the conditions (1) and (2), and hence our completeness-result need not (in fact will not) hold.

In particular this paper

(1) shows how to treat procedures and parameters in Hoare Logic, avoiding renaming issues and substitution rules; sharing (aliasing) of variables causes no problems (We do not at all modify the calculus for λ-terms in order to apply it to imperative languages.),

(2) gives reason to believe that the Hoare Calculus for λ-terms is the core of Hoare Calculi for arbitrary finitely typed languages, hence a unifying framework of a major part of Hoare Logic,

(3) indicates how to obtain Hoare Calculi being for Herbrand definable interpretations complete in the sense of Cook for languages allowing higher type procedures and functions (functions occurring on right-hand sides of assignments), thus answering positively the question raised by Trakhtenbrot et al.[17] on page 497.

We start the presentation of details in section 1 by extending the calculus for λ-terms and our completeness result[9, 10] to the many-sorted case, which is necessary because we translate imperative programs into many-sorted λ-terms: We need at least one sort for the store (store is a base type, cf. above), one for the individuals, one for the Boolean values. We hope to enhance readability of this paper by treating first the simple *While* (section 2) and then Clarke's L_4 (section 3).

1 The Hoare Calculus for λ-terms, many sorted

Let a fixed set of base types be given by $\{ind_0, ind_1, \ldots, ind_N, bv\}$. The ind_k stand for different sets of individuals, bv for the set of Boolean values. The set of types consists of all functional (non-cartesian) types over $ind_0, \ldots, ind_N$, bv.

Moreover we have a signature of operation and relation symbols over the base types and an interpretation I of the signature as usual. The base types are interpreted by a family of sets of individuals I with

$$I = (I^\tau | \tau \text{ base type}) \text{ and } I^{bv} = \{tt, ff\}.$$

Totally analogous to the author's papers[9, 10] we define the Hoare Calculus for λ-terms and get the following results: The calculus is correct, i. e. only valid formulae are derivable. If the interpretation is such, that a family of strongest assertions exists (cf. Goerdt[9], definition 2.2; this condition corresponds to the expressiveness condition normally used) any valid formula t p, t being a closed λ-term of first-order type, p being an assertion of the same type, is derivable (with the first-order theory of the interpretation supplied as oracle).

Which conditions on our fixed interpretation I entail the existence of a family of strongest assertions? For Herbrand definable, finite interpretations we can find a family of strongest assertions as in the case of only two base types, ind, bv, treated by the author[10]. (Herbrand definable means, that every individual can be described by a variable free simple expression of operation symbols and constants.) As to infinite interpretations the situation is more complicated than in the case of only two base types, ind, bv. The example of Bergstra et al.[1] showing that a many-sorted interpretation consisting of two independent copies of $\mathbb{N}$ is not expressive with respect to *While* can be transferred to our situation. The example is interesting in view of the fact that $\mathbb{N}$ itself is expressive[9, 10] and also has a family of strongest assertions:

Assume our base types are given by ind_1, ind_2, bv and let $I^{ind_1} = \mathbb{N} = I^{ind_2}$. We have the usual arithmetical operations and relations available on I^{ind_1}, and I^{ind_2}, we do not have any operations or relations with arguments from I^{ind_1} *and* I^{ind_2}. The following term t computes the identity function $I^{ind_1} \rightarrow I^{ind_2}$ (superscripts indicate the sort of the symbols):

```
t = fix λF.λy¹.if y¹ = 0¹ then 0² else
        |   |  F(y¹ - 1¹) +² 1² fi
        |   |  └─────────────────────┘
        |  ind₁       Type ind₂
   Type ind₁ → ind₂
```

The existence of a family of strongest assertions for the present interpretation would entail the existence of a predicate $p(u^1, u^2)$ with: $\models p(i^1, i^2)$ (i. e. $p(u^1, u^2)$ is valid if we bind i^1 to u^1 and i^2 to u^2) iff $i^1 = i^2$. p describes the semantics of t. As proved in Bergstra et al.[1] such a predicate cannot exist, hence there is no family of strongest assertions for the present interpretation.

We define the notion "strongly arithmetic" for our many-sorted interpretation such, that it implies the existence of a family of strongest assertions.

1.1 Definition Our given interpretation is strongly arithmetic iff there is a $k \in \{1, \ldots, N\}$ and a bijection $\varepsilon: \mathbb{N} \rightarrow I^{ind_k}$ such that the following two statements hold:

(1) There are predicates over our interpretation, which describe operations on I^{ind_k} making I^{ind_k} under ε isomorphic to arithmetic. (That is just the definition of strongly arithmetic in the not many-sorted case, cf. **Clarke** et al.[3].)

(2) For any base type τ there is a numbering

$\varepsilon^\tau: \mathbb{N} \rightarrow D^\tau$, with $D^\tau = I^\tau \cup \{\perp\}$ and $\varepsilon^\tau(0) = \perp$,

such that $(D^\tau, \varepsilon^\tau)$ is an effective domain[15, 10]. Moreover this numbering can be described by a predicate, i. e. there is a predicate $D^\tau(u, outp)$, u individual variable of type ind_k, outp individual variable of type τ such that for all $i \in I^{ind_k}$ (k as above), $j \in I^\tau$ holds:

$$\models D^\tau(i, j) \Longleftrightarrow \varepsilon^\tau(\varepsilon^{-1}(i)) = j.$$

$D^\tau(u, outp)$ is a first-order description of ε^τ within our interpretation. (2) makes sure that we can define a sufficient number of relations *between* the I^{ind_1} by predicates, so that the phenomenon described above cannot occur. In the case of only two base types, ind, bv (i. e. the not many-sorted case) the existence of the predicates D^{ind} and D^{bv} follows already from (1). That implies: If we have just two base types, ind_0 , bv, in our signature, the usual notion of strongly arithmetic and the one given here are equivalent.□

Let our interpretation I be strongly arithmetic. Using the theory of effective domains, we can construct a family of strongest assertions as in the case of the base types ind, bv treated by the author[10].

Summing up we get:

1.2 Corollary If the interpretation I is Herbrand definable and finite or strongly arithmetic, the Hoare Calculus for λ-terms can derive any valid formula t p, t a λ-term of first-order type, p an assertion of the same type. □

2 *While*

In the following we have to carefully distinguish the level of imperative languages (objects of this level are marked by the suffix -imp) and the level of λ-terms (marked by -lam).

The operation and relation symbols occurring in the *While* programs are given by families

$$Opsymimp = (Opsymimp^{(n)} \mid n \in \mathbb{N}),$$
$$Relsymimp = (Relsymimp^{(n)} \mid n \in \mathbb{N}),$$

n denoting the arity of the symbols. We assume equality to be a two-ary relation symbol. Let the fixed interpretation *Iimp* be given by:

$$Iimp = (Iimp, \varphi_{Opsimp}, \varphi_{Relimp}),$$

Iimp a set of individuals, the φ's interpreting the operation and relation symbols as usual. Let *Indvarimp* be a set of individual variables ranging over elements from *Iimp*. *Predimp* is the set of first-order predicates over *Opsymimp*, *Relsymimp*, and *Indvarimp*.

2.1 The interpretation *Ilam* (1) The set of base types is given by

$$Btype = \{ind, st, bv\},$$

standing for individuals, store, Boolean values. The interpretation *Ilam* interprets these base types by the family of sets

$$Ilam = (Ilam^{\tau} \mid \tau \in Btype)$$

with

$$Ilam^{ind} = Iimp,$$
$$Ilam^{st} = Iimp^{M},$$

the store is modelled by the set of its possible values, the M-fold cartesian product of *Iimp*, M will be the maximum number of storage variables occurring in our *While* programs,

$$Ilam^{bv} = \{tt, ff\}.$$

(2) The *While* program

$$x_1 := x_2 ,$$

a simple assignment, is translated into the λ-term r of type st→st with

$$r = \lambda y.assign_1(y)(pr_2 y)$$

- y: Type st
- $pr_2 y$: Type st→ind (x_2 on the right-hand side)
- $assign_1$: Type st→ind→st (corresponds to x_1 on the left-hand side).

The program

$$x_2 := x_3 + x_4$$

becomes the term s of type st→st with

$$s = \lambda y.assign_2(y)((\lambda y.pr_3 y + pr_4 y)y) .$$

- y: Type st
- $(\lambda y.pr_3 y + pr_4 y)$: Translation of the simple expression $x_3 + x_4$ on the right-hand side.

The program

$$\text{if } x_2 > 3 \wedge x_3 = 4 \text{ then } x_1 := x_2 \text{ else } x_2 := x_3 + x_4 \text{ fi}$$

is translated into

$$\lambda y.\text{if } (\lambda y.\ pr_2 y > 3 \wedge pr_3 y = 4)(y) \text{ then } r(y) \text{ else } s(y) \text{ fi}$$

- $>$: Operation symbol of type ind→ind→bv.
- y: st
- $(\lambda y.\ pr_2 y > 3 \wedge pr_3 y = 4)$: Translation of $x_2 > 3 \wedge x_3 = 4$, type st→bv.

Accordingly we need the following family of operation symbols for the λ-terms:

$$Opsymlam = (Opsymlam^{(w,\tau)} \mid w \in Btype^*,\ \tau \in Btype)$$

with

$$Opsymlam^{(w,\tau)} = \begin{cases} Opsymimp^{(n)} & \text{if } w = ind^n, \tau = ind \\ Relsymimp^{(n)} & \text{if } w = ind^n, \tau = bv \\ \{\wedge\} \text{ (conjunction)} & \text{if } w = bv\,bv, \tau = bv \\ \{\neg\} \text{ (negation)} & \text{if } w = bv, \tau = bv \\ \{tt, ff\} \text{ (Bool. const.)} & \text{if } w = e \text{ (empty word)}, \tau = bv \\ \{pr_k \mid k = 1,\dots,M\} \text{ (projections)} & \text{if } w = st, \tau = ind \\ \{assign_k \mid k = 1,\dots,M\} & \text{if } w = st\ ind, \tau = st \\ \emptyset & \text{otherwise} \end{cases}$$

The interpretation *Ilam* interprets the symbols by the function φ_{Opslam} , the interpretation is as it should be expected, e. g.:

$$\varphi_{Opslam}(\varphi) = \varphi_{Opsimp}(\varphi),\ \varphi \in Opsymimp$$

$$\varphi_{Opslam}(assign_k)(i_1,\dots,i_M)(i) = (i_1,\dots,i,\dots,i_M)$$

where $(i_1,\dots,i_M) \in Ilam^{st}$, $i \in Ilam^{ind}$, and i stands at the k'th position.

(3) The family of relation symbols

$$Relsymlam = (Relsymlam^{w} \mid w \in Btype^*),$$

these symbols are used to build up the predicates and assertions of the Hoare Calculus for λ-terms over *Ilam*, is defined by:

$$Relsymlam^w = \begin{cases} =^\tau & \text{if } w = \tau\tau,\ \tau \in Btype \\ Relsymimp^{(n)} & \text{if } w = \text{ind}^n \\ \emptyset & \text{otherwise} \end{cases}$$

The symbols of *Relsymlam* are interpreted by φ_{Rellam} with

$\varphi_{\text{Rellam}}(\rho) = \varphi_{\text{Relimp}}(\rho)$ for $\rho \in Relsymimp$.

(4) For the rest of this section we consider the Hoare Calculus for λ-terms over the base types ind, bv, st and the interpretation *Ilam*.

Let $Indvarlam = Indvarlam^\tau \mid \tau \in Btype)$ be a family of individual variables, $Indvarlam^\tau$ ranging over $Ilam^\tau$, w. l. o. g. $Indvarlam^{\text{ind}} = Indvarimp$ (cf. beginning of this section). *Predlam* is the set of many-sorted first-order predicates over *Indvarlam*, *Opsymlam* , *Relsymlam*. Because of $Indvarimp \subseteq Indvarlam$, $Opsymimp \subseteq Opsymlam$ and $Relsymimp \subseteq Relsymlam$ we have $Predimp \subseteq Predlam$. □

2.2 Corollary The interpretation *Ilam* satisfies the requirements (1) and (2) from the introductory section.

Proof Requirement (1): Assume *Iimp* is strongly arithmetic. We have to show that *Ilam* is strongly arithmetic in the sense of 1.1. Statement (1) of 1.1 is satisfied with $\text{ind}_k = \text{ind}$: As *Iimp* is strongly arithmetic, we can describe arithmetic by predicates from $Predimp \subseteq Predlam$ on $Iimp = Ilam^{\text{ind}}$. Statement (2) of 1.1 is satisfied: Viewing the arithmetic symbols on $Ilam^{\text{ind}}$ as abbreviations of the appropriate predicates, we define:

$$D^{bv}(u,outp) = (u = 0 \rightarrow \text{false}) \wedge (u = 1 \rightarrow outp = tt) \wedge (u \geq 2 \rightarrow outp = ff)$$

(false: Predicate; ff: Constant of type bv.)

$$D^{st}(u,outp) = (u = 0 \rightarrow \text{false}) \wedge (u > 0 \rightarrow \exists u_1,\dots,u_M.\ PI_1^{(M)}(u-1) = u_1 \wedge \dots \wedge PI_M^{(M)}(u-1) = u_M \wedge outp = (u_1,\dots,u_M))$$

(outp: Type st; $u_1,\dots,u_M$: Type ind.)

$(u_1,\dots,u_M)$ abbreviates the simple expression of type st $\text{assign}_M(\dots\text{assign}_2(\text{assign}_1(v,u_1),u_2),\dots,u_M)$, and the $PI_k^{(M)}$ describe the projection functions of recursion theory, $\pi_k^{(M)}$, in $Ilam^{\text{ind}}$. It is $< \pi_1^{(M)}(n),\dots,\pi_M^{(M)}(n) > = n$.

Now assume *Iimp* is Herbrand definable and finite, then *Ilam* is Herbrand definable and finite. Here it is important that the store is modelled by a *finite* cartesian product. Hence, *Ilam* satisfies requirement (1) from the introduction.

Requirement (2): By checking the signature *Opsymlam*, *Relsymlam* we see that for $p \in Predlam$ holds: $p \in Predimp$ ($\subseteq Predlam$) iff p contains no components of type bv or st. Hence the transformation $\rceil$ has to eliminate all parts of type bv or st from a given $p \in Predlam$, and of course to preserve validity. $\rceil$ starts eliminating the parts of type st:

(1) At first all individual variables of type st are eliminated. We substitute the variable u of type st by the simple expression of type st, $(u_1,\dots,u_M)$, u_k being individual variables of type ind. Again we use that the store is modelled by a *finite* cartesian product.

$$\forall u,v.\ u =^{st} v$$

becomes

$$\forall u_1,\dots,u_M,v_1,\dots,v_M.\ (u_1,\dots,u_M) = (v_1,\dots,v_M).$$

(2) The only relation symbol connected with the type st is $=^{st}$, which can be eliminated using the projection functions pr_k and conjunction. The example is transformed into

$$\forall u_1,\dots,u_M,v_1,\dots,v_M.\ pr_1(u_1,\dots,u_M) = pr_1(v_1,\dots,v_M) \wedge \dots \wedge pr_M(u_1,\dots,u_M) = pr_M(v_1,\dots,v_M).$$

(3) Components of type st occur only in the context $pr_k(e)$. As e cannot be a variable,

$$e = \text{assign}_j(e_1,e_2)$$

Hence,

$$pr_k(e) \text{ reduces to} \begin{cases} e_2 & \text{if } k = j \\ pr_k(e_1) & \text{otherwise.} \end{cases}$$

The example becomes

$$\forall u_1,\dots,u_M,v_1,\dots,v_M.\ u_1 = v_1 \wedge \dots \wedge u_M = v_M.$$

Similarly we can get rid of the type bv and the desired result follows. □

2.3 Convention and corollary We identify $p \in Predlam$ and $\rceil p \in Predimp$ (this identification is effective and independent of the interpretation) and the Hoare Calculus for λ-terms is a calculus, whose interpretation dependent part is the first-order theory of *Iimp*. If *Iimp* is strongly arithmetic or Herbrand definable and finite, every valid formula t p, t a term of first-order type, p an assertion of the same type is derivable. □

2.4 The translation functions Λ for *While*

(1) The function Λ translating *While* programs into λ-terms of type st→st should be clear from the examples under 2.1 (2). The while loop is translated as follows:

$$\Lambda\text{while b do S od} = \text{fix}\lambda F.\lambda y.\text{if}(\Lambda b)(y) \text{ then } F((\Lambda S)(y)) \text{ else } y \text{ fi},$$

(F: st→st)

where Λb is the translation of b into a λ-term of type st→bv.

Note that we assume that the only storage variables in the *While* programs are from the set $\{x_1,\dots,x_M\} \subseteq Indvarimp$, as to M cf. 2.1 (1). The operation and relation symbols are taken from *Opsymimp* and *Relsymimp*.

(2) The partial correctness formulae of *While* are translated into formulae of the calculus for λ-terms by

$$\Lambda\{p\}S\{q\} = \Lambda S \; ((p[pr_1 inp/x_1,\dots,pr_M inp/x_M])_{inp},\; q[pr_1 outp/x_1,\dots,pr_M outp/x_M]_{outp}).$$

(Assertion of type st→st)

inp, outp are individual variables of type st, $p[pr_k inp/x_k]$ denotes the substitution of x_k by $pr_k inp$ in p. The equivalence of $\{p\}S\{q\}$ and $\Lambda\{p\}S\{q\}$

follows from the definition of the semantics of the assertions of the calculus for λ-terms, cf. definition 1.1 (b) of the author's paper[9].

(2) Finally we identify $\{p\}S\{q\}$ and $\Lambda\{p\}S\{q\}$ (this identification is effective and independent of the interpretation) and the calculus for λ-terms is a Hoare Calculus for *While* being complete if *Iimp* is Herbrand definable finite or strongly arithmetic, hence[16], complete in the sense of Cook for Herbrand definable interpretations. □

With the classical Hoare Calculus for *While* we now have two calculi to derive partial correctness formulae of *While*. These calculi are effectively equivalent:

2.5 Theorem (1) The axioms and rules of the classical Hoare Calculus for *While* are derivable in the calculus obtained here. The way the rules and axioms are derived does not depend on the interpretation.

(2) From a given derivation of a partial correctness formula of *While* in the calculus for λ-terms we can effectively and independently of the interpretation find a derivation of the formula in the classical Hoare Calculus for *While*.

The proof of this theorem can be found in Goerdt[10]. □

For any programming language the programs of which can be translated into λ-terms over the present *Ilam* we can obtain a Hoare Calculus in the same way as for *While*. This applies in particular to languages with parameterless procedures (recursive) and to languages with higher type procedures, as long as no reference parameters or local variables occur. An interpretation *Ilam* to treat languages with reference parameters is introduced in the next section.

3 Clarke's language L_4

The language called L_4 by Clarke[2] is characterized by higher type procedures and reference parameters (parameters standing for locations). In the past some researchers tried to construct a sufficiently complete Hoare Calculus for languages like L_4 [4, 6, 7, 8, 12, 13, 14] but only the calculus presented by German et al.[7, 8] makes do with the first-order theory of the interpretation as oracle, the remaining calculi have stronger oracles. Here we show, that a Hoare Calculus for L_4 being for Herbrand definable interpretations as complete as the calculus by German et al. can be derived from our calculus for λ-terms in the same way as we derived the calculus for *While* in the last section.

The basic notions here are the same as at the beginning of section 2. We omit the steps totally analogous to the *While*-case and can start directly with the interpretation *Ilam* for L_4.

3.1 The interpretation *Ilam* (1) Consider the following example of an L_4 program:

$$\underbrace{\text{proc } P(y_1, y_2) = y_1 := y_2 \text{ corp}}_{\text{Procedure declaration}}\ \underbrace{P(x_1, x_2); P(x_2, x_2)}_{\text{Procedure calls}}$$

y_1, y_2 are reference parameters, x_1, x_2 are storage variables (locations). If we supply the procedure P with two storage variables as argument, we get a storage transformation, an object of type st→ st. Accordingly P itself is an object of type loc→ loc→ st→ st (loc standing for locations) Hence, in order to translate L_4-pograms into λ-terms, we need a base type loc and a corresponding set of individuals (a semantic domain!)

$$\{x_1,\dots,x_M\}$$

where $x_1,\dots,x_M$ will again be the set of storage variables occurring in our programs.

The set of base types is given by

$$Btype = \{\text{ind, st, loc, bv}\}$$

and

$$Ilam^{loc} = \{x_1,\dots,x_M\},$$

for the remaining definitions see 2.1 (1).

(2) In procedure declarations assignments like

$$y_1 := y_2,$$

y_1, y_2 formal reference parameters, can occur. Such assignments cannot as in section 2 be translated into terms like

$$\lambda \underset{\text{Type st}}{y}.\text{assign}_k(y)(\text{pr}_1 y)$$

because we do not know whether y_1 stands for the k'th location and y_2 for the l'th. Instead of the symbols assign_k, pr_k we include only the symbols assign and pr (without index) in our signature. The index is then provided by an additional argument of type loc. Thus

$$y_1 := y_2$$

becomes

$$\lambda \overset{\text{st}}{y}.\text{assign}(\overset{\text{loc}}{y_1})(y)\overbrace{(\text{pr}(y_2)(y))}^{\text{ind}},$$

the formal parameters y_1, y_2 are transformed into free variables of type loc.

The family of operation symbols

$$Opsymlam = (Opsymlam^{(w,\tau)} \mid w \in Btype^*, \tau \in Btype)$$

is defined by:

$$Opsymlam^{(w,\tau)} = \begin{cases} \text{assign} & \text{if } w = \text{loc st ind}, \tau = \text{st} \\ \text{pr} & \text{if } w = \text{loc st}, \tau = \text{ind} \\ \{x_1,\dots,x_M\} & \text{if } w = e \text{ (empty word)}, \tau = \text{loc} \\ \emptyset & \text{if } w = \text{st}, \tau = \text{ind} \text{ or } w = \text{st ind}, \tau = \text{st} \\ \text{as in 2.1 (2) otherwise} \end{cases}$$

The interpretation of the symbols from 2.1 (2) remains unchanged. The new symbols are interpreted by:

$$\varphi_{Opslam}(\text{assign})(\underset{\in Ilam^{loc}}{x_k})(i_1,\dots,i_M)(\underset{\in Ilam^{ind}}{i}) = \overbrace{(i_1,\dots,\underset{\text{k'th posit.}}{i},\dots,i_M)}^{\in Ilam^{st}}$$

$\varphi_{Opslam}(pr)(x_k)(i_1,\dots,i_M) = i_k$

$\varphi_{Opslam}(x_k) = x_k \in Ilam^{loc}$

$\in Opsymlam$ (e, loc)

(3) The family of relation symbols, *Relsymlam* and the interpretation φ_{Rellam} is defined analogously to 2.1 (3). In particular

$$Relsymlam^{loc\,loc} = \{=^{loc}\}.$$

(4) From now on we consider the calculus for λ-terms over the signature and the interpretation *Ilam* defined here. The notions and denotations from 2.1 (4) are transferred to the present context. □

As $Ilam^{loc}$ is finite and every element of $Ilam^{loc}$ can be described by a simple expression (x_k corresponds to the expression x_k) we get, extending the proof of 2.2:

3.2 Corollary *Ilam* defined here satisfies the requirements (1) and (2) from the introductory section and we can identify $p \in Predlam$ and $\rceil p \in Predimp$. □

3.3 The translation functions for L_4 The translation of L_4-programs into λ-terms over *Ilam* is illustrated by way of example: The program from the beginning of 3.1,

proc $P(y_1, y_2) = y_1 := y_2$ corp $P(x_1, x_2); P(x_2, x_2)$,

is translated as follows: The body, consisting of the two procedure calls becomes the term t of type st→st with the free variable P of type loc→loc→st→st, y is of type st, x_1, x_2 are constants of type loc,

$$t = \lambda y.P(x_2)(x_2)\underbrace{(P(x_1)(x_2)(y))}_{\text{Type st}}.$$

The body of the declaration becomes the term r of type st→st, with free variables of type loc, y_1, y_2; y is of type st,

$$r = \lambda y.assign(y_1)(y)\underbrace{(pr(y_2)(y))}_{\text{Type ind}}.$$

The declaration as a whole is translated into the term s, P is a variable of type loc→loc→st→st, note that in general the declaration might be recursive, therefore the fixpoint,

$$s = fix\ \lambda P.\underbrace{\lambda y_1.\lambda y_2.t}_{\text{Type loc}\to\text{loc}\to\text{st}\to\text{st}}.$$

And the above program is translated into

$(\lambda P.t)(s)$.

A more typical declaration of L_4 is

```
proc Q(y1)(y2) = if y2 = 0
                   then y2 := y2
                   else y2 := y2 - 1;
                        Q(y1)(y2);
                        y1
                 fi,
corp
```

where y_1 stands for a parameterless procedure (is a formal procedure parameter of type st→st) and y_2 is a reference parameter (is a formal parameter of type loc). Hence, Q is of type (st→st)→loc→st→st. Let y_1, y_2, Q be term variables of the same type as mentioned, let y of type st, then the term

$$t = fix\ \lambda Q.\lambda y_1.\lambda y_2.\lambda y.$$

$$\left.\begin{array}{l}\text{if } pr(y_2)(y) = 0\\ \quad\text{then } assign(y_2)(y)(pr(y_2)(y))\\ \quad\text{else } y_1(Q(y_1)(y_2)(assign(y_2)(y)\\ \qquad\qquad((pr(y_2)(y)) - 1)))\end{array}\right]\text{Type st}$$

is semantically equal to Q. Assume we are given in addition a declaration of the paramterless procedure P being translated into the term s, then the program

$$Q(P)(x_2)$$

becomes just

$$(\lambda Q.\lambda P.Q(P)(x_2))(t)(s).$$

Note that mutually recursive declarations can also be translated into λ-terms (cf. theorem 5.3 in Scott's report[15]) and that nested declarations can be treated by naturally extending our translation method above.

By the same procedure as in the *While*-case we get a Hoare Calculus for L_4 being complete in the sense of Cook for Herbrand definable interpretations (cf. 3.2). □

It should be clear, that we can get Hoare Calculi for languages even more complex than L_4 using the same *Ilam* as for L_4, e. g. for languages with higher type function calls on right-hand sides of assignments, thus solving positively the question by Trakhtenbrot et al.[17], page 497.

It would be interesting to examine languages for which according to Clarke[2] no Hoare Calculus exists, which is complete in the sense of Cook (even if we restrict attention to Herbrand definable interpretations) with the method presented here. We assume, that in order to treat L_4 plus the possibility to declare local variables (the language Clarke considered) the store cannot any more be modelled by a finite cartesian product, so that the calculi obtained will have weaker completeness properties than the calculi in this paper, cf. Halpern's paper[11].

References

[1] J. A. Bergstra and J. V. Tucker, Hoare's Logic for programming languages with two data types, *Theoretical Computer Science*, pp. 215 - 221, vol. 28, 1984.

[2] E. M. Clarke, Programming languages for which it is impossible to obtain good Hoare-like axioms, *Journal of the ACM*, pp. 129 - 147, vol. 26, 1979.

[3] E. M. Clarke, S. M. German, and J. Y. Halpern, Effective axiomatizations of Hoare Logics,

Journal of the ACM, pp. 612 - 636, vol. 30, 1983.

[4] W. Damm and B. Josko, A sound and relatively* complete Hoare Logic for a language with higher type procedures, *Acta Informatica*, pp. 59 - 101, vol. 20, 1983.

[5] J. W. deBakker, J. W. Klop, and J.-J. Ch. Meyer, Correctness of programs with function procedures, Proceedings Logics of Programs 1981, *Lecture Notes in Computer Science*, pp. 94 - 112, vol. 134, 1982.

[6] E. W. Ernst, J. K. Navlakha, and W. F. Ogden, Verification of programs with procedure type parameters, *Acta Informatica*, pp. 149 - 169, vol. 18, 1982.

[7] S. M. German, E. M. Clarke, and J. Y. Halpern, Reasoning about procedures as parameters, Proceedings Logics of Programs 1983, *Lecture Notes in Computer Science*, pp. 206 - 220, vol. 164, 1984.

[8] —, True relative completeness of an axiom system for the language L_4, Proceedings Logic in Computer Science 1986, pp. 11 - 25, 1986.

[9] A. Goerdt, A Hoare Calculus for functions defined by recursion on higher type, Proceedings Logics of Programs 1985, *Lecture Notes in Computer Science*, pp. 106 - 117, vol. 193, 1985.

[10] —, Ein Hoare Kalkül für die Sprache der getypten Lambda-Terme - Korrektheit, Vollständigkeit, Anwendungen, Thesis, Technische Hochschule (RWTH) Aachen, 1986.

[11] J. Y. Halpern, A good Hoare axiom system for an Algol-like language, Proceedings 11th Conference on Principles of Programming Languages, pp. 262 - 271, 1983.

[12] B. Josko, Über einen Hoare-Kalkül für Algol-ähnliche Programmiersprachen mit Prozeduren endlicher Art, Thesis, Technische Hochschule (RWTH) Aachen, 1984.

[13] H. Langmaack, Aspects of programs with finite modes, Proceedings International Conference on Foundations of Computing Theory 1983, *Lecture Notes in Compter Science*, pp.241 - 254, vol. 158, 1983.

[14] E. R. Olderog, Correctness of programs with Pascal-like procedures without global variables, *Theoretical Computer Science*, pp. 49 - 90, vol. 30, 1984.

[15] D. Scott, Lectures on a mathematical theory of Computation, report no. PRG-19, Oxford University Computing Laboratory, 1981.

[16] P. Urzyczyn, A necessary and sufficient condition in order that a Herbrand interpretation is expressive relative to recursive programs, *Information and Control*, pp. 212 - 219, vol. 56, 1983.

[17] B. A. Trakhtenbrot, J. Y. Halpern, and A. R. Meyer, From denotational to operational and axiomatic semantics for Algol-like languages: an overview, Proceedings Logics of Programs 1983, *Lecture Notes in Computer Science*, pp. 474 - 500, vol 164, 1984.

Session 8

Chair

G. Longo

Universita Di Pisa

Kripke-style models for typed lambda calculus

John C. Mitchell
AT&T Bell Labs

Eugenio Moggi
University of Edinburgh

Abstract

The semantics of typed lambda calculus is usually described using classical models, consisting of set-theoretic functions over some ground domains, or cartesian closed categories. We discuss Kripke-style models which are more general than classical models, and may be regarded as "semantic" but not necessarily concrete cartesian closed categories. We show that the traditional inference system, while incomplete for classical models which may have empty types, is complete for Kripke models. Furthermore, in contrast to the classical situation, every set of equations that is closed under semantic implication is the theory of a single model. We also develop some properties of logical relations over Kripke structures, showing that every theory is the theory of a model determined by a Kripke equivalence relation over a classical lambda model.

1 Introduction

Lambda calculus is a calculus of functions: we read the lambda term $\lambda x{:}\sigma.M$ as, "the function defined by treating the expression M as a function of the variable x," where $\lambda x{:}\sigma$ specifies that the domain of this function is type σ. Formalizing this reading, it is natural to base a mathematical semantics of typed lambda calculus on sets of functions. When terms are given functional types in the usual way, it is easy to see how each term defines a set-theoretic function with the appropriate domain and range. However, when we base our understanding of typed terms on classical set theory, we adopt some subtle semantic properties which are slightly at odds with the traditional axiom system.

One way to see the influence of classical principles on the semantic properties of terms is to consider an implication presented in [MMMS87]. Suppose a and b are types and f is a function $f:(a \to a \to a) \to b$ mapping Curried two-argument functions on a into b. Since the two functions

$$\pi_1 ::= \lambda x{:}a.\lambda y{:}a.x$$
$$\pi_2 ::= \lambda x{:}a.\lambda y{:}a.y$$

both have type $a \to a \to a$, we can apply f to either one. We will show, by a simple case analysis, that

$$(*) \quad \lambda x{:}a.f\pi_1 = \lambda x{:}a.f\pi_2 \text{ implies } f\pi_1 = f\pi_2.$$

In words, we will show that if the two constant functions $\lambda x{:}a.f\pi_1$ and $\lambda x{:}a.f\pi_2$ are equal, then their values $f\pi_1$ and $f\pi_2$ must be equal. The first case to consider is when the type a has no elements. If this happens, then we have $\pi_1 = \pi_2$, since both expressions denote the empty function, and so it must be that $f\pi_1 = f\pi_2$. The second case is a not empty, and so there is some element u of type a. We can apply both functions in the antecedent to u, and since "equals applied to equals produces equals," we obtain $f\pi_1 = f\pi_2$. Thus regardless of whether a is empty, the implication above is semantically sound.

Although the traditional axiom system is complete for proving the equations that hold in all classical models, there is a slightly complicated relationship between axioms for typed lambda calculus and semantic implication. In the traditional axiom system, there is no provision for reasoning by cases, and so the argument above cannot be formalized. However, it has been common to assume that no type is empty. When we make this simplifying assumption, we eliminate one case, and the inference is easily carried out within the appropriate axiom system. This leads to the completeness theorems of [Fri75,Hen50,Sta85a]. The drawback, however, is that in many computer science applications it is not appropriate to assume every type is inhabited (nonempty). This point is discussed in [MMMS87], and related discussions of multi-sorted equational logic appear in [GM82,GM86]. When we reject the nonemptiness assumption and allow types to be empty, we are led to non-equational principles, as in [MMMS87], which formalize reasoning by cases as above. The extended axiom system of [MMMS87] is semantically complete, but it has a very different flavor from the traditional system. For example, some useful connections between equational theories and β, η-conversion fail[1]. In addition, we give up the usual "minimal model" property of lambda calculus and equational logic: with empty types allowed, there is a set of equations which is closed under semantic implication, but not the theory of any single model.

It is worth noting that these comments hold true whether we describe models using the language of set theory or category theory. As proposed in [Sco80, Section 2], one might choose *concrete* cartesian closed categories, those satisfying

$$f = g : A \rightarrow B \text{ iff } f \circ a = g \circ a \text{ all } a : 1 \rightarrow A,$$

as "models." However, since any object A of a concrete category may be identified with the set of arrows $a: 1 \rightarrow A$ from the terminal object, our discussion of classical models above applies to concrete cartesian closed categories as well. In particular, the traditional inference system is not complete for semantic implication over concrete cartesian closed categories when "empty" objects are allowed.

The goal of the present paper is to give a natural set-like semantic account of the traditional inference system. To do this, we must find a semantics which does not support the classically valid justification of $(*)$. Since the argument assumes that either a is empty or a is not empty, the law of the excluded middle is used in a critical way. Thus one might expect an intuitionistic semantics to provide a completeness theorem. Since categorical logic is essentially intuitionistic, the equivalence between typed lambda theories (defined using the traditional axiom system) and arbitrary cartesian closed categories could be considered an intuitionistic completeness theorem (see, e.g., [Fou77,Lam80,LS86]). However, we prefer the stronger completeness theorem using Kripke models for several reasons. For one, Kripke models are relatively easy to picture, and they seem to support a set-like intuition about the lambda terms better than arbitrary cartesian closed categories. In addition, predicate logic may be interpreted over Kripke lambda models, while there is no analogous interpretation in arbitrary cartesian closed categories (except indirectly via the Yoneda embedding). A practical advantage is that it is often easy to devise Kripke counter-models to implications like $(*)$. Furthermore, the useful techniques of logical relations generalize to Kripke lambda models without much difficulty and provide an easy way to construct Kripke lambda models from classical models.

We define Kripke lambda models in Section 2 and describe the axiom system and the semantics of terms in Section 3. In Section 4, we discuss the relationship between Kripke lambda models and cartesian closed categories (CCC's): every Kripke model determines a CCC, and (as pointed out to us by Edmund Robinson and Pino Rosolini) every small CCC may be embedded in a Kripke model. We prove soundness and completeness theorems in Section 5, along with a correspondence between nonempty types and intuitionistically valid propositional formulas. Finally, in Section 6, we turn our attention to logical relations. We describe some general properties of Kripke logical relations, which are closely related to *I-relations* [Plo80], and show that a general class of Kripke models may be obtained as Kripke quotients of classical models. As an application of Kripke quotients, we construct a counter-model to the implication $(*)$ given in the second paragraph of the paper.

While we began our study of Kripke lambda models by working out a definition from first principles, our model definition and many of our results may be developed using a paradigm that is well-known to researchers in category theory and logic. We are grateful to Edmund Robinson and Pino Rosolini for some helpful discussion of this point of view, and refer the reader to [Fou77,Sco80,LS86] for related discussion. In short, the usual definition of semantics of typed lambda calculus, as in [Bar84,Fri75,Hen50], may be formalized in the language of set theory: a model is a collection of sets satisfying several properties easily described by logical formulas. While we usually interpret this definition in the "standard classical model" of set theory, other interpretations are possible. In particular, our definition of Kripke lambda model may be viewed as an explicit description of the meaning of *typed lambda model* in a class of Kripke-style interpretations of set theory. In categorical terms, the interpretations of set theory we consider are functor (or presheaf) categories $Set^{\mathscr{C}}$, where we assume $\mathscr{C}$ is

[1] Here is one example, based on the results of [Jac75]. We write $M \overset{U,V}{\longleftrightarrow} N$ if there is a term P with $PUV =_{\beta,\eta} M$ and $PVU =_{\beta,\eta} M$. Then in the traditional inference system for typed lambda calculus, we have $U = V \vdash M = N$ iff $M \overset{U,V}{\longleftrightarrow} \ldots \overset{U,V}{\longleftrightarrow} N$. This fails when the new inference rules for empty types are added.

a poset. Since much of the development seems entirely routine from this point of view, we will use the Kripke interpretation of logical formulas to motivate part of the model definition. We should emphasize, to avoid possible confusion, that it is standard in topos theory to use the name "Kripke model" for a presheaf category over a poset. However, our Kripke lambda models are *not* presheaf categories, but lambda models "inside" these categories, as will become clear from the discussion in Sections 2 and 4.

2 Kripke lambda models

As with other Kripke-style semantics, a Kripke lambda model will include a partially-ordered set $\mathcal{W}$ of "possible worlds." Instead of having a set of elements of each type, a Kripke lambda model will have a set of elements of each type, for each possible world $w \in \mathcal{W}$. The relationship between elements of type σ at world w and at world w' is that if $w \leq w'$, then every $a{:}\sigma$ *at* w will be associated with some $a'{:}\sigma$ *at* w'. Informally, using the common reading of $\leq$ as relation in time, this means that every element of σ at w will continue to be an element of σ in every possible $w' \geq w$. As we move from w to a possible future world w', two things are allowed to happen: we may acquire more elements, and distinct elements may become identified. These changes may be explained by saying that as time progresses, we may become aware of (or construct) more elements of our universe, and we may come to know more "properties" of elements. In our case, the properties of interest are equations, and so we may have more equations in future worlds. Since a type σ may be empty at some world w and then become nonempty at $w' \geq w$, some types may be neither "globally" empty nor nonempty.

Kripke lambda models will be defined precisely using the subsidiary notion of applicative structure. A *Kripke applicative structure* $\mathfrak{A} = \langle \mathcal{W}, \leq, \{A_w^\sigma\}, \{App_w^{\sigma,\tau}\}, \{i_{w,w'}^\sigma\}\rangle$ consists of

- a set $\mathcal{W}$ of "possible worlds" partially-ordered by $\leq$,
- a family $\{A_w^\sigma\}$ of sets indexed by types σ and worlds $w \in \mathcal{W}$,
- a family $\{App_w^{\sigma,\tau}\}$ of "application maps" $App_w^{\sigma,\tau}: A_w^{\sigma\to\tau} \times A_w^\sigma \to A_w^\tau$ indexed by pairs of types σ, τ and worlds $w \in \mathcal{W}$,
- a family $\{i_{w,w'}^\sigma\}$ of "transition functions" $i_{w,w'}^\sigma: A_w^\sigma \to A_{w'}^\sigma$ indexed by types σ and pairs of worlds $w \leq w'$

subject to the following conditions. We want the transition from A_w^σ to A_w^σ to be the identity

$$(id) \qquad i_{w,w}^\sigma: A_w^\sigma \to A_w^\sigma \text{ is the identity,}$$

and other transition functions to compose

$$(comp)\ i_{w',w''}^\sigma \circ i_{w,w'}^\sigma = i_{w,w''}^\sigma \quad \text{all } w \leq w' \leq w''$$

so that there is exactly one mapping of A_w^σ into $A_{w'}^\sigma$ given for $w \leq w'$. We also require that application and transition commute in a natural way

$$(nat) \qquad \forall f \in A_w^{\sigma\to\tau}.\forall a \in A_w^\sigma.$$

$$i_{w,w'}^\tau(App_w^{\sigma,\tau}(f, a)) = App_{w'}^{\sigma,\tau}((i_{w,w'}^{\sigma\to\tau} f), (i_{w,w'}^\sigma a)),$$

which may be drawn

$$\begin{array}{ccc}
A_{w'}^{\sigma\to\tau} \times A_{w'}^\sigma & \xrightarrow{App_{w'}^{\sigma,\tau}} & A_{w'}^\tau \\
\uparrow \langle i^{\sigma\to\tau}, i^\sigma\rangle & & \uparrow i^\tau \\
A_w^{\sigma\to\tau} \times A_w^\sigma & \xrightarrow[App_w^{\sigma,\tau}]{} & A_w^\tau
\end{array}$$

and will be described informally below. This completes the definition.

If $a \in A_w^\sigma$ and $w \leq w'$, then we can read $i_{w,w'}^\sigma a \in A_{w'}^\sigma$ as "a viewed at world w'." The purpose of the application map $App_w^{\sigma,\tau}$ is to associate a function $App_w^{\sigma,\tau}(f, \cdot)$ from A_w^σ to A_w^τ with each each element $f \in A_w^{\sigma\to\tau}$. Since we can view $f \in A_w^{\sigma\to\tau}$ as an element at any future world $w' \geq w$, the application map at world w' also associates a function with $i_{w,w'}^{\sigma\to\tau} f$ at w'. The condition *(nat)* is intended to give a degree of coherence to the functions associated with different views of f. Basically, *(nat)* says that if we apply f to argument a at world w, and and then regard the result as an element of a later world $w' \geq w$, this gives the same result as first regarding f and a as elements of world w', and then applying f to a.

Kripke applicative structures can also be defined using category-theoretic concepts. The usual definition of applicative structure (also called a *prestructure*; see [Fri75,Sta85a]) may be understood in any cartesian category. The usual definition of applicative structure is a pair $\langle\{A^\sigma\}, \{App^\sigma\}\rangle$, where $\{A^\sigma\}$ is a family of sets A^σ indexed by types and $\{App^\sigma\}$ is a family of application functions

$$App^{\sigma,\tau}: A^{\sigma\to\tau} \times A^\sigma \to A^\tau$$

indexed by pairs of types. We may see this definition "inside" a category $\mathcal{C}$ by interpreting the word "set" as meaning "object from $\mathscr{C}$" and "function" as meaning "morphism from $\mathscr{C}$". More precisely, an applicative structure in $\mathscr{C}$ is a collection of objects $\{C^\sigma\}$ indexed by types and a collection of morphisms $\{App^{\sigma,\tau}\}$ indexed by pairs σ, τ of types such that $App^{\sigma,\tau}$ has the domain and codomain given above. To derive our definition of Kripke applicative structure from this general idea, we regard a poset $\langle \mathscr{W}, \leq \rangle$ as a category in the usual way (see Section 4), and consider the category $Set^{\langle \mathscr{W}, \leq \rangle}$ of functors from $\langle \mathscr{W}, \leq \rangle$ to sets. If we work out what *applicative structure* means in $Set^{\langle \mathscr{W}, \leq \rangle}$, taking "set" to mean functor and "function" to mean natural transformation, we end up with exactly the conditions spelled out above. We will say a little more about functors and natural transformations in Section 4; some related details may be found in [Sco80, Section 4] and [LS86, Example 9.5 of Part II].

It is often convenient to omit the application map *App*, writing fx for $App_w^{\sigma,\tau}(f, x)$ when this does not seem confusing.

It is relatively easy to use Kripke applicative structures to interpret a predicate logic with quantification over all types. A brief discussion of logic at this point will make it easier to motivate the further conditions needed to define Kripke lambda models. We will use the notation

$$w \Vdash \phi\,[\eta]$$

for formula ϕ holding at world w relative to variable assignment (environment) η, and let $\mathfrak{A} \Vdash \phi$ mean $w \Vdash \phi\,[\eta]$ for every w and η. Equations between expressions without λ are easily interpreted, and we will see how to interpret equations between typed lambda terms in the next section. If we take equations as atomic formulas, then conjunction, disjunction and existential quantification are straightforward. For example,

$$w \Vdash \phi \wedge \psi\,[\eta] \text{ iff } w \Vdash \phi\,[\eta] \text{ and } w \Vdash \psi\,[\eta].$$

Negation is interpreted by taking $\neg\phi \equiv \phi \supset \bot$, where $\bot$ never holds. As in Kripke semantics of propositional or first-order logic, implication and quantification make use of the partial ordering. For example,

$$w \Vdash \phi \supset \psi\,[\eta] \text{ iff } \forall w' \geq w.\ w' \Vdash \phi\,[\eta] \text{ implies } w' \Vdash \psi\,[\eta].$$

(For this to make sense, we need to construe a variable assignment at w as a variable assignment at $w' \geq w$, a technical detail we will address below.) We will give an example of universal quantification below. These conditions are well-known and may be found in [Sco80,LS86]. If we define a Kripke applicative structure to be an applicative structure in a topos of presheaves, then this is just the standard interpretation of logic in the topos.

A classical applicative structure may fail to be a model for two reasons, and these reasons apply to Kripke applicative structures as well. The first possibility is that we may not have enough elements. For example, $\sigma \rightarrow \sigma$ might be empty, making it impossible to give meaning to the identity function $\lambda x\!:\!\sigma.x$. The second problem is that application may not be extensional, i.e., we may have two distinct elements of functional type which have the same functional behavior. Consequently, the meaning of a lambda term $\lambda x\!:\!\sigma.M$ may not be determined uniquely.

The usual statement of extensionality is that $f = g$ whenever $fx = gx$ for all x of the appropriate type. In Kripke applicative structures, we are concerned not only with the behavior of elements $f, g \in A_w^{\sigma\rightarrow\tau}$ as functions from A_w^σ to A_w^τ, but also as functions from $A_{w'}^\sigma$ to $A_{w'}^\tau$ for all $w' \geq w$. Therefore, we want to say that for all $f, g \in A_w^{\sigma\rightarrow\tau}$,

$$f = g \quad \text{whenever} \quad \forall w' \geq w. \forall a \in A_{w'}^\sigma.\ (i_{w,w'}^{\sigma\rightarrow\tau} f)\, a = (i_{w,w'}^{\sigma\rightarrow\tau} g)\, a.$$

This can be said a little more simply by appealing to the interpretation of predicate logic described above. Specifically, we will say that a Kripke applicative structure $\mathfrak{A}$ is *extensional* if

$$(ext) \qquad \mathfrak{A} \Vdash (\forall x\!:\!\sigma.\ f\ x = g\ x) \supset f = g$$

where the variables f and g have type $f, g\!:\!\sigma\rightarrow\tau$. (We will discuss the typing of free variables in the next section.) It is a routine calculation to see that (*ext*) is equivalent to the more elaborate statement with explicit quantification over possible worlds.

We make sure an applicative structure has enough elements to interpret lambda terms by requiring elements K and S of appropriate types (cf. [Bar84, Chapter 5] or [Mey82]). For Kripke applicative structures, the description of K and S is simplified by introducing the notion of global element. A *global element* $a\!:\!\sigma$ of $\mathfrak{A}$ is a mapping $w \mapsto a_w$ from worlds to elements such that $a_w \in A_w^\sigma$ and, whenever $w \leq w'$, we have $i_{w,w'}^\sigma a_w = a_{w'}$. Constant symbols in logical formulas are interpreted as global elements, and we interpret a constant at world w using the element a_w at w. We say a Kripke applicative structure $\mathfrak{A}$ *has combinators* if, for any types ρ, σ, τ there exist global elements K and S of types $\sigma\rightarrow\tau\rightarrow\sigma$ and $(\rho\rightarrow\sigma\rightarrow\tau)\rightarrow(\rho\rightarrow\sigma)\rightarrow\rho\rightarrow\tau$ such that

$$(K) \qquad \mathfrak{A} \Vdash K\ x\ y = x$$

$$(S) \qquad \mathfrak{A} \Vdash S\ x\ y\ z = x\ z\ (y\ z).$$

where we assume variables x, y, z are given the appropriate types, e.g., $x\!:\!\sigma$ and $y\!:\!\tau$ in (K). In more detail, (K) means that for every world w and all elements $a \in A^{\sigma}_{w}, b \in A^{\tau}_{w}$, we have $w \Vdash K_w\ a\ b = a$. Condition (S) may be spelled out in a similar way.

We define a *Kripke lambda model* to be a Kripke applicative structure $\mathfrak{A}$ which is extensional and has combinators.

3 Terms, Equations and Interpretation

3.1 Syntax

As usual in typed lambda calculus, we will be interested in equations between terms of the same type, but not concerned with equations between types. Since we wish to allow empty types, we will be explicit about the types assigned to variables (see [MMMS87]). Consequently, terms and their types are defined using the subsidiary notion of type assignment. A *type assignment* $\mathcal{A}$ is a finite set of formulas $x{:}\tau$, with no x occurring twice in $\mathcal{A}$. The formula $x{:}\tau$ may be read "the variable x has type τ." We write $\mathcal{A}, x{:}\sigma$ for the type assignment

$$\mathcal{A}, x{:}\sigma = \mathcal{A} \cup \{x{:}\sigma\},$$

where, in writing this, we assume that x does not appear in $\mathcal{A}$. Terms will be written in the form $\mathcal{A}|M{:}\tau$, which may be read, "M has type τ relative to $\mathcal{A}$." Since open terms may define "partial," or "nonglobal elements," there may be some confusion about what it means to use a variable. In contrast to the logic of partial elements of [Fou77], for example, all of our expressions will have existential import. When we write $x{:}\sigma$ in a type assignment, we mean that x is defined, or "exists," and has type σ. The vertical bar "|" may be considered implication with respect to existence, so that $x{:}\sigma|M{:}\tau$ will mean that whenever x denotes an element of type σ at world w, the meaning of M will be defined at w and denote an element of type τ.

The well-typed terms are defined as follows.

$$(var) \qquad x{:}\tau|x{:}\tau$$

$$(\to E) \qquad \frac{\mathcal{A}|M{:}\sigma\to\tau,\ \mathcal{A}|N{:}\sigma}{\mathcal{A}|MN{:}\tau}$$

$$(\to I) \qquad \frac{\mathcal{A}, x{:}\sigma|M{:}\tau}{\mathcal{A}|\lambda x{:}\sigma.M{:}\sigma\to\tau}$$

$$(add\ var) \qquad \frac{\mathcal{A}|M{:}\tau}{\mathcal{A}, x{:}\sigma|M{:}\tau}$$

Given this formulation of terms, it is natural to write equations in the form

$$\mathcal{A}\,|\,M = N\ :\ \tau$$

where we assume that $\mathcal{A}|M{:}\tau$ and $\mathcal{A}|N{:}\tau$.

We have the usual axioms for renaming bound variables, evaluating function application by substitution, and equating extensionally equal functions.

$$(\alpha)\ \mathcal{A}\,|\,\lambda x{:}\sigma.M = \lambda y{:}\sigma[y/x]M]\ ,\ \text{for } y \notin FV(M)$$

$$(\beta) \qquad \mathcal{A}\,|\,(\lambda x{:}\sigma.M)N = [N/x]M$$

$$(\eta) \qquad \mathcal{A}\,|\,\lambda x{:}\sigma.Mx = M\ ,\ \text{for } x \notin FV(M)$$

The inference rules are symmetry and transitivity

$$(sym) \qquad \frac{\mathcal{A}\,|\,M = N : \sigma}{\mathcal{A}\,|\,N = M : \sigma}$$

$$(trans) \qquad \frac{\mathcal{A}\,|\,M = N : \sigma,\ \mathcal{A}\,|\,N = P : \sigma}{\mathcal{A}\,|\,M = P : \sigma}$$

as well as congruence with respect to application and lambda abstraction

$$(cong) \qquad \frac{\mathcal{A}\,|\,M_1 = M_2 : \sigma\to\tau,\ \ \mathcal{A}\,|\,N_1 = N_2 : \sigma}{\mathcal{A}\,|\,M_1N_1 = M_2N_2 : \tau}$$

$$(\xi) \qquad \frac{\mathcal{A}, x{:}\sigma\,|\,M = N : \tau}{\mathcal{A}\,|\,\lambda x{:}\sigma.M = \lambda x{:}\sigma.N : \sigma\to\tau}.$$

Since type assignments are explicitly included in equations, we also need the rule

$$(add\ var) \qquad \frac{\mathcal{A}\,|\,M = N : \sigma}{\mathcal{A}, x{:}\tau\,|\,M = N : \sigma}$$

This lets us add additional typing hypotheses to equations. We write $\Gamma \vdash \mathcal{A}\,|\,M = N : \sigma$ if the equation $\mathcal{A}\,|\,M = N : \sigma$ is provable from the equations in the set Γ. To emphasize the difference between our proof system and the proof rules that apply when types are assumed not empty, we point out that we do *not* have the rule

$$(nonempty) \frac{\mathcal{A}, x{:}\sigma\,|\,M = N : \tau}{\mathcal{A}\,|\,M = N : \tau}\ \ x \notin FV(M, N)$$

since this rule is sound only if empty types are not allowed.

3.2 Environments and meanings of terms

An *environment* η for a Kripke applicative structure $\mathfrak{A}$ is a partial mapping from variables and worlds to elements of $\mathfrak{A}$ such that

(*env*) If $\eta x w \in A^{\sigma}_{w}$ and $w' \geq w$, then

$$\eta x w' = i^{\sigma}_{w,w'}(\eta x w).$$

Intuitively, an environment η maps a variable x to a "partial element" ηx which may exist (or be defined) at some worlds, but not necessarily all worlds. Since a type may be empty at one world and then nonempty later, we need to have environments such that $\eta x w$ is undefined at some w, and then "becomes" defined at a later $w' \geq w$. We will return to this point after defining the meanings of terms.

If η is an environment and $a \in A_w^\sigma$, we write $\eta[a/x]$ for the environment identical to η on variables other than x, and with

$$(\eta[a/x])xw' = i_{w,w'}^\sigma a$$

for all $w' \geq w$. We take $(\eta[a/x])xw'$ to be undefined for w' not $\geq w$.

If η is an environment for applicative structure $\mathfrak{A}$, and $\mathscr{A}$ is a type assignment, we say w *satisfies* $\mathscr{A}$ *at* η, written $w \Vdash \mathscr{A}\,[\eta]$ if

$$\eta x w \in A_w^\sigma \text{ for all } x\!:\!\sigma \in \mathscr{A}.$$

Note that if $w \Vdash \mathscr{A}\,[\eta]$ and $w' \geq w$, then $w' \Vdash \mathscr{A}\,[\eta]$.

For any Kripke model $\mathfrak{A}$ and environment $w \Vdash \mathscr{A}\,[\eta]$, we define the meaning $[\![\mathscr{A}|M\!:\!\sigma]\!]\eta w$ of term $\mathscr{A}|M\!:\!\sigma$ in environment η at world w by induction on the structure of terms.

$[\![\mathscr{A}|x\!:\!\sigma]\!]\eta w = \eta x w$
$[\![\mathscr{A}|MN\!:\!\tau]\!]\eta w =$
$\quad App_w^{\sigma,\tau}\ [\![\mathscr{A}|M\!:\!\sigma\!\to\!\tau]\!]\eta w\ [\![\mathscr{A}|N\!:\!\sigma]\!]\eta w$
$[\![\mathscr{A}|\lambda x\!:\!\sigma.M\!:\!\sigma\!\to\!\tau]\!]\eta w = d \in A_w^{\sigma\to\tau}$ such that
$\quad$ for all $a \in A_{w'}^\sigma$ and $w' \geq w$,
$\quad App_{w'}^{\sigma,\tau}(i_{w,w'}^{\sigma\to\tau} d)a = [\![\mathscr{A}, x\!:\!\sigma|M\!:\!\tau]\!]\eta[a/x]\ w'$

The combinators and extensionality guarantee that in the $\mathscr{A}|\lambda x\!:\!\sigma.M\!:\!\sigma\!\to\!\tau$ case, d exists and is unique. We can see the importance of partial environments by looking at the lambda abstraction case in a little more detail. The meaning of a lambda abstraction in environment η at w is determined by "patched" environments $\eta[a/x]$ for all $a \in A_{w'}^\sigma$ with $w' \geq w$. If A_w^σ is empty and $A_{w'}^\sigma$ is not, then every environment $\eta[a/x]$ with $a \in A_{w'}^\sigma$ must be partial since there is no possible value for x at w.

We write $w \Vdash (\mathscr{A}\,|M = N : \sigma)\ [\eta]$ if, whenever $w \Vdash \mathscr{A}\,[\eta]$, we have

$$[\![\mathscr{A}|M\!:\!\sigma]\!]\eta w = [\![\mathscr{A}|N\!:\!\sigma]\!]\eta w.$$

This is the base case of the inductive definition of $w \Vdash \phi\,[\eta]$ given earlier. It is an easy exercise, which we leave to the interested reader, to work out the complete definition of $w \Vdash \phi\,[\eta]$ when type assignments are included in formulas.

4 Kripke lambda models and cartesian closed categories

It is easy to extend the definitions of Kripke applicative structure and lambda model to include cartesian product types $\sigma \times \tau$ and a terminal type 1 with one element at each world. In this section, we will see that any Kripke model $\mathfrak{A}$ with products and a terminal type determines a cartesian closed category $C_{\mathfrak{A}}$. As one would hope, the categorical interpretation of a term in $\mathscr{A}|M\!:\!\sigma$ in $C_{\mathfrak{A}}$ coincides with the meaning of $\mathscr{A}|M\!:\!\sigma$ in $\mathfrak{A}$ given above. We also sketch a way to embed any small cartesian closed category into a Kripke lambda model.

We regard a partially-ordered set $\langle \mathscr{W}, \leq \rangle$ as a category in the usual way, writing $\ell_{w,w'}$ for the unique "less-than-or-equal-to" arrow

$$\ell_{w,w'}\!: w \to w'$$

whenever $w \leq w'$. Given a Kripke applicative structure $\mathfrak{A}$, it is easy to see that each type σ determines a functor Φ_σ from $\langle \mathscr{W}, \leq \rangle$ to sets. Specifically, we take

$$\begin{aligned}\Phi_\sigma(w) &= A_w^\sigma \\ \Phi_\sigma(\ell_{w,w'}) &= i_{w,w'}^\sigma\end{aligned}$$

and use conditions *(id)* and *(comp)* to show that this map is a functor. While it may seem simplest to use functors Φ_σ as objects of $C_{\mathfrak{A}}$, this leads to some technical complications when two types determine the same functor. Therefore, we take the type expressions as the objects of $C_{\mathfrak{A}}$.

Since each type determines a functor, the morphisms of $C_{\mathfrak{A}}$ will be natural transformations. For every pair of types σ and τ, condition *(nat)* says that the map $w \mapsto App_w^{\sigma,\tau}$, which we shall write simply as $App^{\sigma,\tau}$, is a natural transformation from $\Phi_{\sigma\to\tau} \times \Phi_\sigma$ to Φ_τ. Using $App^{\sigma,\tau}$, we can see that every global element a of type $\sigma\!\to\!\tau$ induces a natural transformation ν from Φ_σ to Φ_τ, namely

$$\nu_w\ b \quad = \quad App_w^{\sigma,\tau}(a_w, b)$$

We let the morphisms from σ to τ in $C_{\mathfrak{A}}$ be the natural transformations $\nu\!: \Phi_\sigma \!\to\! \Phi_\tau$ induced by global elements of $\mathfrak{A}$ of type $\sigma\!\to\!\tau$. We let composition of morphisms be composition of natural transformations in $Set^{\langle \mathscr{W}, \leq \rangle}$.

A routine calculation shows that if $\mathfrak{A}$ is a Kripke lambda model, then $C_{\mathfrak{A}}$ is a category, and there is a one-one correspondence between global elements of type $\sigma\!\to\!\tau$ and morphisms from σ to τ. In addition, it is easy to show that this category is cartesian closed if $\mathfrak{A}$ has products and a terminal object. The relationship between the categorical interpretation of terms, as in

[Sco80][2], and the meaning function we have given is summarized in the following theorem. Note that with product types, any $\mathcal{A}|M:\tau$ is easily transformed into a semantically equivalent $x:\sigma|M':\tau$ with only one free variable. (Roughly speaking, we replace the tuple of variables in $\mathcal{A}$ by a single variable of the appropriate product type.)

Theorem 4.1 *If $\mathfrak{A}$ is a Kripke lambda model with products and terminal type, then the interpretation of $x:\sigma|M:\tau$ in $C_{\mathfrak{A}}$, as defined in [Sco80], is the natural transformation from Φ_σ to Φ_τ induced by the global element $w \mapsto [\![\lambda x:\sigma.M:\sigma\rightarrow\tau]\!]\emptyset w$, where $\emptyset$ is the empty environment.*

Therefore an equation is valid in $\mathfrak{A}$ iff it is valid in $C_{\mathfrak{A}}$.

We now sketch a method for defining a Kripke lambda model from any small cartesian closed category. Specifically, we show that for any categorical interpretation of typed lambda calculus (in the sense of [Sco80]) in a small D, there exists a Kripke lambda model $\mathfrak{B}$ satisfying the same equations. If we take the internal language of D (interpreted in the usual way) as our categorical interpretation of typed lambda calculus, then this construction gives us a Kripke lambda model $\mathfrak{B}$ with a faithful functor from D to $C_{\mathfrak{B}}$ preserving products and function spaces. However, this functor may not be full in general.

There are three steps from a small CCC to a Kripke lambda model. The first step transforms a categorical interpretation in D into a categorical interpretation in $Set^{D^{op}}$, the topos of presheaves over D. The second takes any categorical interpretation in a topos of presheaves $Set^{D^{op}}$ and produces an applicative structure in the same category that satisfies (K), (S) and extensionality. Finally, the third step finds an elementarily equivalent applicative structure in Set^W, where W is a poset.

Let D be a small CCC. Any categorical interpretation of the lambda calculus in D can be considered a categorical interpretation in the topos of presheaves over D, via the Yoneda embedding Y_D (this is spelled out in [Sco80]). For instance, if d is the interpretation of the base type σ in D, then we use $Y_D(d)$ as the interpretation of σ in the topos of presheaves, and similarly for the interpretations of constants. Since Y_D preserves the cartesian closed structure, the interpretation of any type and term in the topos of presheaves is the image (via Y_D) of its interpretation in D.

A categorical interpretation in the topos of presheaves over D gives us an applicative structure $\mathfrak{A}$ in the same topos. Specifically, $\mathfrak{A}$ is the applicative structure with the type σ interpreted as a functor Φ_σ from D^{op} to Set, and $App^{\sigma,\tau}$ as the evaluation morphism $eval_{\Phi_\sigma,\Phi_\tau}$ from $(\Phi_\sigma\rightarrow\Phi_\tau)\times\Phi_\sigma$ to Φ_τ. (Here we have $\Phi_{\sigma\rightarrow\tau}\cong\Phi_\sigma\rightarrow\Phi_\tau$.) Moreover, the applicative structure $\mathfrak{A}$ satisfies the axioms (K), (S) and the extensionality condition *(ext)*, according to the Kripke-Joyal semantics of formulas in $Set^{D^{op}}$ (cf. [LS86]).

We now have a lambda model in $Set^{D^{op}}$, but not necessarily a *Kripke* lambda model since D^{op} may not be a poset. The third step of the construction bridges this gap using facts about the Diaconescu cover, described in [Joh80] (see Example 2.8 and Corollary 3.3). Given an applicative structure $\mathfrak{A}$ in $Set^{D^{op}}$ we may show that there exists a poset W with $\mathfrak{A}$ elementarily equivalent to an applicative structure $\mathfrak{B}$ in Set^W. (We omit the details.) In particular, $\mathfrak{A}$ and $\mathfrak{B}$ satisfy the same equations between typed lambda terms. As a note of caution, it seems worth mentioning that if $\mathfrak{A}$ is induced by a categorical interpretation of lambda terms, it does not follow that $\mathfrak{B}$ is also induced by such an interpretation. (Further discussion, and a verification of this construction will appear in later versions of this paper.)

5 Soundness, Completeness and Inhabitation

Using the relationships between Kripke lambda models and cartesian closed categories described in the last section, the soundness and completeness theorems for Kripke lambda models may be derived from the corresponding theorems for cartesian closed categories, which are well known. However, we will sketch a direct completeness proof since it is quite straightforward and the construction has other uses.

Lemma 5.1 *(Soundness) Let Γ be a set of well-typed equations. If $\Gamma \vdash \mathcal{A}\,|\,M = N : \sigma$, then every model satisfying Γ also satisfies $\mathcal{A}\,|\,M = N : \sigma$.*

Theorem 5.2 *(Completeness) Let Γ be any set of equations closed under $\vdash$. There is a Kripke lambda model $\mathfrak{A}$ with $\mathfrak{A} \Vdash \mathcal{A}\,|\,M = N : \sigma$ iff $\mathcal{A}\,|\,M = N : \sigma \in \Gamma$.*

Proof Sketch: The completeness theorem is proved by constructing a term model $\mathfrak{A} = \langle \mathcal{W}, \leq, \{A_w^\sigma\}, \{App_w^{\sigma,\tau}\}, \{i_{w,w'}^\sigma\}\rangle$ in the following way.

[2] There is a minor source of confusion in [Sco80, page 413]. In assigning an arrow of a category to an open term M, we must decide which variables to consider free in M. In particular, we may want to consider some variables "vacuously" free. Scott's slightly informal discussion does not address this point, but since we write terms with explicit type assignments, there is no ambiguity. It is easy to see, when we write out the meaning function explicitly, that it is best to treat all variables in $\mathcal{A}$ as occurring free in $\mathcal{A}|M:\sigma$.

- $\mathcal{W}$ is the poset of finite type assignments $\mathcal{A}$ ordered by inclusion. In what follows, we will write $\mathcal{A}$ for an arbitrary element of $\mathcal{W}$
- $A^\sigma_{\mathcal{A}}$ is the set of equivalence classes $[\mathcal{A}|M:\sigma]$ where $\mathcal{A}|M:\sigma$ is well-typed, and $[\mathcal{A}|M:\sigma] = \{\mathcal{A}|N:\sigma \mid \Gamma \vdash \mathcal{A} \mid M = N : \sigma\}$
- $App^{\sigma,\tau}_{\mathcal{A}}([\mathcal{A}|M:\sigma\to\tau], [\mathcal{A}|N:\sigma]) = [\mathcal{A}|MN:\tau]$
- $i^\sigma_{\mathcal{A},\mathcal{A}'}([\mathcal{A}|M:\sigma]) = [\mathcal{A}'|M:\sigma]$ for $\mathcal{A} \subseteq \mathcal{A}'$

It is easy to check that the definition make sense, and that we have global elements K and S at all appropriate types. The proof of extensionality is a little more interesting. Suppose that $[\mathcal{A}|M:\sigma\to\tau]$ and $[\mathcal{A}|N:\sigma\to\tau]$ have the same functional behavior, i.e., for at any $\mathcal{A}' \geq \mathcal{A}$, we have

$$[\mathcal{A}'|MP:\tau] = [\mathcal{A}'|NP:\tau] \text{ all } \mathcal{A}'|P:\sigma.$$

Then, in particular, for $\mathcal{A}' \equiv \mathcal{A}, x:\sigma$ with x not in $\mathcal{A}$, we have

$$[\mathcal{A}, x:\sigma|Mx:\tau] = [\mathcal{A}, x:\sigma|Nx:\tau]$$

and so by rule (ξ) and axiom (η), we have $[\mathcal{A}|M:\sigma\to\tau] = [\mathcal{A}|N:\sigma\to\tau]$. The remaining steps of the proof are straightforward, and proceed in the same manner as the completeness proof in [Mey82], for example. ■

One important property of the model we construct in the completeness proof is that A^σ_w is nonempty for all $w \in \mathcal{W}$ iff σ is an intuitionistically provable proposition. Our interest in this stems from a well-known syntactic correspondence between typed lambda calculus and intuitionistic logic, called the *formulas-as-types principle*, or *analogy* [How80,Lau65,Lau70]. In this analogy, types correspond to logical formulas and terms correspond to proofs. We read basic types as atomic propositions and read the type $\sigma\to\tau$ of functions from σ to τ as the formula "σ implies τ." The crucial part of this analogy is that since lambda terms are a notational variant of intuitionistic natural deduction proofs, there is a closed term of type σ iff σ is an intuitionistically provable formula. Based on this syntactic correspondence between terms and proofs, we might expect there to be a semantic interpretation in which the nonempty types correspond to the intuitionistically provable formulas. The term model construction may be used to prove the following correspondence between provability and type inhabitation.

Theorem 5.3 *(Inhabitation) Let Σ be a set of typed constants and Th an equational theory over Σ. There is a Kripke lambda model $\mathfrak{A}$ for Th with the following property: A^σ_w is nonempty for all $w \in \mathcal{W}$ iff the type σ, when viewed as an implicational formula, is intuitionistically provable from the types of constants in Σ.*

This theorem stands in sharp contrast to the correspondence we achieve with classical models. To construct a classical model with only the provable types nonempty, we must begin with each base type nonempty, since no atomic proposition is provable. It is easy to see that if σ and τ each have at most one element, then $\sigma\to\tau$ has at most one element, and so a straightforward induction shows that our model must have at most one element of each type. Consequently, every well-typed equation will be satisfied.

6 Kripke Logical Relations

6.1 Relations over applicative structures

Logical relations have proven useful in the study of classical lambda models. For example, we may prove the completeness of pure β,η-conversion (without equational hypotheses) for many specific classical models, and characterize the lambda definable elements of certain models using logical relations [Plo80,Sta82,Sta85b,Sta85a]. In [Plo80], Plotkin introduced *I-relations*, which are families of typed relations over a classical lambda model, indexed by possible worlds. In this section, we will consider Kripke logical relations, which are the straightforward generalization of I-relations to Kripke lambda models.

In the classical model theory of typed lambda calculus, a logical relation is a family of relations indexed by types which satisfies a condition implying closure under application and lambda abstraction. The generalization to Kripke applicative structures involves indexing relations by both types and possible worlds. We will simplify our presentation by assuming a fixed structure $\langle\mathcal{W}, \leq\rangle$ throughout Section 6.

A *Kripke logical relation* over Kripke applicative structures $\mathfrak{A}$ and $\mathfrak{B}$ (using the same $\langle\mathcal{W}, \leq\rangle$) is a family $\mathcal{R} = \{R^\sigma_w\}$ of relations $R^\sigma_w \subseteq A^\sigma_w \times B^\sigma_w$ indexed by types σ and worlds $w \in \mathcal{W}$ satisfying the following two conditions. The first is a monotonicity condition

(mon) $\quad R^\sigma_w(a, b)$ implies

$$R^\sigma_{w'}(i^\sigma_{w,w'}a, i^\sigma_{w,w'}b) \text{ for all } w \leq w',$$

which says that when $w \leq w'$, the relation R^σ_w is contained in $R^\sigma_{w'}$, modulo the transition functions. The second condition

$(cmpre)$ $\quad R^{\sigma\to\tau}_w(f, g)$ iff $\forall w' \geq w. \forall a, b.$

$$R^\sigma_{w'}(a, b) \text{ implies } R^\tau_{w'}((i^{\sigma\to\tau}_{w,w'} f)a, (i^{\sigma\to\tau}_{w,w'} g)b),$$

called "comprehension", says that relative to the functions available from $\mathfrak{A}$ and $\mathfrak{B}$, the relation $R_w^{\sigma\to\tau}$ contains all functions mapping related arguments to related results. Kripke logical relations are a generalization of Plotkin's I-relations to Kripke structures, and the basic facts about Kripke logical relations are proved as in [Plo80].

We say environments η_a, η_b are *related by* $\mathcal{R}$ *on* $\mathcal{A}$ *at* w if $R_w^\tau(\eta_a x w, \eta_b x w)$ for all $x\colon\tau$ in $\mathcal{A}$.

Lemma 6.1 *(Fundamental Lemma) If $\mathcal{R} \subseteq \mathfrak{A} \times \mathfrak{B}$ is a Kripke logical relation over models $\mathfrak{A}$ and $\mathfrak{B}$, and environments η_a, η_b are related by $\mathcal{R}$ on $\mathcal{A}$ at w, then for every term $\mathcal{A}|M\colon\sigma$, we have* $R_w^\sigma(\mathfrak{A}[\![\mathcal{A}|M\colon\sigma]\!]\eta_a w, \mathfrak{B}[\![\mathcal{A}|M\colon\sigma]\!]\eta_b w)$

As with many of our other definitions, the definition of Kripke logical relation may be derived by interpreting the usual definition in the topos $Set^{\langle\mathcal{W},\leq\rangle}$. The usual definition of logical relation $\mathcal{R} \subseteq \mathfrak{A} \times \mathfrak{B}$ is a family of relations $R^\sigma \subseteq A^\sigma \times B^\sigma$ such that

$$(usual) \qquad R^{\sigma\to\tau}(f, g) \text{ iff}$$

$$\forall x \in A^\sigma. \forall y \in B^\sigma.\ R^\sigma(x, y) \supset R^\tau(fx, gy).$$

To re-interpret this condition, we must first say what Kripke relations are. As we have seen, a type, or "Kripke set," is a family $A = \{A_w\}$ of sets indexed by worlds, with transition functions $i_{w,w'}^A$ for each $w \leq w'$. (Or, equivalently, a functor from $\langle\mathcal{W}, \leq\rangle$ to sets.) If we have two such Kripke sets $A = \{A_w\}$ and $B = \{B_w\}$, then a *Kripke relation* $R \subseteq A \times B$ is a subset of $A \times B = \{A_w \times B_w\}$, i.e., a family $R = \{R_w\}$ of relations $R_w \subseteq A_w \times B_w$ such that

$$R_w(a, b) \text{ implies } R_{w'}(i_{w,w'}^A a, i_{w,w'}^B b) \text{ for all } w \leq w'.$$

If we now say that a Kripke logical relation over $\mathfrak{A}$ and $\mathfrak{B}$ should be a family of Kripke relations $R^\sigma \subseteq A^\sigma \times B^\sigma$ satisfying *(usual)* above, then we can see that we must have a set R_w^σ for each type σ and world w, and that condition *(mon)* follows from the definition of Kripke relation (relation in a presheaf topos). When we work out the Kripke interpretation of the classical comprehension condition *(usual)*, we obtain *(compre)*.

6.2 Partial equivalence relations and quotients

A *Kripke logical partial equivalence relation* $\mathcal{R} \subseteq \mathfrak{A} \times \mathfrak{A}$ is a Kripke logical relation such that each R_w^σ is symmetric and transitive. The name partial equivalence relation comes from the fact that if R_w^σ is symmetric and transitive, then R_w^σ is an equivalence relation on the set of a with $R_w^\sigma(a, a)$. We will abbreviate the cumbersome phrase "Kripke logical partial equivalence relation" to KLPER. If

$$\mathfrak{A} = \langle\mathcal{W}, \leq, \{A_w^\sigma\}, \{App_w^{\sigma,\tau}\}, \{i_{w,w'}^\sigma\}\rangle$$

is a Kripke applicative structure and $\mathcal{R} \subseteq \mathfrak{A} \times \mathfrak{A}$ is a KLPER, then we define the *quotient applicative structure*

$$\mathfrak{A}/\mathcal{R} = \langle\mathcal{W}, \leq, \{A_w^\sigma / R_w^\sigma\}, \{App_w^{\sigma,\tau}/\mathcal{R}\}, \{i_{w,w'}^\sigma/\mathcal{R}\}\rangle$$

as follows.

- $A_w^\sigma / R_w^\sigma = \{\, [a]_\mathcal{R} \mid R_w^\sigma(a, a)\,\}$, where $[a]_\mathcal{R}$ is the *equivalence* class
  $[a]_\mathcal{R} = \{\, a' \in A_w^\sigma \mid R_w^\sigma(a, a')\,\}$
- $(App_w^{\sigma,\tau}/\mathcal{R})\ [a]_\mathcal{R}\ [b]_\mathcal{R} = [App_w^{\sigma,\tau}\ a\ b]_\mathcal{R}$
- $(i_{w,w'}^\sigma/\mathcal{R})\ [a]_\mathcal{R} = [i_{w,w'}^\sigma\ a]_\mathcal{R}$

It is a simple exercise to verify that the quotient structure is well-defined, and a Kripke applicative structure.

Lemma 6.2 *If $\mathcal{R} \subseteq \mathfrak{A} \times \mathfrak{A}$ is a* KLPER *over Kripke lambda model $\mathfrak{A}$, then $\mathfrak{A}/\mathcal{R}$ is a Kripke lambda model such that for every environment η with $R_w^\tau(\eta x w, \eta x w)$ for all $x\colon\tau$ in $\mathcal{A}$, we have*

$$(\mathfrak{A}/\mathcal{R})[\![\mathcal{A}|M\colon\sigma]\!]\eta_\mathcal{R} w = [\,\mathfrak{A}[\![\mathcal{A}|M\colon\sigma]\!]\eta w\,]_\mathcal{R},$$

where the environment $\eta_\mathcal{R}$ for $\mathfrak{A}/\mathcal{R}$ is defined by taking $\eta_\mathcal{R} x w = [\eta x w]_\mathcal{R}$ for all x and w.

In short, the meaning of a term M in the quotient model $\mathfrak{A}/\mathcal{R}$ is the equivalence class of the meaning of M in $\mathfrak{A}$.

6.3 Kripke logical relations over classical applicative structures

We consider Kripke logical relations over classical structures by viewing classical structure as Kripke structures. Let $\mathfrak{A} = \langle\{A^\sigma\}, \{App^{\sigma,\tau}\}\rangle$ be a classical applicative structure, i.e., $\{A^\sigma\}$ is a collection of sets indexed by types and $\{App^{\sigma,\tau}\}$ is a collection of application functions. We define the Kripke structure

$$\mathfrak{A}^\mathcal{W} = \langle\mathcal{W}, \leq, \{A_w^\sigma\}, \{App_w^{\sigma,\tau}\}, \{i_{w,w'}^\sigma\}\rangle$$

by taking sets $A_w^\sigma = A^\sigma$, application functions $App_w^{\sigma,\tau} = App^{\sigma,\tau}$ and transition functions $i_{w,w'}^\sigma =$ *identity*. It is easy to check that $\mathfrak{A}^\mathcal{W}$ is a Kripke lambda model whenever $\mathfrak{A}$ is a classical lambda model, and that the meaning of a term M in $\mathfrak{A}^\mathcal{W}$ is the same as the meaning of M in $\mathfrak{A}$. In categorical terms, $\mathfrak{A}^\mathcal{W}$ is the inclusion of classical $\mathfrak{A}$ into the category of presheaves over $\langle \mathcal{W}, \leq \rangle$, and may be called an "applicative structure of constant presheaves."

We say $\mathcal{R} = \{R_w^\sigma\}$ is a *Kripke logical relation over classical applicative structures* $\mathfrak{A}$ and $\mathfrak{B}$ if $\mathcal{R}$ is a Kripke logical relation over $\mathfrak{A}^W$ and $\mathfrak{B}^W$. This amounts to the same thing as Plotkin's definition of *I-relation*. By Lemma 6.2, we can produce Kripke models by taking Kripke quotients of classical models.

Corollary 6.3 *If* $\mathfrak{A}$ *is a classical typed lambda model and* $\mathcal{R}$ *is a* KLPER *over* $\mathfrak{A}$*, then* $\mathfrak{A}/\mathcal{R}$ *is a Kripke lambda model.*

This gives us a fairly simple class of models with intuitionistic properties. In fact, we can show that every theory is the theory of a model of this form.

Theorem 6.4 *Let* Γ *be any set of equations closed under* $\vdash$. *There exists a classical lambda model* $\mathfrak{A}$ *and a Kripke partial equivalence relation* $\mathcal{R}$ *such that* $\mathfrak{A}/\mathcal{R}$ *satisfies precisely those equations that belong to* Γ.

However, we can show that some Kripke lambda models are not isomorphic to any Kripke quotient of any classical applicative structure.

Theorem 6.5 *There is a Kripke lambda model* $\mathfrak{B}$ *which is not elementarily equivalent to* $\mathfrak{A}/\mathcal{R}$*, for any classical applicative structure* $\mathfrak{A}$ *and partial equivalence relation* $\mathcal{R}$.

Proof Sketch: We give a formula ϕ in the predicate logic for applicative structures with base types p and q which is valid in all quotients $\mathfrak{A}/\mathcal{R}$ but is not valid in every Kripke lambda model $\mathfrak{B}$. Intuitively, ϕ is the formula that says:

- if $empty(p)$ and $\neg\neg inhabited(p \to q)$, then $inhabited(p \to q)$,

  where $inhabited(\tau) \equiv (\exists x{:}\tau.x = x)$ and $empty(\tau) \equiv \neg inhabited(\tau)$

It is easy to check that this formula is valid in a quotient of a classical applicative structure, and we can give a Kripke lambda model which does not satisfy ϕ. ■

6.4 A counter-model to implication (∗)

As an application of Kripke quotients, we show how to construct a counter-model to the implication (∗) given in the second paragraph of the paper. We will construct a classical model $\mathfrak{A}$ with base types a and b and give a Kripke logical partial equivalence relation $\mathcal{R} \subseteq \mathfrak{A} \times \mathfrak{A}$ such that in the quotient model $\mathfrak{A}/\mathcal{R}$, we will have

$$\lambda x{:}a.f\pi_1 = \lambda x{:}a.f\pi_2 \text{ but not } f\pi_1 = f\pi_2.$$

We let $\mathfrak{A}$ be a classical term model. More specifically, we choose an infinite type assignment $\mathcal{A}$ which provides infinitely many variables of each type, and take β, η-equivalence classes $[\mathcal{A}|M{:}\sigma]$ as elements of type σ. (There is a slight abuse of notation here; we write $\mathcal{A}|M{:}\sigma$ if M is well-typed in some finite subset of $\mathcal{A}$.) Since f appears in the equations above, we include terms with constant $f{:}(a \to a \to a) \to b$ in constructing $\mathfrak{A}$. More details of term model constructions may be found in [Fri75].

It remains to define the relation $\mathcal{R}$ at base types, since this will determine $\mathcal{R}$ at higher types. Since the justification of (∗) depends on type a being either globally empty or globally nonempty, we will make a empty at one world and nonempty at another. We let $\mathcal{W} = \{0, 1\}$ with $0 \leq 1$ and take $R_0^a = \emptyset$ and R_1^a the identity relation A^a. Now, we want to satisfy equation

$$(E) \qquad \lambda x{:}a.f\pi_1 = \lambda x{:}a.f\pi_2$$

at both worlds. This is easy at world 0, since a is empty. We can take R_0^b to be the identity relation on A^b. To satisfy (E) at world 1 where a is not empty, we need to equate $f\pi_1$ and $f\pi_2$. An easy way to do this is just to take $R_1^b = A^b \times A^b$ so that A^b/R_1^b has only one element. It is easy to verify that

$$R_w^{a \to b}(\lambda x{:}a.f\pi_1,\ \lambda x{:}a.f\pi_2)$$

at both worlds $w = 0, 1$, and so these terms are equal in the quotient model. However, since $f\pi_1$ and $f\pi_2$ are not β, η-equivalent, they are not related by R_0^b, and so the equation $f\pi_1 = f\pi_2$ does not hold at world 0 in the quotient model. Consequently, $\mathfrak{A}/\mathcal{R}$ satisfies (E), but not $f\pi_1 = f\pi_2$.

7 Conclusion and directions for further investigation

While the traditional axiom system is not complete for semantic implication over classical models, we have completeness for Kripke models. This may be interpreted as evidence that typed lambda calculus is basically an intuitionistic system rather than a classical one. In addition, we have a straightforward correspondence between provable propositions and nonempty types, which suggests that Kripke models may be useful for studying systems like Martin-Löf's type theory (cf. [Bee82]). It is easy to see that Kripke lambda models are more general than classical lambda models, since any classical lambda model may be be regarded as a Kripke lambda model over a set $\mathcal{W}$ consisting of a single possible world. Kripke models with products $\sigma \times \tau$ and a terminal type 1 are also a special kind of cartesian closed category and, conversely, any cartesian closed category may be embedded in a Kripke model. It is worth emphasizing that since Kripke lambda models differ from classical lambda models in some significant ways, and Kripke lambda models are a special case of cartesian closed categories, classical models are actually quite different from arbitrary cartesian closed categories.

Although we defined Kripke models without using much category theory, one way to view our development is as a "worked example" in the use of the internal language of a topos. Specifically, our Kripke lambda models result from interpreting the standard classical definition of typed lambda model in a topos of presheaves over a poset. In addition, as pointed out to us by Edmund Robinson and Pino Rosolini, our completeness theorem may also be derived using connections between cartesian closed categories and presheaf topoi. Our study of Kripke logical relations may also be viewed this way using the standard notion of relation inside a topos of presheaves over a poset.

Our brief investigation of Kripke logical relations suggests that many classical model-theoretic techniques may be adapted to Kripke lambda models, and demonstrates that Plotkin's I-relations provide a useful class of intuitionistic lambda models. We have shown that every typed lambda theory is the theory of some Kripke quotient of a classical lambda models, but that this does not carry over to quantified formulas. Specifically, we found a formula ϕ which is valid in Kripke quotient models, but not in all Kripke lambda models.

In general, our main focus has been on theoretical aspects of Kripke lambda models. Having found Kripke models relatively natural and easy to work with, it is worth asking whether Kripke lambda models are appropriate to computer science applications. For example, do Kripke-like models arise naturally in the semantics of programming languages? One suggestion that they do comes from the study of storage allocation in Algol-like languages. John Reynolds and Frank Oles have proposed functors over "store-shapes" as a mathematical semantics for languages which admit stack-structured storage allocation [Rey81,Ole85]. (Some related discussion appears in [Ten85].) In addition to taking "storage maps" as possible worlds, some other possibilities might be sets of declarations (as in our completeness proof), program contexts, or their meanings. Given the differences between classical models and functor categories, it seems worthwhile to reconsider carefully which are most natural for the semantics of programs.

Acknowledgments: We are grateful to Edmund Robinson and Pino Rosolini for very helpful discussion on the relationship between cartesian closed categories and Kripke lambda models.

References

[Bar84] H.P. Barendregt. *The Lambda Calculus: Its Syntax and Semantics*. North Holland, 1984.

[Bee82] M. Beeson. Recursive models for constructive set theories. *Ann. Mathematical Logic*, 23:127–178, 1982.

[Fou77] M.P. Fourman. The logic of topoi. In *Handbook of Mathematical Logic*, pages 1053–1090, North-Holland, 1977.

[Fri75] H. Friedman. Equality between functionals. In R. Parikh, editor, *Logic Colloquium*, pages 22–37, Springer-Verlag, 1975.

[GM82] J. Goguen and J. Meseguer. Completeness of many-sorted equational logic. *SIGPLAN Notices*, 17:9–17, 1982.

[GM86] J. Goguen and J. Meseguer. Remarks on remarks on many-sorted equational logic. *Bulletin EATCS*, 30:66–73, 1986.

[Hen50] L. Henkin. Completeness in the theory of types. *Journal of Symbolic Logic*, 15(2), June 1950. pages 81-91.

[How80] W. Howard. The formulas-as-types notion of construction. In *To H.B. Curry: Essays on Combinatory Logic, Lambda-Calculus and Formalism*, pages 479–490, Academic Press, 1980.

[Jac75] G. Jacopini. A condition for identifying two elements of whatever model of combinatory logic. In C. Bohm, editor, *Lambda Calculus and Computer Science Theory*, pages 213–219, Springer-Verlag, 1975.

[Joh80] P. Johnstone. Open maps of toposes. *Manuscripta Mathematica*, 31:217–247, 1980.

[Lam80] J. Lambek. From lambda calculus to cartesian closed categories. In *To H.B. Curry: Essays on Combinatory Logic, Lambda Calculus and Formalism*, pages 375–402, Academic Press, 1980.

[Lau65] H. Läuchli. Intuitionistic propositional calculus and definably non-empty terms (abstract). *Journal of Symbolic Logic*, 30, 1965. pages 263.

[Lau70] H. Läuchli. An abstract notion of realizability for which intuitionistic predicate calculus is complete. In Kino Myhill and Vesley, editors, *Intuitionism and Proof Theory: Proc. of the Summer Conference at Buffalo N.Y.*, North Holland, 1970. pages 227-234.

[LS86] J. Lambek and P.J. Scott. *Introduction to Higher-Order Categorical Logic*. Cambridge studies in advanced mathematics 7, 1986.

[Mey82] A.R. Meyer. What is a model of the lambda calculus ? *Information and Control*, 52(1), 1982. pages 87-122.

[MMMS87] A.R. Meyer, J.C. Mitchell, E. Moggi, and R. Statman. Empty types in polymorphic lambda calculus. In *Proc. 14-th ACM Symp. on Principles of Programming Languages*, pages 253–262, 1987.

[Ole85] F.J. Oles. Type algebras, functor categories and block structure. In M. Nivat and J.C. Reynolds, editors, *Algebraic Methods in Semantics*, Cambridge University Press, 1985.

[Plo80] G.D. Plotkin. Lambda definability in the full type hierarchy. In *To H.B. Curry: Essays on Combinatory Logic, Lambda Calculus and Formalism*, pages 363–373, Academic Press, 1980.

[Rey81] J.C. Reynolds. The essence of algol. In de Bakker and van Vliet, editors, *Algorithmic Languages*, pages 345–372, IFIP, North Holland, 1981.

[Sco80] D. Scott. Relating theories of the lambda calculus. In P. Seldin R. Hindley, editor, *To H. B. Curry: essays on combinatory logic, lambda calculus and formalism*, Academic Press, 1980.

[Sta82] R. Statman. Completeness, invariance and lambda-definability. *J. Symbolic Logic*, 47:17–26, 1982.

[Sta85a] R. Statman. Equality between functionals, revisited. In *Harvey Friedman's Research on the Foundations of Mathematics*, North-Holland, 1985.

[Sta85b] R. Statman. Logical relations and the typed lambda calculus. *Information and Control*, 65:85–97, 1985.

[Ten85] R. D. Tennant. Semantical analysis of specification logic. In *Logics of Programs*, pages 373–386, Springer Lecture Notes Computer Science 193, Brooklyn, NY, June 1985.

SOME SEMANTIC ASPECTS OF POLYMORPHIC LAMBDA CALCULUS[1]

PETER FREYD and ANDRE SCEDROV[2]

Department of Mathematics
University of Pennsylvania
Philadelphia, PA 19104-6395

Abstract. A simple relational framework is used in obtaining new characterizations of partial recursive functions and higher-order partial recursive functionals from the point of view of models for polymorphic lambda calculus. This framework also enables us to establish the higher-order expressive power of polymorphic terms.

Introduction

Polymorphic lambda calculus is an extension of the ordinary simple typed lambda calculus obtained by allowing abstraction over types. It was originally introduced by Girard [1971, 1972] as a proof-theoretic tool for obtaining normalization (and thus cut-elimination) for deductions in intuitionistic higher-order predicate logic. The main vehicle in this approach is the Curry-Howard isomorphism or the propositions-as-types analogy, under which a type is a formula of intuitionistic higher-order predicate logic and a term of type B with free variables of types $A_1,\ldots,A_n$ is a deduction in this logic of the conclusion B from the premises $A_1,\ldots,A_n$. Thus function types are given by implication and type abstraction is given by universal quantification.

A second-order fragment of this calculus was proposed independently in Reynolds [1974] as a mathematical framework for the parameter-binding mechanisms and data type abstraction in functional programming languages. Such features are present to a certain extent in languages CLU , Ada, ML and HOPE (see Bruce et al. [1985]). This aspect of polymorphic lambda calculus is closely related to recursion-free computation and type-checking.

Over the last several years, there has been considerable interest in semantic investigation of polymorphic lambda calculus (e.g., McCracken [1979], Bruce et al. [1985], Amadio et al. [1986], Girard [1986]), based to some extent on the semantics of untyped lambda calculus introduced by D. Scott [1976, 1982]. In all such models the structure of function types is rather involved. In fact, Reynolds [1984] proved that a non-trivial standard set-theoretic interpretation of polymorphic types is impossible. A categorist who considers types and terms as objects and morphisms in a category is thus reminded of the fact that a small category with equalizers and small products must be a poset, and hence that it must identify any two terms that have the same type and the same free variables.

Moggi and Hyland have recently shown, however, that the straightforward set-theoretic interpretation of polymorphic lambda calculus <u>is</u> possible if the

---

[1] Each author is partially supported by N.S.F.

[2] ARPANET: Andre@cis.upenn.edu

ambient category of sets is formulated in intuitionistic logic. Then the set of natural numbers **N** may be isomorphic to $[N \to 2] \to 2$ and the full category of all double-negation closed subquotients of **N** is a small category with equalizers and all small products, but it is not a poset (see e.g. Rosolini [1986]). In the Moggi-Hyland approach the relevant semantic framework for an intuitionistic theory of sets is given by toposes. (The connections between toposes and intuitionistic type theory are discussed e.g. in Lambek-Scott [1986].) In particular, the topos used in the Moggi-Hyland example is the <u>Effective topos</u> studied in Hyland [1982]. This topos is based on the partial applicative structure on the natural numbers given by partial recursive functions. The Moggi-Hyland interpretation of polymorphic lambda calculus is thus closely related to the HEO_2 interpretation given in Girard [1972] and Troelstra [1973], and to the PER-models described in Mitchell [1986].

We present a simple relational framework that includes the Moggi-Hyland setting as a special case, but does not depend on partial applicative algebras. In fact, we show that such applicative structures are forced by some basic operations on relations that correspond to the formation of function types and to type abstraction. We are thus able to give semantic characterizations of partial recursive functions of each finite type (or order) [Kleene 1959] in terms of toposes and in terms of models for polymorphic lambda calculus. (In the case of order 1, that is, for partial recursive numerical functions, our characterization is related to axiomatic descriptions given by Wagner [1969], Strong [1968] and Friedman [1971].) Furthermore, when our framework is considered in a suitably chosen ambient topos, it may be used to obtain a higher-order extension of the standard results regarding the expressive power of polymorphic terms as provably recursive functions in type theory [Girard 1972] (see also Statman [1981] and Leivant [1983]).

1. **Basic construction**

Our construction is given in three steps. Let **A** be an infinite set and let $(\ ,\ ): \mathbf{A}\times\mathbf{A} \dashrightarrow \mathbf{A}$ and $\ell, r: \mathbf{A} \dashrightarrow \mathbf{A}\times\mathbf{A}$ be such that $\ell(a,a') = a$, $r(a,a') = a'$ for all $a, a' \in \mathbf{A}$ (that is, a <u>pairing system</u> on **A**). Let **K** be a set of partial endofunctions on **A** that contains the identity and such that a composition of two functions in **K** is a restriction of a function in **K** . We shall also assume that **K** is closed under substitution with respect to the given pairing and unpairing.

As the first step of our construction, consider the category whose objects are sets and whose morphisms $X \dashrightarrow Y$ are named by **A**-indexed families of relations from X to Y . (Some prefer to think of a relation from X to Y as a subset of $X\times Y$; we prefer to tabulate it as an ordered pair of maps $f: Z \to X$, $g: Z \to Y$.) We require that $R,S: X \dashrightarrow Y$ name the same morphism iff there are f , g in **K** such that for each $x\in X$, $y\in Y$, and $a\in\mathbf{A}$:

If $xR_a y$, then $f(a)$ is defined and $xS_{f(a)}y$,

and

If $xS_a y$, then $g(a)$ is defined and $xR_{g(a)}y$.

We write $R \subset S$ and $S \subset R$, respectively. Morphisms will be referred to by their names. A reciprocal of a morphism $R: X \dashrightarrow Y$ is the morphism $R^o: Y \dashrightarrow X$, where $(R^o)_a$ is the reciprocal relation of R_a for each $a \in \mathbf{A}$. The composition of $R: X \dashrightarrow Y$ and $S: Y \dashrightarrow Z$ is given by $RS: X \dashrightarrow Z$, where for each $a,b \in \mathbf{A}$, the coordinate given by the pair code $(a,b) \in \mathbf{A}$ is the composition of relations R_a and S_b. In short, $(RS)_{(a,b)} = R_a S_b$. A morphism R is called symmetric iff $R^o = R$, and idempotent iff $RR = R$.

The second step in the construction is the splitting of all symmetric idempotents. In other words, we consider a new category whose objects are pairs (X,I) where $I: X \dashrightarrow X$ is a symmetric idempotent in the first category, and whose morphisms $R: (X,I) \dashrightarrow (Y,J)$ are those morphisms $R: X \dashrightarrow Y$ in the first category for which $IR = R = RJ$. This is the category $\mathbf{K}^+$.

The last step is the restriction to the subcategory whose objects are those of $\mathbf{K}^+$, but whose morphisms are only those morphisms $R: (X,I) \dashrightarrow (Y,J)$ in $\mathbf{K}^+$ that are "maps", that is:

$$I \subset RR^o \qquad \text{(total)}$$

and

$$R^oR \subset J \qquad \text{(single-valued)}$$

This is the category $\mathbf{K}^*$.

The construction is a special case of the relational framework introduced by Freyd [1974] and developed in Freyd-Scedrov [1988] and in Carboni-Walters [1985].

2. The main results

We refer only to those classes $\mathbf{K}$ of partial endofunctions on $\mathbf{A}$ that satisfy the conditions given in section 1. Let $\mathbf{N}^{[0]} = \mathbf{N}$ (the set of natural numbers), $\mathbf{N}^{[k+1]} = \mathbf{N}^{[k]} \rightarrow \mathbf{N}$. For any $j \leq k$, we recall the explicit surjections $\mathbf{N}^{[k]} \dashrightarrow \mathbf{N}^{[j]}$ and their sections $\mathbf{N}^{[j]} \dashrightarrow \mathbf{N}^{[k]}$ from Kleene [1959]. Recall also that any pairing system on $\mathbf{N}$ naturally induces a pairing system on $\mathbf{N}^{[k]}$ for each k. In turn, for each $i,j \leq k$ these data induce functions $\theta_{ij}: \mathbf{N}^{[i]} \times \mathbf{N}^{[j]} \dashrightarrow \mathbf{N}^{[k]}$, $\phi_{ij}: \mathbf{N}^{[k]} \dashrightarrow \mathbf{N}^{[i]}$ and $\psi_{ij}: \mathbf{N}^{[k]} \dashrightarrow \mathbf{N}^{[j]}$ such that for all $a \in \mathbf{N}^{[i]}$ and $b \in \mathbf{N}^{[j]}$, one has $\phi(\theta(a,b)) = a$ and $\psi(\theta(a,b)) = b$. For any $i,j_1,\ldots,j_n \leq k$, one is thus allowed to consider any partial function from $\mathbf{N}^{[j_1]} \times \ldots \times \mathbf{N}^{[j_n]}$ to $\mathbf{N}^{[i]}$ as a partial endofunction on $\mathbf{N}^{[k]}$.

THEOREM 1. Fix $k \geq 0$. Let $\mathbf{A} = \mathbf{N}^{[k]}$ and let a pairing system on $\mathbf{A}$ be induced by an explicit pairing system on $\mathbf{N}$ (given, say, by a quadratic polynomial). Consider a class $\mathbf{K}$ of partial endofunctions on $\mathbf{A}$ satisfying the following properties:

(i) $\mathbf{K}$ contains constant zero, the successor, and the conditionals $\delta(n) = k_0$ if $n=0$ else k_1 (for each $k_0,k_1 \in \mathbf{N}$); all considered as functions with possible other arguments,

(ii) $\mathbf{K}$ is closed under numerical substitution and under substitution with respect to θ_{ij}, ϕ_{ij}, and ψ_{ij} for all $i,j \leq k$,

(iii) If $k \geq j+1$, $\mathbf{K}$ contains evaluations $\mathbf{N}^{[j+1]} \times \mathbf{N}^{[j]} \dashrightarrow \mathbf{N}$ and all partial functions obtained from them by substitutions of $\mathbf{N}^{[j]}$-valued partial functions that belong to $\mathbf{K}$.

Then the class of partial recursive endofunctions on $\mathbf{N}^{[k]}$ [Kleene 1959] is the least class $\mathbf{K}$ satisfying (i), (ii), and (iii) such that $\mathbf{K}^*$ is a topos. ■

In fact, the proof of the interesting direction involves the structure of the category of relations $\mathbf{K}^+$ that is more canonical than the topos structure on $\mathbf{K}^*$. In particular, one of the necessary requirements on $\mathbf{K}^+$ is that for any two morphisms R: A ---> B , S: C ---> B there exists a unique residual morphism R/S: A ---> C maximal among all morphisms Q: A → C for which $QS \subset R$ (more precisely, $QS \subset R$ iff $Q \subset (R/S)$). It may be shown that this condition implies the existence of a partial endofunction $\Phi \in \mathbf{K}$ such that for any $g \in \mathbf{K}$ there exists $g' \in \mathbf{K}$ for which $g(a,b) \simeq \Phi(g'(a),b)$ for all $a,b \in \mathbf{A}$ (that is, one side is defined iff the other is, in which case they are equal). This forces the enumeration property. The s-m-n property is forced by the following derived property of residuation: given T: D ---> C , $(R/(TS))T \subset (R/S)$. (If A = B = C , R/S may be thought of as S => R .)

Seely [1986] introduced a categorical description of higher-order polymorphic lambda calculus (PL-categories) that includes both the syntactic calculus itself as well as the models defined by Bruce et al. [1985]. PL-categories may be used to strengthen Theorem 1 as follows.

THEOREM 2. Under the assumptions of Theorem 1, there exists an object Σ in $\mathbf{K}^*$ such that $\mathbf{K}^*$ is a topos iff the fibration given by the contravariant functor $\mathbf{C}(-,\Sigma)$ on the full subcategory $\mathbf{C}$ of $\mathbf{K}^*$ with finite products and generated by Σ is a PL-category. ■

One may also adapt the examples of our construction that were used in Scedrov [1986]. The free topos with the natural number object is chosen as the ambient topos. One lets $\mathbf{K}$ be the set of all partial recursive functions of order n+1 , each uniform in some parameter of order n . (The proof is inductive on n .) It follows by the Curry-Howard isomorphism between intuitionistic higher-order arithmetic and the calculus OFA^{ω} [Girard 1972] that:

THEOREM 3. Closed terms of type [...[N → N] → ... N] → N (k+1 arrows) of higher-order polymorphic lambda calculus OFA^{ω} may be identified with definable recursive functionals of order k+1 that are given together with proofs of totality in intuitionistic higher-order arithmetic. ■

REFERENCES

Amadio R., Bruce K.B., Longo G. [1986], The finitary projection model for second order lambda calculus and solutions to higher order domain equations. Proc. 1st IEEE Symp. "Logic in Computer Science", Cambridge, Mass., pp. 122-130.

Bruce K.B., Meyer A.R., Mitchell J.C. [1985], The semantics of second-order lambda calculus. Information and Control, to appear.

Carboni A., Walters R.F.C. [1985], Cartesian bicategories I. J. Pure Appl. Algebra, to appear.

Freyd P.J. [1974], On functorializing model theory, or: on canonizing category theory. Unpublished preprint.

Freyd P.J., Scedrov A. [1988], "Geometric logic" to appear.

Friedman H. [1971], Axiomatic recursive function theory. In: "Logic Colloquium '69", ed. R.O. Gandy and C.M.E. Yates, North-Holland, Amsterdam.

Girard J.Y. [1971], Une extension de l'interprétation fonctionelle de Gödel à l'analyse et son application à l'élimination des coupures dans l'analyse et la théorie des types. In: "Proc. 2nd Scandinavian Logic Symp.", ed. J.E. Fenstad, North-Holland, Amsterdam.

Girard J.Y. [1972], "Interprétation fonctionelle et élimination des coupures de l'arithmetique d'ordre superieur". Thèse de Doctorat d'Etat, Université Paris VII.

Girard J.Y. [1986], The system F of variable types, fifteen years later. Theoretical Computer Science, 45 (1986), pp. 159-192.

Hyland J.M.E. [1982], The effective topos. In: The L.E.J. Brouwer Centenary Symp., ed. by A.S. Troelstra and D. van Dalen, North-Holland, pp. 165-216.

Kleene S.C. [1959], Recursive functionals and quantifiers of finite types I. Trans. Amer. Math. Soc. 91, pp. 1-52.

Lambek, J., Scott P.J. [1986], "Introduction to higher order categorical logic". Cambridge Univ. Press.

Leivant D. [1983], Reasoning about functional programs and complexity classes associated with type disciplines. 24th Annual IEEE Symp. Foundations of Computer Science.

McCracken N. [1979], "An investigation of a programming language with a polymorphic type structure". Ph.D. Dissertation, Syracuse University.

Mitchell J.C. [1986], A type-inference approach to reduction properties and semantics of polymorphic expressions. In: Symp. on Lisp and Funct. Prog.

Reynolds J.C. [1974], Towards a theory of type structure. In: Springer LNCS 19, pp. 408-425.

Reynolds J.C. [1984], Polymorphism is not set-theoretic. In: Springer LNCS 173, pp. 145-156.

Rosolini G. [1986], About modest sets. Preprint.

Scedrov A. [1986], Kleene computable functionals and the higher order existence property. J. Pure Appl. Algebra, to appear. Preliminary report in J. Symbolic Logic 51, pp. 1089-1090.

Scott D.S. [1976], Data types as lattices. SIAM J. Comp. 5, pp. 522-587.

Scott D.S. [1982], Domains for denotational semantics. In: ICALP 82, Springer LNCS 140.

Seely R.A.G. [1986], Categorical semantics for higher order polymorphic lambda calculus. Preprint.

Statman R. [1981], Number theoretic functions computable by polymorphic programs. 22nd Annual IEEE Symp. Foundations of Computer Science.

Strong H. [1968], Algebraically generalized recursive function theory. I.B.M. Journal of R&D 12, pp. 465-475.

Troelstra A.S. [1973], "Metamathematical investigation of intuitionistic arithmetic and analysis". Springer LNM 344.

Wagner E. [1969], Uniformly reflective structures: on the nature of godelizations and relative computability. Trans. A.M.S. 144, pp. 1-41.

X-SEPARABILITY AND LEFT-INVERTIBILITY IN λ-CALCULUS *

C. Böhm and E. Tronci**

Dipartimento di Matematica, Istituto "G.Castelnuovo",
Università degli Studi "La Sapienza", P.le Aldo Moro 5,
I-00185 Roma, Italy.

Abstract

The separability problem is: given a finite set $\mathcal{F} \equiv \{M_1, \ldots, M_n\}$ of λ-terms to find a context C[ ] such that $C[M_i] = y_i$ (i=1,...,n), where the y_i are arbitrary variables. Solvability of such a problem has been fully studied ten years ago. Replacing free variables belonging to a set X of cardinality w by suitable terms throughout $\mathcal{F}$ is the same as using only contexts having the structure

$$\Delta_{\vec{X}}[\,] \equiv (\lambda \vec{X}.[\,])\,\Delta_1 \ldots \Delta_w.$$

This induces a new problem: the X-separability problem which solvability is constructively characterized in the paper for a class of λ-terms. The major difficulty surmounted is the treatment of self-application. A typical result arises if $\mathcal{F}$ consists of mutually distinct β-η-normal closed forms. In such a case not only Δ exists such that $\Delta M_i = y_i$ (i=1,...,n) (this is Böhm's theorem) but also such that $\Delta\Delta = y_0$! Another example of self-recognition is exhibited in the paper. The problem of the β-η-left-invertibility is also faced and a class of λ-terms has been recognized which are β-η-left-invertible iff a related set of terms is β-η-X-separable.

Keywords: pure λ-calculus, self-application, self-recognition, left-invertibility.

0. Motivations

Pure λ-calculus (Λ) seems to have inspired for some decades lively and fascinating research in Computer Science. Let us see how the present work started up. It is known [Bar 84, pag. 184] that the set of closed λ-terms (Λ^0) possesses some singleton basis {Δ} (namely an infinity). An example is $\Delta = \lambda u.u\ \mathbf{S(S(KK)K)}$ with the property $\Delta\Delta = \mathbf{K}$ and $\Delta\mathbf{K} = \mathbf{S}$. No systematic method is given in the literature to solve such kind of equations. Searching for a singleton basis or sub-basis of Λ^0 becomes then a special case of a self-recognition problem. A solution will be done here (Cor. 3.7) for all finite sets of pairwise distinct closed β-η-normal terms of Λ, extending Böhm's theorem [Böh 68] and its generalization [BDPR 78]. Generalizing the previous set of equations to more than one unknown λ-term brought us to a strenghtened notion of separability for finite subsets of Λ, namely of separability by means of a context having the structure $(\lambda x_1 \ldots x_w.[\,])\,\Delta_1 \ldots \Delta_w$ where the number w of unknown terms is given a priori. Putting X for $\{x_1, \ldots, x_w\}$ let us call this notion X-separability. Does a family of proper subsets of Λ exist such that any finite and distinct [CDR 78, Bar 84] set of λ-terms included in some of those subsets is X-separable ? The answer is positive (Theor. 3.4). The problem of the β-η-left-invertibility is also faced and a class of λ-terms has been recognized which are β-η-left-invertible iff a related set of terms is β-η-X-separable. (Theor. 4.1).

1. Definitions and preliminary results

We assume that the reader is familiar with the principal notions of the λ-β-(η)-calculus.

We will denote by $\mathcal{V}$ the set of variables, by M any term of Λ and by BT(M) its Böhm tree [Bar 84, Chapt.10].

If M reduces to a *head normal form* (hnf)

$$\lambda z_1 \ldots z_n.\zeta M_1 \ldots M_m$$

we will write

M∈ SOL (M is *solvable*)

and define

$$\mathrm{ord}(M) = n,\ \deg(M) = m,\ \mathrm{head}(M) = \zeta$$

and we will have

BT(M) =

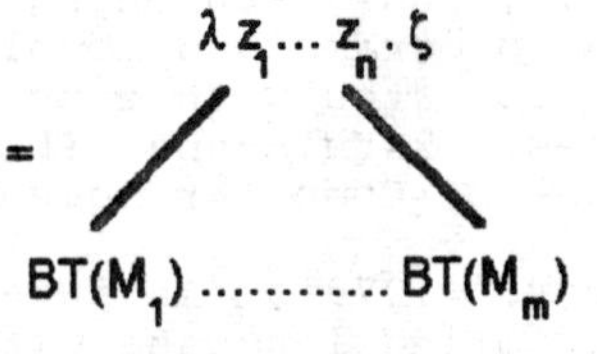

otherwise

$$BT(M) = \mathrm{head}(M) = \perp \text{ and }^{\dagger}$$
$$\mathrm{ord}(M) = \deg(M) = 0\,.$$

A path α starting from the root of BT(M) is a sequence of positive integers (α ∈ Seq) uniquely identifying a subtree of BT(M) and we will write α∈ BT(M).

<> will be used for the empty path and * as a concatenation symbol.

* This research has been supported by Grants of the Ministry of Public Education, Italy.

** Developing a master thesis in Ingegneria on these topics under supervision of C.Böhm.

† Throughout the paper an undefined BT will be represented by the unsolvable λ-term $\Omega \equiv (\lambda u.uu)\lambda u.uu$.

1.0 Let $M \in \Lambda$ and $\alpha \in BT(M)$. $M\alpha$ is recursively defined by

$$M<> \equiv M$$
$$M<i> * \beta \equiv M_i \beta$$

if $\lambda z_1 \ldots z_n . \zeta M_1 \ldots M_m$ is the hnf of M. □

If we allow η–expansions, new paths in the BT may be generated. Next definitions may clarify this matter:

1.0.0 $\beta < \alpha \equiv \exists \gamma \neq <> . \ \beta * \gamma = \alpha$

1.0.1 $\alpha \in_\eta BT(M) \equiv \forall \beta < \alpha . \ \beta \in BT(M) \Rightarrow M\beta \in SOL$

1.0.2 If $\alpha \in_\eta BT(M)$ then M^α is the least η–expansion of M s.t. $\alpha \in BT(M^\alpha)$. □

We may extend the notation $M\alpha$ also in the case of η–expansions.

1.0.3 Let $M \in \Lambda$ and $\alpha \in_\eta BT(M)$. Then $M\alpha \equiv M^\alpha \alpha$. □

Let $\mathfrak{F} \subset \Lambda$ and finite, $w \in N^+$ and

$$X \equiv \{x_1, \ldots, x_w\} \subset \mathcal{V}, \ \vec{X} \equiv x_1 \ldots x_w.$$

$\Lambda^0(X)$ is the extension of Λ^0 using (possibly) free variables only in X.

FV(M) is the set of free variables in M and FV($\mathfrak{F}$) is the set of free variables in $\mathfrak{F}$; similarly for BT($\mathfrak{F}$) and $\mathfrak{F}\alpha$. We may then extend definitions 1.0.1 and 1.0.2 to $\mathfrak{F}$:

1.0.4 $\alpha \in_\eta BT(\mathfrak{F}) \equiv \forall M \in \mathfrak{F} . \ \alpha \in_\eta BT(M)$

1.0.5 If $\alpha \in_\eta BT(\mathfrak{F})$ then $\mathfrak{F}^\alpha \equiv \{ M^\alpha \mid M \in \mathfrak{F}\}$ □

In the sequel, unless otherwise stated, if we consider M_α or pairs $(\mathfrak{F},\alpha)$ we will always assume that

$$\alpha \in_\eta BT(M) \text{ or } \alpha \in_\eta BT(\mathfrak{F}).$$

Let us now recall two equivalence relations $\sim$ [Böh 68] [Bar 84, § 10.2.19] and $\sim_\alpha$ [CDR 78] [Bar 84, § 10.2.21] between pairs P,Q of terms:

$$P \sim Q \equiv head(P) = head(Q) \wedge$$
$$\wedge \ deg(P) - ord(P) = deg(Q) - ord(Q)$$
$$P \sim_\alpha Q \equiv P_\alpha \sim Q_\alpha$$

The next two relations for $(\mathfrak{F},\alpha)$ are in [Bar 84] and the third is conceived to put a limit to the number of feasible η–expansions inside $\mathfrak{F}$.

1.0.6 $\mathfrak{F}$ *agrees up to* α i.e.

$(\mathfrak{F},\alpha) \in AGT \equiv \forall M,N \in \mathfrak{F} . \forall \beta < \alpha . \ M \sim_\beta N.$

1.0.7 α *is useful for* $\mathfrak{F}$ i.e.

$(\mathfrak{F},\alpha) \in USF \equiv \mathfrak{F}\alpha \subset SOL \wedge \exists M,N \in \mathfrak{F} . \ M \not\sim_\alpha N.$

1.0.8 α *is adherent to* $\mathfrak{F}$ i.e.

$(\mathfrak{F},\alpha) \in ADH \equiv \exists M \in \mathfrak{F} . \alpha \in BT(M)$

that is: for at least one term M of $\mathfrak{F}$ α belongs to the original BT(M). □

A path α useful for $\mathfrak{F}$ splits $\mathfrak{F}$ into a family $\mathfrak{F}/\sim_\alpha$ of equivalence classes. This fact has been used the first time by [CDR 78] (and it is also reported in [Bar 84, § 10.4.12]) to define recursively the $\mathfrak{F}$-distinction attribute.

1.1 Definition ($\mathfrak{F}$-distinction)

Let $\mathfrak{F} \subset \Lambda$. $\mathfrak{F}$ is *distinct* iff Card($\mathfrak{F}$)=1 or $\exists \alpha$ s.t.

(i) α is useful for $\mathfrak{F}$

(ii) All elements of $\mathfrak{F}/\sim_\alpha$ are distinct.

1.1.0 Examples

(i) $\{x_1 U^2{}_1, x_1 x_1\}$ is distinct since $U^2{}_1 \not\sim x_1$

(ii) $\{x_1, x_1 x_1\}$ is distinct since $x_1 \not\sim x_1 x_1$

(iii) $\mathfrak{F} \equiv \{x_1 \Omega U^2{}_1 (x_1 U^2{}_1), x_1 U^2{}_1 \Omega (x_1 U^1{}_1), x_1 U^2{}_2 U^2{}_2 (x_1 \Omega)\}$

is not distinct. Notice however that the elements of $\mathfrak{F}$ are pairwise distinct. □

Let us now define the maximum degree of bound subterms depending on (M, α) and on ($\mathfrak{F}$, α).

1.1.1 $bdg(M,\alpha) = \max\{ deg(M\beta) \mid \beta \le \alpha \wedge M\beta \in SOL \wedge \wedge head(M\beta) \notin FV(M\beta)\}$

1.1.2 $BDG(\mathfrak{F}, \alpha) = \max\{ bdg(M,\alpha) \mid M \in \mathfrak{F}\}$ □

Following results will be given without proof and used later:

1.1.3 a) $(\mathfrak{F}, \alpha) \in USF \cap AGT \Rightarrow (\mathfrak{F}, \alpha) \in ADH \cap AGT$

b) $(\mathfrak{F}, \alpha) \in ADH \cap AGT \Rightarrow BDG(\mathfrak{F}^\alpha, \alpha) = BDG(\mathfrak{F}, \alpha)$.

The meaning is: if we stop a path as soon as it becomes useful then BDG($\mathfrak{F}$, α) does not change even if we have done a not redundant number of η–expansions in order to find that path. □

C[ ] will denote any *context* i.e. any λ-term with one *hole* in it. C[M] (C[$\mathfrak{F}$]) is the term (set of terms) obtained filling the hole(s) with M (each element of $\mathfrak{F}$).

1.2 Ad hoc definitions

The aim of section 1 is to introduce a class $\Lambda_{X,e}$ of subsets of Λ and a class of contexts $\Delta_{\vec{X},q}[\ ]$ such that filling the holes with $\mathfrak{F} \subset \Lambda_{X,e}$ the distinction of $\mathfrak{F}$ will be preserved.

Notice that every (approximant of a) term M will belong to some $\Lambda_{X,e}$ (namely to an infinity) and the same is true for any finite $\mathfrak{F}$ if we agree to possibly renaming some free variable; hence introducing $\Lambda_{X,e}$ exerts no coercion on terms if we disregard counting.

1.2.0 Definition (of $\Lambda_{X,e}$)

Let $e: X \to N^+$. From now on we will only consider terms M whose bound variables are not in X (which is no restriction at all).

$$M \in \Lambda_{X,e} \equiv \text{For all subterms } M\alpha \text{ of } M:$$
$$head(M\alpha) = x \in X \Rightarrow deg(M\alpha) < e(x)$$ □

Previous definition needs obviously to be tested only on paths $\alpha \in BT(M)$.

1.2.0.0 Proposition

$(\mathfrak{F}, \alpha) \in ADH \cap AGT \Rightarrow (\mathfrak{F} \subset \Lambda_{X,e} \Rightarrow \mathfrak{F}^\alpha \subset \Lambda_{X,e})$ □

The contexts we are introducing are modelled on $\Lambda_{X,e}$ and have two parameter functions. The second function is more important.

1.2.1 <u>Definition</u> (of $\Delta_{\vec{X},q}[\ ]$)

We will introduce two new functions m, q: $X \to N^+$ by means of some majorations .

(i) $\forall x \in X.\ m(x) \geq e(x)$.

The function q will be tailored on a pair $(\mathcal{F},\alpha)$:

(ii) q is injective and $\forall x \in X.\ q(x) > BDG(\mathcal{F},\alpha)$.

Let $\Omega^p \equiv \Omega \ldots \Omega$ an Ω-string of length p and let define $n: X \to N^+$ s.t. $n(x) \equiv q(x) + m(x) - e(x)$.

Then

(iii) $\Delta_{\vec{X},q}[\ ] \equiv (\lambda \vec{X}.[\ ])\Delta_{x_1,q} \ldots \Delta_{x_w,q}$ where

$\Delta_{x,q} \equiv \lambda t_1 \ldots t_{e(x)} \cdots t_{m(x)} \cdot t_{e(x)}\ \Omega^{n(x)-1}(\lambda u.\ u\ t_1 \ldots t_{e(x)} \cdots t_{m(x)})$ □

1.2.2 <u>Lemma</u>

Let $\mathcal{F} \subset \Lambda_{X,e}$. Then $\exists\ \Delta_{\vec{X},q}[\ ]\ .\ \forall M \in \mathcal{F}$

$$M \in SOL \Leftrightarrow \Delta_{\vec{X},q}[M] \in SOL.$$

<u>Proof</u> Easy from the definition of $\Lambda_{X,e}$. □

Secondly we prove that the ~-relation is also preserved under similar constraints.

1.2.3 <u>Lemma</u>

Let $\mathcal{F} \subset \Lambda_{X,e}$.

Then

$\exists\ \Delta_{\vec{X},q}[\ ]\ |\ \forall M,N \in \mathcal{F}\ .\ M \sim N \ \Leftrightarrow\ \Delta_{\vec{X},q}[M] \sim \Delta_{\vec{X},q}[N]$.

<u>Proof</u> (See Appendix 0) □

The next lemma inspects the internal change of terms produced by the given contexts.

1.2.4 <u>Definition</u> (A path transformation)

(i) Let $hd_{X,q}: \Lambda \to Seq$ be defined:

$hd_{X,q}(M) =$ **if** head(M) $\in X$ **then** $\langle n(x)\rangle$ **else** $\langle\rangle$.

(ii) Let $\delta_{X,q}: \Lambda \times Seq \to Seq$ be recursively defined:

$\delta_{X,q}(M,\langle\rangle) = \langle\rangle$

$\delta_{X,q}(M,\langle j\rangle * \beta) = hd_{X,q}(M) * \langle j\rangle * \delta_{X,q}(M,\beta)$ □

1.2.5 <u>Lemma</u>

Let $\mathcal{F} \subset \Lambda_{X,e}$ and $(\mathcal{F},\alpha) \in ADH \cap AGT$.

Then

$\exists q.\ \forall M \in \mathcal{F}.\ \Delta_{\vec{X},q}[M\alpha] = \Delta_{\vec{X},q}[M]\ \delta_{X,q}(M,\alpha)$.

<u>Proof</u>

We may suppose that $\alpha \in BT(\mathcal{F})$

(otherwise thanks to 1.1.0.0 we may reason about $\mathcal{F}^{\alpha}$).

Let q satisfy 1.2.1. (ii) for $(\mathcal{F},\alpha)$ - by 1.1.2 b the same will hold for $(\mathcal{F}^{\alpha},\alpha)$ - and let us proceed by induction on the length of α.

$\alpha = \langle\rangle$. Obvious.

$\alpha = \langle j\rangle * \beta$.

Notice that q satisfies 1.2.1. (ii) for $(\mathcal{F}\langle j\rangle,\beta)$.

Then by inductive assumption on the l.h.s. $\forall M \in \mathcal{F}$:

$$\Delta_{\vec{X},q}[M(\langle j\rangle * \beta)] = \Delta_{\vec{X},q}[M\langle j\rangle]\ \delta_{X,q}(M\langle j\rangle,\beta).$$

Moreover from the r.h.s.

$\Delta_{\vec{X},q}[M]\ \delta_{X,q}(M,\alpha) = (\Delta_{\vec{X},q}[M]\ \delta_{X,q}(M,\langle j\rangle))\ \delta_{X,q}(M\langle j\rangle,\beta)$.

Hence we need only to prove that

$$\forall M \in \mathcal{F}.\ \Delta_{\vec{X},q}[M\langle j\rangle] = \Delta_{\vec{X},q}[M]\ \delta_{X,q}(M,\langle j\rangle).$$

In such a case $\mathcal{F} \subset SOL$ and we may assume that

$$M = \lambda z_1 \ldots z_j.\ u\ M_1 \ldots M_k$$

Case 1. $u \equiv x \in X$.

Then

$$\delta_{X,q}(M,\langle j\rangle) = \langle n(x), j\rangle ,$$

$$\Delta_{\vec{X},q}[M] = \lambda z_1 \ldots z_j\ t_{k+1} \cdots t_{m(x)} \cdot t_{e(x)}\ \Omega^{n(x)-1}$$
$$(\lambda u.\ u\ \Delta_{\vec{X},q}[M_1] \ldots \Delta_{\vec{X},q}[M_k]\ t_{k+1} \cdots t_{m(x)}).$$

and the conclusion easily follows.

Case 2. $u \notin X$.

Then

$$\delta_{X,q}(M,\langle j\rangle) = \langle j\rangle$$

and the case is settled. □

In the next lemma we will still assume $(\mathcal{F},\alpha) \in AGT$.

Then

$$\forall M,N \in \mathcal{F}.\ \delta_{X,q}(M,\alpha) = \delta_{X,q}(N,\alpha)$$

and we may write

$\delta_{X,q}(\mathcal{F},\alpha)$ instead of $\delta_{X,q}(M,\alpha)$ for $M \in \mathcal{F}$.

1.2.6 <u>Lemma</u>

Let $\mathcal{F} \subset \Lambda_{X,e}$ and $(\mathcal{F},\alpha) \in ADH \cap AGT$.

Then $\exists q$ s. t.

(i) $\forall M,N \in \mathcal{F}.\ M\alpha \sim N\alpha \Leftrightarrow$

$\Leftrightarrow \Delta_{\vec{X},q}[M]\ \delta_{X,q}(\mathcal{F},\alpha) \sim \Delta_{\vec{X},q}[N]\ \delta_{X,q}(\mathcal{F},\alpha)$

(ii) $\forall M \in \mathcal{F}$.

$M\alpha \in SOL \Leftrightarrow \Delta_{\vec{X},q}[M]\ \delta_{X,q}(\mathcal{F},\alpha) \in SOL$.

<u>Proof</u>

Notice that if q satisfies 1.2.1. (ii) for $(\mathcal{F},\alpha)$ then the same holds for $(\mathcal{F}\alpha,\langle\rangle)$.

(i) Using Lemmas 1.2.3 and 1.2.5:

$M\alpha \sim N\alpha \Leftrightarrow \Delta_{\vec{X},q}[M\alpha] \sim \Delta_{\vec{X},q}[N\alpha]\ ) \Leftrightarrow$

$\Leftrightarrow \Delta_{\vec{X},q}[M]\ \delta_{X,q}(\mathcal{F},\alpha) \sim \Delta_{\vec{X},q}[N]\ \delta_{X,q}(\mathcal{F},\alpha)$.

(ii) Using Lemmas 1.2.2 and 1.2.5:

$M\alpha \in SOL \Leftrightarrow \Delta_{\vec{X},q}[M\alpha] \in SOL \Leftrightarrow$

$\Leftrightarrow \Delta_{\vec{X},q}[M]\ \delta_{X,q}(\mathcal{F},\alpha) \in SOL$.

□

1.2.7 <u>Lemma</u>

Let $\mathcal{F} \subset \Lambda_{X,e}$ .Then

$\exists q\ .\ \mathcal{F}$ is distinct $\Rightarrow \Delta_{\vec{X},q}[\mathcal{F}]$ is distinct.

<u>Proof</u>

The distinction of $\mathcal{F}$ may be tested by using only paths stopped as soon as they become useful. Hence if $\mathcal{F}'$ is some equivalence class generated during the partition process and if α is useful for $\mathcal{F}'$ then for $(\mathcal{F}',\alpha)$ 1.1.3 a) will hold. Choosing q satisfying 1.2.1. (ii) for $(\mathcal{F}',\alpha)$ and using lemma 1.2.6 the conclusion easily follows. □

2. Separability by blooming contexts

In this section we will show that the features of $\Delta_{\vec{X},q}[\ ]$ will be inherited by the contexts originated by the blooming of each Ω (considered as gem) toward an arbitrary solvable λ-term. The achieved gain of freedom enables to state a lemma strengthening the separability theorem [CDR 78, theor. 3].

2.0 Definition [CDR 78]

A finite set

$\mathcal{F} \subset \Lambda$ is *separable* iff $\exists C[\ ].\ \forall M \in \mathcal{F}.\ C[M] = y_M$, where $y_M \in \mathcal{V}$. □

It is suitable to assume that the variables y_M are pairwise distinct and $FV(C[\ ]) \cap FV(\mathcal{F}) = \Phi$.

2.1 Definition (Blooming contexts)

$$\Delta[\ ] \in \mathcal{U}(\Delta_{\vec{X},q}[\ ]) = \Delta[\ ] = (\lambda\vec{X}.[\ ])\Delta_1 \dots \Delta_w \wedge \wedge \forall i \in \{1,\dots,w\}.\ \Delta_{x_i,q} \sqsubseteq \Delta_i .$$

2.2 Main Lemma

Let $\mathcal{F} \subset \Lambda_{X,e}$ and $\mathcal{F}$ be distinct.

Then

$\exists q.\ \exists C[\ ].\ \forall \Delta[\ ] \in \mathcal{U}(\Delta_{\vec{X},q}[\ ]).\forall M \in \mathcal{F}.\ C[\Delta[M]] = y_M.$

Proof

We choose q as in 1.2.7.Then $\Delta_{\vec{X},q}[\mathcal{F}]$ is distinct. From Theorem 3 [CDR 78]

$$\forall M \in \mathcal{F}.\ C[\Delta_{\vec{X},q}[M]] = y_M.$$

Since

$$\forall \Delta[\ ] \in \mathcal{U}(\Delta_{\vec{X},q}[\ ]).\forall M \in \mathcal{F}.\ \Delta_{\vec{X},q}[M] \sqsubseteq \Delta[M]$$

the conclusion follows from the continuity of C[ ]. □

The next two lemmas apply the same ideas developed in the main lemma to some special $\mathcal{F}$'s to be used in the next section. The results are essential to break the self-application of unknown terms unavoidably occurring in the X-separability problem.

2.3 Lemma

Let

$$\mathcal{F} \subset (\Lambda_{X,e} \cap \Lambda^0(X))$$

and $\mathcal{F}$ be distinct.

Then

$\exists q.\ \exists F \in \Lambda.\ \forall \Delta[\ ] \in \mathcal{U}(\Delta_{\vec{X},q}[\ ]).\forall M \in \mathcal{F}.\ F\Delta[M] = y_M.$

Proof

The only difference from the main lemma is that here

$$\Delta_{\vec{X},q}[\mathcal{F}] \in \Lambda^0;$$

hence C[ ] cannot bind free variables:

$\forall M \in \mathcal{F}.\ C[\Delta_{\vec{X},q}[M]] = (\lambda t.C[t])\Delta_{\vec{X},q}[M] = F\Delta_{\vec{X},q}[M].$

(continuation as in 2.2) □

2.4 Lemma

Let

$$t \in \mathcal{V} - X,$$

$$\mathcal{F} = \{t M_{i,1} \dots M_{i,r} \mid i = 1,\dots,p\} \subset \Lambda_{X,e}$$

and

$$M_{i,j} \in \Lambda^0(X) \qquad (i = 1,\dots,p \quad j = 1,\dots,r).$$

Then if $\mathcal{F}$ is distinct

$$\exists q.\ \exists G \in \Lambda.\ \forall \Delta[\ ] \in \mathcal{U}(\Delta_{\vec{X},q}[\ ])$$

$$G\ \Delta[M_{i,1}] \dots \Delta[M_{i,r}] = y_i \qquad (i = 1,\dots,p).$$

Proof

By induction on Card $(\mathcal{F})$:

If Card $(\mathcal{F}) = 1$

then

$$G = \lambda z_1 \dots z_r . y_1 .$$

Let

Card $(\mathcal{F}) > 1$ and $(\mathcal{F},\alpha) \in USF \cap AGT$:

clearly is

$$\alpha \neq \langle\rangle,$$

let's say

$$\alpha = \langle j \rangle * \beta .$$

Then

$$\mathcal{F}/\sim_\alpha = \{\mathcal{F}_1,\dots,\mathcal{F}_b\} .$$

Let

$$I_h = \{i \in N \mid t M_{i,1},\dots,M_{i,r} \in \mathcal{F}_h\} \qquad (h = 1,\dots,b).$$

By inductive assumption

$$\forall h \in \{1,\dots,b\}.\ \exists G_h \in \Lambda.\ \forall \Delta[\ ] \in \mathcal{U}(\Delta_{\vec{X},q}[\ ])$$

$$G_h\ \Delta[M_{i,1}] \dots \Delta[M_{i,r}] = y_{h,\ i} \qquad (i \in I_h)$$

Choosing q satisfying 1.2.1. (ii) for $(\mathcal{F}\langle j \rangle,\beta)$ and reasoning similarly to 2.3 we obtain

$$\exists F \in \Lambda.\ \forall h \in \{1,\dots,b\}.\ \forall \Delta[\ ] \in \mathcal{U}(\Delta_{\vec{X},q}[\ ]).\forall M \in \mathcal{F}_h$$

$$F\ \ \Delta[M\langle j \rangle] = G_h .$$

Setting

$$G = \lambda z_1 \dots z_r . F\ z_j\ z_1 \dots z_r$$

the conclusion follows. □

2.4.0 Example

Let $X = \{x\}$ and let e, m,q replace e(x), m(x), q(x).

$\mathcal{F} = \{t\,x(x(x\Omega))\Omega,\ t\,x(xx)x,\ t\,x(xx)(U^2_1(xx))\}$.

Let e = 2 ; we have then $\mathcal{F} \subseteq \Lambda_{X,2}$.

It is easy to see that we may choose m=3 and q=2 .

We wish to find a $G \in \Lambda$ such that

$$G\ \ \Delta_{X,q}[x]\ \ \Delta_{X,q}[x(x\,\Omega)]\ \ \Delta_{X,q}[\Omega] \quad = y_1$$

$$G\ \ \Delta_{X,q}[x]\ \ \Delta_{X,q}[xx] \qquad \Delta_{X,q}[x] \quad = y_2$$

$$G\ \ \Delta_{X,q}[x]\ \ \Delta_{X,q}[xx] \qquad \Delta_{X,q}[U^2_1(xx)] = y_3.$$

A possible solution is

$$G = \lambda v_1 v_2 v_3 .\ G_0\ v_2 v_1 v_2 v_3 ,$$

$$G_0 = \langle U^3_3 , a_1 , U^3_1 , (U^8_1\ y_1) , (U^6_1\ G_1) , a_2 \rangle$$

and

$$G_1 = \langle (U^4_1\ y_2) , U^3_3 , a_3 , U^3_1 , a_4 , (U^4_1\ y_3) , a_5 \rangle .$$ □

3. X - Separability

We are ready to introduce a new notion of separability for finite sets $\mathcal{F}$ of λ-terms admitting solving contexts only of a given shape.

3.0 Definition (of (β–η–)X-separability)

Let $w \in N^+$, $X \equiv \{x_1, \dots, x_w\}$, $\vec{X} \equiv x_1 \dots x_w$.

A finite set $\mathcal{F} \subset \Lambda$ is

(β–η–) X-separable iff $\exists \Delta_{\vec{X}}[\ ].\ \forall M \in \mathcal{F}.\ \Delta_{\vec{X}}[M] = y_M$,

where $y_M \in \mathcal{V}$. ◻

It is suitable to assume that the variables y_M are pairwise distinct and $FV(\Delta_{\vec{X}}[\ ]) \cap FV(\mathcal{F}) = \Phi$.

Remark Notice that previous definition is stronger that separability in [CDR 78, Bar 84]:

$$\mathcal{F}_0 = \{x_1, x_1 x_1\}$$

is separable , namely separable by

$$C[\ ] \equiv (\lambda x_1.[\ ])\, U^2_1\, U^1_1\, y_1\, y_0,$$

where

$$U^n_i \equiv \lambda v_1 \dots v_n . v_i,$$

but obviously not $\{x_1\}$-separable.

Another example (to be treated in 3.7.1) is

$$\mathcal{F}_1 = \{x_1 x_1, x_1 x_2, x_2 x_1, x_2 x_2\}$$

which is $\{x_1, x_2\}$-, but not $\{x_1\}$-separable. ◻

We will now make some assumptions on the finite set $\mathcal{F}$.

3.1 Definition (X- distinction)

Let $\mathcal{F}_\Omega \in \Lambda^0(X)$ be obtained from $\mathcal{F}$ by replacing any occurrence of free variable $v \in FV(\mathcal{F}) - X$ by Ω. Then

$\mathcal{F}$ is X-distinct $\equiv \mathcal{F}_\Omega \subset SOL\ \wedge$

$\wedge \forall M \in \mathcal{F}.\ head(M) \in X\ \wedge$

$\wedge\ \mathcal{F}_\Omega$ is distinct ◻

3.2 Proposition

Let $\mathcal{F} \in \Lambda$. Then

$\mathcal{F}$ is (β–η–)X-separable $\Rightarrow \mathcal{F}$ is X- distinct ◻

The X- distinction is not , in general, sufficient for the X-separability (see previous remark). We will now define a class of λ-terms inside which X-distinction implies X-separability.

3.3 Main definition ($\Lambda_{X,e,m}$)

Let $e, m : X \to N^+$. Then

$M \in \Lambda_{X,e,m} \Leftrightarrow M \equiv x M_1 \dots M_{e(x)} \dots M_{m(x)} \wedge x \in X\ \wedge$

$\wedge\ M_{e(x)} \in SOL \wedge head(M_{e(x)}) \in FV(M) \Rightarrow head(M_{e(x)}) \in X\ \wedge$

$\wedge \forall i = \{1, \dots, m(x)\}\ M_i \in \Lambda_{X,e}$ ◻

3.3.0 Examples

Let $X \equiv \{x\}$, and let e , m replace e(x) , m(x) . Then

(i) $x(\lambda t.x)(\lambda t.z) \in \Lambda_{X,1,2}$

(ii) $x(\lambda t.zx) \notin \Lambda_{X,1,1}$

(iii) $x(\lambda t.zx)U^1_1 \in \Lambda_{X,2,2}$

(iv) $x(\lambda t.xxxx)U^1_1 \notin \Lambda_{X,2,2}$ and $\notin \Lambda_{X,1,2}$

(v) $x(\lambda t.zx)U^1_1 \notin \Lambda_{X,1,2}$

(vi) $x(\lambda t.xx)\, U^1_1 \in \Lambda_{X,2,2}$ and $\notin \Lambda_{X,1,2}$. ◻

3.4 Theorem (characterizing X-separability)

Let $\mathcal{F} \subset \Lambda_{X,e,m}$. Then

$\mathcal{F}$ is X-separable iff $\mathcal{F}$ is X-distinct.

Proof (⇒) Easy.

(⇐)

Let $\mathcal{F}_\Omega$ be defined as in 3.1.

We shall show that $\mathcal{F}_\Omega$ is X-separable.

Step 0. First we split $\mathcal{F}$ into atmost w classes:

Let $\mathcal{F}_x \equiv \{M \in \mathcal{F}_\Omega \mid head(M) \equiv x\}$

We split then $\mathcal{F}_x$ possibly into two more classes

$\mathcal{F}^0_{x,h} \equiv \{x M_1 \dots M_{e(x)} \dots M_{m(x)} \in \mathcal{F}_x \mid head(M_{e(x)}) \in X\ \wedge$

$\wedge\ ord(M_{e(x)}) + e(head(M_{e(x)})) - deg(M_{e(x)}) = h\}$

$\mathcal{F}^1_{x,h} \equiv \{x M_1 \dots M_{e(x)} \dots M_{m(x)} \in \mathcal{F}_x \mid M_{e(x)} =$

$= \lambda z_1 \dots z_p.\ z_h Q_1 \dots Q_r$ where p, r, h ∈ N and h ≤ p }.

Clearly $\mathcal{F}^0_{x,h} \cap \mathcal{F}^1_{x,h} \equiv \Phi$.

Let $\mathcal{F}_{x,h} \equiv \mathcal{F}^0_{x,h} \cup \mathcal{F}^1_{x,h}$

and $L(x) \equiv \{h \in N \mid \mathcal{F}_{x,h} \not\equiv \Phi\}$; we may compute now

$r^0_x = \max\{\max\{ord(M_{e(x)}) + m(head(M_{e(x)})) - deg(M_{e(x)}) \mid$

$x M_1 \dots M_{e(x)} \dots M_{m(x)} \in \mathcal{F}^0_{x,h}\} \mid h \in L(x)\}$

$r^1_x = \max\{\max\{ord(M_{e(x)}) \mid x M_1 \dots M_{e(x)} \dots M_{m(x)} \in \mathcal{F}^1_{x,h}\} \mid$

$h \in L(x)\}$; $r_x = \max\{r^0_x, r^1_x\}$.

It is clear that $\max L(x) \le r_x$.

Step 1.

We can choose n(x) such that

$$\forall x \in X\ n(x) > r_x$$

and sufficiently large to make possible the following reasonings .

Step 2.

We have

$$\forall x \in X\ \forall h \in L(x):$$

$$I(x,h) = \{i \in N \mid x M_{i,1} \dots M_{i,e(x)} \dots M_{i,m(x)} \in \mathcal{F}_{x,h}\}$$

Let $t \in (\mathcal{V} - X)$ and

$$\mathcal{F}'_{x,h} \equiv \{t M_{i,1} \dots M_{i,e(x)} \dots M_{i,m(x)} \mid i \in I(x,h)\}.$$

Since $\mathcal{F}_{x,h}$ is distinct then $\mathcal{F}'_{x,h}$ is distinct .

Then according to the lemma 2.4

$$\exists G_{x,h} \in \Lambda.\ \forall \Delta[\ ] \in \mathcal{U}(\Delta_{\vec{X},q}[\ ]).\ \forall i \in I(x,h)$$

$$G_{x,h}\ \Delta[M_{i,1}] \dots \Delta[M_{i,m(x)}] = y_{x,h,i}$$

Let

$$x M_{i,1} \dots M_{i,e(x)} \dots M_{i,m(x)} \in \mathcal{F}_x$$

and

$g(x,i) =$ **if** $head(M_{i,e(x)}) \in X$

then $n(x) + n(head(M_{i,e(x)})) - m(head(M_{i,e(x)})) +$
$+ deg(M_{i,e(x)}) - ord(M_{i,e(x)}) + 1$

else $n(x) + deg(M_{i,e(x)}) - ord(M_{i,e(x)}) + 1$.

We are interested to find $G^*_{x,h}$ such that

$\forall\Delta[\ ] \in \mathcal{U}(\Delta_{\vec{x},q}[\ ])$. $\forall\, i \in I(x,h)$

$G^*_{x,h}\, \Delta[M_{i,1}\ ]\ldots\Delta[M_{i,m(x)}] = \quad U^{g(x,i)}_1\, y_{x,h,i}$

Indeed it is sufficient to choose

$G^*_{x,h} \equiv G_{x,h}[\, U^{g(x,i)}_1\, y_{x,h,i} / y_{x,h,i}$ for $i \in I(x,h)]$

Let

$$\forall x \in X\ \forall h \in \{1,\ldots n(x)\}$$

$\Delta_{x,h}$ = **if** $h \in L(x)$ **then** $G^*_{x,h}$ **else** arbitrary

$$\Delta_x = \lambda t_1 \ldots t_{e(x)} \ldots t_{m(x)}.t_{e(x)}(\Delta_{x,1} t_1 \ldots t_{e(x)} \ldots t_{m(x)}) \ldots$$
$$\ldots(\Delta_{x,n(x)-1}\, t_1 \ldots t_{e(x)} \ldots t_{m(x)})$$
$$(\lambda u.\, u\, t_1 \ldots t_{e(x)} \ldots t_{m(x)})$$

and

$$\Delta^*[\ ] \equiv (\lambda\vec{x}.\,[\ ])\, \Delta_{x_1} \ldots \Delta_{x_w}$$

It is clear that

$$\Delta^*[\ ] \in \mathcal{U}(\Delta_{\vec{x},q}[\ ])$$

and it can be verified that

$$\forall M \in \mathcal{F}.\ \Delta^*[M] = y_M.$$

Step 3. (checking) See Appendix 1. □

<u>3.4.0 Example</u> (2.4.0 continued)

Let $x = \{x\}$ and

$$\mathcal{F} = \{xx(x(x\Omega))z,\ xx(xx)x,\ xx(xx)(U^2_1(xx))\}$$

(Notice the similarity with 2.4.0).

Since

$$\mathcal{F}_\Omega = \{xx(x(x\Omega))\Omega,\ xx(xx)x,\ xx(xx)(U^2_1(xx))\}$$

is distinct, it follows that it is X-separable.

Let G be as in 2.4.0, and choosing

$$C[\ ] = (\lambda y_1 y_2 y_3.[\ ])(U^5_1 y_1)(U^5_1 y_2)(U^5_1 y_3)$$

let

$$G' \equiv C[G].$$

Let $\Delta_{\vec{x}}[\ ]$ be defined by

$$\Delta_{\vec{x}}[\ ] \equiv (\lambda\vec{x}.\,[\ ])\,\Delta$$

such that

$$\Delta \equiv \lambda t_1 t_2 t_3.t_2\,(G'\, t_1 t_2 t_3)\,\Omega < t_1, t_2, t_3 > .$$

Comparing this Δ with that one of 2.4.0 and remembering lemma 2.4 it is easy to see that

$$\Delta\Delta(\Delta(\Delta\Omega))z = y_1$$
$$\Delta\Delta(\Delta\Delta)\Delta = y_2$$
$$\Delta\Delta(\Delta\Delta)(U^2_1(\Delta\Delta)) = y_3.$$ □

3.5 <u>Remark</u>

Let $\mathcal{F} \subset \Lambda_{X,e,m}$.

Then $\mathcal{F}$ is β-η-X-separable iff $\mathcal{F}$ is X-distinct

iff $\mathcal{F}$ is X-separable. □

3.6 <u>Corollary</u> ({x}-separability and {x}-distinction)

Let

$$\mathcal{F} = \{x\,x,\ x\,M_1, \ldots, x\,M_n\}$$

and

$$FV(M_1 \ldots M_n) \cap \{x\} = \Phi.$$

Then

$\mathcal{F}$ is {x}-separable iff $\mathcal{F}$ is {x}-distinct.

<u>Proof</u> ($\Rightarrow$) Obvious.

($\Leftarrow$) $\mathcal{F}$ is {x}-distinct implies

$$\mathcal{F} \subset \Lambda_{\{x\},e,m}$$

where

$$e(x) = m(x) = 1.$$

We apply then Theor. 3.4. □

Next proposition, as announced in section 0, is valid in Λ^0 and it is not a consequence of [CDR 78].

3.7 <u>Corollary</u> (self - recognition)

Let $\{M_1, \ldots, M_n\} \subset \beta\text{-}\eta\text{-}NF^0$

and $y_i \in \mathcal{V}$ (i=0,1,...,n).

Then $\exists\Delta \in \Lambda$ s.t.

$$\Delta\,\Delta = y_0$$

and

$\Delta\, M_i = y_i$ (i=1,...,n) iff $M_1, \ldots, M_n$ are pairwise distinct.

<u>Proof</u>

Let

$$\mathcal{F} = \{x\,x,\ x\,M_1, \ldots, x\,M_n\}.$$

Since Def 3.2 applies $\mathcal{F}$ is X-distinct. The result follows directly from Cor. 3.6. □

3.7.0 <u>Example</u>

Let $\mathcal{F} = \{\omega\}$.

Since ω is (vacuously) pairwise distinct then

$\exists\Delta$ s.t. $\Delta\Delta = y_0$ and $\Delta\,\omega = y_1$.

A possible choice for Δ is

$$\Delta \equiv \lambda t.t(t\ U^3_3\,(U^5_1\, y_0)\,(U^3_1\, y_1))\,\Delta_2$$

with arbitrary Δ_2.

Notice that last component of Δ i.e. $\lambda u.ut$ is needed only if we have to use in the BT a path of positive length. □

3.7.1 <u>Example</u> In the realm of self-application and self-recognition even more may be done. We are able to find two terms each recognizing itself and eachother.

In fact

$$\{x_1x_1,\ x_1x_2,\ x_2\,x_1,\ x_2\,x_2\}$$

is $\{x_1, x_2\}$-separable and a possible solution is

$$\Delta_{\vec{x}}[\ ] \equiv (\lambda x_1 x_2.\,[\ ])\,\Delta_1\Delta_2$$

where

$$\Delta_1 \equiv \lambda t.t(G_1\, t) \text{ and } \Delta_2 \equiv \lambda t.t(G_2\, t)\,\Delta_{2,2}$$

with arbitrary $\Delta_{2,2}$ and where

$G_1 \equiv C_1[G]$, $G_2 \equiv C_2[G]$ and $G \equiv < U^3_3,\ U^2_1 y_2,\ y_1 >$

with

$$C_1[\ ] \equiv (\lambda y_1\, y_2.[\ ])\,(U^2_1 y_1)\,(U^3_1 y_2)$$

and

$$C_2[\ ] \equiv (\lambda y_1\, y_2.[\ ])\,(U^3_1 y_3)\,(U^4_1 y_4).$$ □

4. Left-invertibility

β–one-side invertibility for Λ was characterized in [BD 74] and [MZ 83] whereas full β–η–invertibility for Λ was settled in [Dez 76].

4.0 <u>Definition</u> (left-invertibility)
M∈Λ is said
β–η–left-invertible iff $\exists L \in \Lambda . L(M y) =_\eta y$,
where $y \notin FV(LM)$. □

4.1 <u>Theorem</u> (left-invertibility and X- separability)
Let

$$M = \lambda x_0\vec{x}.\, x_0 (M_1 x_0\vec{x})\ldots(M_n x_0\vec{x}).$$

Then
M is β–η–left-invertible iff

$$\{M_1 x_0\vec{x}, \ldots, M_n x_0\vec{x}\} \text{ is } \beta\text{–}\eta\text{–X–separable.}$$

<u>Proof</u>
(⇒) Let L s.t.

$$L(M y) =_\eta y.$$

Then

$$L(\lambda\vec{x}.\, y(M_1 y\vec{x})\ldots(M_n y\vec{x})) =_\eta y.$$

For some p, r∈N and $L_i \in \Lambda$ (i=1,...,r) it follows that

$$L =_\eta \lambda t_0\vec{t}.\, t_0(L_1 t_0\vec{t})\ldots(L_r t_0\vec{t}),$$

where $\vec{t} \equiv t_1\ldots t_p$.
Then

$$L(M y) =_\eta \lambda\vec{t}.(\lambda\vec{x}.\, y(M_1 y\vec{x})\ldots(M_n y\vec{x}))(L_1(M y)\vec{t})\ldots$$
$$\ldots(L_r(M y)\vec{t}).$$

Case 1. w > r

$$L(M y) =_\eta \lambda\vec{t}\, t_{p+1}\ldots t_{p+w-r}\, y(M_1 y(L_1(M y)\vec{t})\ldots$$
$$\ldots(L_r(M y)\vec{t})t_{p+1}\ldots t_{p+w-r})\ldots$$
$$\ldots(M_n y(L_1(M y)\vec{t})\ldots$$
$$\ldots(L_r(M y)\vec{t})t_{p+1}\ldots t_{p+w-r}) =_\eta$$
$$=_\eta y$$

where n=p+w-r.
Hence ∀i ∈{1,...,n}

$$M_i y(L_1(M y)\vec{t})\ldots(L_r(M y)\vec{t})t_{p+1}\ldots t_{p+w-r} =_\eta t_i.$$

Choosing now $\Delta_k = L_k(M x_0)\vec{t}$ for k = 1,..., r
$\Delta_k = t_{p+k-r}$ for k = r+1,..., w
and

$$\Delta[\ ] = (\lambda\vec{x}.[\ ])\Delta_1\ldots\Delta_w$$

it follows that

$$\forall i \in\{1,\ldots,n\}.\ \Delta[M_i x_0\vec{x}] =_\eta t_i,$$

hence

$$\{M_1 x_0\vec{x}, \ldots, M_n x_0\vec{x}\}$$

is β–η–X–separable.
Case 2. w ≤ r

$$L(M y) =_\eta \lambda\vec{t}.\, y(M_1 y(L_1(M y)\vec{t})\ldots(L_w(M y)\vec{t}))\ldots$$
$$\ldots(M_n y(L_1(M y)\vec{t})\ldots(L_w(M y)\vec{t}))\ldots$$
$$\ldots(L_{w+1}(M y)\vec{t})\ldots(L_r(M y)\vec{t}) =_\eta$$
$$=_\eta y.$$

Hence

$$\forall i \in\{1,\ldots,n\}.\ M_i y(L_1(M y)\vec{t})\ldots(L_w(M y)\vec{t}) =_\eta t_i.$$

Choosing now $\Delta_k = L_k(M x_0)\vec{t}$ for k = 1,..., w
we join case 1.
(⇐) Let

$$\Delta[\ ] = (\lambda\vec{x}.[\ ])\Delta_1\ldots\Delta_w$$

such that

$$\forall i \in\{1,\ldots,n\}\ \Delta[M_i x_0\vec{x}] =_\eta t_i.$$

We choose $L = \lambda z_0 z_1\ldots z_n.\, z_0\Delta_1\ldots\Delta_w$.
Then

$$L(M y) =_\eta \lambda z_1\ldots z_n.\, M y\Delta_1\ldots\Delta_w =_\eta$$
$$=_\eta \lambda z_1\ldots z_n.\, y(M_1 y\Delta_1\ldots\Delta_w)\ldots(M_n y\Delta_1\ldots\Delta_w) =_\eta$$
$$=_\eta \lambda z_1\ldots z_n.\, y z_1\ldots z_n =_\eta$$
$$=_\eta y.$$

□

4.2 <u>Corollary</u> (Left invertibility and X-distinction)
Let

$$M = \lambda x_0 x_1\ldots x_w.\, x_0 M_1\ldots M_n$$

and

$$\mathcal{F} = \{M_1, \ldots, M_n\} \subset \Lambda_{x,e,m}$$

for some e,m: X→N.
Then
M is β–η–left-invertible iff $\mathcal{F}$ is X-distinct.

<u>Proof</u>
From 4.1
M is β–η–left-invertible iff $\mathcal{F}$ is β–η–X–separable
and from 3.7
$\mathcal{F}$ is β–η–X–separable iff $\mathcal{F}$ is X-distinct. □

4.2.0 <u>Example</u> (2.4.0 end) $=_\eta$ y
Let

$$M = \lambda yx.\, y(xx(x(xy))\Omega)(xx(xx)x)(xx(xx)(\mathbf{U}^2{}_1(xx))).$$

Then $\mathcal{F}_\Omega$, being the same as in 3.4.0, is distinct.
Then a possible choice for L is

$$L = \lambda t y_1 y_2 y_3.t\Delta \text{ with } \Delta \text{ as in 3.4.0.}$$

5. Concluding remark and further development

The results of this paper can be summarized saying that it shows how a self-controlled use of self-application can be embodied in the solution of functional equations without falling into infinite computations.
The next step seems to be trying to enlarge the class of X-separable λ-terms and consequently that one of left - invertible λ–β–η–terms. The handling in a similar way right-invertibility remains an open problem.

Acknowledgements

The authors are grateful to Mariangiola Dezani-Ciancaglini and Adolfo Piperno for helpful discussions on the topics of this paper.

References

[Bar 84] Barendregt, H.P., The lambda calculus, North Holland, 1984

[BD 74] Böhm, C. and Dezani-Ciancaglini, M., Combinatorial problems, combinator equations and normal forms in: Loeckx (ed.) *Aut., Langu. and Progr.*, 2nd Colloquium, LNCS 14, 1974

[BDPR 79] Böhm, C., Dezani-Ciancaglini, Peretti, P. and Ronchi della Rocca, S., A discrimination algorithm inside λ–β–Calculus, *Theor. Comput. Sci.* 8, (1979), pp. 271-291

[Böh 68] Böhm, C., Alcune proprietà delle forme β–η–normali nel λ-K-calcolo, *IAC Publ.* n. 696, Roma, 19 pp., 1968

[CDR 78] Coppo, M., Dezani-Ciancaglini, M. and Ronchi della Rocca, S., (Semi-)separability of finite sets of terms in Scott's D_∞-models of the λ–calculus, in: Ausiello and Böhm (eds.), *Aut., Langu. and Progr.*, 5th Colloq., LNCS 62, 1978

[Dez 76] Dezani-Ciancaglini, M., Characterization of normal forms possessing inverse in the λ–β–η–calculus, *Theor. Comput. Sci.* 2, (1976), pp. 323-337

[MZ 83] Margaria, I., Zacchi, M., Right and Left Invertibility in λ–β–Calculus, *RAIRO Theor. Inf.* 17, (1983), pp. 71-88

Appendix 0

Proof of lemma 1.2.3

Let $M, N \in \mathcal{F}$.

Let q satisfy 1.2.1. (ii) for $(\mathcal{F}, \diamond)$.

The cases where

$$M \notin SOL \text{ or } N \notin SOL$$

are easy.

Let

$$M, N \in SOL.$$

Then

$$M = \lambda z_1 \dots z_j.\, u_1 M_1 \dots M_k,$$

$$N = \lambda z_1 \dots z_r.\, u_2 N_1 \dots N_s.$$

Case 1. $u_1, u_2 \notin X$.

Then

$$\Delta_{\vec{X},q}[M] = \lambda z_1 \dots z_j.\, u_1 \Delta_{\vec{X},q}[M_1] \dots \Delta_{\vec{X},q}[M_k]$$

$$\Delta_{\vec{X},q}[N] = \lambda z_1 \dots z_r.\, u_2 \Delta_{\vec{X},q}[N_1] \dots \Delta_{\vec{X},q}[N_s]$$

and this case is settled.

Case 2. $u_1 = x$, $u_2 = y$ where $x, y \in X$.

Then

$$\Delta_{\vec{X},q}[M] = \lambda z_1 \dots z_j t_{k+1} \dots t_{m(x)} \cdot t_{e(x)}\, \Omega^{n(x)-1} (\lambda u.\, u\, \Delta_{\vec{X},q}[M_1] \dots \Delta_{\vec{X},q}[M_k]\, t_{k+1} \dots t_{m(x)})$$

$$\Delta_{\vec{X},q}[N] = \lambda z_1 \dots z_r t_{s+1} \dots t_{m(y)} \cdot t_{e(y)}\, \Omega^{n(y)-1} (\lambda u.\, u\, \Delta_{\vec{X},q}[N_1] \dots \Delta_{\vec{X},q}[N_s]\, t_{s+1} \dots t_{m(y)}).$$

(⇒)

$$M \sim N \Rightarrow x = y \wedge k-j = s-r \Rightarrow$$

$$\Rightarrow e(x)-k+j = e(y)-s+r \wedge n(x)-m(x)+k-j = n(y)-m(y)+s-r \Rightarrow$$

$$\Rightarrow \Delta_{\vec{X},q}[M] \sim \Delta_{\vec{X},q}[N].$$

(⇐)

$$\Delta_{\vec{X},q}[M] \sim \Delta_{\vec{X},q}[N] \Rightarrow$$

$$\Rightarrow e(x)-k+j = e(y)-s+r \wedge n(x)-m(x)+k-j = n(y)-m(y)+s-r \Rightarrow$$

$$\Rightarrow q(x) = q(y) \wedge n(x)-m(x)+k-j = n(y)-m(y)+s-r \Rightarrow$$

$$\Rightarrow x = y \wedge k-j = s-r \Rightarrow M \sim N$$

Case 3. $u_1 = x \in X$, $u_2 \notin X$. Then

(⇒) Obvious.

(⇐) We prove *per absurdum* that $\Delta_{\vec{X},q}[M] \not\sim \Delta_{\vec{X},q}[N]$.

Let

$$\Delta_{\vec{X},q}[M] \sim \Delta_{\vec{X},q}[N].$$

Then

$$head(N) \notin FV(N);$$

hence

$q(x) > s$. Moreover $\Delta_{\vec{X},q}[M] \sim \Delta_{\vec{X},q}[N] \Rightarrow$

$$\Rightarrow e(x)-k+j \leq r \wedge n(x)-m(x)+k-j = s-r \Rightarrow$$

$$\Rightarrow q(x) \leq s.$$

Absurd. □

Appendix 1

Step 3 (Checking) of theorem 3.4

Since

$$\mathcal{F}_\Omega \equiv \bigcup_{x \in X} \bigcup_{h \in L(x)} \mathcal{F}_{x,h}$$

it remains to show that

$$\forall x \in X.\, \forall h \in L(x).\, \forall i \in I_{x,h}.\, \Delta^*[M_i] = y_{x,h,i}\,.$$

Case 1. $M_i \in \mathcal{F}^0_{x,h}$.

$$\Delta^*[M_i] = \Delta_x\, \Delta^*[M_{i,1}] \dots \Delta^*[M_{i,m(x)}] =$$

$$= \Delta^*[M_{i,e(x)}] (\Delta_{x,1}\ \Delta^*[M_{i,1}] \dots \Delta^*[M_{i,m(x)}]) \dots$$

$$\dots (\Delta_{x,n(x)-1}\, \Delta^*[M_{i,1}] \dots \Delta^*[M_{i,m(x)}])$$

$$(\lambda u.\, u\ \ \Delta^*[M_{i,1}] \dots \Delta^*[M_{i,m(x)}]) =$$

$$= (\lambda z_1 \dots z_{p(i)}.\, \Delta_{x'} (\Delta^*[Q_{i,1}]\, z_1 \dots z_{p(i)}) \dots (\Delta^*[Q_{i,b(i)}]\, z_1 \dots z_{p(i)}))$$

$$(\Delta_{x,1}\ \ \Delta^*[M_{i,1}] \dots \Delta^*[M_{i,m(x)}]) \dots$$

$$\dots (\Delta_{x,n(x)-1}\, \Delta^*[M_{i,1}] \dots \Delta^*[M_{i,m(x)}])$$

$$(\lambda u.\, u\ \ \Delta^*[M_{i,1}] \dots \Delta^*[M_{i,m(x)}]) =$$

$$= \Delta_{x'} (\Delta^*[Q_{i,1}] (\Delta_{x,1}\ \Delta^*[M_{i,1}] \dots \Delta^*[M_{i,m(x)}]) \dots$$

$$\dots (\Delta_{x,p(i)}\, \Delta^*[M_{i,1}] \dots \Delta^*[M_{i,m(x)}])) \dots$$

$$\dots (\Delta^*[Q_{i,b(i)}] (\Delta_{x,1}\ \Delta^*[M_{i,1}] \dots \Delta^*[M_{i,m(x)}]) \dots$$

$$\dots (\Delta_{x,p(i)}\, \Delta^*[M_{i,1}] \dots \Delta^*[M_{i,m(x)}]))$$

$$(\Delta_{x,p(i)+1}\ \ \Delta^*[M_{i,1}] \dots \Delta^*[M_{i,m(x)}]) \dots$$

$$\dots (\Delta_{x,n(x)-1}\ \ \Delta^*[M_{i,1}] \dots \Delta^*[M_{i,m(x)}])$$

$$(\lambda u.\, u\, \Delta^*[M_{i,1}] \dots \Delta^*[M_{i,m(x)}]) =$$

$$= \Delta_{x,p(i)+e(x')-b(i)}\, \Delta^*[M_{i,1}] \dots \Delta^*[M_{i,m(x)}]$$

$$(\Delta_{x',1} (\Delta^*[Q_{i,1}] (\Delta_{x,1}\ \Delta^*[M_{i,1}] \dots \Delta^*[M_{i,m(x)}]) \dots$$

$$\dots (\Delta_{x,p(i)}\, \Delta^*[M_{i,1}] \dots \Delta^*[M_{i,m(x)}])) \dots$$

$$\dots (\Delta^*[Q_{i,b(i)}] (\Delta_{x,1}\ \Delta^*[M_{i,1}] \dots \Delta^*[M_{i,m(x)}]) \dots$$

$$\dots (\Delta_{x,p(i)}\, \Delta^*[M_{i,1}] \dots \Delta^*[M_{i,m(x)}]))$$

$$(\Delta_{x,p(i)+1}\ \ \Delta^*[M_{i,1}] \dots \Delta^*[M_{i,m(x)}]) \dots$$

$$\dots (\Delta_{x,p(i)+m(x')-b(i)}\ \ \Delta^*[M_{i,1}] \dots \Delta^*[M_{i,m(x)}])) \dots$$

$$\dots (\Delta_{x',n(x')-1} (\Delta^*[Q_{i,1}] (\Delta_{x,1}\ \Delta^*[M_{i,1}] \dots \Delta^*[M_{i,m(x)}]) \dots$$

$$\ldots(\Delta_{x,p(i)}\,\Delta^*[M_{i,1}]\ldots\Delta^*[M_{i,m(x)}]))\ldots$$
$$\ldots(\Delta^*[Q_{i,b(i)}](\Delta_{x,1}\;\Delta^*[M_{i,1}]\ldots\Delta^*[M_{i,m(x)}])\ldots$$
$$\ldots(\Delta_{x,p(i)}\,\Delta^*[M_{i,1}]\ldots\Delta^*[M_{i,m(x)}]))$$
$$(\Delta_{x,p(i)+1}\;\;\Delta^*[M_{i,1}]\ldots\Delta^*[M_{i,m(x)}])\ldots$$
$$\ldots(\Delta_{x,p(i)+m(x')-b(i)}\;\Delta^*[M_{i,1}]\ldots\Delta^*[M_{i,m(x)}]))$$
$$(\lambda u.\, u\,(\Delta^*[Q_{i,1}]\,(\Delta_{x,1}\;\;\Delta^*[M_{i,1}]\ldots\Delta^*[M_{i,m(x)}])\ldots$$
$$\ldots(\Delta_{x,p(i)}\,\Delta^*[M_{i,1}]\ldots\Delta^*[M_{i,m(x)}]))\ldots$$
$$\ldots(\Delta^*[Q_{i,b(i)}](\Delta_{x,1}\;\Delta^*[M_{i,1}]\ldots\Delta^*[M_{i,m(x)}])\ldots$$
$$\ldots(\Delta_{x,p(i)}\,\Delta^*[M_{i,1}]\ldots\Delta^*[M_{i,m(x)}]))$$
$$(\Delta_{x,p(i)+1}\;\;\Delta^*[M_{i,1}]\ldots\Delta^*[M_{i,m(x)}])\ldots$$
$$\ldots(\Delta_{x,p(i)+m(x')-b(i)}\;\Delta^*[M_{i,1}]\ldots\Delta^*[M_{i,m(x)}]))$$
$$(\Delta_{x,p(i)+m(x')-b(i)+1}\;\Delta^*[M_{i,1}]\ldots\Delta^*[M_{i,m(x)}])\ldots$$
$$\ldots(\Delta_{x,n(x)-1}\;\Delta^*[M_{i,1}]\ldots\Delta^*[M_{i,m(x)}])$$
$$(\lambda u.\, u\;\;\;\Delta^*[M_{i,1}]\ldots\Delta^*[M_{i,m(x)}]).$$

Since

$$p(i) + e(x') - b(i) = h$$

and

$$\Delta_{x,h} = G^*{}_{x,h}$$

we obtain

$$\Delta^*[M_i] = y_{x,h,i}\,.$$

Case 2. $M_i \in \mathcal{F}^1{}_{x,h}$.

$$\Delta^*[M_i] =$$
$$= (\lambda z_1 \ldots z_{p(i)}.\, z_h\,(\Delta^*[Q_{i,1}]\,z_1\ldots z_{p(i)})\ldots(\Delta^*[Q_{i,b(i)}]\,z_1\ldots z_{p(i)}))$$
$$(\Delta_{x,1}\;\;\Delta^*[M_{i,1}]\ldots\Delta^*[M_{i,m(x)}])\ldots$$
$$\ldots(\Delta_{x,n(x)-1}\Delta^*[M_{i,1}]\ldots\Delta^*[M_{i,m(x)}])$$
$$(\lambda u.\, u\;\;\Delta^*[M_{i,1}]\ldots\Delta^*[M_{i,m(x)}]) =$$
$$= \Delta_{x,h}\;\;\Delta^*[M_{i,1}]\ldots\Delta^*[M_{i,m(x)}]$$
$$(\Delta^*[Q_{i,1}]\,(\,\Delta_{x,1}\;\;\Delta^*[M_{i,1}]\ldots\Delta^*[M_{i,m(x)}])\ldots$$
$$\ldots(\,\Delta_{x,p(i)}\;\Delta^*[M_{i,1}]\ldots\Delta^*[M_{i,m(x)}]))\ldots$$
$$\ldots(\Delta^*[Q_{i,b(i)}](\Delta_{x,1}\;\;\Delta^*[M_{i,1}]\ldots\Delta^*[M_{i,m(x)}])\ldots$$
$$\ldots(\Delta_{x,p(i)}\,\Delta^*[M_{i,1}]\ldots\Delta^*[M_{i,m(x)}]))$$
$$(\Delta_{x,p(i)+1}\;\;\;\Delta^*[M_{i,1}]\ldots\Delta^*[M_{i,m(x)}])\ldots$$
$$\ldots(\Delta_{x,n(x)-1}\Delta^*[M_{i,1}]\ldots\Delta^*[M_{i,m(x)}])$$
$$(\lambda u.\, u\;\;\;\Delta^*[M_{i,1}]\ldots\Delta^*[M_{i,m(x)}]) = y_{x,h,i}\,.$$

(Since $\Delta_{x,h} = G^*{}_{x,h}$). □

Session 9

Chair

J.-P. Jouannaud

Universite Paris-Sud-Orsay

INFERENCE RULES FOR
REWRITE-BASED FIRST-ORDER THEOREM PROVING

Leo Bachmair
Department of Computer Science
SUNY at Stony Brook
Stony Brook, New York 11794

Nachum Dershowitz
Department of Computer Science
University of Illinois at Urbana-Champaign
Urbana, IL 61801

Abstract. In this paper we present a complete inference system for first-order theorem proving that is based on a canonical system for Boolean algebra. We also present a technique for proving the completeness of rewrite-based proof methods.

1. Introduction

Equational formalisms have been applied to many problems in computer science, including specifications of abstract data types and equational programming. The ability to reason about equations is therefore of importance. Many equational reasoning methods are based on the concept of simplification by rewriting.

Rewrite systems are sets of directed equations used to compute by repeatedly substituting equal terms in an expression until a simplest possible form (a normal form) is obtained. Knuth and Bendix (1970) developed a method for constructing a canonical (i.e. terminating Church-Rosser) rewrite system for a given equational theory. A (finite) canonical system provides a decision procedure for the validity problem in the corresponding theory: two terms are equivalent if and only if they reduce to identical normal forms. Since there are (finitely-based) equational theories for which the word problem is undecidable, the Knuth-Bendix completion method must fail for certain inputs. Completion can be used for theorem proving in purely equational theories (Huet 1981), but has the drawback that it may fail. Extensions of completion that do not fail, and therefore constitute semi-decision procedures for purely equational theories, have been described by Bachmair, Dershowitz, and Plaisted (1987) and Hsiang and Rusinowitch (1987).

Within resolution provers, rewriting (known as demodulation; Wos, et al. 1967) is usually used in an incomplete, ad-hoc way, though some completeness results have been derived by Slagle (1974). Hsiang (1985) has extended the completion method to first-order theorem proving, on the basis of a canonical rewrite system for Boolean algebra. This method can be applied to sets of formulas in clausal form. Rewriting has also been investigated by Kapur and Narendran (1985), in the context of polynomial theory.

Conventional techniques for establishing completeness, such as semantic trees, are inadequate for rewrite-based proof methods. In fact, the completeness of the proof methods by Hsiang (1985) and Kapur and Narendran (1985) is an open problem. In this paper, we present a complete inference system for first-order predicate calculus that is based on a canonical system for Boolean algebra. The method is not restricted to clausal format and includes various forms of simplification by rewriting. Our completeness proof is based on the application of proof ordering techniques (Bachmair, Dershowitz, and Hsiang, 1986) to first-order theorem proving.

2. Canonical Simplification for Boolean Algebra

Our proof method is based on the following rewrite system BA for Boolean algebra (Hsiang 1985):

$$\begin{array}{rcl} x+0 & \to & x \\ x+x & \to & 0 \\ x*0 & \to & 0 \\ x*1 & \to & x \\ x*x & \to & x \\ (x+y)*z & \to & (x*z)+(y*z) \\ x \vee y & \to & (x*y)+(x+y) \\ x \supset y & \to & (x*y)+(x+1) \\ x \equiv y & \to & (x+y)+1 \\ \neg x & \to & x+1 \end{array}$$

The constants 1 and 0 represent *true* and *false*, respectively. The operators + and * denote exclusive disjunction and conjunction, respectively. They are associative and commutative. By AC we denote the corresponding set of axioms

$$\begin{aligned}(x+y)+z &= x+(y+z)\\ x+y &= y+x\\ (x*y)*z &= x*(y*z)\\ x*y &= y*x\end{aligned}$$

We write $A \rightarrow_{BA} B$ to indicate that A can be rewritten to B by application of a rewrite rule in BA. Note that associative-commutative matching is employed for rewriting with BA. For example, the Boolean expression $q + 0 * p$ can be reduced to $q + 0$ in BA.

The rewrite system BA is canonical. That is, any Boolean expression has a unique normal form (up to associativity and commutativity) with respect to BA. Consequently, BA provides a decision procedure for the word problem in propositional calculus: two Boolean expressions are equivalent if and only if they reduce to identical normal forms. For example, $\neg(p \vee q)$ and $\neg p * \neg q$ both have the normal form $p*q + p + q + 1$; hence are equivalent.

The first six rules in BA form a canonical system for Boolean rings. We denote this rewrite system by BR. By BN we denote the canonical system consisting of the first five rules.

In general, the rewrite system BA can be used to normalize any (quantifier-free) first-order formula A. A formula in normal form can be written as a *sum* $P_1 + \cdots + P_m$ of *products* $a_1 * \cdots * a_n$ of atoms. (An atom is an expression $p(t_1, \ldots, t_n)$, where p is a predicate symbol and, for $1 \leq i \leq n$, t_i is a (first-order) term possibly containing variables. In addition, 0 and 1 are atoms.) Of course, a sum of products need not necessarily be in normal form. For example, $p+p+q$ reduces to $0+p$. A formula that contains no variables is called *ground.* A ground formula is valid if and only if it reduces to 1; and unsatisfiable if and only if it reduces to 0.

We use the symbols a, b, $\cdots$ to denote atoms; P, Q, $\cdots$ to denote products; and A, B, $\cdots$ to denote sums of products or, occasionally, arbitrary first-order formulas. We usually abbreviate $a_1 * \cdots * a_n$ by $a_1 \cdots a_n$ and, for notational convenience, use aA and PA, where A is a sum $P_1 + \cdots + P_n$, as abbreviations for $aP_1 + \cdots + aP_n$ and $PP_1 + \cdots + PP_n$, respectively.

We will present a proof method for manipulating equations $A = B$ between sums of products. We do not distinguish between equations that differ only in their respective distribution of products to left and right-hand sides. For instance, $A+B+C=0$, $A+B=C$, and $A=B+C$ are considered identical. Equations are implicitly universally quantified. Through Skolemization and normalization with respect to BA any arbitrary set A of (first-order) formulas can be transformed into a set of equations E, such that A is satisfiable if and only if E is satisfiable. For an algorithm for such a translation see Kapur and Narendran (1985), for instance.

Two basic concepts are employed in our proof method: *unification* of products and *orderings* on terms and atoms.

We say that two products $a_1 \cdots a_n$ and $b_1 \cdots b_n$ can be *unified,* if there is a substitution σ, such that $\{a_1\sigma, \ldots, a_n\sigma\}$ and $\{b_1\sigma, \ldots, b_n\sigma\}$ are equal multisets. An algorithm for computing the set of most general unifiers of two products is given in Hsiang (1985).

A (strict partial) ordering is a transitive and irreflexive binary relation. An ordering $>$ on terms and atoms is *stable* if (a) $s > t$ implies $s\sigma > t\sigma$ and (b) $a > b$ implies $a\sigma > b\sigma$, for all terms s and t, atoms a and b, and substitutions σ. The ordering is *monotonic* if $s > t$ implies (a) $u[s] > u[t]$ and (b) $a[s] > a[t]$, for all terms s, t, and u, and all atoms a. A *reduction ordering* is a well-founded ordering that is stable and monotonic. A *strong reduction ordering* is a reduction ordering that is total on the set of ground terms and ground atoms.

We will consider reduction orderings $>$ on terms and atoms for which $a > 1 > 0$, for all atoms a distinct from 0 and 1. Such an ordering can be extended to products of atoms, by defining $a_1 \cdots a_m > b_1 \cdots b_n$ *if and only if* $\{a_1, \ldots, a_m\} \gg \{b_1, \ldots, b_n\}$. (The symbol $\gg$ denotes the extension of $>$ to multisets.) Similarly, the ordering can be extended to sums of products by defining $P_1 + \cdots + P_m > Q_1 + \cdots + Q_n$ *if and only if* $\{P_1, \ldots, P_m\} \gg \{Q_1, \ldots, Q_n\}$. Any such ordering contains BN, i.e. $A \rightarrow_{BN} B$ implies $A > B$, for all sums of products A and B.

3. Inference Rules for First-Order Theorem Proving

Let $>$ be an ordering on terms and atoms. The corresponding extension to sums of products is also denoted by $>$. The following inference rules can be applied to any set E of equations $A = B$ between sums of products:

$$\text{From } PP' = A \text{ and } QQ' = B \quad \text{infer } (Q'A)\sigma = (P'B)\sigma \tag{1}$$

if σ is a most general unifier of P and Q, $A \not> PP'$, and $B \not> QQ'$.

$$\text{From } P + Q = A \text{ infer } A\sigma = 0 \tag{2}$$

if σ is a most general unifier of P and Q, $A \not> P$, and $A \not> Q$.

$$\text{From } abP = A \text{ infer } (aP)\sigma = A\sigma \tag{3}$$

if σ is a most general unifier of a and b and $A \not> abP$.

$$\text{From } aP = A \text{ infer } aA = A \tag{4}$$

if $A \not> aP$.

Note that the above inference rules depend only on the maximal products in a sum. Thus, the ordering $>$ effectively restricts the number of equational consequences that have to be considered.

The *soundness* of the above inference rules can be readily established. For instance, let $PP' = A$ and $QQ' = B$ be equations and σ be a unifier of P and Q. In $(Q'PP')\sigma$ we can either replace $(PP')\sigma$ by $A\sigma$, to obtain $(Q'A)\sigma$; or replace $(Q'P)\sigma$, which by assumption is the same as $(Q'Q)\sigma$, by $B\sigma$ to obtain $(P'B)\sigma$. The resulting equation is $(Q'A)\sigma = (P'B)\sigma$. The second inference rule can be derived from the nilpotency axiom $x + x = 0$ and the identity axiom $x + 0 = x$. Rules (3) and (4) follow from the idempotency axiom $x * x = x$. For instance, rule (4) is obtained from $A = aP$, $aP = aaP$, and $aaP = aA$.

The following inference rules can be used to simplify or delete equations. An equation $A = 0$ *subsumes* $B = 0$, if B is $A\sigma$. For technical reasons, we assume that $1 = 0$ subsumes any other equation.

Normalization

$$\text{Replace } A = 0 \text{ by } B = 0 \text{ if } A \rightarrow_{BN} B \tag{5}$$

Subsumption

Delete any equation that is subsumed by another equation. (6)

Since we consider sums of products only, the system BN suffices for normalization of equations. By **P** we denote the inference system consisting of rules (1)-(6).

4. Completeness

An inference system is *refutationally complete* if a contradiction, namely the equation $1 = 0$, can be derived from any unsatisfiable set of formulas E.

Let **P** be an inference system. We write $E \vdash_{\mathbf{P}} E'$ if E' can be obtained from E by application of an inference rule in **P**. A *derivation* in **P** is a (possibly infinite) sequence $E_0, E_1, \cdots$ such that $E_{i-1} \vdash_{\mathbf{P}} E_i$, for all $i > 0$. The *limit* E^∞ of a derivation is the set $\bigcup_i \bigcap_{j \geq i} E_j$ of all *persisting equations*.

A derivation in **P** is *fair* if (a) every equation $A = 0$ in E^∞ is irreducible with respect to BN, and (b) any equation that can be obtained from E^∞ by application of an inference rule of **P** is contained in some set E_i.

THEOREM 1. *Let* **P** *be an inference system. Suppose that the ordering* $>$ *associated with* **P** *can be extended to a strong reduction ordering. Let* $\{A_1, \ldots, A_n\}$ *be an unsatisfiable set of (quantifier-free) formulas irreducible with respect to* BA, *and let* E *be the set of equations* $\{A_1 = 1, \ldots, A_n = 1\}$. *If* $E, E_1, E_2, \cdots$ *is a fair derivation in* **P**, *then* E^∞ *contains the equation* $1 = 0$.

Theorem 1 not only shows that **P** is refutationally complete, but also that fairness characterizes a class of derivations that produce a refutation.

The ordering $>$ is part of the inference system **P**. The completeness result holds for any ordering that can be extended to a strong reduction ordering. Most of the orderings used in practice, e.g. recursive path orderings and polynomial interpretations, satisfy this requirement; see Dershowitz (1985) for details. The ordering $>$ may also be empty. The strong reduction ordering extending $>$ is not part of the inference system, but is an important tool for proving completeness. The completeness proof is based on the concept of *proof ordering* (Bachmair, Dershowitz, and Hsiang 1986).

Let E be a set of equations and A and B be sums of products. We write $A \leftrightarrow_E B$ if and only if A can be written as $P(A'\sigma) + C$ and B as $P(B'\sigma) + C$, for some equation $A' = B'$ in E.

If $P = A$ is an equation and σ is a substitution for which $P\sigma > A\sigma$, then the rewrite rule $P\sigma \rightarrow A\sigma$ is called an *orientable instance* of $P = A$. (Obviously, $P\sigma > A\sigma$ implies $A \not> P$; hence P has to be a maximal product in $P = A$.) By $R(E)$ we denote the set of all orientable instances of E. We write $A \rightarrow_{R(E)} B$ to indicate that A is $QP\sigma + D$ and B is $QC\sigma + D$, for some rule

$P\sigma \rightarrow C\sigma$ in $R(E)$.

A *proof* of $A_1 = A_n$ in $BN \cup E \cup R(E)$ is a sequence $A_1, A_2, \ldots, A_n$, such that, for $1 < i \leq n$, one of $A_{i-1} \leftrightarrow_{BN} A_i$, $A_{i-1} \leftrightarrow_E A_i$, or $A_{i-1} \leftrightarrow_{R(E)} A_i$ holds. For each replacement step, one has to specify the equation and the substitution used in the replacement. The notation $A_1 \overset{*}{\leftrightarrow}_{BN \cup E \cup R(E)} A_n$ is used for proofs.

Let M be a proof $A_1, A_2, \ldots, A_n$. The *complexity* C_M of M is the multiset $\{c(A_1, A_2), \ldots, c(A_{n-1}, A_n)\}$, where $c(A, B)$ is

$$(\{A, B\}, n, -, -, -) \quad \text{if } A \leftrightarrow_E B \text{ by } P_1 + \cdots + P_n = 0$$

$$(\{A\}, 1, -, -, -) \quad \text{if } A \rightarrow_{BN} B$$

$$(\{A\}, 0, P\sigma, P, B) \quad \text{if } A \rightarrow_{R(E)} B \text{ by } P\sigma \rightarrow C\sigma$$

($P\sigma \rightarrow C\sigma$ is an orientable instance of $P = C$.)

To compare two elements $c(A, B)$ we use the lexicographic combination $>^c$ of the multiset ordering $\gg$, the greater-than relation on the natural numbers, the proper subterm ordering, the proper subsumption ordering, and the given ordering $>$. All these orderings are well-founded; hence their lexicographic combination is well-founded, too. (A is bigger than B in the proper subsumption ordering, if and only if it is an instance of B, but B is not an instance of A.) The ordering $>_{\mathbf{P}}$ is defined by $P >_{\mathbf{P}} P'$ *if and only if* $M_c \gg^c M_c'$. This ordering is well-founded.

Proof of Theorem 1. Let $\mathbf{P}$ and $A_1, \ldots, A_n$ be as described in Theorem 1. Let $>$ be the ordering associated with $\mathbf{P}$. The strong reduction ordering containing $>$ is also denoted by $>$.

We first show that there is a proof of $1 = 0$ in $BN \cup E \cup R(E)$. Then, we prove that the application of inference rules of $\mathbf{P}$ induces a simplification relation on proofs, and that eventually a simplest proof $1 \leftrightarrow_E 0$, i.e. a refutation, will be produced.

Let $\{A_1, \ldots, A_n\}$ be an unsatisfiable set of formulas in normal form. By Herbrand's Theorem, there is an unsatisfiable set of ground instances $A_1^1, \ldots, A_{k_1}^1, \ldots, A_1^n, \ldots, A_{k_n}^n$. Let A be the conjunction of all ground formulas A_j^i. The formula A can be transformed into a sum of products A' by repeatedly applying the distributivity rule $x*(y+z) \rightarrow x*y + x*z$ (written $A \overset{*}{\rightarrow}_D A'$). Both A and A' are unsatisfiable; hence $A' \overset{*}{\rightarrow}_{BN} 0$.

On the other hand, $A_j^i \leftrightarrow_E 1$, for all i and j. Thus, $A \overset{*}{\leftrightarrow}_E (1 * \cdots * 1)$. The two relations $\rightarrow_D$ and $\leftrightarrow_E$ commute, i.e. $A' \overset{*}{\leftarrow}_D A \overset{*}{\leftrightarrow}_E B$ implies $A' \overset{*}{\leftrightarrow}_E B' \overset{*}{\leftarrow}_D B$. In our case B is the product $1 * \cdots * 1$, which is irreducible with respect to distributivity. Thus, we have $A' \overset{*}{\leftrightarrow}_E (1 * \cdots * 1)$. In summary, there is a proof

$$1 \overset{*}{\leftarrow}_{BN} (1 * \cdots * 1) \overset{*}{\leftrightarrow}_E A' \overset{*}{\rightarrow}_{BN} 0.$$

We next show that the application of inference rules induces a simplification relation on proofs. More precisely, whenever $E_{i-1} \vdash_{\mathbf{P}} E_i$ and M_{i-1} is a proof in $BN \cup E_{i-1} \cup R(E_{i-1})$, then there is a proof M_i in $BN \cup E_i \cup R(E_i)$ for which $M_{i-1} \geq_{\mathbf{P}} M_i$.

Suppose $E_{i-1} \vdash_{\mathbf{P}} E_i$, and let M_{i-1} be a proof in $BN \cup E_{i-1} \cup R(E_{i-1})$. If E_i is obtained from E_{i-1} by application of one of inference rules (1)-(4), then M_{i-1} is a proof in $BN \cup E_i \cup R(E_i)$, and the assertion holds trivially. For the subsumption rule the assertion is also obvious. If inference rule (5) is applied to replace an equation $A = B$ by $A = C$, then M_i is obtained from M_{i-1} by replacing all proof steps that use $A = B$ by proof steps involving $A = C$. More specifically, $A \leftrightarrow_{E_{i-1}} B$ can be replaced by $A \leftrightarrow_{E_i} C \leftarrow_{BN} B$; $A \rightarrow_{R(E_{i-1})} B$ can be replaced by $A \rightarrow_{R(E_i)} C \leftarrow_{BN} B$; and $A \leftarrow_{R(E_{i-1})} B$ can be replaced by $A \leftrightarrow_{E_i} C \leftarrow_{BN} B$. In each case, the new proof is simpler than the old proof in the ordering $>_{\mathbf{P}}$.

Let $E, E_1, \cdots$ be a fair derivation. We prove that there is a sequence $M_0, M_1, \cdots$ of proofs of $1 = 0$, such that whenever M_i is not of the form $1 \leftrightarrow_{E_i} 0$, then there is a proof M_j, for some $j \geq i$, with $M_i >_{\mathbf{P}} M_j$.

Suppose M_i is not a proof the form $1 \leftrightarrow_{E_i} 0$. First of all, we may assume that all proof steps in M_i persist, i.e. use equations in E^∞ or rules in BN or $R(E^\infty)$, for otherwise application of one of the simplification rules (4) or (5) will result in a simpler proof. Now, any proof containing an equality step $A \leftrightarrow_{E_i} B$ can be replaced by a simpler proof (with respect to $>_{\mathbf{P}}$). For instance, suppose that A is $PC\sigma + A'$ and B is $PD\sigma + A'$, for some equation $C = D$ and substitution σ. Since $C\sigma + D\sigma$ is a ground formula, its products are totally ordered by the strong reduction ordering $>$. (a) If $C = D$ can be written as $Q + C' = D$, where $Q\sigma > C'\sigma + D\sigma$, then $Q\sigma \rightarrow C'\sigma + D\sigma$ is an orientable instance of $C = D$. The equality step

$$PQ\sigma + PC'\sigma + A' \leftrightarrow_{E_i} PD\sigma + A'$$

can be replaced by

$$PQ\sigma + PC'\sigma + A' \rightarrow_{R(E_i)}$$
$$PC'\sigma + PD\sigma + PC'\sigma + A' \overset{*}{\rightarrow}_{BN} PD\sigma + A'$$

The new proof is simpler than the old one. (b) Suppose that $C = D$ can be written as $Q + C' = Q' + D'$, where both Q and Q' are maximal products and $Q\sigma$ and $Q'\sigma$ are identical. Then Q and Q' are unifiable. By fairness, application of (2) will produce an new equation that subsumes $C'\sigma = D'\sigma$. This equation can be used instead of $C = D$ to prove $A \leftrightarrow_{E_k} B$. The new proof step is simpler than the old one, since the new equation, subsuming $C'\sigma = D'\sigma$, contains fewer products than $C = D$. (c) The case where $C = D$ can be written as $Q + Q' + C' = D$, with Q and Q' maximal products that unify, can be handled in a similar way.

Next suppose that M_i contains a *peak* $B \leftarrow_{BN \cup R(E_i)} A \rightarrow_{BN \cup R(E_i)} C$. By standard arguments from rewrite theory, any peak in which the two rewrite steps do not *overlap* can be resolved, i.e. replaced by a rewrite proof $B \overset{*}{\rightarrow}_{BN \cup R(E_i)} D \overset{*}{\leftarrow}_{BN \cup R(E_i)} C$. The new rewrite proof is simpler than the original peak.

Let us consider overlaps. (a) Overlaps between rules in BN can be resolved because BN is canonical. (b) Overlaps between rules in $R(E_i)$ are of the form $(Q'A)\sigma \leftarrow_{R(E_i)} (Q'PP')\sigma \rightarrow_{R(E_i)} (P'B)\sigma$, where $PP' \rightarrow A$ and $QQ' \rightarrow B$ are orientable instances of equations in E_i and σ is a most general unifier of P and Q. Fairness guarantees that eventually inference rule (1) will be applied, yielding a new equation that allows us to replace the overlap by a simpler equality step $(Q'A)\sigma \leftrightarrow_{E_j} (P'B)\sigma$. (c) Overlaps between a rule in BN and a rule in R can be resolved by the use of inference rules (3), (4), or (5).

By well-foundedness of $>_{\mathbf{P}}$, we can infer that for some k, M_k is of the form $1 \leftrightarrow_{E_k} 0$. Since 1 and 0 are the smallest atoms, E_k must contain the equation $1 = 0$, which concludes the proof. □

5. Simplification

The essential characteristic of rewrite rules is their use for simplification. The rewrite system BA allows us to normalize first-order formulas. The following inference rules describe simplification by orientable instances of equations.

Replace $QP\sigma = A$ *by* $QB\sigma = A$ (7.1)

if $P = B$ is an equation in E and $P\sigma > B\sigma$.

Replace $P\sigma = A$ *by* $B\sigma = A$ (7.2)

if $P = B$ is an equation in E, $P\sigma > B\sigma$, and P and $P\sigma$ are not identical up to renaming of variables.

Replace $P\sigma = A$ *by* $B\sigma = A$ (7.3)

if $P = B$ is an equation in E, $P\sigma > B\sigma$, $A > B\sigma$, and σ is a renaming of variables.

The inference rules are obviously sound. They can be added to **P** without destroying refutation completeness. Whenever an equation is simplified, any proof using it can be replaced by a simpler proof using the new equation. For example, suppose that $QP\sigma = A$ is simplified to $QB\sigma + A$ by $P\sigma \rightarrow B\sigma$. Any equality step $QP\sigma + A_1 \leftrightarrow_E A_2$, where A is $A_1 + A_2$, can be replaced by $QP\sigma + A_1 \rightarrow_{R(E)} QB\sigma + A_1 \leftrightarrow_E A_2$. The new proof is simpler with respect to the proof ordering $>_{\mathbf{P}}$.

Simplification is most effective with rules $P \rightarrow 0$ (e.g. Hsiang 1985). In general, any equation $A = B$, where A is a sum $P_1 + \cdots + P_n$, can be used as a rewrite rule $A \rightarrow B$, if $A > B$. Such rewrite rules necessitate more complicated matching with respect to distributivity of * over +, though. For example, $PA + QA$ can be simplified to A by $P + Q \rightarrow 0$, since $PA + QA$ is equivalent, under distributivity, to $(P + Q)A$. This kind of simplification is utilized by Kapur and Narendran (1985).

Equations are often used for describing or defining a specific domain of objects. Abstract data type specifications are of this kind, for instance. Canonical sets of equations constitute a decision procedure for the word problem in the corresponding domain. A canonical system R (defining an equational theory on terms) can be combined with a first-order inference system **P**, if it is contained in the ordering $>$ associated with **P**. The following inference rules apply to sets of equations E:

Term simplification

Replace $A[s] = 0$ *by* $A[t] = 0$ *if* $s \rightarrow_R t$. (8)

Narrowing

From $A[t] = 0$ *infer* $A[r]\sigma = 0$, (9)

if σ is a most general unifier of l and t, t is not a variable, and $l \rightarrow r$ is a rewrite rule in R.

Term simplification allow us to keep terms in normal form with respect to the canonical system R. Narrowing provides the link between simplification of terms and the first-order inference rules. Narrowing was introduced by Slagle (1974).

The completeness of the inference system consisting of **P** and the additional inference rules (8) and (9) is straightforward with the proof ordering techniques described above. (In modifying the proof of Theorem 1, inference rule (8) is dealt with in a similar way as rule (5); rule (9) is needed for elimination of overlaps $B \leftarrow_{R(E)} A \rightarrow_R C$ between orientable instances of equations and rewrite rules in R.) In the completeness proof we only have to reason about ground proofs, therefore it is sufficient to require that R be ground confluent. More advanced rewrite techniques (Bachmair, Dershowitz, and Plaisted 1987; Hsiang and Rusinowitch 1987) can be used to deal with unorientable equations on terms.

6. Comparison With Other Approaches

A rewrite-based method for first-order predicate calculus was first designed by Hsiang (1985). This method—the *N-strategy*—is a particular strategy based on the inference system **P**. It can be applied to sets of input formulas in *clausal* form. Using the canonical system BA, a set of clauses is converted into a set of equations between sums of products. The main mechanism for generating new formulas is a restricted version of inference rule (1), which only applies to pairs of equations in which at least one equation is an *N-rule*, i.e. an equation $P = 0$. An N-rule $a_1 \cdots a_n = 0$ corresponds to a disjunction $\neg a_1 \vee \cdots \vee \neg a_n$ of negative literals. Any unsatisfiable set of clauses must contain at least one such clause.

The simplification rules (4) and (5), and restricted versions of (7.1)-(7.3) (in which only N-rules are used to simplify other equations) are also part of the standard N-strategy. The basic method, without simplification, essentially corresponds to resolution. (However, inference rules (2) and (3) are not used in the N-strategy; hence factoring is not done.) Simplification of equations by N-rules may destroy the clausal structure of a formula; hence has no equivalent in the resolution framework. For example, the clauses $\neg a \vee b \vee c$ and $\neg b \vee \neg c$ are represented by equations $abc + ab + ac + a = 0$ and $bc = 0$, respectively. Simplifying the first equation by the second yields a new equation $ab + bc + a = 0$ that does not correspond to a clause. Completeness of the full N-strategy, with simplification, has not been established yet. Canonical rewrite systems for equational theories can be built into the N-strategy in a natural way (Hsiang 1985).

A different approach to first-order theorem proving, also equational in nature, was proposed by Kapur and Narendran (1985). This method also operates on equations between sums of products. Sums of products are called *first-order polynomials*, a notion that, together with a corresponding algebraic framework of first-order rings and first-order ideals, has been introduced by Kapur and Narendran (1985). First-order polynomials differ from ordinary polynomials in that atoms take the role of indeterminates. The set of indeterminates is therefore infinite and can not be totally ordered, in general. In analogy to ordinary polynomial ideal theory, Kapur and Narendran present a method for constructing a canonical basis, called a *Gröbner basis*, for the ideal defined by a given set of first-order polynomials. Any set of first-order polynomials that represents an unsatisfiable set of formulas, generates the trivial ideal, whose canonical basis consists just of the equation $1 = 0$. Thus, any correct method for constructing a canonical basis will generate a refutation $1 = 0$, when provided with an unsatisfiable set of input formulas. The correctness of the Gröbner basis method for first-order rings has not been proved yet.

Conceptually, the major difference between the polynomial ideal approach and our approach is in the respective notions of rewriting. In the polynomial approach, every equation $A = 0$ is converted into a rewrite rule $A_1 \rightarrow A_2$, where A_1 is the sum of all maximal products of A, and A_2 the sum of the remaining products. In our approach, $A = 0$ represents a set of rewrite rules, namely the set of all orientable instances $P\sigma \rightarrow A'\sigma$. The more refined concept of orientable instances of equations, which is the key to our completeness proof, has no analogy in polynomial ideal theory.

Hsiang (1985b) discusses the polynomial approach and compares it with the N-strategy. He points out several disadvantages of the polynomial method. The use of rewrite rules $A \rightarrow B$, for instance, requires matching with respect to distributivity of * over + for rewriting. Furthermore, mutual simplification of polynomials is obligatory for generating a canonical ideal basis.

Construction of a Gröbner basis also necessitates computation of equations (polynomials) that are irrelevant for refutational theorem proving. For example, let $P = A$ and $Q = B$ be equations in which P and Q are maximal. The equation $QA = PB$, obtained from a peak $QA \leftrightarrow_E PQ \leftrightarrow_E PB$, is obviously redundant in deriving a refutation: the two proof steps do not overlap, therefore any ground instance of the peak can be resolved by rewriting with orientable instances of equations. For construction of a Gröbner basis, however, the polynomial representing $QA = PB$ is needed, whenever A and B contain additional maximal products aside from P and Q. In other words, for any two formulas containing m and n maximal products (m, $n > 1$), respectively, $m \times n$ (redundant) formulas have to be added! This is highly impractical, indicating that the polynomial ideal method may not be optimal for theorem proving, in general.

7. Summary

We have presented a complete inference system for rewrite-based first-order theorem proving. The method is not restricted to clausal input and can be combined with rewrite methods for purely equational theories, such as completion without failure (Bachmair, Dershowitz, and Plaisted 1987; Hsiang and Rusinowitch 1987). We have proved the completeness of our proof system by generalizing proof techniques for purely equational rewriting (Bachmair, Dershowitz, and Hsiang 1986) to first-order theorem proving. These techniques should also be useful for establishing the completeness of other proof methods.

The inference system presented above, in particular inference rule (4), is not practical in its full generality. The inference rules are general enough for constructing sets of equations that satisfy a certain Church-Rosser property on ground terms. For refutational theorem proving, however, it is sufficient to establish a Church-Rosser property on (ground) terms that are equivalent to 1 or 0 (see also Hsiang 1985b), or to phrase it differently, it suffices to compute enough equations so that any (ground) proof of $1 = 0$ can be transformed into a refutation. We conjecture that inference rule (4) is not needed for refutation completeness.

Acknowledgements. We wish to thank Jieh Hsiang for his comments and suggestions.

References

[1] Bachmair, L., Dershowitz, N., and Hsiang, J. (1986). Orderings for equational proofs. *Proc. IEEE Symp. Logic in Computer Science,* Cambridge, Massachussetts, 346-357.

[2] Bachmair, L., Dershowitz, N., and Plaisted, D.A. (1987). Completion without failure. To appear in *Proc. Coll. on Resolution of Equations in Algebraic Structures,* Lakeway, Texas.

[3] Dershowitz, N. (1985). Termination. *Rewriting Techniques and Applications,* J.-P. Jouannaud, ed., Lect. Notes in Comp. Sci., vol. 202, Springer-Verlag, Berlin, 180-224. (Revised version to appear in *J. of Symbolic Computation.*)

[4] Hsiang, J. (1985). Refutational theorem proving using term-rewriting systems. *Artificial Intelligence* 25, 255-300.

[5] Hsiang, J. (1985). Two results in term rewriting theorem proving. *Rewriting Techniques and Applications,* J.-P. Jouannaud, ed., Lect. Notes in Comp. Sci., vol. 202, Springer-Verlag, Berlin, 301-324.

[6] Hsiang, J., and Rusinowitch, M. (1987). On word problems in equational theories. To appear in *Proc. ICALP 87,* Karlsruhe, Germany.

[7] Huet, G. (1981). A complete proof of correctness of the Knuth and Bendix completion algorithm. *J. Comp. and System Sciences* 23, 11-21.

[8] Kapur, D., and Narendran, P. (1985). An equational approach to theorem proving in first-order predicate calculus. Rep. 84CRD322, General Electric Corporate Research and Development, Schenectady, New York.

[9] Knuth, D., and Bendix, P. (1970). Simple word problems in universal algebras. *Computational Problems in Abstract Algebra,* J. Leech, ed., Pergamon Press, 263-297.

[10] Slagle, J. R. (1974). Automated theorem proving for theories with simplifiers, commutativity, and associativity. *J. ACM* 21, 622-642.

[11] Wos, L.T., Robinson, G.A., Carson, D.F., Shalla, L. (1967). The concept of demodulation in theorem proving. *J. ACM* 14, 698-709.

THEOREM PROVING USING RIGID E-UNIFICATION EQUATIONAL MATINGS

Jean H. Gallier, Stan Raatz, and Wayne Snyder
Department of Computer and Information Science
University of Pennsylvania
Philadelphia, Pa 19104

1 Introduction

In this paper, we show that the method of matings due to Andrews [1], can be extended to (first-order) languages with equality, and prove that this extension is both sound and complete. Recall that the method of matings applies to formulae in negation normal form, and that it was introduced with two motivations in mind: to avoid breaking a formula into parts, which can result in loss of information about the global structure, and to avoid transforming it to clausal form, which can result in an exponential increase in the number of literals due to the repeated use of the distributive law $(P \vee (Q \wedge R)) \equiv ((P \vee Q) \wedge (P \vee R))$.

The extension to *equational matings* is nontrivial, and requires proving a generalization of Andrews's version of the Skolem-Herbrand-Gödel theorem. It also requires considering matings which consist of sets of literals consisting of several positive equations and a single negated equation (rather than pairs of literals as in Andrews's case), and a form of unification modulo equational theories, or E-unification, first studied by Plotkin [18]. The method is an *analytic* proof procedure in the sense of Smullyan [19], and, even though Andrews did not present it in terms of Gentzen or Tableaux systems [20,3,19], it can easily be presented in any of these formalisms. For example, Fitting's method of tableaux [2] is close in spirit to the method of matings. We use these generalizations to prove a theorem which suggests a refutation procedure for finding equational matings.

An interesting and apparently hard problem comes up in trying to automate the process of finding equational matings. This problem, which is central to this method, is a restricted version of unification modulo equations. Let $E = \{(s_1 \doteq t_1), \ldots, (s_m \doteq t_m)\}$ be a finite set of equations, and $(u \doteq v)$ any equation.

Problem: It is decidable whether there is some substitution θ such that the set

$$\{\theta(s_1 \doteq t_1), \ldots, \theta(s_m \doteq t_m), \neg\theta(u \doteq v)\}$$

is unsatisfiable? Equivalently, denoting by $\overset{*}{\Longleftrightarrow}_{\theta(E)}$ the least congruence induced by $\theta(E)$, treating the equations in $\theta(E)$ as ground equations, does $\theta(u) \overset{*}{\Longleftrightarrow}_{\theta(E)} \theta(v)$ hold, for some substitution θ?[1]

Note that any substitution θ satisfying the above property is an E-unifier of u and v. However, the equations in E are used in a restricted fashion. Contrary to E-unification, in which there is no bound on the number of instances of the equations in E used to show that $\theta(u) \overset{*}{\Longleftrightarrow}_E \theta(v)$, in our situation, *only* the m instances in $\theta(E)$ can be used. For this reason, we call a substitution satisfying our problem a *rigid E-unifier*.

We conjecture that rigid E-unification is decidable. This conjecture is supported by the fact that we have been able to show that the problem is NP-complete in some nontrivial subcases:

(1) The equations in E are either ground or regular (an equation $s \doteq t$ is regular iff $Var(s) = Var(t)$), and one of u, v is ground.

(2) Any two equations in E have disjoint sets of variables, $Var(u \doteq v) \cap Var(E) = \emptyset$, and there is a

This research was partially supported by the National Science Foundation under Grant No. DCR-86-07156.

[1] Given θ, since the equations in $\theta(E)$ are considered ground, $\theta(u) \overset{*}{\Longleftrightarrow}_{\theta(E)} \theta(v)$ can be decided (in polynomial time) by the congruence closure method, [11,12,17,3].

sequence of rewrite steps $\theta(u) \overset{*}{\longleftrightarrow}_{\theta(E)} \theta(v)$, such that, every nonground equation $\theta(s \doteq t)$ is used at most once. We will call such substitutions *strong* E-unifiers.

Case (2) is a significant extension of a result of Kozen, who has shown that the problem is NP-complete when all equations in E are ground, [13]. We also show that even when u, v are ground, and, all equations in E, except one regular equation, are ground, the problem is NP-complete.

Rigid E-unification is exciting because it suggests strategies for eliminating one of the two aspects of undecidability associated with the method, namely, that of E-unification. This is particularly important here, since even if E-unification is decidable for the set of all equations occurring in a formula in nnf, it is necessary to consider subsets of this set of equations, and the E-unification problem for any subset can be undecidable. At present, we have been able to show that the method of equational matings is complete using strong E-unification, which is decidable, for arbitrary first-order equational formulae in nnf, and, that the method is complete using rigid E-unification for the subclasses mentioned above, which, for these classes, is also decidable. The method is also complete for arbitrary first-order equational formulae in nnf using standard E-unification, but this is not as interesting, because standard E-unification is undecidable.

2 Equational Matings

In order to generalize matings to equational languages, it is necessary to consider sets of literals rather than pairs, as in Andrews's case, [1]. As in Andrews, without loss of generality, we consider formulae in *negation normal form* (for short, in *nnf*, see [1], or [3]).

Let A be a quantifier-free formula, and let the set of variables occurring in A be $\{x_1, \ldots, x_n\}$. The *universal closure of* A is denoted as $\forall A$. The crucial observation due to Andrews, is that a quantifier-free formula in nnf is satisfiable iff some conjunction of literals occurring in A is satisfiable.

Definition 2.1 Given a quantifier-free formula A in nnf, the set $vp(A)$ of *vertical paths* in A is the set of sets of literals defined inductively as follows:

If A is a literal, then $vp(A) = \{\{A\}\}$;

If $A = (B \wedge C)$, then $vp(A) = \{\pi_1 \cup \pi_2 \mid \pi_1 \in vp(B), \pi_2 \in vp(C)\}$;

If $A = (B \vee C)$, then $vp(A) = vp(B) \cup vp(C)$.

The following simple lemma shows the crucial role played by vertical paths.

Lemma 2.2 Given a quantifier-free formula A in nnf, A is unsatisfiable iff every vertical path in A is unsatisfiable.

Note that every vertical path π can be interpreted as a conjunction of literals. Furthermore, a criterion for the unsatisfiability of a conjunction of literals based on the concept of congruence closure is known. In order to explain this criterion, it is convenient to view our language as a two-sorted language, containing the constant $\top$, interpreted as **true**. Then, every atomic formula $Pt_1 \ldots t_n$ can be expressed as the equation $(Pt_1 \ldots t_n \doteq \top)$. Hence, we can assume that all atomic formulae are equations, those of sort *bool* being the nonequational atoms.

Given a vertical path π, let us arrange the literals in π by grouping positive and negative literals together, to form a conjunction C_π of the form

$$(s_1 \doteq t_1) \wedge \ldots \wedge (s_m \doteq t_m) \wedge \neg(s'_1 \doteq t'_1) \wedge \ldots \wedge \neg(s'_n \doteq t'_n).$$

Let $\overset{*}{\cong}_E$ be the congruence closure ([11,12,17]) on the graph $G(C_\pi)$ of the relation

$$E = \{(s_1, t_1), \ldots, (s_m, t_m)\}.$$

The following result is well known (see [11,17], or [3]).

Lemma 2.3 π is unsatisfiable iff for some j, $1 \leq j \leq n$, $s'_j \overset{*}{\cong}_E t'_j$.

We are now in a position to define equational matings.

Definition 2.4 Let A be a quantifier-free formula in nnf. An *equational mating* $\mathcal{M}$ *for* A is a pair $\langle MS, \sigma \rangle$, where MS is a set of sets of literals called *mated sets* and σ is a substitution, such that, each mated set is a subset of some vertical path $\pi \in vp(A)$ and is of the form

$$\{(s_1 \doteq t_1), \ldots, (s_m \doteq t_m), \neg(s \doteq t)\} \subseteq \pi,$$

where $m \geq 0$,[2] and, for every mated set

$$\{(s_1 \doteq t_1), \ldots, (s_m \doteq t_m), \neg(s \doteq t)\} \in MS,$$

[2] The case $m = 0$ is indeed possible when $\sigma(s) = \sigma(t)$, i.e., when σ is a unifier of s and t.

the set of literals $\{\sigma(s_1 \doteq t_1), \ldots, \sigma(s_m \doteq t_m), \neg\sigma(s \doteq t)\}$ is unsatisfiable. The substitution associated with the mating $\mathcal{M}$ is also denoted as $\sigma_{\mathcal{M}}$. We will also say (with a slight abuse of notation) that a mated set belongs to $\mathcal{M}$.

An equational mating $\mathcal{M}$ is a *refutation mating* iff $\sigma_{\mathcal{M}}(A)$ is unsatisfiable.

An equational mating $\mathcal{M}$ is *path acceptable*[3] (for short, *p-acceptable*), iff, for every path $\pi \in vp(A)$, there is some mated set $\{(s_1 \doteq t_1), \ldots, (s_m \doteq t_m), \neg(s \doteq t)\} \in \mathcal{M}$, such that

$$\{(s_1 \doteq t_1), \ldots, (s_m \doteq t_m), \neg(s \doteq t)\} \subseteq \pi.$$

A number of remarks are in order:

(1) Given the substitution σ, the mating condition can be tested using the congruence closure method. As mentioned earlier, we conjecture that it is decidable whether a mating substitution exists, however, this is an NP-hard problem.

(2) If A does not contain equations, each mated set contains some atom which unifies with the negated atom.

Lemma 2.5 Given a quantifier-free formula A in nnf, the following properties hold:

(1) Given a substitution θ, if $\theta(A)$ is unsatisfiable, then there is a p-acceptable mating $\mathcal{M}$ for A.

(2) A p-acceptable mating for A is a refutation mating for A.

(3) If $\mathcal{M}$ is a refutation mating for A with associated substitution $\sigma_{\mathcal{M}}$, then $\sigma_{\mathcal{M}}(A)$ is unsatisfiable.

Let us give an example illustrating the use of the previous lemma.

Example 2.6 Consider the following Horn formula A, where x, y, z denote variables:

$$\begin{array}{l}(a \doteq b) \wedge \\ ((f^3x \doteq x) \vee \neg(fx \doteq fb)) \wedge \\ \quad (Qa \vee \neg(f^3a \doteq a)) \wedge \\ ((f^5y \doteq y) \vee \neg Qy) \wedge \\ \quad (Ra \vee \neg(fa \doteq a) \vee \neg Pfa) \wedge \\ \quad \neg Rfz \wedge \\ \quad Pa\end{array}$$

[3] A path acceptable mating is also called a *spanning mating* by Miller, [16].

There are 24 vertical paths in A. Let $\theta = [a/x, a/y, a/z]$. It is easy to see that 21 of the vertical paths in $\theta(A)$ are unsatisfiable. These are the vertical paths containing the sets of literals $\{(f^3a \doteq a), \neg(f^3a \doteq a)\}$, $\{Qa, \neg Qa\}$, and $\{(a \doteq b), \neg(fa \doteq fb)\}$. A p-acceptable mating for A is given by θ and the following set of 6 sets of literals:

$$\begin{array}{c}\{\{(f^3x \doteq x), \neg(f^3a \doteq a)\}, \\ \{Qa, \neg Qy\}, \\ \{(a \doteq b), \neg(fx \doteq fb)\}, \\ \{(f^5y \doteq y), (f^3x \doteq x), Ra, \neg Rfz\}, \\ \{(f^5y \doteq y), (f^3x \doteq x), \neg(fa \doteq a)\}, \\ \{(f^5y \doteq y), (f^3x \doteq x), Pa, \neg Pfa\}\}.\end{array}$$

The above set is a mating because $(fa \doteq a)$ is equationally provable from $(f^3a \doteq a)$ and $(f^5a \doteq a)$. Indeed, $(f^3a \doteq a)$ implies $(f^4a \doteq fa)$, which implies $(f^5a \doteq f^2a)$, which, by transitivity, implies $(f^2a \doteq a)$. In turn, $(f^2a \doteq a)$ implies $(f^3a \doteq fa)$, and by one more application of transitivity, this implies $(fa \doteq a)$. According to lemma 2.5, $\theta(A)$ is unsatisfiable. Since $\models \forall x \forall y \forall z A \supset \theta(A)$, the universal closure $\forall A$ of A is also unsatisfiable.

Unfortunately, in general, a universal sentence $\forall A$ may be unsatisfiable, but there may not be any substitution θ such that $\theta(A)$ is unsatisfiable. However, a version of the Skolem-Herbrand-Gödel theorem for first-order languages with equality ensures that some substitution instance of an *amplification* of A (a formula obtained from A by duplicating some universal subformulae of A) is unsatisfiable. It is the notion of amplification (due to Andrews, [1]), that will allow us to apply the method of matings to arbitrary universal sentences in nnf.

3 A Skolem-Herbrand-Gödel Theorem

First, we need the definition of a compound instance, due to Andrews, [1].

3.1 Compound Instances

From now on, it is assumed that we are dealing with *rectified formulae*.[4]

[4] A formula A is *rectified* iff no variable occurs both free and bound in A, and distinct occurrences of quantifiers bind distinct variables. It is well known that every formula is equivalent to a rectified formula (see Gallier, [3]).

Definition 3.1 Let A be a rectified universal sentence in nnf (i.e, every variable occurring in A is universally quantified). The set of *compound instances* (for short, *c-instances*) of A is defined inductively as follows:

(i) If A is either a ground atomic formula B or the negation $\neg B$ of a ground atomic formula, then A is its only c-instance;

(ii) If A is of the form $(B * C)$, where $* \in \{\vee, \wedge\}$, for any c-instance H of B and c-instance K of C, $(H * K)$ is a c-instance of A;

(iii) If A is of the form $\forall x B$, for any k closed terms $t_1, \ldots, t_k$, if H_i is a c-instance of $B[t_i/x]$ for $i = 1, \ldots, k$, then $H_1 \wedge \ldots \wedge H_k$ is a c-instance of A.

The importance of c-instances lies in the following version of the Skolem-Herbrand-Gödel theorem, which is a generalization of a theorem of Andrews to first-order languages with equality. For stating this theorem, we assume (without loss of generality) that there is a least one constant symbol in the language.

Theorem 3.2 (Skolem-Herbrand-Gödel theorem) Given a universal sentence A in nnf, A is unsatisfiable iff some c-instance C of A is unsatisfiable.

Proof: It is nontrivial. A proof is given in Gallier, [3], theorem 7.6.1, page 364. Showing that if some compound instance C is unsatisfiable implies that A is unsatisfiable is straightforward, because it is easily shown that $\models A \supset C$ (Gallier, [3], theorem 7.6.1). The proof of the converse is much harder. In Gallier, [3], this is derived proof-theoretically as a consequence of a sharpened Gentzen-like Hauptsatz ([3], theorem 7.4.1, page 334, theorem 7.4.2, page 337, and lemma 7.6.2, page 360). A semantic proof in the line of Andrews's proof can also be given. □

The connection between matings and compound instances is established through the notion of amplification, also due to Andrews, [1].

3.2 Amplifications and Compound Instances

Let A, B, C, and D be universal sentences in nnf.

Definition 3.3 We say that a sentence C is obtained from a sentence B by *quantifier duplication* iff C results from B by replacing some subformula of B of the form $\forall x M$ by $(\forall x M \wedge \forall x M)$. If there is a sequence $\langle C_1, \ldots, C_n \rangle$, $n \geq 1$, of formulae, such that, $B = C_1$, $C = C_n$, and C_{i+1} is obtained from C_i by quantifier duplication, for every i, $1 \leq i < n$, we say that C is obtained from B by some *sequence of quantifier duplications*.

If B is obtained from A by some sequence of quantifier duplications, C is a rectified sentence equivalent to B, and D is obtained from C by deleting the quantifiers in C, we say that D is an *amplification* of A. The following result can be shown easily.

Lemma 3.4 Given a universal sentence A in nnf, C is a c-instance of A iff there is some amplification D of A and some (ground) substitution θ such that $C = \theta(D)$.

We can now state one of the four main theorems of this paper.

Theorem 3.5 Given a universal sentence A in nnf, A is unsatisfiable iff some amplification of A has a p-acceptable mating.

Proof: First, assume that some amplification D of A has a p-acceptable mating $\mathcal{M}$. Let B be obtained by some sequence of quantifier duplications from A, C the rectified formula equivalent to B, and D the result of deleting quantifiers from C. Let $\forall x_1, \ldots, \forall x_n$ be the quantifiers of C, in the left-to-right order in which they occur in C. It is easy to show that $\models A \equiv B$, $\models B \equiv C$, $\models C \equiv \forall x_1 \ldots \forall x_n D$, and $\models \forall x_1 \ldots \forall x_n D \supset \sigma_{\mathcal{M}}(D)$. Since $\mathcal{M}$ is a p-acceptable mating, by lemma 2.5, it is a refutation mating, and so $\sigma_{\mathcal{M}}(D)$ is unsatisfiable. Hence, A is also unsatisfiable.

Now, suppose that A is unsatisfiable. By the Skolem-Herbrand-Gödel theorem (theorem 3.2), there is some c-instance C of A which is unsatisfiable. By lemma 3.4, there is some amplification D of A and a substitution θ such that $C = \theta(D)$. By lemma 2.5, since $\theta(D)$ is unsatisfiable and D is quantifier free, there is some p-acceptable mating $\mathcal{M}$ for D. □

For the reader's convenience, an example illustrating theorem 3.5 is given in the appendix.

3.3 Outermost Quantifier Duplication

Since the complexity of the search for an acceptable mating grows exponentially as the number of occurrences of literals in the amplification D increases, it is important to keep this number small. A systematic scheme for duplicating quantifiers that both minimizes to some extent the number of occurrences of literals, and guarantees completeness, is to duplicate *outermost* quantifiers. It is easy to see that Andrews's proof of the following lemma still holds for equational languages.

Lemma 3.6 Let A be a universal sentence in nnf. Then, A is unsatisfiable iff there is a refutation mating for some amplification D of A, such that, in forming D from A, only outermost quantifier duplications are performed.

4 Rigid E-unifiers

We have already noted in remark (1) after definition 2.4 that one of the conditions in the definition of a mating, namely, that for a mated set

$$\{(s_1 \doteq t_1), \ldots, (s_m \doteq t_m), \neg(s \doteq t)\} \in \mathcal{M},$$

the set $\{\sigma(s_1 \doteq t_1), \ldots, \sigma(s_m \doteq t_m), \neg\sigma(s \doteq t)\}$ is unsatisfiable, implies that σ is an E-unifier of s and t modulo the set of equations $\{(s_1 \doteq t_1), \ldots, (s_m \doteq t_m)\}$. Actually, a much stronger condition holds.

Definition 4.1 Let $E = \{(s_1 \doteq t_1), \ldots, (s_m \doteq t_m)\}$ be a finite set of equations, and let $Var(E) = \bigcup_{(s \doteq t) \in E} Var(s \doteq t)$ denote the set of variables occurring in E.[5] Given any two terms u and v,[6] a substitution θ is a *rigid E-unifier of u and v modulo E* iff

(1) (idempotence) $I(\theta) \cap D(\theta) = \emptyset$, and $D(\theta) \subseteq Var(E) \cup Var(u) \cup Var(v)$;

(2) The set $\{\theta(s_1 \doteq t_1), \ldots, \theta(s_m \doteq t_m), \neg\theta(u \doteq v)\}$ is unsatisfiable. Equivalently, the equation $\theta(u \doteq v)$ is a consequence of the set $\{\theta(s_1 \doteq t_1), \ldots, \theta(s_m \doteq t_m)\}$ by the congruence closure method.

Note that a rigid E-unifier is an E-unifier, but the converse is not true, as shown by the following example.

Example 4.2 Let $E = \{(f(a) \doteq a)\ (1), (f(a) \doteq x)\ (2)\}$, $u = x$ and $v = g(x)$. The substitution $\sigma = [g(a)/x]$ is a rigid unifier of u and v, because,

$$\begin{aligned} g(g(a)) &\Longrightarrow g(f(a)) && \text{by (2)} \\ &\Longrightarrow g(a). && \text{by (1)} \end{aligned}$$

The substitution $[a/x]$ is an E-unifier of u and v (rename x as y in the equation $(f(a) \doteq x)$), but it is *not* a rigid E-unifier.

The property of being a rigid E-unifier constrains the use of the equations considerably. For E-unification, there is no bound on the number of instances of equations in E used in showing that $\theta(u)$ and $\theta(v)$ are congruent modulo E. On the other hand, for rigid E-unification, only the equations in the set $\{\theta(s_1 \doteq t_1), \ldots, \theta(s_m \doteq t_m)\}$ can be used (as ground equations). This is the reason why we conjecture that rigid E-unification is decidable, whereas E-unification is undecidable in general. Actually, we shall prove that rigid E-unification is NP-complete in a number of nontrivial cases.

A special case of rigid E-unification has been investigated by Kozen, the case in which the equations in E are all *ground*.[7] In this case, Kozen showed that E-unification is NP-complete. This shows that rigid E-unification is NP-hard. We have developed an approach inspired by the Herbrand-Martelli-Montanari approach to E-unification[8] based on transformations on systems of equations. Our results are nontrivial, and require some new and rather intricate technical lemmas.

We will need the notion of a system in order to give algorithms for finding rigid E-unifiers (in certain decidable cases).

Definition 4.3 A *system* S is a set $\{(u_1, v_1), \ldots, (u_m, v_m)\}$ of pairs of terms. A substitution θ is a *rigid E-unifier of S* iff θ is a rigid E-unifier of every pair (u_i, v_i). A pair $(u, v) \in S$ is *solved* iff u is a *variable*, and this variable occurs *nowhere else* in S. A system S is in *solved form* iff every pair $(u_i, v_i) \in S$ is solved.

---

[5] It is possible that equations have variables in common.

[6] It is possible that u and v have variables in common with the equations in E.

[7] Actually, when E is a set of ground equations, E-unification and rigid E-unification coincide.

[8] It is remarkable that in his thesis, Herbrand gave all the steps of a (nondeterministic) unification algorithm based on transformations on systems of equations. These transformations are given at the end of the section on property A, page 148 of Herbrand [5]. Apparently, this algorithm was rediscovered by a number of people, including Huet [6], Martelli and Montanari [14], and Kozen, [13].

A system S in solved form defines the substitution $\sigma_S = [v_1/u_1, \ldots, v_m/u_m]$ which is a both a E-unifier and a rigid E-unifier of S.

We now give the transformations on systems that will be used to give algorithms for finding rigid E-unifiers in some decidable subcases. The relation $\Rightarrow$ on systems is defined as follows:

Definition 4.4 (Transformations Rules) Let E be a set of m equations, R any system (possibly empty), and u, v be two terms. We have the following transformation rules:

$$\{(u,u)\} \cup R \Rightarrow R \tag{1}$$

$$\{(v,x)\} \cup R \Rightarrow \{(x,v)\} \cup R, \tag{2}$$

where x is a variable, and $x \neq v$;

$$\{(f(u_1,\ldots,u_k), f(v_1,\ldots,v_k))\} \cup R \Rightarrow \{(u_1,v_1),\ldots,(u_k,v_k)\} \cup R \tag{3}$$

$$\{(x,v)\} \cup R \Rightarrow \{(x,v)\} \cup R[v/x], \tag{4}$$

where x is a variable, $x \notin Var(v)$, $x \in Var(R)$, and $R[v/x]$ is the system obtained by substituting v for all occurrences of x in R.

Note: The transformations (1) to (4) are essentially those given by Herbrand [5] and Martelli-Montanari [14]. To deal with equations, we also need:

$$\{(u,v)\} \cup R \Rightarrow \{(u,l_1),(r_1,l_2),\ldots,(r_{n-1},l_n),(r_n,v)\} \cup R, \tag{5}$$

where the $(l_i \doteq r_i) \in E \cup E^{-1}$ are $n \leq m$ distinct equations, $1 \leq i \leq n$, and u, v are not variables;

$$\{(x,v)\} \cup R \Rightarrow \{(x, v[\beta \leftarrow t])\} \cup \{(v/\beta, s)\} \cup R, \tag{6}$$

where $|v| \geq 1$, $x \in Var(v)$, β is any address in the set $\{\beta \in dom(v) \mid \exists \gamma \neq e, v(\beta\gamma) = x\}$ of proper prefixes of paths ending in a leaf labeled with the variable x, $(s \doteq t)$ is an equation in $E \cup E^{-1}$, $Var(s,t) \cap (Var(v) \cup Var(R)) = \emptyset$, and $v[\beta \leftarrow t]$ denotes the term obtained by replacing the subterm at address β in v with t.

When rule (5) is applied, it is never applied again to any pair in the set $\{(u,l_1),(r_1,l_2),\ldots,(r_{n-1},l_n),(r_n,v)\}$. Case (6) is the difficult case. It corresponds to the situation where the *occur check* fails. The purpose of rule (6) is to eliminate occurrences of the variable causing the occur check situation. A variant of rule (6) is also used in Martelli, Moiso, and Rossi [15], but in the more restrictive context of confluent and Noetherian rewrite rules.

Let $\Rightarrow^*$ be the reflexive and transitive closure of the relation $\Rightarrow$ on systems. It is not difficult to prove the soundness of the transformations.

Lemma 4.5 Given a set E of equations and a system S, if $S \Rightarrow^* S'$ and S' is in solved form, then, the substitution $\sigma_{S'}$ associated with S' is a rigid E-unifier of S.

Although we are not able to prove the completeness of the transformations in the general case, we have obtained the following decidability results.

Theorem 4.6 Assume that the equations in E are either ground or regular (an equation $s \doteq t$ is regular iff $Var(s) = Var(t)$), and that we consider systems such that for every pair $(u,v) \in S$, one of u, v is ground. Then, rigid E-unification is NP-complete. Furthermore, if S has a rigid E-unifier, there is a system S' in solved form such that, $S \Rightarrow^* S'$, for every pair $(u,v) \in S'$, u is ground, and the substitution $\sigma_{S'}$ is a rigid E-unifier of S.

Using an idea of Kozen [11], we can show that rigid E-unification is NP-hard even when E is a set of ground and regular equations, and both u, v are ground.

Theorem 4.7 Rigid E-unification is NP-hard when E is a set of ground and regular equations and both u, v are ground.

Proof: The satisfiability problem is reduced to rigid E-unification as follows. Let the set of function symbols consist of $\wedge$, $\vee$, $\neg$, and the constants $\top$ and $\bot$. Write down the set E_{bool} of 10 ground equations corresponding to the truth tables for $\wedge$, $\vee$, $\neg$. Given any clause A, if $Var(A) = \{x_1, \ldots, x_n\}$, let

$$B_A = (x_1 \wedge x_2 \wedge \ldots \wedge x_n \wedge \bot).$$

Finally, let $E_A = E_{bool} \cup \{A \doteq B_A\}$, $u = \top$ and $v = \bot$. It is easy to see that a substitution σ such that $\top$ and $\bot$ are congruent modulo $\sigma(E_A)$ exists iff A is satisfiable, since B_A is false for every truth assignment. Hence, satisfiability is reduced to rigid E-unification. □

In order to state our second decidability result, we make the following definition.

Definition 4.8 Given a pair (u, v) of terms and a set E of equations, assume that any two equations in E have disjoint sets of variables, and that $Var(u \doteq v) \cap Var(E) = \emptyset$. A substitution θ is a *strong* E-unifier of u and v iff there is a sequence of rewrite steps $\theta(u) \overset{*}{\Longleftrightarrow}_{\theta(E)} \theta(v)$, such that, every nonground equation $\theta(s \doteq t)$ is used at most once. The definition is extended to systems in the obvious way.

Strong E-unifiers are interesting because the method of matings is complete using strong E-unifiers. Unfortunately, using strong E-unifiers, the method also requires many more duplications of quantifiers.

Lemma 4.9 If the amplification D of a universal sentence A in nnf has a mating found using rigid E-unification, then there is some (further) amplification D' of A which has a mating found using strong E-unification.

Our second decidability result reads as follows.

Theorem 4.10 Strong E-unification is NP-complete. Furthermore, if S has a strong E-unifier, there is a system S' in solved form such that, $S \Rightarrow^* S'$, and the substitution $\sigma_{S'}$ is a strong E-unifier of S.

The following example illustrates the use of the transformations in the case of strong E-unification.

Example 4.11 Let $E = \{(f(g(u)) \doteq h(u))\ (1), (h(v) \doteq f(v))\ (2), (f(w) \doteq w)\ (3)\}$, and $S = \{\langle g(f(x)), x\rangle\}$. The following sequence of transformations leads to a system in solved form.

$$
\begin{aligned}
\{\langle g(f(x)), x\rangle\} &\Rightarrow_2 \{\langle x, g(f(x))\rangle\}\\
&\Rightarrow_6 \{\langle x, g(h(u))\rangle, \langle f(x), f(g(u))\rangle\}\\
&\Rightarrow_3 \{\langle x, g(h(u))\rangle, \langle x, g(u)\rangle\}\\
&\Rightarrow_4 \{\langle x, g(h(u))\rangle, \langle g(h(u)), g(u)\rangle\}\\
&\Rightarrow_3 \{\langle x, g(h(u))\rangle, \langle h(u), u\rangle\}\\
&\Rightarrow_5 \{\langle x, g(h(u))\rangle, \langle h(u), h(v)\rangle, \langle f(v), f(w)\rangle, \langle w, u\rangle\}\\
&\Rightarrow_3 \{\langle x, g(h(u))\rangle, \langle u, v\rangle, \langle f(v), f(w)\rangle, \langle w, u\rangle\}\\
&\Rightarrow_2 \{\langle x, g(h(u))\rangle, \langle v, u\rangle, \langle f(v), f(w)\rangle, \langle w, u\rangle\}\\
&\Rightarrow_3 \{\langle x, g(h(u))\rangle, \langle v, u\rangle, \langle v, w\rangle, \langle w, u\rangle\}\\
&\Rightarrow_4 \{\langle x, g(h(u))\rangle, \langle v, u\rangle, \langle u, w\rangle, \langle w, u\rangle\}\\
&\Rightarrow_2 \{\langle x, g(h(u))\rangle, \langle v, u\rangle, \langle w, u\rangle\}.
\end{aligned}
$$

Hence, $[g(h(u))/x, u/v, u/w]$ is a strong E-unifier of S.

The rest of the full paper is devoted to the methods used to prove theorems 4.6 and 4.10, whose proofs are quite complex and sometimes tedious, and to the sketch of a refutation procedure for identifying equational matings. The basic idea of such a procedure is straightforward, as suggested by theorem 3.5: compute incrementally amplifications of a formula in nnf, and at each stage, test whether such an amplification has a p-acceptable mating. The efficiency related issues here are the same as in Andrews's non-equational case, except that they are harder: in addition to efficient data structures which save information between stages, we must identify mated sets instead of mated pairs, and use a form of E-unification instead of standard unification, either rigid or strong E-unification.

There has been quite a lot of recent work on E-unification procedures, including the work by Kirchner and Kirchner [8,9,10], Gallier and Snyder [4], and Martelli, Moiso, and Rossi [15], that might be applicable in designing rigid and strong E-unification procedures. While implementation issues are of importance for a practical procedure, we don't feel they are as new as the ideas of equational matings and rigid E-unification, and save their presentation for the full paper.

5 Appendix

The following example illustrates theorem 3.5.

Example 5.1 Let A be the following (equational) sentence:

$$
\begin{aligned}
&\forall x \forall y \forall z(*(x, *(y, z)) \doteq *(*(x, y), z)) \land && (1)\\
&\forall u(*(u, 1) \doteq u) \land && (2)\\
&\forall v(*(1, v) \doteq v) \land && (3)\\
&\forall w(*(w, w) \doteq 1) \land && (4)\\
&\neg(*(a, b) \doteq *(b, a)). && (5)
\end{aligned}
$$

The first three equations are the axioms for monoids (a binary operation $*$ which is associative and has an identity element 1), the fourth equation asserts that the square of every element is the identity, and the fifth asserts the commutativity of $*$ (A is the result of a Skolemization). The unsatisfiability of A asserts that any monoid such that the square of every element is the identity is commutative.

Consider the following amplification D of A and the

set MS consisting of one set of literals.

$$\begin{aligned}D =&(*(u_1,1) \doteq u_1)\\ &\wedge\ (*(w_1,w_1) \doteq 1)\\ &\wedge\ (*(x_1,*(y_1,z_1)) \doteq *(*(x_1,y_1),z_1)))\\ &\wedge\ (*(x_2,*(y_2,z_2)) \doteq *(*(x_2,y_2),z_2)))\\ &\wedge\ (*(w_2,w_2) \doteq 1)\\ &\wedge\ (*(1,v_1) \doteq v_1)\\ &\wedge\ (*(x_3,*(y_3,z_3)) \doteq *(*(x_3,y_3),z_3)))\\ &\wedge\ (*(x_4,*(y_4,z_4)) \doteq *(*(x_4,y_4),z_4)))\\ &\wedge\ (*(w_3,w_3) \doteq 1)\\ &\wedge\ \neg(*(a,b) \doteq *(b,a)).\end{aligned}$$

$$\begin{aligned}MS = \{\{&(*(u_1,1) \doteq u_1),\\ &(*(w_1,w_1) \doteq 1),\\ &(*(x_1,*(y_1,z_1)) \doteq *(*(x_1,y_1),z_1))),\\ &(*(x_2,*(y_2,z_2)) \doteq *(*(x_2,y_2),z_2))),\\ &(*(w_2,w_2) \doteq 1),\\ &(*(1,v_1) \doteq v_1),\\ &(*(x_3,*(y_3,z_3)) \doteq *(*(x_3,y_3),z_3))),\\ &(*(x_4,*(y_4,z_4)) \doteq *(*(x_4,y_4),z_4))),\\ &(*(w_3,w_3) \doteq 1),\\ &\neg(*(a,b) \doteq *(b,a))\}\}.\end{aligned}$$

Let θ be the substitution

$$\begin{aligned}&[a/u_1,(a*b)/w_1,a/x_1,(a*b)/y_1,(a*b)/z_1,\\ &a/x_2,a/y_2,b/z_2,a/w_2,b/v_1,\\ &b/x_3,(a*b)/y_3,b/z_3,a/x_4,b/y_4,b/z_4,b/w_3].\end{aligned}$$

We claim that $\langle MS,\theta\rangle$ is a mating for D. For simplicity of notation let adopt infix notation, and denote $*(s,t)$ as $s*t$. Then, we have:

$$\begin{aligned}a*b=&\\ &=\{a*1\}*b && \text{by (2)}\\ &=\{a*[(a*b)*(a*b)]\}*b && \text{by (4)}\\ &=\{[a*(a*b)]*(a*b)\}*b && \text{by (1)}\\ &=\{[(a*a)*b]*(a*b)\}*b && \text{by (1)}\\ &=\{[1*b]*(a*b)\}*b && \text{by (4)}\\ &=\{b*(a*b)\}*b && \text{by (3)}\\ &=b*\{(a*b)*b\} && \text{by (1)}\\ &=b*\{a*(b*b)\} && \text{by (1)}\\ &=b*\{a*1\} && \text{by (4)}\\ &=(b*a), && \text{by (2)}\end{aligned}$$

which shows that $\langle MS,\theta\rangle$ is a p-acceptable mating for D (there is a single vertical path in D). Note that equation (2) instantiated by the substitution $[a/u_1]$ is used twice.

6 References

[1] Andrews, P. Theorem Proving via General Matings. *J.ACM* 28(2), 193-214, 1981.

[2] Fitting, M. A Tableaux Based Automated Theorem Prover for Classical Logic. Technical Report, CUNY, June 1986.

[3] Gallier, J. H. *Logic for Computer Science: Foundations of Automatic Theorem Proving*. New York: Harper and Row, 1986.

[4] Gallier, J. H. and Snyder, W. A General Complete E-Unification Procedure, to be presented at *RTA'87*, Bordeaux, France, May 1987.

[5] Herbrand, J. *Logical Writings*. Hingham, MA: Reidel Publishing Company, 1971.

[6] Huet, G. Résolution d'Equations dans les Langages d'Ordre $1,2,\ldots,\omega$. Thèse d'Etat, Université de Paris VII, 1976.

[7] Huet, G. and Oppen, D. C. Equations and Rewrite Rules: A Survey. In: R. V. Book (ed.), *Formal Languages: Perspectives and Open Problems*, Academic Press, NY, 1982.

[8] Kirchner, C. Méthodes et Outils de Conception Systematique d'Algorithmes d'Unification dans les Theories Equationnelles, Thèse d'Etat. Université de Nancy I, 1985.

[9] Kirchner, C. Computing Unification Algorithms. *1st IEEE Symposium on Logic in Computer Science*, Cambridge, Massachusetts, 206-216, June 1986.

[10] Kirchner, H. Preuves Par Completion dans les Varietés d'Algèbres. Thèse d'Etat, Université de Nancy I, 1985.

[11] Kozen, D. Complexity of Finitely Presented Algebras, Technical Report TR 76-294, Department of Computer Science, Cornell University, Ithaca, NY, 1976.

[12] Kozen, D. Complexity of Finitely Presented Algebras, *9th STOC Symposium*, Boulder Colorado, 164-177, May 1977.

[13] Kozen, D. Positive First-Order Logic is NP-Complete. *IBM Journal of Research and Development*, 25(4), 327-332, 1981.

[14] Martelli, A. and Montanari, U. An Efficient Unification Algorithm. *TOPLAS* 4(2), 258-282, 1982.

[15] Martelli, A., Moiso, C., and Rossi, G.F. An Algorithm for Unification in Equational Theories. *3rd IEEE Symposium on Logic Programming*, Salt Lake City, Utah, 180-186, Sept. 1986.

[16] Miller, D. A. Expansion Trees and Their Conversion to Natural Deduction Proofs. In *7th International Conference on Automated Deduction, Napa, CA*, edited by R.E. Shostak, L.N.C.S, No. 170, New York: Springer Verlag, 1984.

[17] Nelson G. and Oppen, D. C. Fast Decision Procedures Based on Congruence Closure. *J. ACM* 27(2), 356-364, 1980.

[18] Plotkin, G., Building in Equational Theories, in: *Machine Intelligence* 7: 73-90, 1972.

[19] Smullyan, R. M. *First-order Logic*. Berlin, Heidelberg, New York: Springer-Verlag, 1968.

[20] Szabo, M. E. *The Collected Papers of Gerhard Gentzen*. Studies in Logic. New York: Elsevier North-Holland, 1970.

SOLVING DISEQUATIONS

Claude Kirchner
Pierre Lescanne

Centre de Recherche en Informatique de Nancy,
CNRS UA 262 and INRIA-Lorraine,
Campus Scientifique, BP 239,
54506 VANDŒUVRE-LES-NANCY, FRANCE
E-mail: mcvax!inria!crin!(ckirchner lescanne)

Abstract

We present a general study of equations (objects of form $s = t$ and disequations (objects of form $s \neq t$) solving. The problem is approached from its fully general mathematical definition clearly separating universally and existentially quantified variables. In addition it is showed to have many connections with unification in equational theories like associativity commutativity, in particular methods similar to those used to solve equational unification problem works in solving disequations. This abstract framework is then applied to study the sufficient completeness of a rewrite rule based definition of a function.

1 The Problem

Solving equations in the algebra of terms is well-known in the computer science community as unification. In this paper, we study the dual problem of solving disequations which is finding solutions to problems of the form $s \neq t$. As we will see this cannot be dissociated from solving equations, thus we study the general question of computing solutions for a combination of equations and disequations. This problem has many connections with the now classical one of unification in theories, like unification in associative and commutative theories. First, the basis of the set of solutions which is a set of substitutions contains usually more than one element. Second, methods proposed for unification, namely decomposition , merging and mutation [12].

A first explicit reference to this problem is due to A. Colmerauer [3,2]. He indeed introduces disequations in Prolog II and proposes algorithms to solve them. But he studies solutions in infinite trees, as our method solves a combination of equations and disequations in the empty theory, i.e., in the finite terms algebra without axioms. Moreover, in some problems we are looking for solutions in the initial algebra only, i.e., the theory of ground terms. As another fundamental difference, we solve disequations containing free variables and Bürckert [1] has shown in the case of unification this is a deeply different problem, same thing happens here. Mention to this problem exists also in [14].

In addition to the theorical interest of solving disequation, a main motivation of this work was to propose tools for proving the sufficient completeness of an algebraic specification [4] or for checking inductive reducibility [11]. The sufficient completeness is the fact that the definition of a function by a set of rewrite rules is complete in the sense that this function is defined on any possible pattern. This is useful for checking the correctness of a specification. We show that our framework for solving a combination of equations and disequations applies precisely to check sufficient completeness and, in the case of an incomplete definition, to give the set of patterns where the function is undefined. The inductive reducibility is the reducibility of all the ground instances of a term. It plays an important role in the so-called inductionless induction method. In the next section, we define the kind of problem we address in this work : equational problems. Section 3 deals with the rules we are using in order to decompose an equational problem into a simpler one. In Section 4, the main result is stated : the rules of Section 3 are terminating and the normal forms of an equational problem is a equational problems in solved form. In Section 5, we show how to get ride of disequalities when they are solved in the initial algebra. Section 6 shows how the problems of sufficient completeness and inductive reducibility can be reduced to our notion of equational problems. Examples of applications are given in Section 7 and we conclude in Section 8.

2 Equational Problems

In the remainder of this work, we assume the reader familiar with equational logic and equational unification. References can be found respectively in [10] and [13,12].

A **system** is a conjunction of pairs of terms written $s = t$ and called **equations** or written $s \neq t$ and called **disequations**. Note that a disequation is not an *inequation* (usualy denoted $x < y$ in arithmetic or in algebraic semantics [6]) and that we intentionaly choose a different name, following a terminology proposed by J.A.Goguen and J.Meseguer [7]. An **equational problem** P in the unknowns $y_1, \ldots, y_n$ is a **disjunction of systems**. We denote by $Evar(P)$, the set

*This research was partly supported by the GRECO of programmation (CNRS).

of Existentially quantified variables $\{y_1, y_2, \ldots, y_n\}$. Outside the unknowns, an equational problem P contains a set $Uvar(P)$ of Universally quantified variables. Actually the problem should be written,

$$\exists y_1, y_2, ..., y_n \in M(F,X), \forall x_1, x_2, ..., x_m \in M(F,X): \\ P(y_1, y_2, ..., y_n, x_1, x_2, ..., x_m)$$

In order to make clearer the difference between the two kinds of variables we use x's for universally quantified variables and y's for existentially quantified variables or unknowns.

A classical unification problem is of the form

$$\exists y_1, \ldots, y_n,\ t(y_1, y_2, \ldots, y_n) = t'(y_1, y_2, \ldots, y_n),$$

and recently Bückert [1] has studied the notion of *restricted unification*, that is a problem of the form,

$$\exists y_1, \ldots, y_n, \forall x_1, \ldots, x_m \\ t(y_1, \ldots, y_n, x_1, \ldots, x_m) = t'(y_1, \ldots, y_n, x_1, \ldots, x_m),$$

He shows that the universally quantified variables cannot be equivalently replaced by new constants. In particular, if one knows a unification algorithm for a theory T, this does not imply necessarily the existence of a matching algorithm for T.

Actually, only the existentially quantified variables can be instantiated and one says that a substitution σ, s.t. $D(\sigma) \subseteq \{x_1, x_2, \ldots, x_n\}$, is a **solution** of a problem $P = S_1 \vee \ldots \vee S_n$, if there exists a system S_i such that, for all equations $s = t$ in S_i, $\sigma(s) = \sigma(t)$ and, for all disequations $s \neq t$ in S_i, $\sigma(s) \neq \sigma(t)$.

3 Rules

We are now going to describe a set of rules for solving a mixture of equations and disequations. By solving we mean to reduce an equational problem to a simpler form, from which the set of solutions can be easily deduced. So the purpose of these rules is to simplify an equational problem in such a way that the set of solutions is preserved. For a precise inside into the problem of equivalence of equational problems see [12].

For readibility, the set of rules is divided into different classes, one of them deals with **decomposition** and **clash**. There are two types of decomposition and clash according to the kind of pairs which is decomposed. The decomposition of an equation or =-decomposition is the same as the decomposition used in unification, it transforms an equation into a conjunction of equations. The decomposition of a disequation or $\neq$-decomposition transforms a disequation into a disjunction of conjunctions of disequations. An operation called **sliding** transforms a pair of an equation of the form $y = s$ and a disequation of the form $y \neq t$ into the equation $y = s$ and the disequation $s \neq t$. The rules are presented as a set of premisses and a conclusion. Both part are separated by an arrow $\mapsto$. An inference rule presentation is also possible.

Warning: The x's are quantified variables, the y's are the unknowns of the problem and, the ξ's are indifferently universally and existentially quantified variables. To emphasize this convention, universal quantifiers are explicitely written.

3.1 Basic rules

The disequation $\xi \neq \xi$ is trivially never satisfied:

$$\{\xi \neq \xi\} \mapsto false \tag{1}$$

Similarly the equation $\xi = \xi$ is always satisfied:

$$\{\xi = \xi\} \mapsto true \tag{2}$$

3.2 Anteposition

In what follows we transform each equation of the form $s = \xi$ into an equation of the form $\xi = s$. The same thing is done for disequations. Colmerauer has called this rule anteposition.

$$s = \xi \mapsto \xi = s \text{ if } s \text{ is not a variable} \tag{3}$$

The same rule for disequation is also interesting,

$$s \neq \xi \mapsto \xi \neq s \text{ if } s \text{ is not a variable} \tag{4}$$

3.3 Quantifiers rules

The following rules are classical and useful:

$$\forall x(P \vee Q) \mapsto (\forall x P) \vee Q \text{ if } x \notin Var(Q) \tag{5}$$
$$\forall x(Q \wedge R) \mapsto (\forall x Q \wedge \forall x R) \tag{6}$$

3.4 Occur checks

We define first an ordering on the equations of a system S [9,16] by $(\xi = t) \prec_S (\xi' = t')$ if and only if t and t' are non variable terms such that $\xi \in Var(t')$, $(\xi = t) \in S$ and $(\xi' = t') \in S$.

If there is a cycle in the system S for the transitive closure $\prec_S^+$, then S is never satisfied:

$$S \mapsto false \text{ if } S \ni (\xi = s) \text{ s.t. } (\xi = s) \prec_S^+ (\xi = s) \tag{7}$$

Something similar can happen with equations and disequations. If $\xi \in Var(s)$ and $\xi \neq s$ or there is a path in the system for the transitive and reflexive closure $\prec_S^+$ that can be prolonged into a cycle by the disequation working like an equation, then $\xi \neq s$ is always satisfied:

$$S \wedge \xi \neq s \mapsto S \text{ if } C \tag{8}$$

where C is the following condition: $\xi \in Var(s)$ and s is not a variable or there exists $(\xi' = s') \prec_S^+ (\xi'' = s'')$, with $\xi'' \in Var(s)$ *and* $\xi \in Var(s')$.

3.5 Clashes and Decompositions

If the top operators are different in a disequation, then this disequation is always satisfied.
[≠-clash]

$$f(u_1, ..., u_m) \neq g(v_1, ..., v_m) \quad \mapsto \quad true \tag{9}$$

If the the top operators are different in an equation, then this equation is never satisfied.
[=-clash]

$$f(u_1, ..., u_m) = g(v_1, ..., v_m) \quad \mapsto \quad false \tag{10}$$

If the top operators are similar in a disequation, this disequation can be transformed into a disjunction of disequations.
[≠-decomposition]

$$f(u_1, ..., u_m) \neq f(v_1, ..., v_m) \quad \mapsto \quad \bigvee_{1 \le i \le m} u_i \neq v_i \tag{11}$$

If the top operators are similar in an equation, this equation can be transformed in a conjunction of equations.
[=-decomposition]

$$f(u_1, ..., u_m) = f(v_1, ..., v_m) \quad \mapsto \quad \bigwedge_{1 \le i \le m} (u_i = v_i) \tag{12}$$

By using the basic rule and these rules, one gets $s = s \overset{*}{\mapsto} true$ and $s \neq s \overset{*}{\mapsto} false$.

3.6 Sliding

If $\xi = s$ and $\xi \neq t$, obviously $s \neq t$, similary if $\xi = s$ and $\xi = t$, then $s = t$. So doing we may continue to solve the problem by a clash or a decomposition. This corresponds to the merging in [12].

$$\xi = s \wedge \xi \neq t \quad \mapsto \quad \xi = s \wedge s \neq t \text{ if } s, t \text{ are not } \xi \tag{13}$$

For instance, using this rule and $s \neq s \overset{*}{\mapsto} false$ one gets $\xi = s \wedge \xi \neq s \overset{*}{\mapsto} false$.

$$\xi = s \wedge \xi = t \quad \mapsto \quad \xi = s \wedge s = t \text{ if } s, t \text{ are not } \xi \tag{14}$$

For instance, using this rule and $s = s \overset{*}{\mapsto} true$ one gets $\xi = s \wedge \xi = s \overset{*}{\mapsto} \xi = s$.

3.7 Boolean rules

The following rules are classical when dealing with boolean expressions. We give only some of them. In addition, it is assumed that the operators $\vee$ and $\wedge$ are associative and commutative.

$p \wedge false \mapsto p$	
$p \wedge p \mapsto p$	*Idempotence*
$q \vee (s \wedge q) \mapsto q$	*Absorption*
$p \vee (s \wedge q) \mapsto (p \wedge s) \vee (p \wedge q)$	*Distributivity*
$\ldots \mapsto \ldots$	

3.8 Substitution.

Consider the formula $\forall x((P \wedge \{x \neq s\}) \vee Q(x))$ where x does not occur in s. We have the following sequence of equivalences: (note that $\forall x\{x \neq s\}$ is always false if $x \notin Var(s)$)

$$\begin{aligned} & \forall x((P \wedge \{x \neq s\}) \vee Q(x)) \\ \equiv\ & \forall x[(P \vee Q(x)) \wedge (x \neq s \vee Q(x))] \\ \equiv\ & \forall x(P \vee Q(x)) \wedge \forall x(x \neq s \vee Q(x)) \\ \equiv\ & \forall x(P \vee Q(x)) \wedge Q(s) \\ \equiv\ & \forall x[(P \wedge Q(s)) \vee (Q(x) \wedge Q(s))] \end{aligned}$$

Therefore we state the following rule,

$$\begin{gathered} \forall x((P \wedge \{x \neq s\}) \vee Q(x)) \mapsto \\ \forall x[(P \wedge Q(s)) \vee (Q(x) \wedge Q(s))] \text{ if } x \notin Var(s) \end{gathered}$$

The goal of this rule is to get ride of disequations of the form $x \neq s$. It has specific variants when P or Q is empty.

$$\begin{aligned} \forall x(\{x \neq s\} \vee Q(x)) &\quad \mapsto \quad Q(s) \text{ if } x \notin Var(s) \\ \forall x\{x \neq s\} &\quad \mapsto \quad false \text{ if } x \notin Var(s) \end{aligned}$$

Example: we may apply a previous rule to derive $s \neq t$ from $\forall x(x \neq s \vee x \neq t)$, when $x \notin Var(s)$. Indeed in this case, P is empty and Q is $x \neq t$.

4 Problems in Normal Form

A problem is said to be in normal form, if all the systems it contains are made of disequations of the form $y \neq s$ and of equations of the form $y = s$. In addition, if there is an equation of the form $y = s$, there is no equation of the form $y = t$ or disequation of the form $y \neq u$. Problems in normal form determine the solutions of the problem by values to attribute to existential variables or sets of values to forbid to these variables. Disequations of the form $y \neq s$ are called *constraints* by H.Comon. The previous rules are powerful enough to allow reducing each problem into a problem in normal form as stated by the following theorem.

Theorem 1 *Given an equational problem P, there exists always an equational problem P' in normal form such that*

$$P \overset{*}{\mapsto} P'.$$

Proof: (sketch) Equations and disequations of the from $s = t$ or $s \neq t$ disappear by decompositions or clashes. Equations of the form $x = s$ disappear by sliding or by a basic rule, if they occur with equations or disequations with the same left-hand side. Disequations of the form $x \neq s$ disappear by substitution. If there are two equations $y = s$ and $y = t$, one of them disappear by sliding, the same if the second is $x \neq t$ instead. Equations or disequations of the form $s = \xi$ or $s \neq \xi$ are transformed by anteposition. These processes produce always an expression which is smaller w.r.t. the following well-founded ordering,

$$P \gg P'$$
$$\Leftrightarrow$$
$$(\phi(P) > \phi(P')) \ or \ (\phi(P) = \phi(P') \ and \ P >_{rpo} P')$$

where $\phi(P)$ is the number of variables ξ in position $\xi = s$ or $\xi \neq s$ plus twice the number of variables in position $s = \xi$ or $s \neq \xi$ and $>_{rpo}$ is the recursive path ordering [5] described by the precedence

$$\{=, \neq\} > \wedge > \vee > \{true, false\}$$

◇

Note that the normalization proposed in the previous proof does not use the occur check and that the following example issued from [3] is in normal form since the substitution rule does not apply:

$$\exists y_1, y_2, (y_1 = f(y_1)) \wedge (y_2 = f(f(y_2))) \wedge (y_1 \neq y_2).$$

The following theorem says that restricted to problems that contain only equations, the rules of the previous section provide a unification algorithm .

Theorem 2 *If P contains only equalities, then P' contains only equalities. If P contains only disequalities, then P' contains only disequalities.*

5 Getting rid of disequalities

The following rule is really important since is allows getting rid of disequalities in some cases and to transform them into equalities. Usually this fully determines the substitutions that are solutions. This rule differs from the others in the sense that it refers to a specific model, namely the initial algebra. This means that when one uses it, solutions are not anymore true in any algebra, but only in the initial algebra $T(C)$ where C is the set of constructors or generators of the initial algebra. This also means that the quantifications, essentially the universal quantifications, are taken over the initial algebra. Another interesting aspect of this rule is that it introduces new existential variables. This fact is not very surprising, since a similar property appears for example in associative commutative unification. The rule means that if y does not match some patterns of the form $f_i(...)$ for $i \in I$, there exists a pattern of the form $f_j(...)$ for $i \in C - I$, that y has to match.

[Disequations to equations]

$$\exists y'_1, \ldots, \exists y'_m, \forall x'_1, \ldots, \forall x'_n$$
$$(R \vee \forall x_{1,1}, \ldots, \forall x_{i,k} \in T(C)(Q \wedge \textstyle\bigwedge_{i \in I} y \neq f_i(\underline{x}_i)))$$
$$\mapsto$$
$$\exists y'_1, \ldots, \exists y'_m, \exists y_{1,1}, \ldots, \exists y_{j,h}, \forall x'_1, \ldots, \forall x'_n$$
$$(R \vee (Q \wedge \textstyle\bigvee_{j \notin C-I} y = f_j(\underline{y}_j)))$$

A more general form of this rule could be given using the complementary, as described in [15].

6 Disequations, Sufficient Completeness, Inductive Reducibility

H.Comon [4] has shown how disequations can be used to solve the problem of sufficient completeness [8] and recently Jouannaud and Kounalis [11] introduced the concept of inductive reducibility.

A term is said to be **inductively reducible** by a term rewriting system R if all its ground instances are reducible. If R terminates the **sufficient completeness** of the definition of an operator f is just the inductive reducibility by normalized ground instances of the term $f(x_1, \ldots, x_n)$. So we introduce the following property equivalent to inductive reducibility: a term t is **inductively internally reducible** by a term rewriting system R if all its ground instances by normalized substitutions are reducible.

Let t be a term and $Sub(t)$ the set of its subterms. If $T^N(C)$ is the set of normalized ground terms, inductive internal reducibility of t can be written:

$$\forall y_{1,1} \in T^N(C) \ldots \forall y_{j,h} \in T^N(C)$$
$$\exists x_{1,1} \in T(C) \ldots \exists x_{i,k} \in T(C) \ldots$$
$$\textstyle\bigvee_{s \in Sub(t)} \bigvee_{(l \rightarrow g \in R)} s(\underline{y}_j) = l(\underline{x}_i)$$

Indeed, the internal reducibility means there exists a non variable subterm (disjunction on the subterms) that matches (existence of a values $x_{i,k} \in T(C)$) the left-hand-side of a rule (disjunction on the rules). The inductive internal reducibility means that this has to be satisfied for each ground instance by normalised substitutions (universal quantification over $y_{j,h} \in T^N(C)$). This is not a unification problem because of the quantifiers: in a unification the existential quantifier $\exists$ is in first position. Its negation is,

$$\exists y_{1,1} \in T^N(C) \ldots \exists y_{j,h} \in T^N(C)$$
$$\forall x_{1,1} \in T(C) \ldots \forall x_{i,k} \in T(C) \ldots$$
$$\textstyle\bigwedge_{s \in Sub(t)} \bigwedge_{(l \rightarrow g \in R)} s(\underline{y}_j) \neq l(\underline{x}_i)$$

This has now a flavor of unification, since the existential quantifier is in first position. It can be decomposed into a two steps process: (1) find the solutions (or better, a representation of the set of solutions) of the problem above where $\exists y_{1,1} \in T^N(C) \ldots \exists y_{j,h} \in T^N(C)$ has been replaced by $\exists y_{1,1} \in T(C) \ldots \exists y_{j,h} \in T(C)$ and then (2) check that the solutions are in normal form. This last check is of course trivial if there is no solution.

This states the inductive internal reducibility partly as an equational problem without providing a specific strategy to get the solution. A brute force strategy is then provided by the application of the inference rules, but it can be very inefficient because of the size of the equational problem to solve. This could be a starting point for the study of efficient algorithm testing the inductive reducibility.

7 Examples

In these examples we are not going to write the existential quantifiers systematically

Example 1

Let us first solve a problem posed by H.Comon [4]. This is a problem in y and z,

$$\forall x_1, \forall x_2\ a(x_1, x_1) \neq a(y, z) \wedge a(f(x_1, x_2), x_1) \neq a(y, z).$$

By decomposing the first disequation we get,

$$\begin{array}{ll} \forall x_1, \forall x_2 & [x_1 \neq y \wedge a(f(x_1, x_2), x_1) \neq a(y, z))] \\ \vee & [x_1 \neq z \wedge a(f(x_1, x_2), x_1) \neq a(y, z))] \end{array}$$

By decomposing the second disequation we get,

$$\begin{array}{ll} \forall x_1, \forall x_2 & [x_1 \neq y \wedge f(x_1, x_2) \neq y] \\ \vee & [x_1 \neq y \wedge x_1 \neq z] \\ \vee & [x_1 \neq z \wedge f(x_1, x_2) \neq y] \\ \vee & [x_1 \neq z \wedge x_1 \neq z] \end{array}$$

which simplifies to

$$\forall x_1, \forall x_2 < [x_1 \neq y \wedge f(x_1, x_2) \neq y] \vee x_1 \neq z.$$

By using the substitution rule, this gives,

$$\begin{array}{l} [z \neq y \wedge \forall x_2 f(z, x_2) \neq y] \\ \quad \vee \forall x_1, \forall x_2 [x_1 \neq y \wedge f(x_1, x_2) \neq y], \end{array}$$

and using the second quantifier rule and the last basic rule,

$$(z \neq y) \wedge (\forall x_2, f(z, x_2) \neq y).$$

Example 2

Let us solve a problem of sufficient completeness. Suppose one wants to prove that the definition

$$\{ \quad eq(0, s(x_1)) = false \qquad eq(s(x_2), 0) = false \\ eq(s(x_3), s(x_4)) = eq(x_3, x_4) \qquad eq(x_5, x_5) = true \quad \}$$

is sufficiently complete. This can be stated as proving,

$$\begin{array}{ll} \multicolumn{2}{l}{\forall y, z \in T(\{s, 0\})\ \exists x_1, x_2, x_3, x_4, x_5 \in T(\{s, 0\})} \\ & eq(0, s(x_1)) = eq(y, z) \\ \vee & eq(s(x_2), 0) = eq(y, z) \\ \vee & eq(s(x_3), s(x_4)) = eq(y, z) \\ \vee & eq(x_5, x_5) = eq(y, z). \end{array}$$

whose negation is,

$$\begin{array}{ll} \multicolumn{2}{l}{\exists y, z \in T(\{s, 0\})\ \forall x_1, x_2, x_3, x_4, x_5 \in T(\{s, 0\})} \\ & eq(0, s(x_1)) \neq eq(y, z) \\ \wedge & eq(s(x_2), 0) \neq eq(y, z) \\ \wedge & eq(s(x_3), s(x_4)) \neq eq(y, z) \\ \wedge & eq(x_5, x_5) \neq eq(y, z). \end{array}$$

This leads to look for a possible assignment of values to y and z in the following problem.

$$\begin{array}{ll} \multicolumn{2}{l}{\forall x_1, x_2, x_3, x_4, x_5 \in T(\{s, 0\})} \\ & eq(0, s(x_1)) \neq eq(y, z) \\ \wedge & eq(s(x_2), 0) \neq eq(y, z) \\ \wedge & eq(s(x_3), s(x_4)) \neq eq(y, z) \\ \wedge & eq(x_5, x_5) \neq eq(y, z). \end{array}$$

The definition of eq is sufficiently complete if there is no such assignment, which means the negation of the sufficient completeness problem is identically *false*. This demonstrates the important difference between *free variables* and *unknows* in an equational problem. In the following we assume quantification are taken over $T(\{s, 0\})$. By decompositions the initial equational problem is equivalent to

$$\begin{array}{c} \forall x_1, x_2, x_3, x_4, x_5, \\ (0 \neq y \vee s(x_1) \neq z) \wedge \\ (s(x_2) \neq y \vee 0 \neq z) \wedge \\ (s(x_3) \neq y \vee s(x_4) \neq z) \wedge \\ (x_5 \neq y \vee x_5 \neq z). \end{array}$$

Using first the quantifier rules one gets

$$\begin{array}{l} (0 \neq y \vee \forall x_1 s(x_1) \neq z) \wedge \\ (\forall x_2 s(x_2) \neq y \vee 0 \neq z) \wedge \\ (\forall x_3 s(x_3) \neq y \vee \forall x_4 s(x_4) \neq z) \wedge \\ (\forall x_5 x_5 \neq y \vee x_5 \neq z). \end{array}$$

By the rule called *disequations to equations*, $\forall x_1 s(x_1) \neq z$ and $\forall\ x_4\ s(x_4) \neq z$ are $0 = z$, $\forall x_2 s(x_2) \neq y$ and $\forall\ x_3\ s(x_3) \neq y$ are $0 = y$, and $\forall x_5 (x_5 \neq y \vee x_5 \neq z)$ is $y \neq z$. So we get,

$$\begin{array}{l} (0 \neq y \vee 0 = z) \wedge (0 = y \vee 0 \neq z) \wedge \\ (0 = y \vee 0 = z) \wedge y \neq z \end{array}$$

which normalizes to the empty disjunction.

Example 3

Let us show now that the resolution of an equational problem can also be used to look for the patterns in which a given function is not defined. If there is no such patterns, the function is completely defined or sufficiently complete. Let us go back to the function eq and suppose we look at the (actually incomplete) definition,

$$\{eq(0, s(x_1)) = false, eq(s(x_2), 0) = false, eq(x_5, x_5) = true\}.$$

Like previously, this can be stated as solving,

$$\begin{array}{l} \exists y, z \forall x_1, x_2, x_5 (eq(0, s(x_1)) \neq eq(y, z) \wedge \\ eq(s(x_2), 0) \neq eq(y, z) \wedge eq(x_5, x_5) \neq eq(y, z)). \end{array}$$

Let us drop the $\exists$ and apply decompositions first,

$$\begin{array}{l} \forall x_1, x_2, x_5 (0 \neq y \vee s(x_1) \neq z) \wedge \\ (s(x_2) \neq y \vee 0 \neq z) \wedge (x_5 \neq y \vee x_5 \neq z). \end{array}$$

By applying the rule on quantifiers one gets,

$$(0 \neq y \vee \forall x_1 s(x_1) \neq z) \wedge$$
$$(0 \neq z \vee \forall x_2 s(x_2) \neq y) \wedge$$
$$(\forall x_5 (x_5 \neq y \vee x_5 \neq z)),$$

by the *disequation to equation* rule,

$$(0 \neq y \vee 0 = z) \wedge (0 = y \vee 0 \neq z) \wedge$$
$$\forall x_5 (x_5 \neq y \vee x_5 \neq z).$$

Using the result of the example given after the substitution rule,

$$(0 \neq y \vee 0 = z) \wedge (0 = y \vee 0 \neq z) \wedge (y \neq z)$$
$$\overset{*}{\mapsto} (0 \neq y \wedge 0 \neq z \wedge y \neq z) \vee (0 = y \wedge 0 = z \wedge y \neq z)$$

Systems of the form $(0 = y \wedge 0 \neq y \wedge y \neq z)$ disappear by sliding. And by sliding on the last expression, one gets,

$$(0 \neq y \wedge 0 \neq z \wedge y \neq z) \vee (0 = y \wedge 0 = z \wedge 0 \neq z)$$
$$\mapsto (0 \neq y \wedge 0 \neq z \wedge y \neq z)$$

By *disequation to equation* (with the convention on existential quantifiers),

$$y = s(x_1) \wedge y = (s_2) \wedge s(y_1) \neq s(y_2)$$
$$\overset{*}{\mapsto} y = s(x_1) \wedge y = (s_2) \wedge y_1 \neq y_2$$

This means the operator *eq* is not sufficiently complete and has to be completed on patterns of the form $y = s(y_1)$ and $y = s(y_2)$ with $y_1 \neq y_2$.

8 Conclusion

Attempts to address the problem of solving inequations in term algebra are not new since we cited already A. Colmerauer [3] and H. Comon [4]. However our approach is original in two respects, we make a clear distinction between roles plaid by variables (existential and universal), and we exhibit a set of inference rules that highlight the basic operations to perform in order to solve disequations. In some sense, this improves the readibility as Martelli and Montanari [16] or G.Huet [9] did for unification or C.Kirchner [12] for equational unification. Our hope is that this axiomatic approach will provide tools for proposing a simple algorithm for solving the decision of inductive reducibility. Next this very general framework has to be extended to equational theories.

References

[1] H. Bürckert. Some relationships between unification, restricted unification and matching. In J. Siekmann, editor, *Proceedings 8th Conference on Automated Deduction, Oxford*, pages 514–524, Springer Verlag, Oxford (England), 1986.

[2] A. Colmerauer. Equations and inequations on finite and infinite trees. In *FGCS'84Proceedings*, pages 85–99, November 1984.

[3] A. Colmerauer. *PROLOG II, Manuel de Référence et Modèle théorique.* Technical Report, GIA, Université Aix-Marseille II, 1982.

[4] H. Comon. Sufficient completeness, term rewriting system and anti-unification. In J. Siekmann, editor, *Proceedings 8th Conference on Automated Deduction, Oxford*, pages 128–140, Springer Verlag, Oxford (England), 1986.

[5] N. Dershowitz. Termination. In *Proceedings 1st Conference on Rewriting Techniques and Applications*, pages 180–224, Springer Verlag, Dijon (France), May 1985.

[6] J. Gallier. The semantics of recursive programs with functions parameters of finite types: n-rational algebras and logic of inequalities. In M. Nivat and Reynolds J.C., editors, *Algebraic Methods in Semantics*, Cambridge University Press, 1985.

[7] J.A. Goguen and J. Meseguer. EQLOG: equality, types and generic modules for logic programming. In D. DeGroot and G. Lindstrom, editors, *Logic Programming. Funstions, relations and equations*, Prentice Hall, 1986.

[8] J.V. Guttag and J.J. Horning. The algebraic specification of abstract data types. *Acta Informatica*, 10:27–52, 1978.

[9] G. Huet. Resolution d'equations dans les langages d'ordre 1,2, ...,ω. Thèse d'état de l'Université de Paris 7, 1976.

[10] G. Huet and D. Oppen. Equations and rewrite rules: a survey. In R. Book, editor, *Formal Language Theory: Perspectives and Open Problems*, Academic Press, 1980.

[11] J.P. Jouannaud and E. Kounalis. Proof by induction in equational theories without constructors. In *Proceeding of the first symposium on Logic In Computer Science, Boston (USA)*, pages 358–366, 1986.

[12] C. Kirchner. Computing unification algorithms. In *Proceeding of the first symposium on Logic In Computer Science, Boston (USA)*, pages 206–216, 1986.

[13] C. Kirchner. Méthodes et outils de conception systématique d'algorithmes d'unification dans les théories équationnelles. Thèse d'état de l'Université de NancyI, 1985.

[14] J-L. Lassez, M.J. Maher, and K. Marriot. *Unification Revisited.* Technical Report, IBM Thomas J. Watson Research Center, 1986.

[15] A. Lazrek, P. Lescanne, and J-J. Thiel. *Proving inductive equalities, Algorithms and Implementation.* Technical Report, Internal Report CRIN 86-R-087, to be published in Information and Control, 1986.

[16] A. Martelli and U. Montanari. An efficient unification algorithm. *ACM Transactions On Programming Languages And Systems*, 4(2):258–282, 1982.

Decidability of the Confluence of Ground Term Rewriting Systems

Max DAUCHET Sophie TISON*
Laboratoire d'Informatique Fondamentale de Lille, UA 369 du CNRS,
Université de Lille-Flandres-Artois,
59655 VILLENEUVE D'ASCQ, FRANCE

Thierry HEUILLARD† Pierre LESCANNE‡
Centre de Recherche en Informatique de Nancy,
CNRS UA 262 and INRIA-Lorraine,
Campus Scientifique, BP 239,
54506 VANDŒUVRE-LES-NANCY, FRANCE

Abstract

The aim of this paper is to propose a simple algorithm to decide the confluence of ground term rewriting systems. A simple view of the problem and its solution is proposed. Let us recall that a ground term rewriting system is a term rewriting system where each rule is a pair of ground terms, i.e., a pair of terms without variables. The confluence is the property that asserts that $u \xleftarrow{*} s \xrightarrow{*} v$ implies there exists a term t such that $u \xrightarrow{*} t \xleftarrow{*} v$. For example, the reader may try to prove that the system $\{f(f(a)) \to f(a),\ g(f(a)) \to f(g(f(a))),\ g(f(a)) \to f(f(a))\}$ is confluent and that the system $\{a \to f(a,b), f(a,b) \to f(b,a)\}$ is not. It is well known the confluence is not decidable for general term rewriting systems, but this paper proves it is for ground term rewriting systems following a conjecture made by Huet and Oppen in their survey. We also sketch a simple algorithm for checking this property. This algorithm is based on tree automata and tree transducers. Here, we regard them as rewriting systems and specialists in automata theory would translate that easily in their language.

1 Introduction

The aim of this paper is to propose a simple algorithm to decide the confluence of ground term rewriting systems. This algorithm is derived from decidability results presented in [1]. Here a simple view of the problem and its solution is proposed. Let us recall that a ground term rewriting system is a term rewriting system where each rule is a pair of ground terms, i.e., a pair of terms without variables. The confluence is the property that asserts that $u \xleftarrow{*} s \xrightarrow{*} v$ implies there exists a term t such that $u \xrightarrow{*} t \xleftarrow{*} v$. For example, the reader may try to prove that the system $\{f(f(a)) \to f(a),\ g(f(a)) \to f(g(f(a))),\ g(f(a)) \to f(f(a))\}$ is confluent and that the system $\{a \to f(a,b), f(a,b) \to f(b,a)\}$ is not. It is well known the confluence is not decidable for general term rewriting systems, but this paper proves it is for ground term rewriting systems following a conjecture made by Huet and Oppen [3] in their survey. We also sketch a simple algorithm for checking this property. This algorithm is based on tree automata and tree transducers. Here, we regard them as rewriting systems and specialists in automata theory would translate that easily in their language.

In the second part of this paper, a new class of tree transducers is introduced: *ground tree transducers, GTT* in short. In the third part, stability of *GTT* relation w.r.t inverse, composition, iteration and precongruence closure of union is proved. In the fourth part, each ground term rewriting system is associated with a *GTT* and the confluence of ground term rewriting system is reduced to the inclusion of *GTT* relations. Part 5 solves the decision problem by encoding *GTT* into rational tree languages.

2 Ground tree transducers

The intuitive idea behind a ground tree transducer is to transform ground terms into ground terms in two steps, with a memory that uses a finite number of values or states. In the first step, one nibbles the term and in the second step one restores a new term. The nibbling consists of transforming some subterms of the term into constants, the states, and the restoration consists of transforming the states into subterms. These operations are rational, this means the relation they define satisfy properties expected for rational relations, namely stability w.r.t. union, composition and iteration.

The steps of nibbling and restoration are described by a tree automaton which is nothing but a ground term rewriting system that works on a set of ground terms enriched by the states as constants. In the following the set of states is named E (or E_G if one wants to refer to a ground term rewriting system G) and its elements are written e. Let F be a finite ranked alphabet. $T(F)$ denotes the set of terms (or trees) on F.

Definition 1 *A relation* $\to$ *is F*-compatible *or is a* precongruence *if*

$$(\forall f \in F) s \to t \Rightarrow f(\ldots,s,\ldots) \to f(\ldots,t,\ldots).$$

Definition 2 *A* tree automaton *G is a rewriting system on* $T(F \cup E_G)$ *which contains only rules of the form:*

$f(e_1,\ldots,e_n) \to e_0$ *called* reduction transitions

and

$e \to e'$ *called* ε-transitions.

for $f \in F$ *and* $e_1,\ldots,e_n,e_0,e,e'$ *in* E_G.

*Supported by Greco Mathématique et Informatique

†currently at LRI, Université de Paris-Sud, Orsay, France, this work was done as student at the Ecole des Mines de Nancy

‡Supported by Greco Programmation

The relation $\overset{*}{\rightarrow}$ is the least reflexive and transitive precongruence on ground terms that contains $\rightarrow$.

Definition 3 *A* ground tree transducer *on $T(F)$ (a GTT in short) is the relation T or (G, D) associated with two tree automata G and D and defined as follows:*

$t \overset{T}{\rightarrow\leftarrow} t'$ iff there exists $u \in T(F \cup E_G \cup E_D)$ such that $t \overset{*}{\rightarrow}_G u \overset{*}{\leftarrow}_D t'$.

In order to produce actual pairs of terms, the set E_G and E_D are supposed non disjoint. $E_G \cap E_D$ is called the *interface.* It could be more intuitive to see u as a term of the form $c(e_1, \ldots, e_n)$ where $c(x_1, \ldots, x_n)$ is a common context of t and t' with $t = c(t_1, \ldots, t_n), t' = c(t'_1, \ldots, t'_n)$ and $t_1 \overset{*}{\rightarrow}_G e_1 \overset{*}{\leftarrow}_D t'_1, \ldots, t_n \overset{*}{\rightarrow}_G e_n \overset{*}{\leftarrow}_D t_n$ (see Figure 1.)

3 Stability of *GTT* relations

From the definition, it is really easy to see that the inverse of a *GTT*-relation is still a *GTT*-relation, we have just to commute the rôle of G and D. The union of two *GTT*-relations R_1 and R_2, is not actually a *GTT*-relation. However the *precongruence closure* of $R_1 \cup R_2$, which is the least precongruence that contains R_1 and R_2, is associated with the *GTT* (G_3, D_3) defined by $G_3 \equiv G_2 \cup G_2$ and $D_3 \equiv D_1 \cup D_2$, where (G_1, D_1) and (G_2, D_2) are the *GTT* associated with R_1 and R_2. This supposes the $E_{G_1} \cup E_{D_1} \neq E_{G_2} \cup E_{D_2}$. So we may state the following proposition.

Proposition 1 *1. The inverse of a GTT-relation is a GTT-relation.*

2. The precongruence closure of the union of two GTT-relations is a GTT-relation.

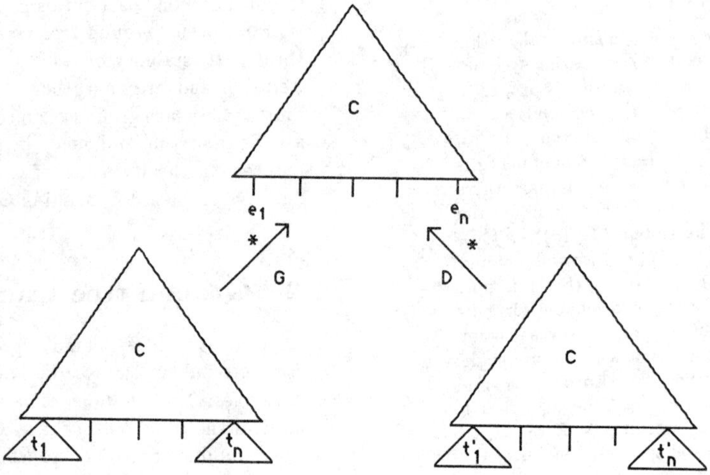

Figure 1: A ground term transduction

A relation associated with a ground term transducer is called a *GTT*-relation. The relation associated with a ground term transducer T is denoted by $R(T)$. We will first prove a useful lemma.

Lemma 1 : *A GTT-relation can always be associated with a GTT without ε-transition.*

Proof: From the *GTT* (G, D) we build the *GTT* (G', D') defined as follows: $E_{G'} = E_G$ and $E_{D'} = E_D$ the rules of G' are of the form:

$$f(e'_n, \ldots, e'_n) \rightarrow_{G'} e'_0$$

if and only if

$$e'_1 \overset{*}{\rightarrow}_G e_1,$$

$$\ldots,$$

$$e'_n \overset{*}{\rightarrow}_G e_n,$$

$$e_0 \overset{*}{\rightarrow}_G e'_0,$$

$$f(e_1, \ldots, e_n) \rightarrow_G e_0.$$

and the same for D. It is easy to see that $t \overset{(G,D)}{\rightarrow\leftarrow} t'$ if and only if $t \overset{(G',D')}{\rightarrow\leftarrow} t'$. □

We are going now to address two other properties of *GTT*-relations namely the stability by composition and the stability by iteration. We will propose two proofs of these properties, one is based on a diamond lemma and the second one, which is more constructive, is based on properties of minimality of some paths that go from one term to another. Given two relations A and B, we define a relation $\rightarrow_{\{A;B\}}$ by the two inference rules of Figure 2.

We will now prove a diamond lemma.

Lemma 2 *If A and B are described by tree automata without ε-transitions and*

$$u_1 \overset{*}{\leftarrow}_{\{A;B\}} t \overset{*}{\rightarrow}_{\{B;A\}} u_2$$

with $t \in T(F \cup E_A \cup E_B)$, there exists $s \in T(F \cup E_A \cup E_B)$, such that

$$u_1 \overset{*}{\rightarrow}_{\{B;A\}} s \overset{*}{\leftarrow}_{\{A;B\}} u_2$$

. In terms of relations we have

$$\overset{*}{\leftarrow}_{\{A;B\}} \circ \overset{*}{\rightarrow}_{\{B;A\}} \subseteq \overset{*}{\rightarrow}_{\{B;A\}} \circ \overset{*}{\leftarrow}_{\{A;B\}}$$

$$\frac{f(e_1,\ldots,e_n)\xrightarrow{*}_A e}{f(e_1,\ldots,e_n)\rightarrow_{\{A;B\}}e}$$

$$\frac{e_0 \xleftarrow{*}_B f(e_1,\ldots,e_n) \& e_1 \xrightarrow{*}_{\{A;B\}} e'_1,\ldots,e_n \xrightarrow{*}_{\{A;B\}} e'_n \& f(e'_1,\ldots,e'_n) \xrightarrow{*}_{\{A;B\}} e'_0}{e_0\rightarrow_{\{A;B\}}e'_0}$$

Figure 2: Definition of $\rightarrow_{\{A;B\}}$

Proof: Note that $\leftarrow_{\{A;B\}}$ and $\rightarrow_{\{B;A\}}$ contain ε-transitions. Note also that if $u\xrightarrow{*}_{\{B;A\}}v$ uses only ε-transitions, then $u \xleftarrow{*}_{\{A;B\}} v$ uses only ε-transitions and vice-versa. Let us write $u \overset{\{A;B\}}{\longleftrightarrow} v$ in this case. The proof of the lemma is by induction on the size of the terms. The basic cases are the following.

First case. $u_1 \overset{\{A;B\}}{\longleftrightarrow} t \xrightarrow{*}_{\{B;A\}} u_2$, then if s is taken to be u_2 then $u_1 \xrightarrow{*}_{\{B;A\}} s \equiv u_2$.

Second case. $u_1 \xleftarrow{*}_{\{A;B\}} t \overset{\{A;B\}}{\longleftrightarrow} u_2$, the proof is as previously with $s \equiv u_1$.

General case. The premise of the general case is a diagram of the form given in Figure 3.

Two cases have to be considered, either the occurrences where A and B are used are different or it is the same. If the occurrences are different, we have,

$$t = c(e_1,\ldots,e_n,f(a_1,\ldots,a_p),g(b_1,\ldots,b_q))$$

and

$$t' = c(e'_1,\ldots,e'_n,f(a'_1,\ldots,a'_p),g(b'_1,\ldots,b'_q))$$

and

$$t_1 = c(e_1,\ldots,e_n,a_0,g(b_1,\ldots,b_q))$$

and

$$t_2 = c(e_1,\ldots,e_n,a_0,g(b'_1,\ldots,b'_q))$$

and

$$t'_1 = c(e'_1,\ldots,e'_n,f(a'_1,\ldots,a'_p),b_0)$$

and

$$t'_2 = c(e'_1,\ldots,e'_n,f(a_1,\ldots,a_p),b_0)$$

where $e_1,\ldots,e_n, e'_1,\ldots,e'_n, a_1,\ldots,a_p, a'_1,\ldots,a'_p, a_0, b_1,\ldots,b_q, b'_1,\ldots,b'_q, b_0$ are in $E_A \cup E_B$.

Let us define

$$s = c(e_1,\ldots,e_n,a_0,b_0)$$

$$s' = c(e'_1,\ldots,e'_n,a_0,b_0)$$

we have $s \overset{\{A;B\}}{\longleftrightarrow} s'$. By induction on the size of the terms, indeed t_1, t'_1, s and s' are of size less than this of t, the diagram can be completed into this of Figure 4.

If the occurrences are the same, we have,

$$t = c(e_1,\ldots,e_n,f(a_1,\ldots,a_p))$$

and

$$t' = c(e'_1,\ldots,e'_n,f(b_1,\ldots,b_p)).$$

We define t_1 and t'_1 as

$$t_1 = c(e_1,\ldots,e_n,a_0)$$

where

$$f(a_1,\ldots,a_p)\xrightarrow{*}_A a_0,$$

and

$$t'_1 = c(e'_1,\ldots,e'_n,b_0)$$

where

$$f(b_1,\ldots,b_p)\xrightarrow{*}_B b_0.$$

We have $t_1 \overset{\{A;B\}}{\longleftrightarrow} t'_1$ from the second inference rule, therefore the diagram can be completed into this of Figure 5. □

The following propositions are consequences of the previous lemma.

Proposition 2 $\xleftarrow{*}_A \circ \xrightarrow{*}_B \subseteq \xrightarrow{*}_{\{B;A\}} \circ \xleftarrow{*}_{\{A;B\}}$

Proof: This is obvious from Lemma 2 and from $\leftarrow_A \subseteq \leftarrow_{\{A;B\}}$ and $\rightarrow_B \subseteq \rightarrow_{\{B;A\}}$. □

Proposition 3 $\xrightarrow{*}_B \circ \xleftarrow{*}_A = \xrightarrow{*}_{\{B;A\}} \circ \xleftarrow{*}_{\{A;B\}}$. *The iteration of a GTT-relation is a GTT-relation.*

Proof: The inclusion $\subseteq$ comes by induction from Proposition 2 and Lemma 2. We have $\xrightarrow{*}_{\{B;A\}} \subseteq (\xrightarrow{*}_B \circ \xleftarrow{*}_A)^*$ and $\xleftarrow{*}_{\{A;B\}} \subseteq (\xrightarrow{*}_B \circ \xleftarrow{*}_A)^*$ then obviously $\xrightarrow{*}_{\{B;A\}} \circ \xleftarrow{*}_{\{A;B\}} \subseteq (\xrightarrow{*}_B \circ \xleftarrow{*}_A)^*$. Since $(\rightarrow_{\{B;A\}}, \leftarrow_{\{A;B\}})$ defines a *GTT*, this provides easily the stability by iteration. □

The next proposition is useful for proving the stability by composition.

Proposition 4 *If $E_A \cap E_B = \emptyset$, then*

$$\rightarrow_B \circ \leftarrow_A \subseteq \leftarrow_A \circ \rightarrow_B$$

and

$$\xrightarrow{*}_{\{B;A\}} \circ \xleftarrow{*}_{\{A;B\}} \subseteq \xleftarrow{*}_A \circ \xrightarrow{*}_B .$$

Proof: Since the sets of states are disjoint, if $\rightarrow_B$ precedes $\leftarrow_A$, the rewritings take place at two different occurrences and, by the way, they commute. Thus, we obtain $\xrightarrow{*}_B \circ \xleftarrow{*}_A \subseteq \xleftarrow{*}_A \circ \xrightarrow{*}_B$. We conclude by Proposition 3. □

Proposition 5 *The composition of two GTT-relations is a GTT-relation.*

Proof: Suppose that the two relations are associated with the *GTT*'s (G, D) and (Γ, Δ) and that the sets of states satisfy the condition $E_D \cap E_\Gamma = \emptyset$. The relation which is the composition of the relations associated with the two *GTT* is given by $\xrightarrow{*}_G \circ \xleftarrow{*}_D \circ \xrightarrow{*}_\Gamma \circ \xleftarrow{*}_\Delta$. From Proposition 2 and Proposition 4, this is equal to $\xrightarrow{*}_G \circ \xrightarrow{*}_{\{\Gamma,D\}} \circ \xleftarrow{*}_{\{D,\Gamma\}} \circ \xleftarrow{*}_\Delta$. By a renaming of the states this can be easily described as a *GTT*. □

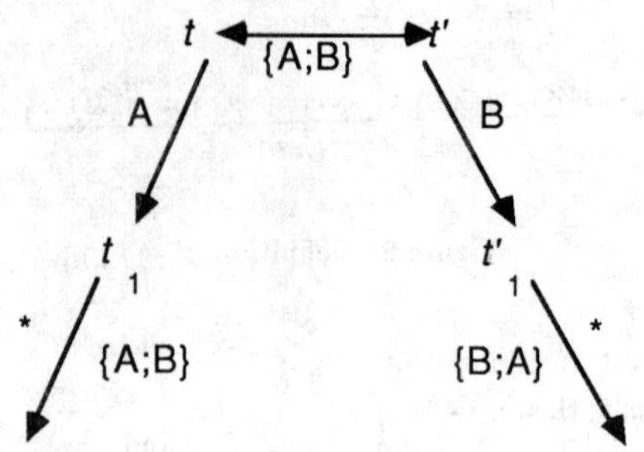

Figure 3: Premise of the general case in Lemma 2.

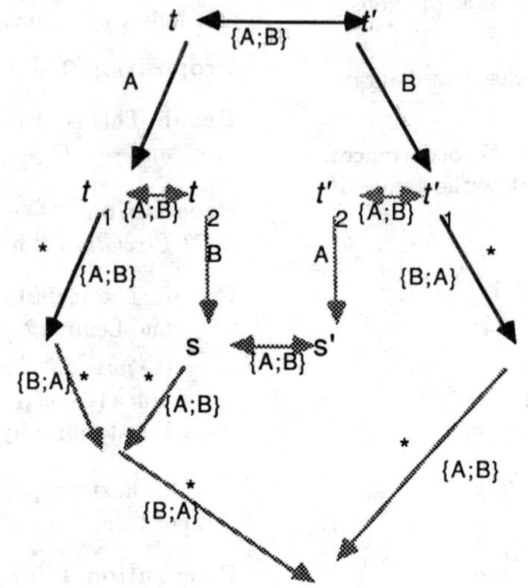

Figure 4: Diagram in the case of different occurrences.

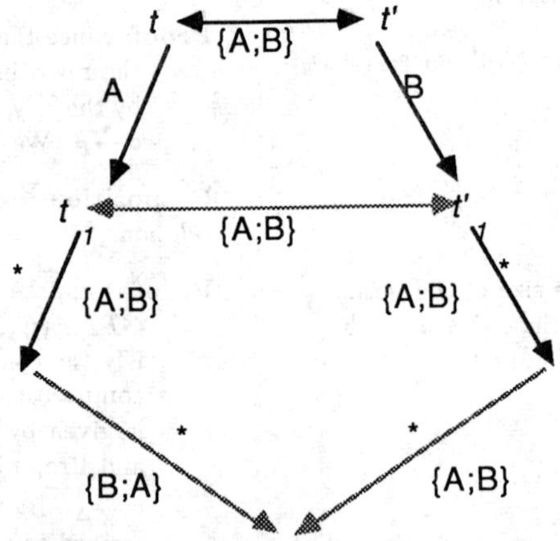

Figure 5: Diagram in the case of the same occurrence.

There is another method for proving the stability based on minimal paths. The idea is to use the relation $\overset{\{A;B\}}{\longleftrightarrow}$. In this relation one can represent transitions of the form $f(e_1,\dots,e_n) \overset{*}{\rightarrow}_{\{A;B\}} e$ by a descending arrow and relation of the form $e_0 \overset{*}{\rightarrow}_{\{A;B\}} e'_0$ by an horizontal arrow. A concave path is a path starting by descending arrows followed by horizontal arrows then followed by ascending arrows (see Figure 6). The size of a path is the sum of the sizes of the terms occurring along the path.

Proposition 6 *The minimal paths in the relation*

$$(\overset{*}{\rightarrow}_{\{B;A\}} \circ \overset{*}{\leftarrow}_{\{A;B\}})^*$$

are concave. This means they belong to $\overset{*}{\rightarrow}_{\{B;A\}} \circ \overset{*}{\leftarrow}_{\{A;B\}}$.

Proof: The principle is by contradiction. The idea is explained in Figure 6, it means that if a path contains a non concave part it is always possible to find a smallest part which is concave. Roughly speaking, if the occurrences where the transitions take place are the same, one can shortcut them by a unique transition, if the occurrences are different, permuting the transitions provides a smaller path because the term below is smaller than the term above. □

4 Term Rewriting Systems, Transducers and Confluence

From the previous section, it is now easy to prove that the rewriting relation deduced from a ground term rewriting system can be described by a *GTT*. First the precongruence that contains a unique rule $s \rightarrow t$ is associated with the *GTT* $(R_s \cup \{e_s \rightarrow e_t\}, R_t)$ where R_s and R_t recognize s and t, which means e_s is a state in R_s and $u \overset{*}{\rightarrow}_{R_s} e_s$ if and only if u is s and the same for t and R_t. The rewriting relation associated with a ground term rewriting system is obtained from the *GTT* associated with each rule, by union and iteration, therefore it is a *GTT*-relation.

The confluence of a rewriting relation $\rightarrow$ can be translated into the inclusion

$$\overset{*}{\leftarrow} \circ \overset{*}{\rightarrow} \subseteq \overset{*}{\rightarrow} \circ \overset{*}{\leftarrow}.$$

From the previous results these two relations are associated with a *GTT*. The decidability of this property will be a consequence of the following section which proves that the inclusion of two *GTT*-relations is decidable.

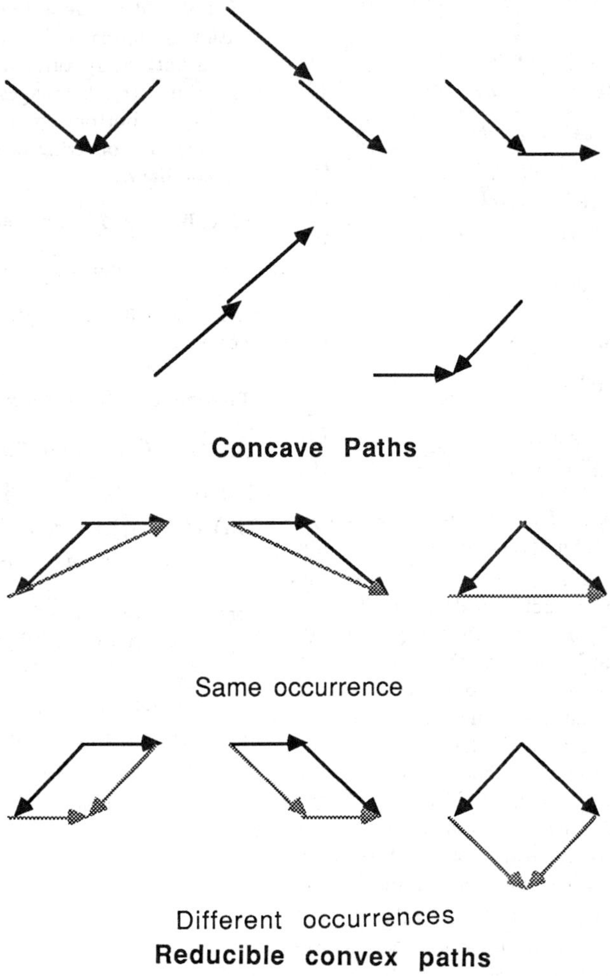

Figure 6: concaveness

5 Decidability of the inclusion of two *GTT*-relations

The idea for deciding the inclusion of two *GTT*-relations is to map each *GTT*-relation onto a regular tree language. Since the map is one-to-one, a language will be included in another language if and only if the associated relations are included one in the other. The map is defined as follows. With each pair

$$t = c(t_1,\ldots,t_n)\xrightarrow{*}_G c(e_1,\ldots,e_n)\xleftarrow{*}_D t' = c(t'_1,\ldots,t'_n)$$

one associates the term $v{\downarrow_\sharp}$, where $v{\downarrow_\sharp}$ is the normal form of the term $v = c(\sharp(t_1,t'_1),\ldots,\sharp(t_n,t'_n))$ for the rewriting system $R_\sharp$ defined by the rules

$$\sharp(f(x_1,\ldots,x_p),f(y_1,\ldots,y_p))\rightarrow_{R_\sharp} f(\sharp(x_1,y_1),\ldots,\sharp(x_p,y_p)).$$

Let us write $\mathcal{L}(T)$ for the language of the $v{\downarrow_\sharp}$'s and let us call it the *tensorial product* of the *GTT* T. Let us show that $\mathcal{L}(T)$ is recognized by a tree automaton $\mathcal{A}(T)$. The set of states is divided into four parts $E_G, E_D^c, \{ok\}$ and $E_G \times E_D^c$. E_D^c is a copy of E_D in order to avoid confusion. $e^c \in E_D^c$ corresponds to $e \in E_D$. ok is the unique final state, in other words, $v \in \mathcal{L}(T)$ if and only if $v \xrightarrow{*}_{\mathcal{A}(T)} ok$. The transitions are those of G, plus those of the form

$$\begin{aligned}
f(e_1^c,\ldots,e_1^c) &\rightarrow e^c &(1)\\
\sharp(e,e^c) &\rightarrow ok &(2)\\
f(ok,\ldots,ok) &\rightarrow ok &(3)\\
\sharp(e',e^c) &\rightarrow \langle e',e^c\rangle &(4)\\
\langle e,e^c\rangle &\rightarrow ok &(5)\\
f(\langle e_1',e_1^c\rangle,\ldots,\langle e_n',e_n^c\rangle) &\rightarrow \langle e',e^c\rangle &(6)
\end{aligned}$$

The first rule corresponds to the rule

$$f(e_1,\ldots,e_n) \rightarrow_D e \qquad (7)$$

The last rule corresponds to the rules

$$\begin{aligned}
f(e_1',\ldots,e_n') &\rightarrow_G e' &(8)\\
f(e_1,\ldots,e_n) &\rightarrow_D e &(9)
\end{aligned}$$

The first transition translates in E_D^c the transitions of E_D, the second one acknowledges a term $\sharp(s,t)$ where s and t are correctly associated by the *GTT T* i.e., $s \xrightarrow{T}\!\!\leftarrow t$, the third one is just for transmitting the previous acknowledgement through the context. Since the system $R_\sharp$ pushes down the $\sharp$'s through terms with the same top, it could be the case that a pair is not completely recognized when $\sharp$ appears. The fourth transition is for allowing the recognition to continue. Since the terms are supposed to have the same top, the recognition of the rest of the two terms of the pairs has to be done on both terms together and the recognition has to work on a pair of terms. This is the rôle of the fifth rule. The last rule corresponds to the second one when one works on a pair of states, it means that what has been recognized till this point is the $R_\sharp$-normal form of a term $\sharp(s,t)$ where $s \xrightarrow{T}\!\!\leftarrow t$. Notice that rules (2) and (3) and rules (5) and (6) make $\mathcal{A}(T)$ non deterministic. The following theorem says that $\mathcal{L}(T)$ and $\mathcal{A}(T)$ are correctly associated.

Theorem 1 *The three following statements are equivalent:*

(i) $c(\sharp(t_1,t'_1),\ldots,\sharp(t_n,t'_n)){\downarrow_\sharp} \in \mathcal{L}(T)$

(ii) $c(t_1,\ldots,t_n) \xrightarrow{T}\!\!\leftarrow c(t'_1,\ldots,t'_n)$

(iii) $c(\sharp(t_1,t'_1),\ldots,\sharp(t_n,t'_n)){\downarrow_\sharp}$ *is recognized by the automaton* $\mathcal{A}(T)$, *in other words* $c(\sharp(t_1,t'_1),\ldots,\sharp(t_n,t'_n)){\downarrow_\sharp} \xrightarrow{*}_{\mathcal{A}(T)} ok$.

Proof: (i) $\Leftrightarrow$ (ii) is a direct consequence of the definition of $\mathcal{L}(T)$. For the proof of (ii) $\Rightarrow$ (iii), let us look at the $\sharp(t_i,t'_i)$ part of $c(\sharp(t_1,t'_1),\ldots,\sharp(t_n,t'_n))$. Its $R_\sharp$-normal form $\sharp(t_i,t'_i){\downarrow_\sharp}$ is of the form $c_i(\sharp(t_{i,1},t'_{i,1}),\ldots,\sharp(t_{i,n},t'_{i,n}))$. If $c(t_1,\ldots,t_n) \xrightarrow{T}\!\!\leftarrow c(t'_1,\ldots,t'_n)$, we have $t_i \xrightarrow{*}_G e_i \xleftarrow{*}_D t'_j$ for a state e_i of $\mathcal{A}(T)$. To recognize $\sharp(t_i,t'_i){\downarrow_\sharp}$, i.e., to get $\sharp(t_i,t'_i){\downarrow_\sharp} \xrightarrow{*}_{\mathcal{A}(T)} ok$ one uses the first rule for deriving $t_{i,j} \xrightarrow{*}_{\mathcal{A}(T)} e_{i,j}$ and $t'_{i,j} \xrightarrow{*}_{\mathcal{A}(T)} e'_{i,j}$, then the fourth rule to get $\sharp(e_{i,j},e'_{i,j})\rightarrow_{\mathcal{A}(T)}\langle e_{i,j}e'_{i,j}\rangle$ then the fifth rule to get

$$c_i(\sharp(t_{i,1},t'_{i,1}),\ldots,\sharp(t_{i,n},t'_{i,n})) \xrightarrow{*}_{\mathcal{A}(T)} \langle e_i,e_i\rangle,$$

then the sixth rule to get $\langle e_i,e_i\rangle\rightarrow_{\mathcal{A}(T)} ok$. So

$$c(\sharp(t_1,t'_1),\ldots,\sharp(t_n,t'_n)){\downarrow_\sharp}\xrightarrow{*}_{\mathcal{A}(T)} ok.$$

by using the third rule.

For the proof of (iii) $\Rightarrow$ (ii), the problem is to rebuild the terms $c(t_1,\ldots,t_n)$ and $c(t'_1,\ldots,t'_n)$ from the recognition of

$$c(\sharp(t_1,t'_1),\ldots,\sharp(t_n,t'_n)){\downarrow_\sharp},$$

in other words to rebuild $c(\sharp(t_1,t'_1),\ldots,\sharp(t_n,t'_n))$ from its $R_\sharp$-normal form. The idea is just to push up the $\sharp$ in the term till the point where the rules $\langle e_i,e_i\rangle\rightarrow_{\mathcal{A}(T)} ok$ is used. □

Since the correspondence between $\mathcal{L}(T)$ and R(T) is one-to-one, the following corollary is an easy consequence of the theorem.

Corollary 1 $R(T) \subseteq R(T')$ *if and only if* $\mathcal{L}(T) \subseteq \mathcal{L}(T')$.

The tree language $\mathcal{L}(T)$ is rational, since it is recognized by the bottom up automaton $\mathcal{A}(T)$. The presentation is a little different of this used in the automata literature, but the reader familiar with this approach can easily convince himself that $\mathcal{A}(T)$ is actually a bottom-up automaton. It is well-known that the inclusion of rational tree languages is decidable. This can be done by extending to bottom-up tree automata the decision procedure for the inclusion of string rational languages. So we have the following corollary.

Corollary 2 *The inclusion of GTT-relations is decidable.*

From the previous section we have the following main corollary.

Corollary 3 *The confluence of a ground tree rewriting system is decidable.*

6 An algorithm for deciding the confluence of ground term rewriting systems

A possible algorithm for deciding the confluence of ground term rewriting system can be divided into three main steps.

- build the *GTT* associated with the term rewriting system, first one makes a *GTT* for the precongruence of each individual rule, then a *GTT* for their union and eventually the iteration of this *GTT*.

- build the *GTT* associated with the relations $\overset{*}{\leftarrow} \circ \overset{*}{\rightarrow}$ and $\overset{*}{\rightarrow} \circ \overset{*}{\leftarrow}$ and then build the rational language associated with these relations.

- decide the inclusion of the rational free languages, by classical tree automata techniques.

7 Conclusion

We have shown that the problem of deciding the confluence of ground term rewriting systems can be reduced to the problem of deciding the inclusion of two rational tree languages, problem which has a well-known decision procedure. In addition, this paper proposes a full algorithm. It should be noticed that this algorithm is essentially interesting for no terminating term rewriting systems, because otherwise a method based on superposition (detection of subterms in this case) similar to the Knuth-Bendix algorithm would work. Notice also that it was known for a long time [2] that the termination of such ground term rewriting systems was decidable.

8 References

1. Dauchet M., S. Tison, *Tree automata and decidability in ground term rewriting systems*, Internal Report, Universit de Lille 1, Laboratoire Associé au CNRS 236 and FCT'85, *Lecture Notes in Computer Science* vol.199, pp 80-84 (1985).

2. Huet G., Lankford, *On the Uniform Halting Problem for Term Rewriting Systems*, Rapport Laboria 283 (1978).

3. Huet G., D. Oppen, *Equations and Rewrite Rules*: A Survey, in Formal Languages: Perspectives and Open Problems, Ed. Book R., Academic Press (1980).

Author Index

NOTES

NOTES

NOTES

NOTES

NOTES

NOTES

NOTES

NOTES

NOTES

NOTES